SECRET SIX

VOLUME 2

MONEY FOR MURDER

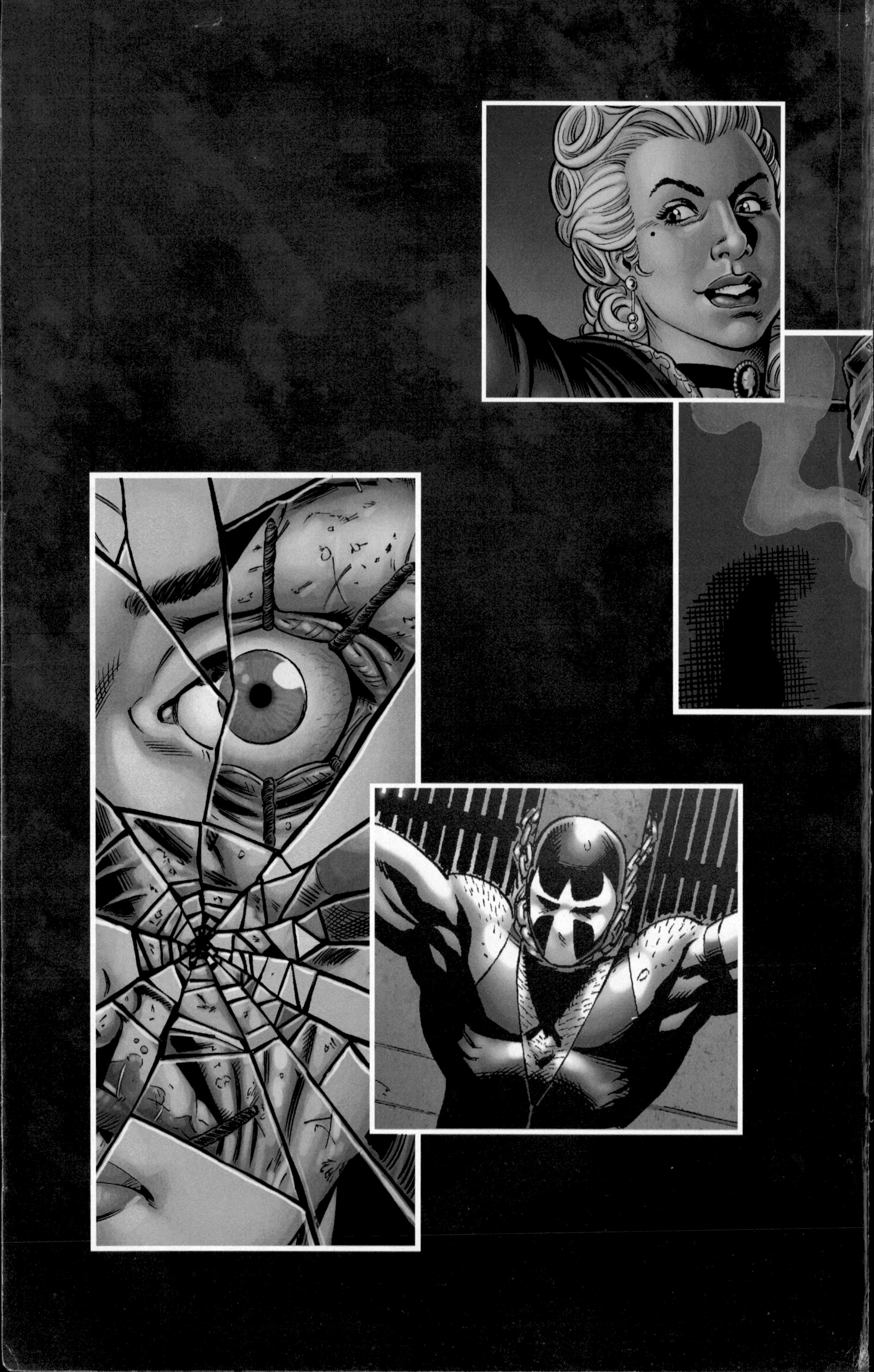

SECRET SIX

VOLUME 2
MONEY FOR MURDER

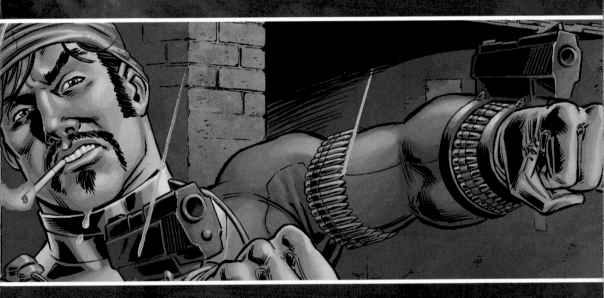

Gail Simone
Mark Waid
Scott Beatty
writers

Nicola Scott
Javier Pina
Carlos Rodriguez
Dale Eaglesham
Freddie E. Williams III
pencillers

Doug Hazlewood
Rodney Ramos
Javier Pina
Bit
Mike Sellers
Mike McKenna
Art Thibert
Freddie E. Williams III

Jason Wright
Alex Sinclair
Hi-Fi
colorist

Steve Wands
Travis Lanham
Sal Cipriano
Rob Clark Jr.
Pat Brosseau
Rob Leigh
Ken Lopez
letterers

Cliff Chiang
collection cover artist

NACHIE CASTRO MATT IDELSON SEAN RYAN Editors – Original Series
RACHEL PINNELAS   Editor
ROBBIN BROSTERMAN   Design Director – Books
SARABETH KETT   Publication Design

BOB HARRAS   Senior VP – Editor-in-Chief, DC Comics

DIANE NELSON   President
DAN DIDIO and JIM LEE   Co-Publishers
GEOFF JOHNS   Chief Creative Officer
AMIT DESAI   Senior VP – Marketing & Franchise Management
AMY GENKINS   Senior VP – Business & Legal Affairs
NAIRI GARDINER   Senior VP – Finance
JEFF BOISON   VP – Publishing Planning
MARK CHIARELLO   VP – Art Direction & Design
JOHN CUNNINGHAM   VP – Marketing
TERRI CUNNINGHAM   VP – Editorial Administration
LARRY GANEM   VP – Talent Relations & Services
ALISON GILL   Senior VP – Manufacturing & Operations
HANK KANALZ   Senior VP – Vertigo & Integrated Publishing
JAY KOGAN   VP – Business & Legal Affairs, Publishing
JACK MAHAN   VP – Business Affairs, Talent
NICK NAPOLITANO   VP – Manufacturing Administration
SUE POHJA   VP – Book Sales
FRED RUIZ   VP – Manufacturing Operations
COURTNEY SIMMONS   Senior VP – Publicity
BOB WAYNE   Senior VP – Sales

SECRET SIX VOLUME 2: MONEY FOR MURDER

DC Comics, 4000 Warner Blvd., Burbank, CA 91522
A Warner Bros. Entertainment Company.
Printed by RR Donnelley, Owensville, MO, USA. 5/1/15. First Printing.
ISBN: 978-1-4012-5537-4

Library of Congress Cataloging-in-Publication Data

Simone, Gail, author.
  Secret Six. Volume 2 / Gail Simone, writer ; Nicola Scott, artist.
    pages cm
  ISBN 978-1-4012-5537-4 (paperback)
  1. Graphic novels. I. Scott, Nicola, illustrator. II. Title.
  PN6727.S51579S5 2015
  741.5'973—dc23

                        2014042084

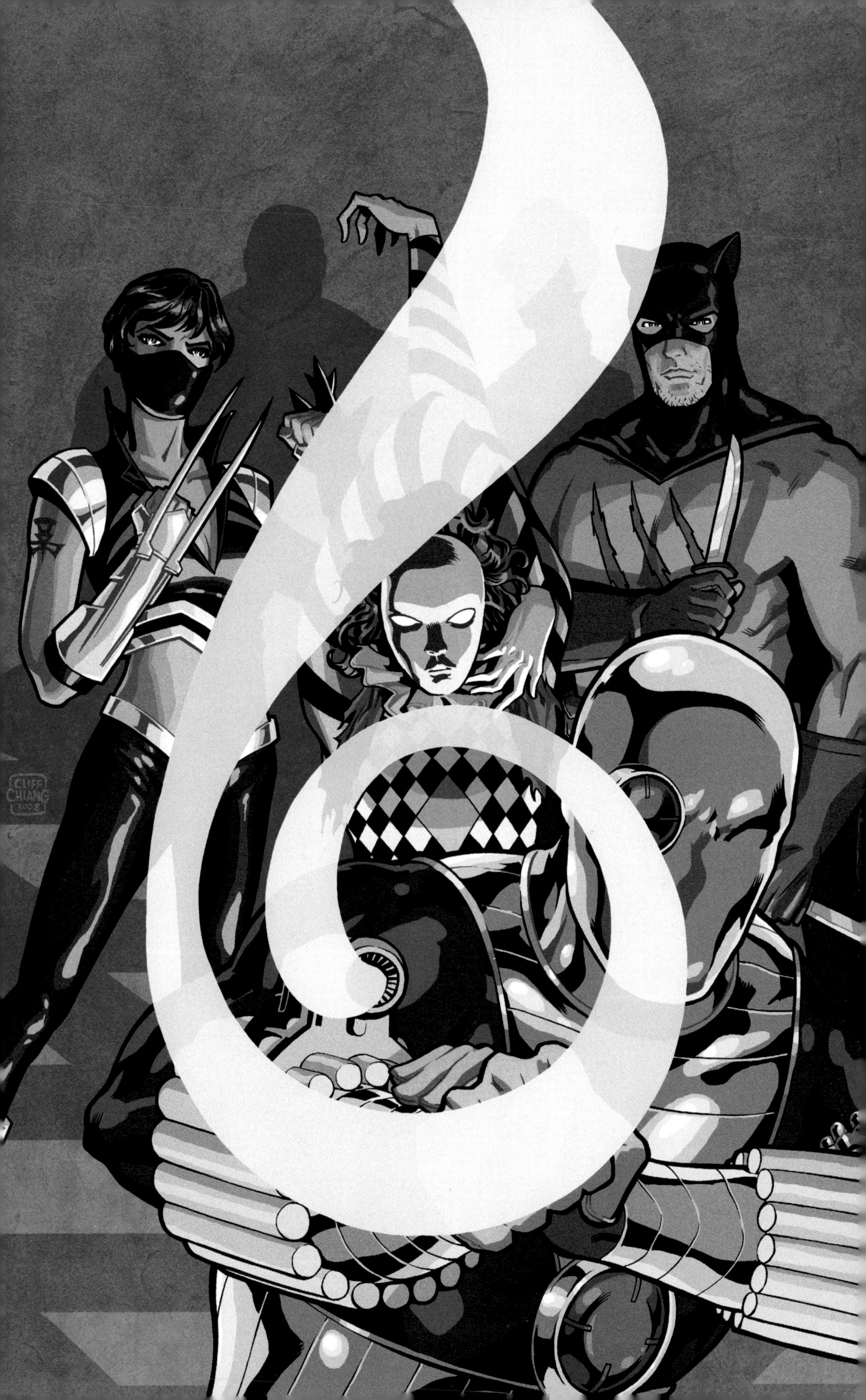
CLIFF
CHIANG
2008

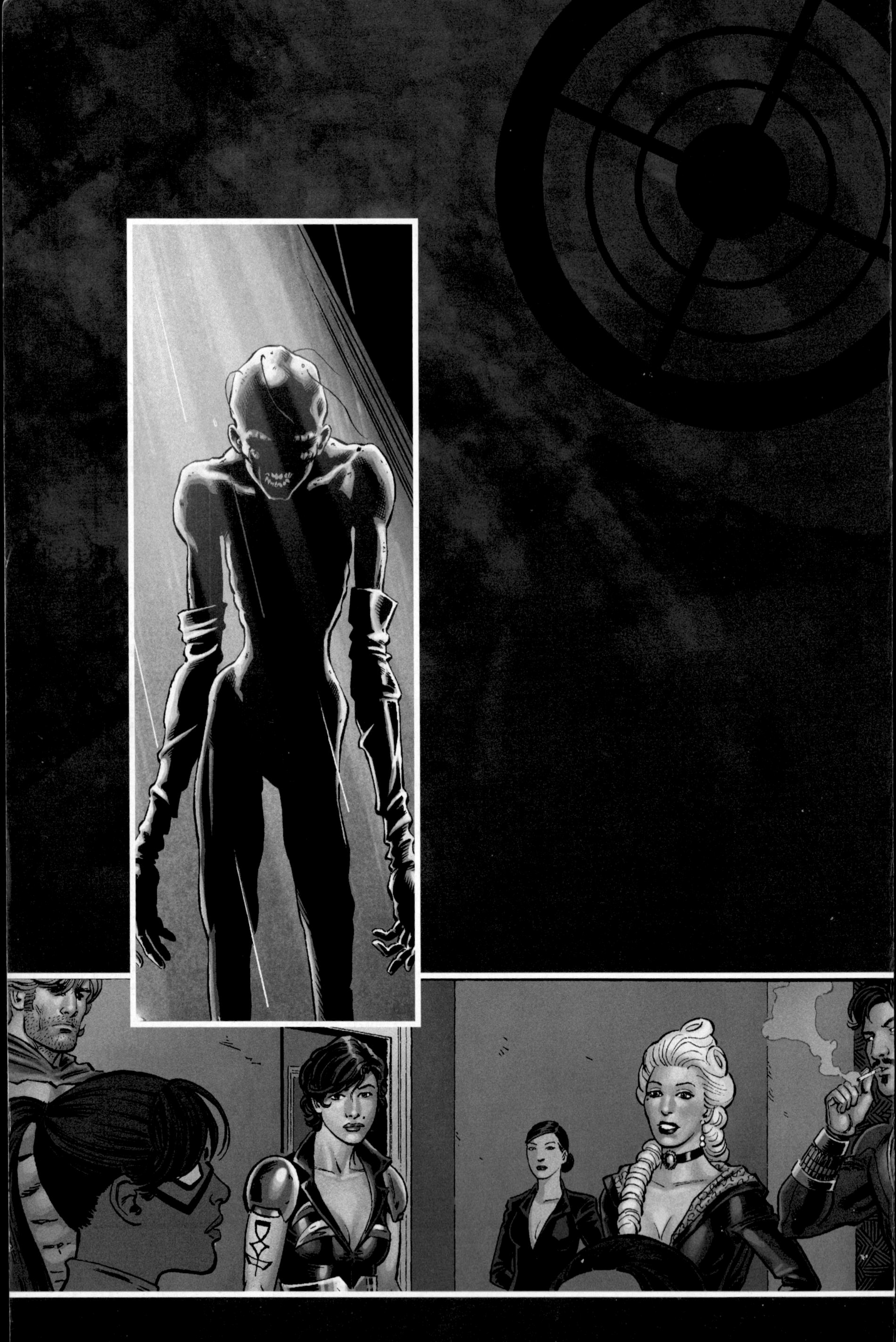

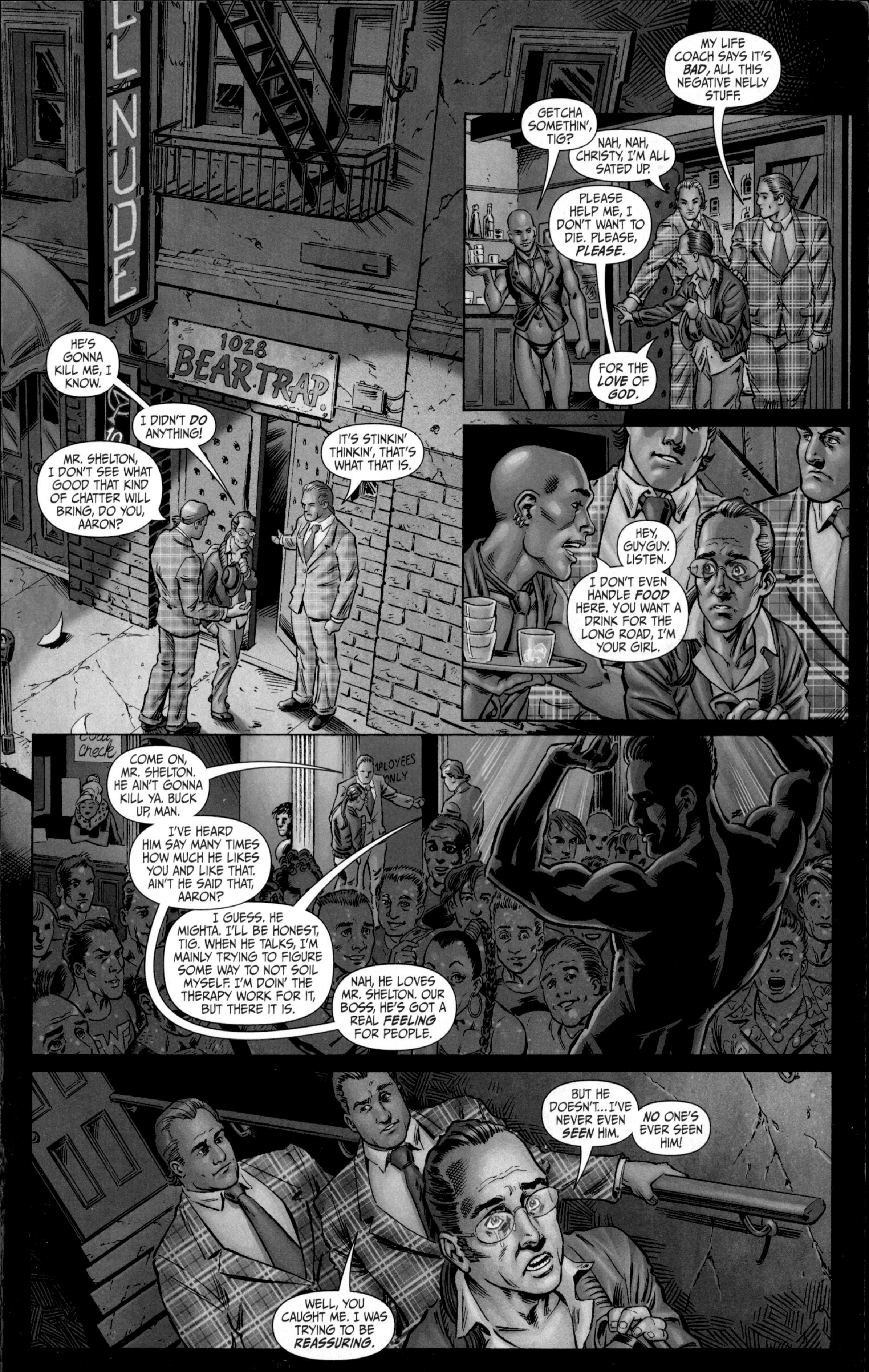

ALL NUDE
1028 BEAR TRAP
HE'S GONNA KILL ME, I KNOW.
I DIDN'T DO ANYTHING!
MR. SHELTON, I DON'T SEE WHAT GOOD THAT KIND OF CHATTER WILL BRING, DO YOU, AARON?
IT'S STINKIN' THINKIN', THAT'S WHAT THAT IS.
MY LIFE COACH SAYS IT'S BAD, ALL THIS NEGATIVE NELLY STUFF.
GETCHA SOMETHIN', TIG?
NAH, NAH, CHRISTY, I'M ALL SATED UP.
PLEASE HELP ME, I DON'T WANT TO DIE. PLEASE, PLEASE.
FOR THE LOVE OF GOD.
HEY, GUYGUY. LISTEN.
I DON'T EVEN HANDLE FOOD HERE. YOU WANT A DRINK FOR THE LONG ROAD, I'M YOUR GIRL.
COAT CHECK
EMPLOYEES ONLY
COME ON, MR. SHELTON. HE AIN'T GONNA KILL YA. BUCK UP, MAN.
I'VE HEARD HIM SAY MANY TIMES HOW MUCH HE LIKES YOU AND LIKE THAT. AIN'T HE SAID THAT, AARON?
I GUESS. HE MIGHTA. I'LL BE HONEST, TIG. WHEN HE TALKS, I'M MAINLY TRYING TO FIGURE SOME WAY TO NOT SOIL MYSELF. I'M DOIN' THE THERAPY WORK FOR IT, BUT THERE IT IS.
NAH, HE LOVES MR. SHELTON. OUR BOSS, HE'S GOT A REAL FEELING FOR PEOPLE.
BUT HE DOESN'T... I'VE NEVER EVEN SEEN HIM.
NO ONE'S EVER SEEN HIM!
WELL, YOU CAUGHT ME. I WAS TRYING TO BE REASSURING.

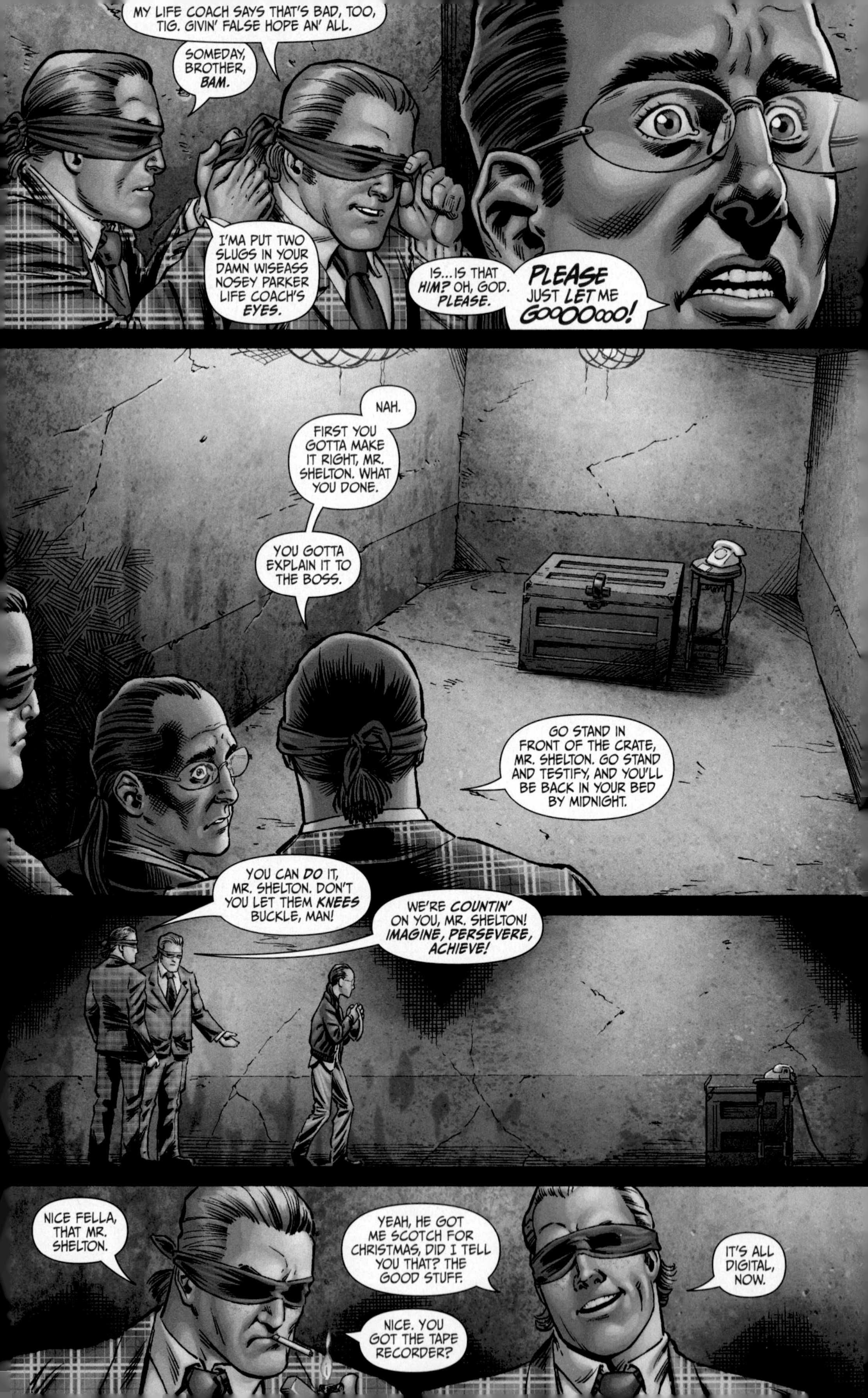
MY LIFE COACH SAYS THAT'S BAD, TOO, TIG. GIVIN' FALSE HOPE AN' ALL.
SOMEDAY, BROTHER, BAM.
I'MA PUT TWO SLUGS IN YOUR DAMN WISEASS NOSEY PARKER LIFE COACH'S EYES.
IS...IS THAT HIM? OH, GOD. PLEASE.
PLEASE JUST LET ME GOOOOooo!
NAH.
FIRST YOU GOTTA MAKE IT RIGHT, MR. SHELTON. WHAT YOU DONE.
YOU GOTTA EXPLAIN IT TO THE BOSS.
GO STAND IN FRONT OF THE CRATE, MR. SHELTON. GO STAND AND TESTIFY, AND YOU'LL BE BACK IN YOUR BED BY MIDNIGHT.
YOU CAN DO IT, MR. SHELTON. DON'T YOU LET THEM KNEES BUCKLE, MAN!
WE'RE COUNTIN' ON YOU, MR. SHELTON! IMAGINE, PERSEVERE, ACHIEVE!
NICE FELLA, THAT MR. SHELTON.
YEAH, HE GOT ME SCOTCH FOR CHRISTMAS, DID I TELL YOU THAT? THE GOOD STUFF.
NICE. YOU GOT THE TAPE RECORDER?
IT'S ALL DIGITAL, NOW.

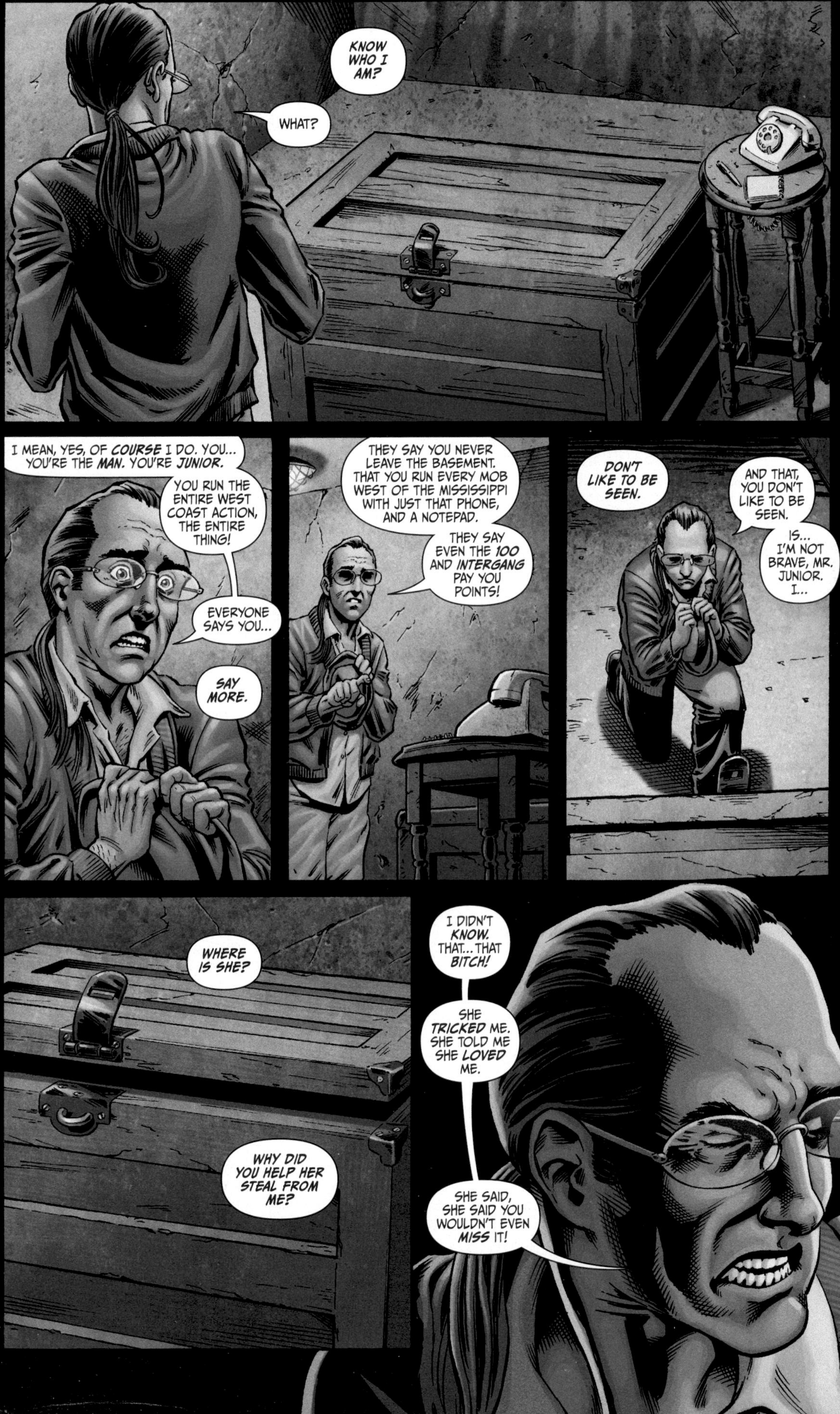
KNOW WHO I AM?
WHAT?
I MEAN, YES, OF COURSE I DO. YOU... YOU'RE THE MAN. YOU'RE JUNIOR.
YOU RUN THE ENTIRE WEST COAST ACTION, THE ENTIRE THING!
EVERYONE SAYS YOU...
SAY MORE.
THEY SAY YOU NEVER LEAVE THE BASEMENT. THAT YOU RUN EVERY MOB WEST OF THE MISSISSIPPI WITH JUST THAT PHONE, AND A NOTEPAD.
THEY SAY EVEN THE 100 AND INTERGANG PAY YOU POINTS!
DON'T LIKE TO BE SEEN.
AND THAT, YOU DON'T LIKE TO BE SEEN.
IS... I'M NOT BRAVE, MR. JUNIOR. I...
WHERE IS SHE?
WHY DID YOU HELP HER STEAL FROM ME?
I DIDN'T KNOW. THAT... THAT BITCH!
SHE TRICKED ME. SHE TOLD ME SHE LOVED ME.
SHE SAID, SHE SAID YOU WOULDN'T EVEN MISS IT!

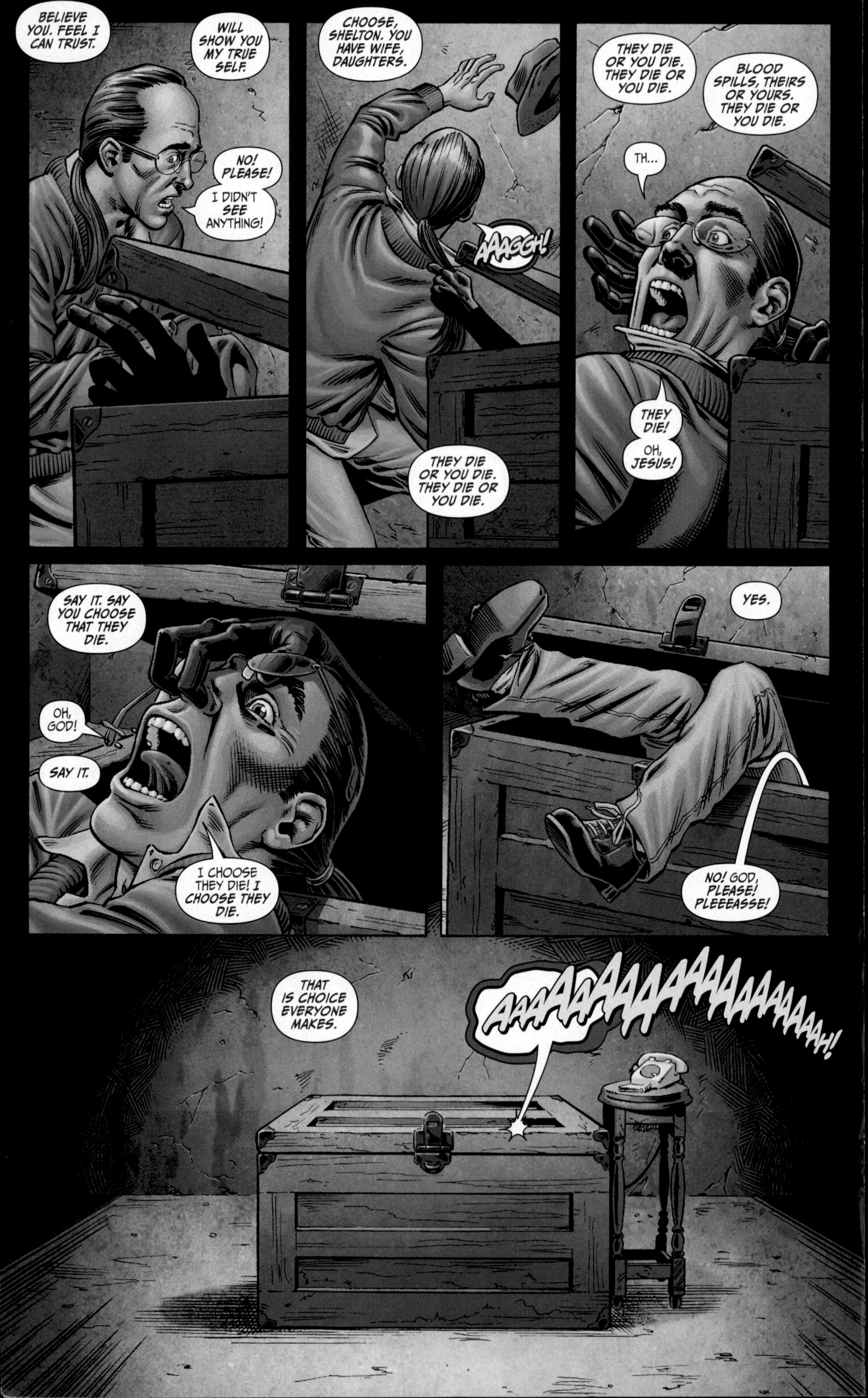
BELIEVE YOU. FEEL I CAN TRUST.
WILL SHOW YOU MY TRUE SELF.
NO! PLEASE!
I DIDN'T SEE ANYTHING!
CHOOSE, SHELTON. YOU HAVE WIFE, DAUGHTERS.
AAAGGH!
THEY DIE OR YOU DIE. THEY DIE OR YOU DIE.
THEY DIE OR YOU DIE. THEY DIE OR YOU DIE.
BLOOD SPILLS, THEIRS OR YOURS. THEY DIE OR YOU DIE.
TH...
THEY DIE!
OH, JESUS!
SAY IT. SAY YOU CHOOSE THAT THEY DIE.
OH, GOD!
SAY IT.
I CHOOSE THEY DIE! I CHOOSE THEY DIE.
YES.
NO! GOD, PLEASE! PLEEEASSE!
THAT IS CHOICE EVERYONE MAKES.
AAAAAAAAAAAAAAAAAAAAAAH!

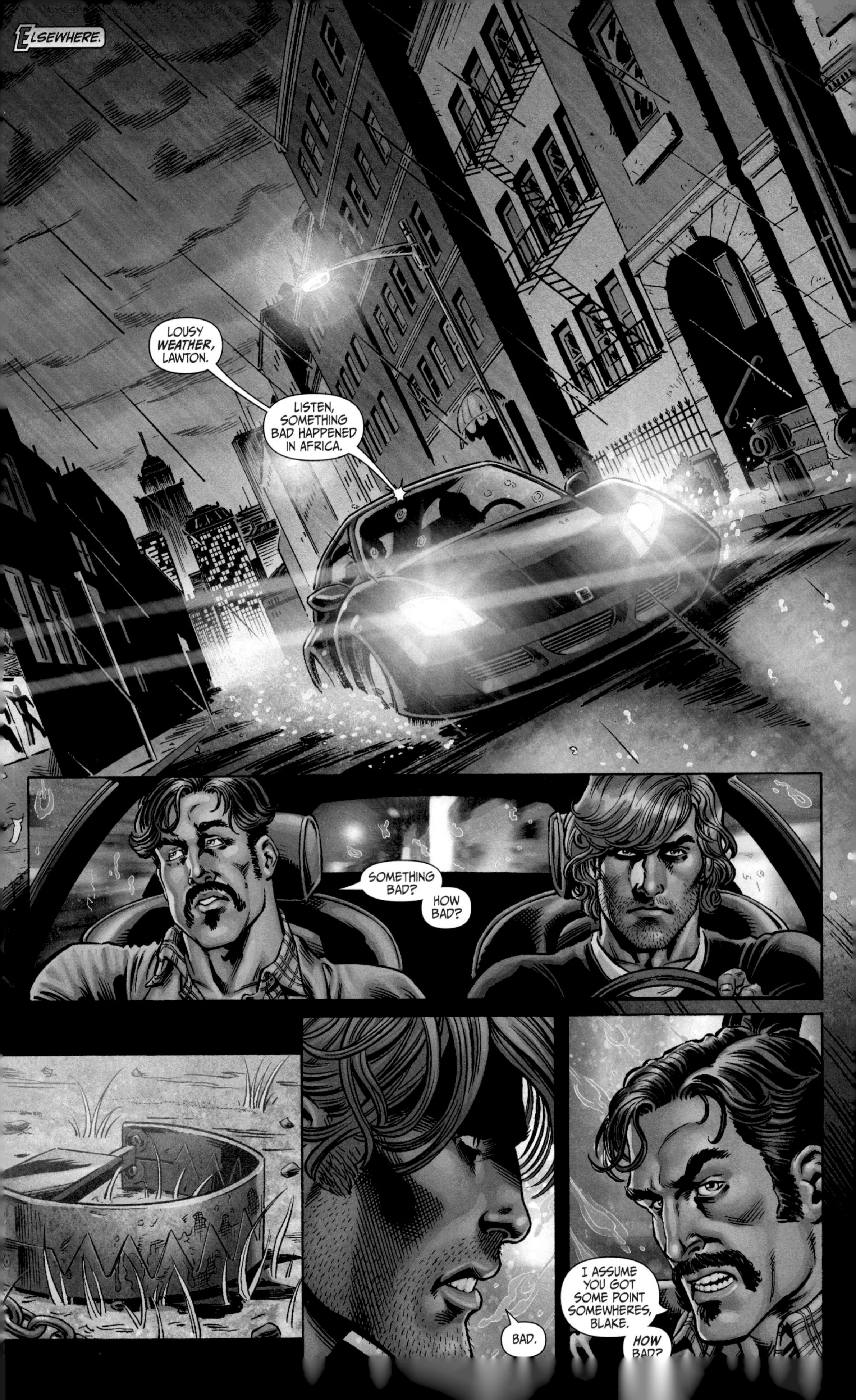
ELSEWHERE.
LOUSY WEATHER, LAWTON.
LISTEN, SOMETHING BAD HAPPENED IN AFRICA.
SOMETHING BAD?
HOW BAD?
BAD.
I ASSUME YOU GOT SOME POINT SOMEWHERES, BLAKE.
HOW BAD?

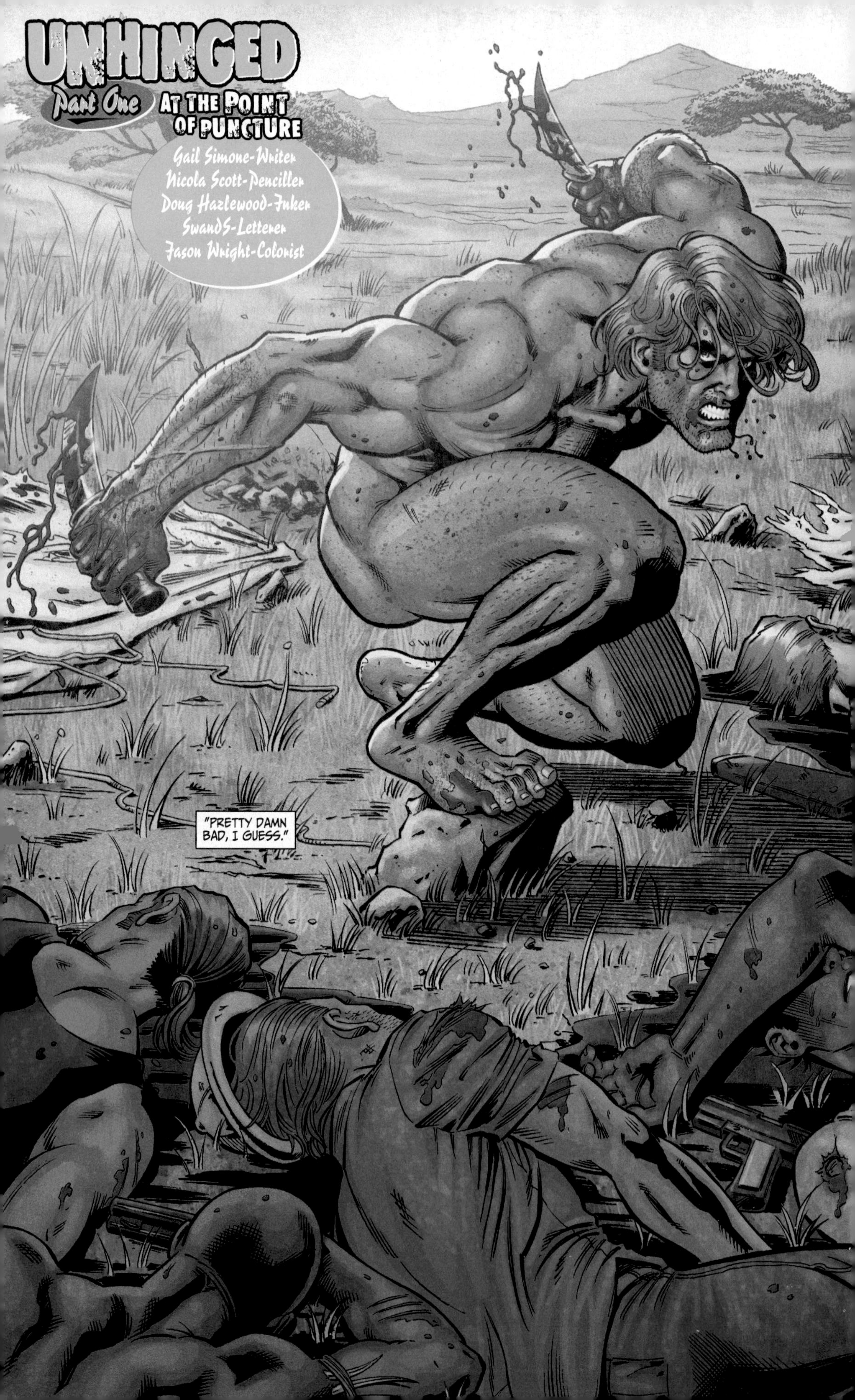
UNHINGED
Part One
AT THE POINT OF PUNCTURE
Gail Simone-Writer
Nicola Scott-Penciller
Doug Hazlewood-Inker
SwandS-Letterer
Jason Wright-Colorist
"PRETTY DAMN BAD, I GUESS."

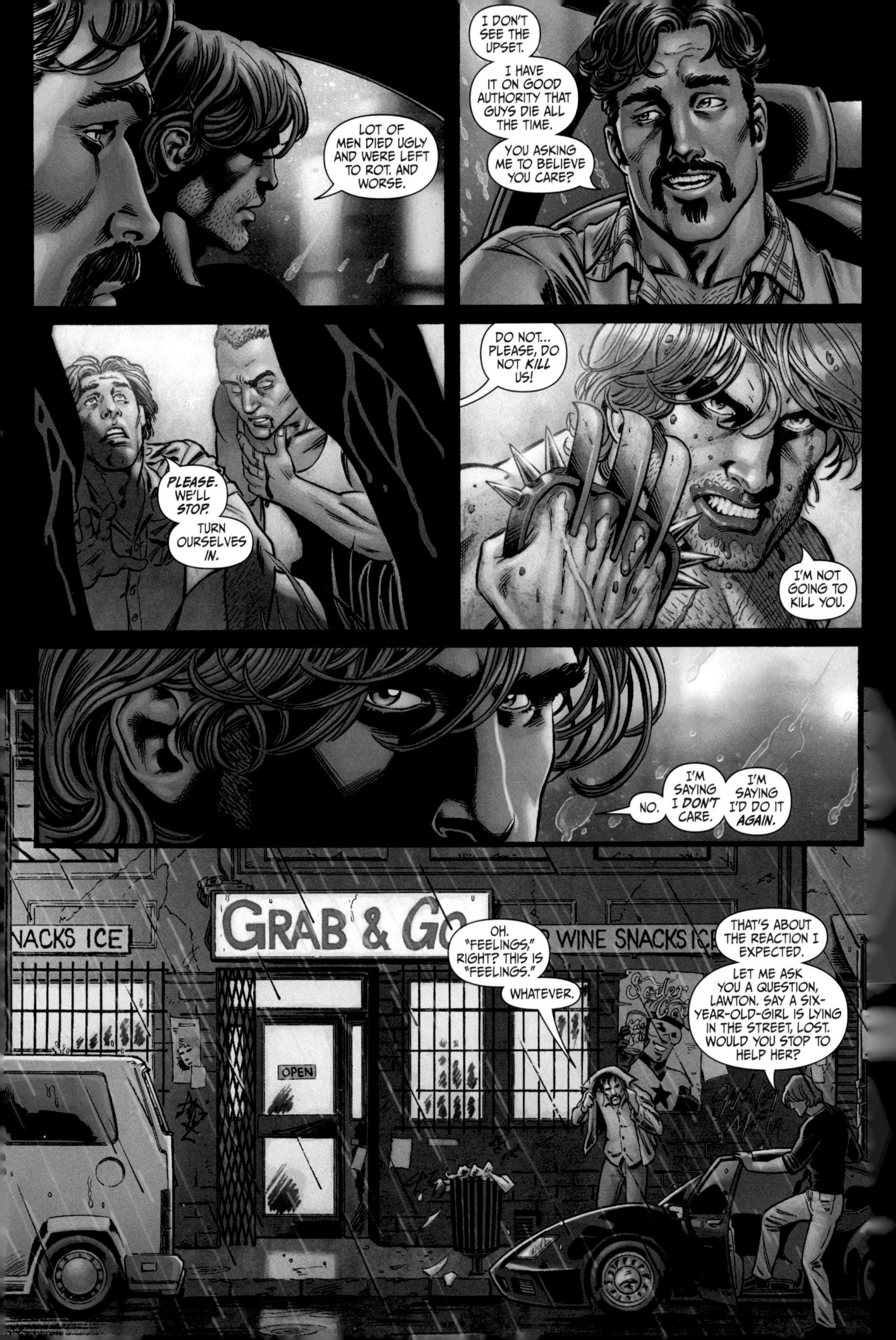
LOT OF MEN DIED UGLY AND WERE LEFT TO ROT. AND WORSE.
I DON'T SEE THE UPSET.
I HAVE IT ON GOOD AUTHORITY THAT GUYS DIE ALL THE TIME.
YOU ASKING ME TO BELIEVE YOU CARE?
PLEASE. WE'LL STOP.
TURN OURSELVES IN.
DO NOT... PLEASE, DO NOT KILL US!
I'M NOT GOING TO KILL YOU.
NO.
I'M SAYING I DON'T CARE.
I'M SAYING I'D DO IT AGAIN.
NACKS ICE
GRAB & GO
WINE SNACKS ICE
OPEN
OH. "FEELINGS," RIGHT? THIS IS "FEELINGS."
WHATEVER.
THAT'S ABOUT THE REACTION I EXPECTED.
LET ME ASK YOU A QUESTION, LAWTON. SAY A SIX-YEAR-OLD-GIRL IS LYING IN THE STREET, LOST. WOULD YOU STOP TO HELP HER?

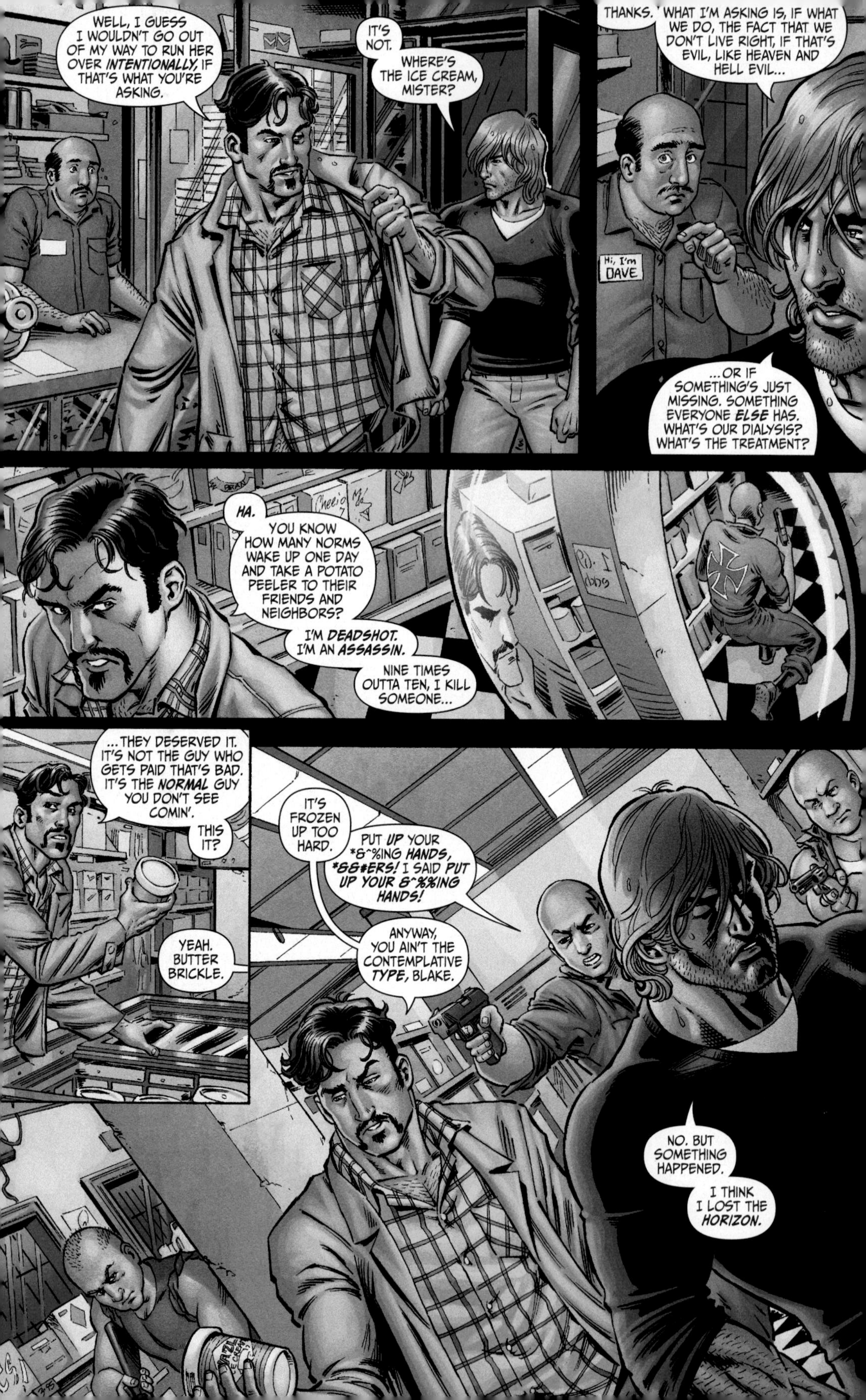
WELL, I GUESS I WOULDN'T GO OUT OF MY WAY TO RUN HER OVER *INTENTIONALLY,* IF THAT'S WHAT YOU'RE ASKING.
IT'S NOT.
WHERE'S THE ICE CREAM, MISTER?
THANKS.
WHAT I'M ASKING IS, IF WHAT WE DO, THE FACT THAT WE DON'T LIVE RIGHT, IF THAT'S EVIL, LIKE HEAVEN AND HELL EVIL...
Hi, I'm DAVE
...OR IF SOMETHING'S JUST MISSING. SOMETHING EVERYONE *ELSE* HAS. WHAT'S OUR DIALYSIS? WHAT'S THE TREATMENT?
HA.
YOU KNOW HOW MANY NORMS WAKE UP ONE DAY AND TAKE A POTATO PEELER TO THEIR FRIENDS AND NEIGHBORS?
I'M *DEADSHOT.* I'M AN *ASSASSIN.*
NINE TIMES OUTTA TEN, I KILL SOMEONE...
...THEY DESERVED IT. IT'S NOT THE GUY WHO GETS PAID THAT'S BAD. IT'S THE *NORMAL* GUY YOU DON'T SEE COMIN'.
THIS IT?
YEAH. BUTTER BRICKLE.
IT'S FROZEN UP TOO HARD.
PUT *UP* YOUR *&^%ING *HANDS,* **&$#ERS!* I SAID *PUT UP YOUR &^%$ING HANDS!*
ANYWAY, YOU AIN'T THE CONTEMPLATIVE *TYPE,* BLAKE.
NO. BUT SOMETHING HAPPENED.
I THINK I LOST THE *HORIZON.*

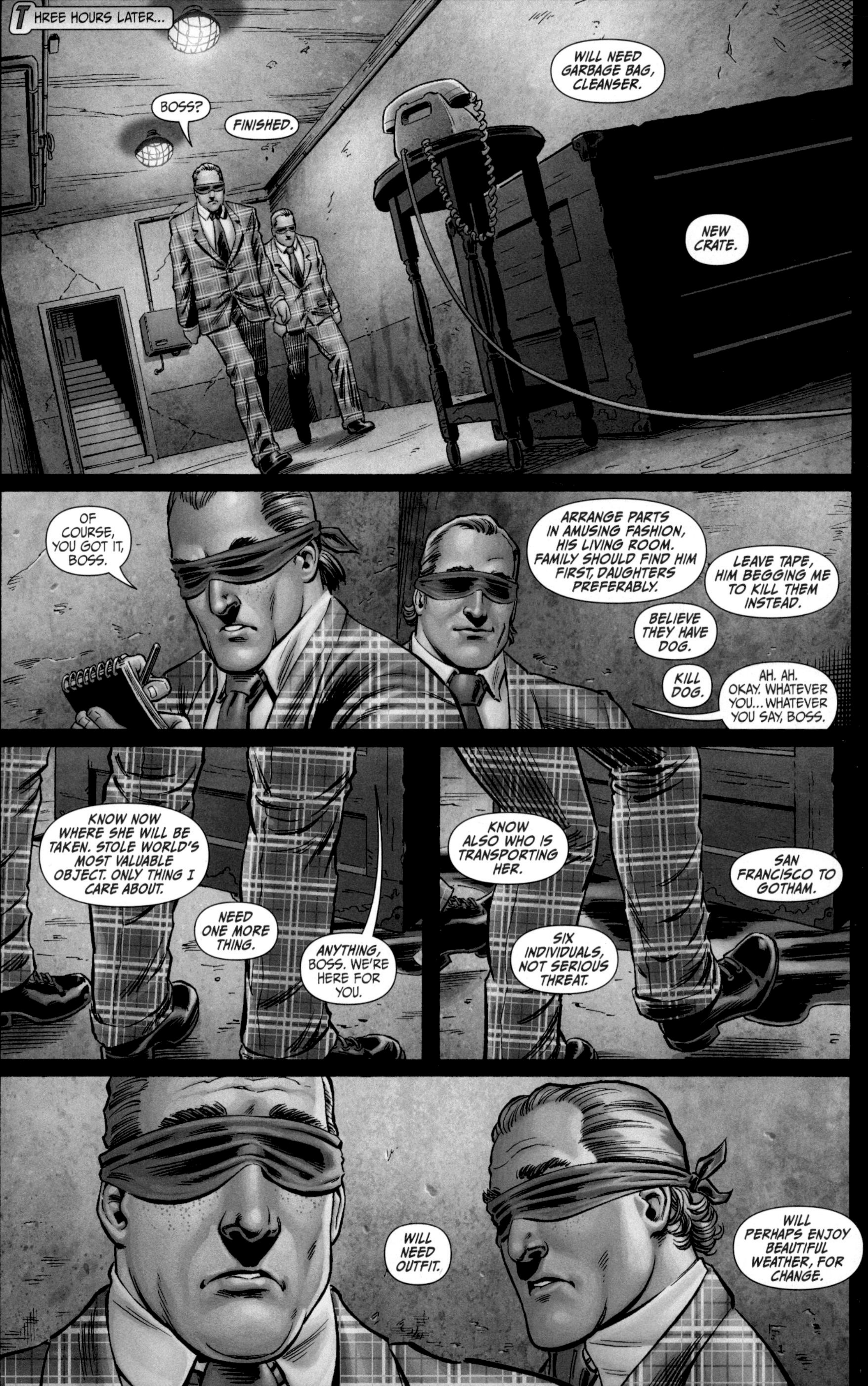
THREE HOURS LATER...
BOSS?
FINISHED.
WILL NEED GARBAGE BAG, CLEANSER.
NEW CRATE.
OF COURSE, YOU GOT IT, BOSS.
ARRANGE PARTS IN AMUSING FASHION, HIS LIVING ROOM. FAMILY SHOULD FIND HIM FIRST, DAUGHTERS PREFERABLY.
LEAVE TAPE, HIM BEGGING ME TO KILL THEM INSTEAD.
BELIEVE THEY HAVE DOG.
KILL DOG.
AH. AH. OKAY. WHATEVER YOU...WHATEVER YOU SAY, BOSS.
KNOW NOW WHERE SHE WILL BE TAKEN. STOLE WORLD'S MOST VALUABLE OBJECT. ONLY THING I CARE ABOUT.
NEED ONE MORE THING.
ANYTHING, BOSS. WE'RE HERE FOR YOU.
KNOW ALSO WHO IS TRANSPORTING HER.
SIX INDIVIDUALS, NOT SERIOUS THREAT.
SAN FRANCISCO TO GOTHAM.
WILL NEED OUTFIT.
WILL PERHAPS ENJOY BEAUTIFUL WEATHER, FOR CHANGE.

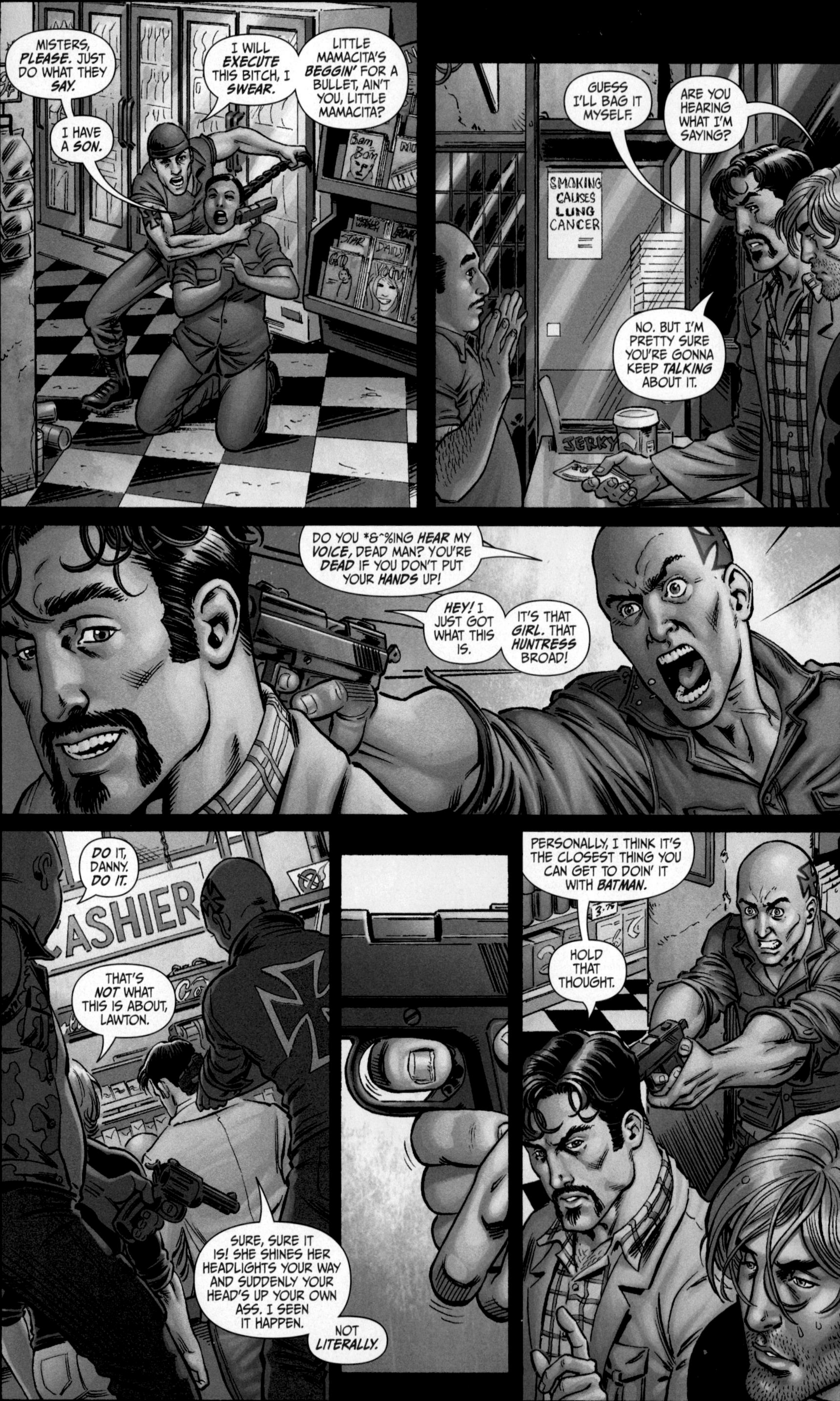
MISTERS, PLEASE. JUST DO WHAT THEY SAY.
I HAVE A SON.
I WILL EXECUTE THIS BITCH, I SWEAR.
LITTLE MAMACITA'S BEGGIN' FOR A BULLET, AIN'T YOU, LITTLE MAMACITA?
GUESS I'LL BAG IT MYSELF.
ARE YOU HEARING WHAT I'M SAYING?
SMOKING CAUSES LUNG CANCER
NO. BUT I'M PRETTY SURE YOU'RE GONNA KEEP TALKING ABOUT IT.
JERKY
DO YOU *&^%ING HEAR MY VOICE, DEAD MAN? YOU'RE DEAD IF YOU DON'T PUT YOUR HANDS UP!
HEY! I JUST GOT WHAT THIS IS.
IT'S THAT GIRL. THAT HUNTRESS BROAD!
DO IT, DANNY. DO IT.
CASHIER
THAT'S NOT WHAT THIS IS ABOUT, LAWTON.
SURE, SURE IT IS! SHE SHINES HER HEADLIGHTS YOUR WAY AND SUDDENLY YOUR HEAD'S UP YOUR OWN ASS. I SEEN IT HAPPEN.
NOT LITERALLY.
PERSONALLY, I THINK IT'S THE CLOSEST THING YOU CAN GET TO DOIN' IT WITH BATMAN.
HOLD THAT THOUGHT.

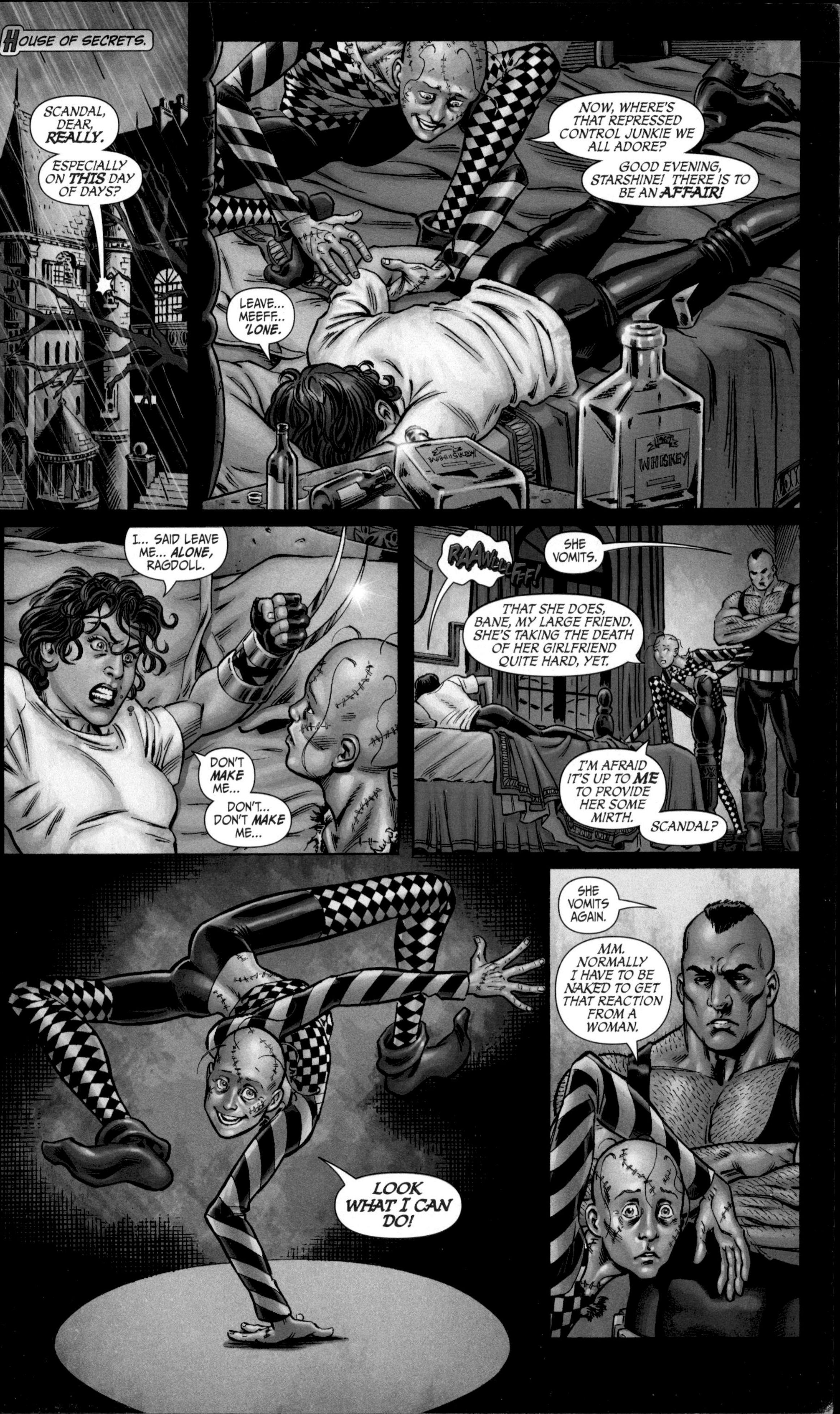
HOUSE OF SECRETS.
SCANDAL, DEAR, REALLY.
ESPECIALLY ON THIS DAY OF DAYS?
NOW, WHERE'S THAT REPRESSED CONTROL JUNKIE WE ALL ADORE?
GOOD EVENING, STARSHINE! THERE IS TO BE AN AFFAIR!
LEAVE... MEEFF... 'LONE.
WHISKEY
I... SAID LEAVE ME... ALONE, RAGDOLL.
DON'T MAKE ME...
DON'T... DON'T MAKE ME...
RAAWLLLFFF!
SHE VOMITS.
THAT SHE DOES, BANE, MY LARGE FRIEND. SHE'S TAKING THE DEATH OF HER GIRLFRIEND QUITE HARD, YET.
I'M AFRAID IT'S UP TO ME TO PROVIDE HER SOME MIRTH.
SCANDAL?
LOOK WHAT I CAN DO!
SHE VOMITS AGAIN.
MM. NORMALLY I HAVE TO BE NAKED TO GET THAT REACTION FROM A WOMAN.

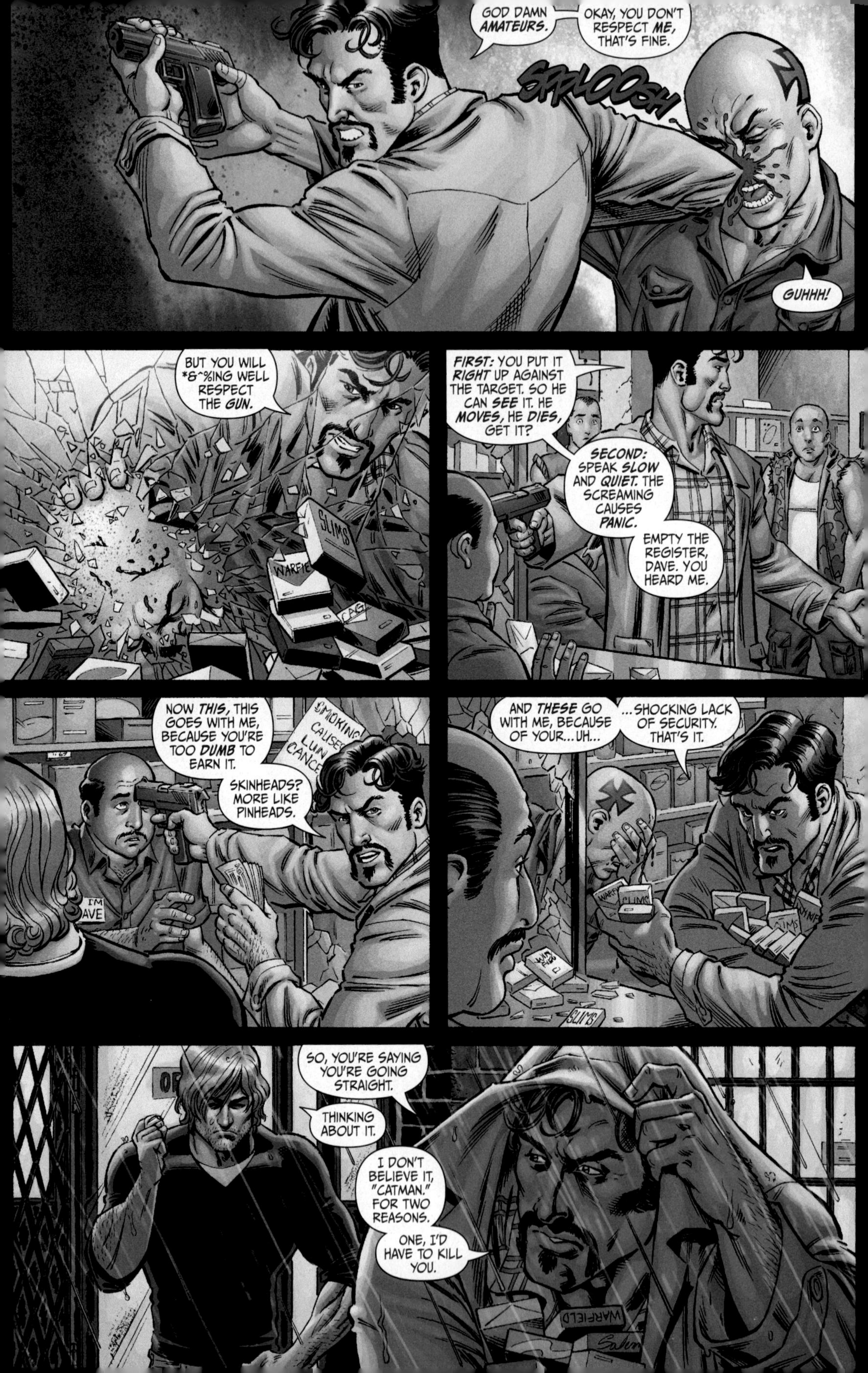
GOD DAMN AMATEURS.
OKAY, YOU DON'T RESPECT ME, THAT'S FINE.
SPPLOOOSH
GUHHH!
BUT YOU WILL *&^%ING WELL RESPECT THE GUN.
SLIMS
WARFIE
FIRST: YOU PUT IT RIGHT UP AGAINST THE TARGET. SO HE CAN SEE IT. HE MOVES, HE DIES, GET IT?
SECOND: SPEAK SLOW AND QUIET. THE SCREAMING CAUSES PANIC.
EMPTY THE REGISTER, DAVE. YOU HEARD ME.
NOW THIS, THIS GOES WITH ME, BECAUSE YOU'RE TOO DUMB TO EARN IT.
SKINHEADS? MORE LIKE PINHEADS.
AND THESE GO WITH ME, BECAUSE OF YOUR...UH...
...SHOCKING LACK OF SECURITY. THAT'S IT.
SO, YOU'RE SAYING YOU'RE GOING STRAIGHT.
THINKING ABOUT IT.
I DON'T BELIEVE IT, "CATMAN." FOR TWO REASONS.
ONE, I'D HAVE TO KILL YOU.
WARFIELD

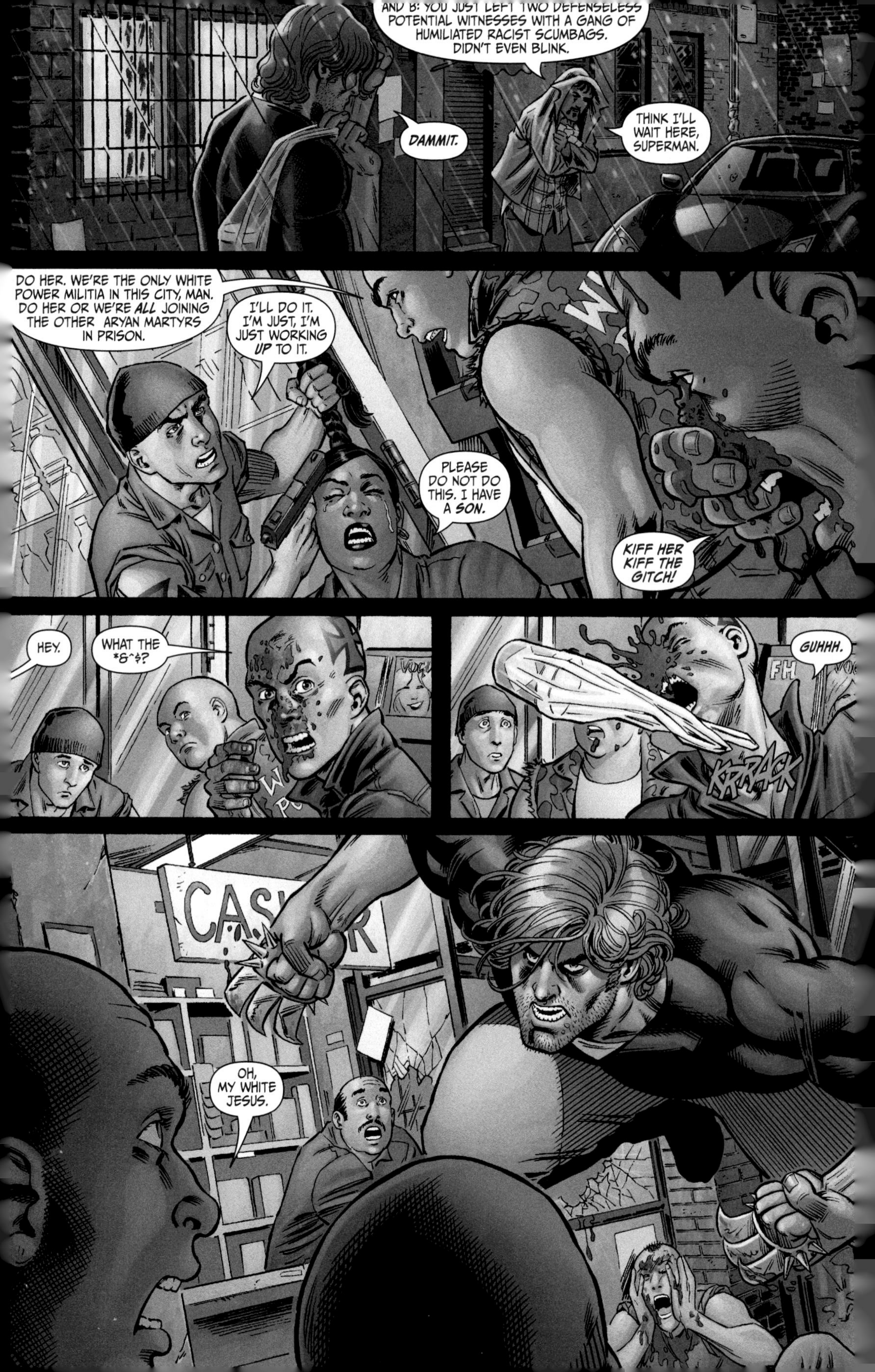
AND B: YOU JUST LEFT TWO DEFENSELESS POTENTIAL WITNESSES WITH A GANG OF HUMILIATED RACIST SCUMBAGS. DIDN'T EVEN BLINK.
DAMMIT.
THINK I'LL WAIT HERE, SUPERMAN.
DO HER. WE'RE THE ONLY WHITE POWER MILITIA IN THIS CITY, MAN. DO HER OR WE'RE ALL JOINING THE OTHER ARYAN MARTYRS IN PRISON.
I'LL DO IT. I'M JUST, I'M JUST WORKING UP TO IT.
PLEASE DO NOT DO THIS. I HAVE A SON.
KIFF HER KIFF THE GITCH!
HEY.
WHAT THE *&^$?
GUHHH.
KRRACK
CASHIER
OH, MY WHITE JESUS.

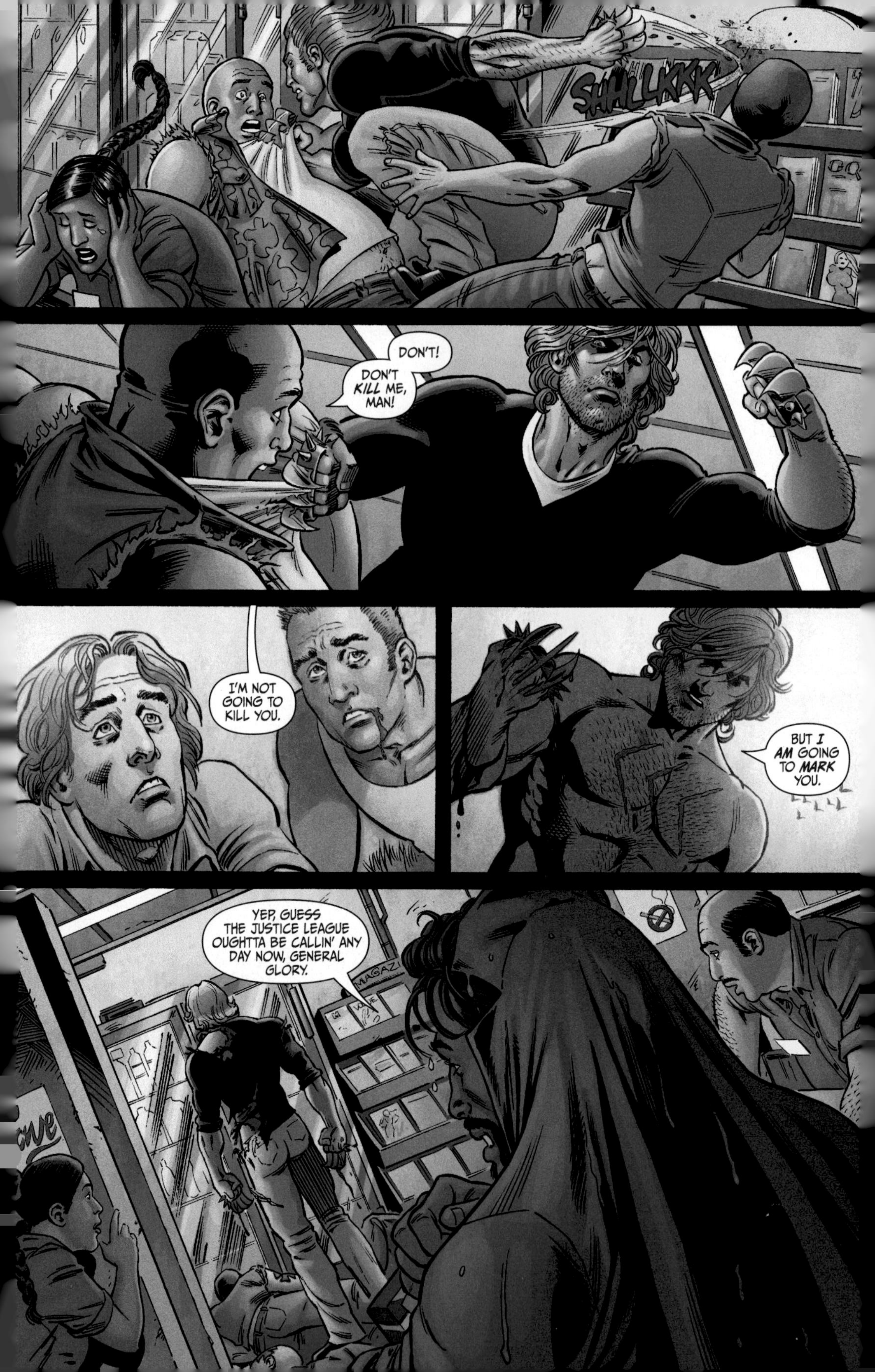
SHHLLKKK
DON'T!
DON'T KILL ME, MAN!
I'M NOT GOING TO KILL YOU.
BUT I AM GOING TO MARK YOU.
YEP, GUESS THE JUSTICE LEAGUE OUGHTTA BE CALLIN' ANY DAY NOW, GENERAL GLORY.

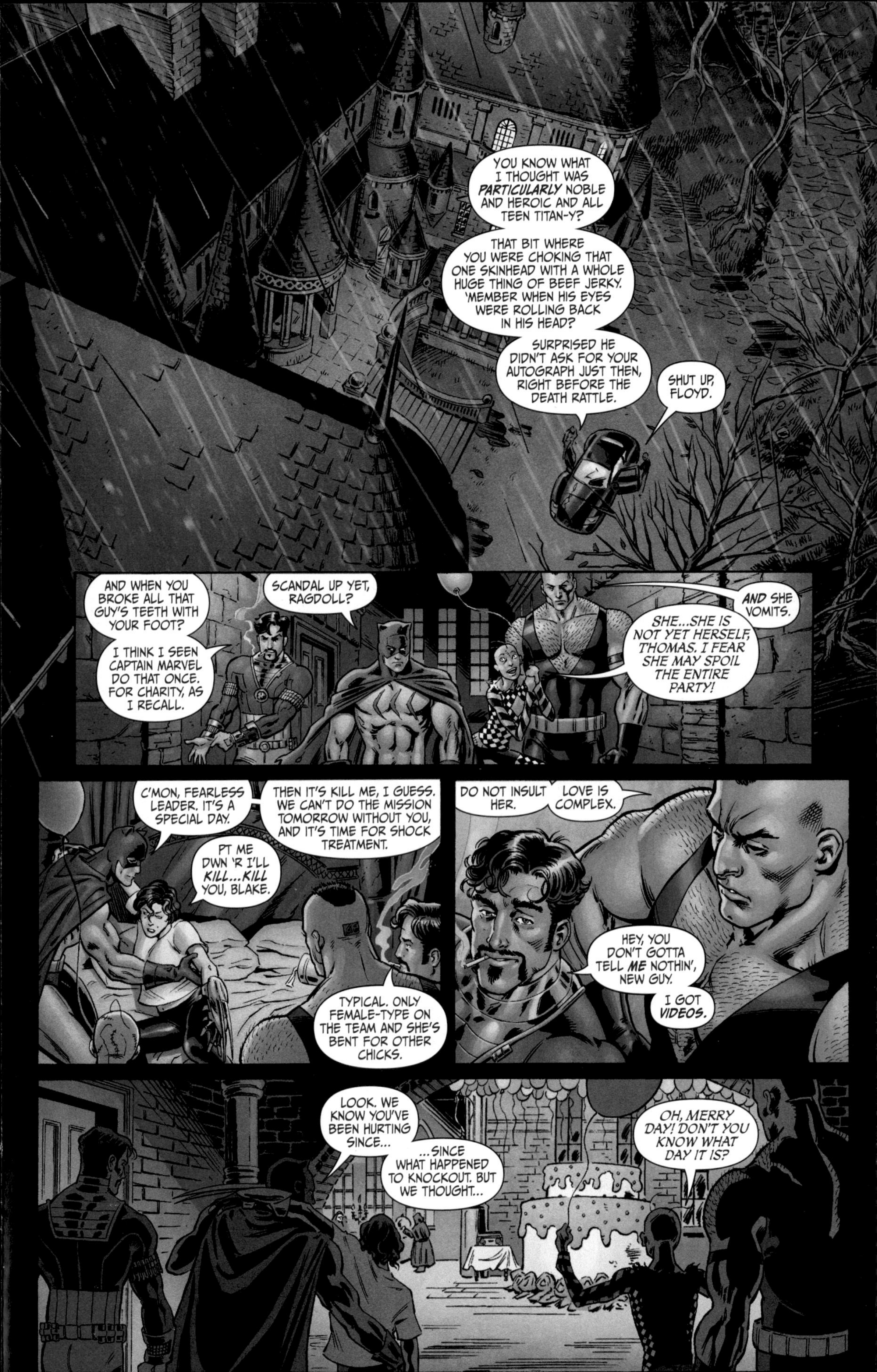
YOU KNOW WHAT I THOUGHT WAS *PARTICULARLY* NOBLE AND HEROIC AND ALL TEEN TITAN-Y?
THAT BIT WHERE YOU WERE CHOKING THAT ONE SKINHEAD WITH A WHOLE HUGE THING OF BEEF JERKY. 'MEMBER WHEN HIS EYES WERE ROLLING BACK IN HIS HEAD?
SURPRISED HE DIDN'T ASK FOR YOUR AUTOGRAPH JUST THEN, RIGHT BEFORE THE DEATH RATTLE.
SHUT UP, FLOYD.
AND WHEN YOU BROKE ALL THAT GUY'S TEETH WITH YOUR FOOT?
I THINK I SEEN CAPTAIN MARVEL DO THAT ONCE. FOR CHARITY, AS I RECALL.
SCANDAL UP YET, RAGDOLL?
AND SHE VOMITS.
SHE...SHE IS NOT YET HERSELF, THOMAS. I FEAR SHE MAY SPOIL THE ENTIRE PARTY!
C'MON, FEARLESS LEADER. IT'S A SPECIAL DAY.
THEN IT'S KILL ME, I GUESS. WE CAN'T DO THE MISSION TOMORROW WITHOUT YOU, AND IT'S TIME FOR SHOCK TREATMENT.
PT ME DWN 'R I'LL *KILL...KILL* YOU, BLAKE.
TYPICAL. ONLY FEMALE-TYPE ON THE TEAM AND SHE'S BENT FOR OTHER CHICKS.
DO NOT INSULT HER.
LOVE IS COMPLEX.
HEY, YOU DON'T GOTTA TELL *ME* NOTHIN', NEW GUY.
I GOT *VIDEOS.*
LOOK. WE KNOW YOU'VE BEEN HURTING SINCE...
...SINCE WHAT HAPPENED TO KNOCKOUT. BUT WE THOUGHT...
OH, MERRY DAY! DON'T YOU KNOW WHAT DAY IT IS?

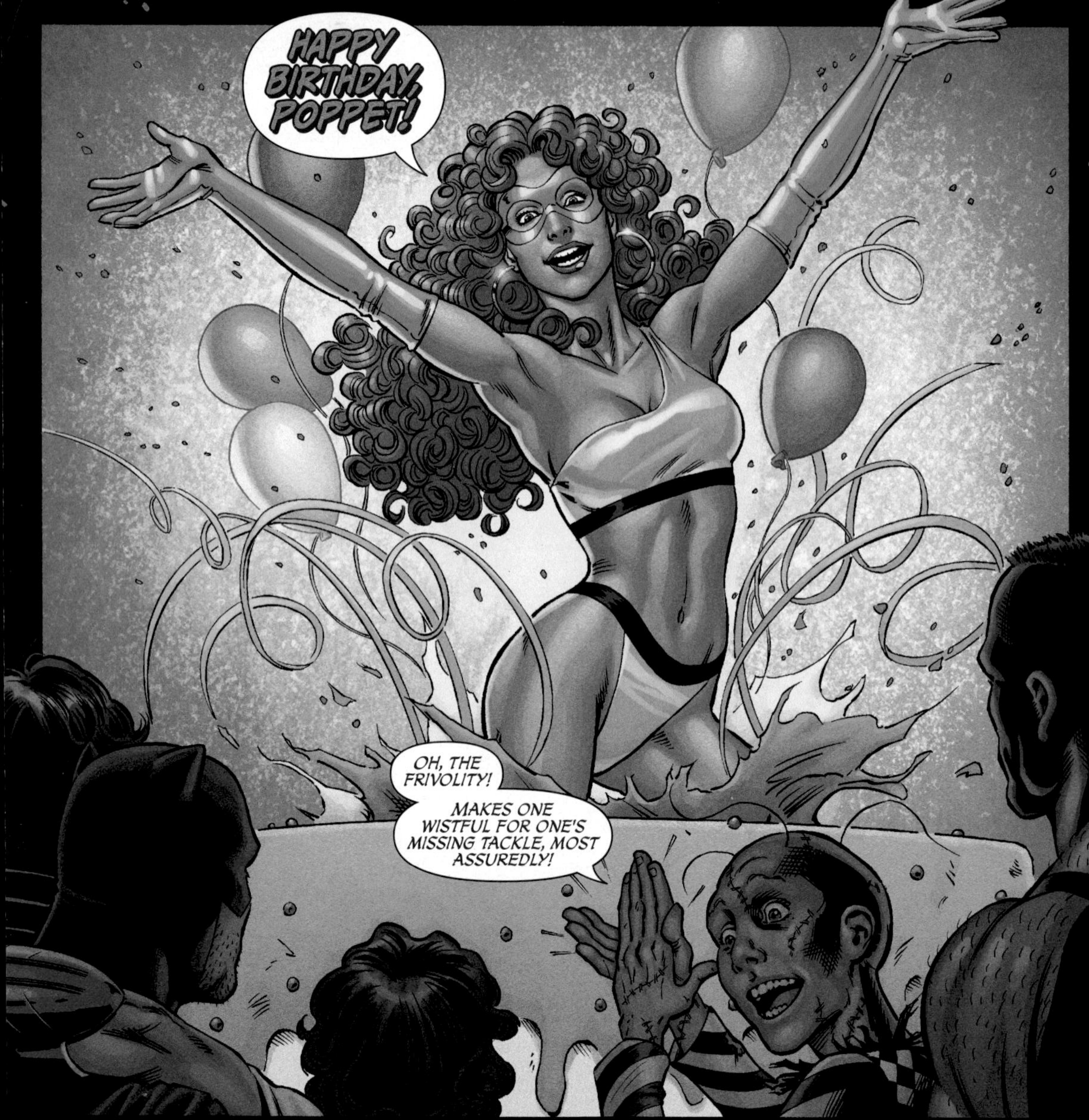
HAPPY BIRTHDAY, POPPET!
OH, THE FRIVOLITY!
MAKES ONE WISTFUL FOR ONE'S MISSING TACKLE, MOST ASSUREDLY!

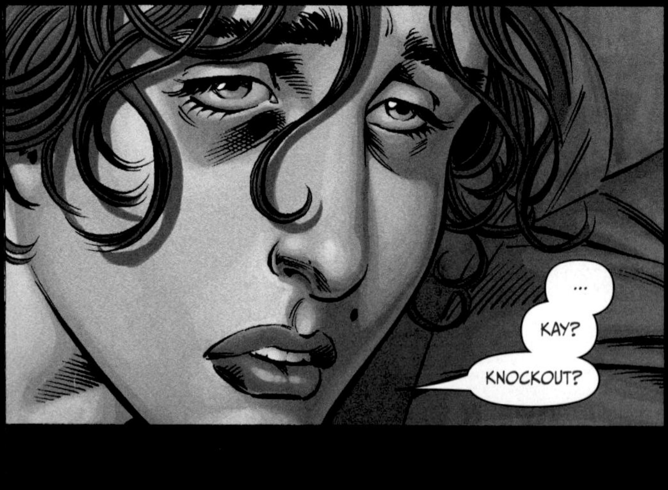
...
KAY?
KNOCKOUT?

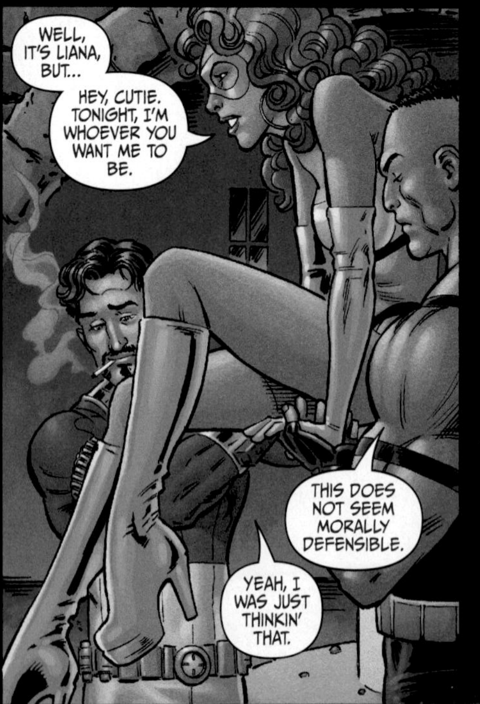
WELL, IT'S LIANA, BUT...
HEY, CUTIE. TONIGHT, I'M WHOEVER YOU WANT ME TO BE.
THIS DOES NOT SEEM MORALLY DEFENSIBLE.
YEAH, I WAS JUST THINKIN' THAT.

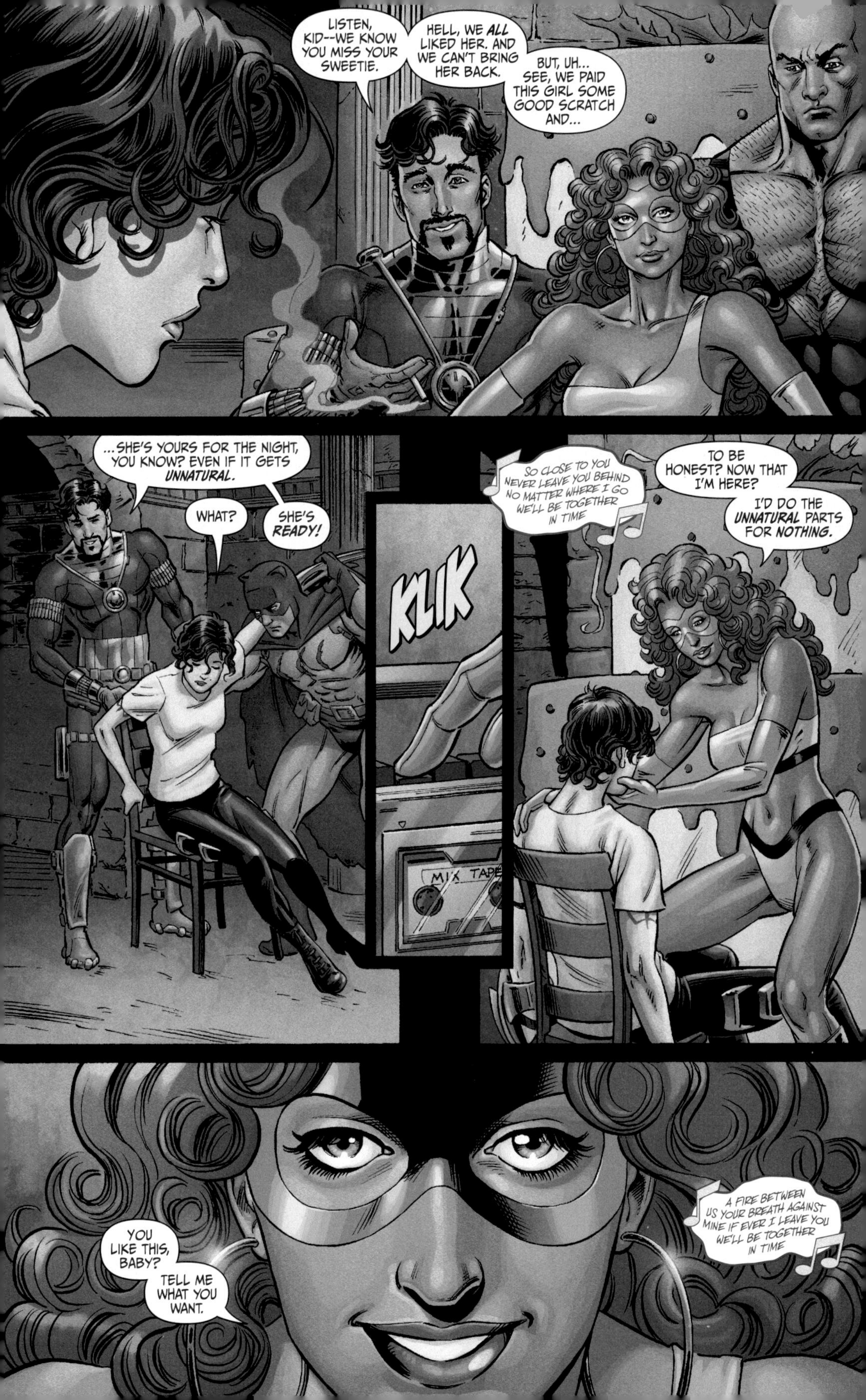
LISTEN, KID--WE KNOW YOU MISS YOUR SWEETIE.
HELL, WE ALL LIKED HER. AND WE CAN'T BRING HER BACK.
BUT, UH... SEE, WE PAID THIS GIRL SOME GOOD SCRATCH AND...
...SHE'S YOURS FOR THE NIGHT, YOU KNOW? EVEN IF IT GETS UNNATURAL.
WHAT?
SHE'S READY!
KLIK
MIX TAPE
SO CLOSE TO YOU NEVER LEAVE YOU BEHIND NO MATTER WHERE I GO WE'LL BE TOGETHER IN TIME
TO BE HONEST? NOW THAT I'M HERE?
I'D DO THE UNNATURAL PARTS FOR NOTHING.
YOU LIKE THIS, BABY?
TELL ME WHAT YOU WANT.
A FIRE BETWEEN US YOUR BREATH AGAINST MINE IF EVER I LEAVE YOU WE'LL BE TOGETHER IN TIME

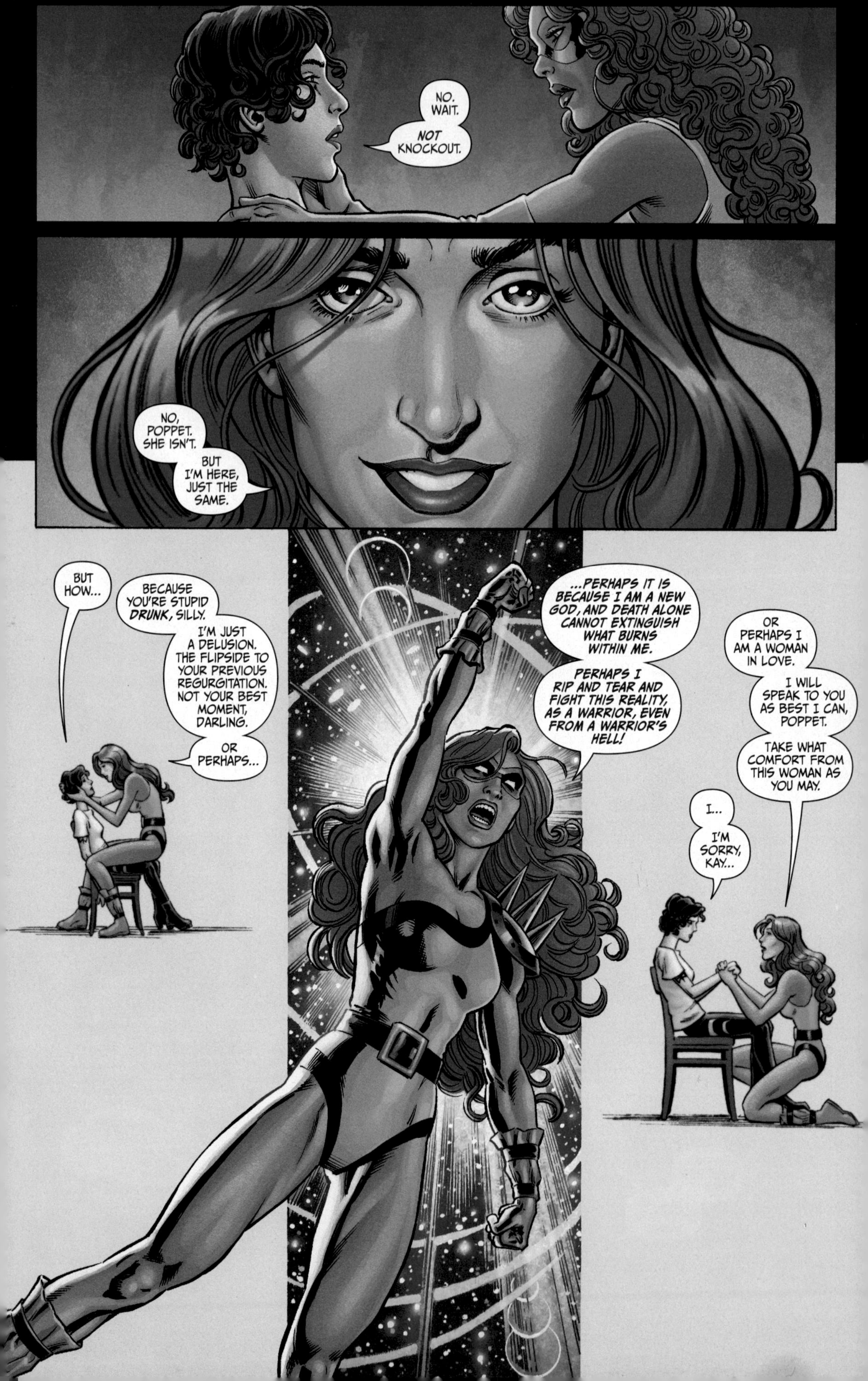

NO. WAIT.
NOT KNOCKOUT.
NO, POPPET. SHE ISN'T.
BUT I'M HERE, JUST THE SAME.
BUT HOW...
BECAUSE YOU'RE STUPID DRUNK, SILLY.
I'M JUST A DELUSION. THE FLIPSIDE TO YOUR PREVIOUS REGURGITATION. NOT YOUR BEST MOMENT, DARLING.
OR PERHAPS...
...PERHAPS IT IS BECAUSE I AM A NEW GOD, AND DEATH ALONE CANNOT EXTINGUISH WHAT BURNS WITHIN ME.
PERHAPS I RIP AND TEAR AND FIGHT THIS REALITY, AS A WARRIOR, EVEN FROM A WARRIOR'S HELL!
OR PERHAPS I AM A WOMAN IN LOVE.
I WILL SPEAK TO YOU AS BEST I CAN, POPPET.
TAKE WHAT COMFORT FROM THIS WOMAN AS YOU MAY.
I...
I'M SORRY, KAY...

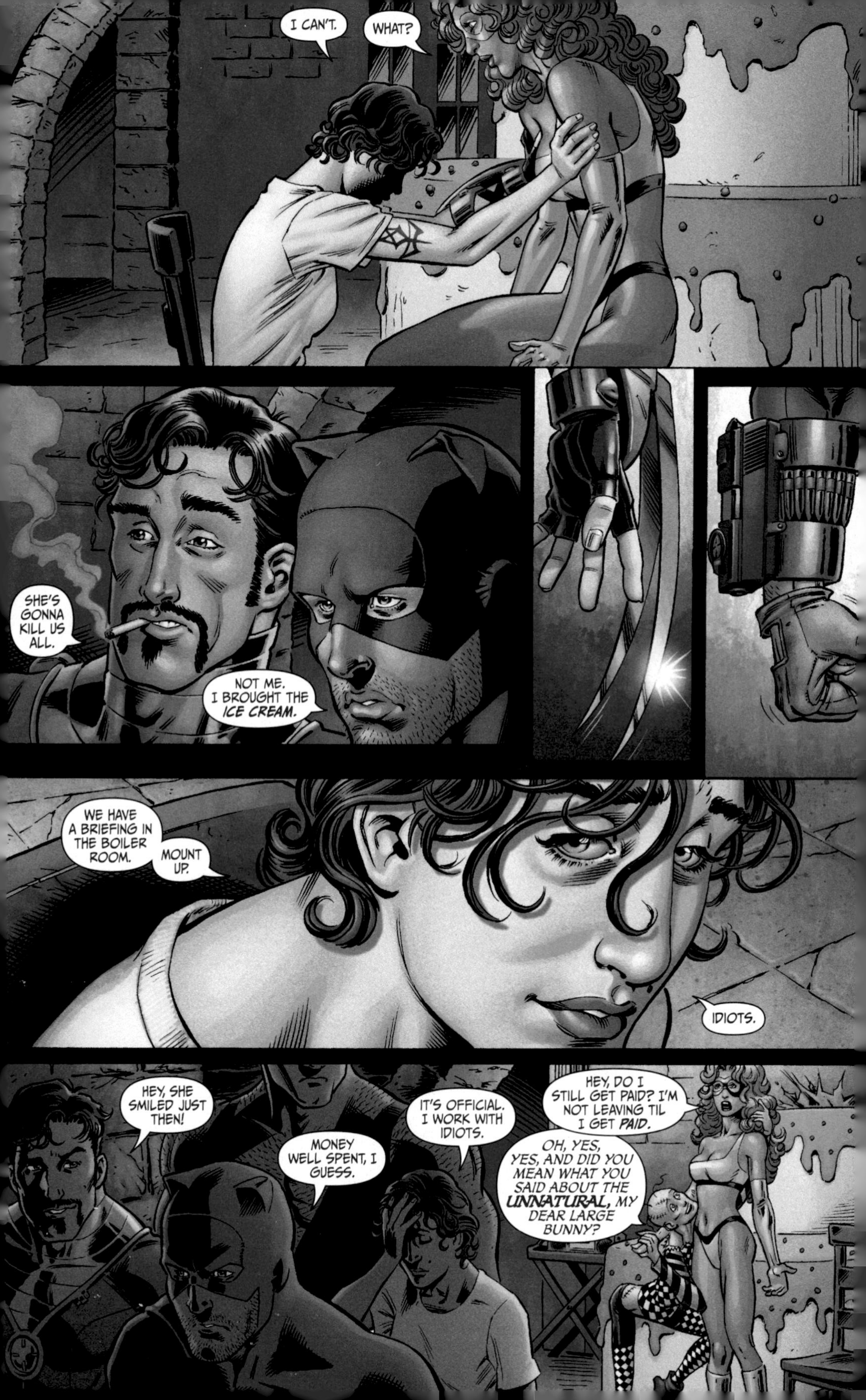
I CAN'T.
WHAT?
SHE'S GONNA KILL US ALL.
NOT ME. I BROUGHT THE *ICE CREAM.*
WE HAVE A BRIEFING IN THE BOILER ROOM.
MOUNT UP.
IDIOTS.
HEY, SHE SMILED JUST THEN!
MONEY WELL SPENT, I GUESS.
IT'S OFFICIAL. I WORK WITH IDIOTS.
HEY, DO I STILL GET PAID? I'M NOT LEAVING TIL I GET *PAID.*
OH, YES, YES, AND DID YOU MEAN WHAT YOU SAID ABOUT THE ***UNNATURAL,*** *MY DEAR LARGE BUNNY?*

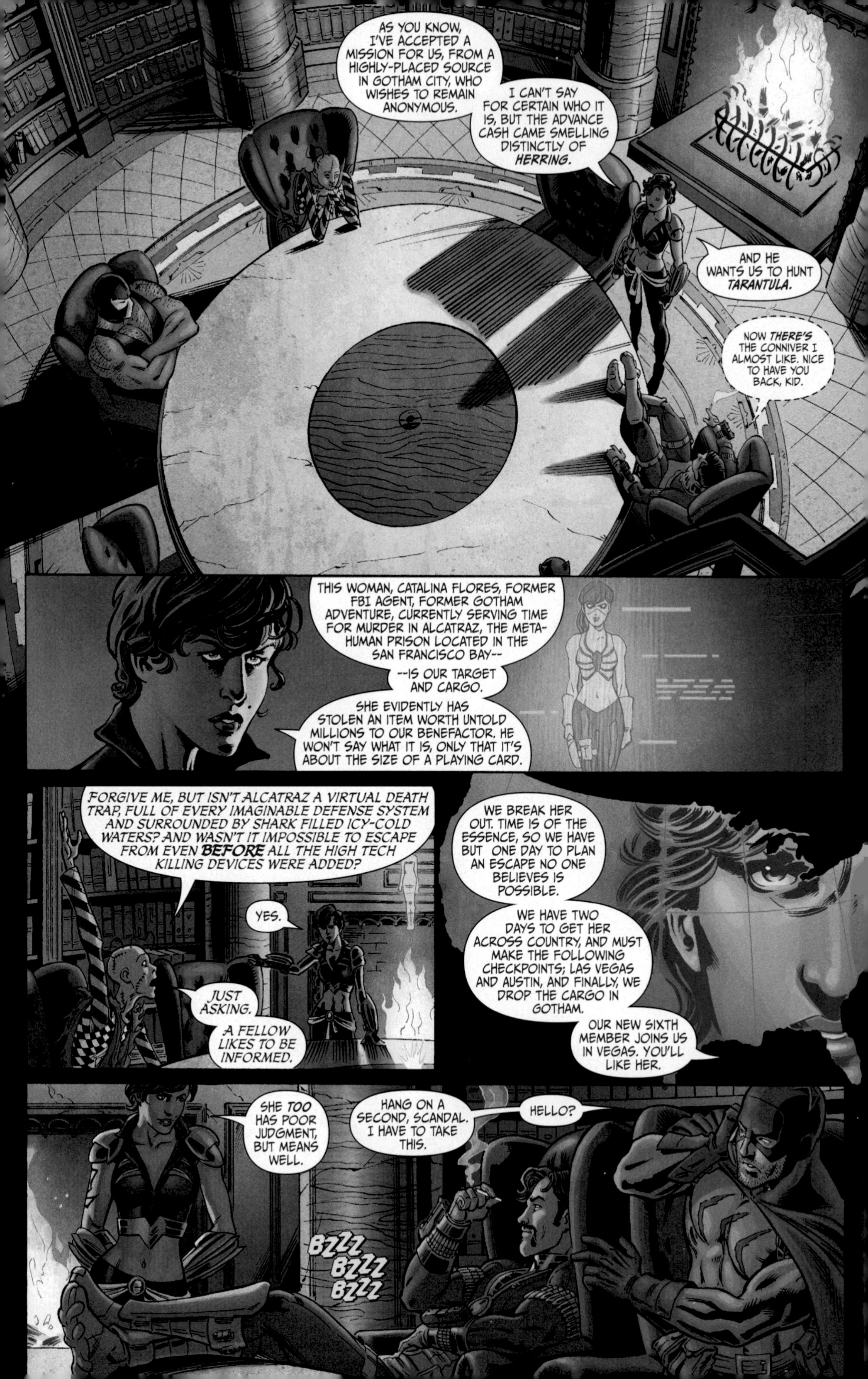
AS YOU KNOW, I'VE ACCEPTED A MISSION FOR US, FROM A HIGHLY-PLACED SOURCE IN GOTHAM CITY, WHO WISHES TO REMAIN ANONYMOUS.
I CAN'T SAY FOR CERTAIN WHO IT IS, BUT THE ADVANCE CASH CAME SMELLING DISTINCTLY OF HERRING.
AND HE WANTS US TO HUNT TARANTULA.
NOW THERE'S THE CONNIVER I ALMOST LIKE. NICE TO HAVE YOU BACK, KID.
THIS WOMAN, CATALINA FLORES, FORMER FBI AGENT, FORMER GOTHAM ADVENTURE, CURRENTLY SERVING TIME FOR MURDER IN ALCATRAZ, THE META-HUMAN PRISON LOCATED IN THE SAN FRANCISCO BAY--
--IS OUR TARGET AND CARGO.
SHE EVIDENTLY HAS STOLEN AN ITEM WORTH UNTOLD MILLIONS TO OUR BENEFACTOR. HE WON'T SAY WHAT IT IS, ONLY THAT IT'S ABOUT THE SIZE OF A PLAYING CARD.
FORGIVE ME, BUT ISN'T ALCATRAZ A VIRTUAL DEATH TRAP, FULL OF EVERY IMAGINABLE DEFENSE SYSTEM AND SURROUNDED BY SHARK FILLED ICY-COLD WATERS? AND WASN'T IT IMPOSSIBLE TO ESCAPE FROM EVEN BEFORE ALL THE HIGH TECH KILLING DEVICES WERE ADDED?
YES.
JUST ASKING.
A FELLOW LIKES TO BE INFORMED.
WE BREAK HER OUT. TIME IS OF THE ESSENCE, SO WE HAVE BUT ONE DAY TO PLAN AN ESCAPE NO ONE BELIEVES IS POSSIBLE.
WE HAVE TWO DAYS TO GET HER ACROSS COUNTRY, AND MUST MAKE THE FOLLOWING CHECKPOINTS; LAS VEGAS AND AUSTIN, AND FINALLY, WE DROP THE CARGO IN GOTHAM.
OUR NEW SIXTH MEMBER JOINS US IN VEGAS. YOU'LL LIKE HER.
SHE TOO HAS POOR JUDGMENT, BUT MEANS WELL.
HANG ON A SECOND, SCANDAL. I HAVE TO TAKE THIS.
HELLO?
BZZZ
BZZZ
BZZZ

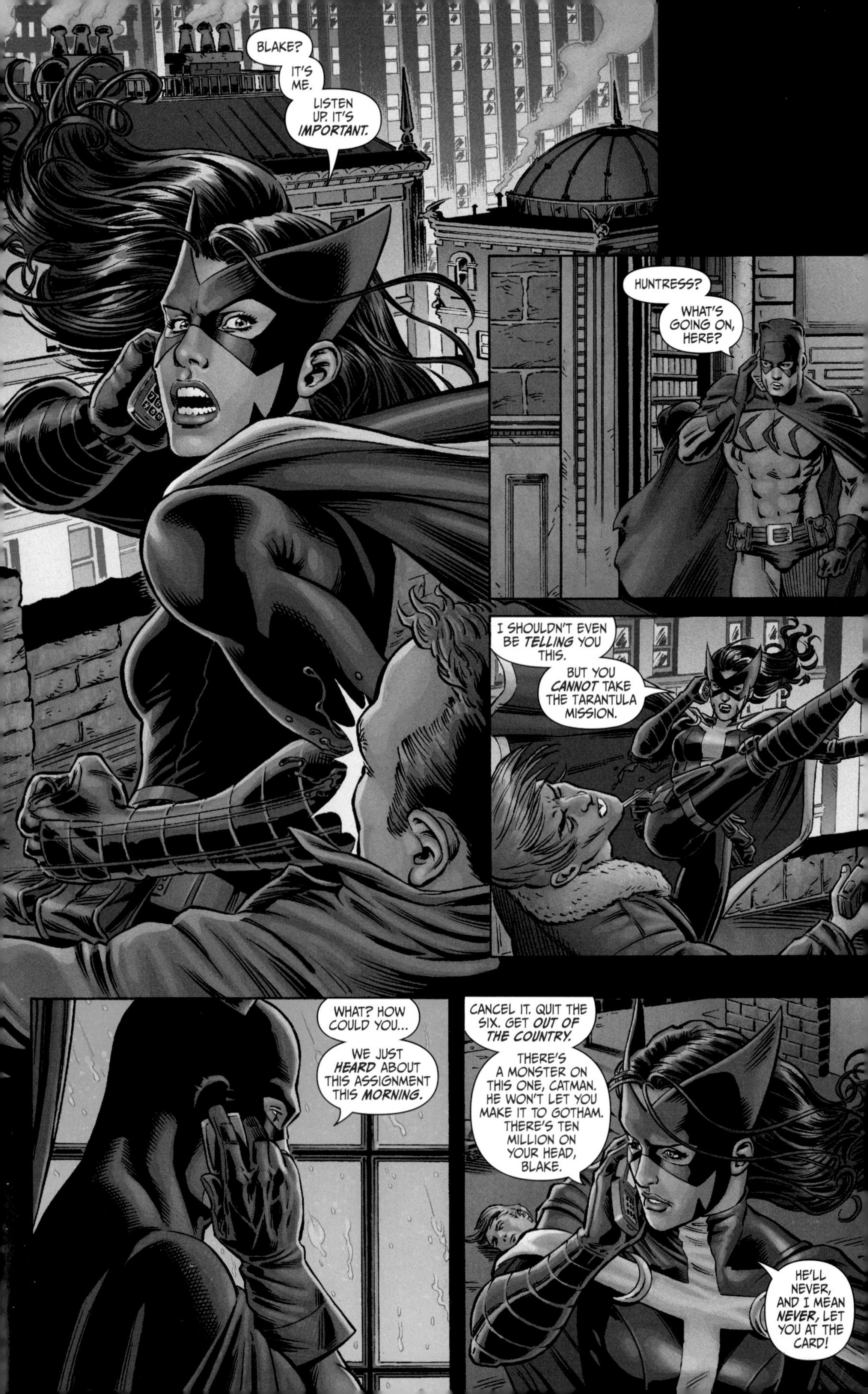
BLAKE?
IT'S ME.
LISTEN UP. IT'S *IMPORTANT.*
HUNTRESS?
WHAT'S GOING ON, HERE?
I SHOULDN'T EVEN BE *TELLING* YOU THIS.
BUT YOU *CANNOT* TAKE THE TARANTULA MISSION.
WHAT? HOW COULD YOU...
WE JUST *HEARD* ABOUT THIS ASSIGNMENT THIS *MORNING.*
CANCEL IT. QUIT THE SIX. GET *OUT OF THE COUNTRY.*
THERE'S A MONSTER ON THIS ONE, CATMAN. HE WON'T LET YOU MAKE IT TO GOTHAM. THERE'S TEN MILLION ON YOUR HEAD, BLAKE.
HE'LL NEVER, AND I MEAN *NEVER,* LET YOU AT THE CARD!

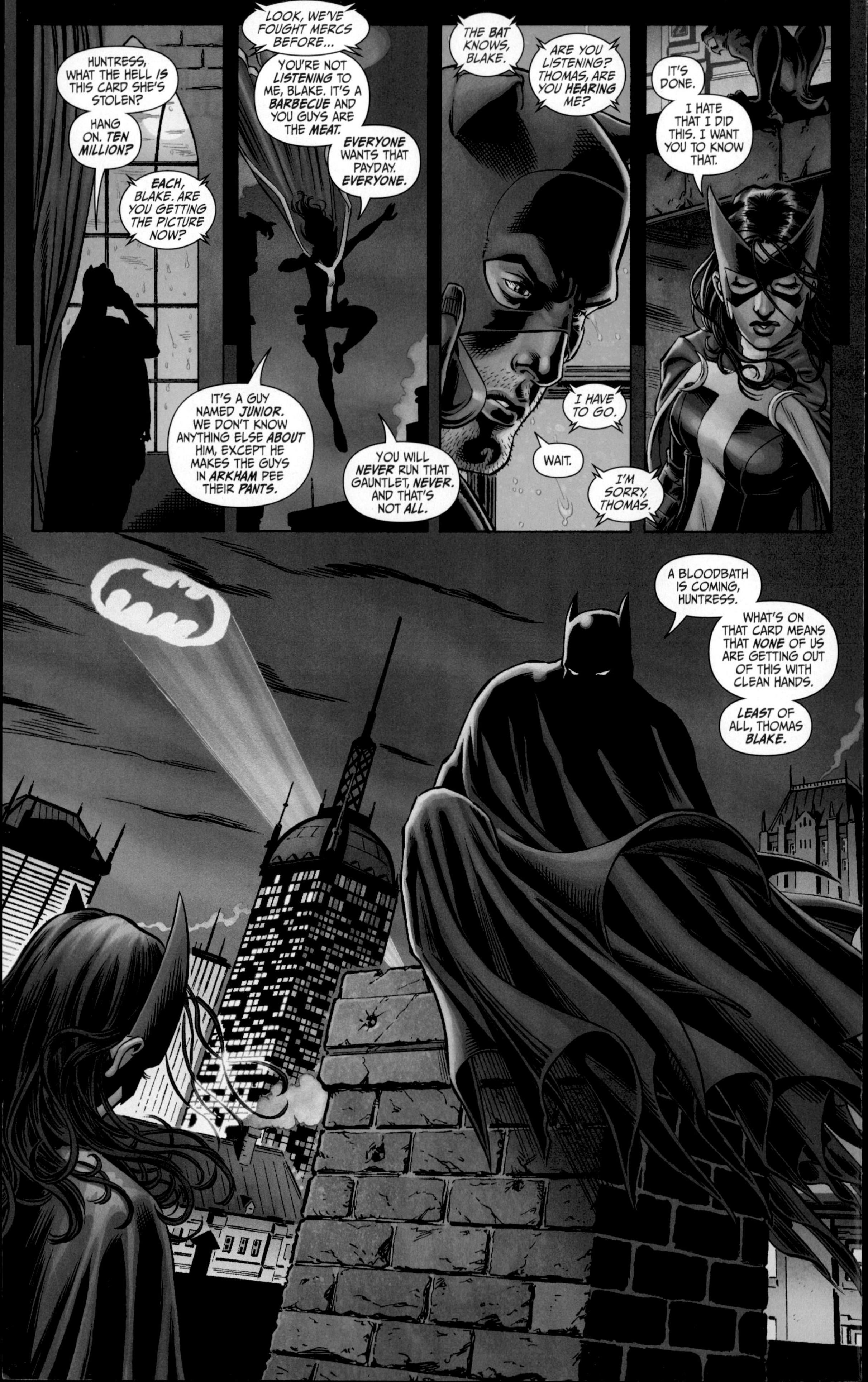
HUNTRESS, WHAT THE HELL IS THIS CARD SHE'S STOLEN?
HANG ON. TEN MILLION?
EACH, BLAKE. ARE YOU GETTING THE PICTURE NOW?
LOOK, WE'VE FOUGHT MERCS BEFORE...
YOU'RE NOT LISTENING TO ME, BLAKE. IT'S A BARBECUE AND YOU GUYS ARE THE MEAT.
EVERYONE WANTS THAT PAYDAY. EVERYONE.
IT'S A GUY NAMED JUNIOR. WE DON'T KNOW ANYTHING ELSE ABOUT HIM, EXCEPT HE MAKES THE GUYS IN ARKHAM PEE THEIR PANTS.
YOU WILL NEVER RUN THAT GAUNTLET, NEVER. AND THAT'S NOT ALL.
THE BAT KNOWS, BLAKE.
ARE YOU LISTENING? THOMAS, ARE YOU HEARING ME?
I HAVE TO GO.
WAIT.
IT'S DONE.
I HATE THAT I DID THIS. I WANT YOU TO KNOW THAT.
I'M SORRY, THOMAS.
A BLOODBATH IS COMING, HUNTRESS.
WHAT'S ON THAT CARD MEANS THAT NONE OF US ARE GETTING OUT OF THIS WITH CLEAN HANDS.
LEAST OF ALL, THOMAS BLAKE.

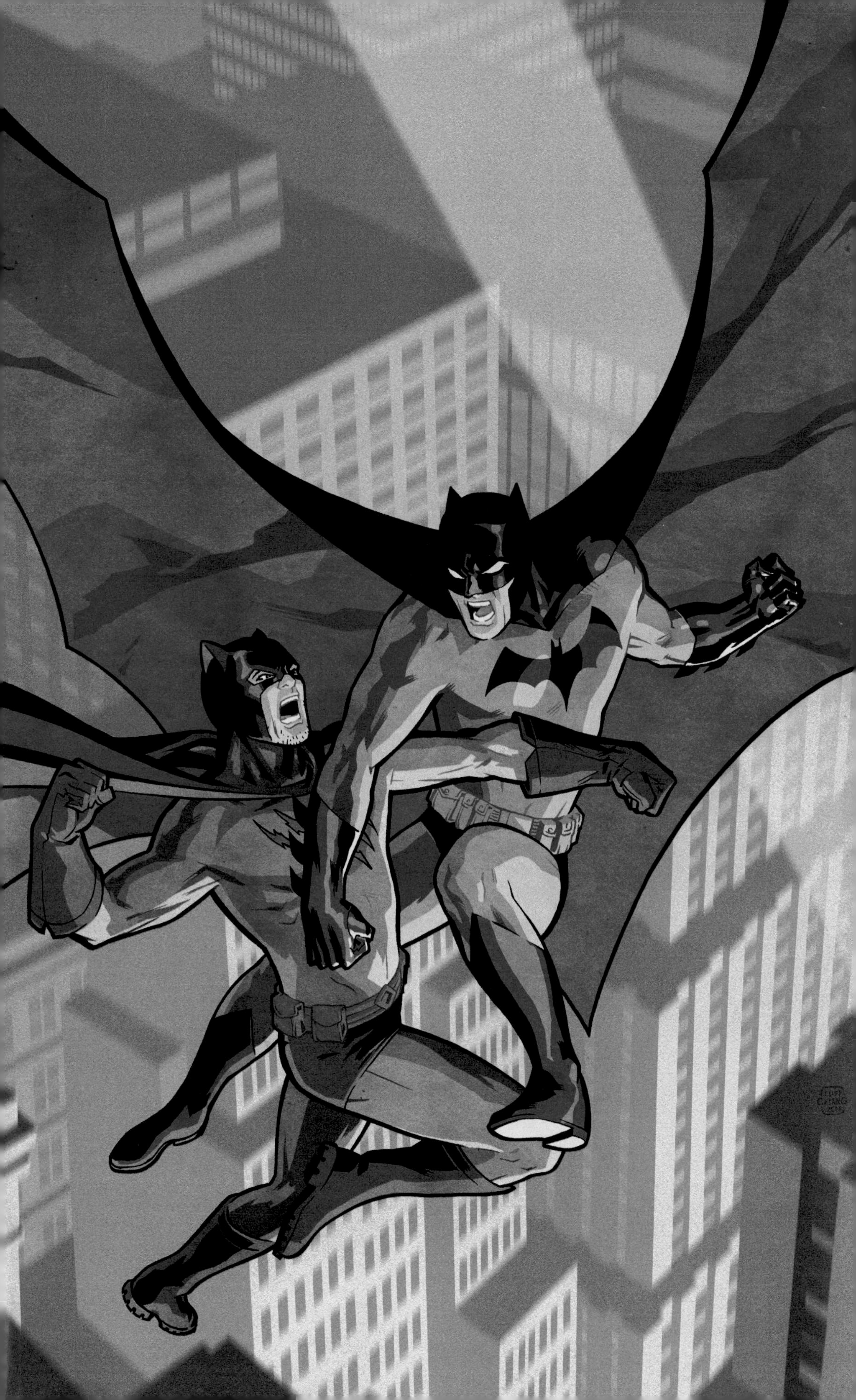

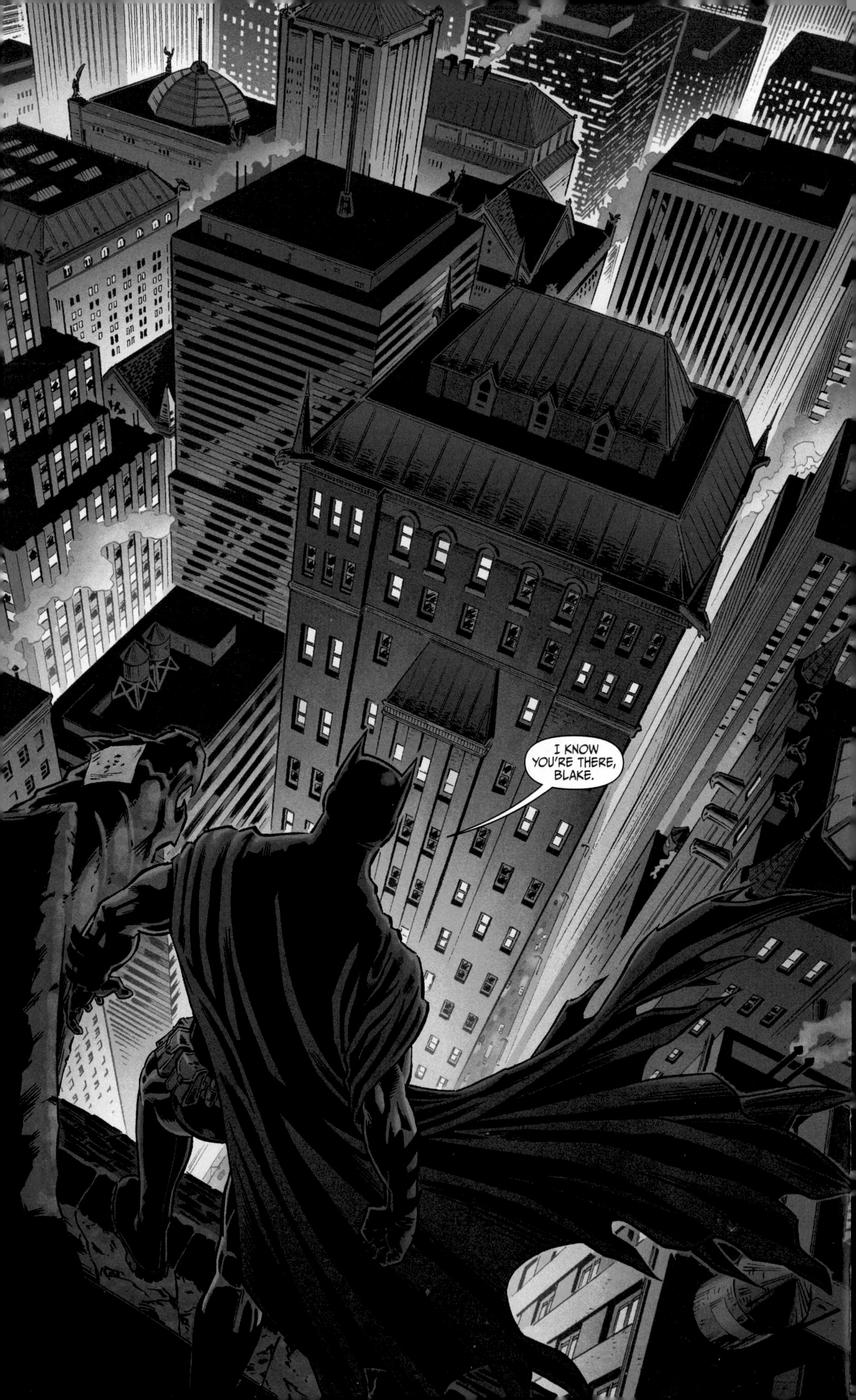
I KNOW YOU'RE THERE, BLAKE.

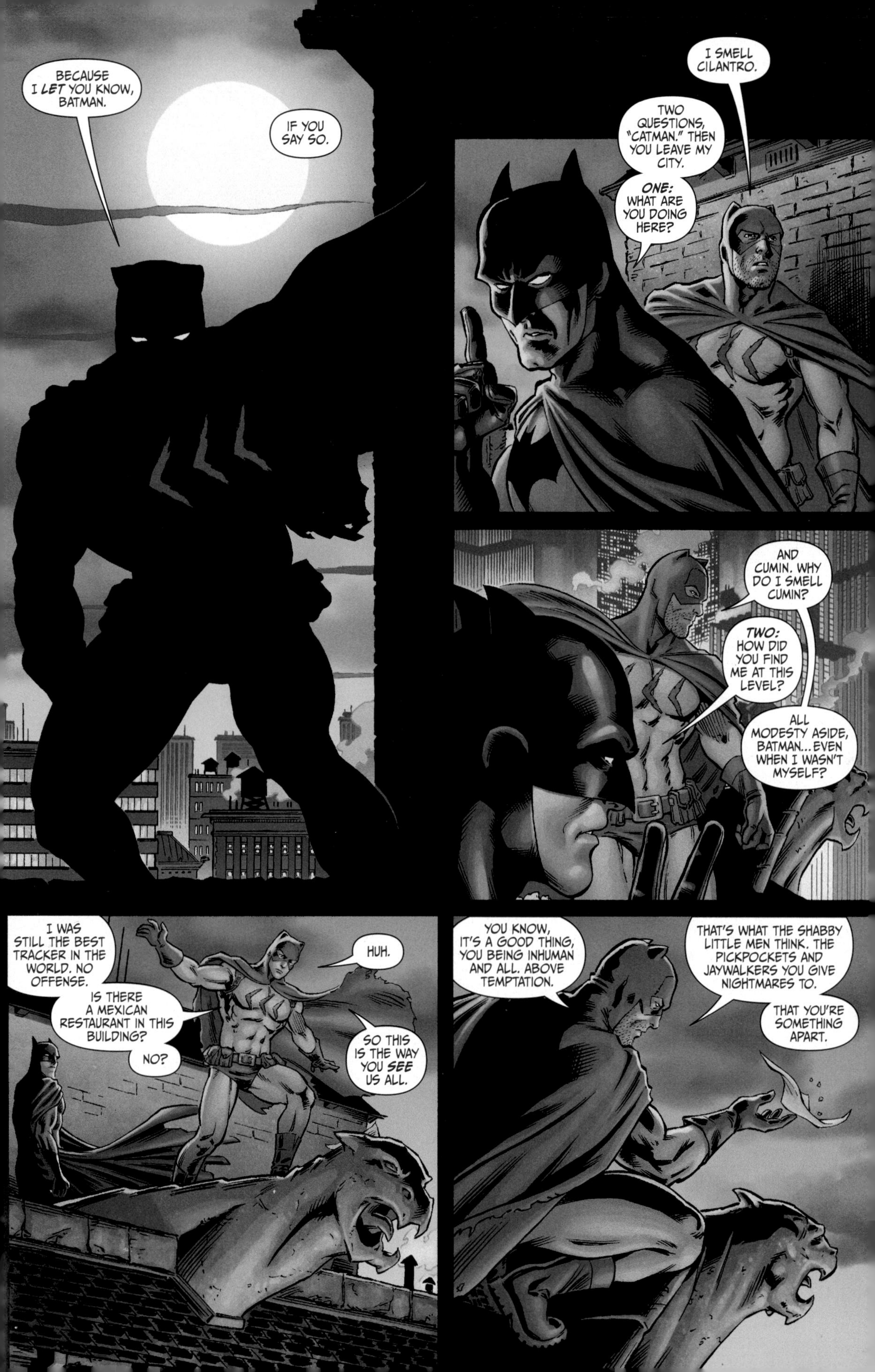
BECAUSE I *LET* YOU KNOW, BATMAN.
IF YOU SAY SO.
I SMELL CILANTRO.
TWO QUESTIONS, "CATMAN." THEN YOU LEAVE MY CITY.
ONE: WHAT ARE YOU DOING HERE?
AND CUMIN. WHY DO I SMELL CUMIN?
TWO: HOW DID YOU FIND ME AT THIS LEVEL?
ALL MODESTY ASIDE, BATMAN...EVEN WHEN I WASN'T MYSELF?
I WAS STILL THE BEST TRACKER IN THE WORLD. NO OFFENSE.
IS THERE A MEXICAN RESTAURANT IN THIS BUILDING?
NO?
HUH.
SO THIS IS THE WAY YOU *SEE* US ALL.
YOU KNOW, IT'S A GOOD THING, YOU BEING INHUMAN AND ALL. ABOVE TEMPTATION.
THAT'S WHAT THE SHABBY LITTLE MEN THINK. THE PICKPOCKETS AND JAYWALKERS YOU GIVE NIGHTMARES TO.
THAT YOU'RE SOMETHING APART.

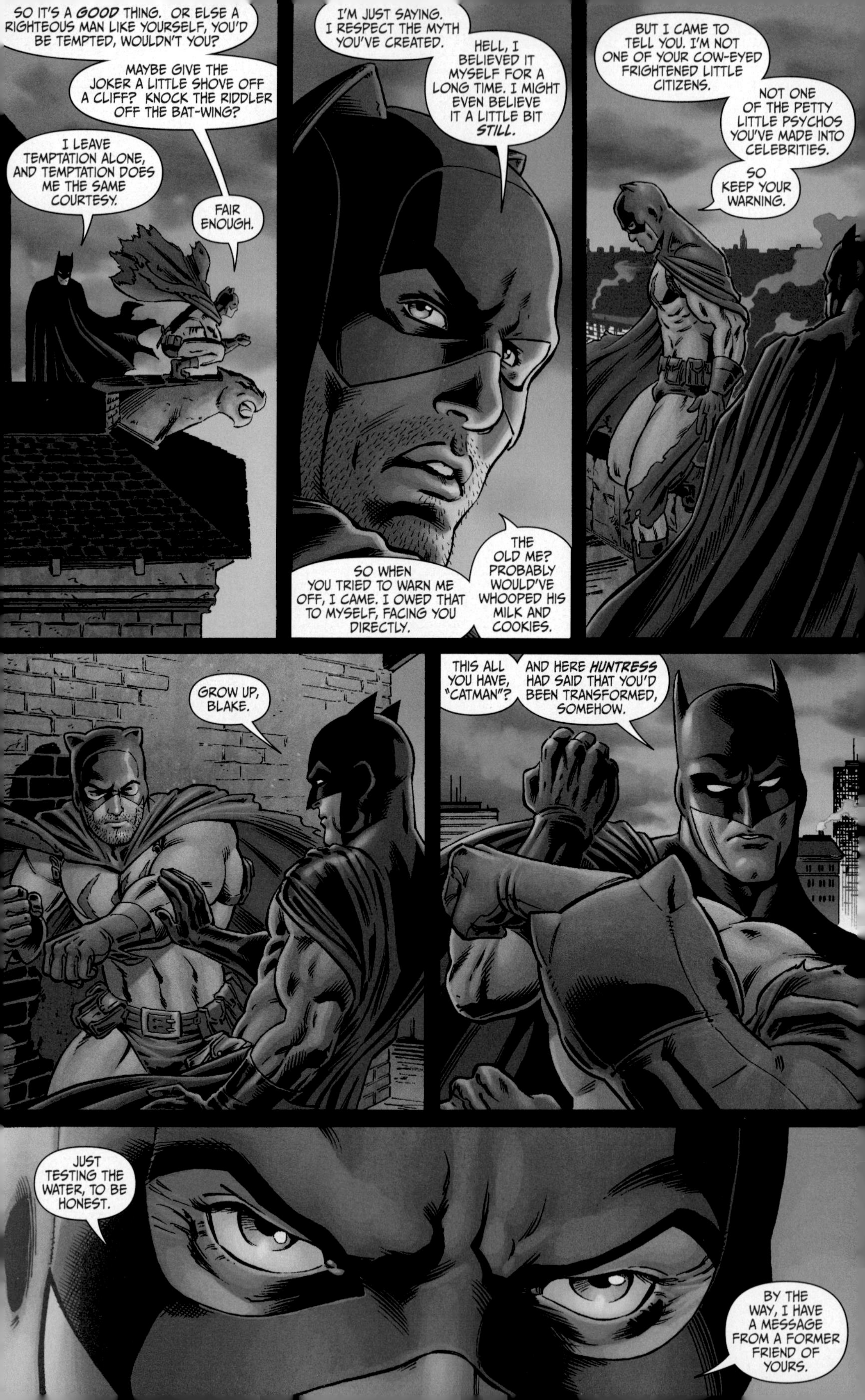
SO IT'S A GOOD THING. OR ELSE A RIGHTEOUS MAN LIKE YOURSELF, YOU'D BE TEMPTED, WOULDN'T YOU?
MAYBE GIVE THE JOKER A LITTLE SHOVE OFF A CLIFF? KNOCK THE RIDDLER OFF THE BAT-WING?
I LEAVE TEMPTATION ALONE, AND TEMPTATION DOES ME THE SAME COURTESY.
FAIR ENOUGH.
I'M JUST SAYING. I RESPECT THE MYTH YOU'VE CREATED.
HELL, I BELIEVED IT MYSELF FOR A LONG TIME. I MIGHT EVEN BELIEVE IT A LITTLE BIT STILL.
SO WHEN YOU TRIED TO WARN ME OFF, I CAME. I OWED THAT TO MYSELF, FACING YOU DIRECTLY.
THE OLD ME? PROBABLY WOULD'VE WHOOPED HIS MILK AND COOKIES.
BUT I CAME TO TELL YOU. I'M NOT ONE OF YOUR COW-EYED FRIGHTENED LITTLE CITIZENS.
NOT ONE OF THE PETTY LITTLE PSYCHOS YOU'VE MADE INTO CELEBRITIES.
SO KEEP YOUR WARNING.
GROW UP, BLAKE.
THIS ALL YOU HAVE, "CATMAN"?
AND HERE HUNTRESS HAD SAID THAT YOU'D BEEN TRANSFORMED, SOMEHOW.
JUST TESTING THE WATER, TO BE HONEST.
BY THE WAY, I HAVE A MESSAGE FROM A FORMER FRIEND OF YOURS.

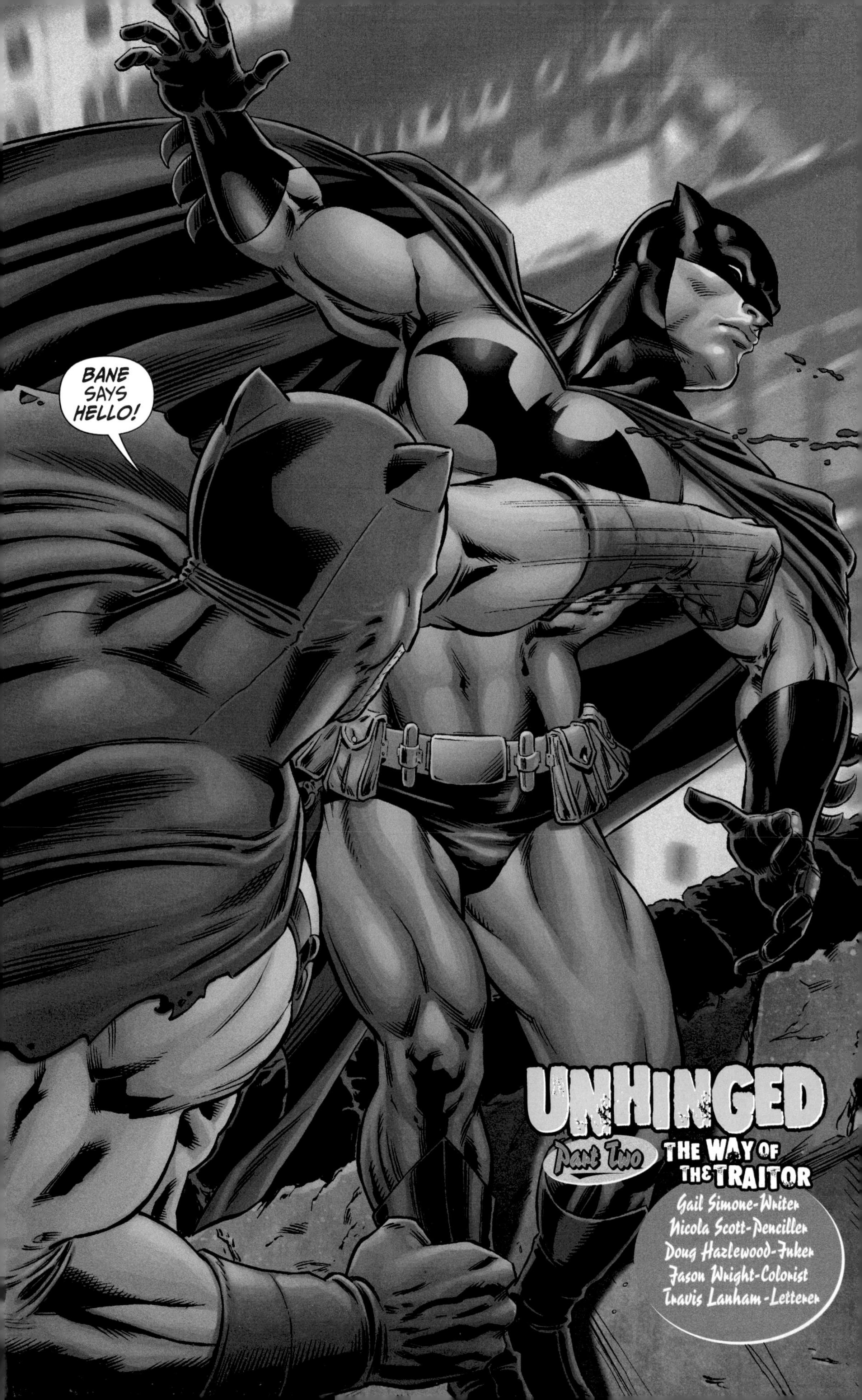
BANE SAYS HELLO!
UNHINGED
Part Two
THE WAY OF THE TRAITOR
Gail Simone-Writer
Nicola Scott-Penciller
Doug Hazlewood-Inker
Jason Wright-Colorist
Travis Lanham-Letterer

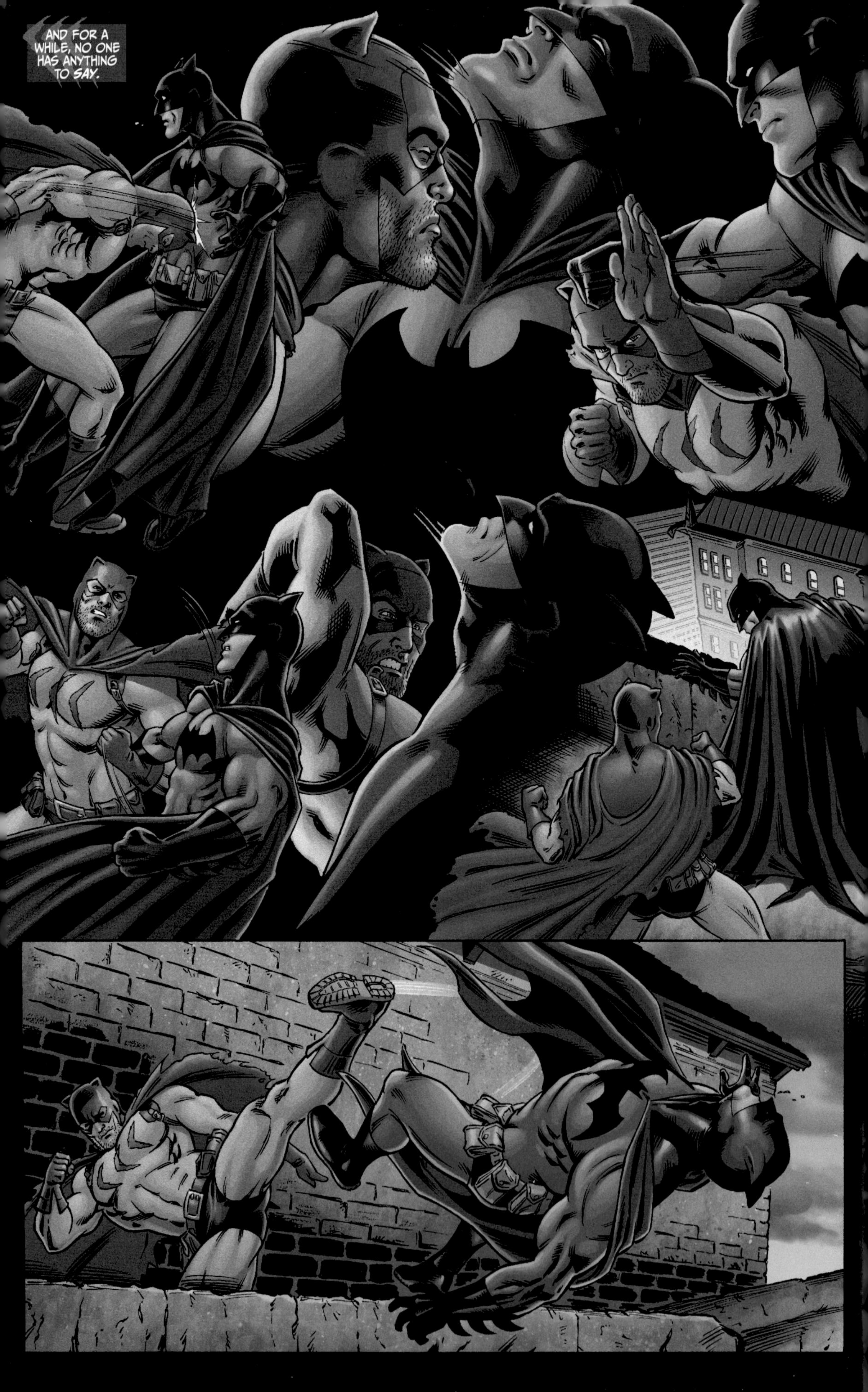
AND FOR A WHILE, NO ONE HAS ANYTHING TO SAY.

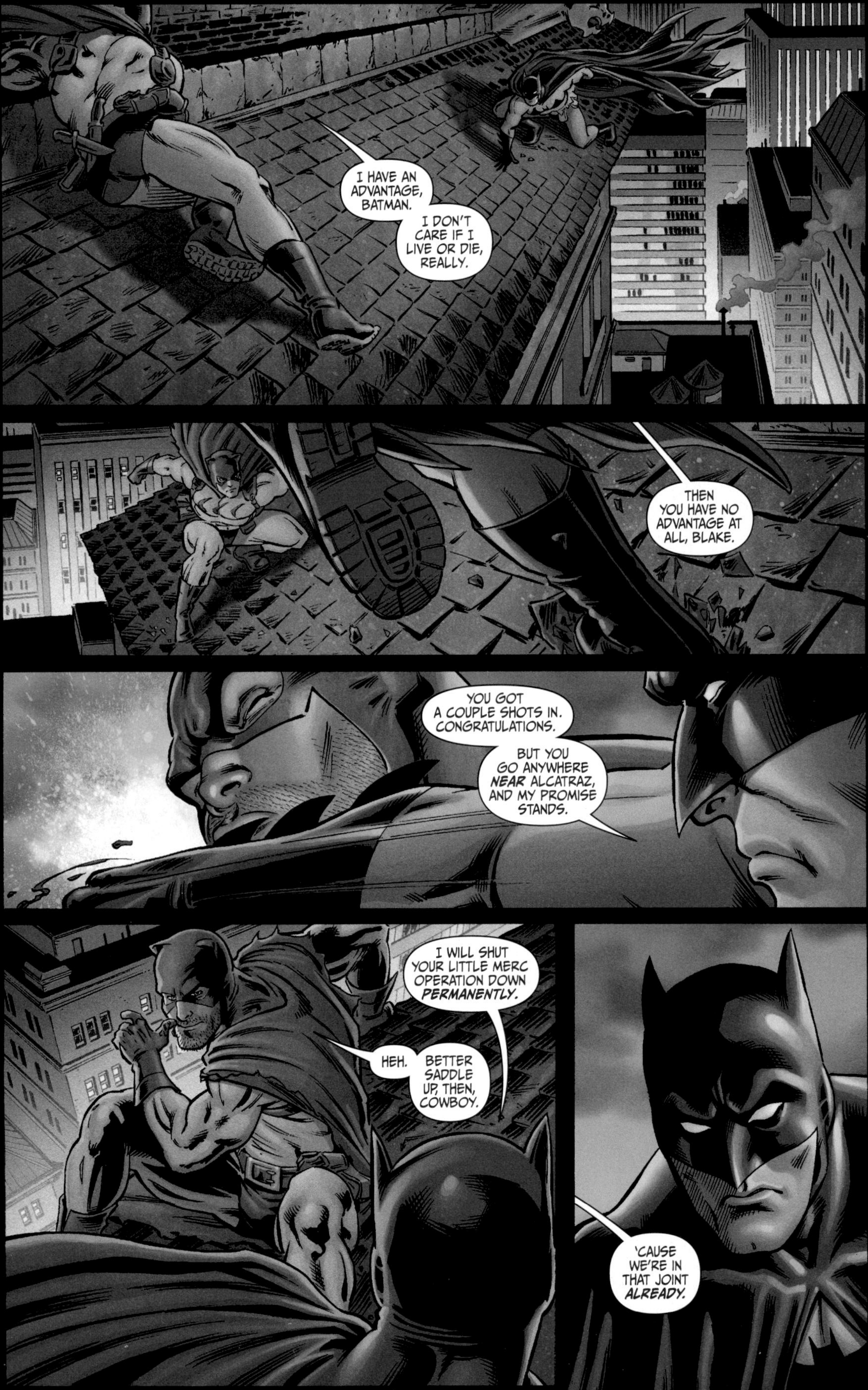
I HAVE AN ADVANTAGE, BATMAN.
I DON'T CARE IF I LIVE OR DIE, REALLY.
THEN YOU HAVE NO ADVANTAGE AT ALL, BLAKE.
YOU GOT A COUPLE SHOTS IN. CONGRATULATIONS.
BUT YOU GO ANYWHERE *NEAR* ALCATRAZ, AND MY PROMISE STANDS.
I WILL SHUT YOUR LITTLE MERC OPERATION DOWN *PERMANENTLY.*
HEH.
BETTER SADDLE UP, THEN, COWBOY.
'CAUSE WE'RE IN THAT JOINT *ALREADY.*

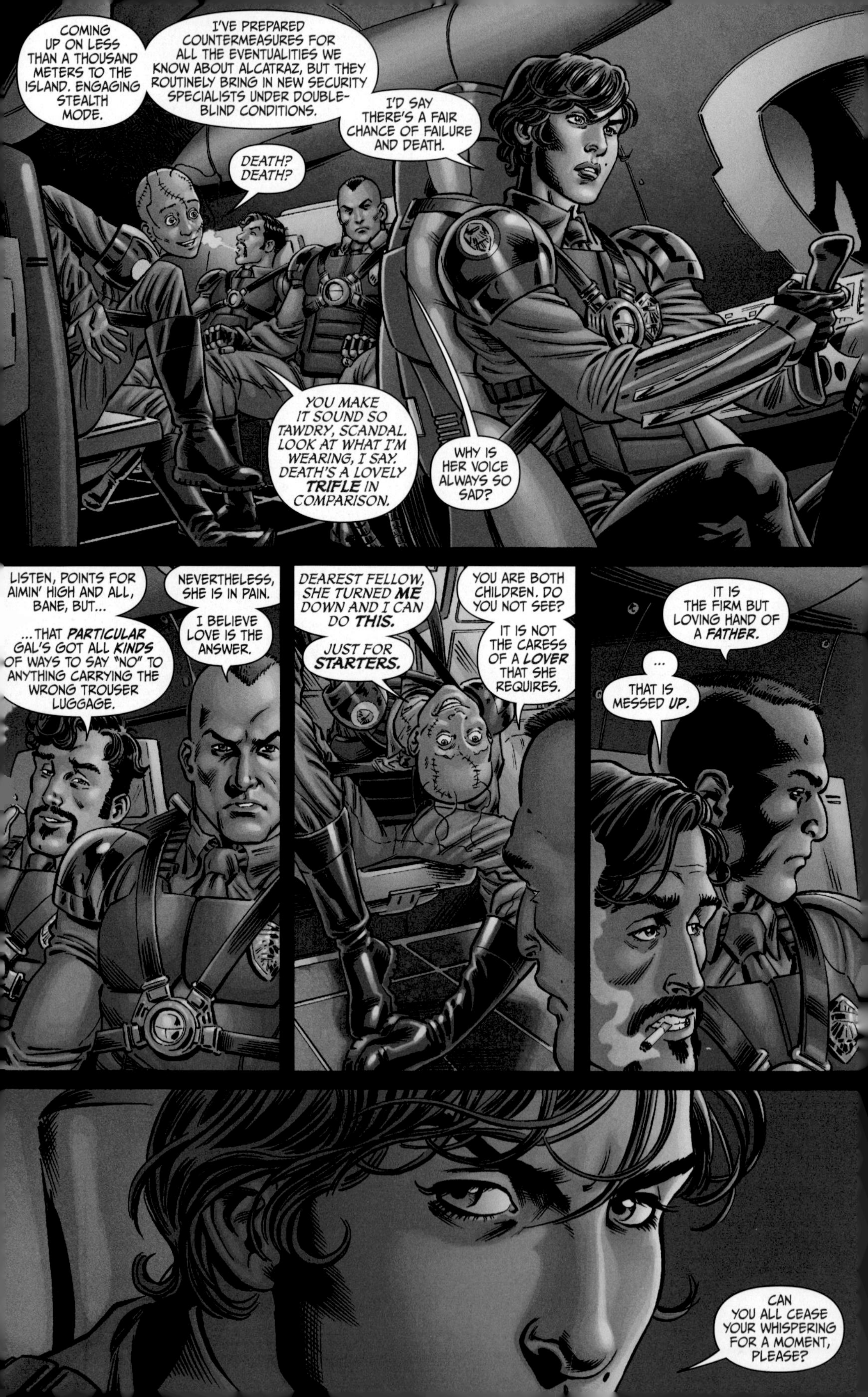
COMING UP ON LESS THAN A THOUSAND METERS TO THE ISLAND. ENGAGING STEALTH MODE.
I'VE PREPARED COUNTERMEASURES FOR ALL THE EVENTUALITIES WE KNOW ABOUT ALCATRAZ, BUT THEY ROUTINELY BRING IN NEW SECURITY SPECIALISTS UNDER DOUBLE-BLIND CONDITIONS.
I'D SAY THERE'S A FAIR CHANCE OF FAILURE AND DEATH.
DEATH? DEATH?
YOU MAKE IT SOUND SO TAWDRY, SCANDAL. LOOK AT WHAT I'M WEARING, I SAY. DEATH'S A LOVELY TRIFLE IN COMPARISON.
WHY IS HER VOICE ALWAYS SO SAD?
LISTEN, POINTS FOR AIMIN' HIGH AND ALL, BANE, BUT...
...THAT PARTICULAR GAL'S GOT ALL KINDS OF WAYS TO SAY "NO" TO ANYTHING CARRYING THE WRONG TROUSER LUGGAGE.
NEVERTHELESS, SHE IS IN PAIN.
I BELIEVE LOVE IS THE ANSWER.
DEAREST FELLOW, SHE TURNED ME DOWN AND I CAN DO THIS.
JUST FOR STARTERS.
YOU ARE BOTH CHILDREN. DO YOU NOT SEE?
IT IS NOT THE CARESS OF A LOVER THAT SHE REQUIRES.
IT IS THE FIRM BUT LOVING HAND OF A FATHER.
...
THAT IS MESSED UP.
CAN YOU ALL CEASE YOUR WHISPERING FOR A MOMENT, PLEASE?

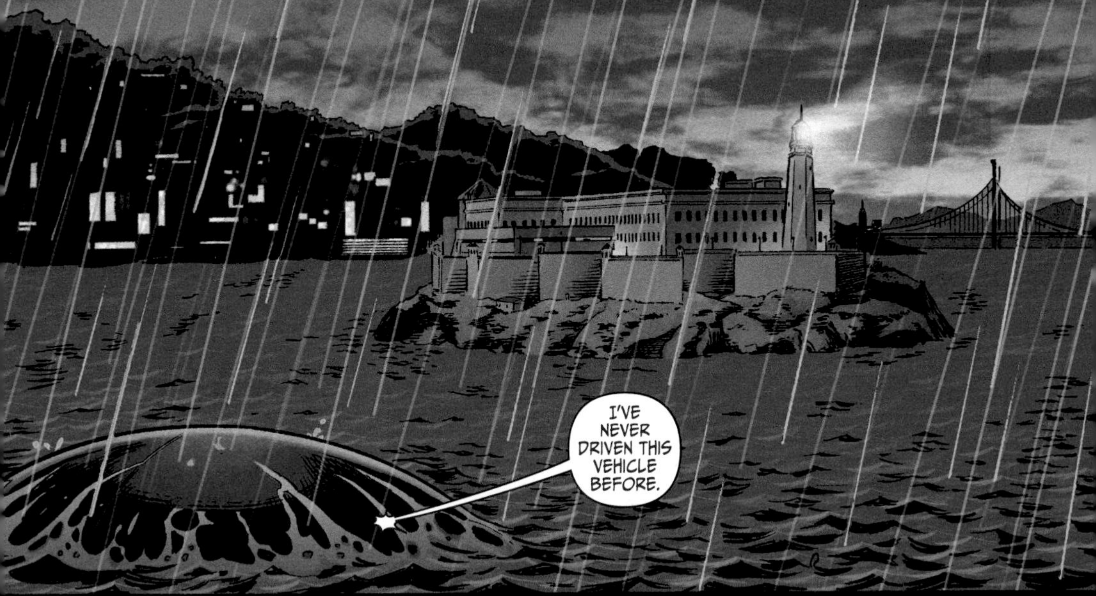
I'VE NEVER DRIVEN THIS VEHICLE BEFORE.

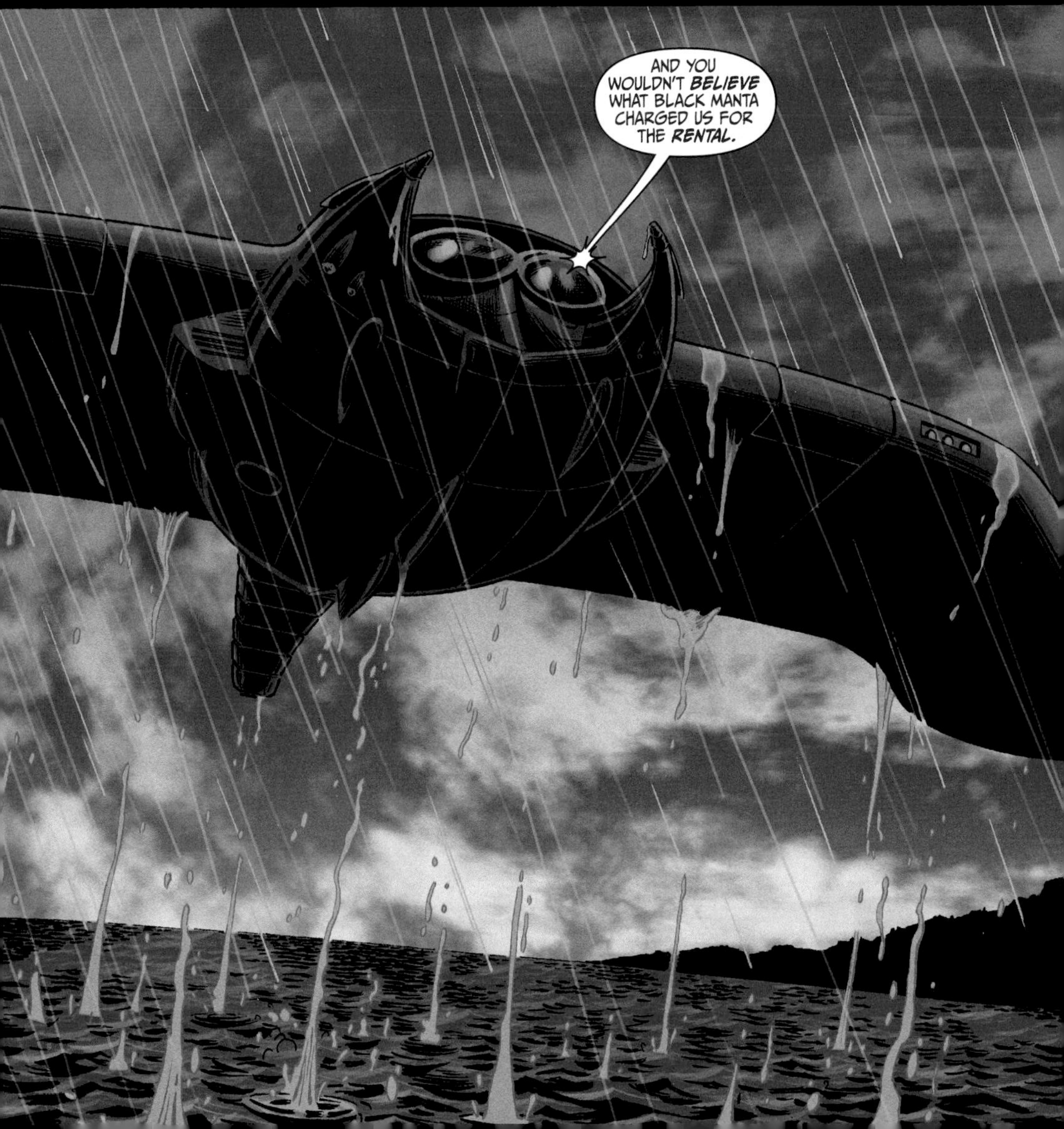
AND YOU WOULDN'T **BELIEVE** WHAT BLACK MANTA CHARGED US FOR THE **RENTAL.**

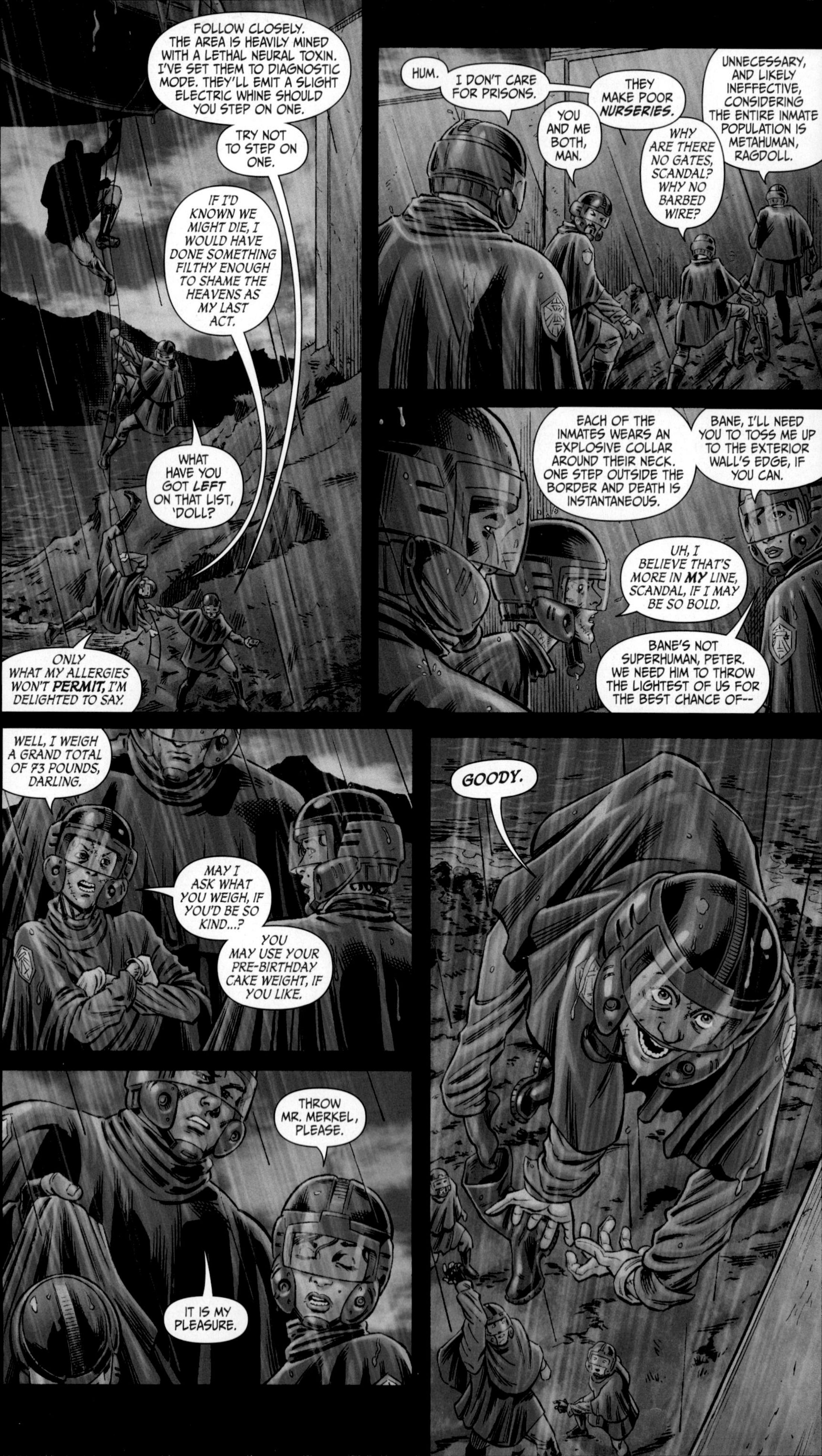
FOLLOW CLOSELY. THE AREA IS HEAVILY MINED WITH A LETHAL NEURAL TOXIN. I'VE SET THEM TO DIAGNOSTIC MODE. THEY'LL EMIT A SLIGHT ELECTRIC WHINE SHOULD YOU STEP ON ONE.
TRY NOT TO STEP ON ONE.
IF I'D KNOWN WE MIGHT DIE, I WOULD HAVE DONE SOMETHING FILTHY ENOUGH TO SHAME THE HEAVENS AS MY LAST ACT.
WHAT HAVE YOU GOT LEFT ON THAT LIST, 'DOLL?
ONLY WHAT MY ALLERGIES WON'T PERMIT, I'M DELIGHTED TO SAY.
HUM.
I DON'T CARE FOR PRISONS.
THEY MAKE POOR NURSERIES.
YOU AND ME BOTH, MAN.
WHY ARE THERE NO GATES, SCANDAL? WHY NO BARBED WIRE?
UNNECESSARY, AND LIKELY INEFFECTIVE, CONSIDERING THE ENTIRE INMATE POPULATION IS METAHUMAN, RAGDOLL.
EACH OF THE INMATES WEARS AN EXPLOSIVE COLLAR AROUND THEIR NECK. ONE STEP OUTSIDE THE BORDER AND DEATH IS INSTANTANEOUS.
BANE, I'LL NEED YOU TO TOSS ME UP TO THE EXTERIOR WALL'S EDGE, IF YOU CAN.
UH, I BELIEVE THAT'S MORE IN MY LINE, SCANDAL, IF I MAY BE SO BOLD.
BANE'S NOT SUPERHUMAN, PETER. WE NEED HIM TO THROW THE LIGHTEST OF US FOR THE BEST CHANCE OF--
WELL, I WEIGH A GRAND TOTAL OF 73 POUNDS, DARLING.
MAY I ASK WHAT YOU WEIGH, IF YOU'D BE SO KIND...?
YOU MAY USE YOUR PRE-BIRTHDAY CAKE WEIGHT, IF YOU LIKE.
THROW MR. MERKEL, PLEASE.
IT IS MY PLEASURE.
GOODY.

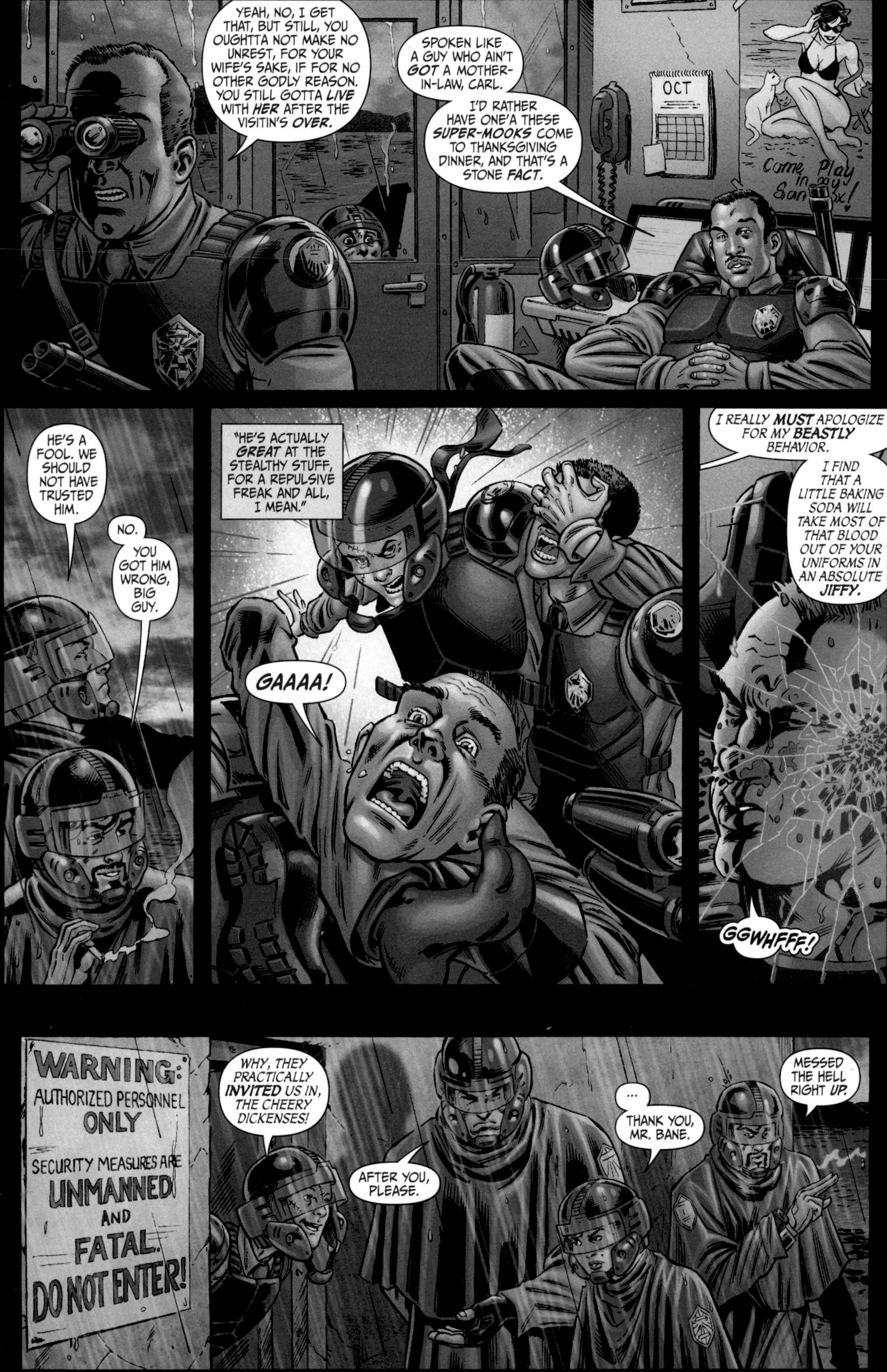
YEAH, NO, I GET THAT, BUT STILL, YOU OUGHTTA NOT MAKE NO UNREST, FOR YOUR WIFE'S SAKE, IF FOR NO OTHER GODLY REASON. YOU STILL GOTTA LIVE WITH HER AFTER THE VISITIN'S OVER.
SPOKEN LIKE A GUY WHO AIN'T GOT A MOTHER-IN-LAW, CARL.
I'D RATHER HAVE ONE'A THESE SUPER-MOOKS COME TO THANKSGIVING DINNER, AND THAT'S A STONE FACT.
OCT
Come Play in my San Box!
HE'S A FOOL. WE SHOULD NOT HAVE TRUSTED HIM.
NO.
YOU GOT HIM WRONG, BIG GUY.
"HE'S ACTUALLY GREAT AT THE STEALTHY STUFF, FOR A REPULSIVE FREAK AND ALL, I MEAN."
GAAAA!
I REALLY MUST APOLOGIZE FOR MY BEASTLY BEHAVIOR.
I FIND THAT A LITTLE BAKING SODA WILL TAKE MOST OF THAT BLOOD OUT OF YOUR UNIFORMS IN AN ABSOLUTE JIFFY.
GGWHFFF!
WARNING: AUTHORIZED PERSONNEL ONLY SECURITY MEASURES ARE UNMANNED AND FATAL. DO NOT ENTER!
WHY, THEY PRACTICALLY INVITED US IN, THE CHEERY DICKENSES!
AFTER YOU, PLEASE.
...
THANK YOU, MR. BANE.
MESSED THE HELL RIGHT UP.

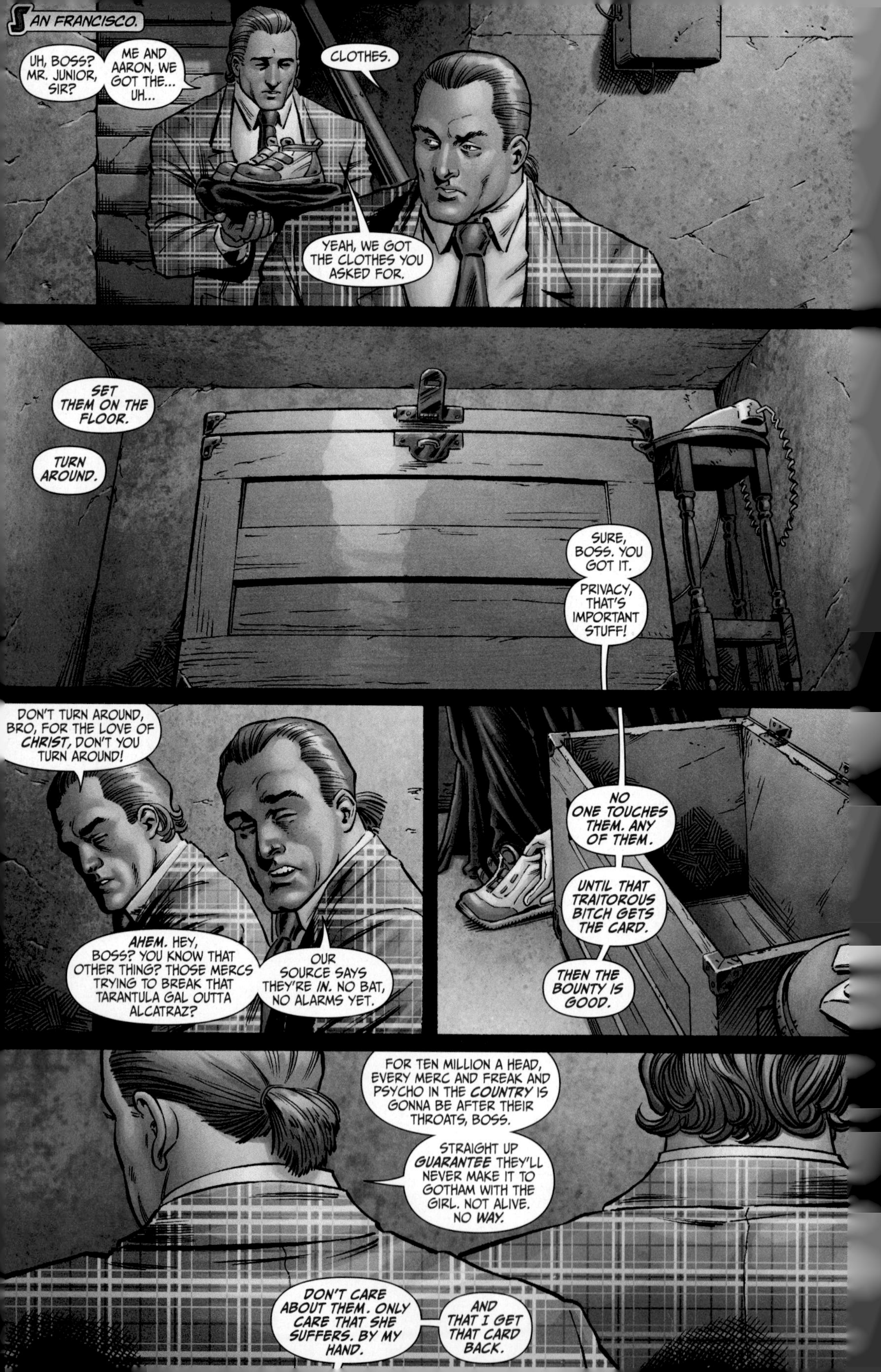
SAN FRANCISCO.
UH, BOSS? MR. JUNIOR, SIR?
ME AND AARON, WE GOT THE... UH...
CLOTHES.
YEAH, WE GOT THE CLOTHES YOU ASKED FOR.
SET THEM ON THE FLOOR.
TURN AROUND.
SURE, BOSS. YOU GOT IT.
PRIVACY, THAT'S IMPORTANT STUFF!
DON'T TURN AROUND, BRO, FOR THE LOVE OF CHRIST, DON'T YOU TURN AROUND!
AHEM. HEY, BOSS? YOU KNOW THAT OTHER THING? THOSE MERCS TRYING TO BREAK THAT TARANTULA GAL OUTTA ALCATRAZ?
OUR SOURCE SAYS THEY'RE IN. NO BAT, NO ALARMS YET.
NO ONE TOUCHES THEM. ANY OF THEM.
UNTIL THAT TRAITOROUS BITCH GETS THE CARD.
THEN THE BOUNTY IS GOOD.
FOR TEN MILLION A HEAD, EVERY MERC AND FREAK AND PSYCHO IN THE COUNTRY IS GONNA BE AFTER THEIR THROATS, BOSS.
STRAIGHT UP GUARANTEE THEY'LL NEVER MAKE IT TO GOTHAM WITH THE GIRL. NOT ALIVE. NO WAY.
DON'T CARE ABOUT THEM. ONLY CARE THAT SHE SUFFERS. BY MY HAND.
AND THAT I GET THAT CARD BACK.

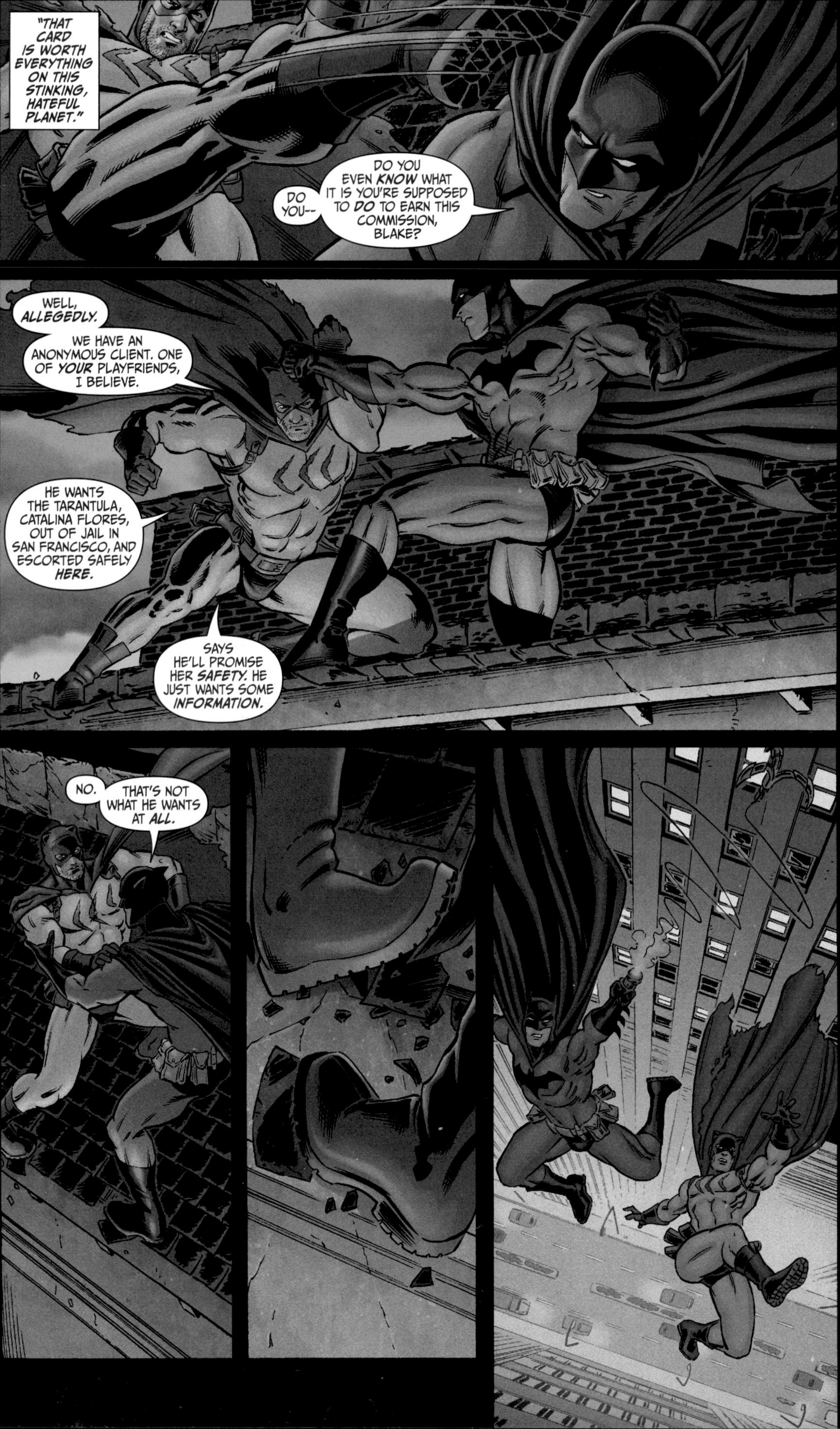
"THAT CARD IS WORTH EVERYTHING ON THIS STINKING, HATEFUL PLANET."
DO YOU--
DO YOU EVEN KNOW WHAT IT IS YOU'RE SUPPOSED TO DO TO EARN THIS COMMISSION, BLAKE?
WELL, ALLEGEDLY.
WE HAVE AN ANONYMOUS CLIENT. ONE OF YOUR PLAYFRIENDS, I BELIEVE.
HE WANTS THE TARANTULA, CATALINA FLORES, OUT OF JAIL IN SAN FRANCISCO, AND ESCORTED SAFELY HERE.
SAYS HE'LL PROMISE HER SAFETY. HE JUST WANTS SOME INFORMATION.
NO.
THAT'S NOT WHAT HE WANTS AT ALL.

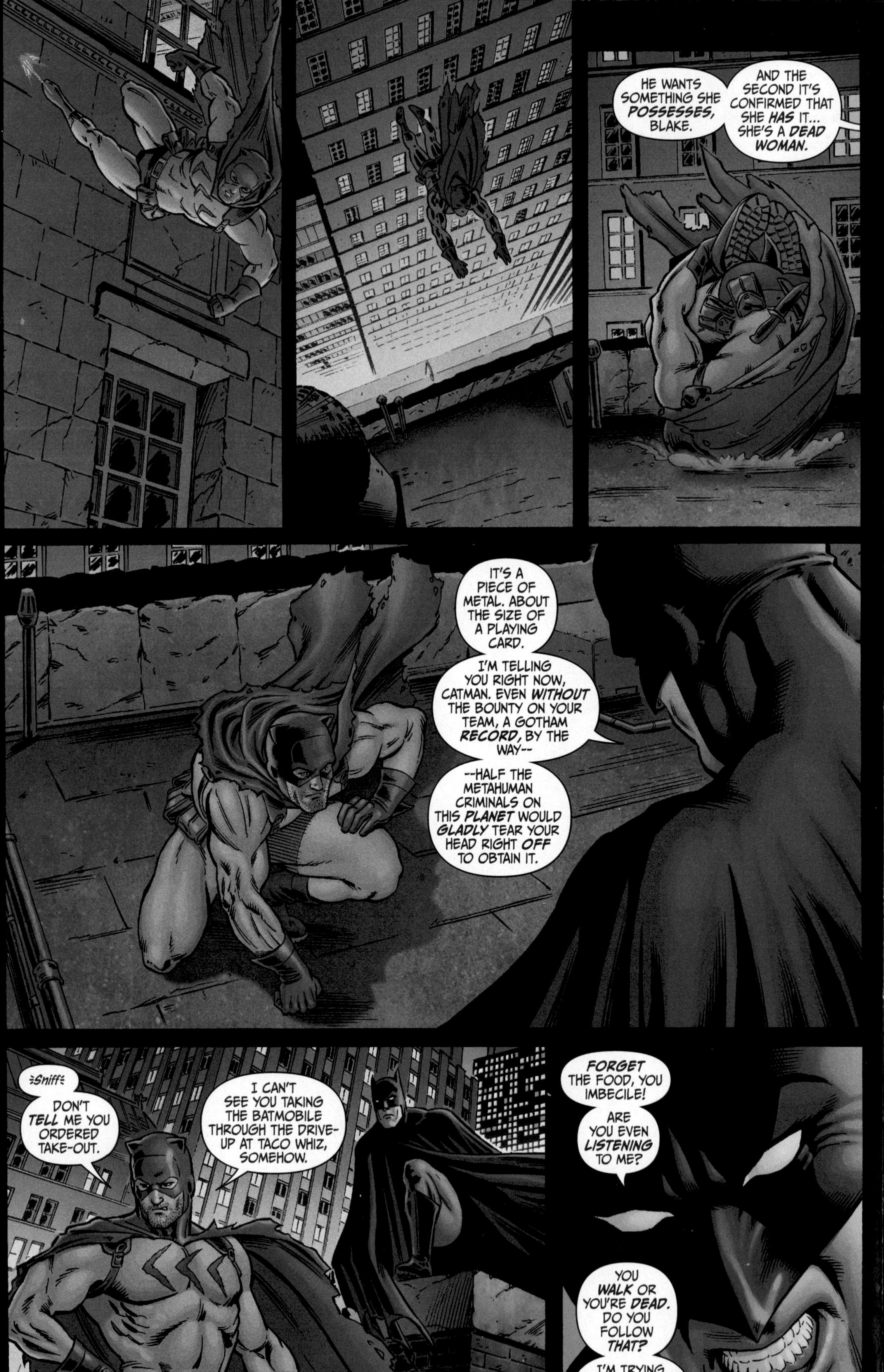
HE WANTS SOMETHING SHE *POSSESSES,* BLAKE.
AND THE SECOND IT'S CONFIRMED THAT SHE *HAS* IT... SHE'S A *DEAD WOMAN.*
IT'S A PIECE OF METAL. ABOUT THE SIZE OF A PLAYING CARD.
I'M TELLING YOU RIGHT NOW, CATMAN. EVEN *WITHOUT* THE BOUNTY ON YOUR TEAM, A GOTHAM *RECORD,* BY THE WAY--
--HALF THE METAHUMAN CRIMINALS ON THIS *PLANET* WOULD *GLADLY* TEAR YOUR HEAD RIGHT *OFF* TO OBTAIN IT.
Sniff
DON'T *TELL* ME YOU ORDERED TAKE-OUT.
I CAN'T SEE YOU TAKING THE BATMOBILE THROUGH THE DRIVE-UP AT TACO WHIZ, SOMEHOW.
KKRRK
FORGET THE FOOD, YOU IMBECILE!
ARE YOU EVEN *LISTENING* TO ME?
YOU *WALK* OR YOU'RE *DEAD.* DO YOU FOLLOW *THAT?*
I'M TRYING TO *SAVE* YOUR FOOLISH, WASTED *LIFE.*

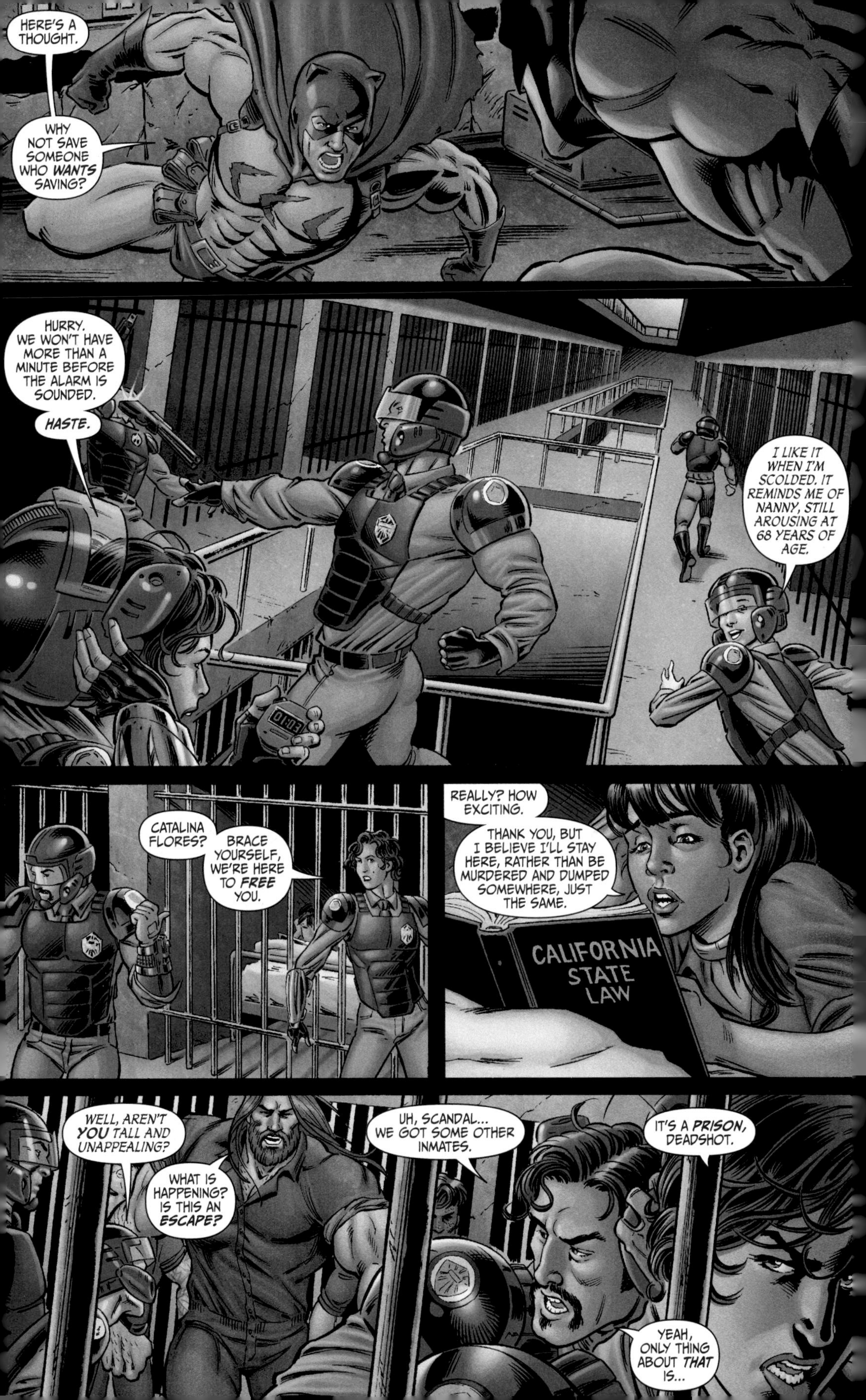
HERE'S A THOUGHT.
WHY NOT SAVE SOMEONE WHO *WANTS* SAVING?
HURRY. WE WON'T HAVE MORE THAN A MINUTE BEFORE THE ALARM IS SOUNDED.
HASTE.
I LIKE IT WHEN I'M SCOLDED. IT REMINDS ME OF NANNY, STILL AROUSING AT 68 YEARS OF AGE.
CATALINA FLORES?
BRACE YOURSELF, WE'RE HERE TO *FREE* YOU.
REALLY? HOW EXCITING.
THANK YOU, BUT I BELIEVE I'LL STAY HERE, RATHER THAN BE MURDERED AND DUMPED SOMEWHERE, JUST THE SAME.
CALIFORNIA STATE LAW
WELL, AREN'T *YOU* TALL AND UNAPPEALING?
WHAT IS HAPPENING? IS THIS AN *ESCAPE?*
UH, SCANDAL... WE GOT SOME OTHER INMATES.
IT'S A *PRISON,* DEADSHOT.
YEAH, ONLY THING ABOUT *THAT* IS...

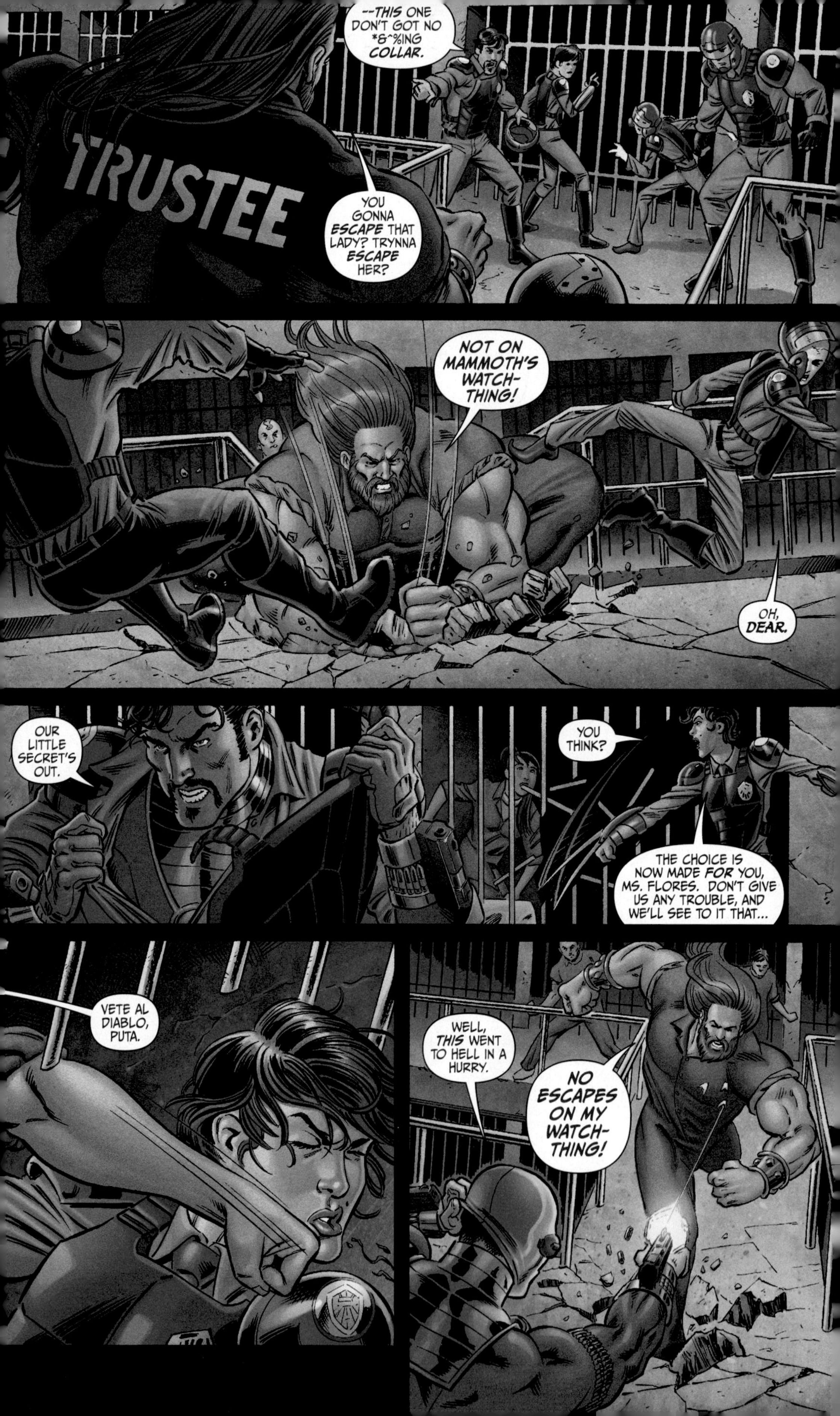
--THIS ONE DON'T GOT NO *&^%ING COLLAR.
TRUSTEE
YOU GONNA ESCAPE THAT LADY? TRYNNA ESCAPE HER?
NOT ON MAMMOTH'S WATCH-THING!
OH, DEAR.
OUR LITTLE SECRET'S OUT.
YOU THINK?
THE CHOICE IS NOW MADE FOR YOU, MS. FLORES. DON'T GIVE US ANY TROUBLE, AND WE'LL SEE TO IT THAT...
VETE AL DIABLO, PUTA.
WELL, THIS WENT TO HELL IN A HURRY.
NO ESCAPES ON MY WATCH-THING!

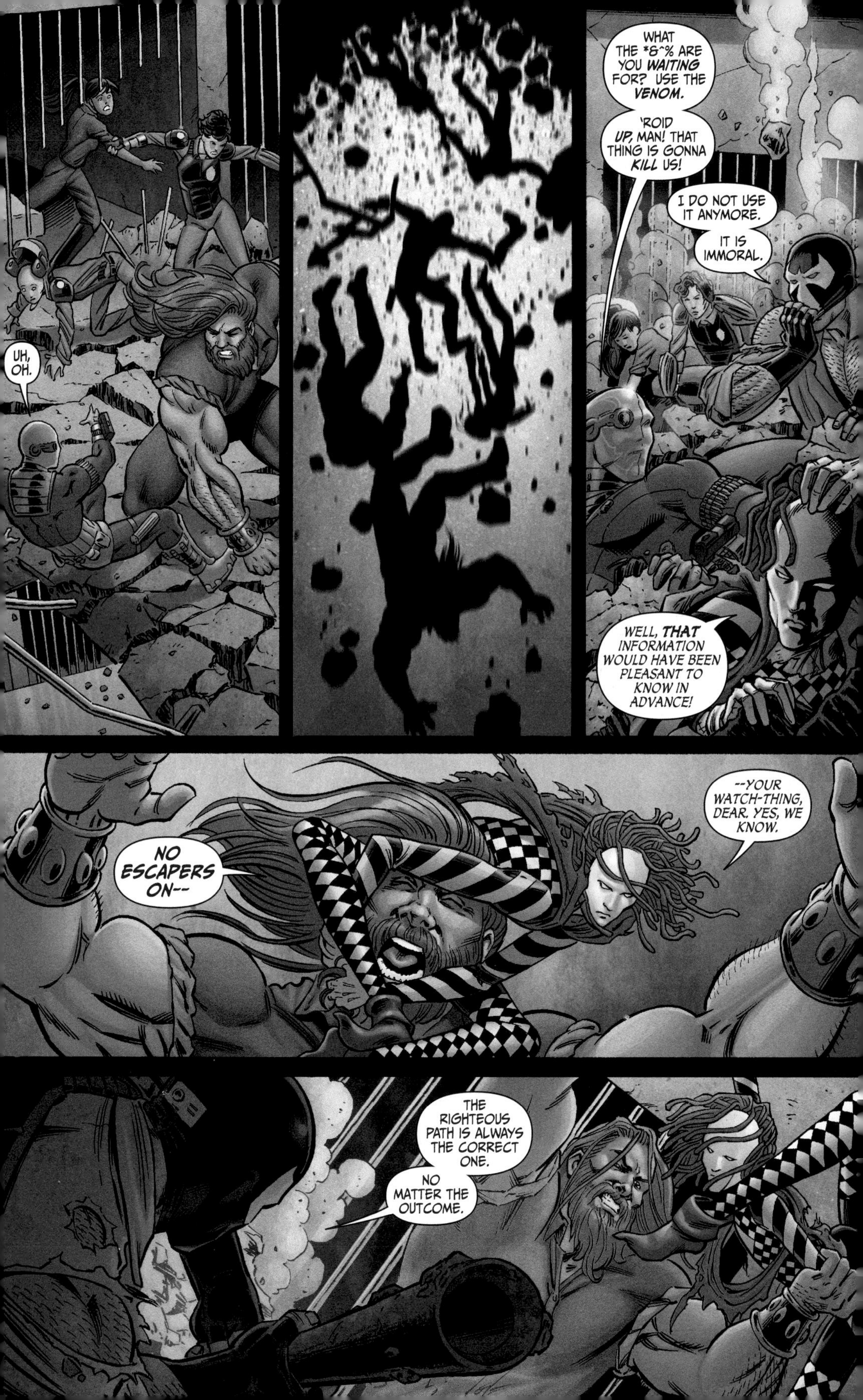
UH, OH.
WHAT THE *&^% ARE YOU WAITING FOR? USE THE VENOM.
'ROID UP, MAN! THAT THING IS GONNA KILL US!
I DO NOT USE IT ANYMORE.
IT IS IMMORAL.
WELL, THAT INFORMATION WOULD HAVE BEEN PLEASANT TO KNOW IN ADVANCE!
NO ESCAPERS ON--
--YOUR WATCH-THING, DEAR. YES, WE KNOW.
THE RIGHTEOUS PATH IS ALWAYS THE CORRECT ONE.
NO MATTER THE OUTCOME.

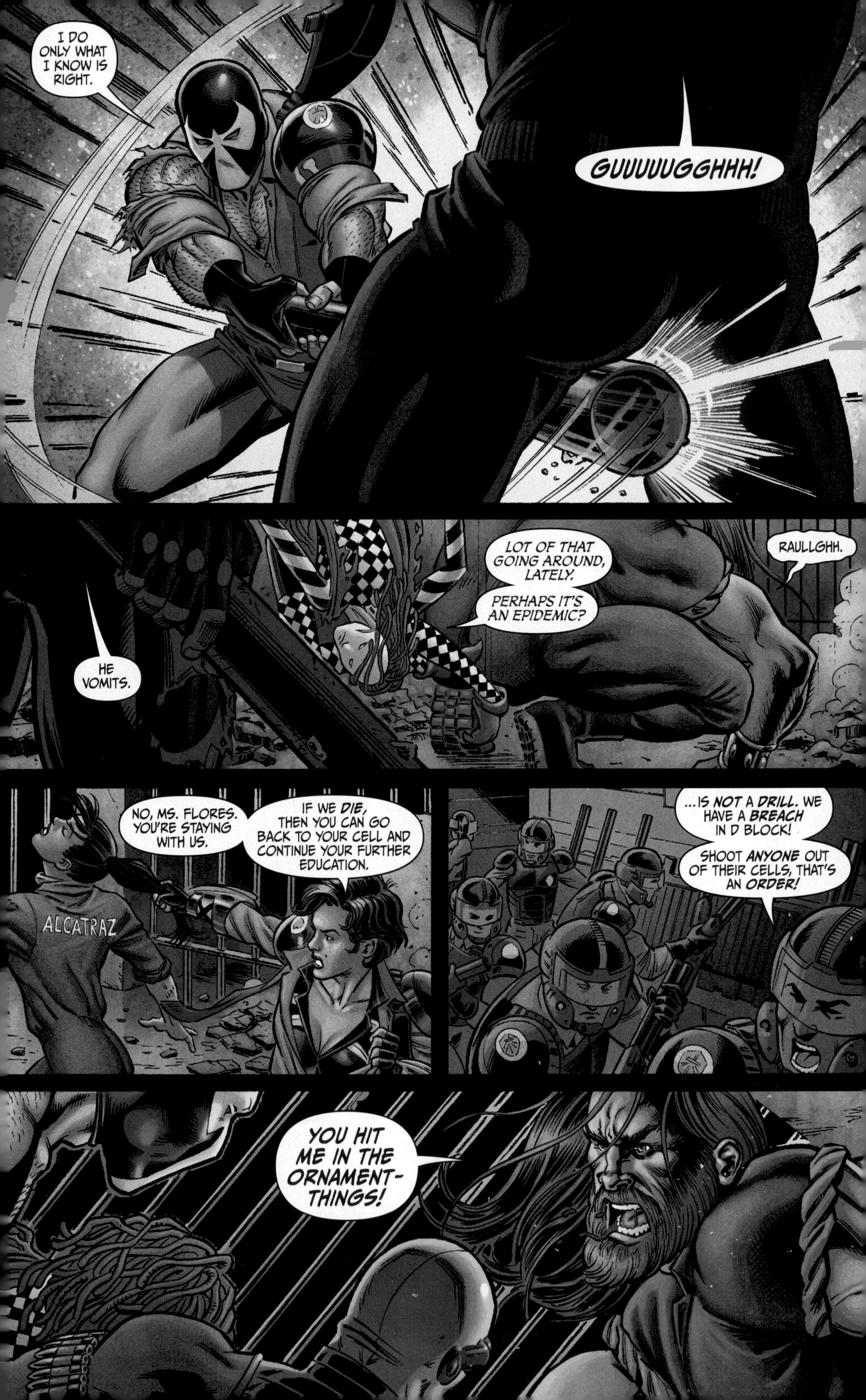
I DO ONLY WHAT I KNOW IS RIGHT.
GUUUUUGGHHH!
HE VOMITS.
LOT OF THAT GOING AROUND, LATELY.
PERHAPS IT'S AN EPIDEMIC?
RAULLGHH.
NO, MS. FLORES. YOU'RE STAYING WITH US.
IF WE DIE, THEN YOU CAN GO BACK TO YOUR CELL AND CONTINUE YOUR FURTHER EDUCATION.
ALCATRAZ
...IS NOT A DRILL. WE HAVE A BREACH IN D BLOCK!
SHOOT ANYONE OUT OF THEIR CELLS, THAT'S AN ORDER!
YOU HIT ME IN THE ORNAMENT-THINGS!

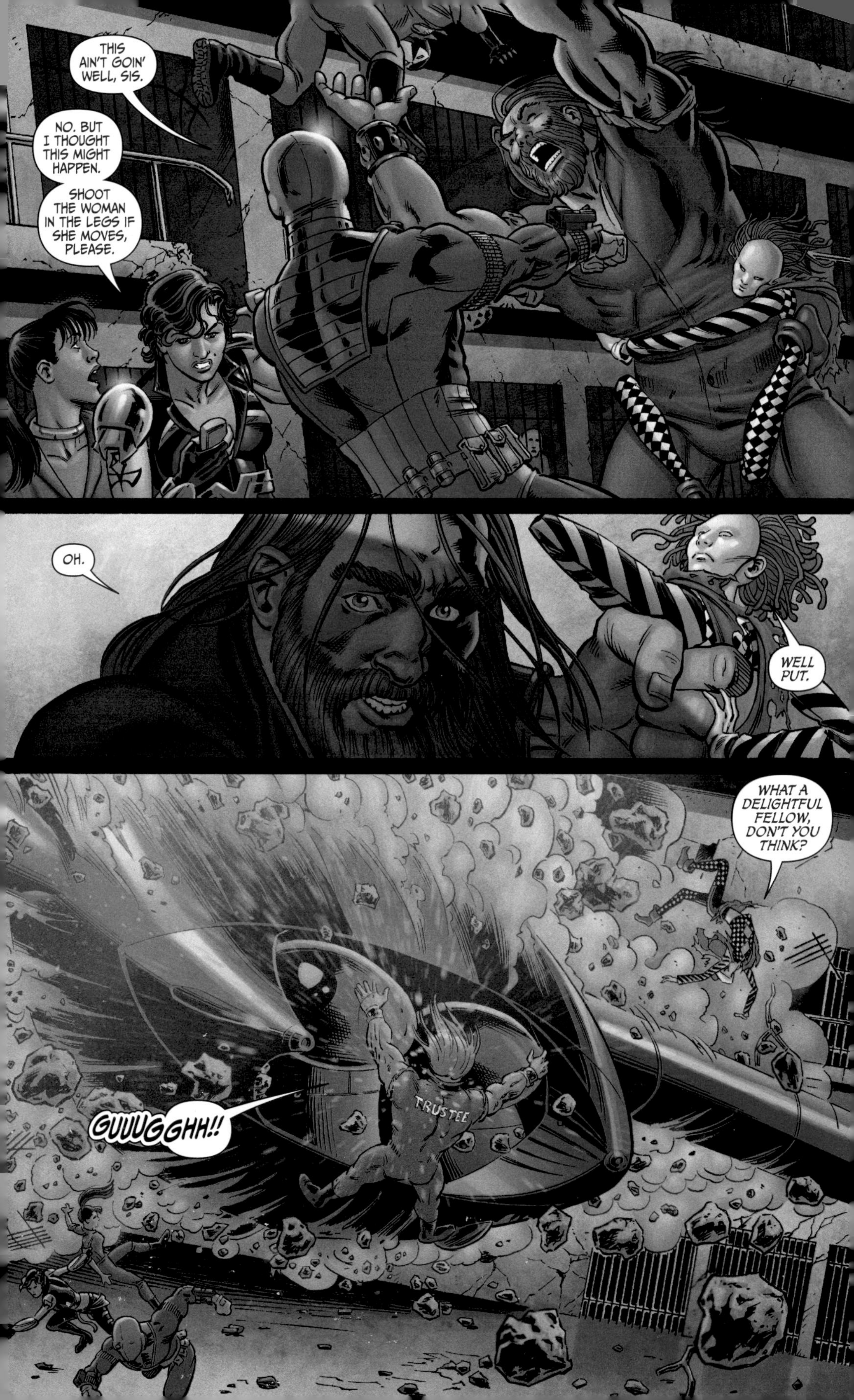
THIS AIN'T GOIN' WELL, SIS.
NO. BUT I THOUGHT THIS MIGHT HAPPEN.
SHOOT THE WOMAN IN THE LEGS IF SHE MOVES, PLEASE.
OH.
WELL PUT.
WHAT A DELIGHTFUL FELLOW, DON'T YOU THINK?
GUUUGGHH!!
TRUSTEE

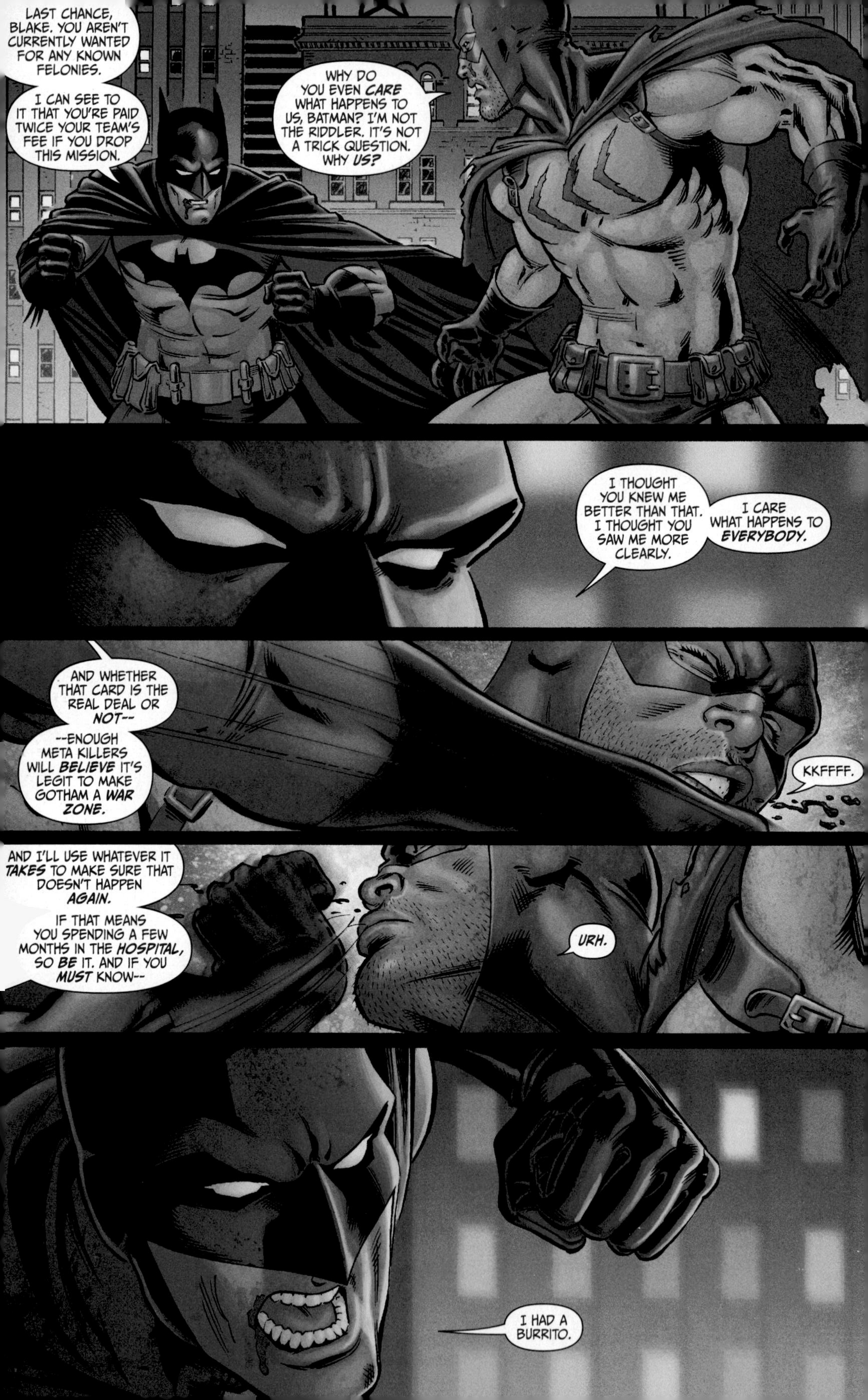
LAST CHANCE, BLAKE. YOU AREN'T CURRENTLY WANTED FOR ANY KNOWN FELONIES.
I CAN SEE TO IT THAT YOU'RE PAID TWICE YOUR TEAM'S FEE IF YOU DROP THIS MISSION.
WHY DO YOU EVEN CARE WHAT HAPPENS TO US, BATMAN? I'M NOT THE RIDDLER. IT'S NOT A TRICK QUESTION. WHY US?
I THOUGHT YOU KNEW ME BETTER THAN THAT. I THOUGHT YOU SAW ME MORE CLEARLY.
I CARE WHAT HAPPENS TO EVERYBODY.
AND WHETHER THAT CARD IS THE REAL DEAL OR NOT--
--ENOUGH META KILLERS WILL BELIEVE IT'S LEGIT TO MAKE GOTHAM A WAR ZONE.
KKFFFF.
AND I'LL USE WHATEVER IT TAKES TO MAKE SURE THAT DOESN'T HAPPEN AGAIN.
IF THAT MEANS YOU SPENDING A FEW MONTHS IN THE HOSPITAL, SO BE IT. AND IF YOU MUST KNOW--
URH.
I HAD A BURRITO.

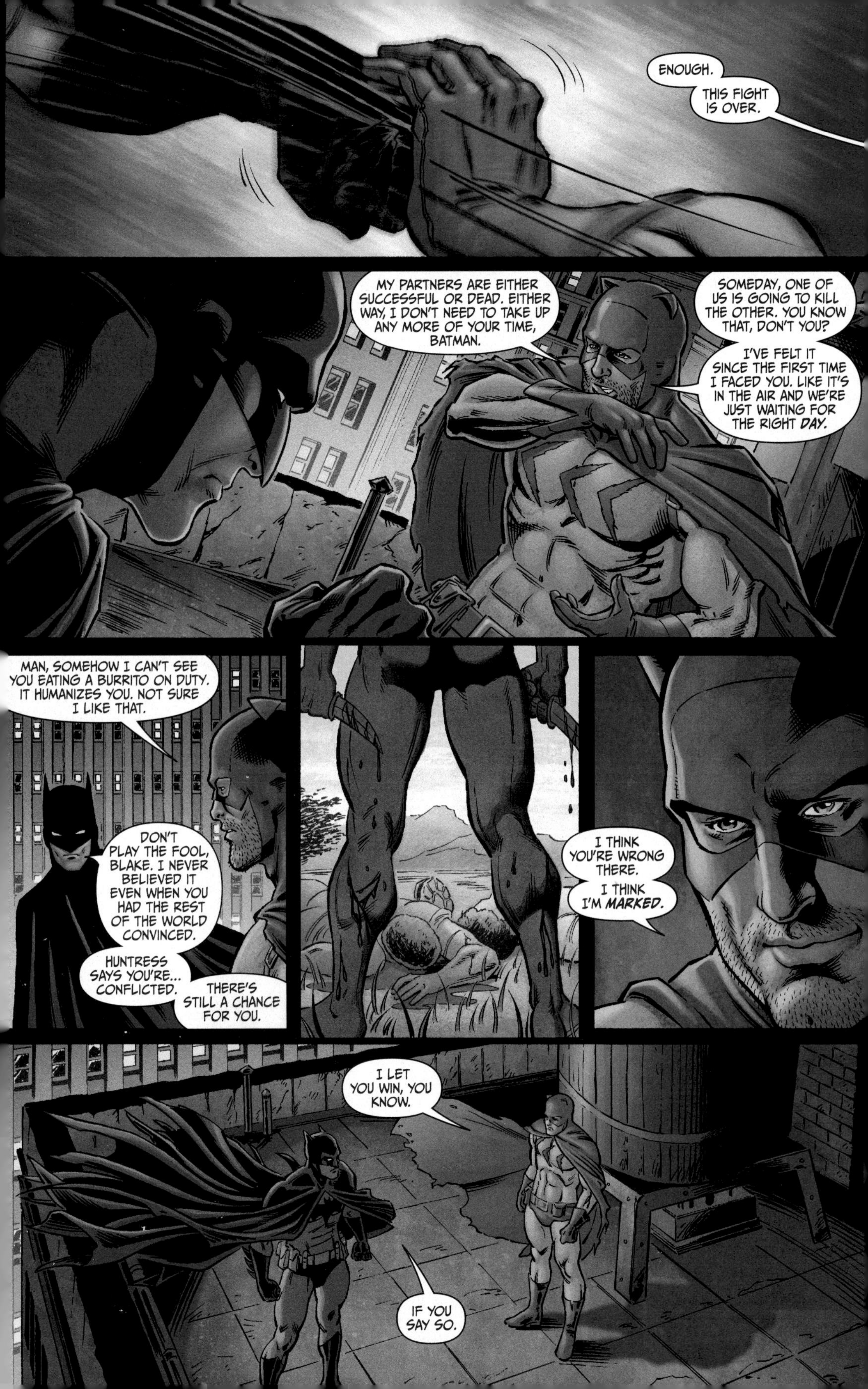

ENOUGH.
THIS FIGHT IS OVER.
MY PARTNERS ARE EITHER SUCCESSFUL OR DEAD. EITHER WAY, I DON'T NEED TO TAKE UP ANY MORE OF YOUR TIME, BATMAN.
SOMEDAY, ONE OF US IS GOING TO KILL THE OTHER. YOU KNOW THAT, DON'T YOU?
I'VE FELT IT SINCE THE FIRST TIME I FACED YOU. LIKE IT'S IN THE AIR AND WE'RE JUST WAITING FOR THE RIGHT *DAY.*
MAN, SOMEHOW I CAN'T SEE YOU EATING A BURRITO ON DUTY. IT HUMANIZES YOU. NOT SURE I LIKE THAT.
DON'T PLAY THE FOOL, BLAKE. I NEVER BELIEVED IT EVEN WHEN YOU HAD THE REST OF THE WORLD CONVINCED.
HUNTRESS SAYS YOU'RE... CONFLICTED.
THERE'S STILL A CHANCE FOR YOU.
I THINK YOU'RE WRONG THERE.
I THINK I'M ***MARKED.***
I LET YOU WIN, YOU KNOW.
IF YOU SAY SO.

HEY, WELCOME, THERE, DISTINGUISHED GUESTS AN' ALL. I'M TIG, AND THIS IS MY BROTHER, AARON.

IT'S A REAL THRILL, AND THAT'S SINCERE.

THE BOSS, HE'S GONNA BE...

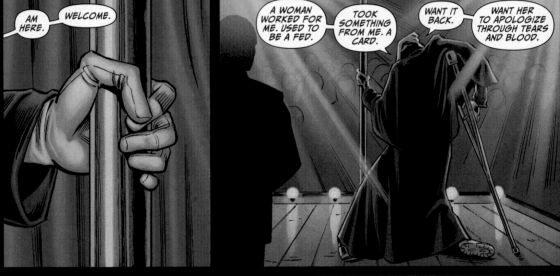

AM HERE.

WELCOME.

A WOMAN WORKED FOR ME. USED TO BE A FED.

TOOK SOMETHING FROM ME. A CARD.

WANT IT BACK.

WANT HER TO APOLOGIZE THROUGH TEARS AND BLOOD.

MOSTLY BLOOD.

WOMAN HAS ESCORTS.

MAKE THEM PAY FOR HELPING HER.

MESSAGE TO OTHERS.

STAKE THEM OUT IN THE SUN.

CUT THEM OPEN.

MAKE THEM DRINK BATTERY ACID.

FILL THEIR EYES WITH RAZORS.

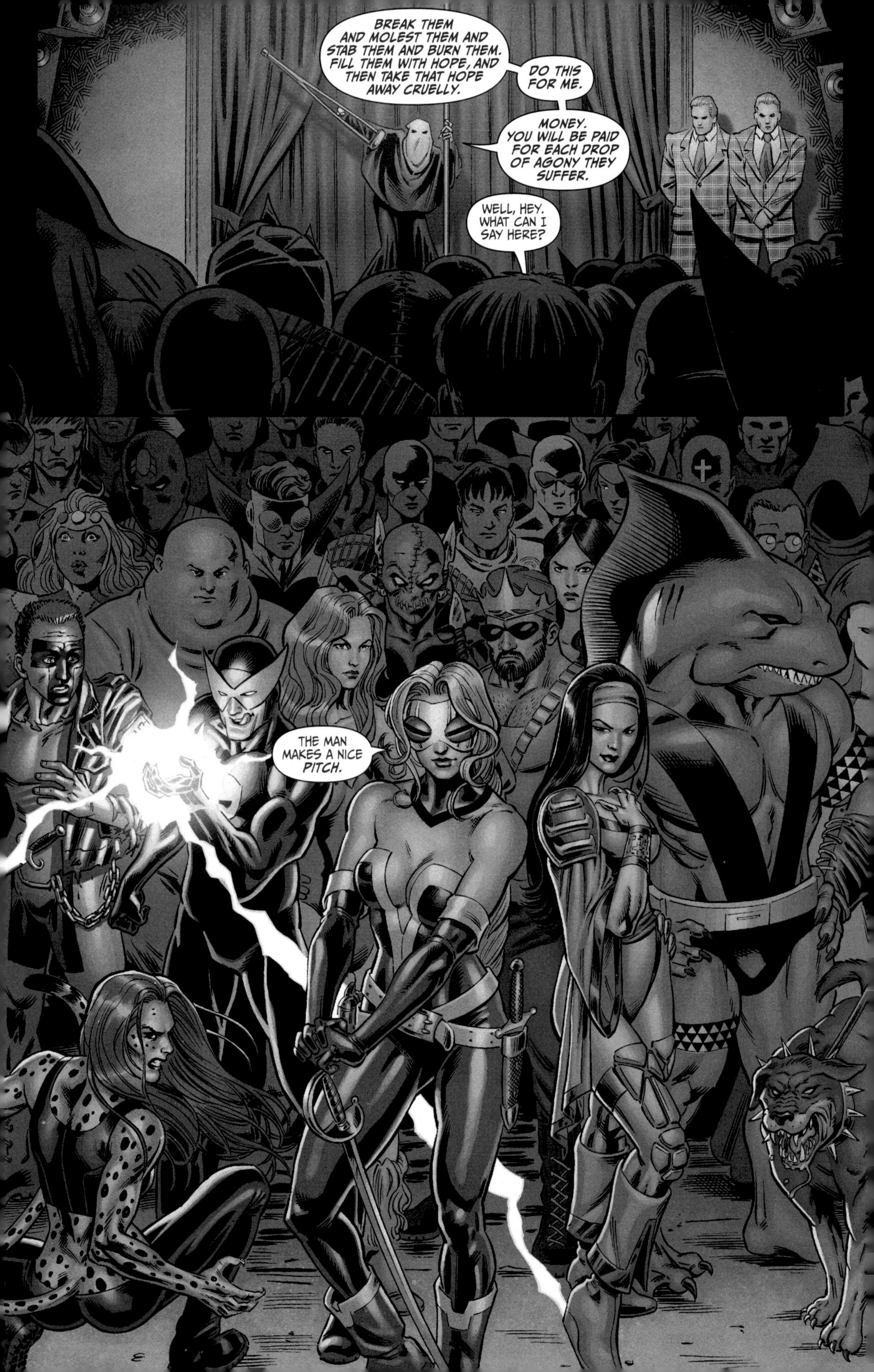
BREAK THEM AND MOLEST THEM AND STAB THEM AND BURN THEM. FILL THEM WITH HOPE, AND THEN TAKE THAT HOPE AWAY CRUELLY.
DO THIS FOR ME.
MONEY. YOU WILL BE PAID FOR EACH DROP OF AGONY THEY SUFFER.
WELL, HEY. WHAT CAN I SAY HERE?
THE MAN MAKES A NICE PITCH.

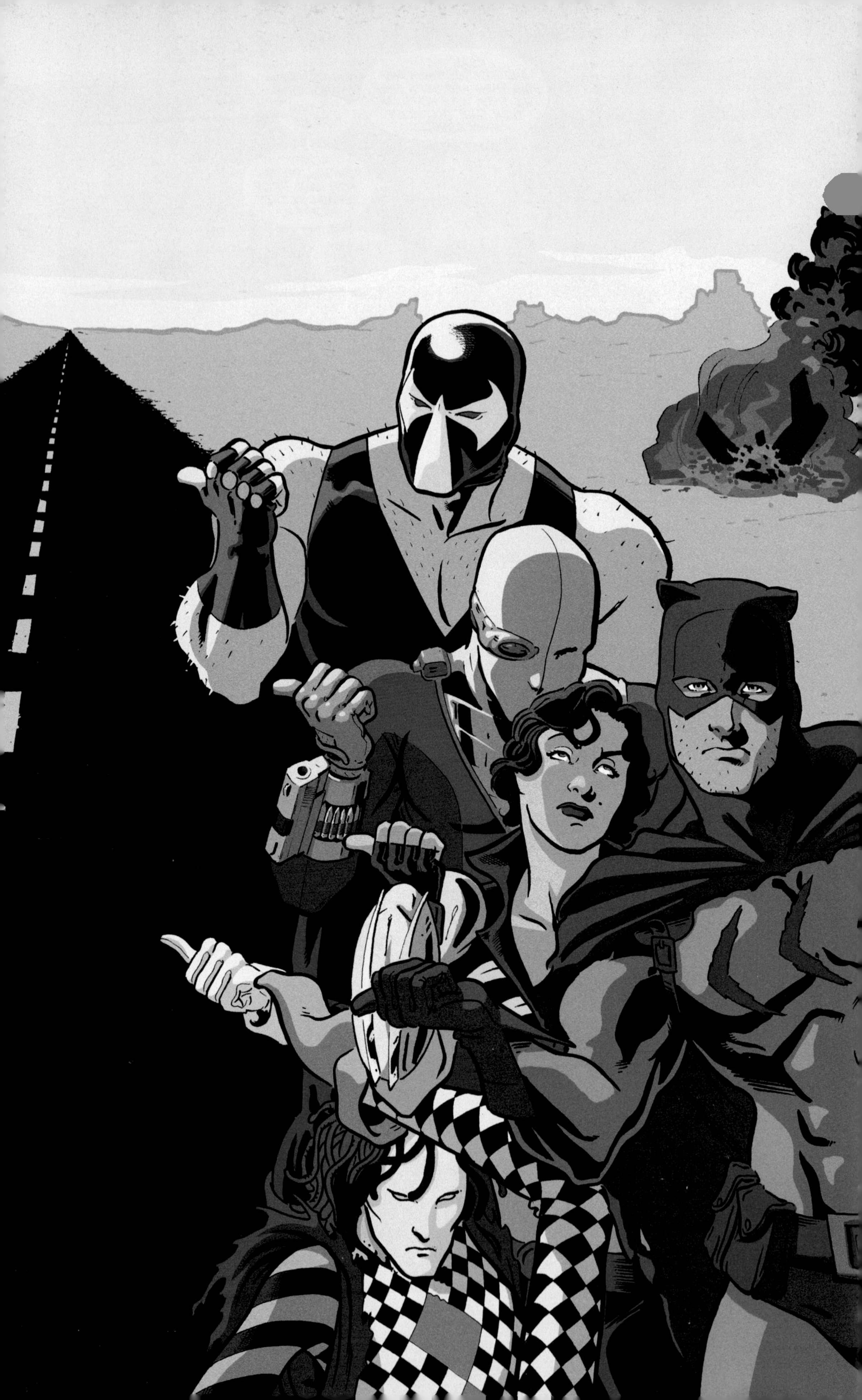

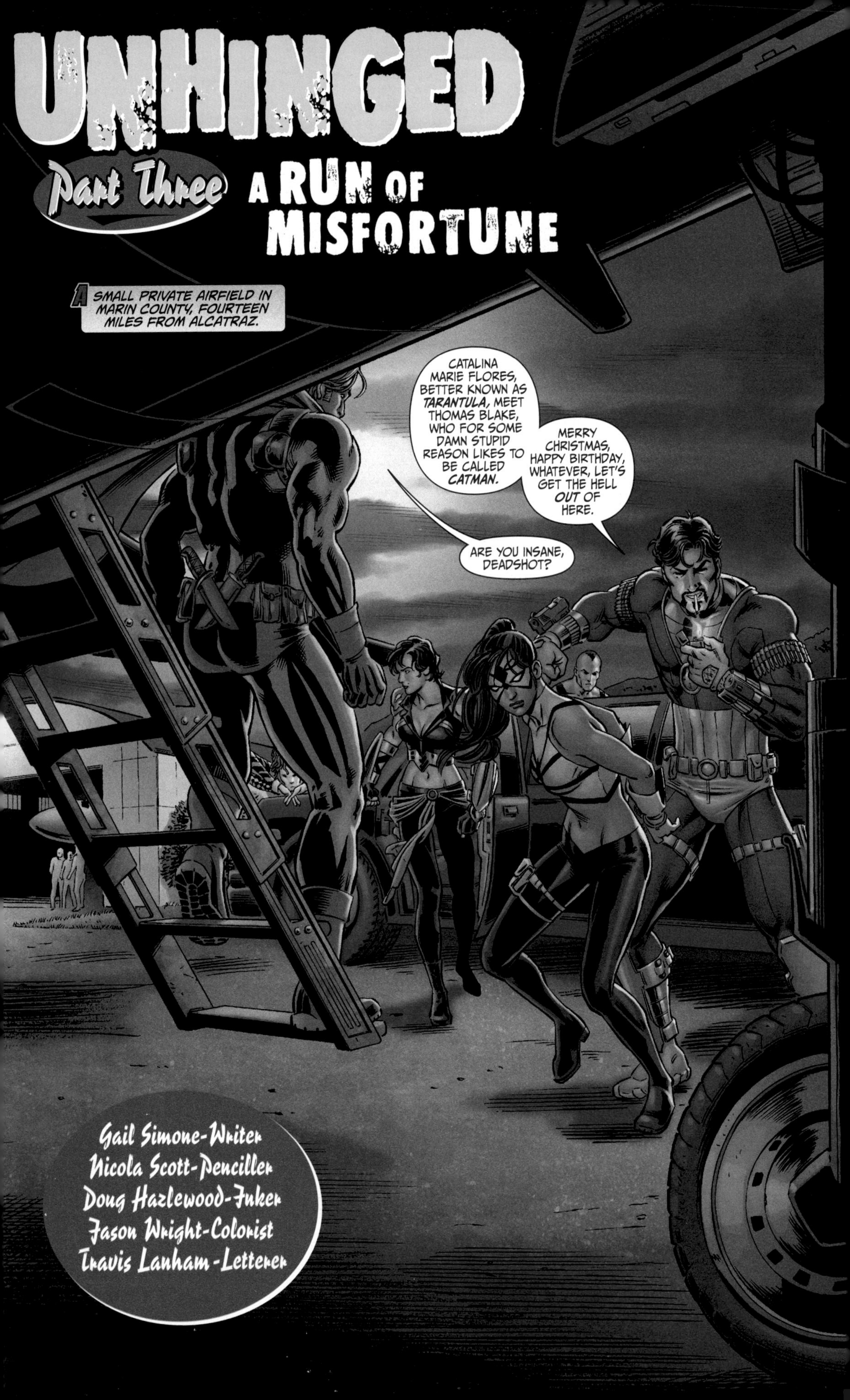
UNHINGED
Part Three A RUN OF MISFORTUNE
A SMALL PRIVATE AIRFIELD IN MARIN COUNTY, FOURTEEN MILES FROM ALCATRAZ.
CATALINA MARIE FLORES, BETTER KNOWN AS TARANTULA, MEET THOMAS BLAKE, WHO FOR SOME DAMN STUPID REASON LIKES TO BE CALLED CATMAN.
MERRY CHRISTMAS, HAPPY BIRTHDAY, WHATEVER, LET'S GET THE HELL OUT OF HERE.
ARE YOU INSANE, DEADSHOT?
Gail Simone-Writer
Nicola Scott-Penciller
Doug Hazlewood-Inker
Jason Wright-Colorist
Travis Lanham-Letterer

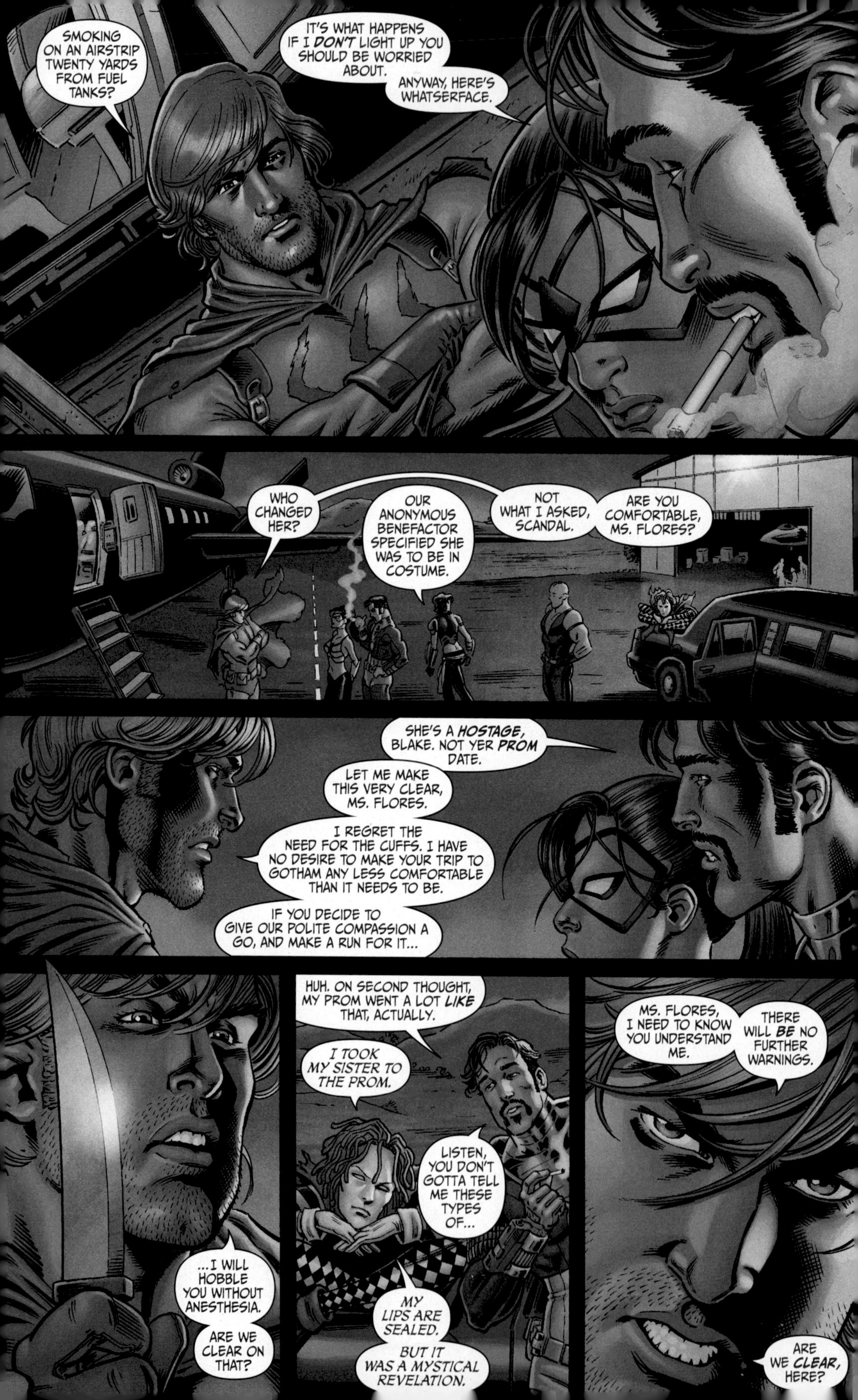
SMOKING ON AN AIRSTRIP TWENTY YARDS FROM FUEL TANKS?
IT'S WHAT HAPPENS IF I *DON'T* LIGHT UP YOU SHOULD BE WORRIED ABOUT.
ANYWAY, HERE'S WHATSERFACE.
WHO CHANGED HER?
OUR ANONYMOUS BENEFACTOR SPECIFIED SHE WAS TO BE IN COSTUME.
NOT WHAT I ASKED, SCANDAL.
ARE YOU COMFORTABLE, MS. FLORES?
SHE'S A ***HOSTAGE,*** BLAKE. NOT YER ***PROM*** DATE.
LET ME MAKE THIS VERY CLEAR, MS. FLORES.
I REGRET THE NEED FOR THE CUFFS. I HAVE NO DESIRE TO MAKE YOUR TRIP TO GOTHAM ANY LESS COMFORTABLE THAN IT NEEDS TO BE.
IF YOU DECIDE TO GIVE OUR POLITE COMPASSION A GO, AND MAKE A RUN FOR IT...
...I WILL HOBBLE YOU WITHOUT ANESTHESIA.
ARE WE CLEAR ON THAT?
HUH. ON SECOND THOUGHT, MY PROM WENT A LOT ***LIKE*** THAT, ACTUALLY.
I TOOK MY SISTER TO THE PROM.
LISTEN, YOU DON'T GOTTA TELL ME THESE TYPES OF...
MY LIPS ARE SEALED.
BUT IT WAS A MYSTICAL REVELATION.
MS. FLORES, I NEED TO KNOW YOU UNDERSTAND ME.
THERE WILL ***BE*** NO FURTHER WARNINGS.
ARE WE ***CLEAR,*** HERE?

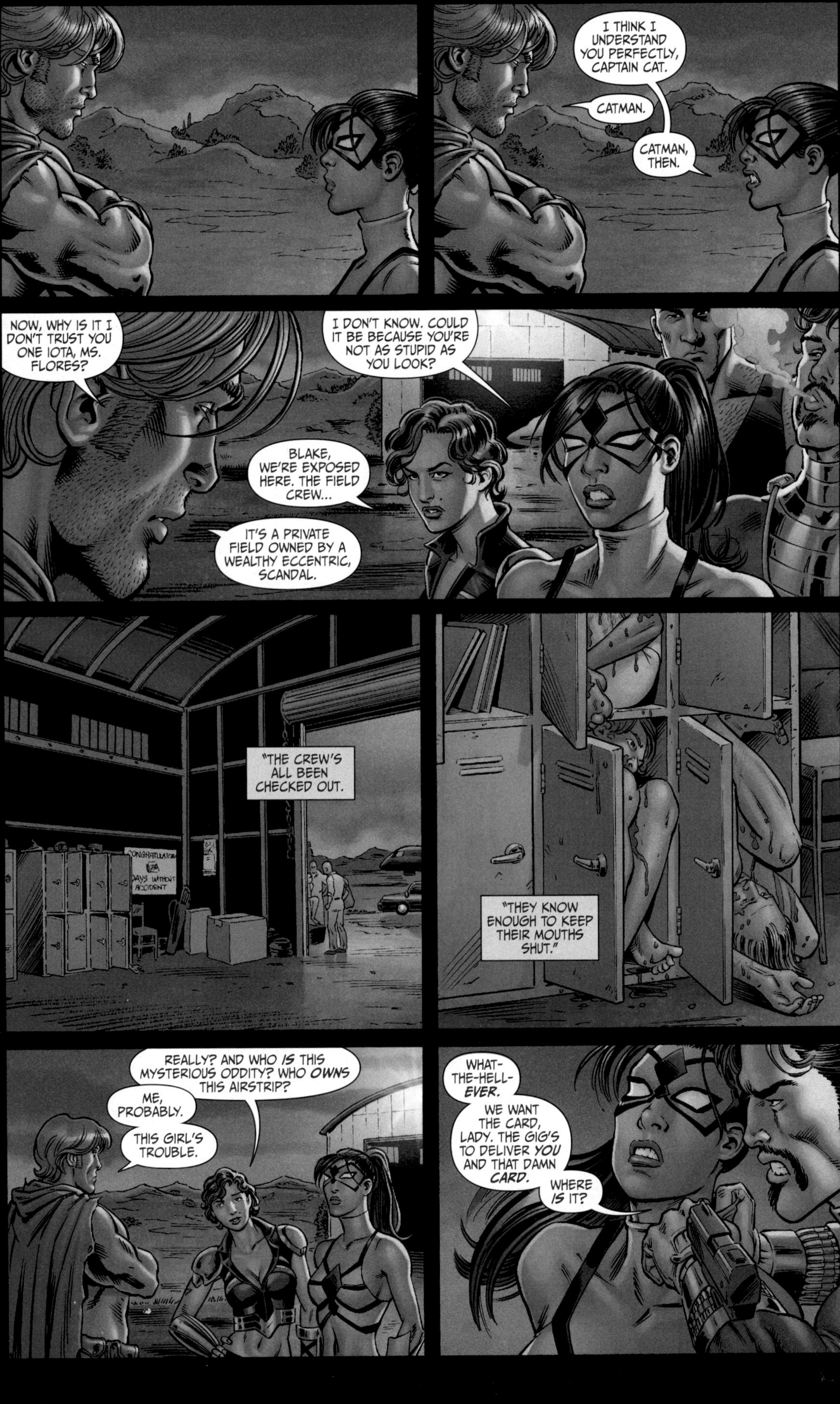

I THINK I UNDERSTAND YOU PERFECTLY, CAPTAIN CAT.
CATMAN.
CATMAN, THEN.
NOW, WHY IS IT I DON'T TRUST YOU ONE IOTA, MS. FLORES?
I DON'T KNOW. COULD IT BE BECAUSE YOU'RE NOT AS STUPID AS YOU LOOK?
BLAKE, WE'RE EXPOSED HERE. THE FIELD CREW...
IT'S A PRIVATE FIELD OWNED BY A WEALTHY ECCENTRIC, SCANDAL.
"THE CREW'S ALL BEEN CHECKED OUT.
"THEY KNOW ENOUGH TO KEEP THEIR MOUTHS SHUT."
REALLY? AND WHO *IS* THIS MYSTERIOUS ODDITY? WHO *OWNS* THIS AIRSTRIP?
ME, PROBABLY.
THIS GIRL'S TROUBLE.
WHAT-THE-HELL-*EVER*.
WE WANT THE CARD, LADY. THE GIG'S TO DELIVER *YOU* AND THAT DAMN *CARD*.
WHERE *IS* IT?

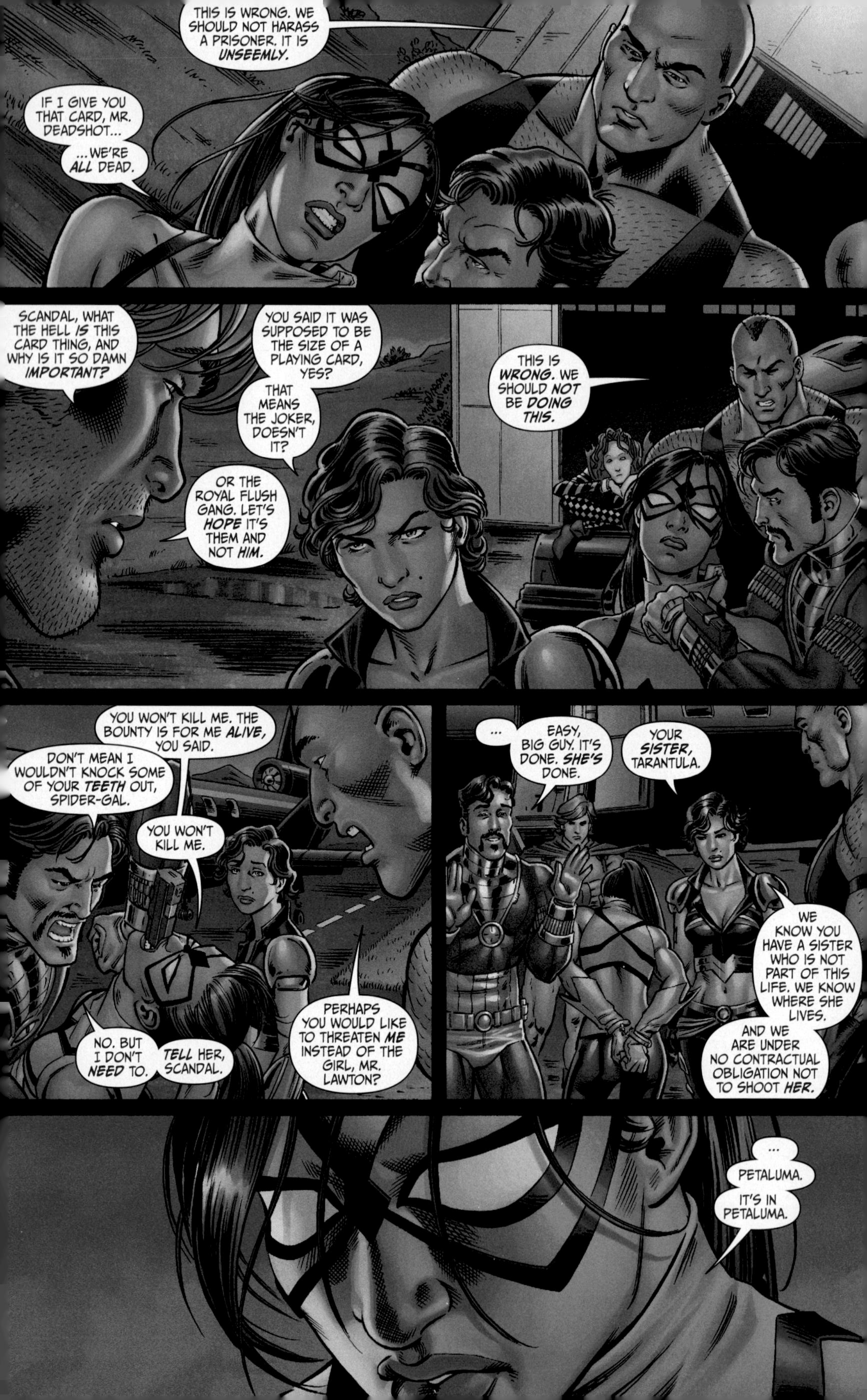
THIS IS WRONG. WE SHOULD NOT HARASS A PRISONER. IT IS UNSEEMLY.
IF I GIVE YOU THAT CARD, MR. DEADSHOT...
...WE'RE ALL DEAD.
SCANDAL, WHAT THE HELL IS THIS CARD THING, AND WHY IS IT SO DAMN IMPORTANT?
YOU SAID IT WAS SUPPOSED TO BE THE SIZE OF A PLAYING CARD, YES?
THAT MEANS THE JOKER, DOESN'T IT?
OR THE ROYAL FLUSH GANG. LET'S HOPE IT'S THEM AND NOT HIM.
THIS IS WRONG. WE SHOULD NOT BE DOING THIS.
YOU WON'T KILL ME. THE BOUNTY IS FOR ME ALIVE, YOU SAID.
DON'T MEAN I WOULDN'T KNOCK SOME OF YOUR TEETH OUT, SPIDER-GAL.
YOU WON'T KILL ME.
NO. BUT I DON'T NEED TO.
TELL HER, SCANDAL.
PERHAPS YOU WOULD LIKE TO THREATEN ME INSTEAD OF THE GIRL, MR. LAWTON?
...
EASY, BIG GUY. IT'S DONE. SHE'S DONE.
YOUR SISTER, TARANTULA.
WE KNOW YOU HAVE A SISTER WHO IS NOT PART OF THIS LIFE. WE KNOW WHERE SHE LIVES.
AND WE ARE UNDER NO CONTRACTUAL OBLIGATION NOT TO SHOOT HER.
...
PETALUMA.
IT'S IN PETALUMA.

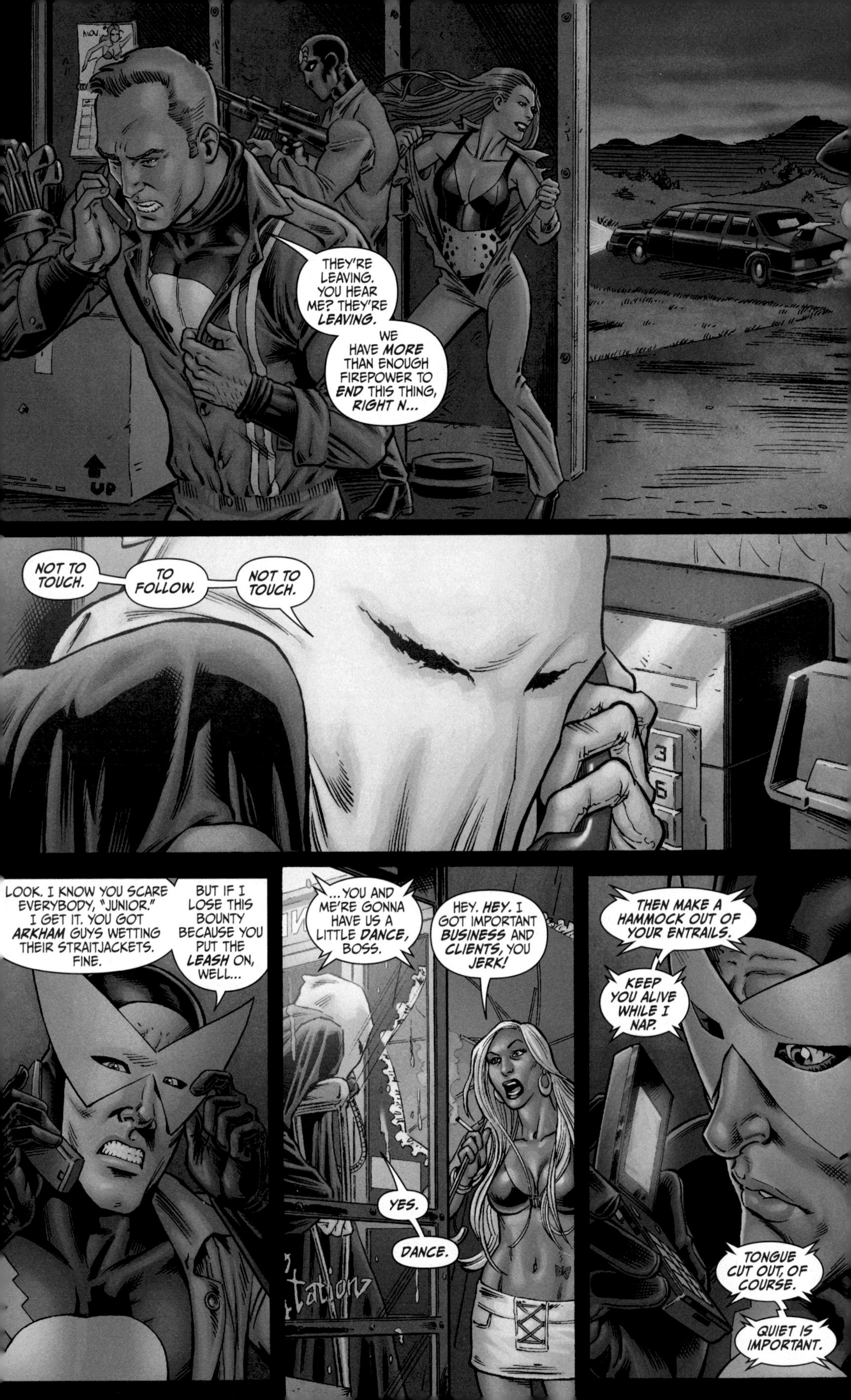
THEY'RE LEAVING. YOU HEAR ME? THEY'RE LEAVING.
WE HAVE MORE THAN ENOUGH FIREPOWER TO END THIS THING, RIGHT N...
NOT TO TOUCH.
TO FOLLOW.
NOT TO TOUCH.
LOOK. I KNOW YOU SCARE EVERYBODY, "JUNIOR." I GET IT. YOU GOT ARKHAM GUYS WETTING THEIR STRAITJACKETS. FINE.
BUT IF I LOSE THIS BOUNTY BECAUSE YOU PUT THE LEASH ON, WELL...
...YOU AND ME'RE GONNA HAVE US A LITTLE DANCE, BOSS.
YES.
DANCE.
HEY. HEY. I GOT IMPORTANT BUSINESS AND CLIENTS, YOU JERK!
THEN MAKE A HAMMOCK OUT OF YOUR ENTRAILS.
KEEP YOU ALIVE WHILE I NAP.
TONGUE CUT OUT, OF COURSE.
QUIET IS IMPORTANT.

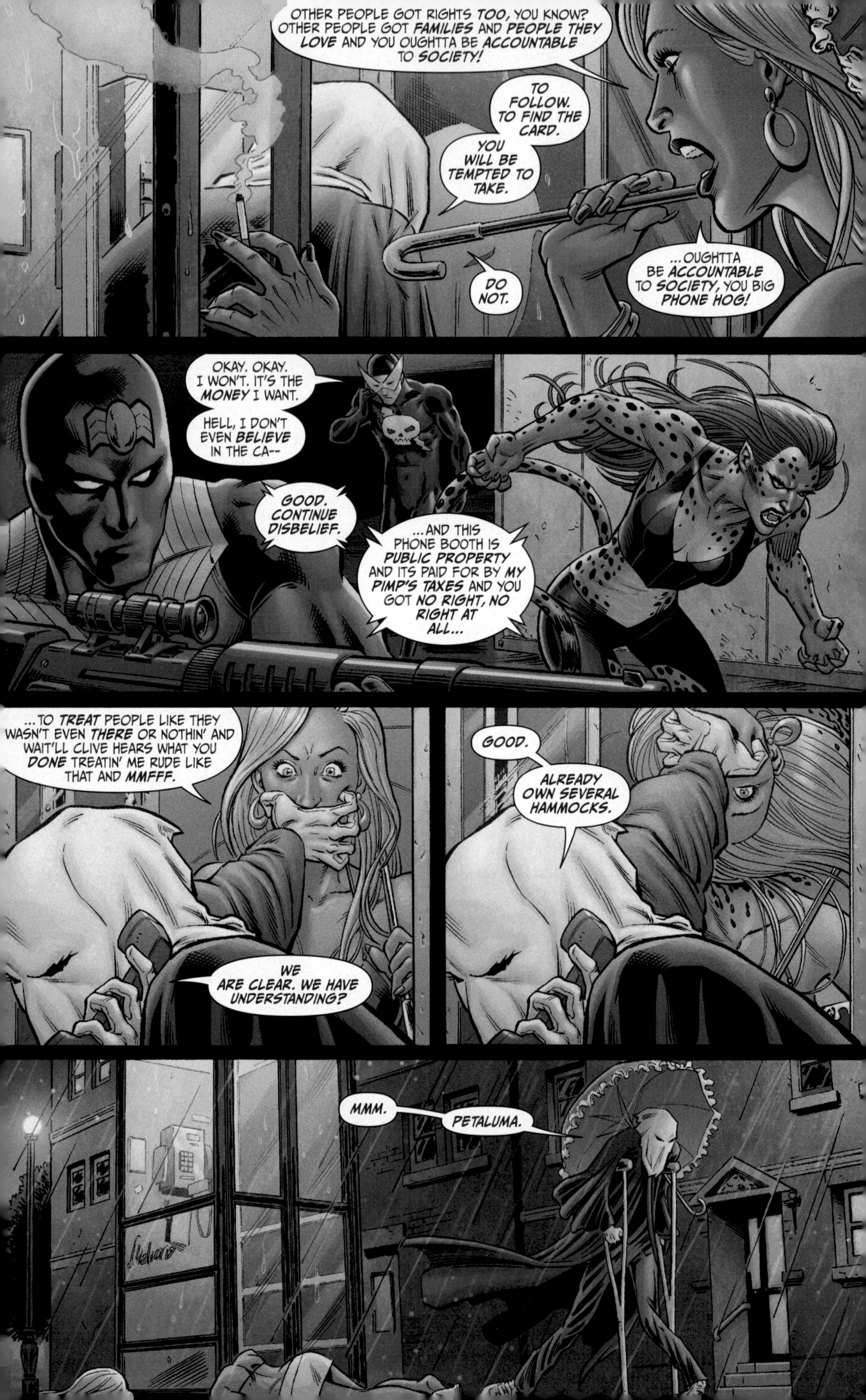
OTHER PEOPLE GOT RIGHTS TOO, YOU KNOW? OTHER PEOPLE GOT FAMILIES AND PEOPLE THEY LOVE AND YOU OUGHTTA BE ACCOUNTABLE TO SOCIETY!
TO FOLLOW. TO FIND THE CARD.
YOU WILL BE TEMPTED TO TAKE.
DO NOT.
...OUGHTTA BE ACCOUNTABLE TO SOCIETY, YOU BIG PHONE HOG!
OKAY. OKAY. I WON'T. IT'S THE MONEY I WANT.
HELL, I DON'T EVEN BELIEVE IN THE CA--
GOOD. CONTINUE DISBELIEF.
...AND THIS PHONE BOOTH IS PUBLIC PROPERTY AND ITS PAID FOR BY MY PIMP'S TAXES AND YOU GOT NO RIGHT, NO RIGHT AT ALL...
...TO TREAT PEOPLE LIKE THEY WASN'T EVEN THERE OR NOTHIN' AND WAIT'LL CLIVE HEARS WHAT YOU DONE TREATIN' ME RUDE LIKE THAT AND MMFFF.
WE ARE CLEAR. WE HAVE UNDERSTANDING?
GOOD.
ALREADY OWN SEVERAL HAMMOCKS.
MMM.
PETALUMA.

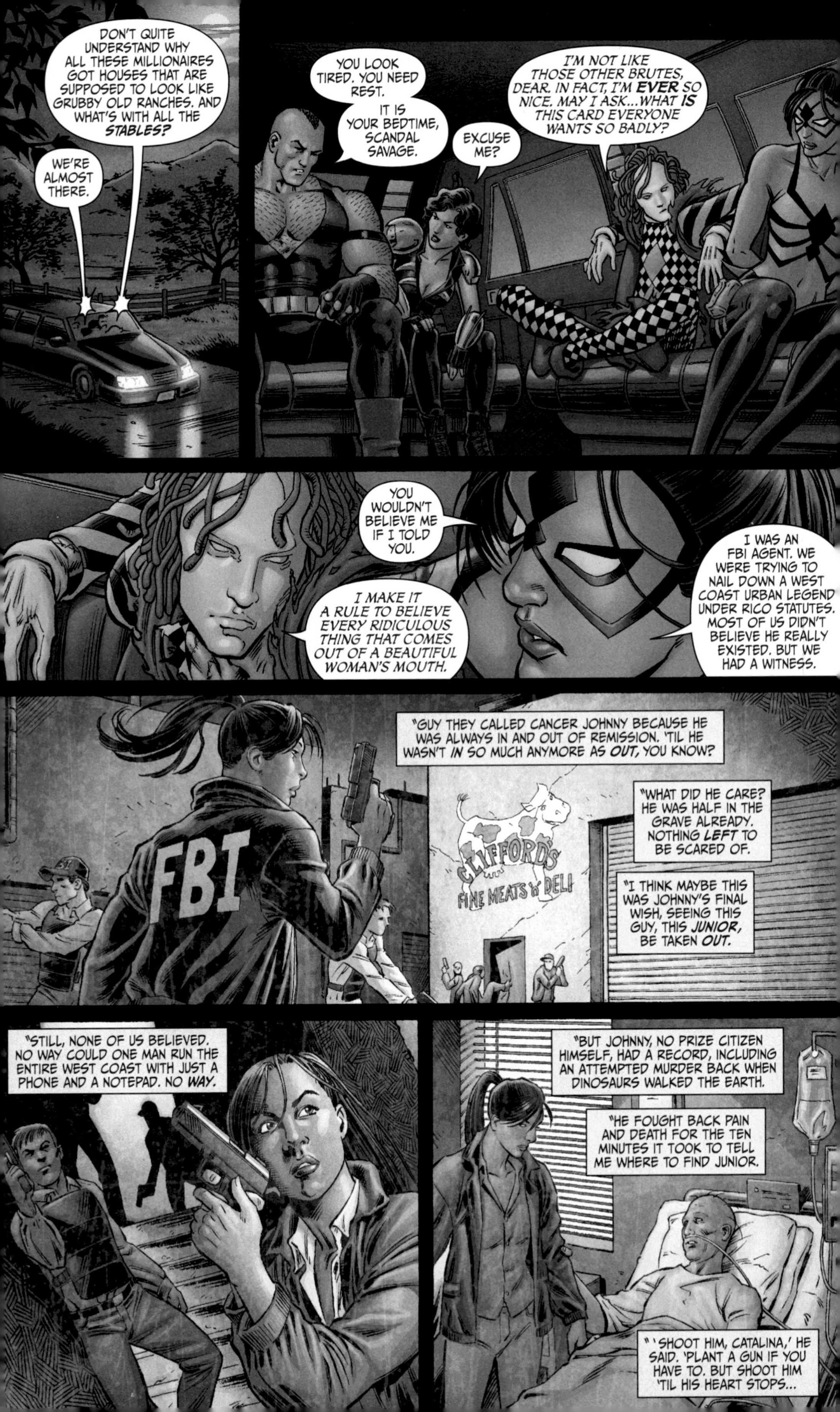
DON'T QUITE UNDERSTAND WHY ALL THESE MILLIONAIRES GOT HOUSES THAT ARE SUPPOSED TO LOOK LIKE GRUBBY OLD RANCHES. AND WHAT'S WITH ALL THE STABLES?
WE'RE ALMOST THERE.
YOU LOOK TIRED. YOU NEED REST.
IT IS YOUR BEDTIME, SCANDAL SAVAGE.
EXCUSE ME?
I'M NOT LIKE THOSE OTHER BRUTES, DEAR. IN FACT, I'M EVER SO NICE. MAY I ASK...WHAT IS THIS CARD EVERYONE WANTS SO BADLY?
YOU WOULDN'T BELIEVE ME IF I TOLD YOU.
I MAKE IT A RULE TO BELIEVE EVERY RIDICULOUS THING THAT COMES OUT OF A BEAUTIFUL WOMAN'S MOUTH.
I WAS AN FBI AGENT. WE WERE TRYING TO NAIL DOWN A WEST COAST URBAN LEGEND UNDER RICO STATUTES. MOST OF US DIDN'T BELIEVE HE REALLY EXISTED. BUT WE HAD A WITNESS.
"GUY THEY CALLED CANCER JOHNNY BECAUSE HE WAS ALWAYS IN AND OUT OF REMISSION. 'TIL HE WASN'T IN SO MUCH ANYMORE AS OUT, YOU KNOW?
FBI
CLIFFORD'S FINE MEATS 'N' DELI
"WHAT DID HE CARE? HE WAS HALF IN THE GRAVE ALREADY. NOTHING LEFT TO BE SCARED OF.
"I THINK MAYBE THIS WAS JOHNNY'S FINAL WISH, SEEING THIS GUY, THIS JUNIOR, BE TAKEN OUT.
"STILL, NONE OF US BELIEVED. NO WAY COULD ONE MAN RUN THE ENTIRE WEST COAST WITH JUST A PHONE AND A NOTEPAD. NO WAY.
"BUT JOHNNY, NO PRIZE CITIZEN HIMSELF, HAD A RECORD, INCLUDING AN ATTEMPTED MURDER BACK WHEN DINOSAURS WALKED THE EARTH.
"HE FOUGHT BACK PAIN AND DEATH FOR THE TEN MINUTES IT TOOK TO TELL ME WHERE TO FIND JUNIOR.
"'SHOOT HIM, CATALINA,' HE SAID. 'PLANT A GUN IF YOU HAVE TO. BUT SHOOT HIM 'TIL HIS HEART STOPS...

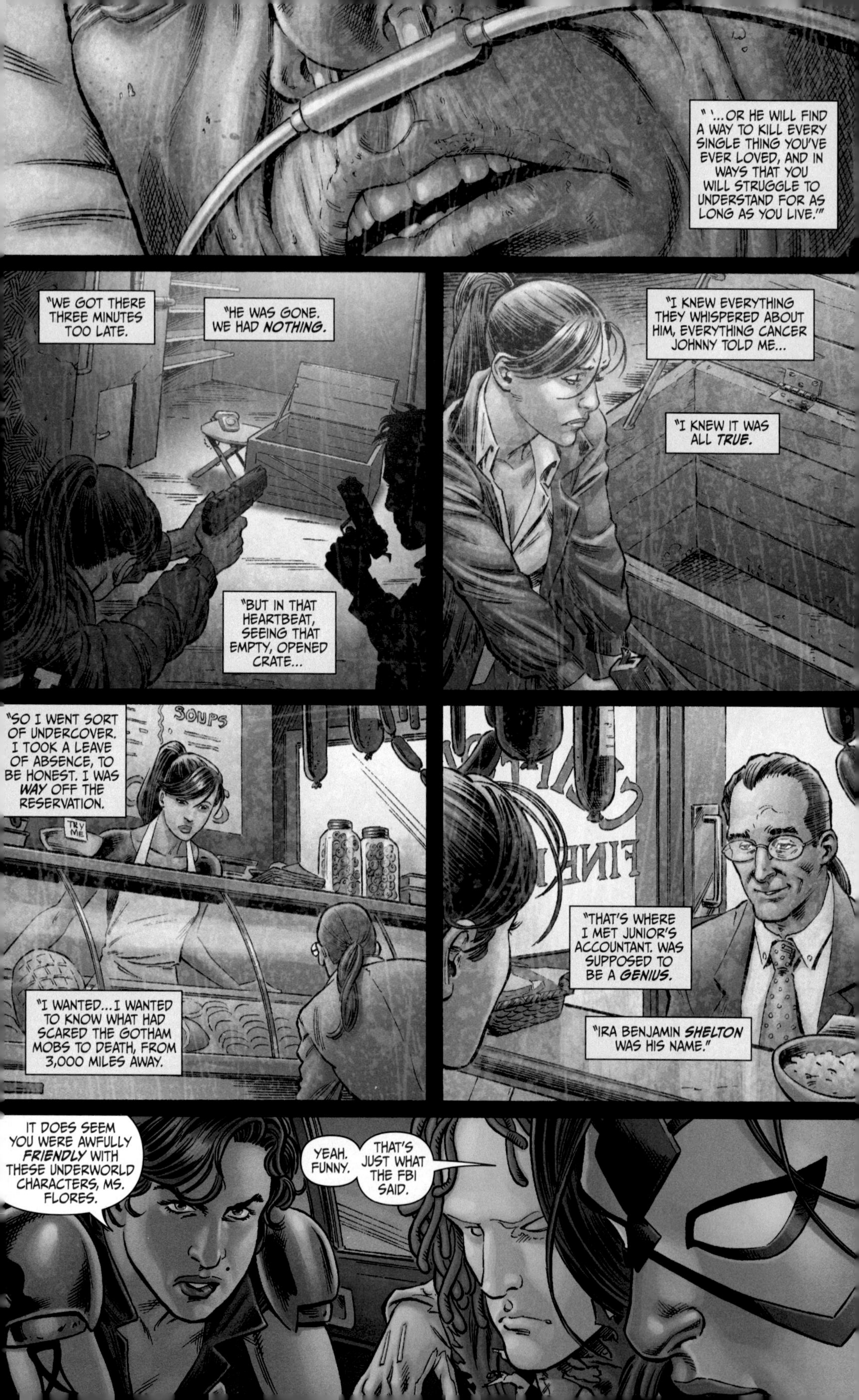
"'...OR HE WILL FIND A WAY TO KILL EVERY SINGLE THING YOU'VE EVER LOVED, AND IN WAYS THAT YOU WILL STRUGGLE TO UNDERSTAND FOR AS LONG AS YOU LIVE.'"
"WE GOT THERE THREE MINUTES TOO LATE.
"HE WAS GONE. WE HAD NOTHING.
"BUT IN THAT HEARTBEAT, SEEING THAT EMPTY, OPENED CRATE...
"I KNEW EVERYTHING THEY WHISPERED ABOUT HIM, EVERYTHING CANCER JOHNNY TOLD ME...
"I KNEW IT WAS ALL TRUE.
SOUPS
"SO I WENT SORT OF UNDERCOVER. I TOOK A LEAVE OF ABSENCE, TO BE HONEST. I WAS WAY OFF THE RESERVATION.
TRY ME
"I WANTED...I WANTED TO KNOW WHAT HAD SCARED THE GOTHAM MOBS TO DEATH, FROM 3,000 MILES AWAY.
"THAT'S WHERE I MET JUNIOR'S ACCOUNTANT. WAS SUPPOSED TO BE A GENIUS.
"IRA BENJAMIN SHELTON WAS HIS NAME."
IT DOES SEEM YOU WERE AWFULLY FRIENDLY WITH THESE UNDERWORLD CHARACTERS, MS. FLORES.
YEAH. FUNNY.
THAT'S JUST WHAT THE FBI SAID.

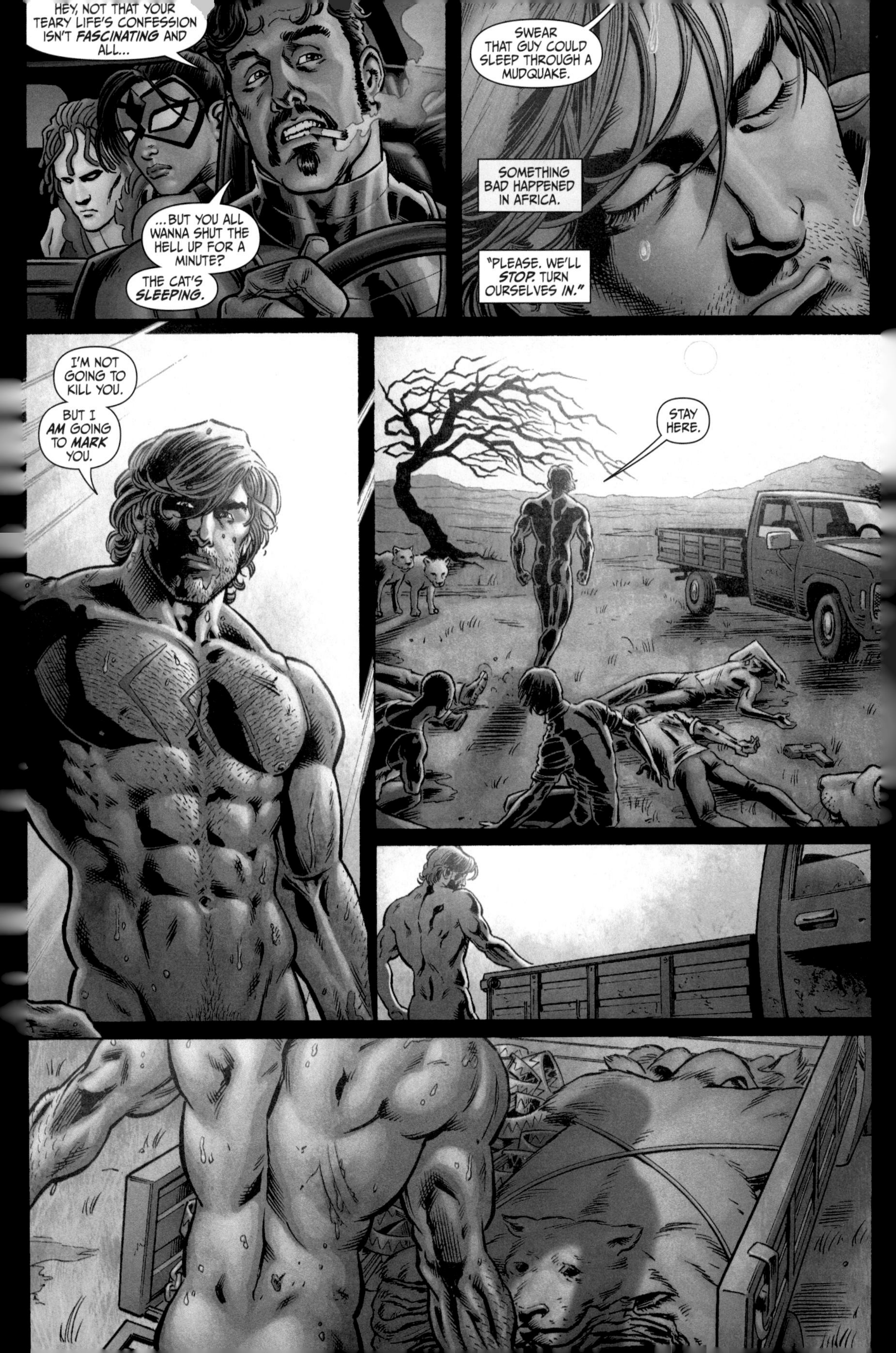
HEY, NOT THAT YOUR TEARY LIFE'S CONFESSION ISN'T FASCINATING AND ALL...
...BUT YOU ALL WANNA SHUT THE HELL UP FOR A MINUTE?
THE CAT'S SLEEPING.
SWEAR THAT GUY COULD SLEEP THROUGH A MUDQUAKE.
SOMETHING BAD HAPPENED IN AFRICA.
"PLEASE. WE'LL STOP. TURN OURSELVES IN."
I'M NOT GOING TO KILL YOU.
BUT I AM GOING TO MARK YOU.
STAY HERE.

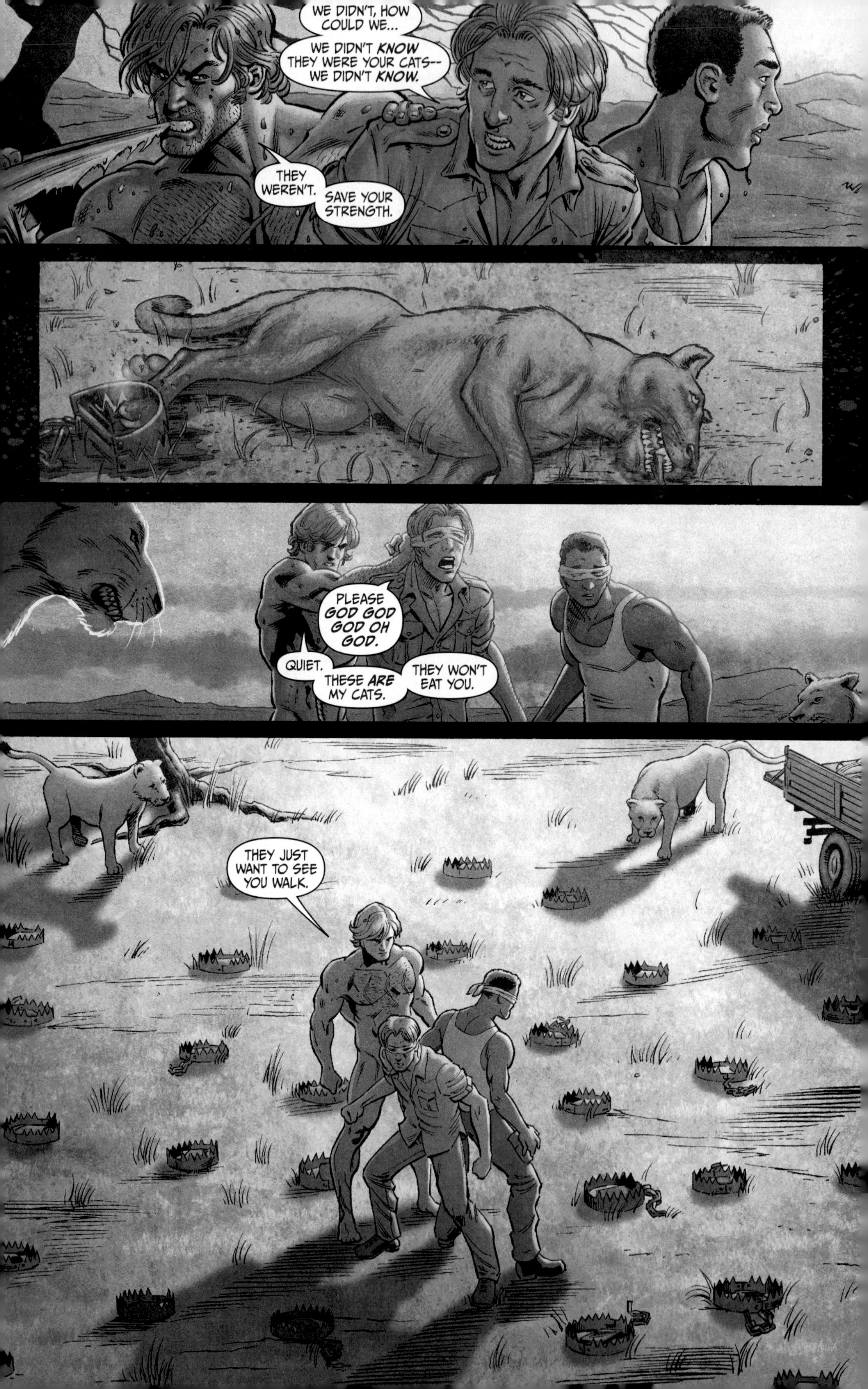
WE DIDN'T, HOW COULD WE...
WE DIDN'T KNOW THEY WERE YOUR CATS-- WE DIDN'T KNOW.
THEY WEREN'T.
SAVE YOUR STRENGTH.
PLEASE GOD GOD GOD OH GOD.
QUIET.
THESE ARE MY CATS.
THEY WON'T EAT YOU.
THEY JUST WANT TO SEE YOU WALK.

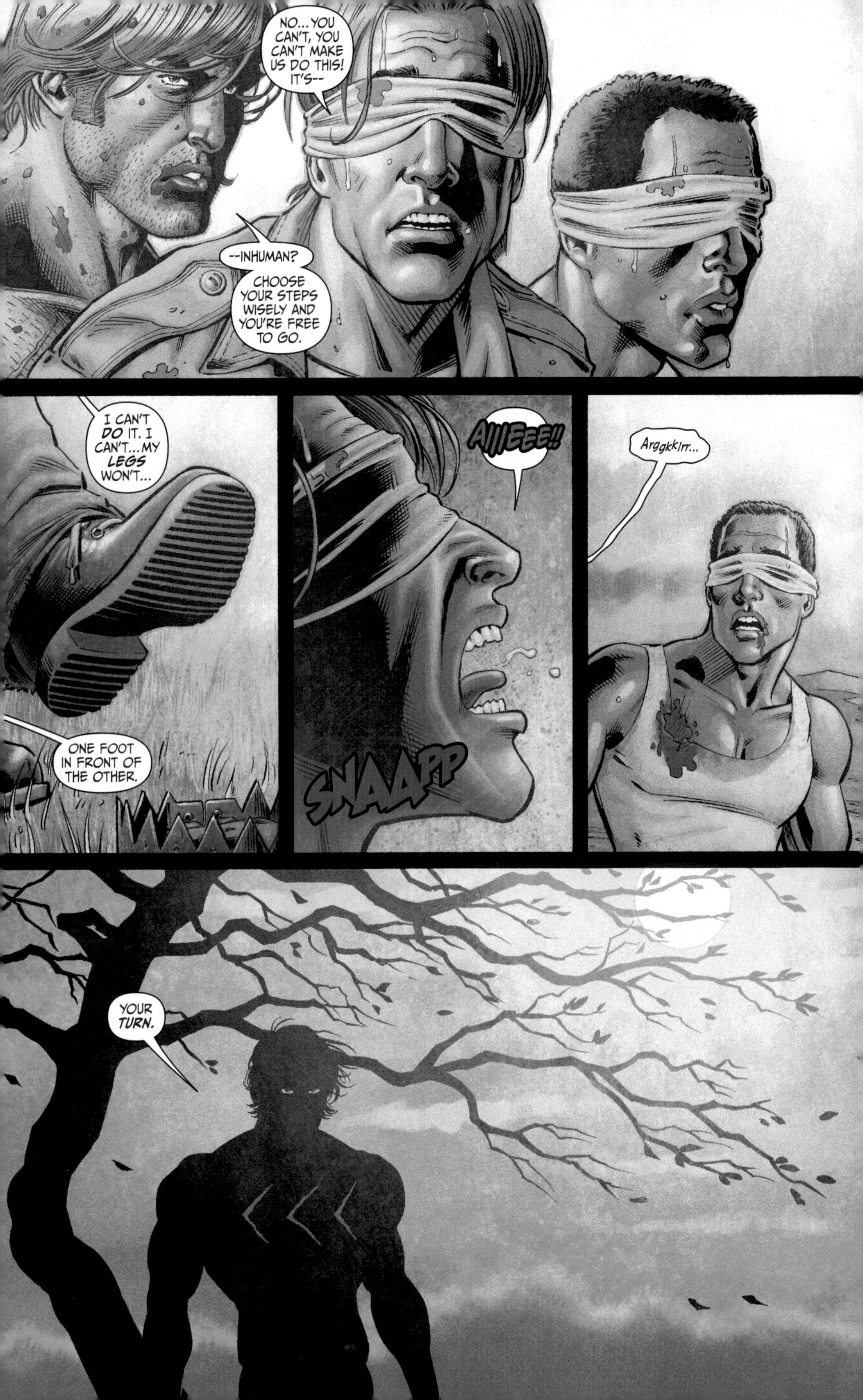
NO... YOU CAN'T, YOU CAN'T MAKE US DO THIS! IT'S--
--INHUMAN?
CHOOSE YOUR STEPS WISELY AND YOU'RE FREE TO GO.
I CAN'T DO IT. I CAN'T... MY LEGS WON'T...
ONE FOOT IN FRONT OF THE OTHER.
AIIIEEE!!
SNAAPP
Arggkklrr...
YOUR TURN.

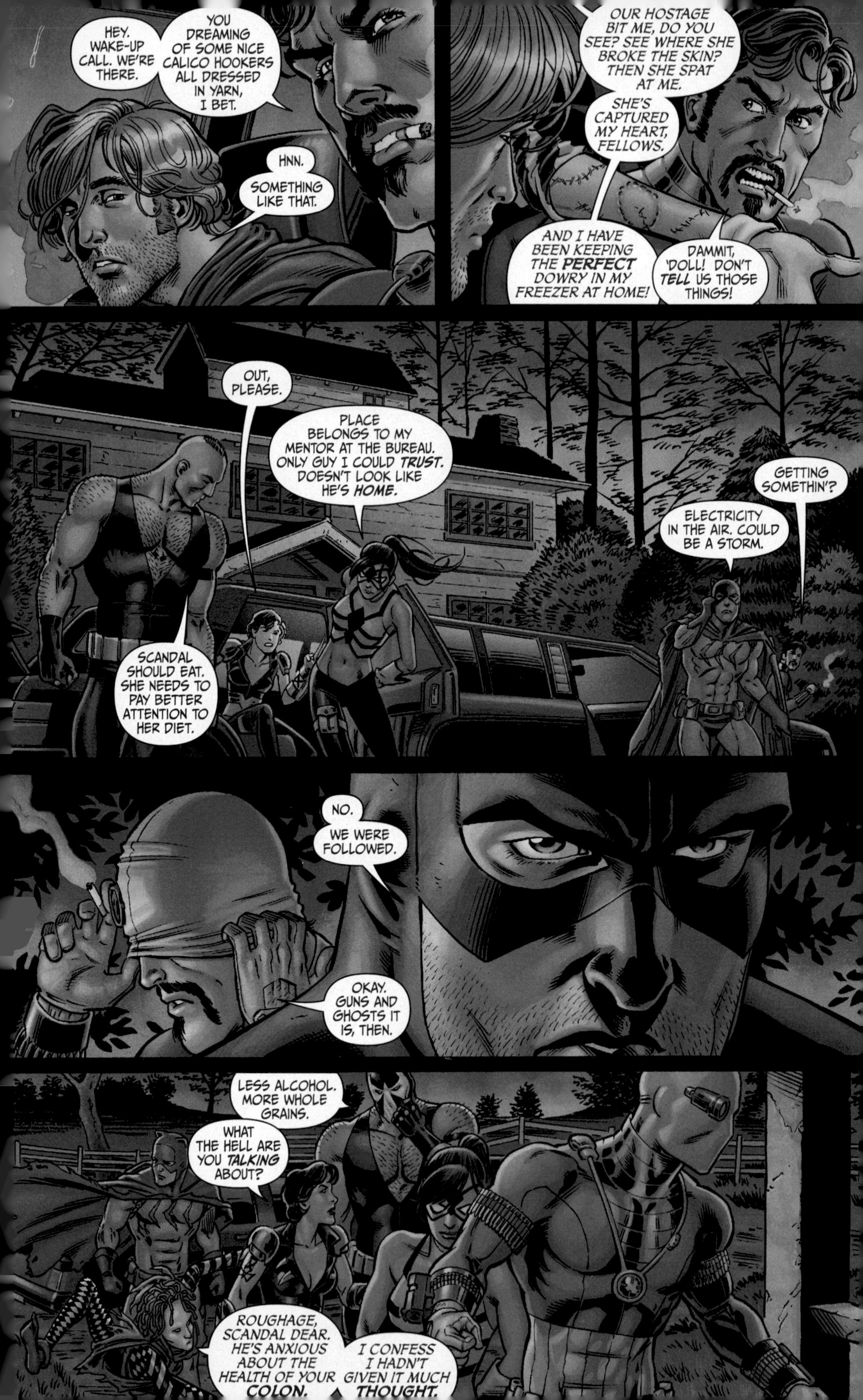
HEY. WAKE-UP CALL. WE'RE THERE.
YOU DREAMING OF SOME NICE CALICO HOOKERS ALL DRESSED IN YARN, I BET.
HNN.
SOMETHING LIKE THAT.
OUR HOSTAGE BIT ME, DO YOU SEE? SEE WHERE SHE BROKE THE SKIN? THEN SHE SPAT AT ME.
SHE'S CAPTURED MY HEART, FELLOWS.
AND I HAVE BEEN KEEPING THE PERFECT DOWRY IN MY FREEZER AT HOME!
DAMMIT, 'DOLL! DON'T TELL US THOSE THINGS!
OUT, PLEASE.
PLACE BELONGS TO MY MENTOR AT THE BUREAU. ONLY GUY I COULD TRUST. DOESN'T LOOK LIKE HE'S HOME.
GETTING SOMETHIN'?
ELECTRICITY IN THE AIR. COULD BE A STORM.
SCANDAL SHOULD EAT. SHE NEEDS TO PAY BETTER ATTENTION TO HER DIET.
NO.
WE WERE FOLLOWED.
OKAY. GUNS AND GHOSTS IT IS, THEN.
LESS ALCOHOL. MORE WHOLE GRAINS.
WHAT THE HELL ARE YOU TALKING ABOUT?
ROUGHAGE, SCANDAL DEAR. HE'S ANXIOUS ABOUT THE HEALTH OF YOUR COLON.
I CONFESS I HADN'T GIVEN IT MUCH THOUGHT.

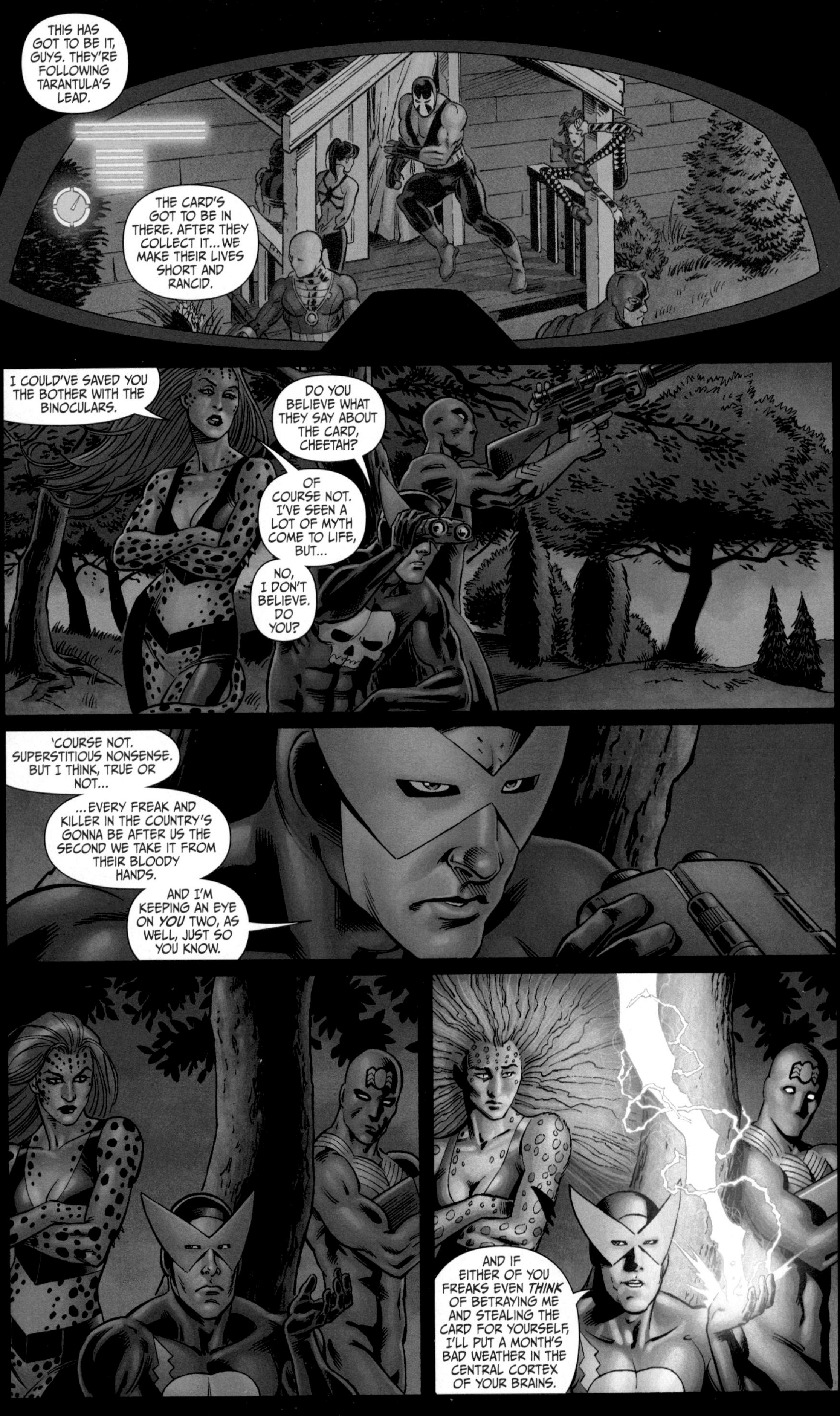
THIS HAS GOT TO BE IT, GUYS. THEY'RE FOLLOWING TARANTULA'S LEAD.
THE CARD'S GOT TO BE IN THERE. AFTER THEY COLLECT IT...WE MAKE THEIR LIVES SHORT AND RANCID.
I COULD'VE SAVED YOU THE BOTHER WITH THE BINOCULARS.
DO YOU BELIEVE WHAT THEY SAY ABOUT THE CARD, CHEETAH?
OF COURSE NOT. I'VE SEEN A LOT OF MYTH COME TO LIFE, BUT...
NO, I DON'T BELIEVE. DO YOU?
'COURSE NOT. SUPERSTITIOUS NONSENSE. BUT I THINK, TRUE OR NOT...
...EVERY FREAK AND KILLER IN THE COUNTRY'S GONNA BE AFTER US THE SECOND WE TAKE IT FROM THEIR BLOODY HANDS.
AND I'M KEEPING AN EYE ON *YOU* TWO, AS WELL, JUST SO YOU KNOW.
AND IF EITHER OF YOU FREAKS EVEN *THINK* OF BETRAYING ME AND STEALING THE CARD FOR YOURSELF, I'LL PUT A MONTH'S BAD WEATHER IN THE CENTRAL CORTEX OF YOUR BRAINS.

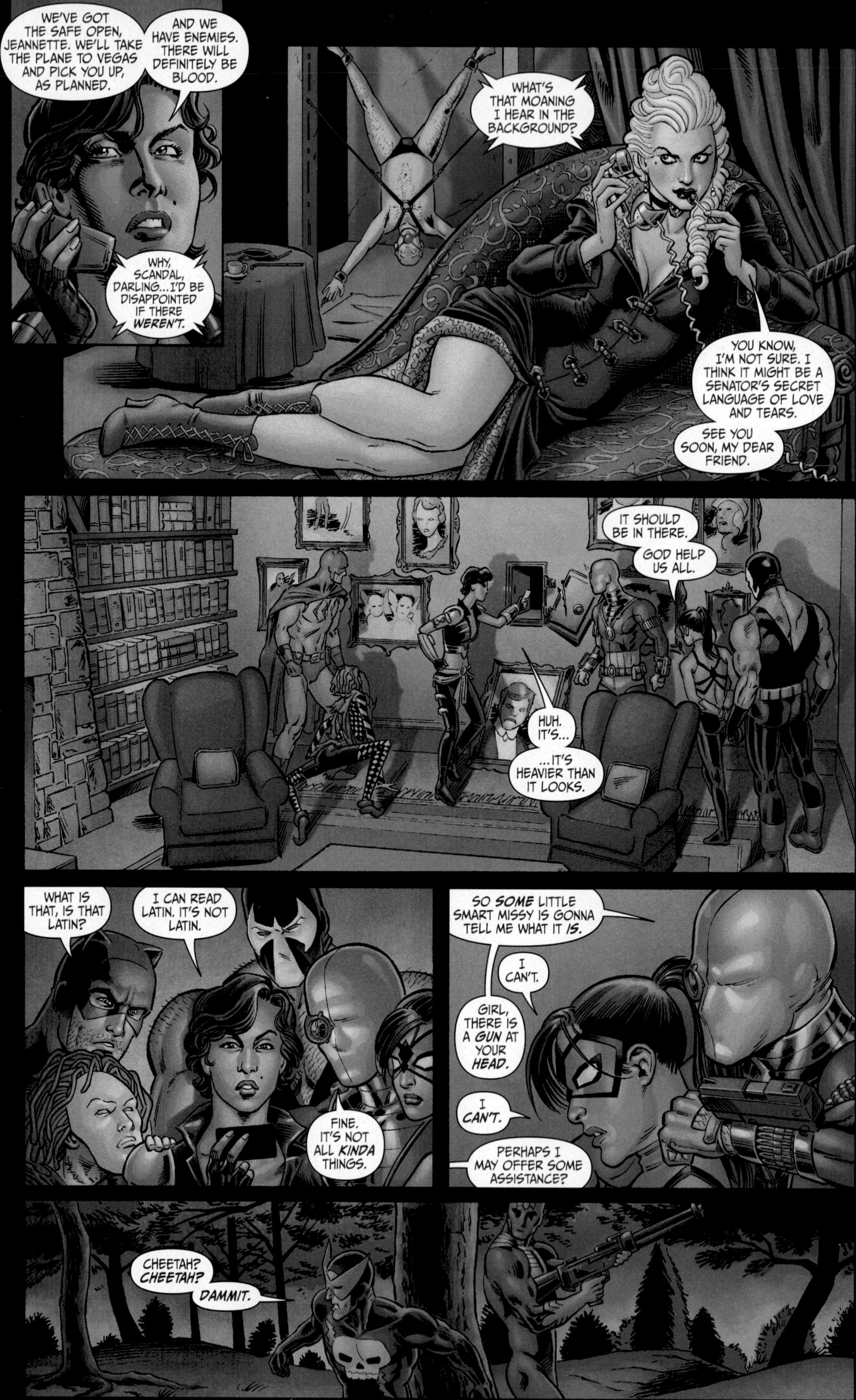
WE'VE GOT THE SAFE OPEN, JEANNETTE. WE'LL TAKE THE PLANE TO VEGAS AND PICK YOU UP, AS PLANNED.
AND WE HAVE ENEMIES. THERE WILL DEFINITELY BE BLOOD.
WHY, SCANDAL, DARLING...I'D BE DISAPPOINTED IF THERE *WEREN'T.*
WHAT'S THAT MOANING I HEAR IN THE BACKGROUND?
YOU KNOW, I'M NOT SURE. I THINK IT MIGHT BE A SENATOR'S SECRET LANGUAGE OF LOVE AND TEARS.
SEE YOU SOON, MY DEAR FRIEND.
IT SHOULD BE IN THERE.
GOD HELP US ALL.
HUH. IT'S...
...IT'S HEAVIER THAN IT LOOKS.
WHAT IS THAT, IS THAT LATIN?
I CAN READ LATIN. IT'S NOT LATIN.
FINE. IT'S NOT ALL *KINDA* THINGS.
SO *SOME* LITTLE SMART MISSY IS GONNA TELL ME WHAT IT *IS.*
I CAN'T.
GIRL, THERE IS A *GUN* AT YOUR *HEAD.*
I *CAN'T.*
PERHAPS I MAY OFFER SOME ASSISTANCE?
CHEETAH? *CHEETAH?*
DAMMIT.

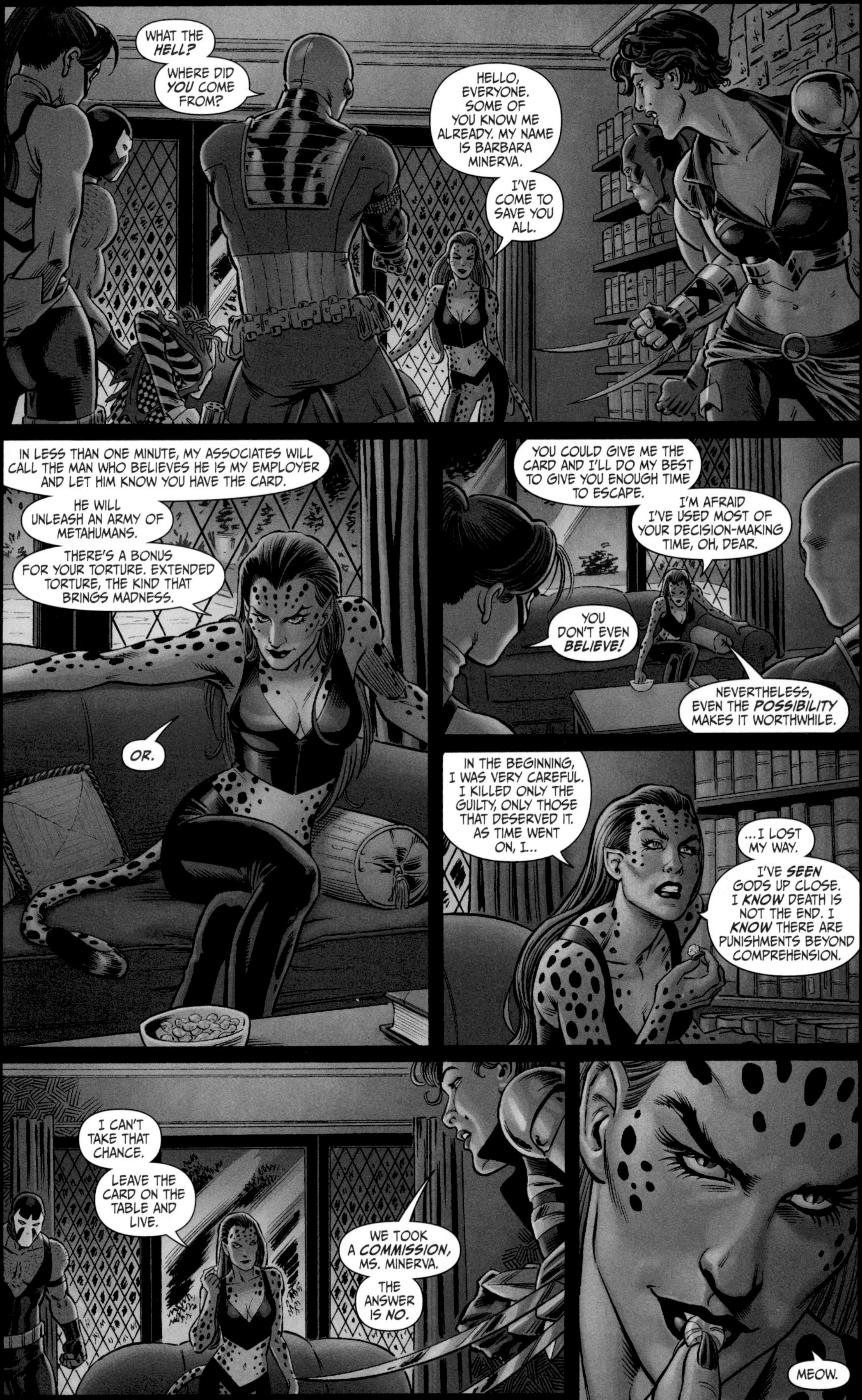
WHAT THE HELL?
WHERE DID YOU COME FROM?
HELLO, EVERYONE. SOME OF YOU KNOW ME ALREADY. MY NAME IS BARBARA MINERVA.
I'VE COME TO SAVE YOU ALL.
IN LESS THAN ONE MINUTE, MY ASSOCIATES WILL CALL THE MAN WHO BELIEVES HE IS MY EMPLOYER AND LET HIM KNOW YOU HAVE THE CARD.
HE WILL UNLEASH AN ARMY OF METAHUMANS.
THERE'S A BONUS FOR YOUR TORTURE. EXTENDED TORTURE, THE KIND THAT BRINGS MADNESS.
OR.
YOU COULD GIVE ME THE CARD AND I'LL DO MY BEST TO GIVE YOU ENOUGH TIME TO ESCAPE.
I'M AFRAID I'VE USED MOST OF YOUR DECISION-MAKING TIME, OH, DEAR.
YOU DON'T EVEN BELIEVE!
NEVERTHELESS, EVEN THE POSSIBILITY MAKES IT WORTHWHILE.
IN THE BEGINNING, I WAS VERY CAREFUL. I KILLED ONLY THE GUILTY, ONLY THOSE THAT DESERVED IT. AS TIME WENT ON, I...
...I LOST MY WAY.
I'VE SEEN GODS UP CLOSE. I KNOW DEATH IS NOT THE END. I KNOW THERE ARE PUNISHMENTS BEYOND COMPREHENSION.
I CAN'T TAKE THAT CHANCE.
LEAVE THE CARD ON THE TABLE AND LIVE.
WE TOOK A COMMISSION, MS. MINERVA.
THE ANSWER IS NO.
MEOW.

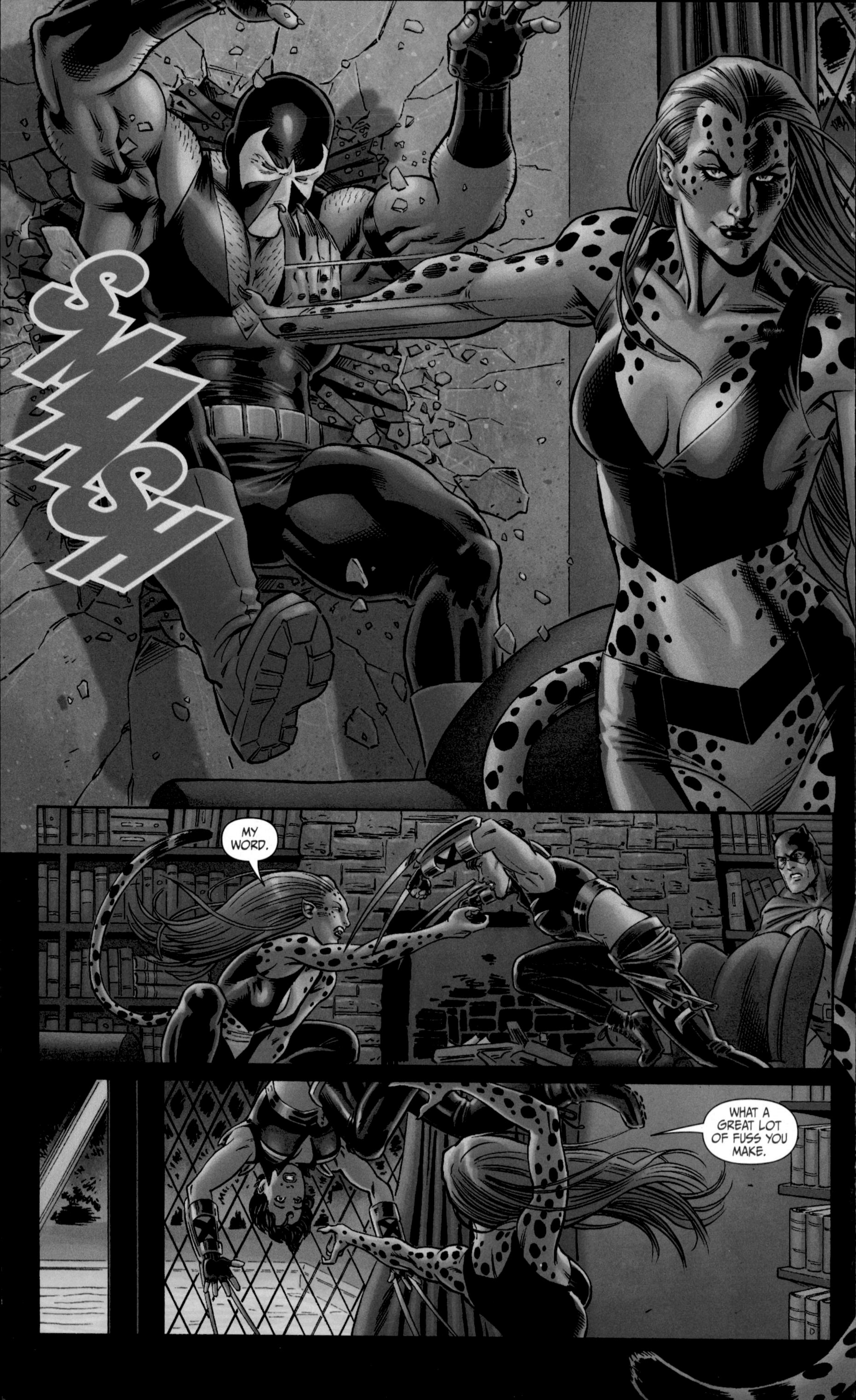
SMASH
MY WORD.
WHAT A GREAT LOT OF FUSS YOU MAKE.

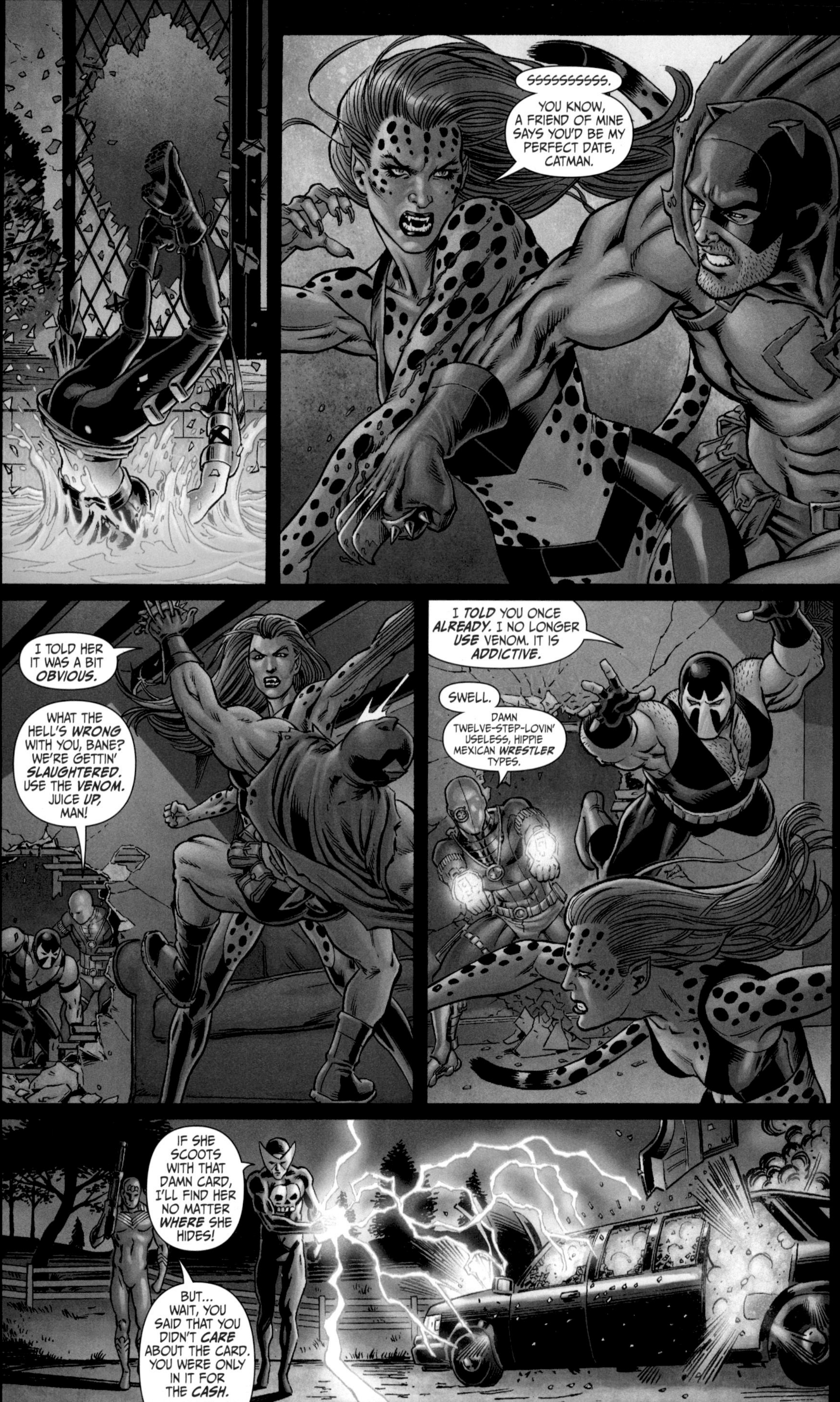
SSSSSSSSSS.
YOU KNOW, A FRIEND OF MINE SAYS YOU'D BE MY PERFECT DATE, CATMAN.
I TOLD HER IT WAS A BIT OBVIOUS.
WHAT THE HELL'S WRONG WITH YOU, BANE? WE'RE GETTIN' SLAUGHTERED. USE THE VENOM. JUICE UP, MAN!
I TOLD YOU ONCE ALREADY. I NO LONGER USE VENOM. IT IS ADDICTIVE.
SWELL.
DAMN TWELVE-STEP-LOVIN' USELESS, HIPPIE MEXICAN WRESTLER TYPES.
IF SHE SCOOTS WITH THAT DAMN CARD, I'LL FIND HER NO MATTER WHERE SHE HIDES!
BUT... WAIT, YOU SAID THAT YOU DIDN'T CARE ABOUT THE CARD. YOU WERE ONLY IN IT FOR THE CASH.

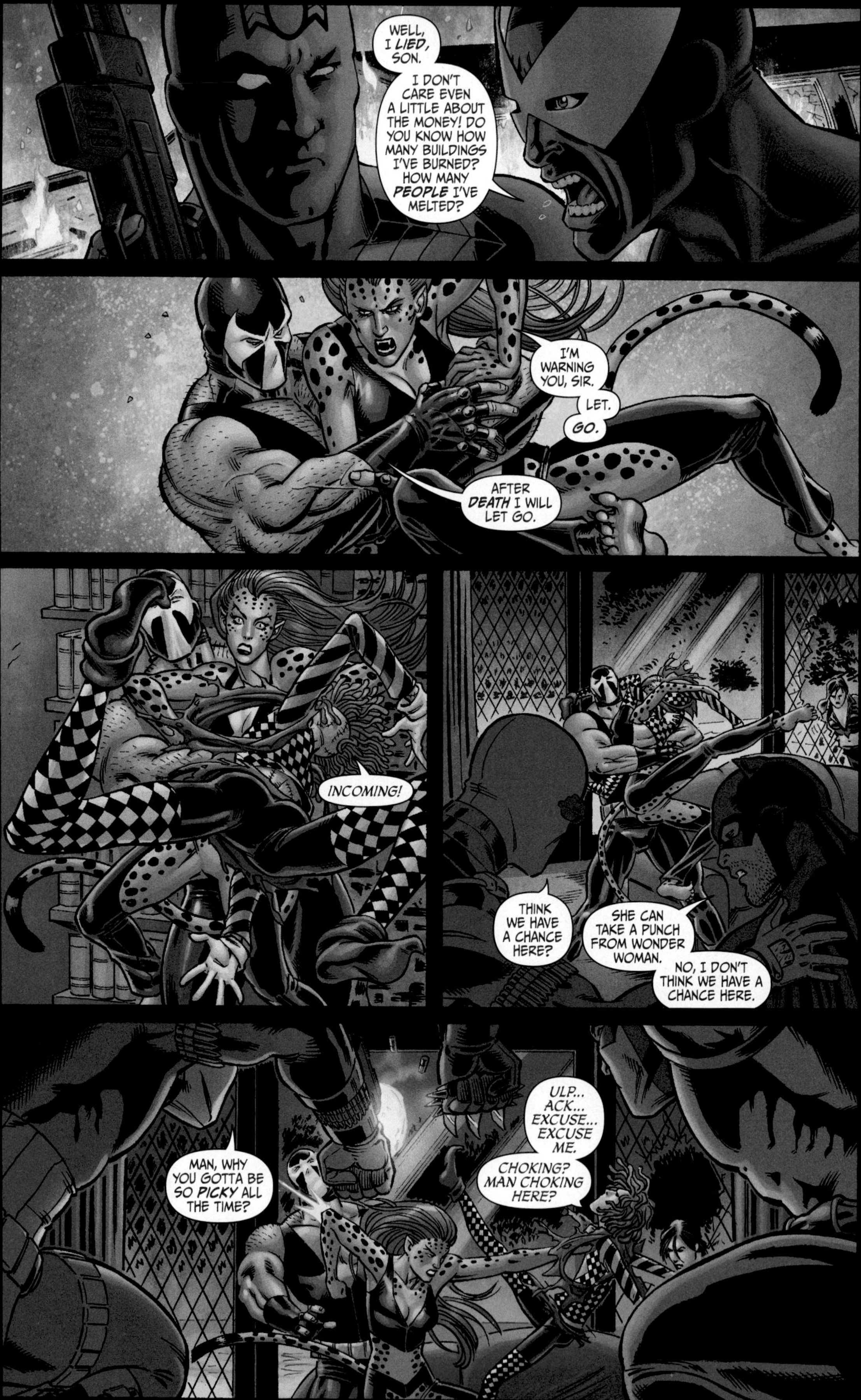

WELL, I *LIED*, SON.
I DON'T CARE EVEN A LITTLE ABOUT THE MONEY! DO YOU KNOW HOW MANY BUILDINGS I'VE BURNED? HOW MANY *PEOPLE* I'VE MELTED?
I'M WARNING YOU, SIR.
LET.
GO.
AFTER *DEATH* I WILL LET GO.
INCOMING!
THINK WE HAVE A CHANCE HERE?
SHE CAN TAKE A PUNCH FROM WONDER WOMAN.
NO, I DON'T THINK WE HAVE A CHANCE HERE.
MAN, WHY YOU GOTTA BE SO *PICKY* ALL THE TIME?
ULP... ACK... EXCUSE... EXCUSE ME.
CHOKING? MAN CHOKING HERE?

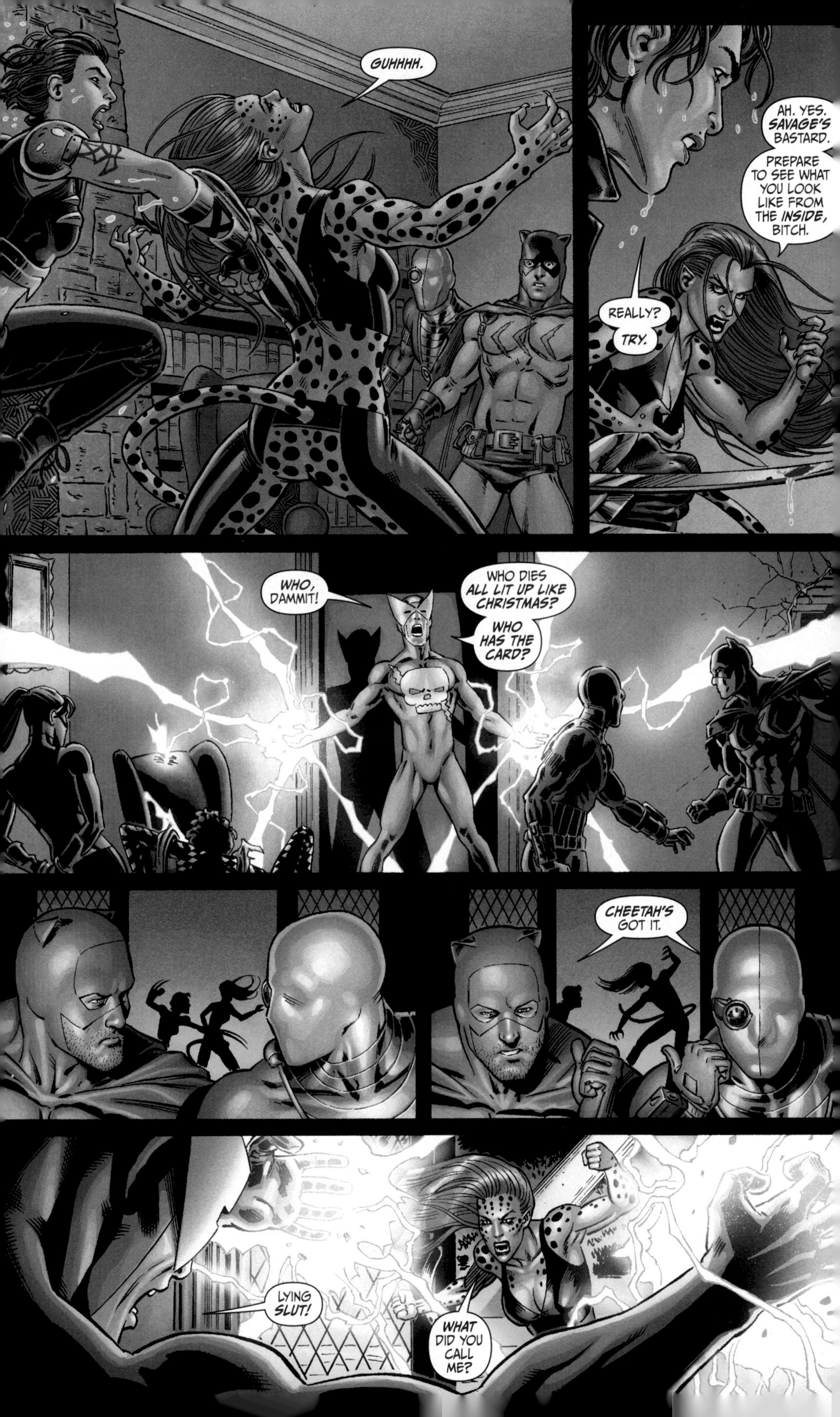
GUHHHH.
AH. YES. SAVAGE'S BASTARD.
PREPARE TO SEE WHAT YOU LOOK LIKE FROM THE INSIDE, BITCH.
REALLY? TRY.
WHO, DAMMIT!
WHO DIES ALL LIT UP LIKE CHRISTMAS? WHO HAS THE CARD?
CHEETAH'S GOT IT.
LYING SLUT!
WHAT DID YOU CALL ME?

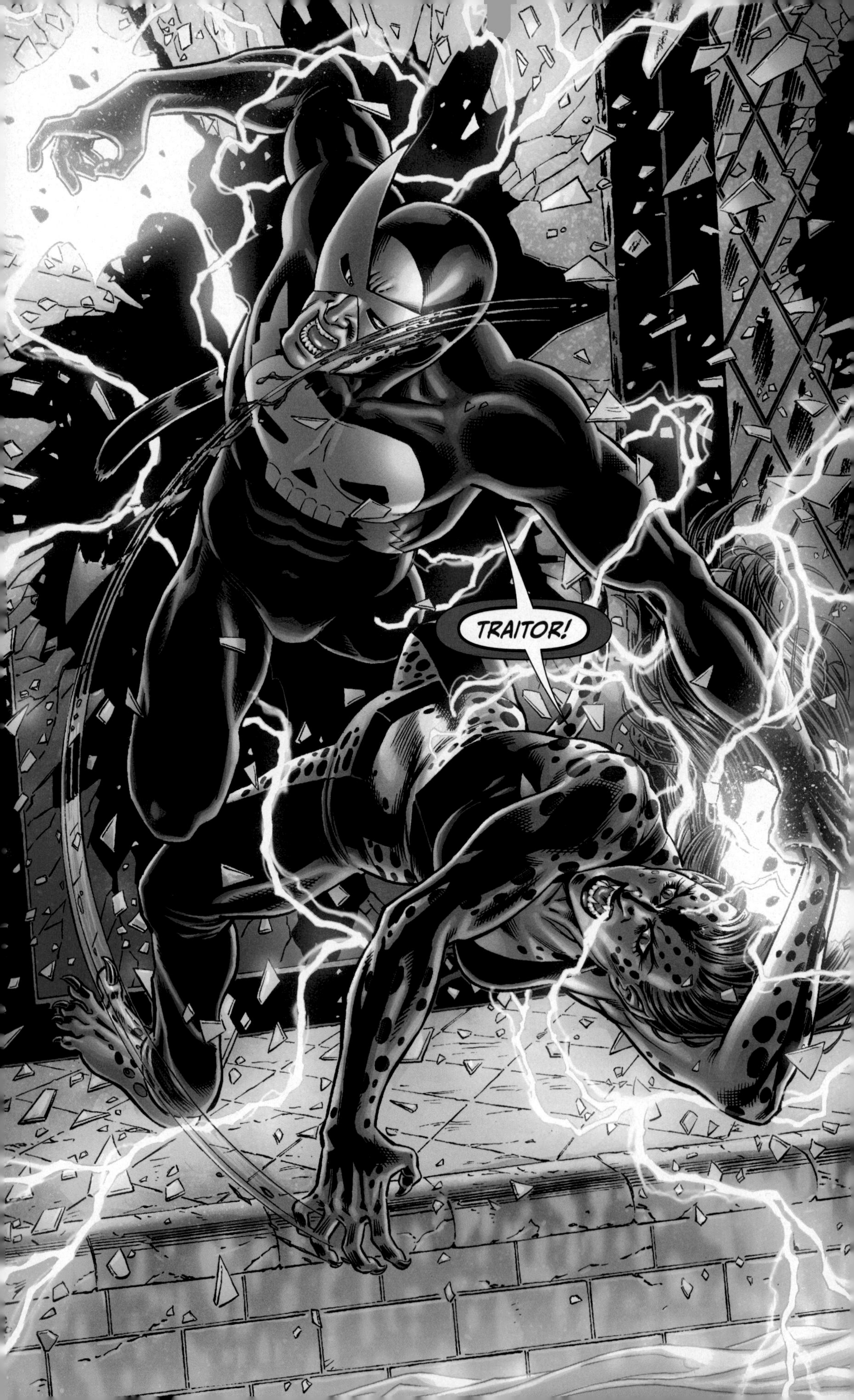
TRAITOR!

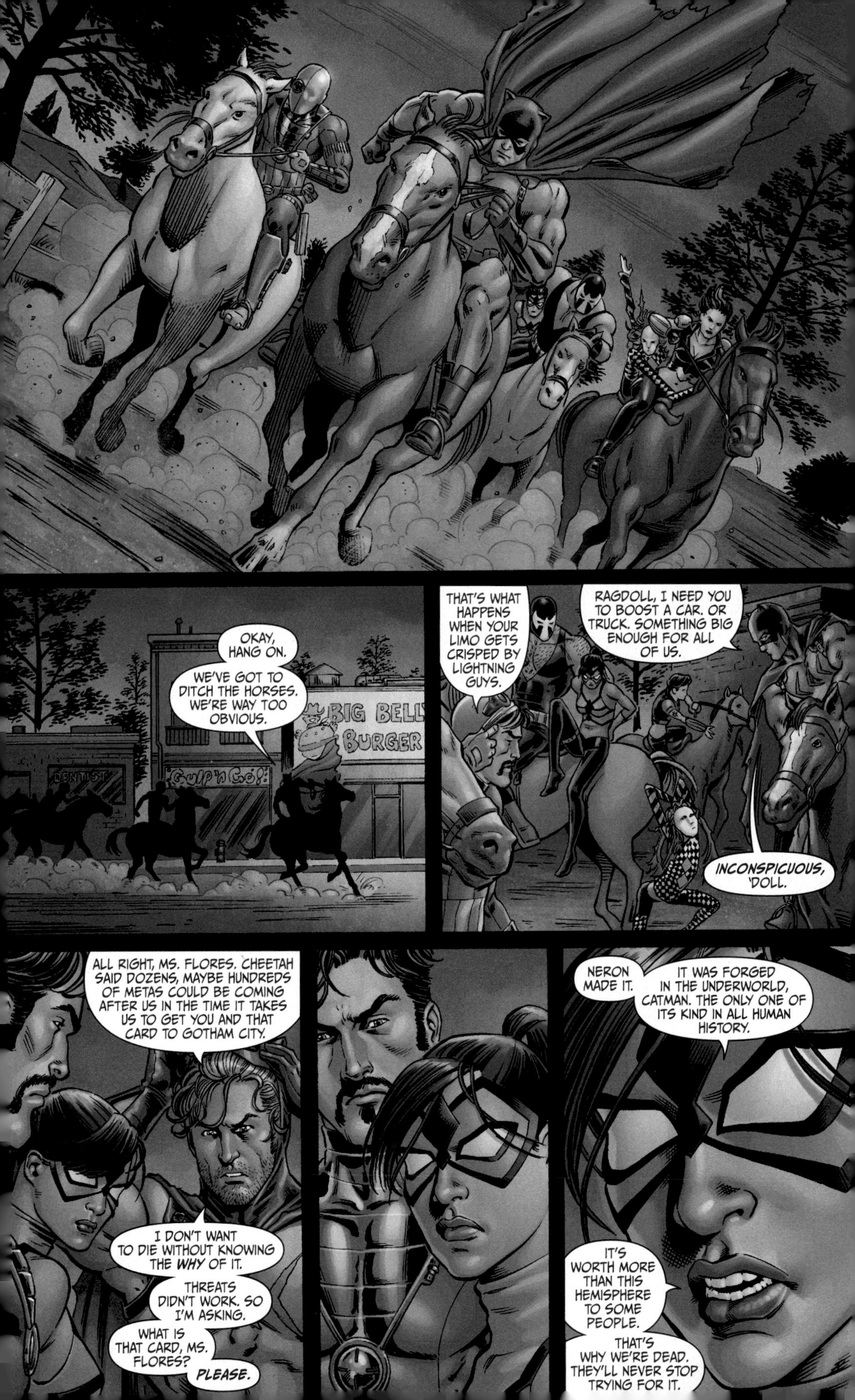
OKAY, HANG ON.
WE'VE GOT TO DITCH THE HORSES. WE'RE WAY TOO OBVIOUS.
BIG BELLY BURGER
DENTIST
Gulp 'n Go!
THAT'S WHAT HAPPENS WHEN YOUR LIMO GETS CRISPED BY LIGHTNING GUYS.
RAGDOLL, I NEED YOU TO BOOST A CAR. OR TRUCK. SOMETHING BIG ENOUGH FOR ALL OF US.
INCONSPICUOUS, 'DOLL.
ALL RIGHT, MS. FLORES. CHEETAH SAID DOZENS, MAYBE HUNDREDS OF METAS COULD BE COMING AFTER US IN THE TIME IT TAKES US TO GET YOU AND THAT CARD TO GOTHAM CITY.
I DON'T WANT TO DIE WITHOUT KNOWING THE *WHY* OF IT.
THREATS DIDN'T WORK. SO I'M ASKING.
WHAT IS THAT CARD, MS. FLORES? ***PLEASE.***
NERON MADE IT.
IT WAS FORGED IN THE UNDERWORLD, CATMAN. THE ONLY ONE OF ITS KIND IN ALL HUMAN HISTORY.
IT'S WORTH MORE THAN THIS HEMISPHERE TO SOME PEOPLE.
THAT'S WHY WE'RE DEAD. THEY'LL NEVER STOP TRYING FOR IT.

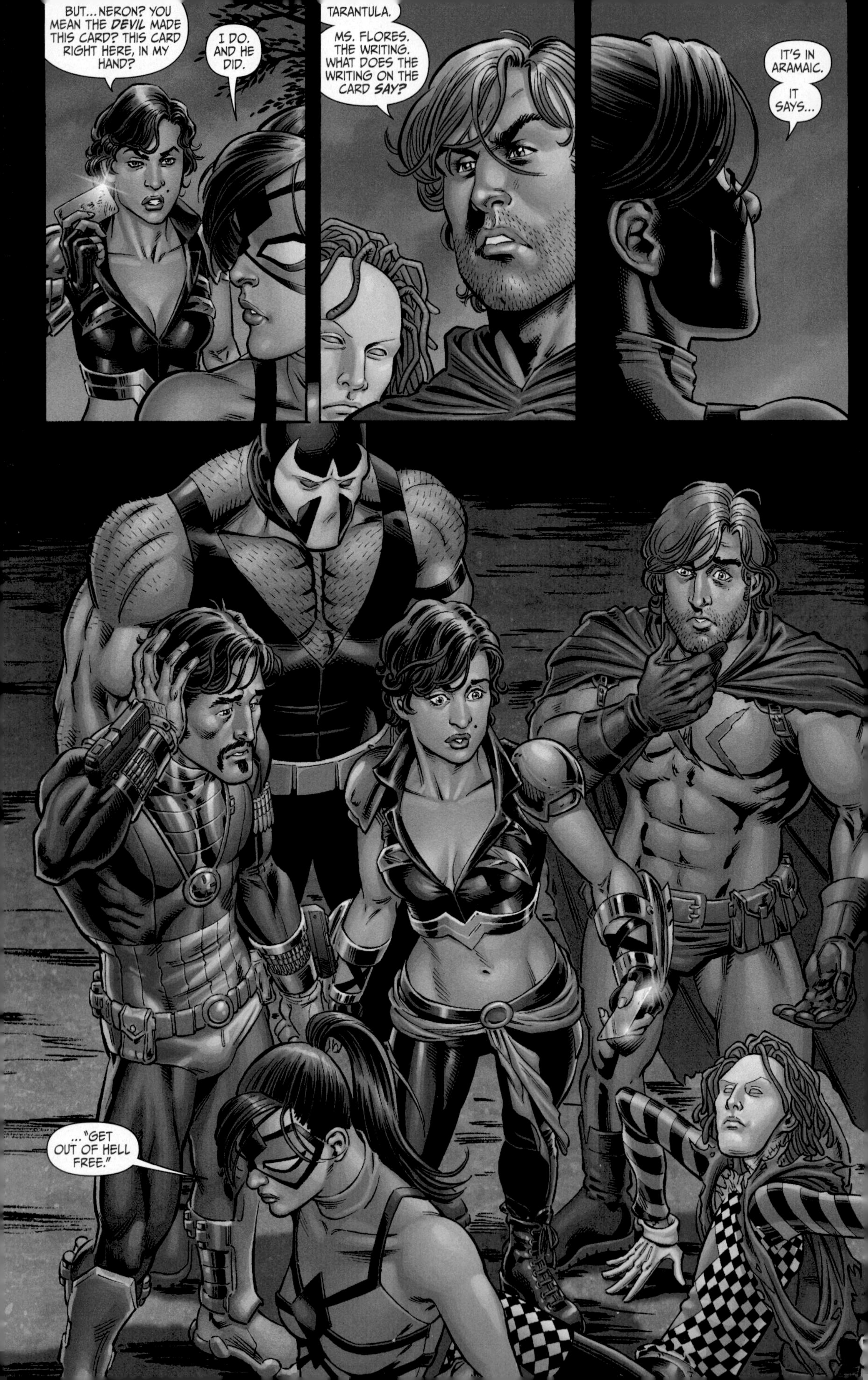

BUT...NERON? YOU MEAN THE DEVIL MADE THIS CARD? THIS CARD RIGHT HERE, IN MY HAND?
I DO. AND HE DID.
TARANTULA.
MS. FLORES. THE WRITING. WHAT DOES THE WRITING ON THE CARD SAY?
IT'S IN ARAMAIC.
IT SAYS...
..."GET OUT OF HELL FREE."

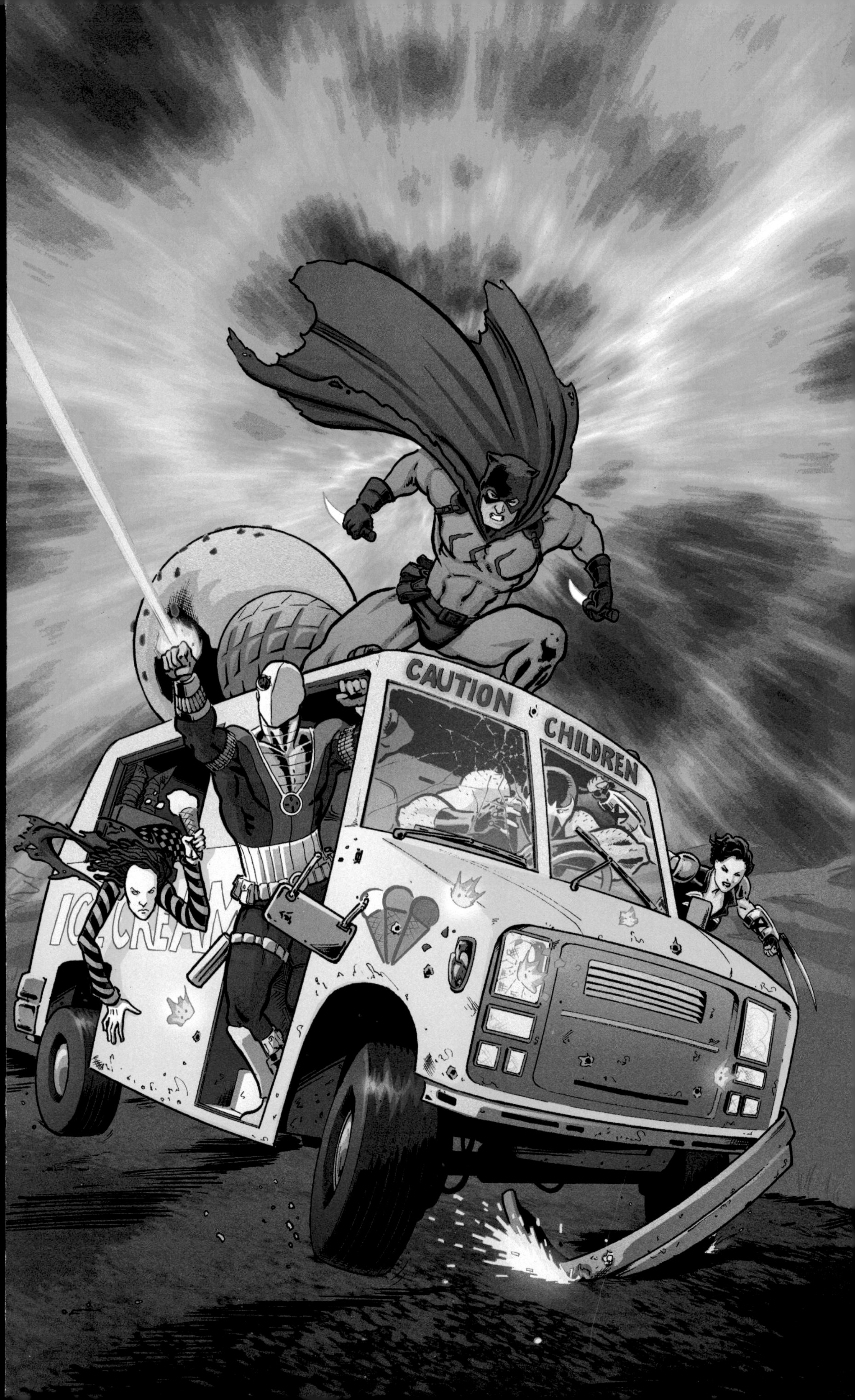
CAUTION CHILDREN

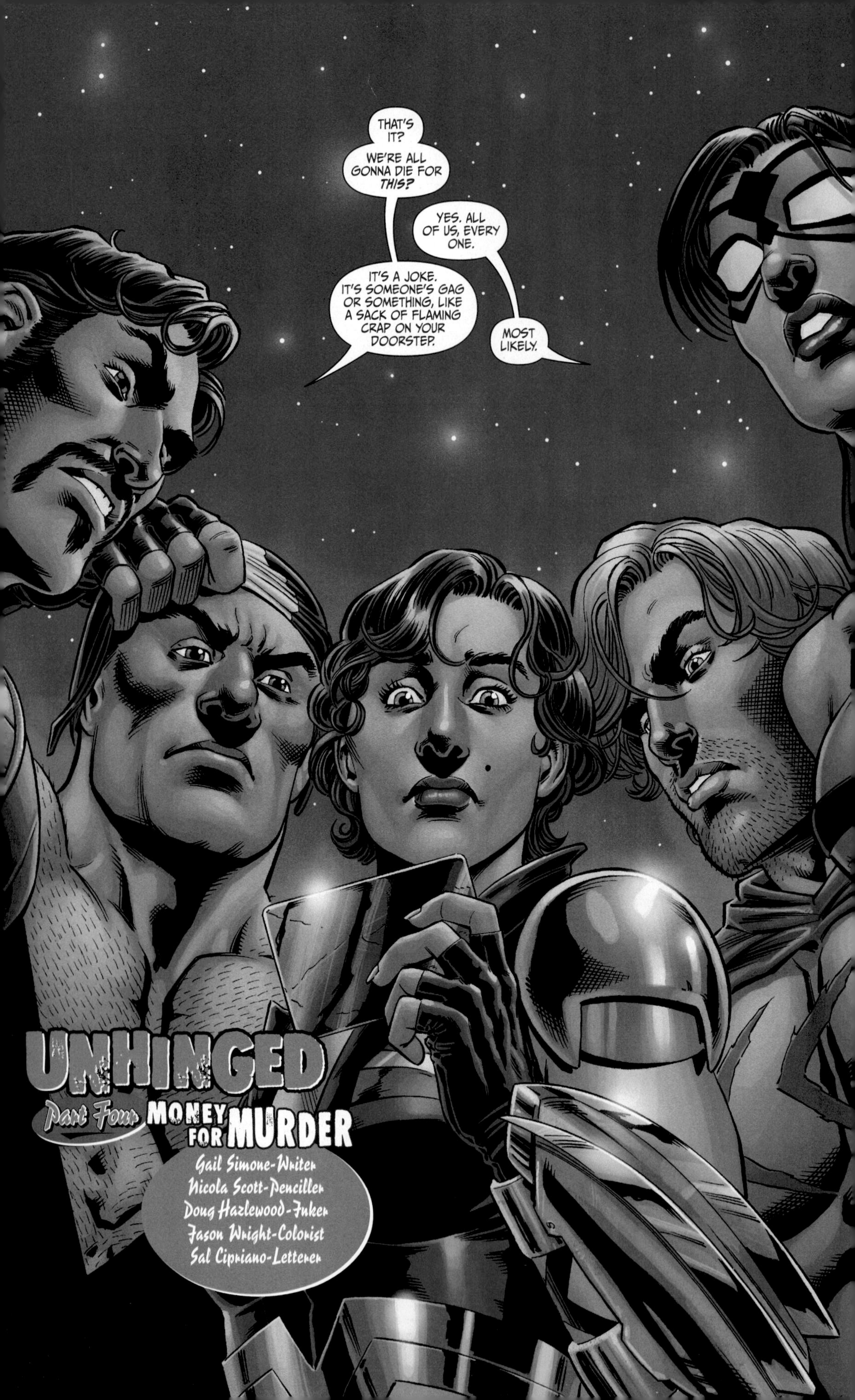
THAT'S IT?
WE'RE ALL GONNA DIE FOR *THIS?*
YES. ALL OF US, EVERY ONE.
IT'S A JOKE. IT'S SOMEONE'S GAG OR SOMETHING, LIKE A SACK OF FLAMING CRAP ON YOUR DOORSTEP.
MOST LIKELY.
UNHINGED
Part Four MONEY FOR MURDER
Gail Simone-Writer
Nicola Scott-Penciller
Doug Hazlewood-Inker
Jason Wright-Colorist
Sal Cipriano-Letterer

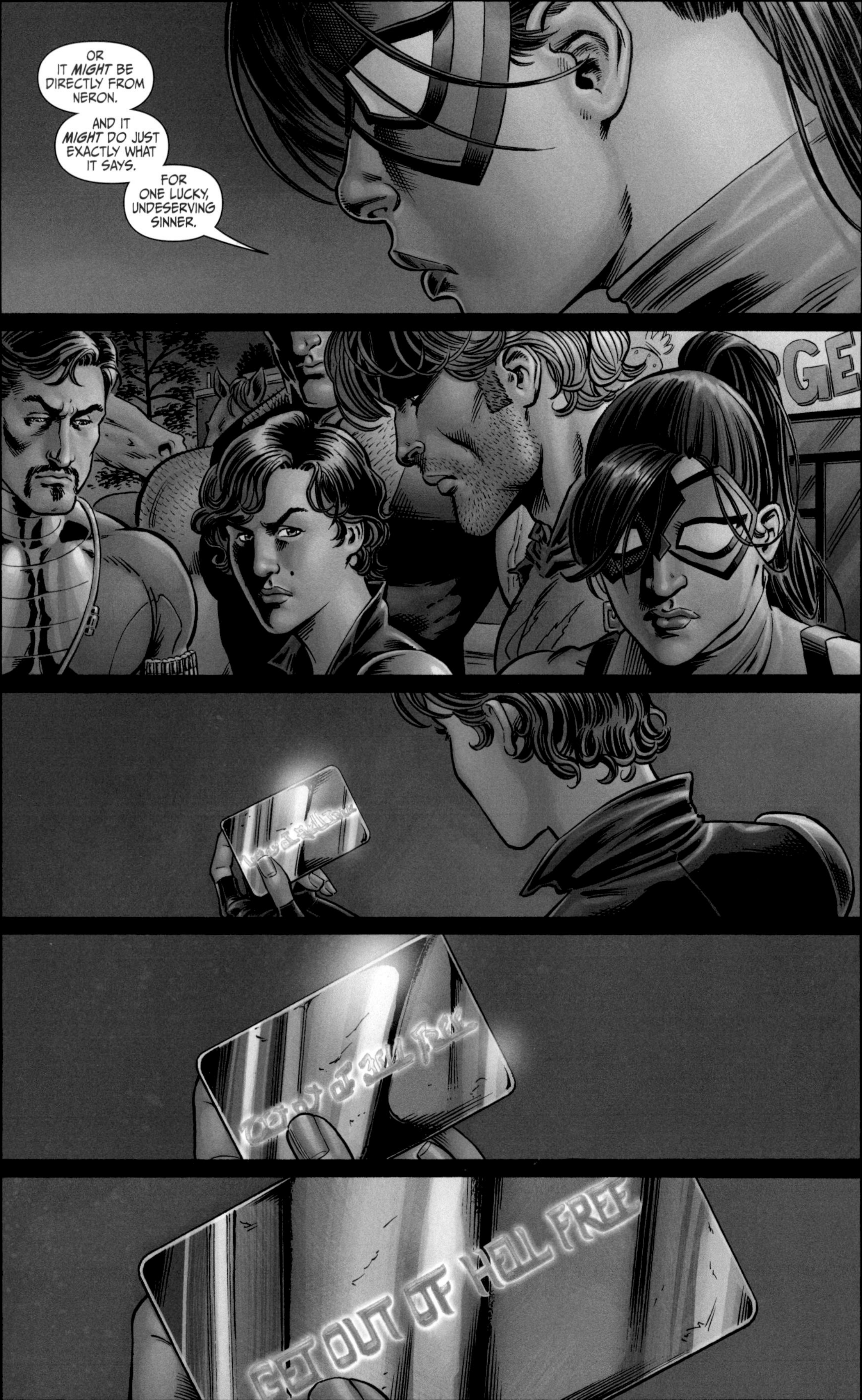
OR IT *MIGHT* BE DIRECTLY FROM NERON.
AND IT *MIGHT* DO JUST EXACTLY WHAT IT SAYS.
FOR ONE LUCKY, UNDESERVING SINNER.
GET OUT OF HELL FREE

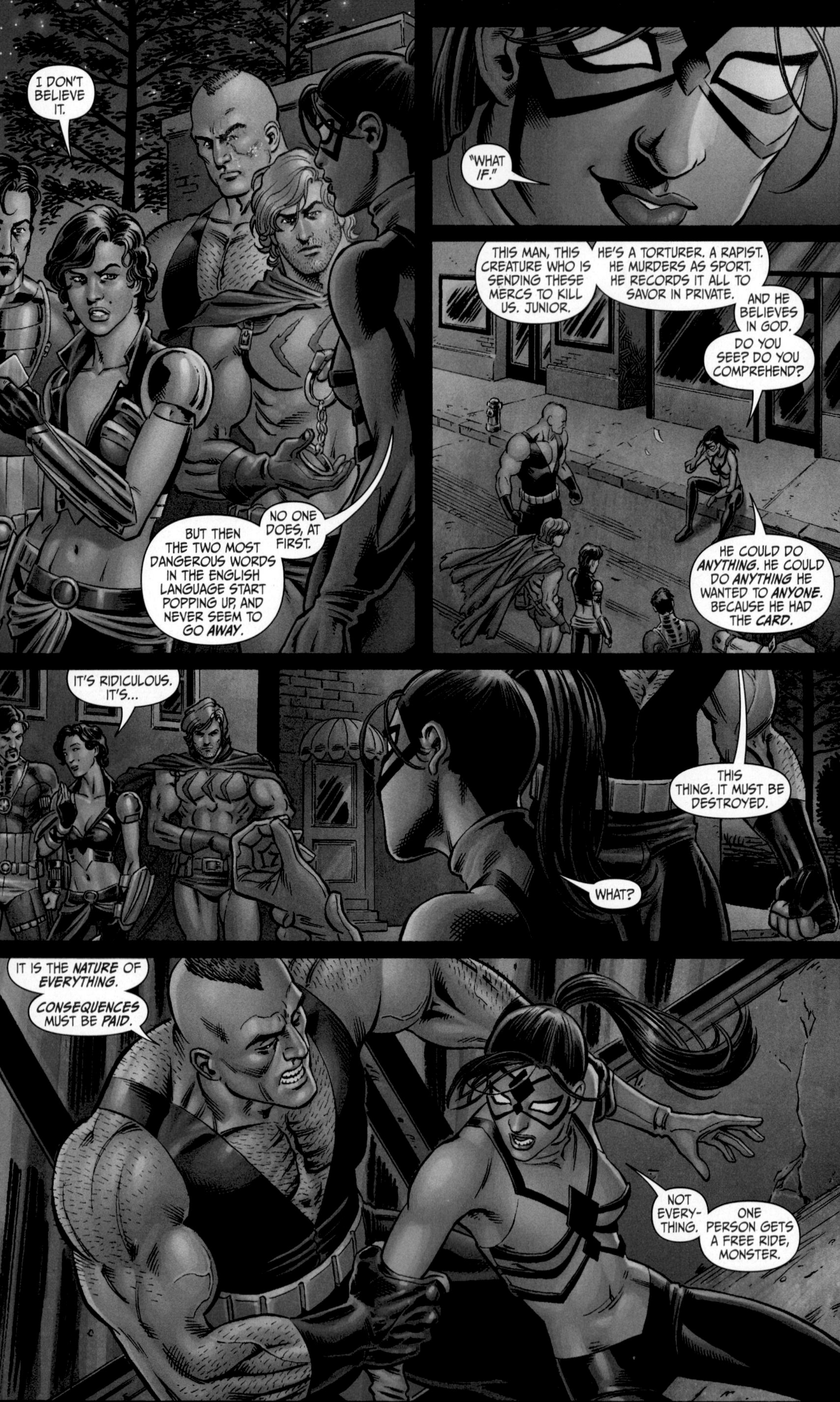
I DON'T BELIEVE IT.
NO ONE DOES, AT FIRST.
BUT THEN THE TWO MOST DANGEROUS WORDS IN THE ENGLISH LANGUAGE START POPPING UP, AND NEVER SEEM TO GO AWAY.
"WHAT IF."
THIS MAN, THIS CREATURE WHO IS SENDING THESE MERCS TO KILL US. JUNIOR.
HE'S A TORTURER. A RAPIST. HE MURDERS AS SPORT. HE RECORDS IT ALL TO SAVOR IN PRIVATE.
AND HE BELIEVES IN GOD.
DO YOU SEE? DO YOU COMPREHEND?
HE COULD DO ANYTHING. HE COULD DO ANYTHING HE WANTED TO ANYONE. BECAUSE HE HAD THE CARD.
IT'S RIDICULOUS. IT'S...
THIS THING. IT MUST BE DESTROYED.
WHAT?
IT IS THE NATURE OF EVERYTHING.
CONSEQUENCES MUST BE PAID.
NOT EVERY-THING.
ONE PERSON GETS A FREE RIDE, MONSTER.

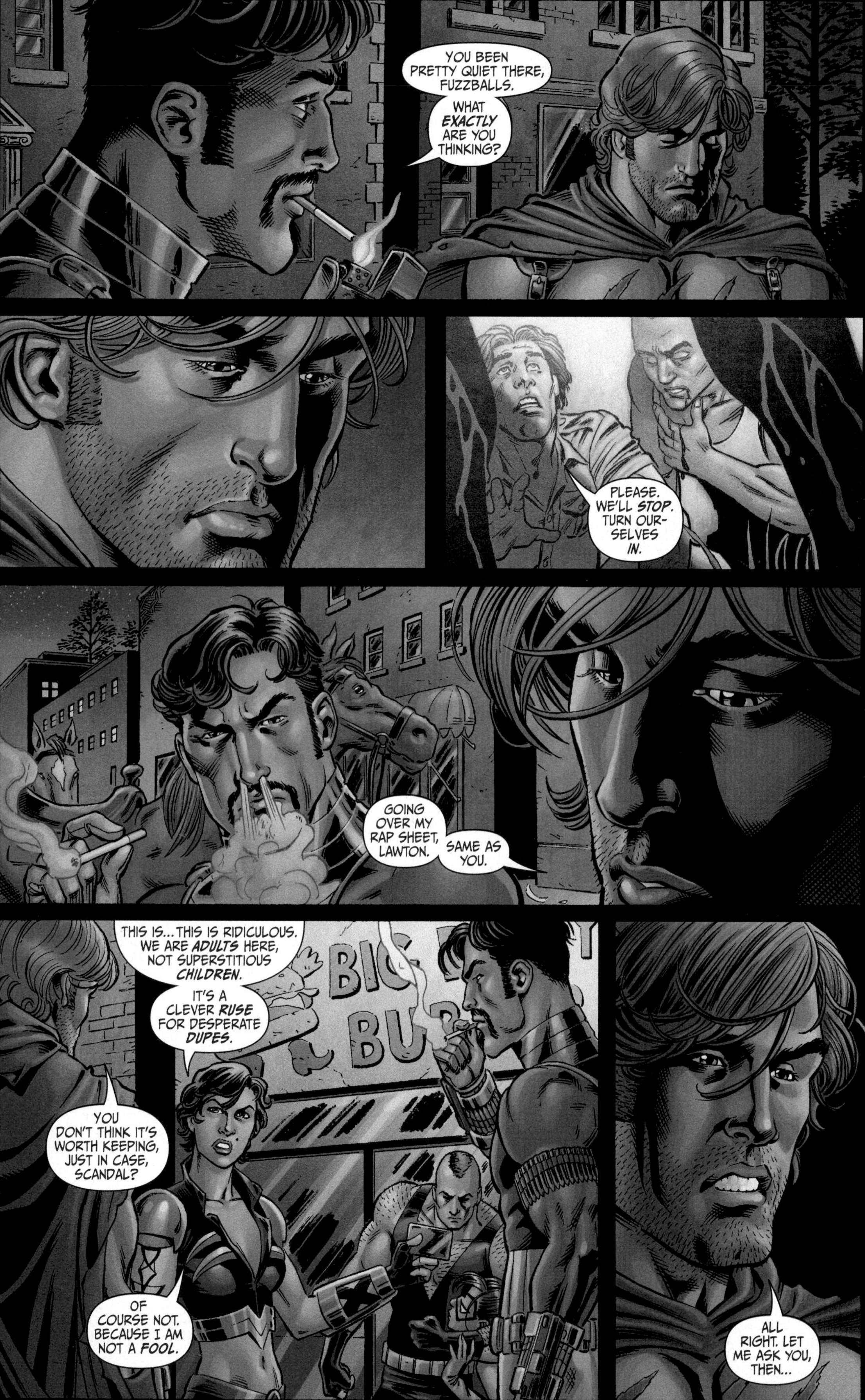

YOU BEEN PRETTY QUIET THERE, FUZZBALLS.
WHAT *EXACTLY* ARE YOU THINKING?
PLEASE. WE'LL *STOP*. TURN OUR-SELVES *IN*.
GOING OVER MY RAP SHEET, LAWTON.
SAME AS YOU.
THIS IS...THIS IS RIDICULOUS. WE ARE *ADULTS* HERE, NOT SUPERSTITIOUS *CHILDREN*.
IT'S A CLEVER *RUSE* FOR DESPERATE *DUPES*.
YOU DON'T THINK IT'S WORTH KEEPING, JUST IN CASE, SCANDAL?
OF COURSE NOT. BECAUSE I AM NOT A *FOOL*.
ALL RIGHT. LET ME ASK YOU, THEN...

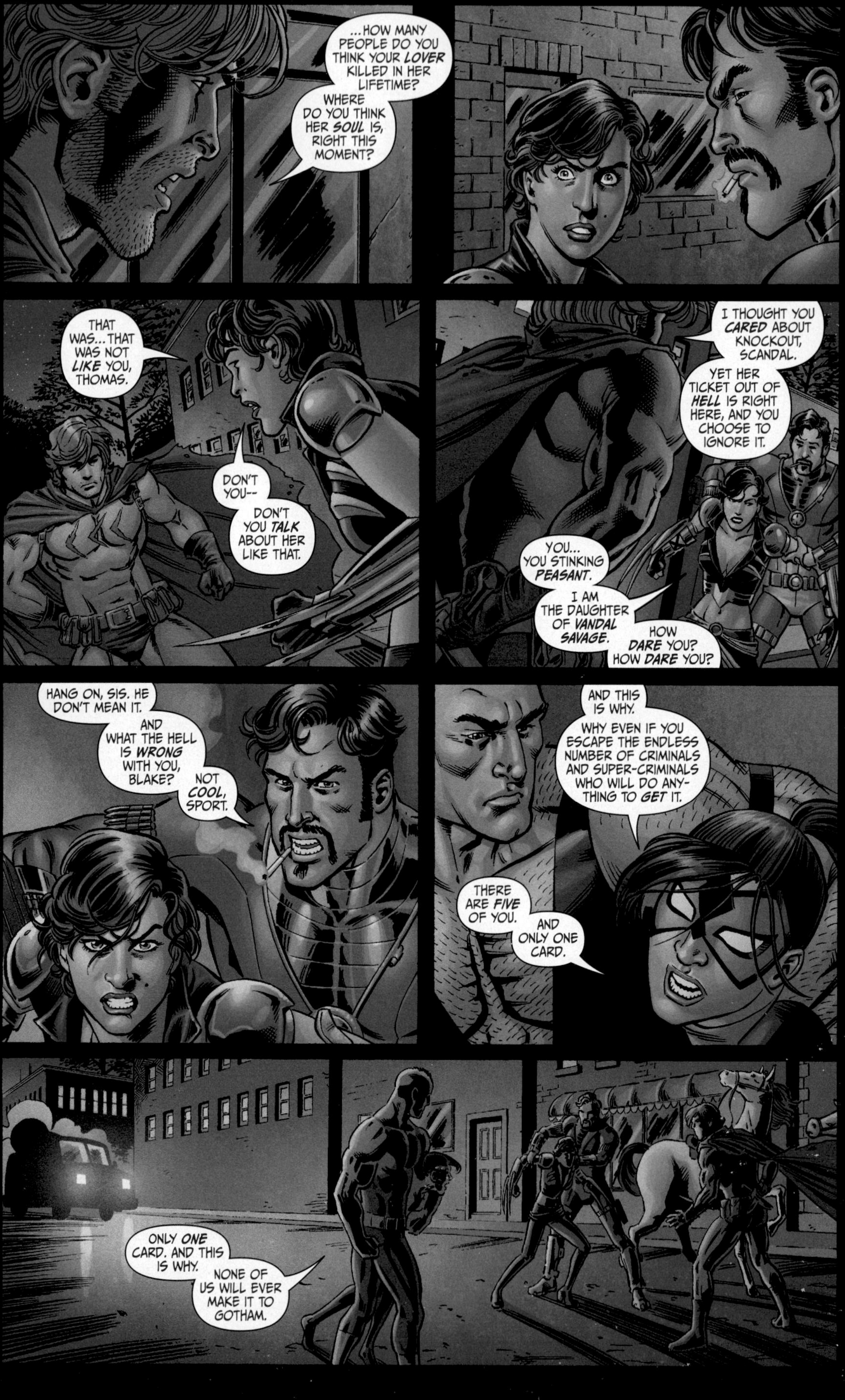
...HOW MANY PEOPLE DO YOU THINK YOUR LOVER KILLED IN HER LIFETIME?
WHERE DO YOU THINK HER SOUL IS, RIGHT THIS MOMENT?
THAT WAS...THAT WAS NOT LIKE YOU, THOMAS.
DON'T YOU--
DON'T YOU TALK ABOUT HER LIKE THAT.
I THOUGHT YOU CARED ABOUT KNOCKOUT, SCANDAL.
YET HER TICKET OUT OF HELL IS RIGHT HERE, AND YOU CHOOSE TO IGNORE IT.
YOU... YOU STINKING PEASANT.
I AM THE DAUGHTER OF VANDAL SAVAGE.
HOW DARE YOU? HOW DARE YOU?
HANG ON, SIS. HE DON'T MEAN IT.
AND WHAT THE HELL IS WRONG WITH YOU, BLAKE?
NOT COOL, SPORT.
AND THIS IS WHY.
WHY EVEN IF YOU ESCAPE THE ENDLESS NUMBER OF CRIMINALS AND SUPER-CRIMINALS WHO WILL DO ANY-THING TO GET IT.
THERE ARE FIVE OF YOU.
AND ONLY ONE CARD.
ONLY ONE CARD. AND THIS IS WHY.
NONE OF US WILL EVER MAKE IT TO GOTHAM.

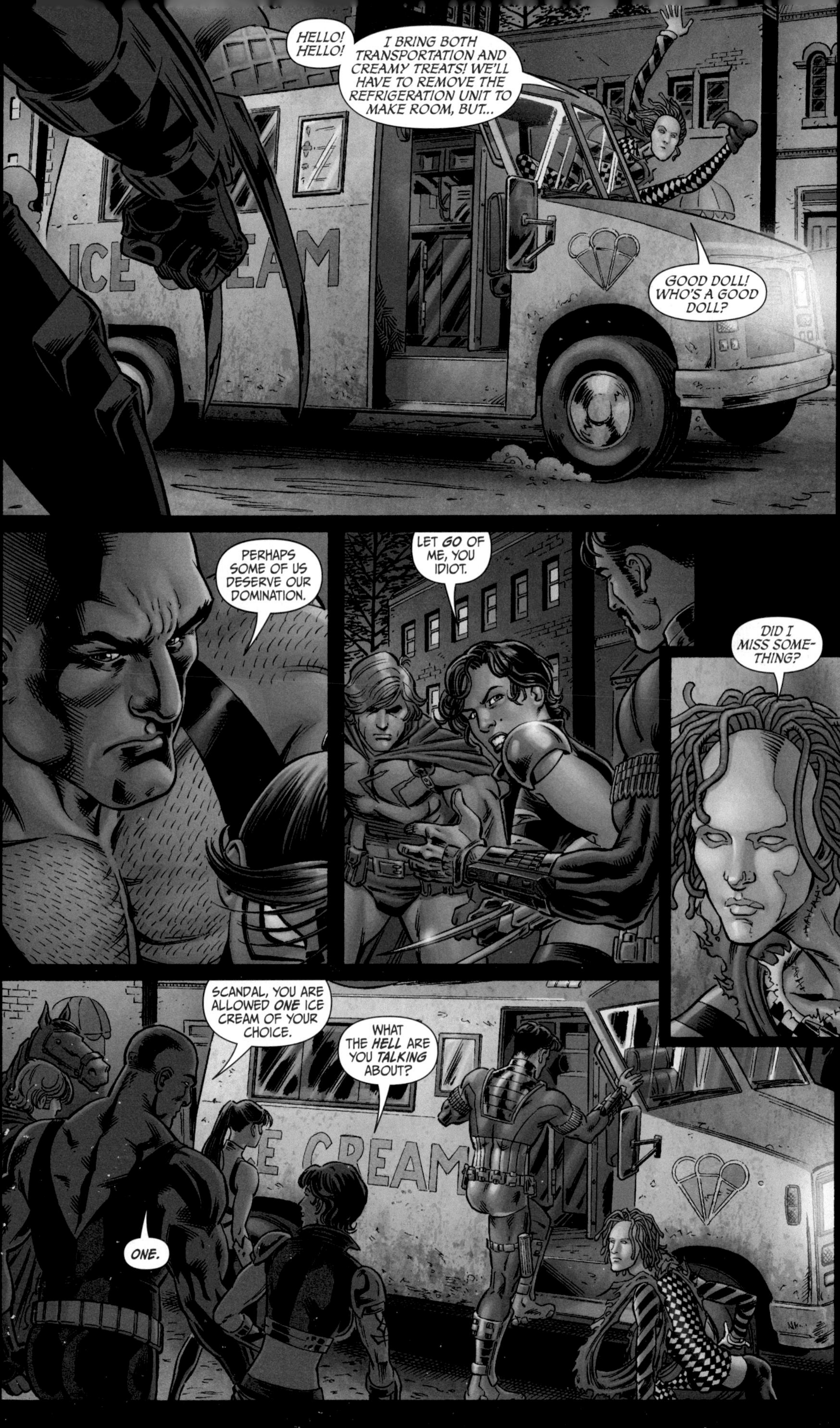
HELLO! HELLO!
I BRING BOTH TRANSPORTATION AND CREAMY TREATS! WE'LL HAVE TO REMOVE THE REFRIGERATION UNIT TO MAKE ROOM, BUT...
ICE CREAM
GOOD DOLL! WHO'S A GOOD DOLL?
PERHAPS SOME OF US DESERVE OUR DOMINATION.
LET GO OF ME, YOU IDIOT.
DID I MISS SOME-THING?
SCANDAL, YOU ARE ALLOWED ONE ICE CREAM OF YOUR CHOICE.
WHAT THE HELL ARE YOU TALKING ABOUT?
ONE.

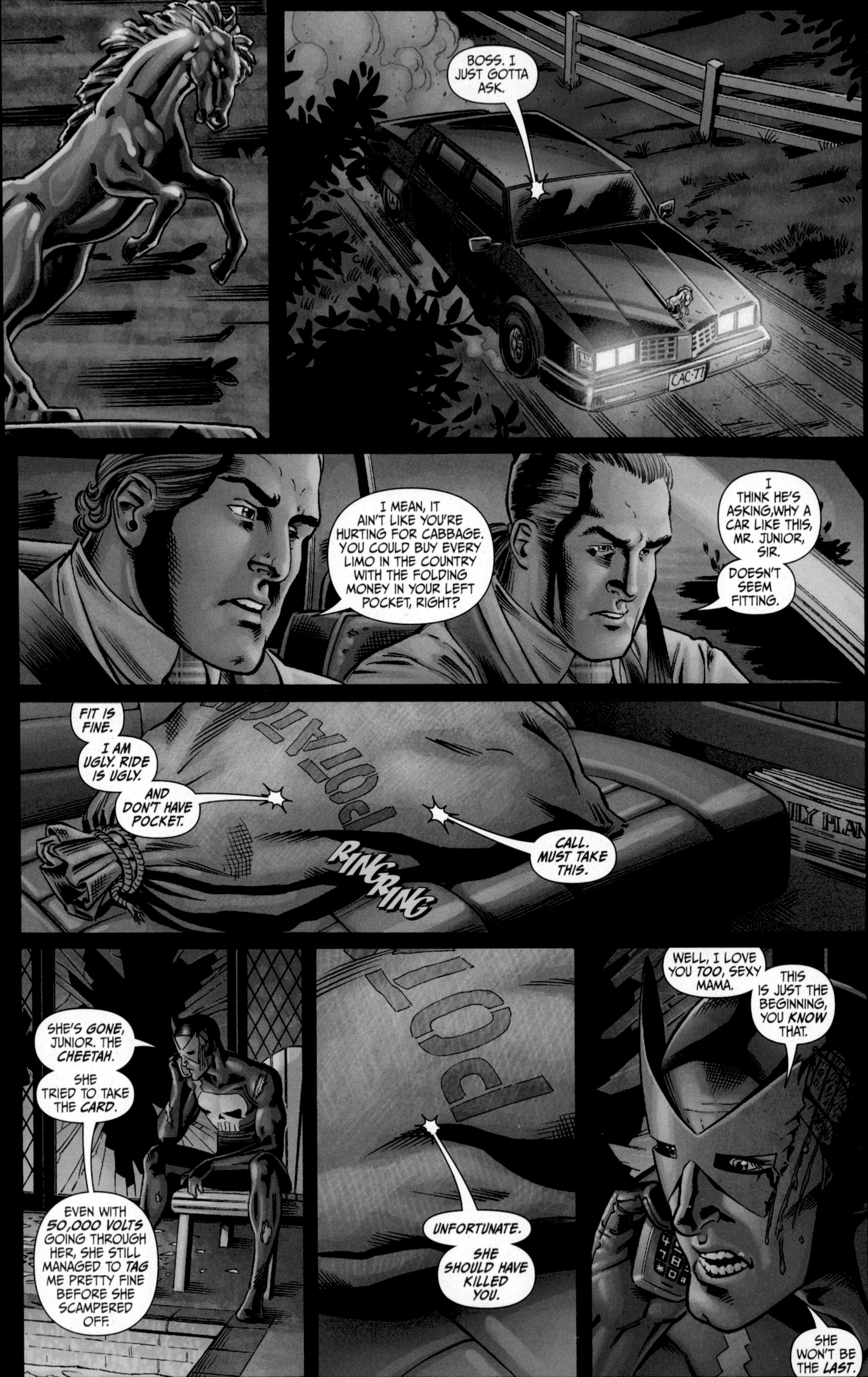
BOSS. I JUST GOTTA ASK.
CAC-77
I MEAN, IT AIN'T LIKE YOU'RE HURTING FOR CABBAGE. YOU COULD BUY EVERY LIMO IN THE COUNTRY WITH THE FOLDING MONEY IN YOUR LEFT POCKET, RIGHT?
I THINK HE'S ASKING,WHY A CAR LIKE THIS, MR. JUNIOR, SIR.
DOESN'T SEEM FITTING.
FIT IS FINE.
I AM UGLY. RIDE IS UGLY.
AND DON'T HAVE POCKET.
RINGRING
CALL. MUST TAKE THIS.
SHE'S GONE, JUNIOR. THE CHEETAH.
SHE TRIED TO TAKE THE CARD.
EVEN WITH 50,000 VOLTS GOING THROUGH HER, SHE STILL MANAGED TO TAG ME PRETTY FINE BEFORE SHE SCAMPERED OFF.
UNFORTUNATE.
SHE SHOULD HAVE KILLED YOU.
WELL, I LOVE YOU TOO, SEXY MAMA.
THIS IS JUST THE BEGINNING, YOU KNOW THAT.
SHE WON'T BE THE LAST.

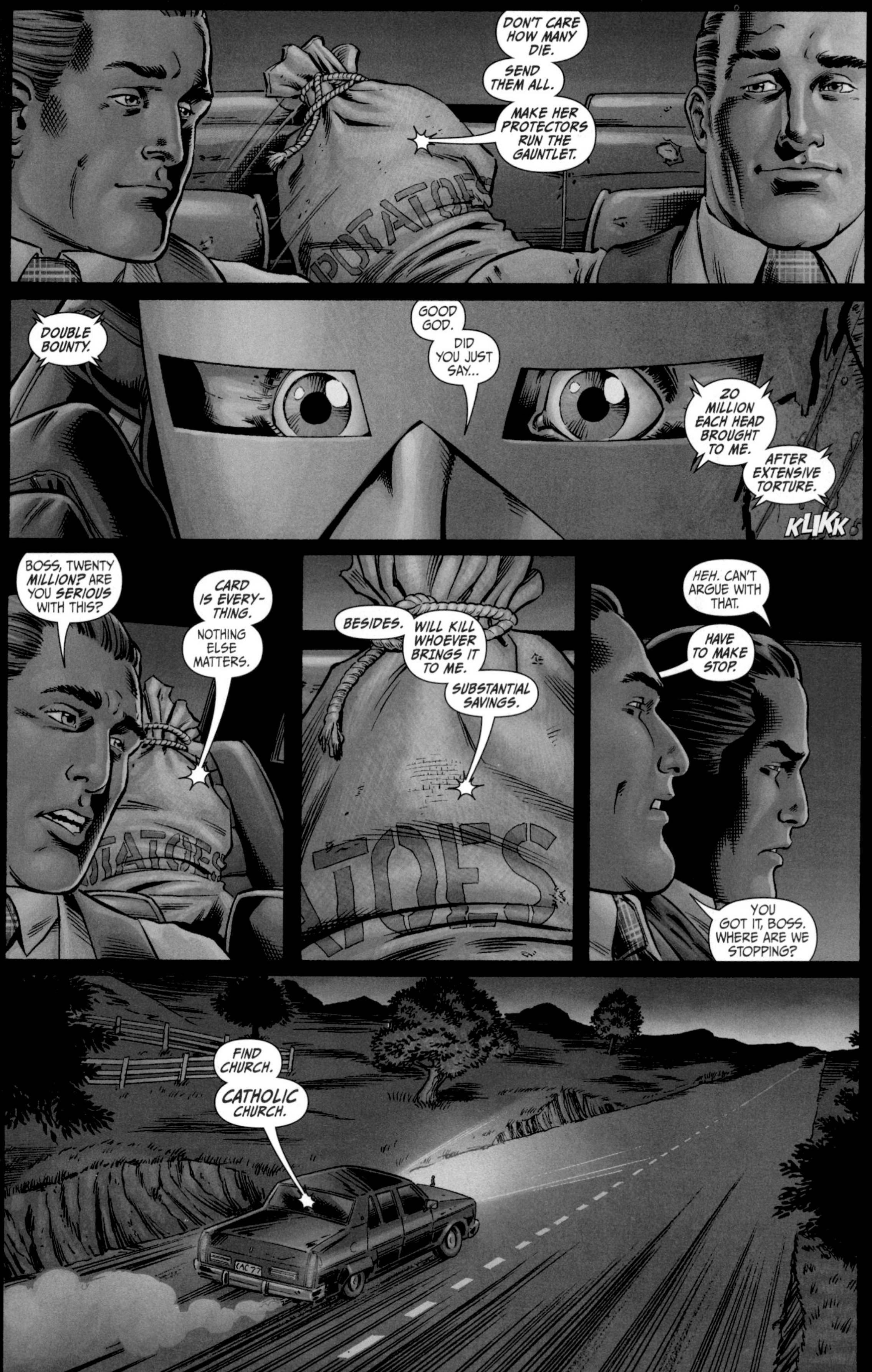
DON'T CARE HOW MANY DIE.
SEND THEM ALL.
MAKE HER PROTECTORS RUN THE GAUNTLET.
POTATOES
DOUBLE BOUNTY.
GOOD GOD.
DID YOU JUST SAY...
20 MILLION EACH HEAD BROUGHT TO ME.
AFTER EXTENSIVE TORTURE.
KLIKK
BOSS, TWENTY MILLION? ARE YOU SERIOUS WITH THIS?
CARD IS EVERYTHING.
NOTHING ELSE MATTERS.
BESIDES.
WILL KILL WHOEVER BRINGS IT TO ME.
SUBSTANTIAL SAVINGS.
HEH. CAN'T ARGUE WITH THAT.
HAVE TO MAKE STOP.
YOU GOT IT, BOSS. WHERE ARE WE STOPPING?
FIND CHURCH.
CATHOLIC CHURCH.

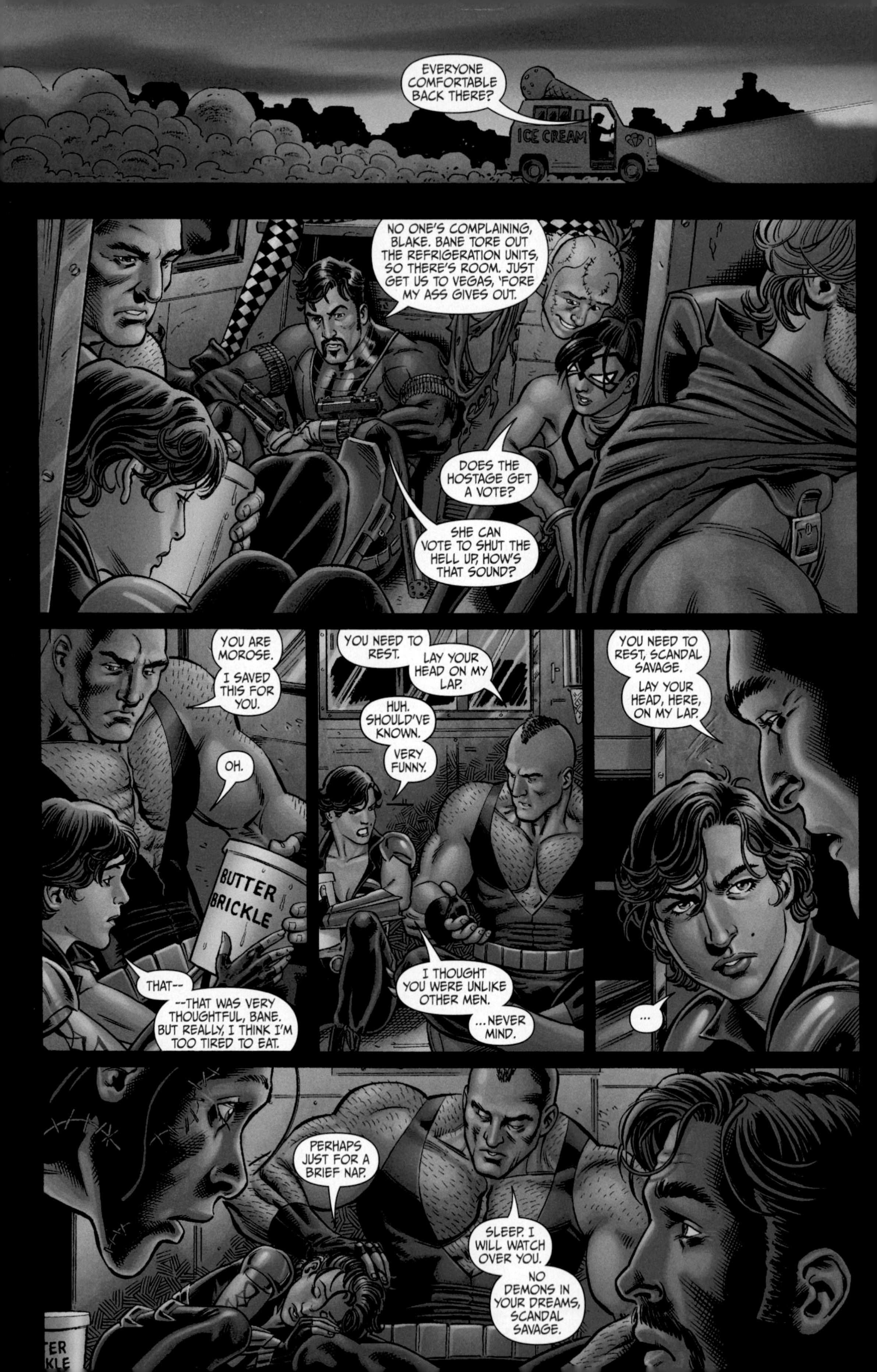
EVERYONE COMFORTABLE BACK THERE?
ICE CREAM
NO ONE'S COMPLAINING, BLAKE. BANE TORE OUT THE REFRIGERATION UNITS, SO THERE'S ROOM. JUST GET US TO VEGAS, 'FORE MY ASS GIVES OUT.
DOES THE HOSTAGE GET A VOTE?
SHE CAN VOTE TO SHUT THE HELL UP, HOW'S THAT SOUND?
YOU ARE MOROSE.
I SAVED THIS FOR YOU.
OH.
BUTTER BRICKLE
THAT--
--THAT WAS VERY THOUGHTFUL, BANE. BUT REALLY, I THINK I'M TOO TIRED TO EAT.
YOU NEED TO REST.
LAY YOUR HEAD ON MY LAP.
HUH. SHOULD'VE KNOWN.
VERY FUNNY.
I THOUGHT YOU WERE UNLIKE OTHER MEN.
...NEVER MIND.
YOU NEED TO REST, SCANDAL SAVAGE.
LAY YOUR HEAD, HERE, ON MY LAP.
...
PERHAPS JUST FOR A BRIEF NAP.
SLEEP. I WILL WATCH OVER YOU.
NO DEMONS IN YOUR DREAMS, SCANDAL SAVAGE.

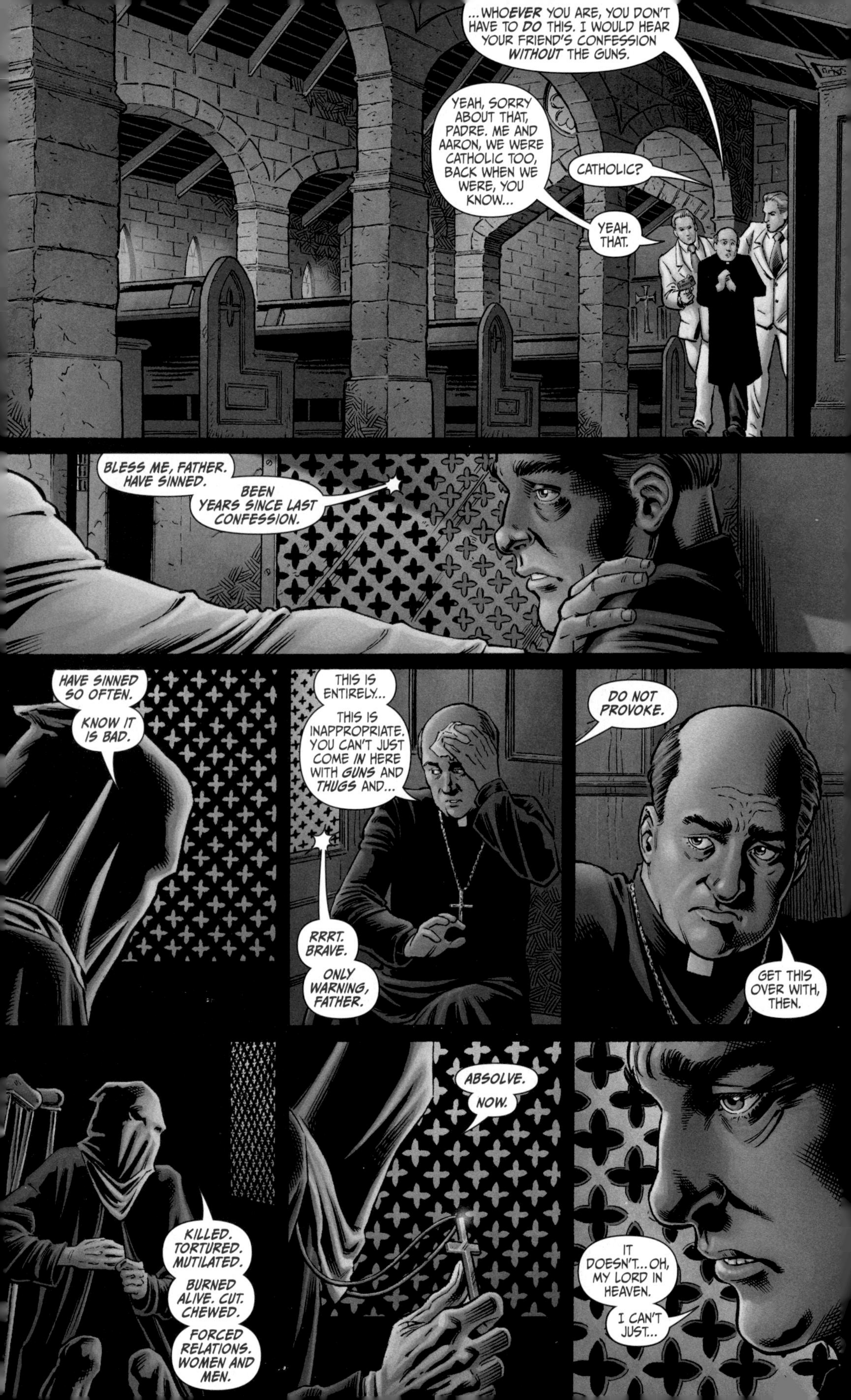
...WHOEVER YOU ARE, YOU DON'T HAVE TO DO THIS. I WOULD HEAR YOUR FRIEND'S CONFESSION WITHOUT THE GUNS.
YEAH, SORRY ABOUT THAT, PADRE. ME AND AARON, WE WERE CATHOLIC TOO, BACK WHEN WE WERE, YOU KNOW...
CATHOLIC?
YEAH. THAT.
BLESS ME, FATHER. HAVE SINNED.
BEEN YEARS SINCE LAST CONFESSION.
HAVE SINNED SO OFTEN.
KNOW IT IS BAD.
THIS IS ENTIRELY...
THIS IS INAPPROPRIATE. YOU CAN'T JUST COME IN HERE WITH GUNS AND THUGS AND...
RRRT. BRAVE.
ONLY WARNING, FATHER.
DO NOT PROVOKE.
GET THIS OVER WITH, THEN.
KILLED. TORTURED. MUTILATED.
BURNED ALIVE. CUT. CHEWED.
FORCED RELATIONS. WOMEN AND MEN.
ABSOLVE.
NOW.
IT DOESN'T...OH, MY LORD IN HEAVEN.
I CAN'T JUST...

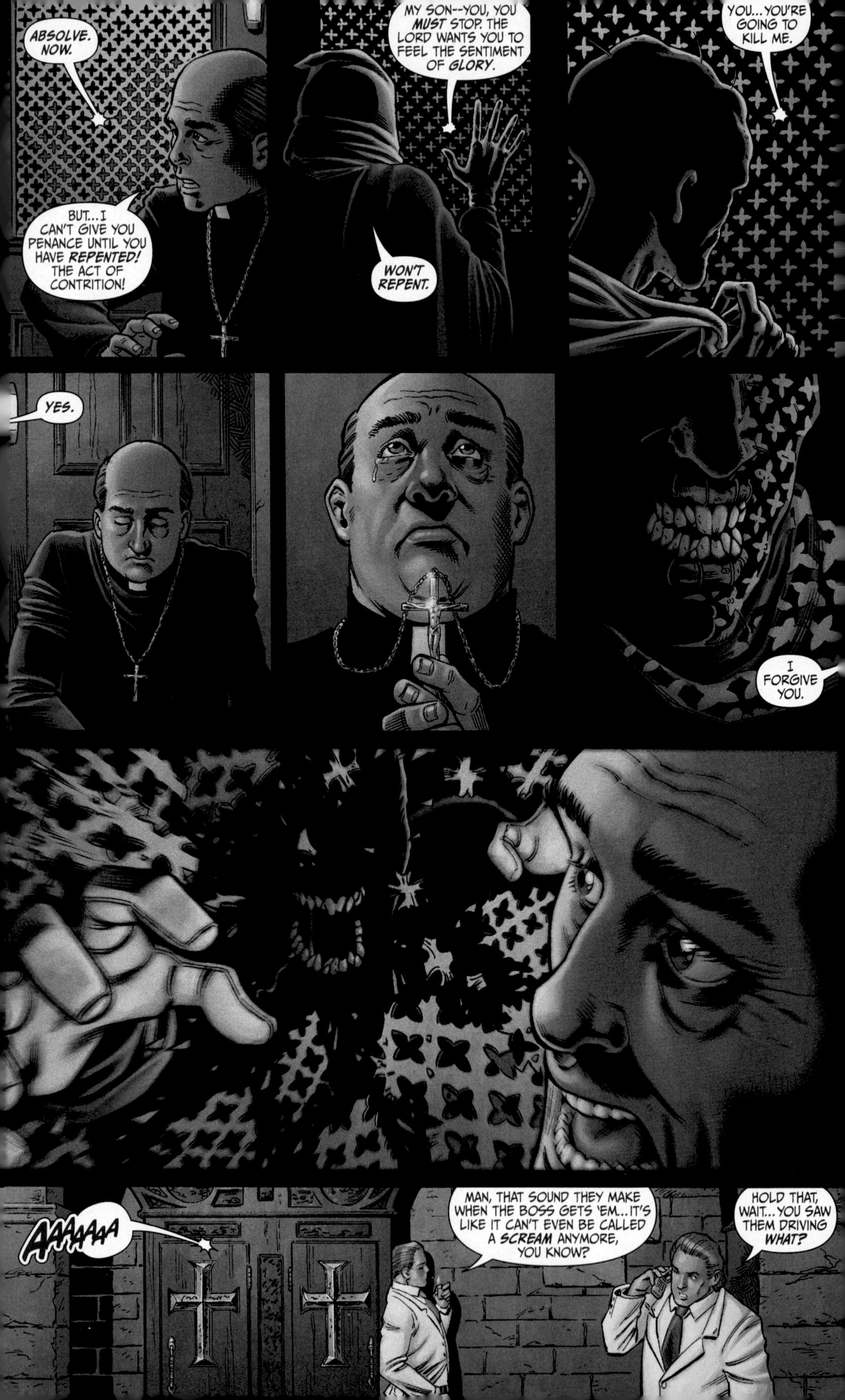
ABSOLVE. NOW.
BUT...I CAN'T GIVE YOU PENANCE UNTIL YOU HAVE *REPENTED!* THE ACT OF CONTRITION!
MY SON--YOU, YOU *MUST* STOP. THE LORD WANTS YOU TO FEEL THE SENTIMENT OF *GLORY*.
WON'T REPENT.
YOU...YOU'RE GOING TO KILL ME.
YES.
I FORGIVE YOU.
AAAAAAA
MAN, THAT SOUND THEY MAKE WHEN THE BOSS GETS 'EM...IT'S LIKE IT CAN'T EVEN BE CALLED A *SCREAM* ANYMORE, YOU KNOW?
HOLD THAT, WAIT...YOU SAW THEM DRIVING *WHAT?*

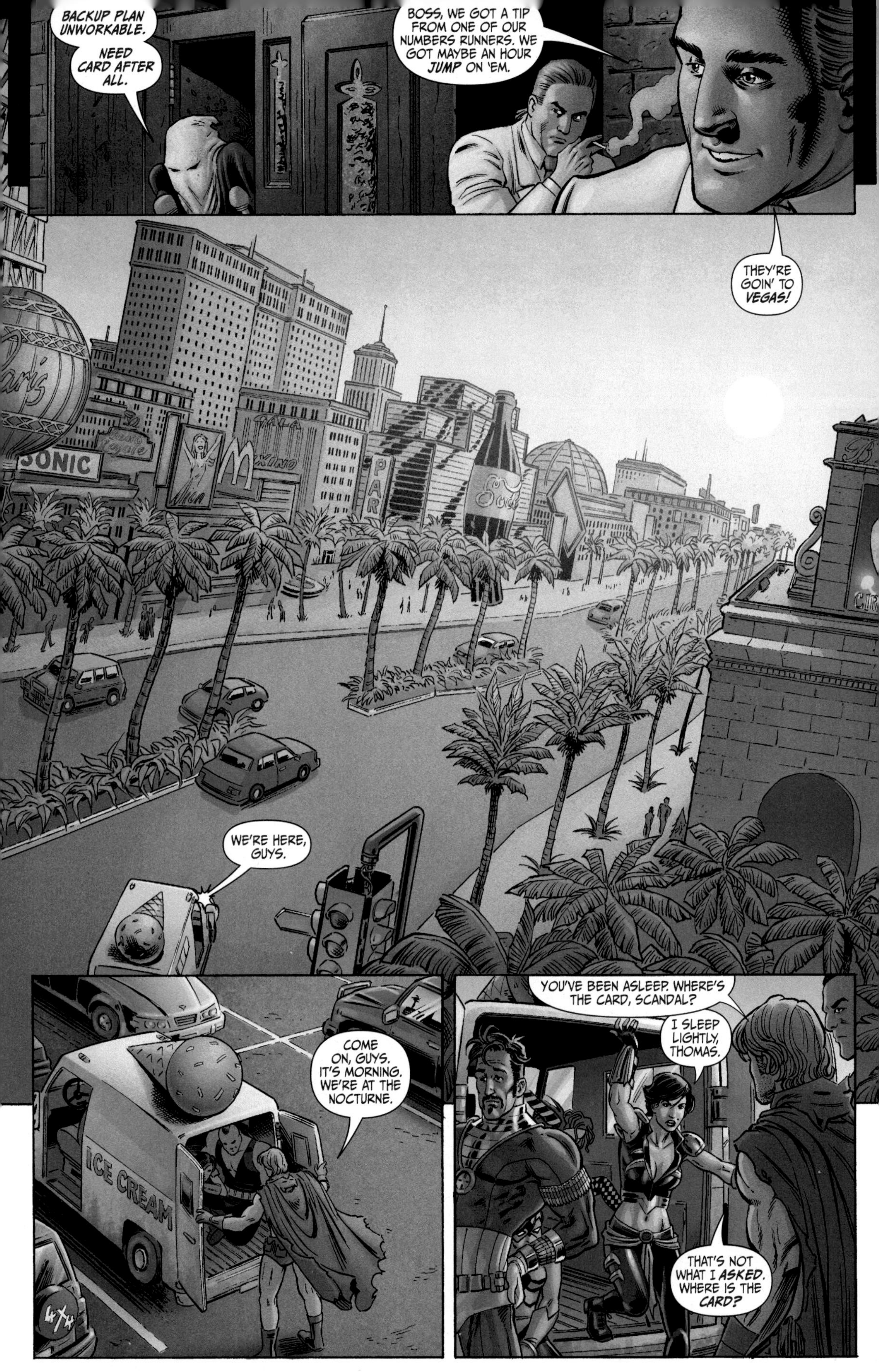
BACKUP PLAN UNWORKABLE.
NEED CARD AFTER ALL.
BOSS, WE GOT A TIP FROM ONE OF OUR NUMBERS RUNNERS. WE GOT MAYBE AN HOUR JUMP ON 'EM.
THEY'RE GOIN' TO VEGAS!
SONIC
WE'RE HERE, GUYS.
COME ON, GUYS. IT'S MORNING. WE'RE AT THE NOCTURNE.
ICE CREAM
YOU'VE BEEN ASLEEP. WHERE'S THE CARD, SCANDAL?
I SLEEP LIGHTLY, THOMAS.
THAT'S NOT WHAT I ASKED. WHERE IS THE CARD?

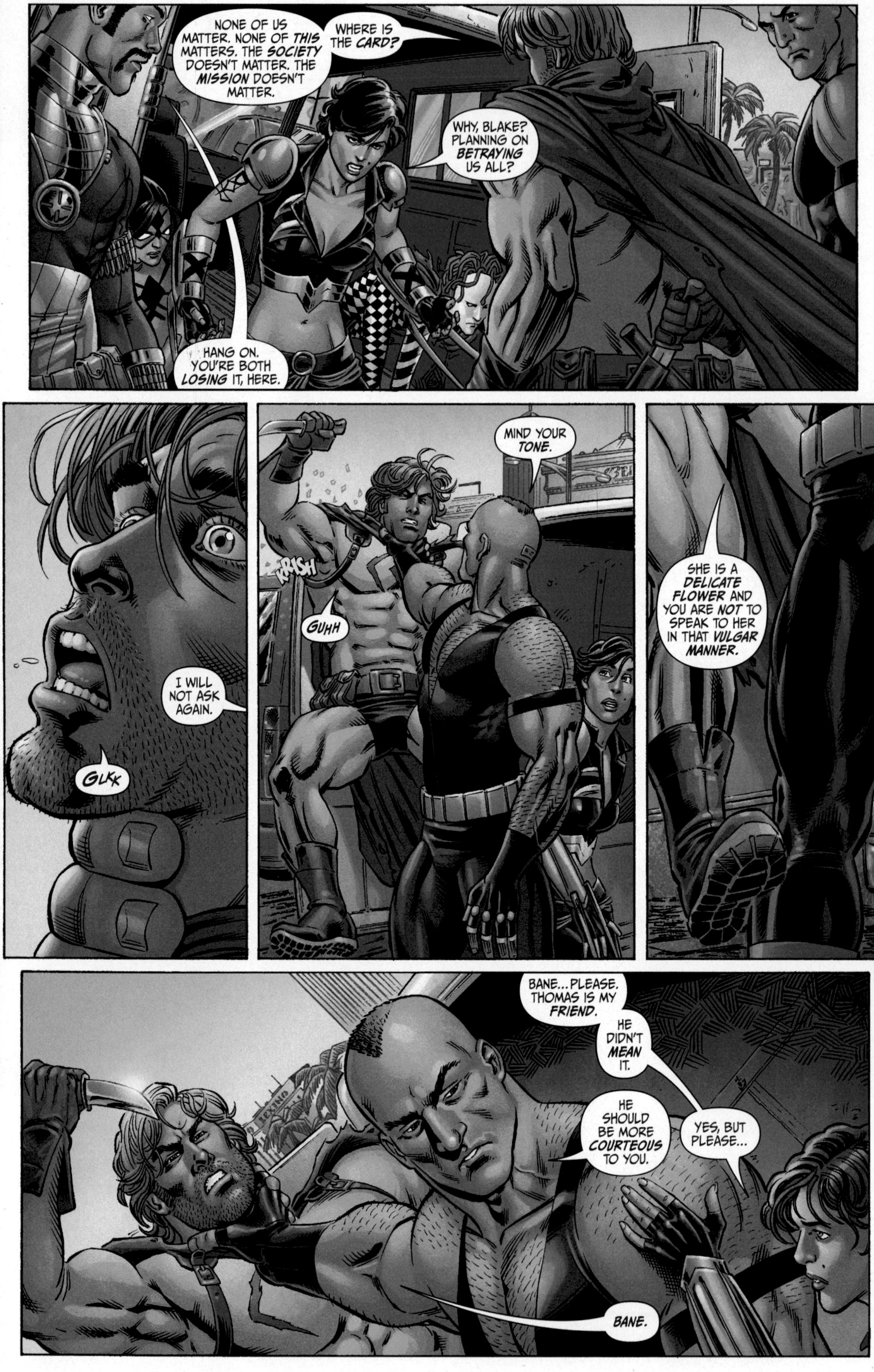
NONE OF US MATTER. NONE OF THIS MATTERS. THE SOCIETY DOESN'T MATTER. THE MISSION DOESN'T MATTER.
WHERE IS THE CARD?
WHY, BLAKE? PLANNING ON BETRAYING US ALL?
HANG ON. YOU'RE BOTH LOSING IT, HERE.
I WILL NOT ASK AGAIN.
GLKK
MIND YOUR TONE.
KRISH
GUHH
SHE IS A DELICATE FLOWER AND YOU ARE NOT TO SPEAK TO HER IN THAT VULGAR MANNER.
BANE...PLEASE. THOMAS IS MY FRIEND.
HE DIDN'T MEAN IT.
HE SHOULD BE MORE COURTEOUS TO YOU.
YES, BUT PLEASE...
BANE.

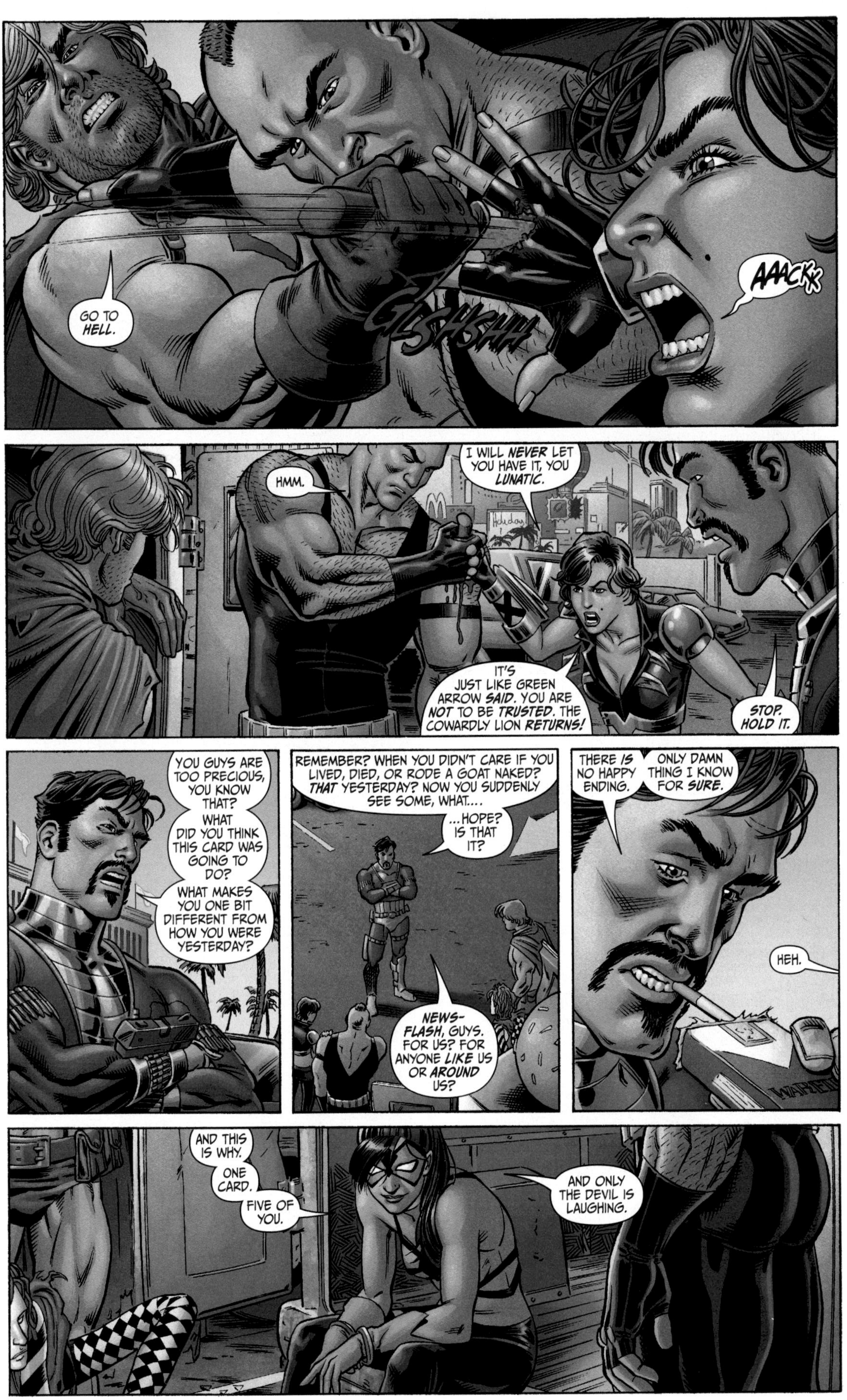
GO TO HELL.
GLSHSHH
AAACKK
HMM.
I WILL NEVER LET YOU HAVE IT, YOU LUNATIC.
IT'S JUST LIKE GREEN ARROW SAID. YOU ARE NOT TO BE TRUSTED. THE COWARDLY LION RETURNS!
STOP. HOLD IT.
YOU GUYS ARE TOO PRECIOUS, YOU KNOW THAT?
WHAT DID YOU THINK THIS CARD WAS GOING TO DO?
WHAT MAKES YOU ONE BIT DIFFERENT FROM HOW YOU WERE YESTERDAY?
REMEMBER? WHEN YOU DIDN'T CARE IF YOU LIVED, DIED, OR RODE A GOAT NAKED? THAT YESTERDAY? NOW YOU SUDDENLY SEE SOME, WHAT....
...HOPE? IS THAT IT?
NEWS-FLASH, GUYS. FOR US? FOR ANYONE LIKE US OR AROUND US?
THERE IS NO HAPPY ENDING.
ONLY DAMN THING I KNOW FOR SURE.
HEH.
AND THIS IS WHY.
ONE CARD.
FIVE OF YOU.
AND ONLY THE DEVIL IS LAUGHING.

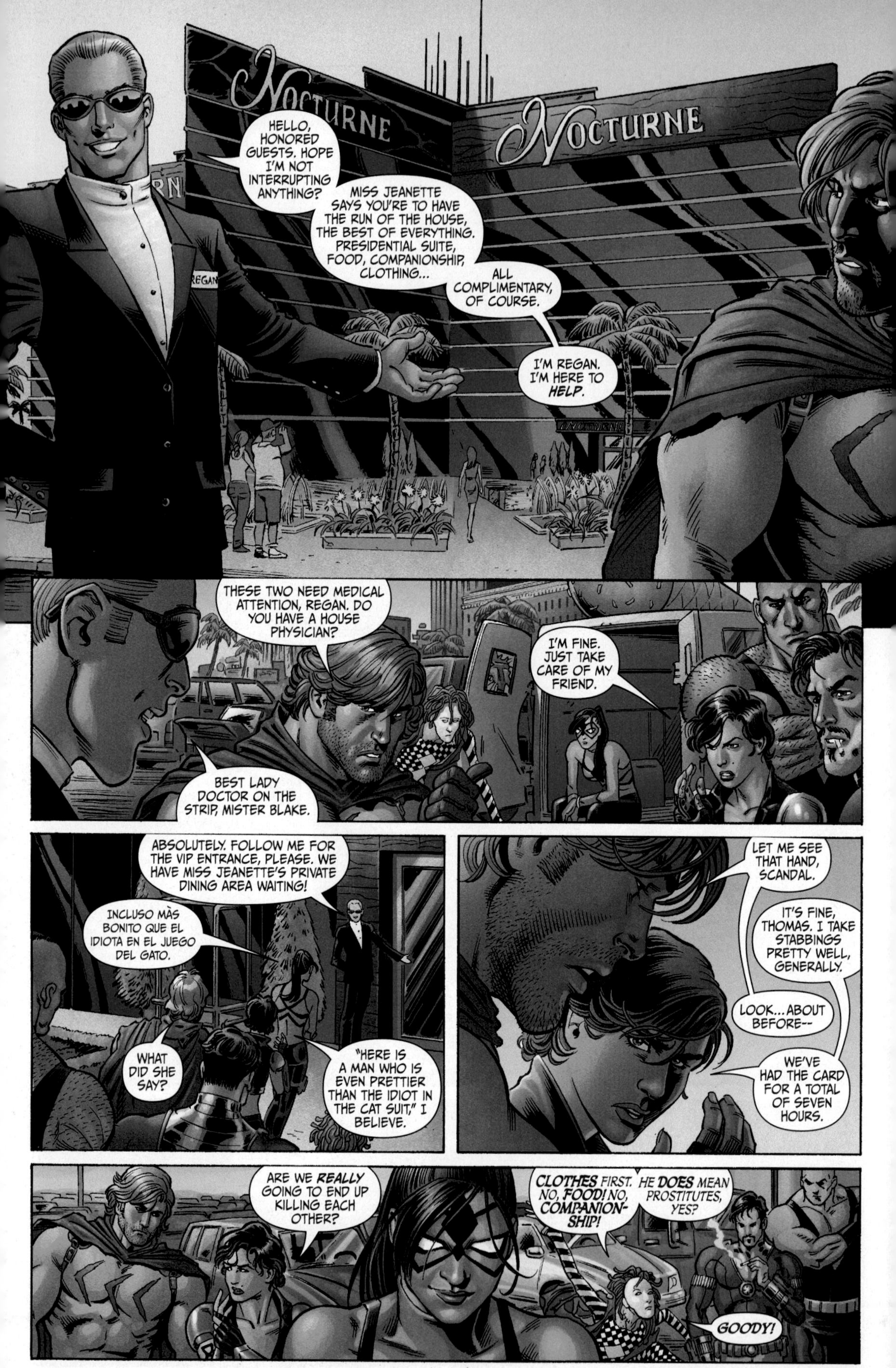

NOCTURNE
NOCTURNE
HELLO, HONORED GUESTS. HOPE I'M NOT INTERRUPTING ANYTHING?
MISS JEANETTE SAYS YOU'RE TO HAVE THE RUN OF THE HOUSE, THE BEST OF EVERYTHING. PRESIDENTIAL SUITE, FOOD, COMPANIONSHIP, CLOTHING...
ALL COMPLIMENTARY, OF COURSE.
I'M REGAN. I'M HERE TO HELP.
REGAN
THESE TWO NEED MEDICAL ATTENTION, REGAN. DO YOU HAVE A HOUSE PHYSICIAN?
I'M FINE. JUST TAKE CARE OF MY FRIEND.
BEST LADY DOCTOR ON THE STRIP, MISTER BLAKE.
ABSOLUTELY. FOLLOW ME FOR THE VIP ENTRANCE, PLEASE. WE HAVE MISS JEANETTE'S PRIVATE DINING AREA WAITING!
INCLUSO MÀS BONITO QUE EL IDIOTA EN EL JUEGO DEL GATO.
WHAT DID SHE SAY?
"HERE IS A MAN WHO IS EVEN PRETTIER THAN THE IDIOT IN THE CAT SUIT," I BELIEVE.
LET ME SEE THAT HAND, SCANDAL.
IT'S FINE, THOMAS. I TAKE STABBINGS PRETTY WELL, GENERALLY.
LOOK...ABOUT BEFORE--
WE'VE HAD THE CARD FOR A TOTAL OF SEVEN HOURS.
ARE WE REALLY GOING TO END UP KILLING EACH OTHER?
CLOTHES FIRST. NO, FOOD! NO, COMPANIONSHIP!
HE DOES MEAN PROSTITUTES, YES?
GOODY!

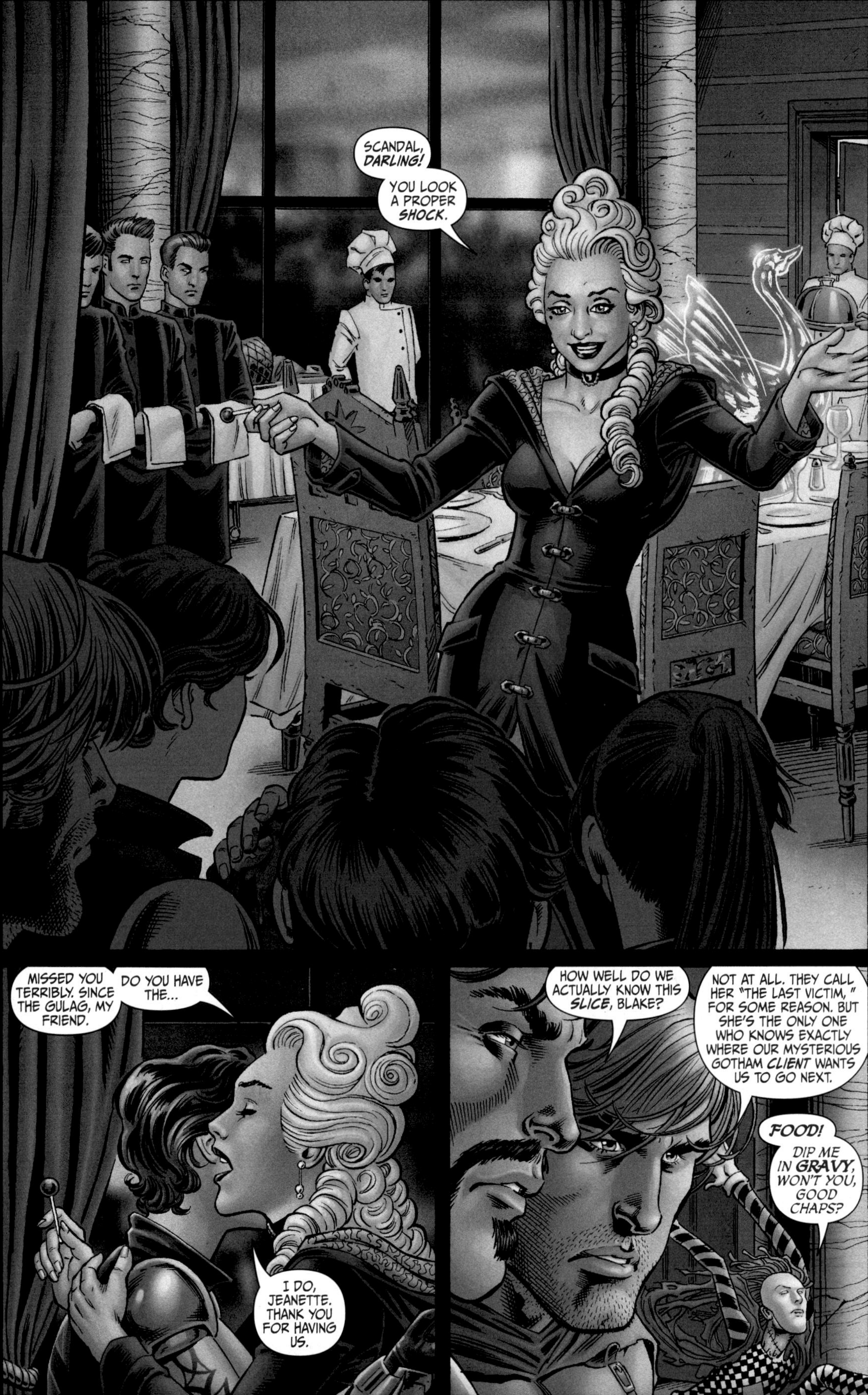
SCANDAL, DARLING!
YOU LOOK A PROPER SHOCK.
MISSED YOU TERRIBLY. SINCE THE GULAG, MY FRIEND.
DO YOU HAVE THE...
I DO, JEANETTE. THANK YOU FOR HAVING US.
HOW WELL DO WE ACTUALLY KNOW THIS SLICE, BLAKE?
NOT AT ALL. THEY CALL HER "THE LAST VICTIM," FOR SOME REASON. BUT SHE'S THE ONLY ONE WHO KNOWS EXACTLY WHERE OUR MYSTERIOUS GOTHAM CLIENT WANTS US TO GO NEXT.
FOOD!
DIP ME IN GRAVY, WON'T YOU, GOOD CHAPS?

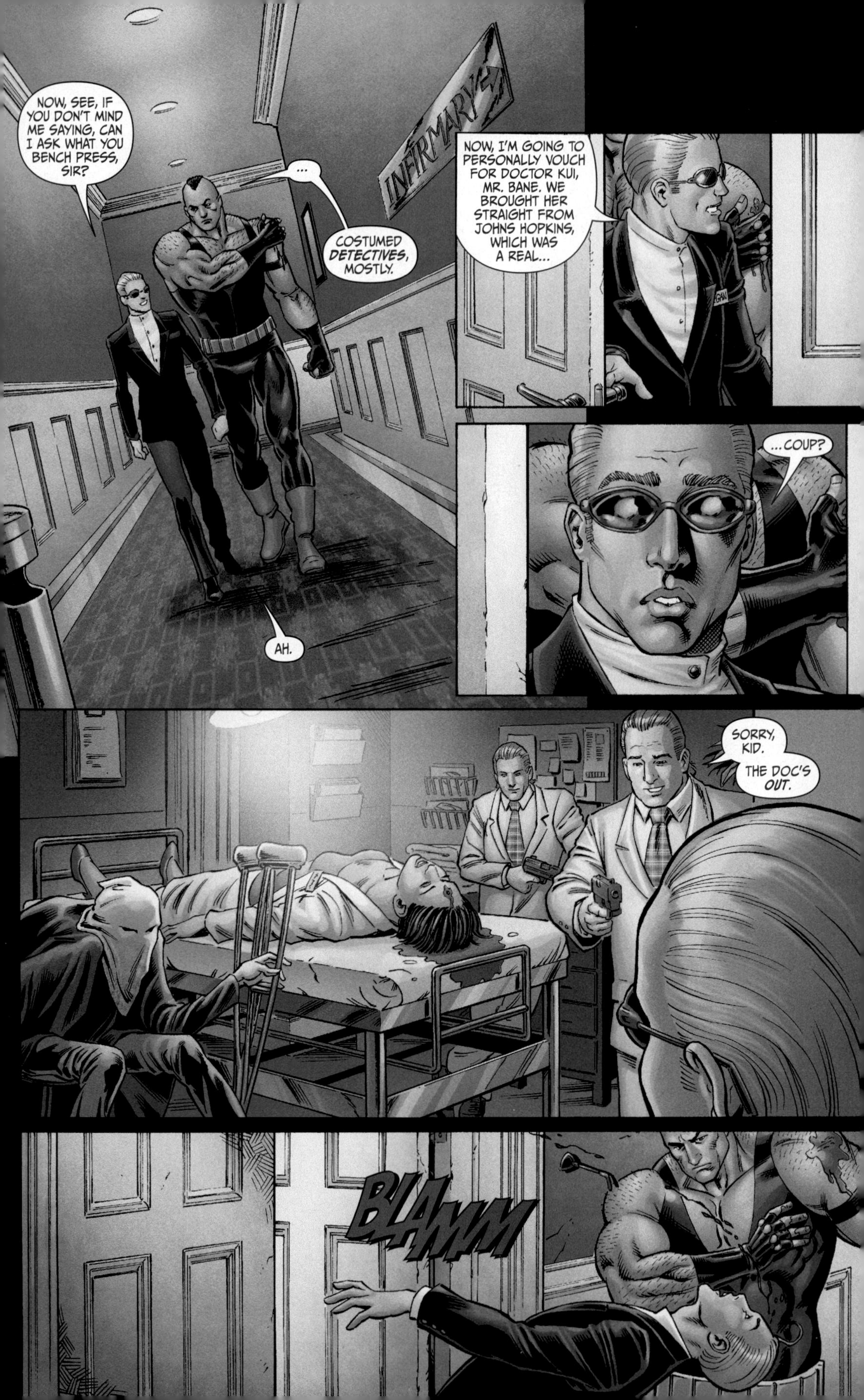

INFIRMARY
NOW, SEE, IF YOU DON'T MIND ME SAYING, CAN I ASK WHAT YOU BENCH PRESS, SIR?
...
COSTUMED *DETECTIVES*, MOSTLY.
AH.
NOW, I'M GOING TO PERSONALLY VOUCH FOR DOCTOR KUI, MR. BANE. WE BROUGHT HER STRAIGHT FROM JOHNS HOPKINS, WHICH WAS A REAL...
...COUP?
SORRY, KID.
THE DOC'S *OUT*.
BLAMM

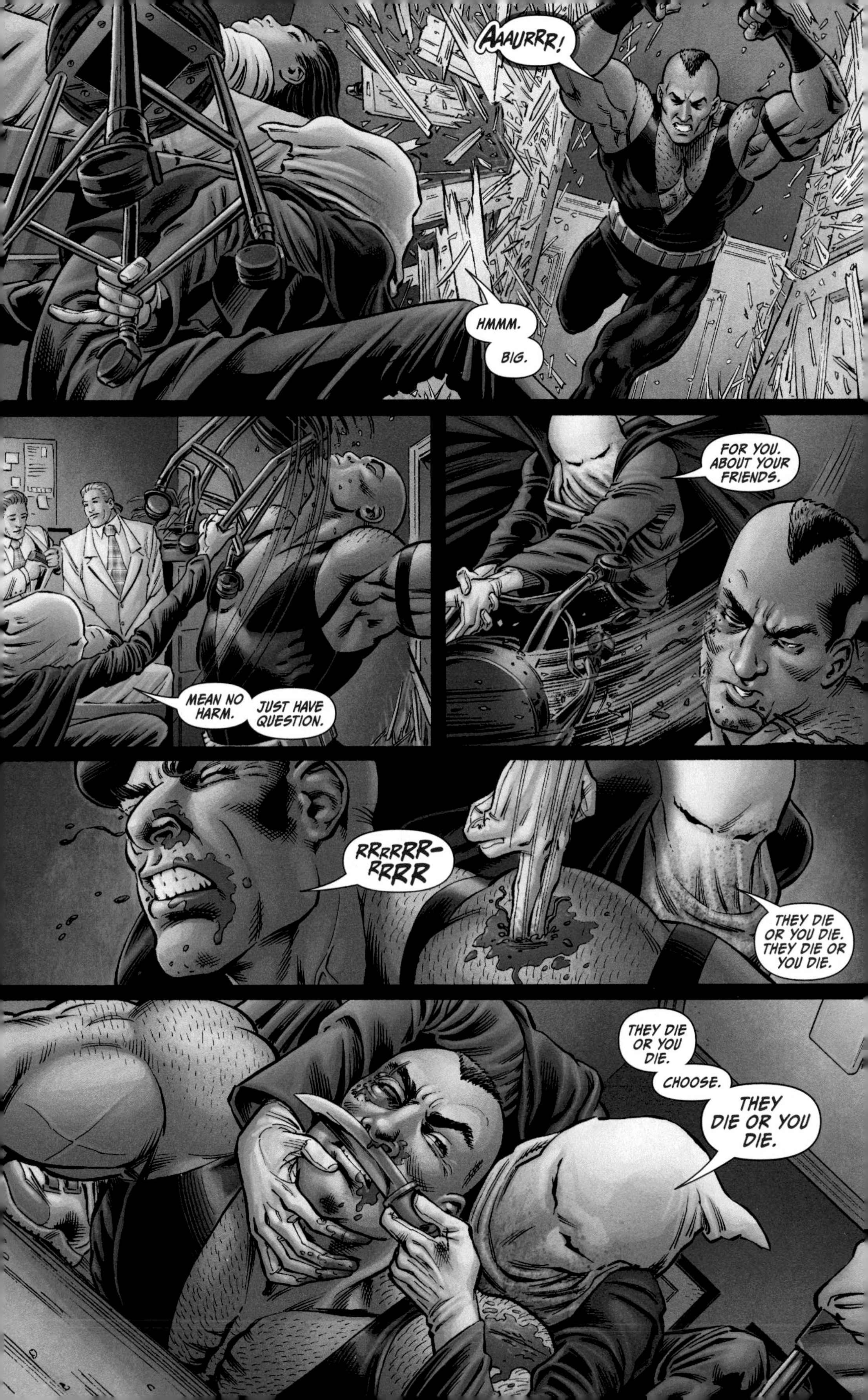
AAAURRR!
HMMM.
BIG.
MEAN NO HARM.
JUST HAVE QUESTION.
FOR YOU. ABOUT YOUR FRIENDS.
RRRRRR-RRRR
THEY DIE OR YOU DIE. THEY DIE OR YOU DIE.
THEY DIE OR YOU DIE.
CHOOSE.
THEY DIE OR YOU DIE.

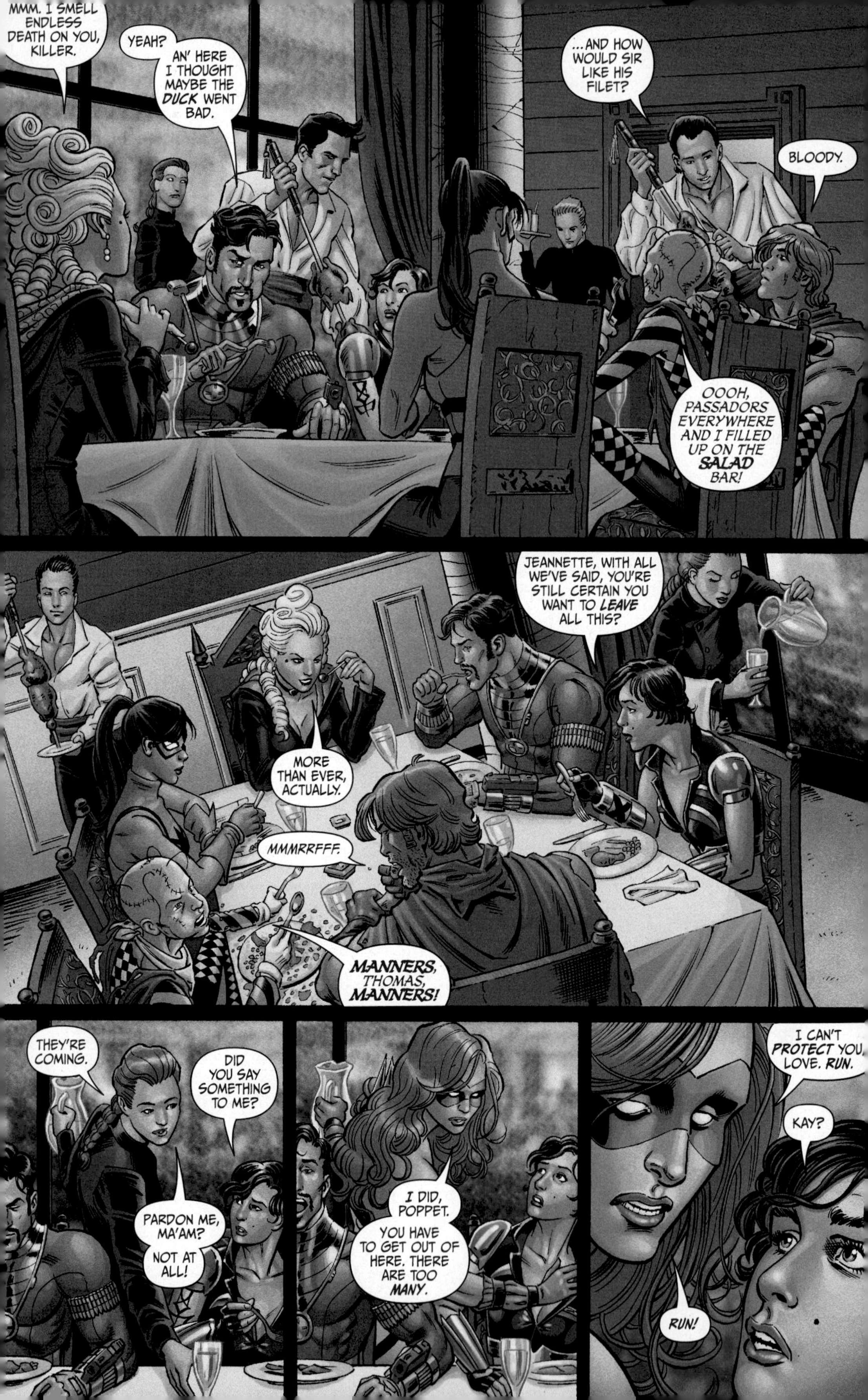
MMM. I SMELL ENDLESS DEATH ON YOU, KILLER.
YEAH?
AN' HERE I THOUGHT MAYBE THE DUCK WENT BAD.
...AND HOW WOULD SIR LIKE HIS FILET?
BLOODY.
OOOH, PASSADORS EVERYWHERE AND I FILLED UP ON THE SALAD BAR!
JEANNETTE, WITH ALL WE'VE SAID, YOU'RE STILL CERTAIN YOU WANT TO LEAVE ALL THIS?
MORE THAN EVER, ACTUALLY.
MMMRRFFF.
MANNERS, THOMAS, MANNERS!
THEY'RE COMING.
DID YOU SAY SOMETHING TO ME?
PARDON ME, MA'AM?
NOT AT ALL!
I DID, POPPET.
YOU HAVE TO GET OUT OF HERE. THERE ARE TOO MANY.
I CAN'T PROTECT YOU, LOVE. RUN.
KAY?
RUN!

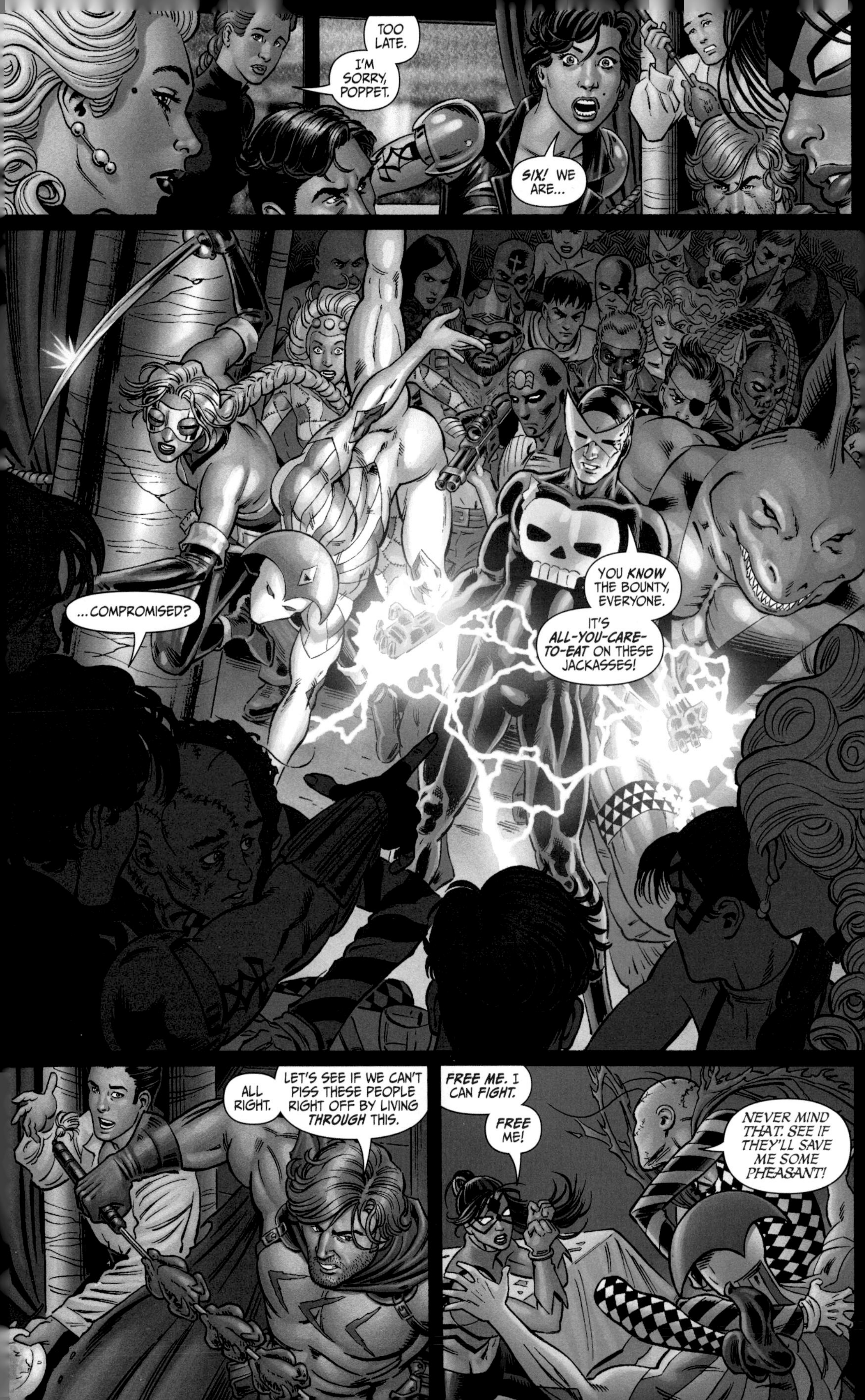
TOO LATE.
I'M SORRY, POPPET.
SIX! WE ARE...
...COMPROMISED?
YOU KNOW THE BOUNTY, EVERYONE.
IT'S ALL-YOU-CARE-TO-EAT ON THESE JACKASSES!
ALL RIGHT.
LET'S SEE IF WE CAN'T PISS THESE PEOPLE RIGHT OFF BY LIVING THROUGH THIS.
FREE ME. I CAN FIGHT.
FREE ME!
NEVER MIND THAT. SEE IF THEY'LL SAVE ME SOME PHEASANT!

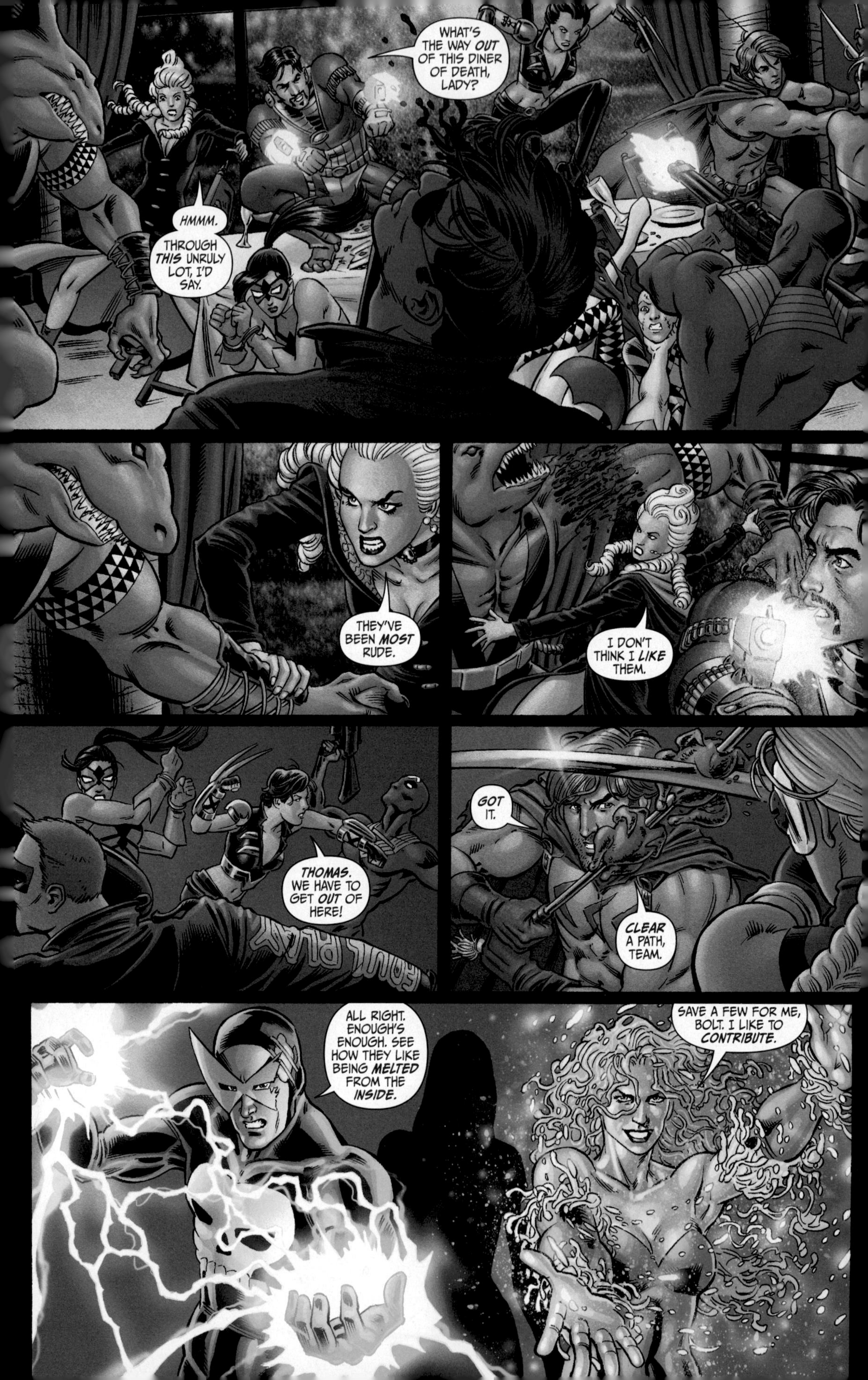
WHAT'S THE WAY *OUT* OF THIS DINER OF DEATH, LADY?
HMMM. THROUGH *THIS* UNRULY LOT, I'D SAY.
THEY'VE BEEN *MOST* RUDE.
I DON'T THINK I *LIKE* THEM.
THOMAS. WE HAVE TO GET *OUT* OF HERE!
FOUL PLAY
GOT IT.
CLEAR A PATH, TEAM.
ALL RIGHT. ENOUGH'S ENOUGH. SEE HOW THEY LIKE BEING *MELTED* FROM THE *INSIDE*.
SAVE A FEW FOR ME, BOLT. I LIKE TO *CONTRIBUTE*.

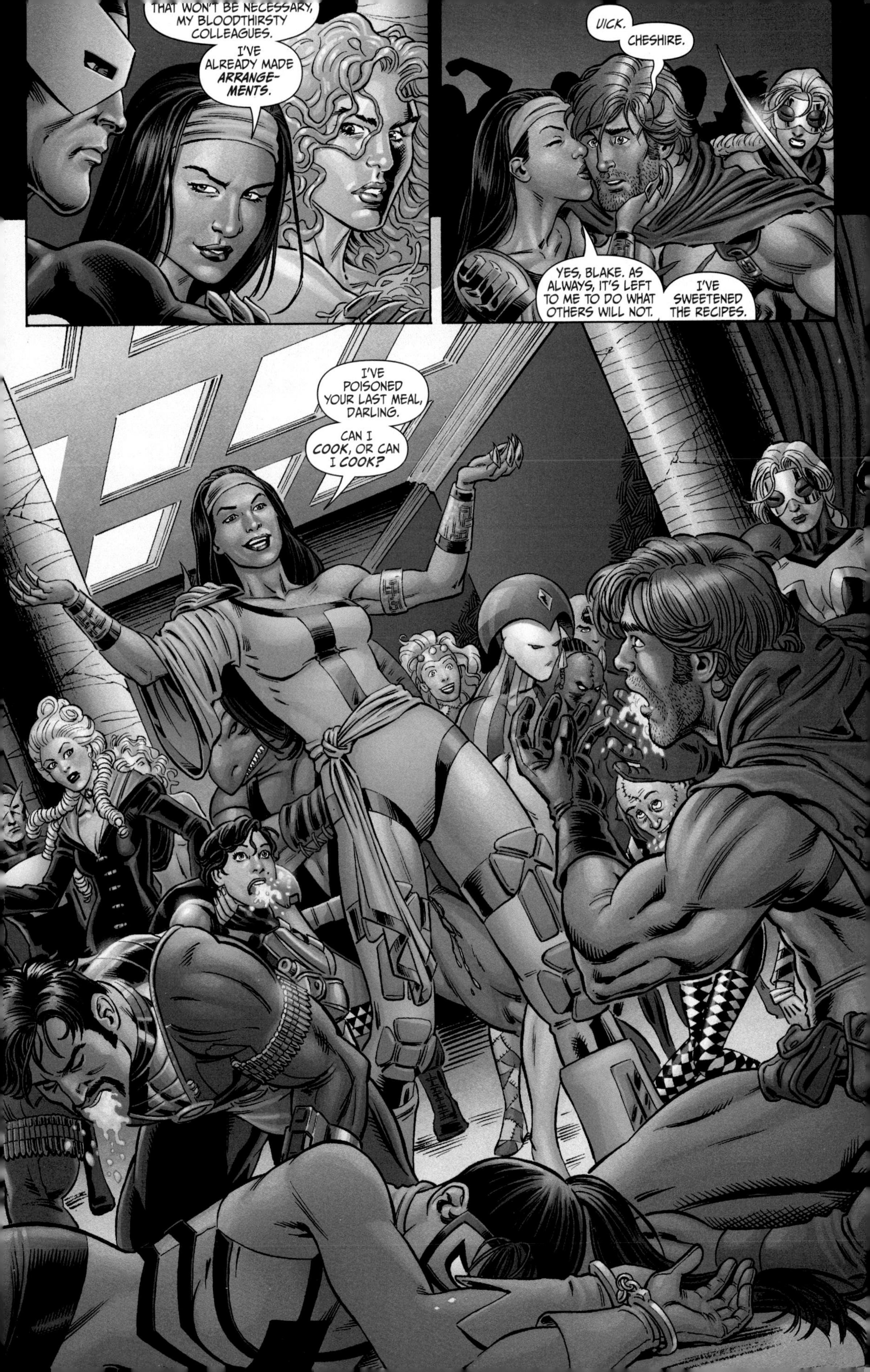
THAT WON'T BE NECESSARY, MY BLOODTHIRSTY COLLEAGUES.
I'VE ALREADY MADE ARRANGE-MENTS.
UICK.
CHESHIRE.
YES, BLAKE. AS ALWAYS, IT'S LEFT TO ME TO DO WHAT OTHERS WILL NOT.
I'VE SWEETENED THE RECIPES.
I'VE POISONED YOUR LAST MEAL, DARLING.
CAN I COOK, OR CAN I COOK?

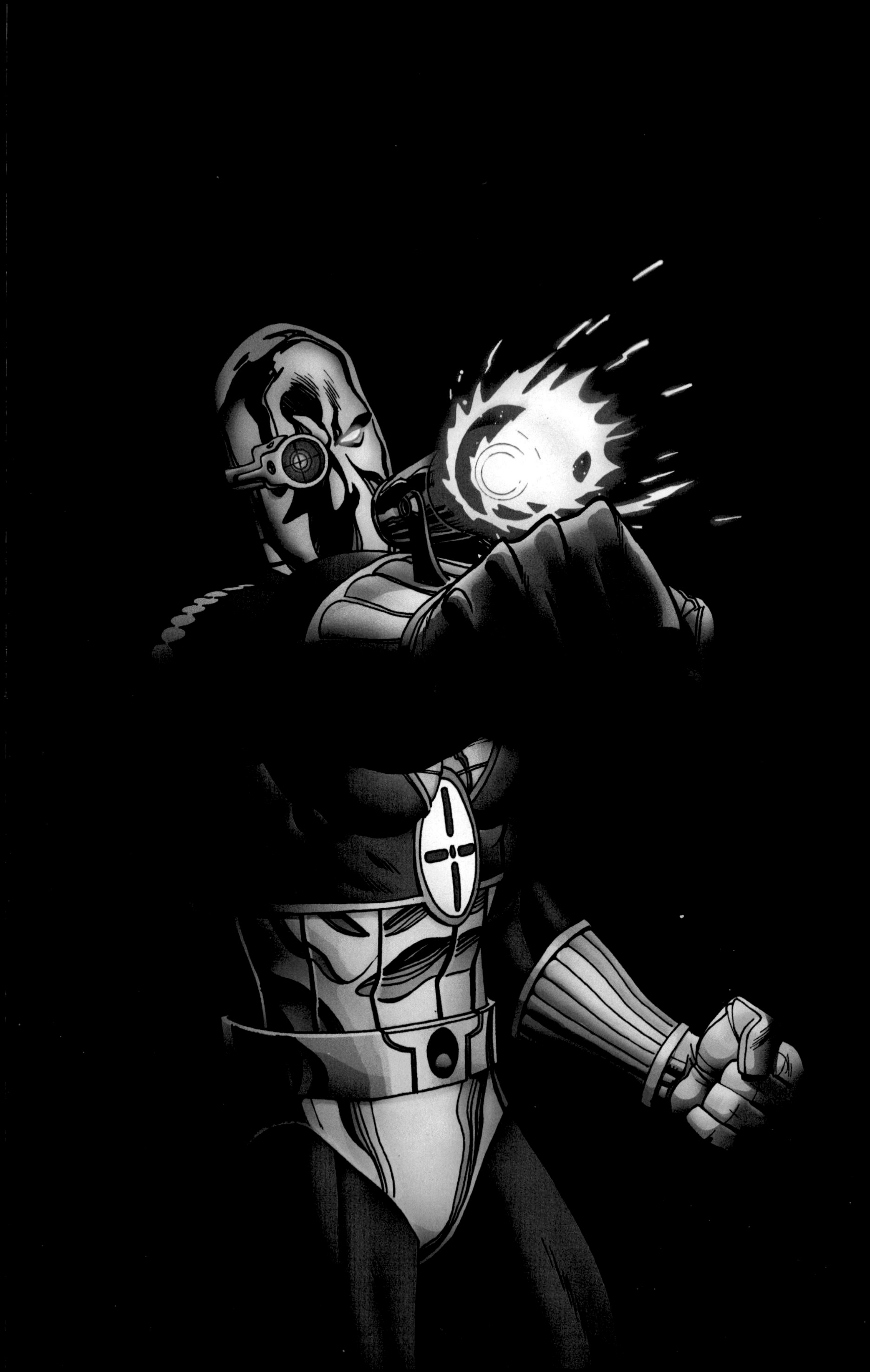

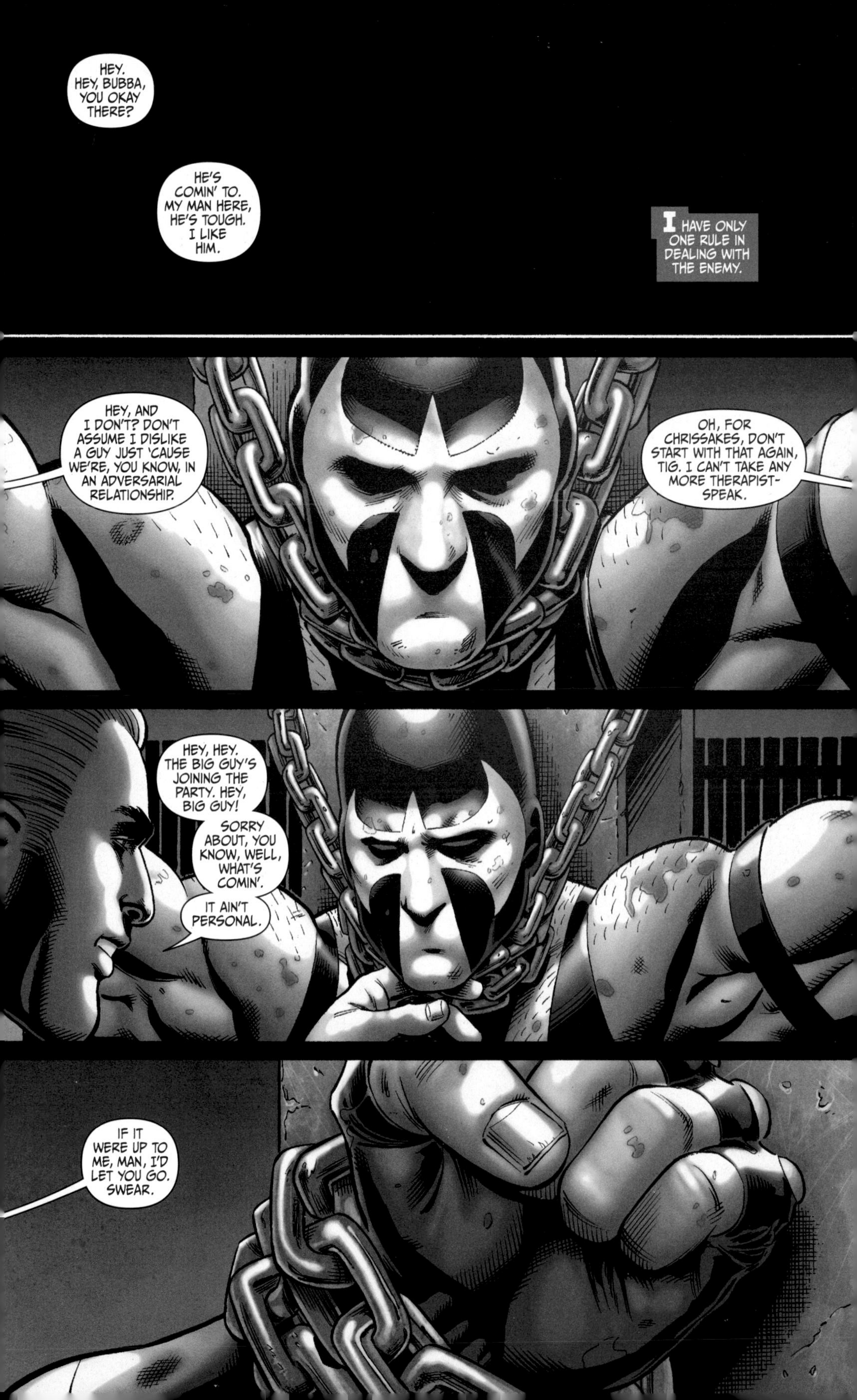
HEY. HEY, BUBBA, YOU OKAY THERE?
HE'S COMIN' TO. MY MAN HERE, HE'S TOUGH. I LIKE HIM.
I HAVE ONLY ONE RULE IN DEALING WITH THE ENEMY.
HEY, AND I DON'T? DON'T ASSUME I DISLIKE A GUY JUST 'CAUSE WE'RE, YOU KNOW, IN AN ADVERSARIAL RELATIONSHIP.
OH, FOR CHRISSAKES, DON'T START WITH THAT AGAIN, TIG. I CAN'T TAKE ANY MORE THERAPIST-SPEAK.
HEY, HEY. THE BIG GUY'S JOINING THE PARTY. HEY, BIG GUY!
SORRY ABOUT, YOU KNOW, WELL, WHAT'S COMIN'.
IT AIN'T PERSONAL.
IF IT WERE UP TO ME, MAN, I'D LET YOU GO. SWEAR.

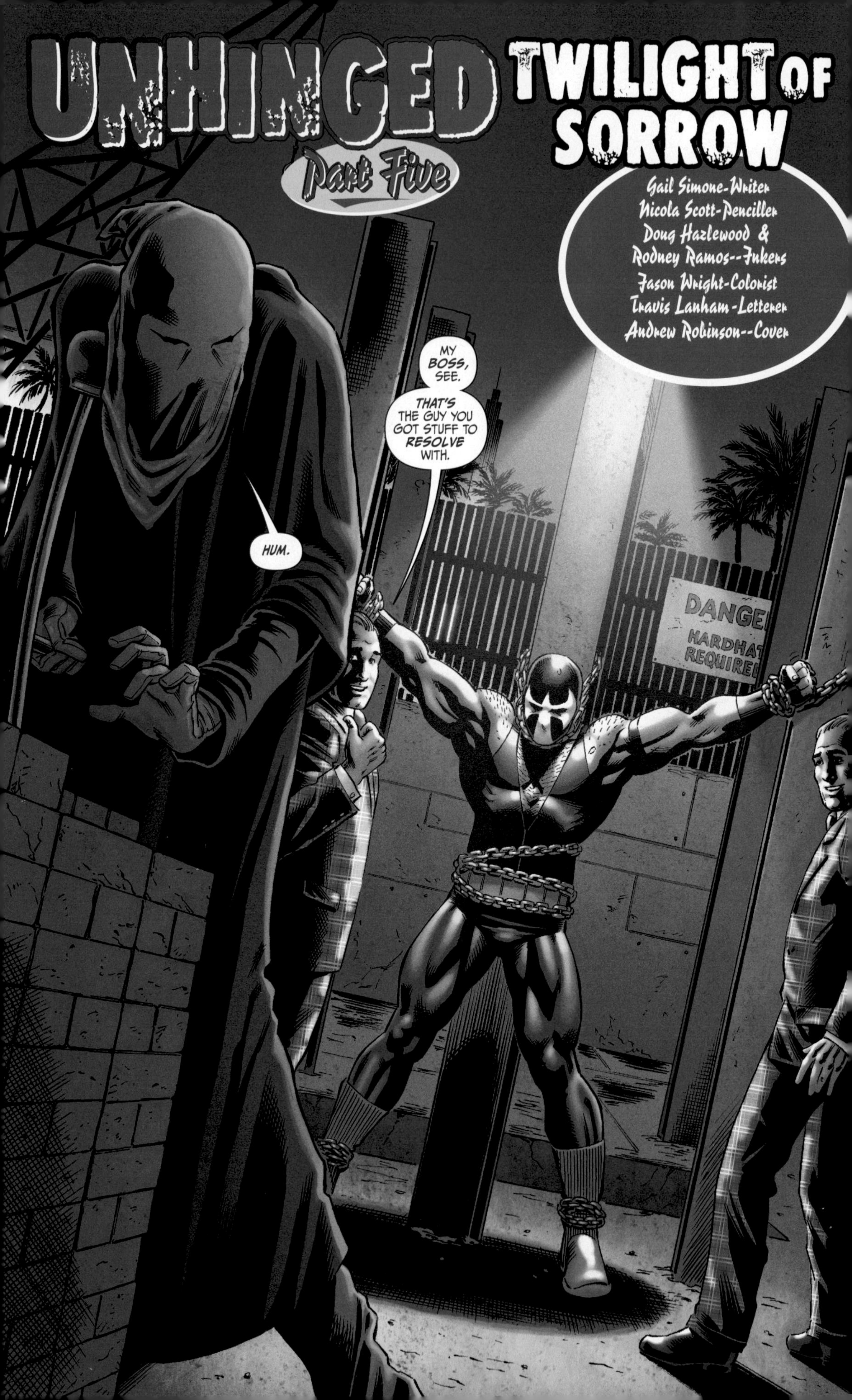

UNHINGED
Part Five
TWILIGHT OF SORROW
Gail Simone-Writer
Nicola Scott-Penciller
Doug Hazlewood &
Rodney Ramos--Inkers
Jason Wright-Colorist
Travis Lanham-Letterer
Andrew Robinson--Cover
MY BOSS, SEE.
THAT'S THE GUY YOU GOT STUFF TO RESOLVE WITH.
HUM.

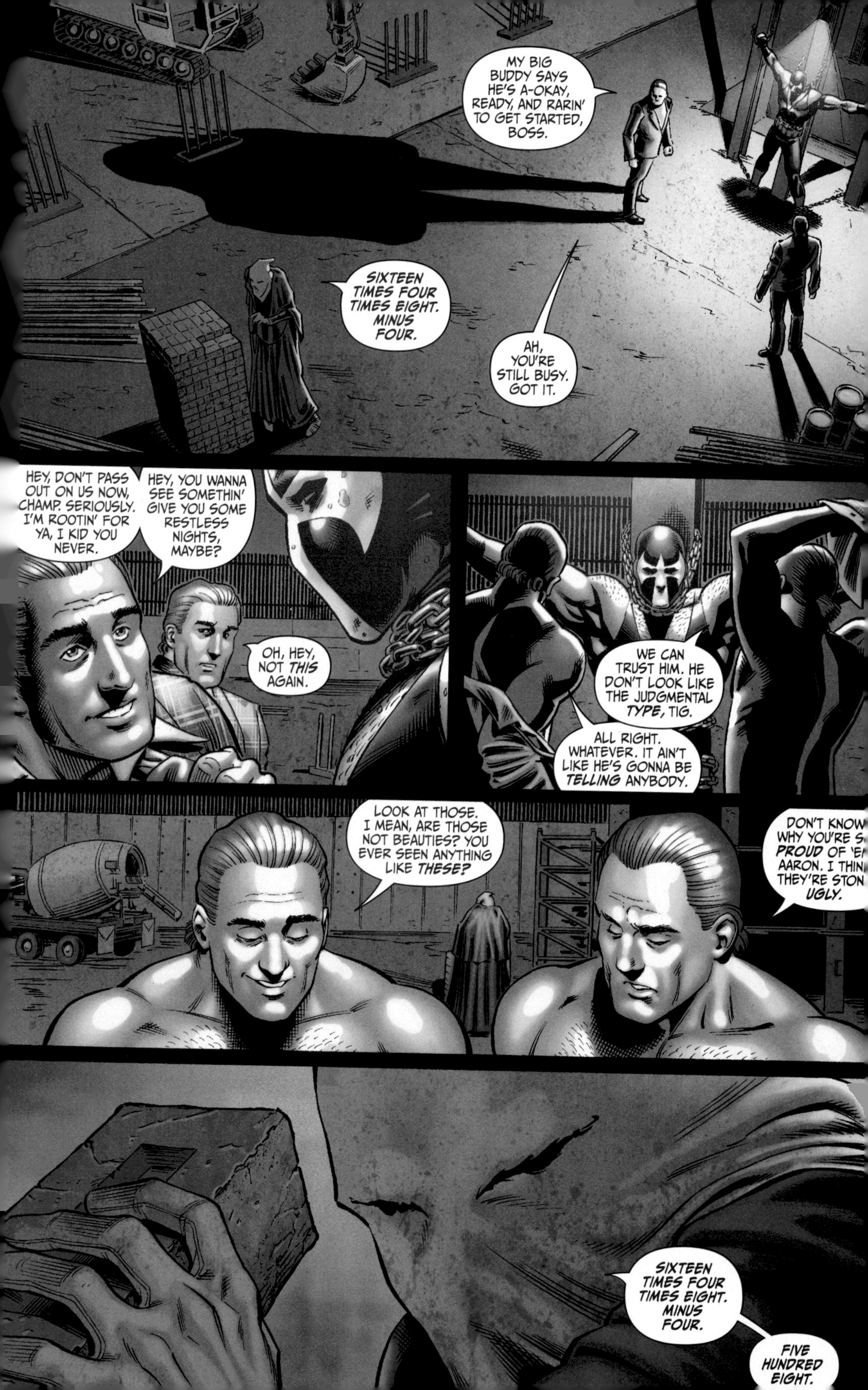
MY BIG BUDDY SAYS HE'S A-OKAY, READY, AND RARIN' TO GET STARTED, BOSS.
SIXTEEN TIMES FOUR TIMES EIGHT. MINUS FOUR.
AH, YOU'RE STILL BUSY. GOT IT.
HEY, DON'T PASS OUT ON US NOW, CHAMP. SERIOUSLY. I'M ROOTIN' FOR YA, I KID YOU NEVER.
HEY, YOU WANNA SEE SOMETHIN' GIVE YOU SOME RESTLESS NIGHTS, MAYBE?
OH, HEY, NOT THIS AGAIN.
WE CAN TRUST HIM. HE DON'T LOOK LIKE THE JUDGMENTAL TYPE, TIG.
ALL RIGHT. WHATEVER. IT AIN'T LIKE HE'S GONNA BE TELLING ANYBODY.
LOOK AT THOSE. I MEAN, ARE THOSE NOT BEAUTIES? YOU EVER SEEN ANYTHING LIKE THESE?
DON'T KNOW WHY YOU'RE S PROUD OF 'E AARON. I THIN THEY'RE STON UGLY.
SIXTEEN TIMES FOUR TIMES EIGHT. MINUS FOUR.
FIVE HUNDRED EIGHT.

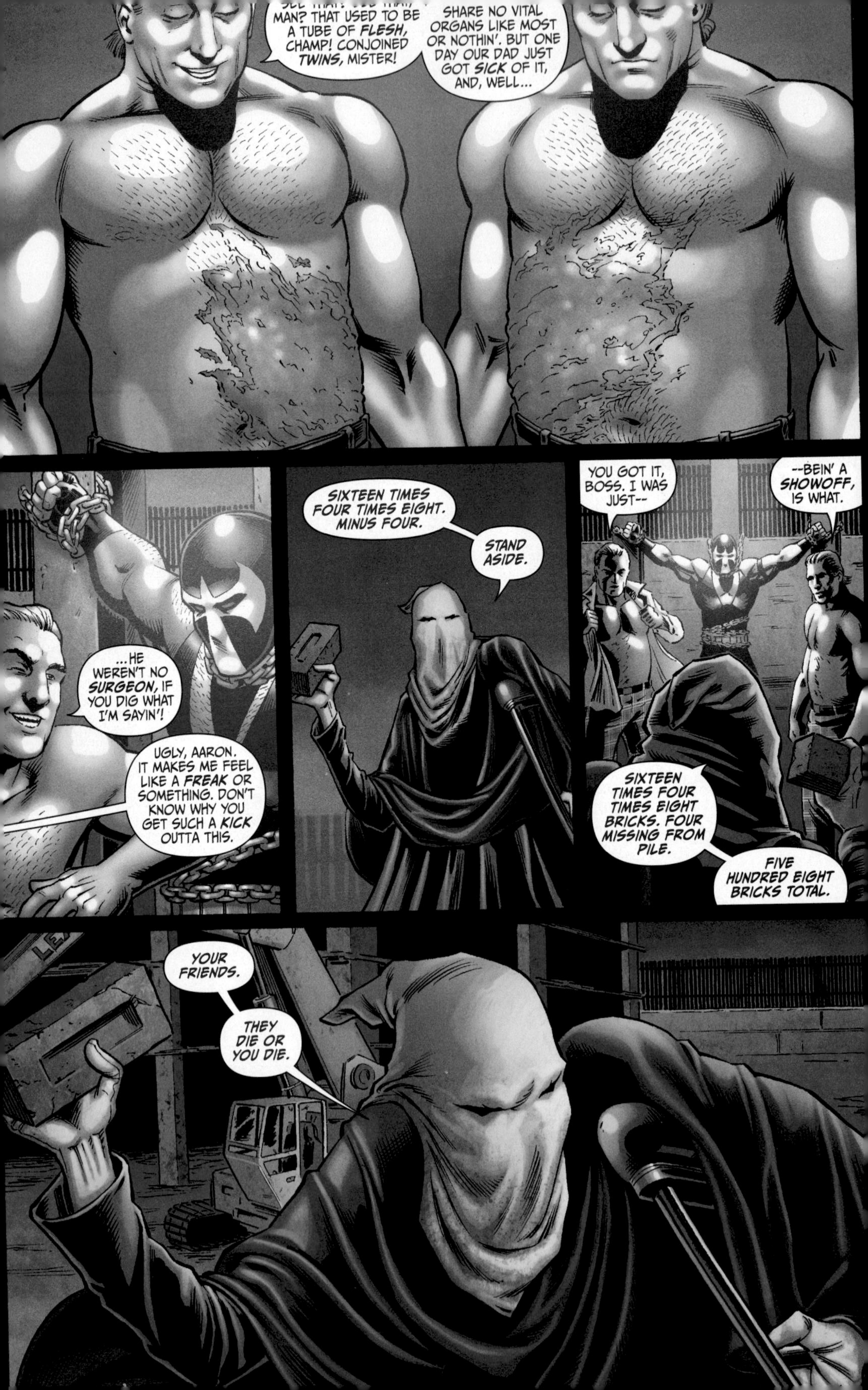

MAN? THAT USED TO BE A TUBE OF FLESH, CHAMP! CONJOINED TWINS, MISTER!
SHARE NO VITAL ORGANS LIKE MOST OR NOTHIN'. BUT ONE DAY OUR DAD JUST GOT SICK OF IT, AND, WELL...
...HE WEREN'T NO SURGEON, IF YOU DIG WHAT I'M SAYIN'!
UGLY, AARON. IT MAKES ME FEEL LIKE A FREAK OR SOMETHING. DON'T KNOW WHY YOU GET SUCH A KICK OUTTA THIS.
SIXTEEN TIMES FOUR TIMES EIGHT. MINUS FOUR.
STAND ASIDE.
YOU GOT IT, BOSS. I WAS JUST--
--BEIN' A SHOWOFF, IS WHAT.
SIXTEEN TIMES FOUR TIMES EIGHT BRICKS. FOUR MISSING FROM PILE.
FIVE HUNDRED EIGHT BRICKS TOTAL.
YOUR FRIENDS.
THEY DIE OR YOU DIE.

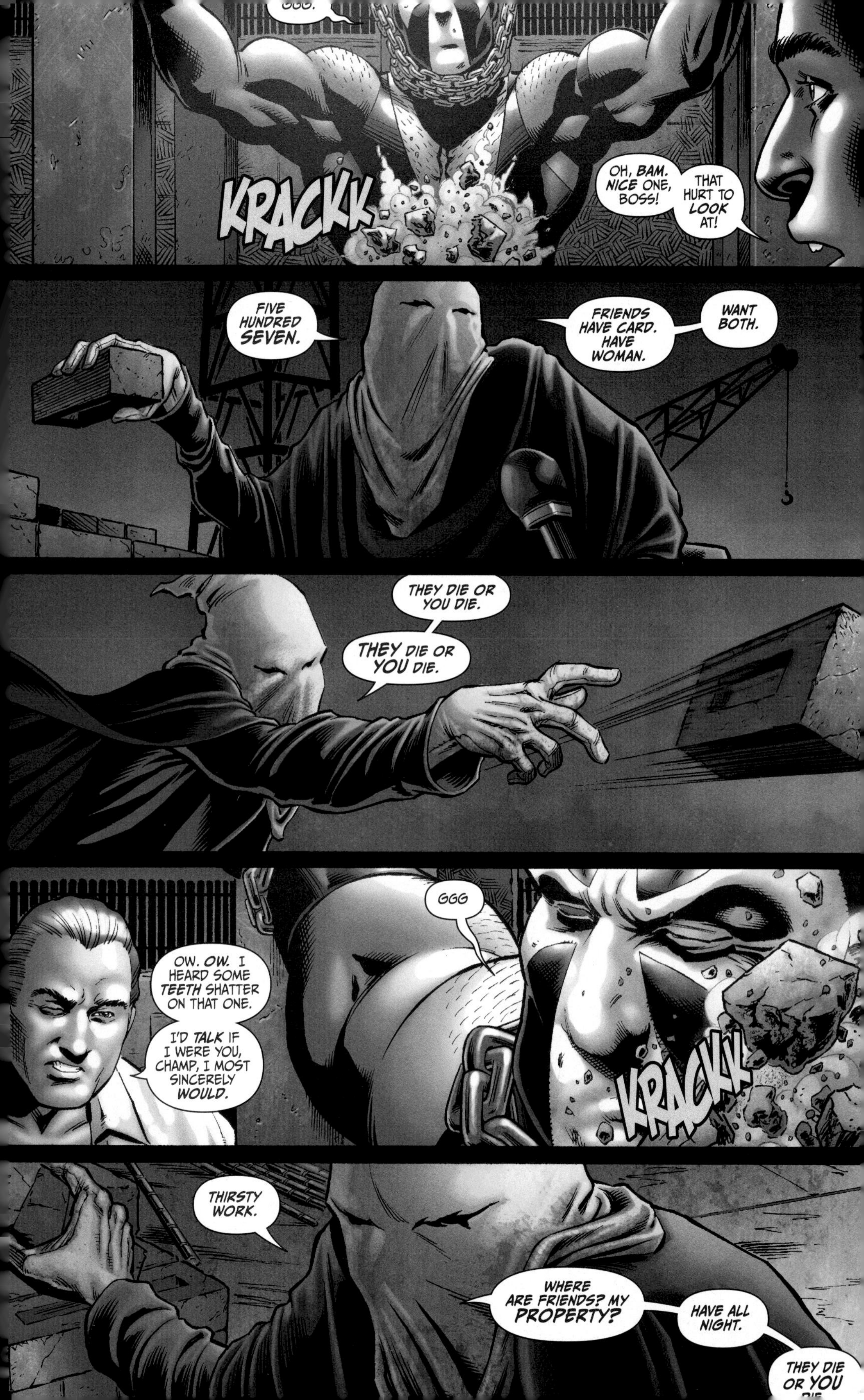
KRACKK
OH, BAM. NICE ONE, BOSS!
THAT HURT TO LOOK AT!
FIVE HUNDRED SEVEN.
FRIENDS HAVE CARD. HAVE WOMAN.
WANT BOTH.
THEY DIE OR YOU DIE.
THEY DIE OR YOU DIE.
OW. OW. I HEARD SOME TEETH SHATTER ON THAT ONE.
I'D TALK IF I WERE YOU, CHAMP, I MOST SINCERELY WOULD.
GGG
KRACKK
THIRSTY WORK.
WHERE ARE FRIENDS? MY PROPERTY?
HAVE ALL NIGHT.
THEY DIE OR YOU

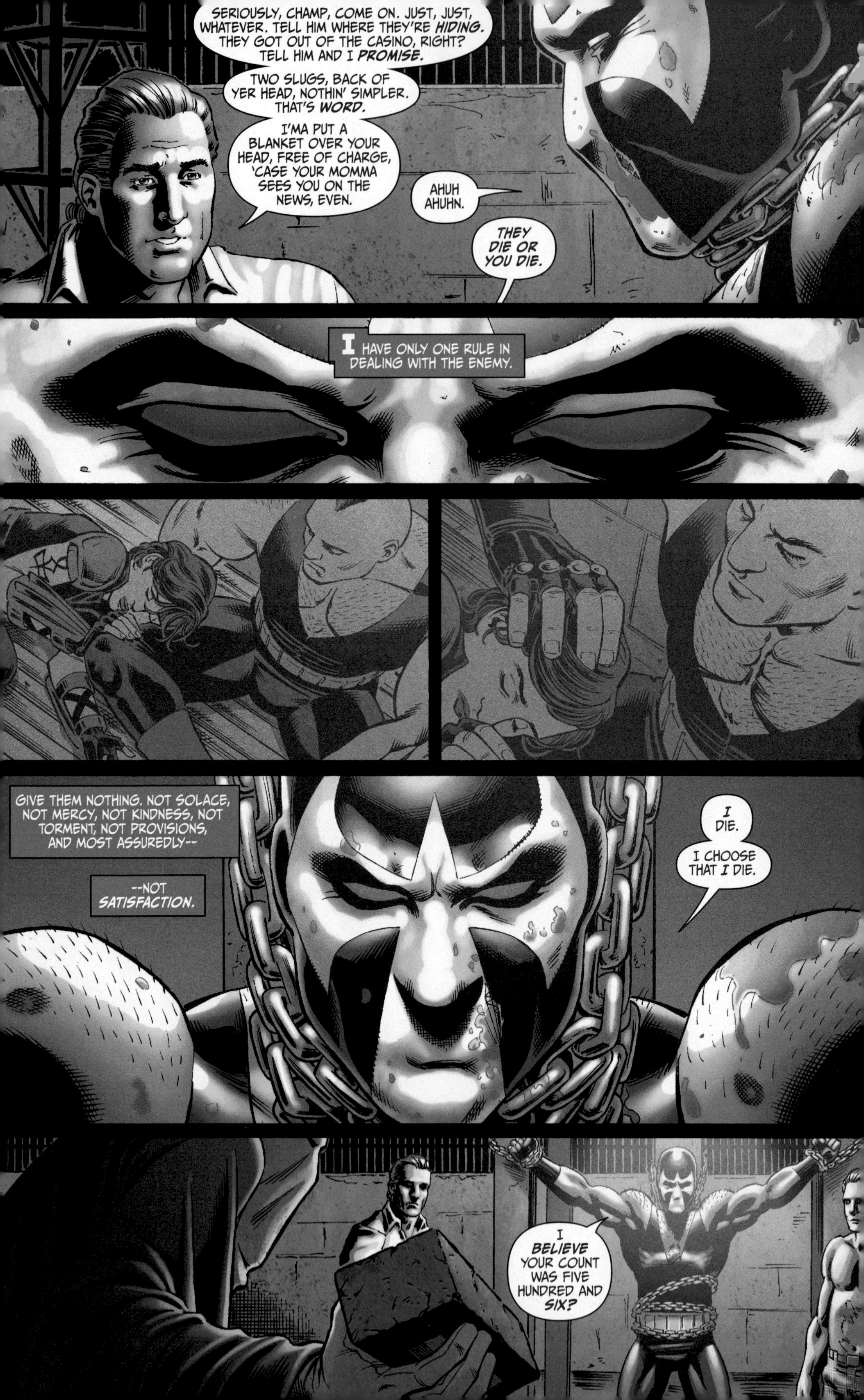
SERIOUSLY, CHAMP, COME ON. JUST, JUST, WHATEVER. TELL HIM WHERE THEY'RE *HIDING*. THEY GOT OUT OF THE CASINO, RIGHT? TELL HIM AND I *PROMISE*.
TWO SLUGS, BACK OF YER HEAD, NOTHIN' SIMPLER. THAT'S *WORD*.
I'MA PUT A BLANKET OVER YOUR HEAD, FREE OF CHARGE, 'CASE YOUR MOMMA SEES YOU ON THE NEWS, EVEN.
AHUH AHUHN.
THEY DIE OR YOU DIE.
I HAVE ONLY ONE RULE IN DEALING WITH THE ENEMY.
GIVE THEM NOTHING. NOT SOLACE, NOT MERCY, NOT KINDNESS, NOT TORMENT, NOT PROVISIONS, AND MOST ASSUREDLY--
--NOT *SATISFACTION*.
I DIE.
I CHOOSE THAT *I* DIE.
I *BELIEVE* YOUR COUNT WAS FIVE HUNDRED AND *SIX?*

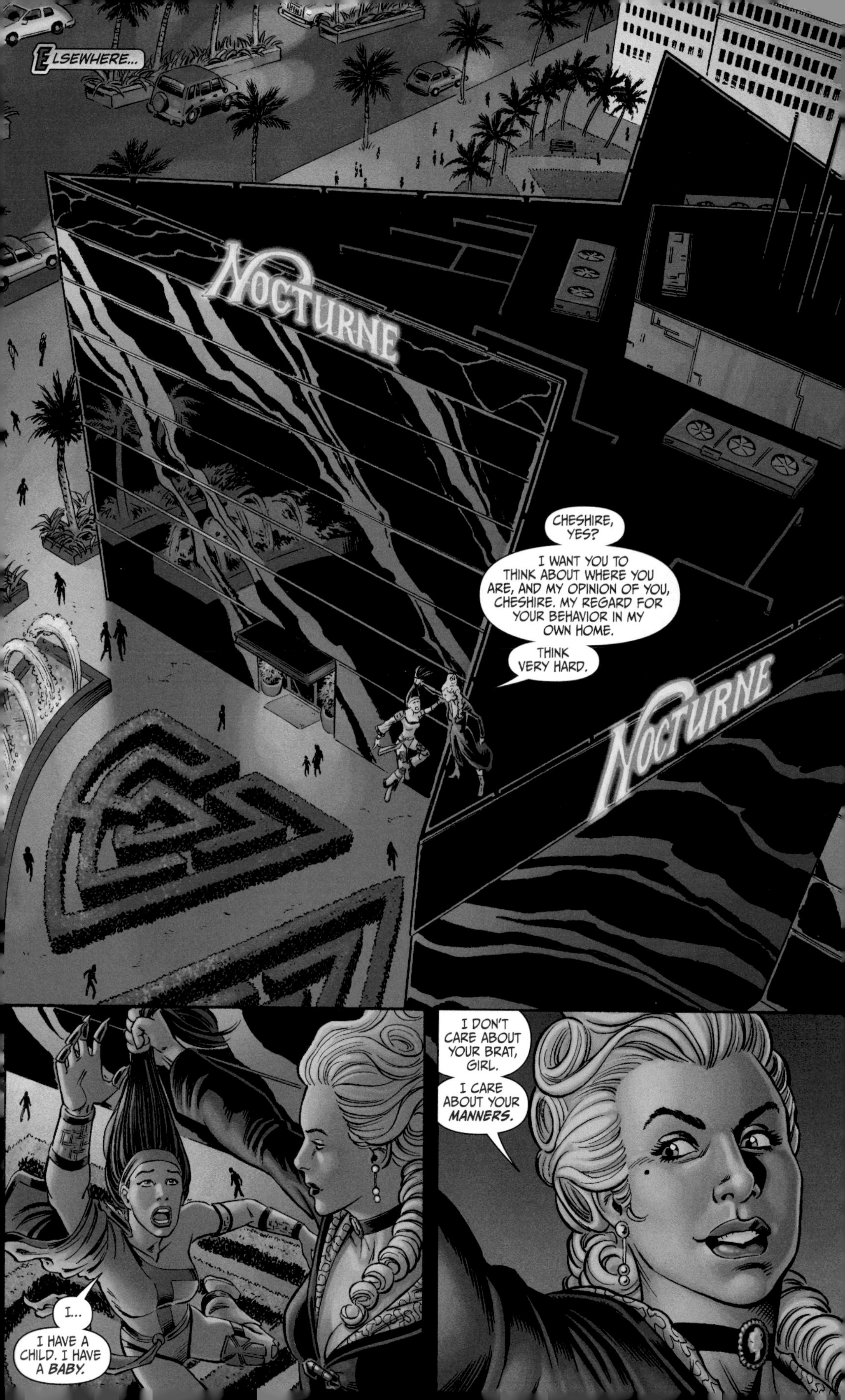
ELSEWHERE...
NOCTURNE
CHESHIRE, YES?
I WANT YOU TO THINK ABOUT WHERE YOU ARE, AND MY OPINION OF YOU, CHESHIRE. MY REGARD FOR YOUR BEHAVIOR IN MY OWN HOME.
THINK VERY HARD.
NOCTURNE
I...
I HAVE A CHILD. I HAVE A BABY.
I DON'T CARE ABOUT YOUR BRAT, GIRL.
I CARE ABOUT YOUR MANNERS.

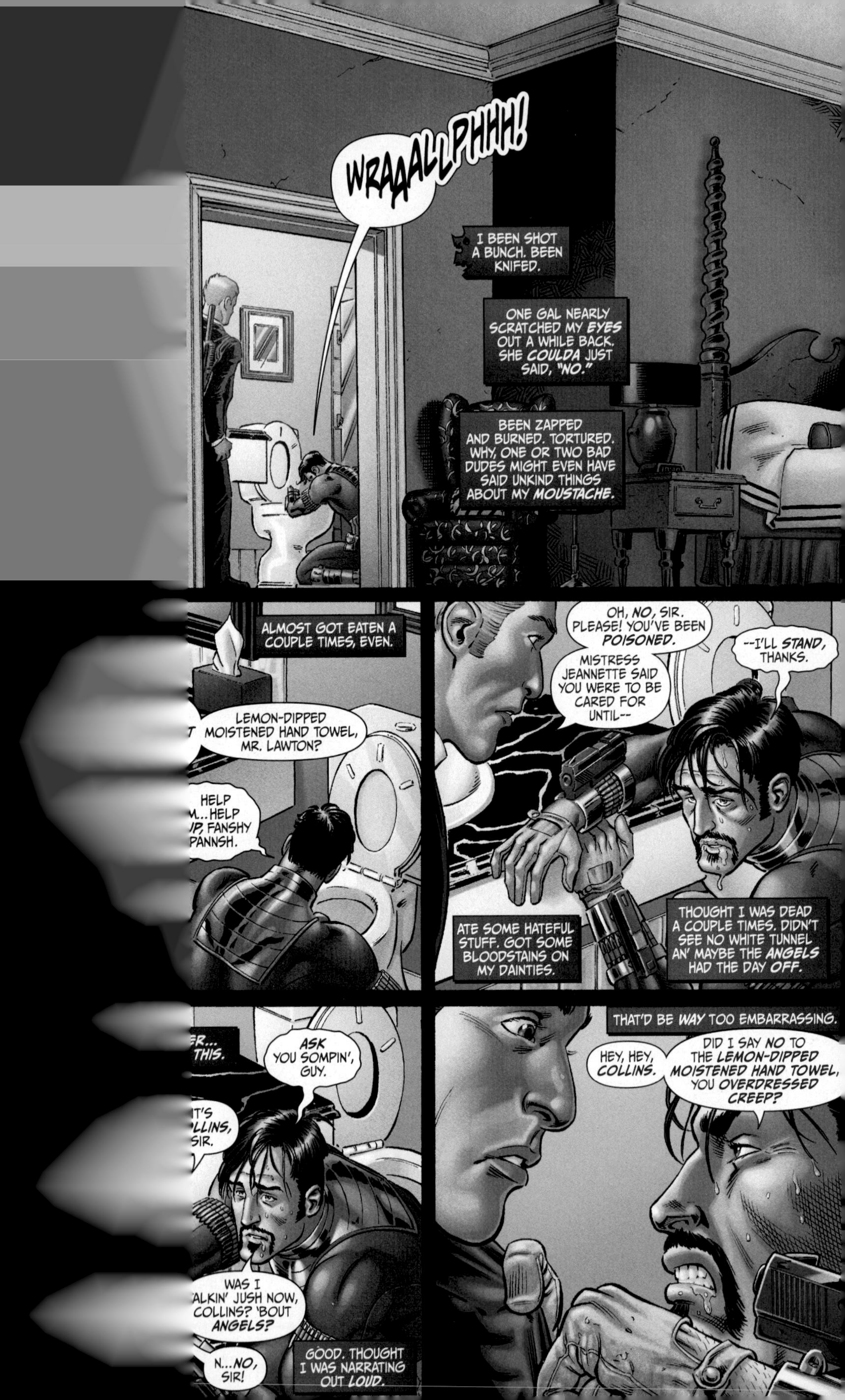
WRAAALLPHHH!
I BEEN SHOT A BUNCH. BEEN KNIFED.
ONE GAL NEARLY SCRATCHED MY EYES OUT A WHILE BACK. SHE COULDA JUST SAID, "NO."
BEEN ZAPPED AND BURNED. TORTURED. WHY, ONE OR TWO BAD DUDES MIGHT EVEN HAVE SAID UNKIND THINGS ABOUT MY MOUSTACHE.
ALMOST GOT EATEN A COUPLE TIMES, EVEN.
LEMON-DIPPED MOISTENED HAND TOWEL, MR. LAWTON?
HELP ...HELP FANSHY PANNSH.
OH, NO, SIR. PLEASE! YOU'VE BEEN POISONED.
MISTRESS JEANNETTE SAID YOU WERE TO BE CARED FOR UNTIL--
--I'LL STAND, THANKS.
ATE SOME HATEFUL STUFF. GOT SOME BLOODSTAINS ON MY DAINTIES.
THOUGHT I WAS DEAD A COUPLE TIMES. DIDN'T SEE NO WHITE TUNNEL AN' MAYBE THE ANGELS HAD THE DAY OFF.
ASK YOU SOMPIN', GUY.
SIR.
WAS I TALKIN' JUSH NOW, COLLINS? 'BOUT ANGELS?
N...NO, SIR!
GOOD. THOUGHT I WAS NARRATING OUT LOUD.
THAT'D BE WAY TOO EMBARRASSING.
HEY, HEY, COLLINS.
DID I SAY NO TO THE LEMON-DIPPED MOISTENED HAND TOWEL, YOU OVERDRESSED CREEP?

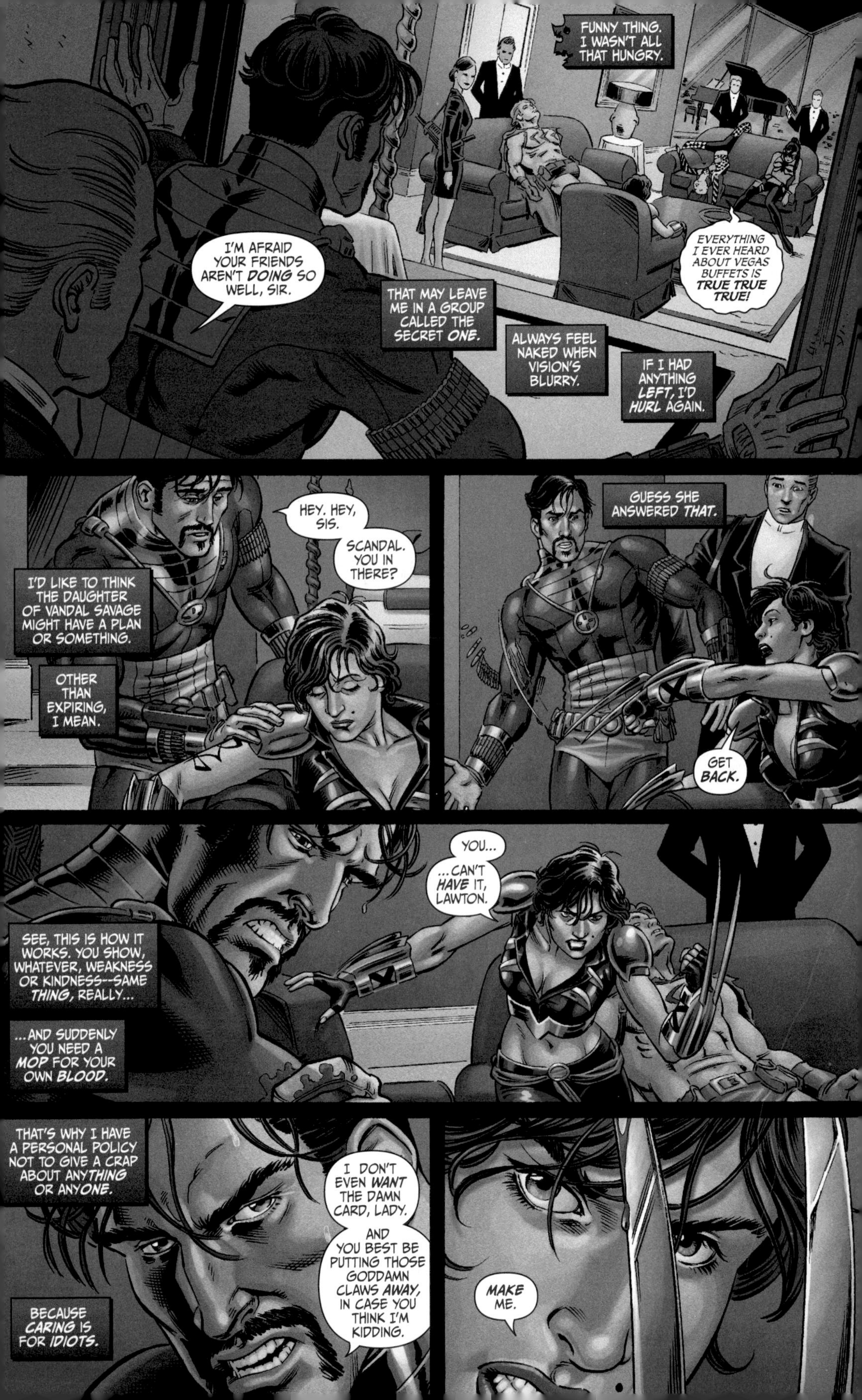
FUNNY THING. I WASN'T ALL THAT HUNGRY.
I'M AFRAID YOUR FRIENDS AREN'T DOING SO WELL, SIR.
THAT MAY LEAVE ME IN A GROUP CALLED THE SECRET ONE.
ALWAYS FEEL NAKED WHEN VISION'S BLURRY.
EVERYTHING I EVER HEARD ABOUT VEGAS BUFFETS IS TRUE TRUE TRUE!
IF I HAD ANYTHING LEFT, I'D HURL AGAIN.
HEY. HEY, SIS.
SCANDAL. YOU IN THERE?
I'D LIKE TO THINK THE DAUGHTER OF VANDAL SAVAGE MIGHT HAVE A PLAN OR SOMETHING.
OTHER THAN EXPIRING, I MEAN.
GUESS SHE ANSWERED THAT.
GET BACK.
YOU...
...CAN'T HAVE IT, LAWTON.
SEE, THIS IS HOW IT WORKS. YOU SHOW, WHATEVER, WEAKNESS OR KINDNESS--SAME THING, REALLY...
...AND SUDDENLY YOU NEED A MOP FOR YOUR OWN BLOOD.
THAT'S WHY I HAVE A PERSONAL POLICY NOT TO GIVE A CRAP ABOUT ANYTHING OR ANYONE.
I DON'T EVEN WANT THE DAMN CARD, LADY.
AND YOU BEST BE PUTTING THOSE GODDAMN CLAWS AWAY, IN CASE YOU THINK I'M KIDDING.
BECAUSE CARING IS FOR IDIOTS.
MAKE ME.

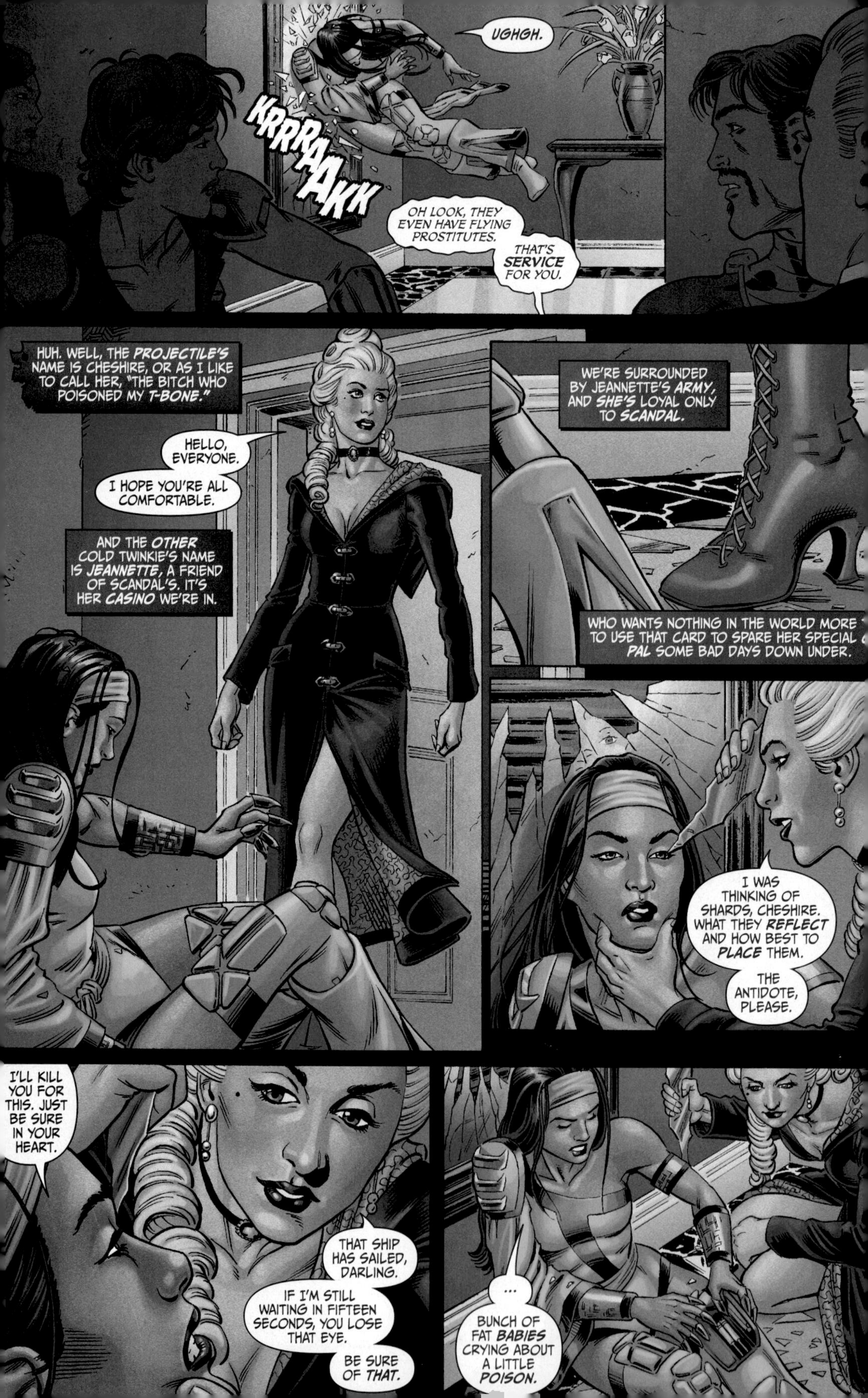
UGHGH.
KRRRAAKK
OH LOOK, THEY EVEN HAVE FLYING PROSTITUTES.
THAT'S SERVICE FOR YOU.
HUH. WELL, THE PROJECTILE'S NAME IS CHESHIRE, OR AS I LIKE TO CALL HER, "THE BITCH WHO POISONED MY T-BONE."
HELLO, EVERYONE.
I HOPE YOU'RE ALL COMFORTABLE.
AND THE OTHER COLD TWINKIE'S NAME IS JEANNETTE, A FRIEND OF SCANDAL'S. IT'S HER CASINO WE'RE IN.
WE'RE SURROUNDED BY JEANNETTE'S ARMY, AND SHE'S LOYAL ONLY TO SCANDAL.
WHO WANTS NOTHING IN THE WORLD MORE TO USE THAT CARD TO SPARE HER SPECIAL PAL SOME BAD DAYS DOWN UNDER.
I WAS THINKING OF SHARDS, CHESHIRE. WHAT THEY REFLECT AND HOW BEST TO PLACE THEM.
THE ANTIDOTE, PLEASE.
I'LL KILL YOU FOR THIS. JUST BE SURE IN YOUR HEART.
THAT SHIP HAS SAILED, DARLING.
IF I'M STILL WAITING IN FIFTEEN SECONDS, YOU LOSE THAT EYE.
BE SURE OF THAT.
...
BUNCH OF FAT BABIES CRYING ABOUT A LITTLE POISON.

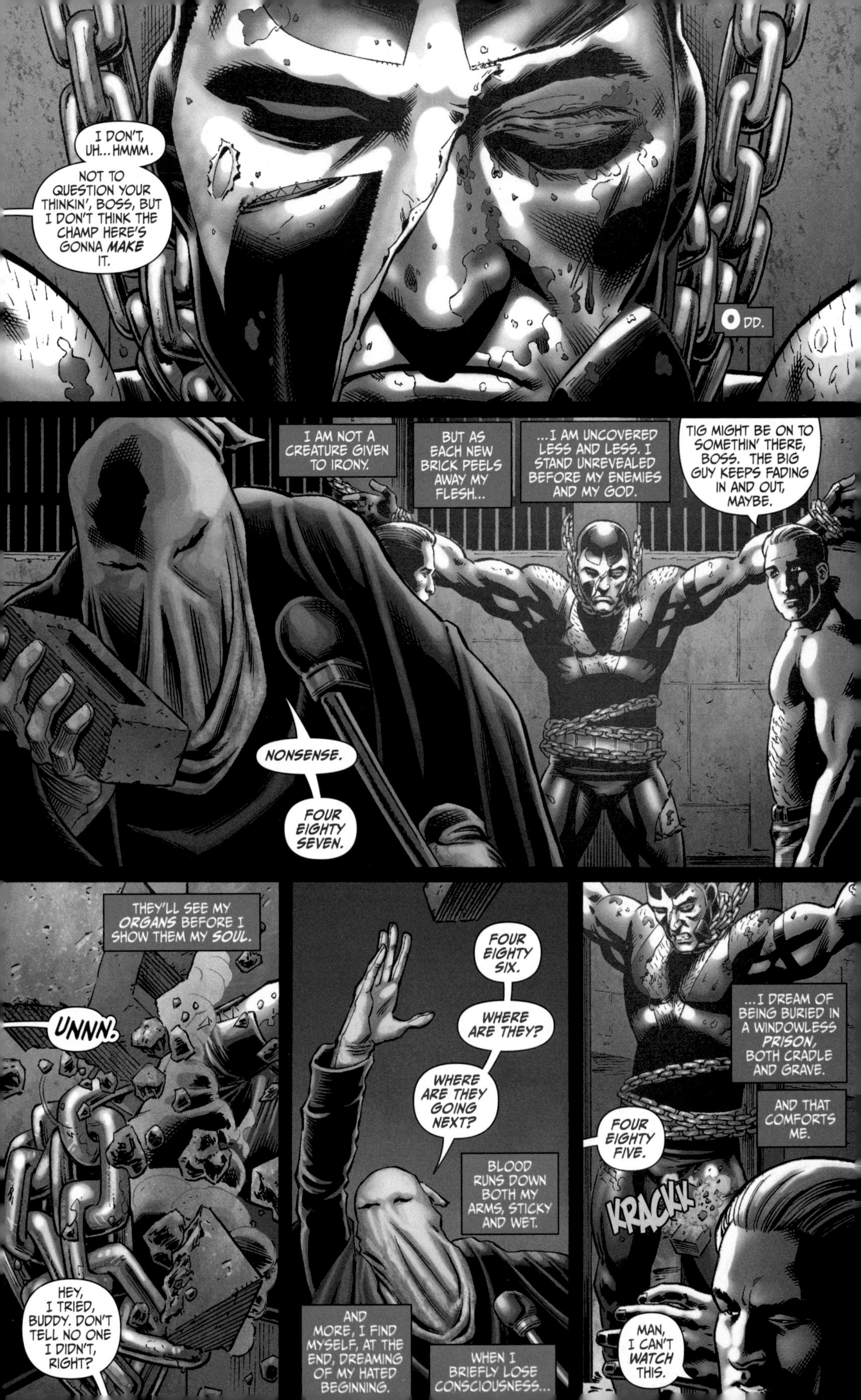
I DON'T, UH...HMMM.
NOT TO QUESTION YOUR THINKIN', BOSS, BUT I DON'T THINK THE CHAMP HERE'S GONNA *MAKE* IT.
ODD.
I AM NOT A CREATURE GIVEN TO IRONY.
BUT AS EACH NEW BRICK PEELS AWAY MY FLESH...
...I AM UNCOVERED LESS AND LESS. I STAND UNREVEALED BEFORE MY ENEMIES AND MY GOD.
TIG MIGHT BE ON TO SOMETHIN' THERE, BOSS. THE BIG GUY KEEPS FADING IN AND OUT, MAYBE.
NONSENSE.
FOUR EIGHTY SEVEN.
THEY'LL SEE MY *ORGANS* BEFORE I SHOW THEM MY *SOUL*.
UNNN.
HEY, I TRIED, BUDDY. DON'T TELL NO ONE I DIDN'T, RIGHT?
FOUR EIGHTY SIX.
WHERE ARE THEY?
WHERE ARE THEY GOING NEXT?
BLOOD RUNS DOWN BOTH MY ARMS, STICKY AND WET.
AND MORE, I FIND MYSELF, AT THE END, DREAMING OF MY HATED BEGINNING.
WHEN I BRIEFLY LOSE CONSCIOUSNESS...
...I DREAM OF BEING BURIED IN A WINDOWLESS *PRISON*, BOTH CRADLE AND GRAVE.
AND THAT COMFORTS ME.
FOUR EIGHTY FIVE.
KRACKK
MAN, I CAN'T *WATCH* THIS.

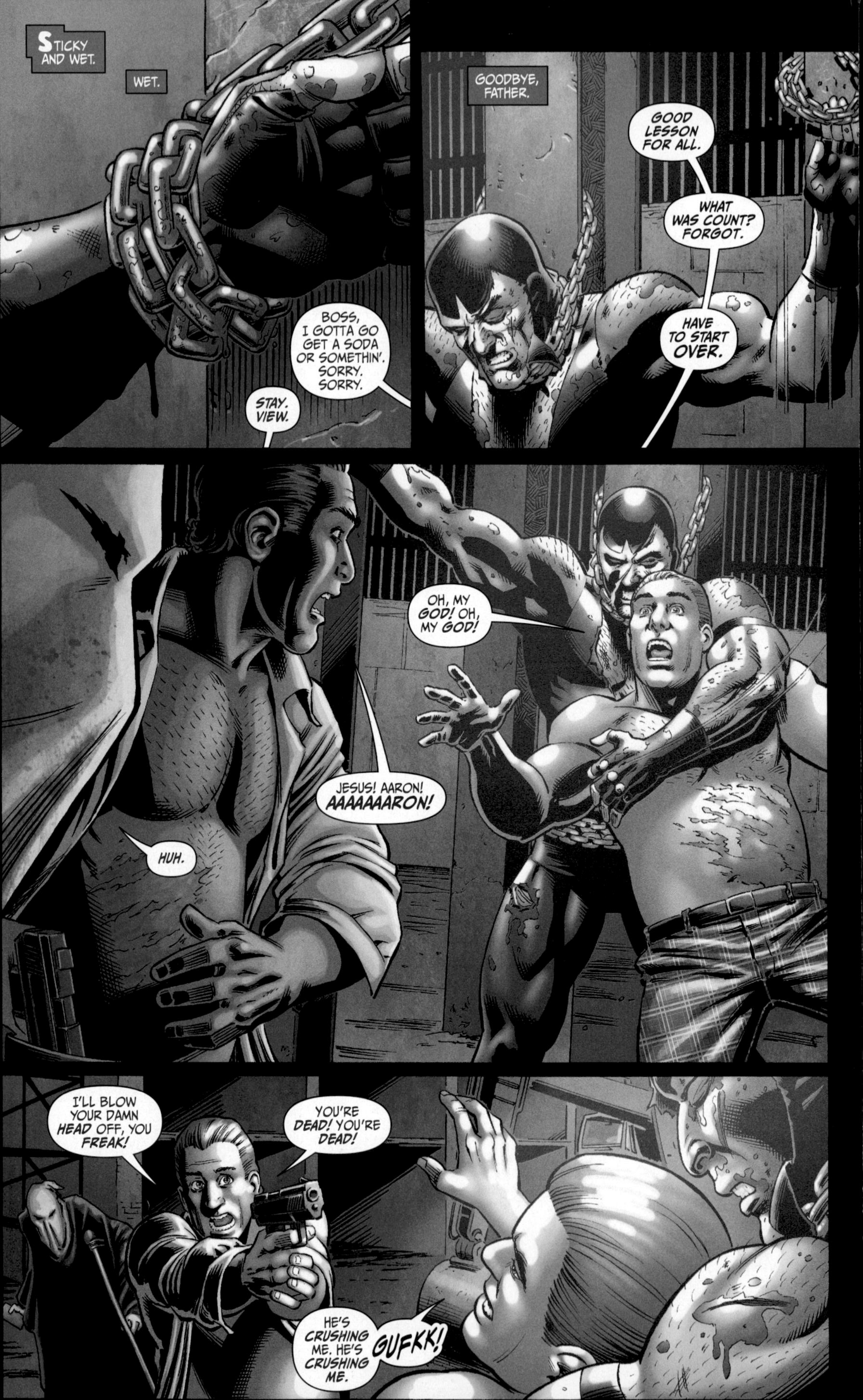
STICKY AND WET.
WET.
BOSS, I GOTTA GO GET A SODA OR SOMETHIN'. SORRY. SORRY.
STAY. VIEW.
GOODBYE, FATHER.
GOOD LESSON FOR ALL.
WHAT WAS COUNT? FORGOT.
HAVE TO START OVER.
OH, MY GOD! OH, MY GOD!
JESUS! AARON! AAAAAAARON!
HUH.
I'LL BLOW YOUR DAMN HEAD OFF, YOU FREAK!
YOU'RE DEAD! YOU'RE DEAD!
HE'S CRUSHING ME. HE'S CRUSHING ME.
GUFKK!

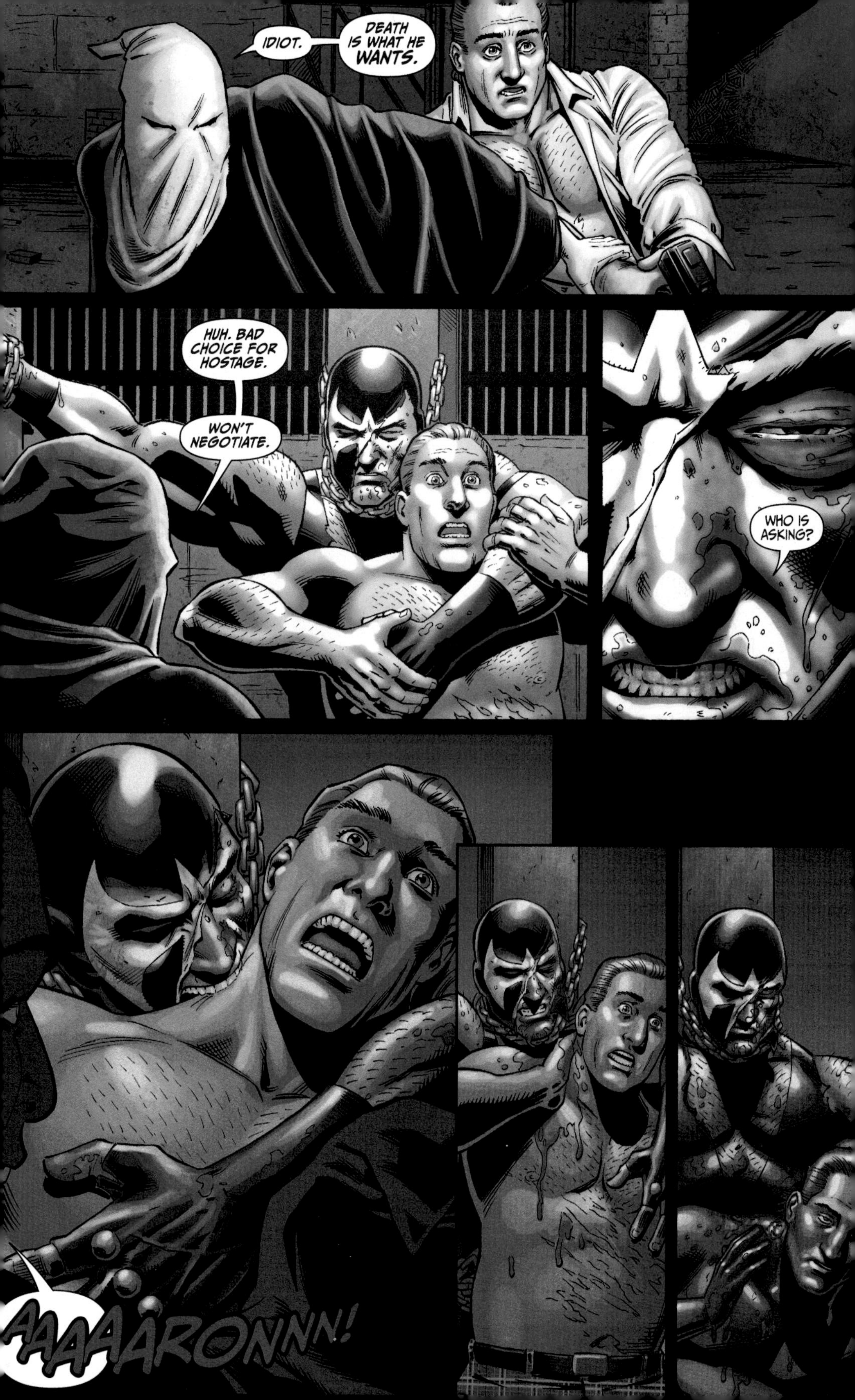
IDIOT.
DEATH IS WHAT HE WANTS.
HUH. BAD CHOICE FOR HOSTAGE.
WON'T NEGOTIATE.
WHO IS ASKING?
AAAAARONNN!

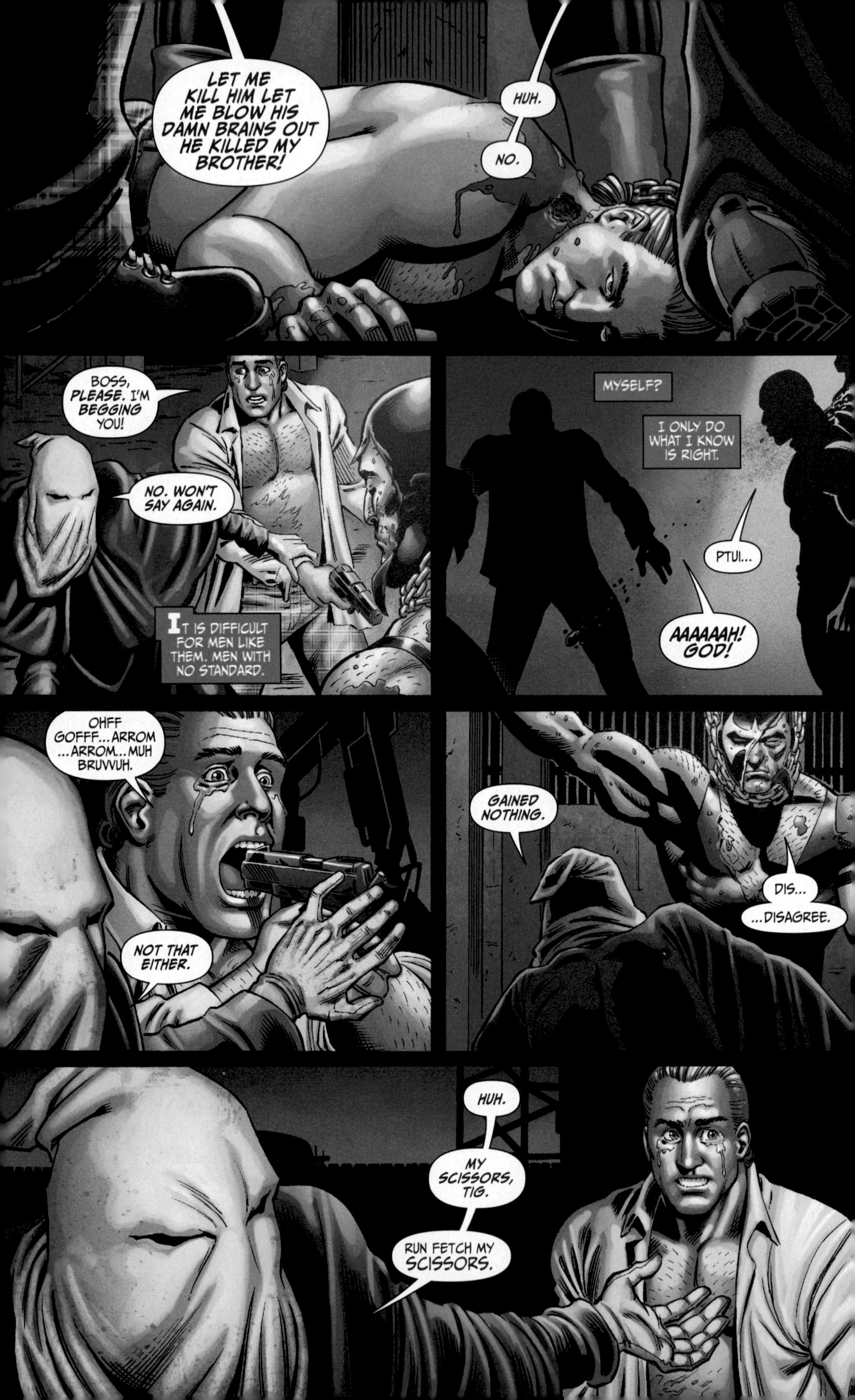
LET ME KILL HIM LET ME BLOW HIS DAMN BRAINS OUT HE KILLED MY BROTHER!
HUH.
NO.
BOSS, PLEASE. I'M BEGGING YOU!
NO. WON'T SAY AGAIN.
IT IS DIFFICULT FOR MEN LIKE THEM. MEN WITH NO STANDARD.
MYSELF?
I ONLY DO WHAT I KNOW IS RIGHT.
PTUI...
AAAAAAH! GOD!
OHFF GOFFF...ARROM ...ARROM...MUH BRUVVUH.
NOT THAT EITHER.
GAINED NOTHING.
DIS...
...DISAGREE.
HUH.
MY SCISSORS, TIG.
RUN FETCH MY SCISSORS.

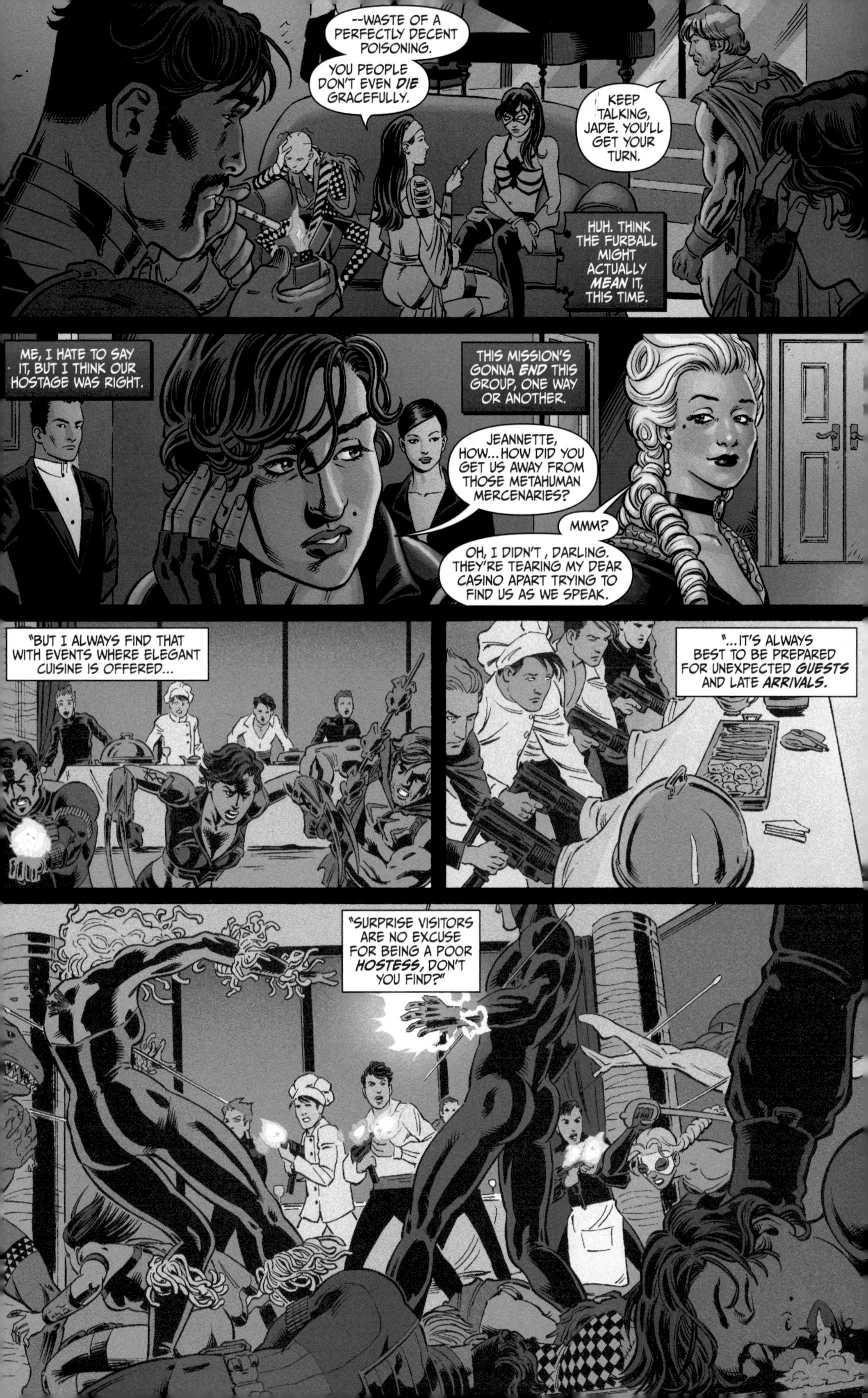
--WASTE OF A PERFECTLY DECENT POISONING.
YOU PEOPLE DON'T EVEN DIE GRACEFULLY.
KEEP TALKING, JADE. YOU'LL GET YOUR TURN.
HUH. THINK THE FURBALL MIGHT ACTUALLY MEAN IT, THIS TIME.
ME, I HATE TO SAY IT, BUT I THINK OUR HOSTAGE WAS RIGHT.
THIS MISSION'S GONNA END THIS GROUP, ONE WAY OR ANOTHER.
JEANNETTE, HOW...HOW DID YOU GET US AWAY FROM THOSE METAHUMAN MERCENARIES?
MMM?
OH, I DIDN'T , DARLING. THEY'RE TEARING MY DEAR CASINO APART TRYING TO FIND US AS WE SPEAK.
"BUT I ALWAYS FIND THAT WITH EVENTS WHERE ELEGANT CUISINE IS OFFERED...
"...IT'S ALWAYS BEST TO BE PREPARED FOR UNEXPECTED GUESTS AND LATE ARRIVALS.
"SURPRISE VISITORS ARE NO EXCUSE FOR BEING A POOR HOSTESS, DON'T YOU FIND?"

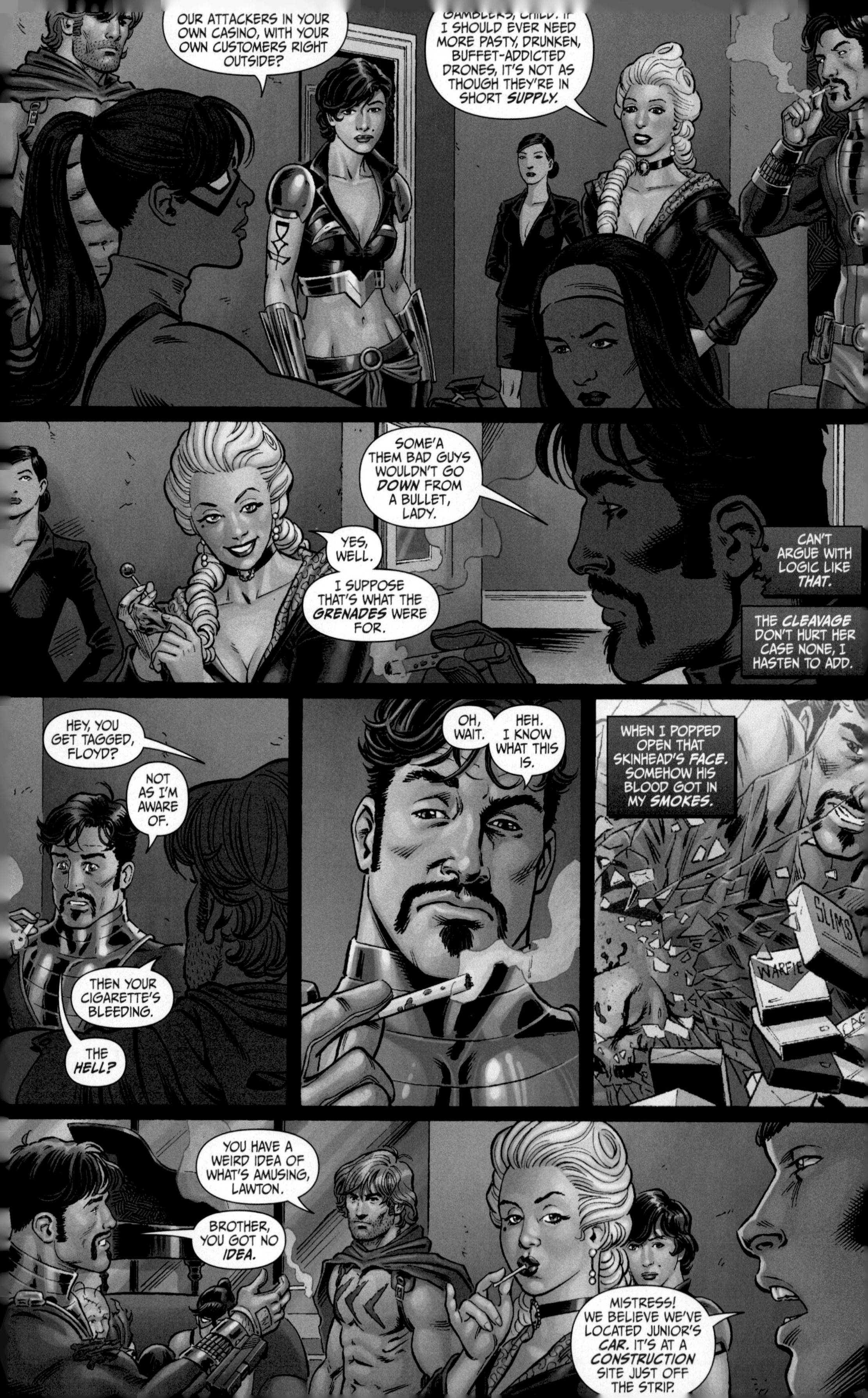

OUR ATTACKERS IN YOUR OWN CASINO, WITH YOUR OWN CUSTOMERS RIGHT OUTSIDE?
I SHOULD EVER NEED MORE PASTY, DRUNKEN, BUFFET-ADDICTED DRONES, IT'S NOT AS THOUGH THEY'RE IN SHORT SUPPLY.
SOME'A THEM BAD GUYS WOULDN'T GO DOWN FROM A BULLET, LADY.
YES, WELL.
I SUPPOSE THAT'S WHAT THE GRENADES WERE FOR.
CAN'T ARGUE WITH LOGIC LIKE THAT.
THE CLEAVAGE DON'T HURT HER CASE NONE, I HASTEN TO ADD.
HEY, YOU GET TAGGED, FLOYD?
NOT AS I'M AWARE OF.
THEN YOUR CIGARETTE'S BLEEDING.
THE HELL?
OH, WAIT.
HEH. I KNOW WHAT THIS IS.
WHEN I POPPED OPEN THAT SKINHEAD'S FACE. SOMEHOW HIS BLOOD GOT IN MY SMOKES.
SLIMS
YOU HAVE A WEIRD IDEA OF WHAT'S AMUSING, LAWTON.
BROTHER, YOU GOT NO IDEA.
MISTRESS! WE BELIEVE WE'VE LOCATED JUNIOR'S CAR. IT'S AT A CONSTRUCTION SITE JUST OFF THE STRIP.

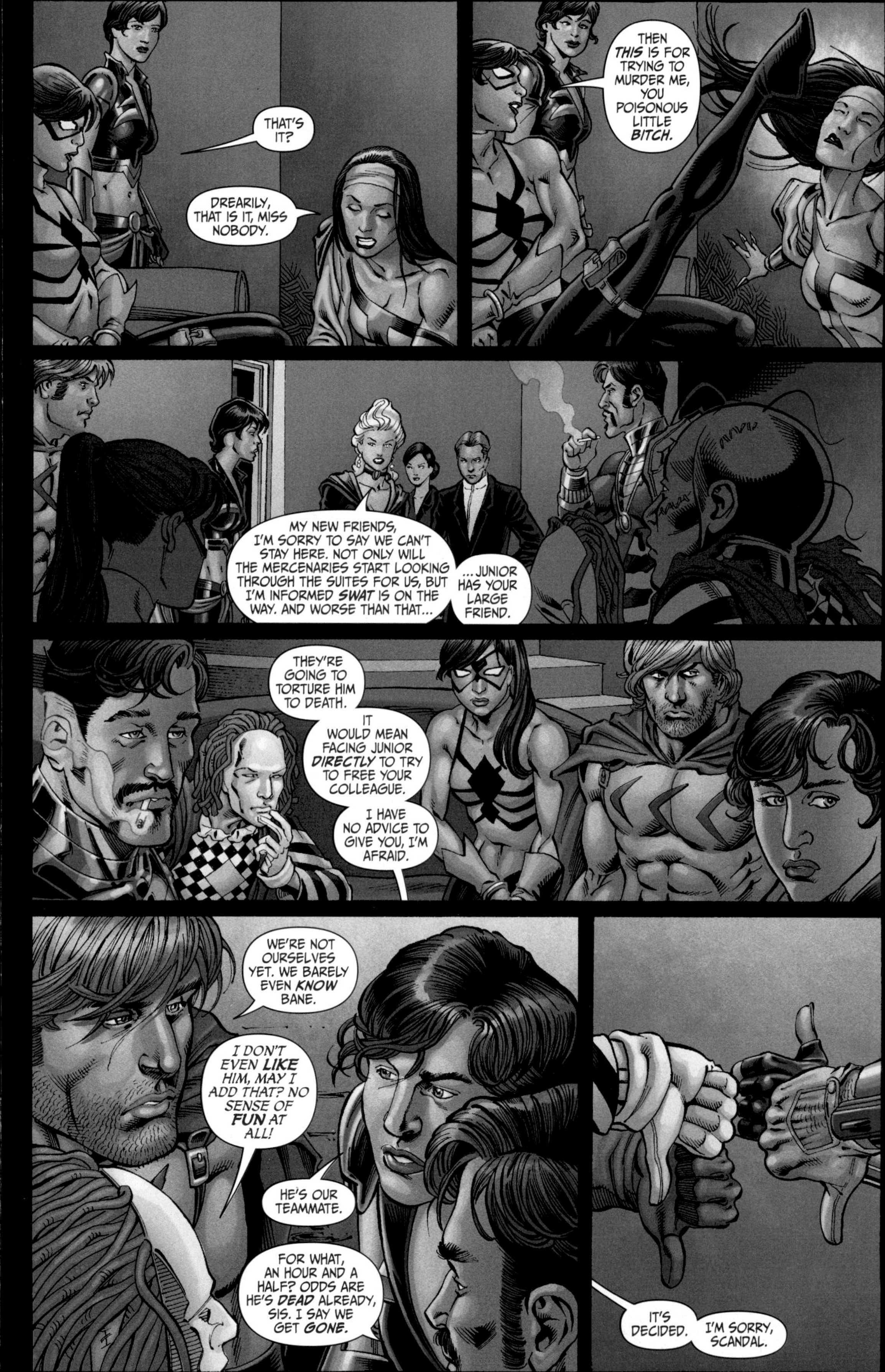
THAT'S IT?
DREARILY, THAT IS IT, MISS NOBODY.
THEN *THIS* IS FOR TRYING TO MURDER ME, YOU POISONOUS LITTLE *BITCH.*
MY NEW FRIENDS, I'M SORRY TO SAY WE CAN'T STAY HERE. NOT ONLY WILL THE MERCENARIES START LOOKING THROUGH THE SUITES FOR US, BUT I'M INFORMED *SWAT* IS ON THE WAY. AND WORSE THAN THAT...
...JUNIOR HAS YOUR LARGE FRIEND.
THEY'RE GOING TO TORTURE HIM TO DEATH.
IT WOULD MEAN FACING JUNIOR *DIRECTLY* TO TRY TO FREE YOUR COLLEAGUE.
I HAVE NO ADVICE TO GIVE YOU, I'M AFRAID.
WE'RE NOT OURSELVES YET. WE BARELY EVEN *KNOW* BANE.
I DON'T EVEN ***LIKE*** *HIM, MAY I ADD THAT? NO SENSE OF* ***FUN*** *AT ALL!*
HE'S OUR TEAMMATE.
FOR WHAT, AN HOUR AND A HALF? ODDS ARE HE'S *DEAD* ALREADY, SIS. I SAY WE GET *GONE.*
IT'S DECIDED.
I'M SORRY, SCANDAL.

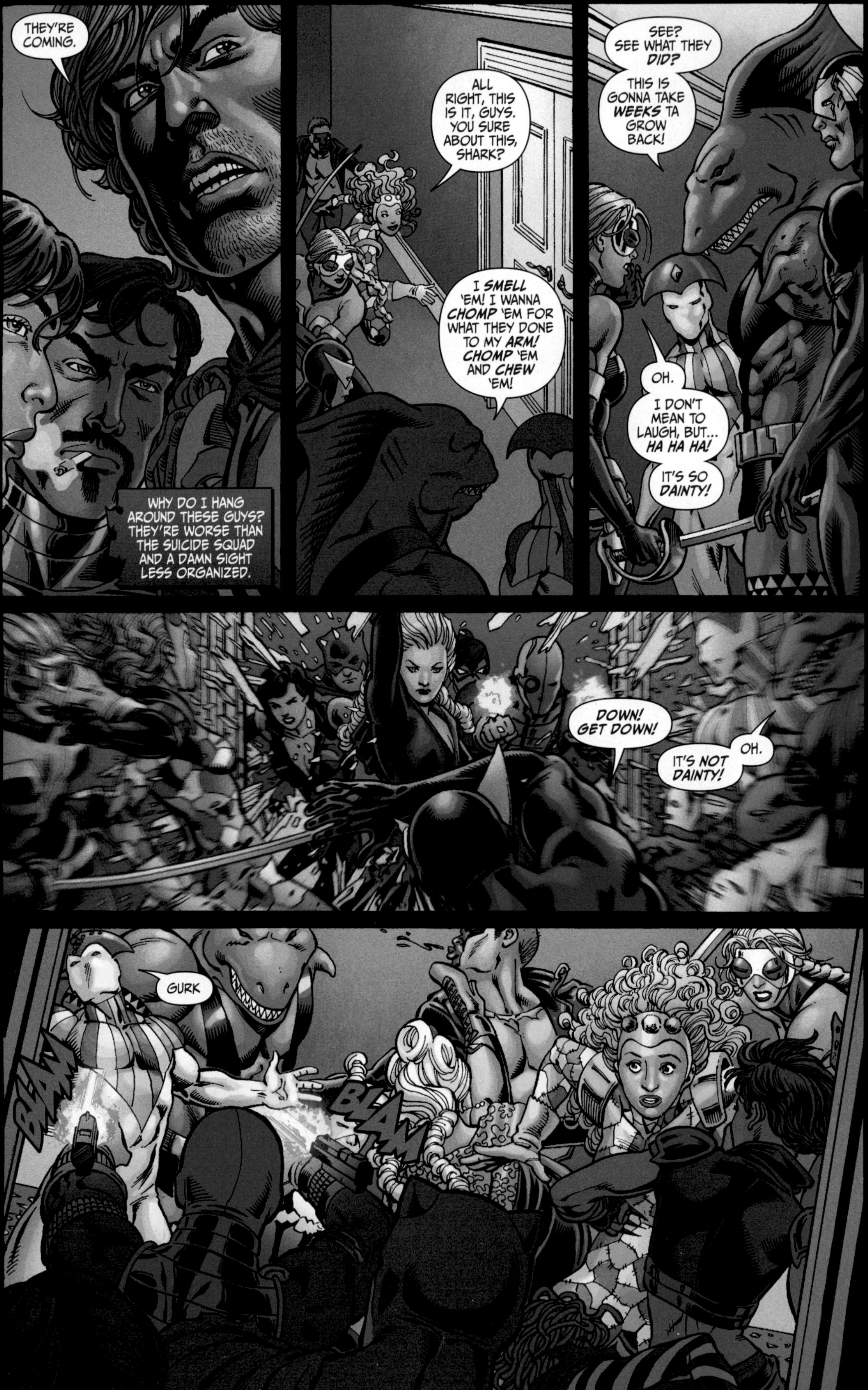
THEY'RE COMING.
WHY DO I HANG AROUND THESE GUYS? THEY'RE WORSE THAN THE SUICIDE SQUAD AND A DAMN SIGHT LESS ORGANIZED.
ALL RIGHT, THIS IS IT, GUYS. YOU SURE ABOUT THIS, SHARK?
I SMELL 'EM! I WANNA CHOMP 'EM FOR WHAT THEY DONE TO MY ARM! CHOMP 'EM AND CHEW 'EM!
SEE? SEE WHAT THEY DID?
THIS IS GONNA TAKE WEEKS TA GROW BACK!
OH.
I DON'T MEAN TO LAUGH, BUT... HA HA HA!
IT'S SO DAINTY!
DOWN! GET DOWN!
OH.
IT'S NOT DAINTY!
GURK
BLAM
BLAM

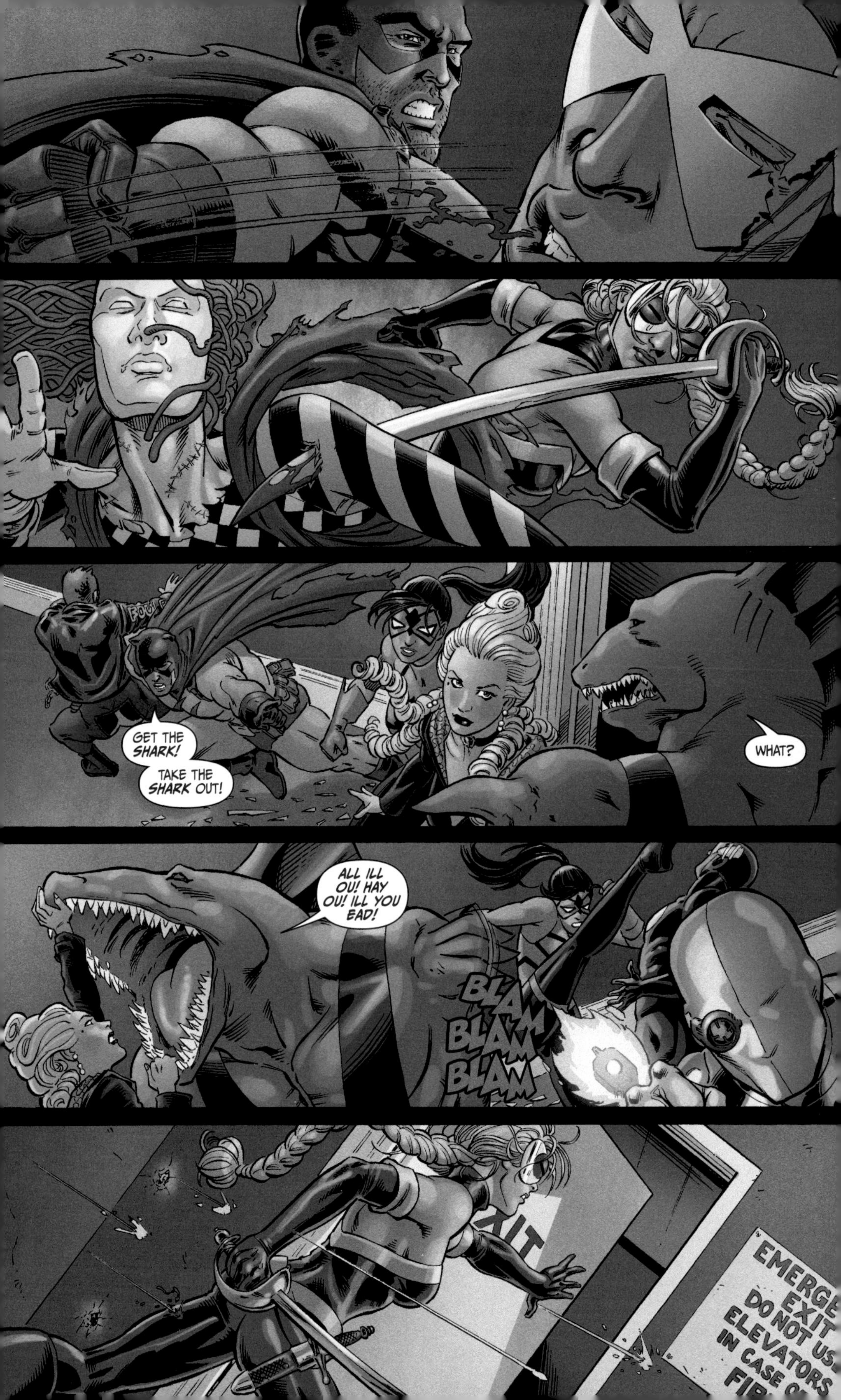
GET THE SHARK!
TAKE THE SHARK OUT!
WHAT?
ALL ILL OU! HAY OU! ILL YOU EAD!
BLAM BLAM BLAM
EXIT
EMERGE EXIT DO NOT US ELEVATORS IN CASE O FIR

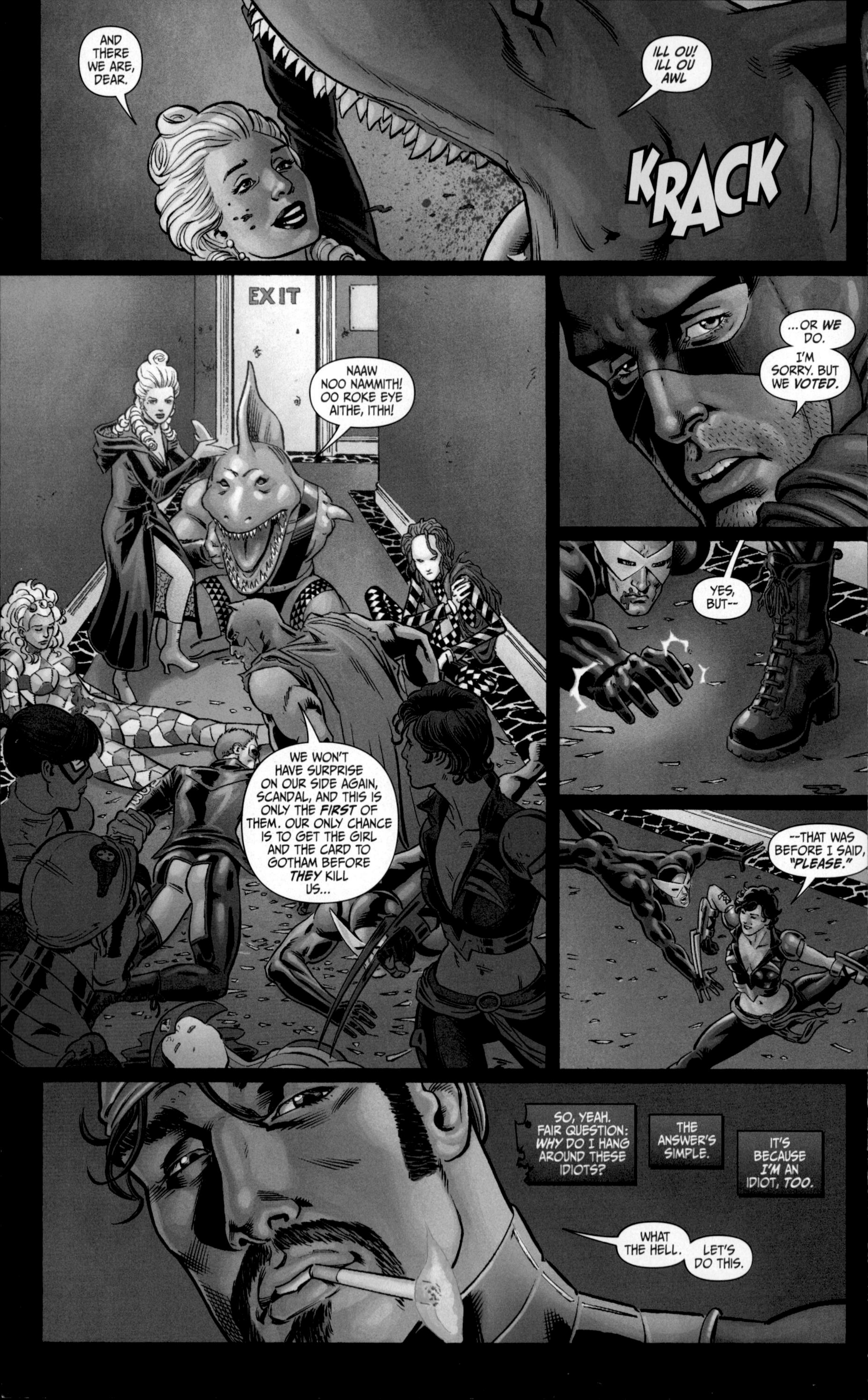
AND THERE WE ARE, DEAR.
ILL OU! ILL OU AWL
KRACK
NAAW NOO NAMMITH! OO ROKE EYE AITHE, ITHH!
WE WON'T HAVE SURPRISE ON OUR SIDE AGAIN, SCANDAL, AND THIS IS ONLY THE FIRST OF THEM. OUR ONLY CHANCE IS TO GET THE GIRL AND THE CARD TO GOTHAM BEFORE THEY KILL US...
EXIT
...OR WE DO. I'M SORRY. BUT WE VOTED.
YES, BUT--
--THAT WAS BEFORE I SAID, "PLEASE."
SO, YEAH. FAIR QUESTION: WHY DO I HANG AROUND THESE IDIOTS?
THE ANSWER'S SIMPLE.
IT'S BECAUSE I'M AN IDIOT, TOO.
WHAT THE HELL.
LET'S DO THIS.

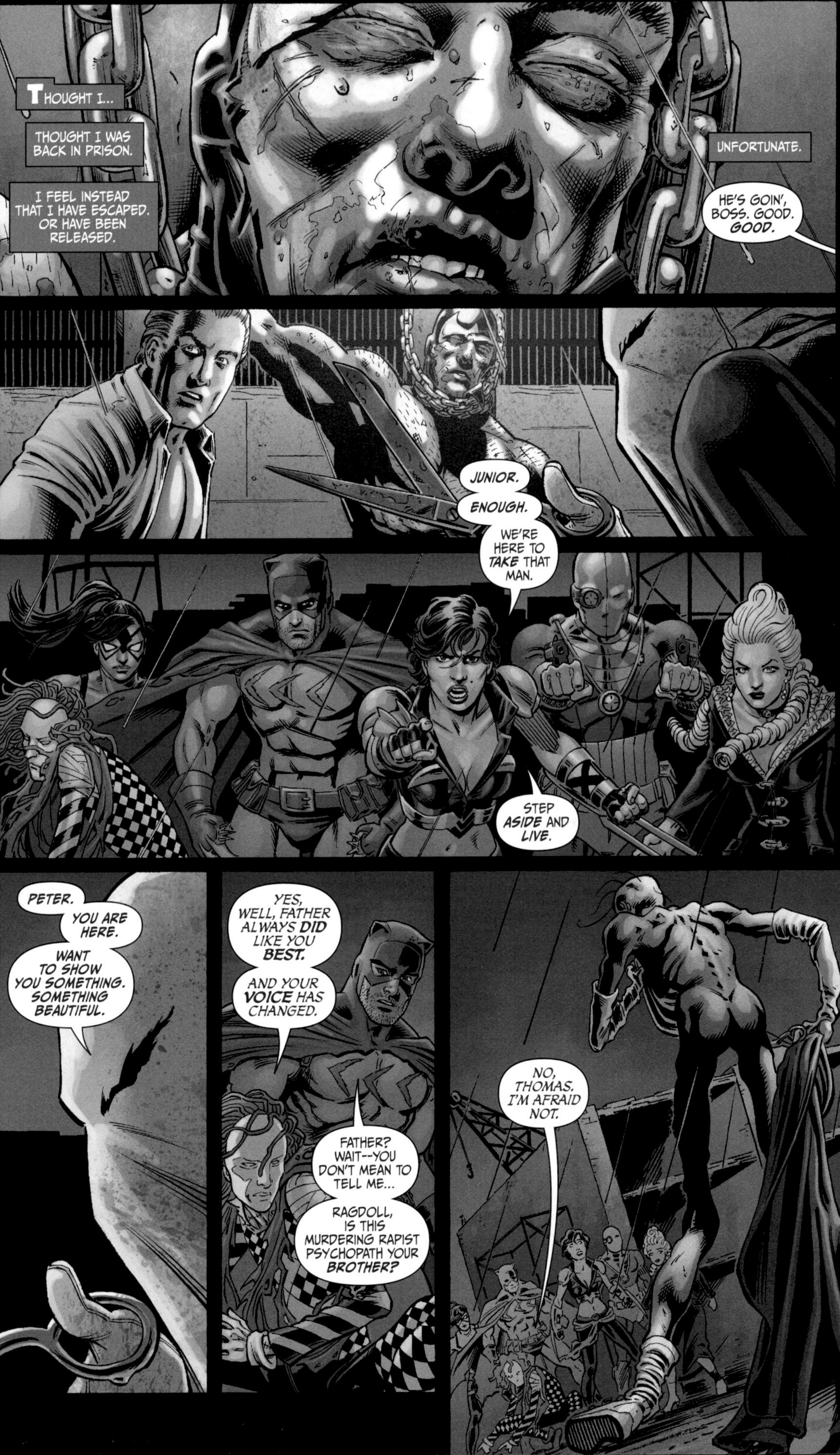
THOUGHT I...
THOUGHT I WAS BACK IN PRISON.
I FEEL INSTEAD THAT I HAVE ESCAPED. OR HAVE BEEN RELEASED.
UNFORTUNATE.
HE'S GOIN', BOSS. GOOD. GOOD.
JUNIOR.
ENOUGH.
WE'RE HERE TO TAKE THAT MAN.
STEP ASIDE AND LIVE.
PETER.
YOU ARE HERE.
WANT TO SHOW YOU SOMETHING. SOMETHING BEAUTIFUL.
YES, WELL, FATHER ALWAYS DID LIKE YOU BEST.
AND YOUR VOICE HAS CHANGED.
FATHER? WAIT--YOU DON'T MEAN TO TELL ME...
RAGDOLL, IS THIS MURDERING RAPIST PSYCHOPATH YOUR BROTHER?
NO, THOMAS. I'M AFRAID NOT.

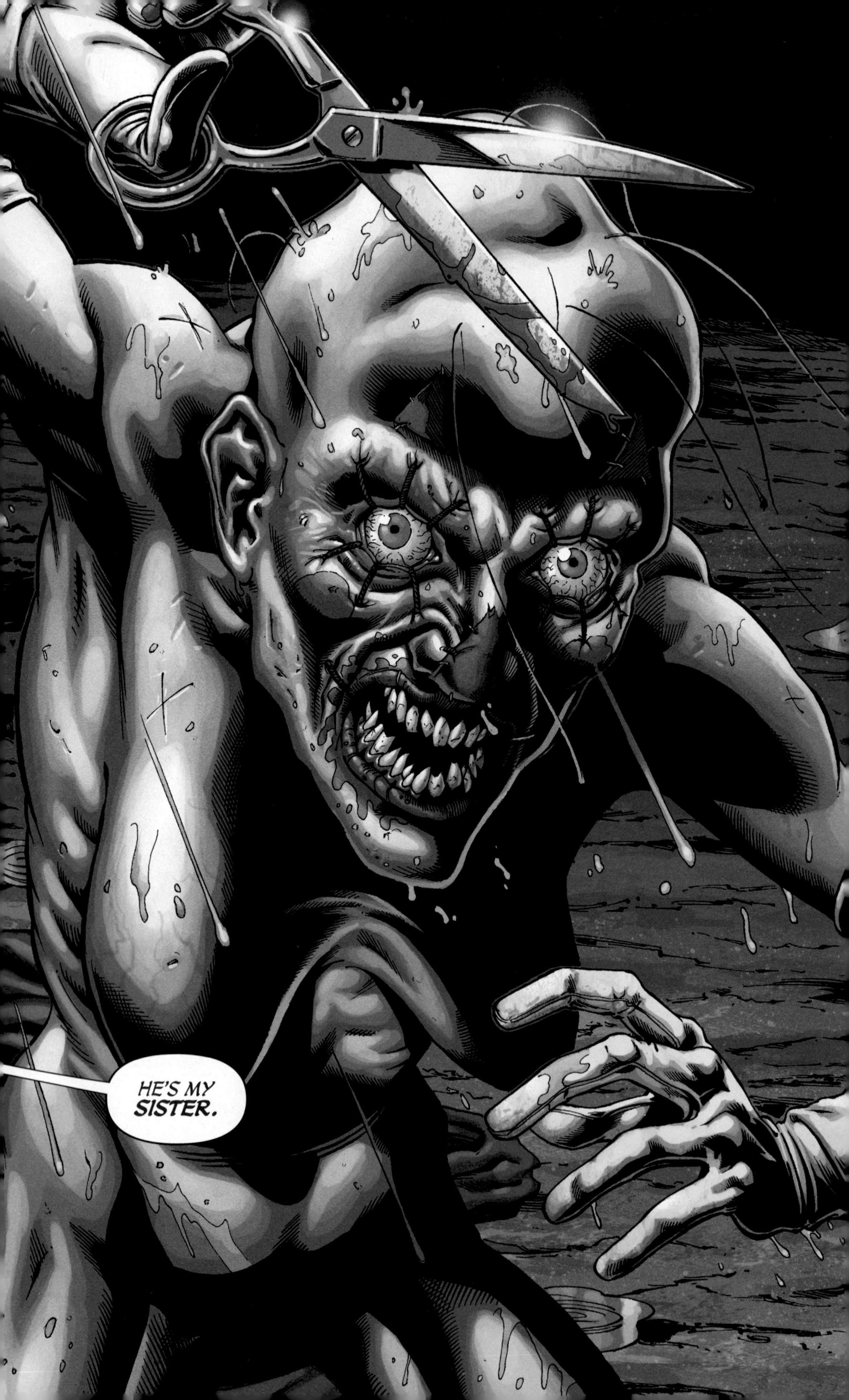
HE'S MY SISTER.

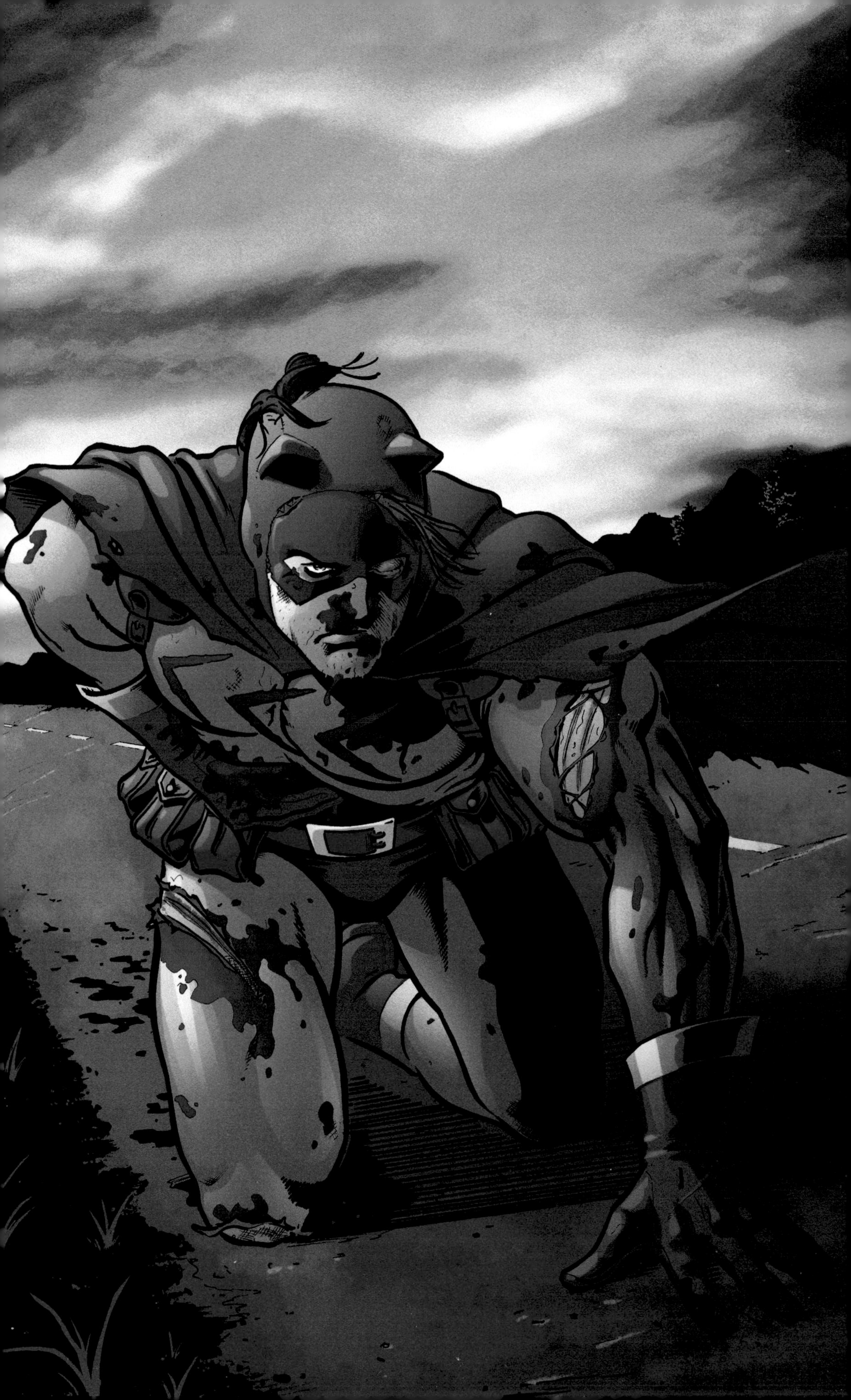

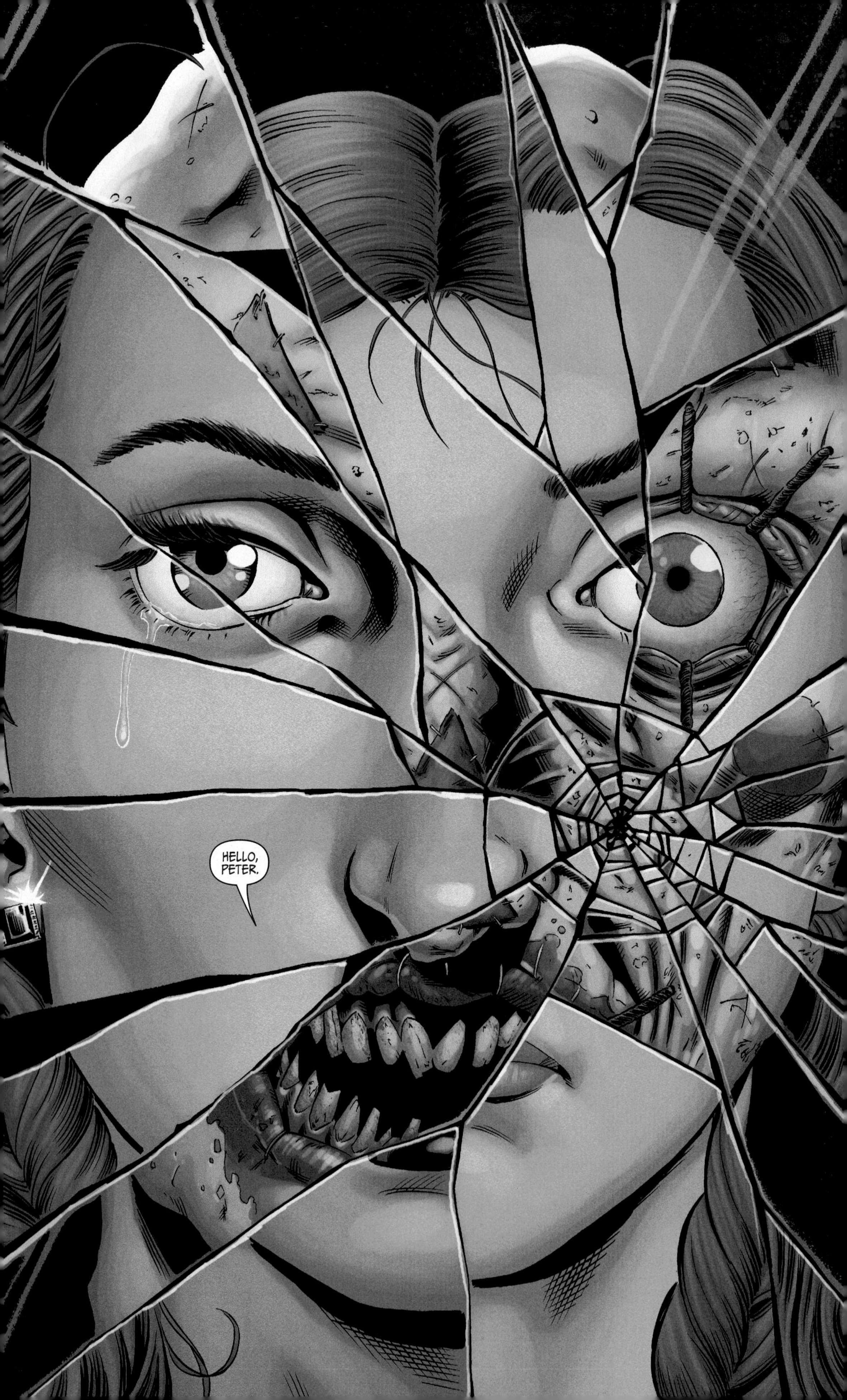
HELLO, PETER.

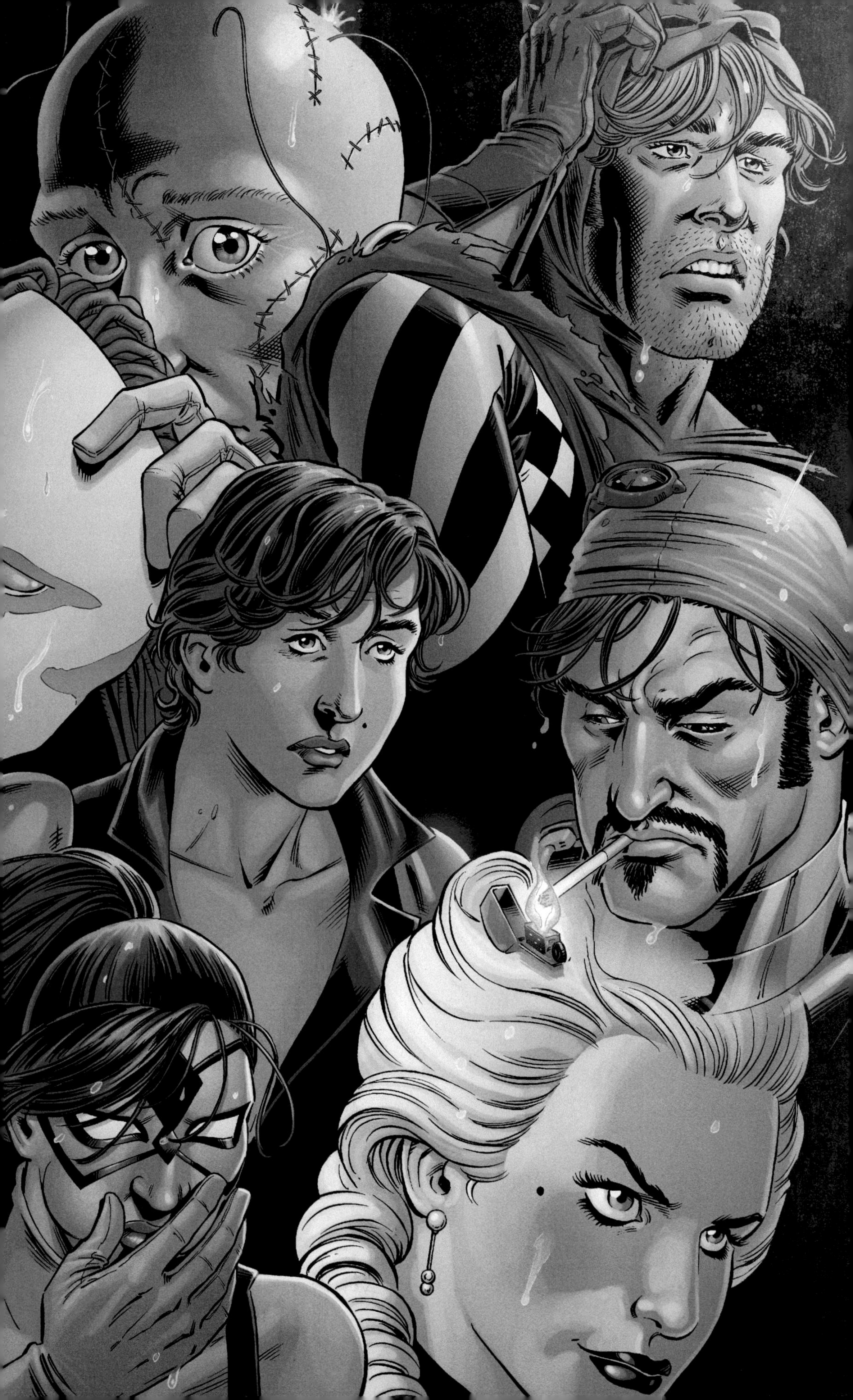

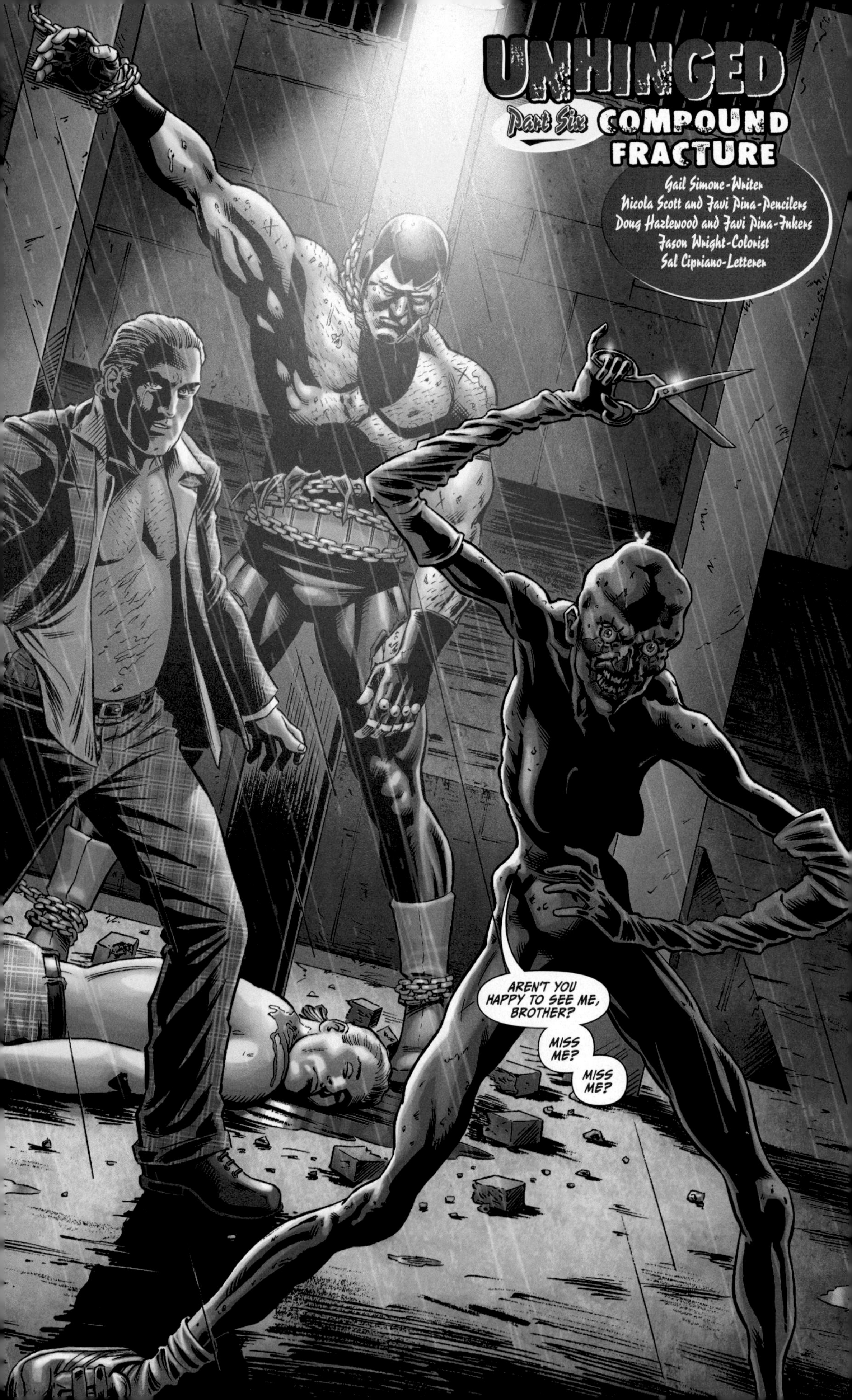
UNHINGED
Part Six COMPOUND FRACTURE
Gail Simone-Writer
Nicola Scott and Javi Pina-Pencilers
Doug Hazlewood and Javi Pina-Inkers
Jason Wright-Colorist
Sal Cipriano-Letterer
AREN'T YOU HAPPY TO SEE ME, BROTHER?
MISS ME?
MISS ME?

SAY THE WORD, BOSS. I DON'T CARE NO MORE.

MAN, I WOULDN'T. I HONEST TO GOD WOULD *NOT*.

BE DOIN' YOU A *FAVOR*, WEARING THAT CRAPSTAIN *JACKET*.

ALEX... DEAR CHILD. MY SWEET SISTER. WHAT HAVE YOU DONE?

YOUR SISTER'S NAMED "ALEX"?

HOLD, TIG. THEY MAY SPEAK.

FATHER WANTED ANOTHER BOY.

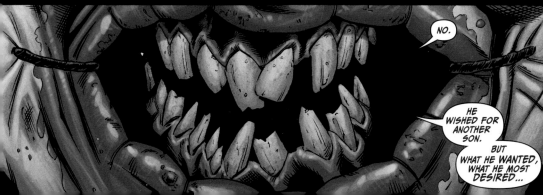

NO.

HE WISHED FOR ANOTHER SON. BUT WHAT HE WANTED, WHAT HE MOST *DESIRED*...

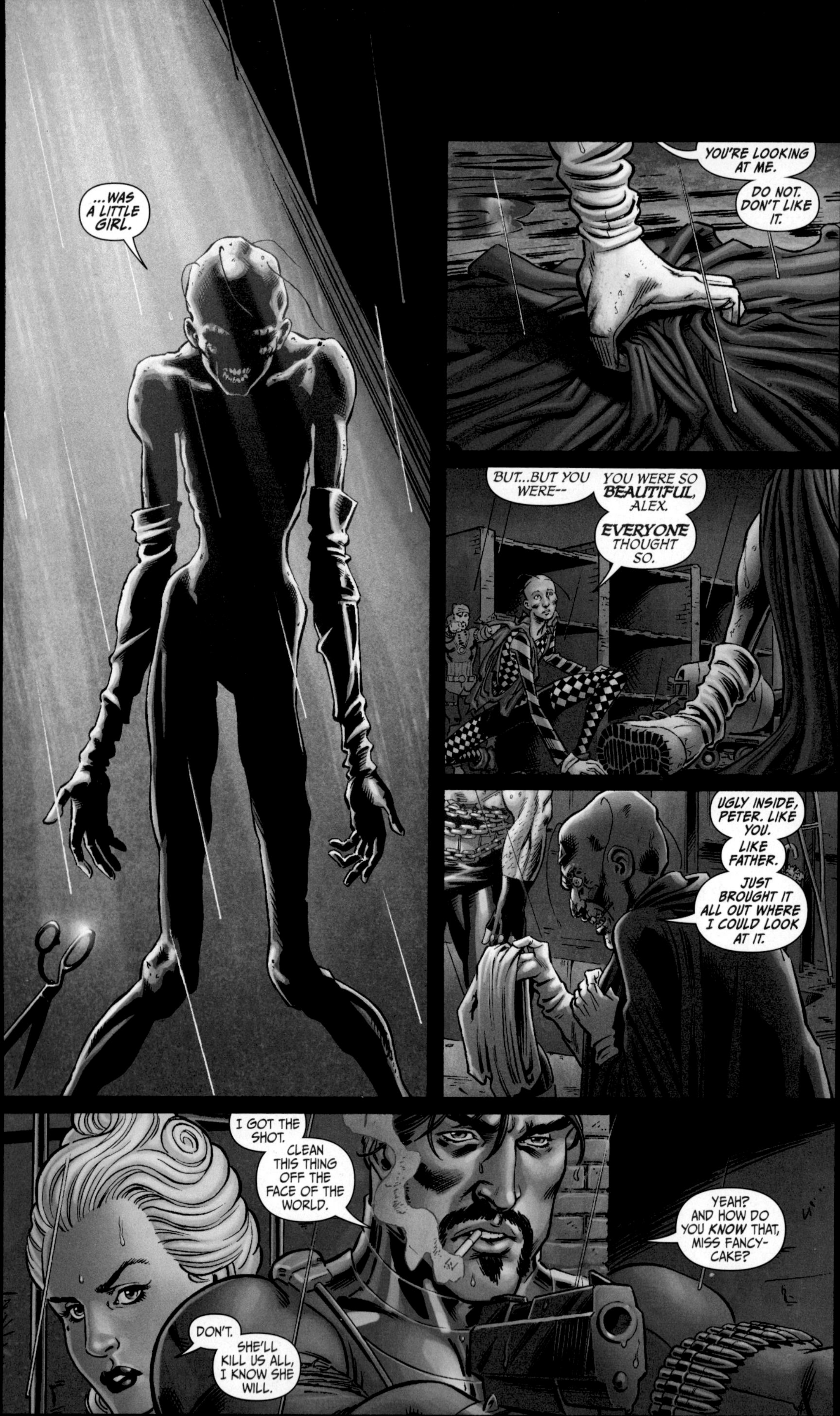
...WAS A LITTLE GIRL.
YOU'RE LOOKING AT ME.
DO NOT. DON'T LIKE IT.
BUT...BUT YOU WERE--
YOU WERE SO BEAUTIFUL, ALEX.
EVERYONE THOUGHT SO.
UGLY INSIDE, PETER. LIKE YOU.
LIKE FATHER.
JUST BROUGHT IT ALL OUT WHERE I COULD LOOK AT IT.
I GOT THE SHOT.
CLEAN THIS THING OFF THE FACE OF THE WORLD.
YEAH? AND HOW DO YOU KNOW THAT, MISS FANCY-CAKE?
DON'T.
SHE'LL KILL US ALL, I KNOW SHE WILL.

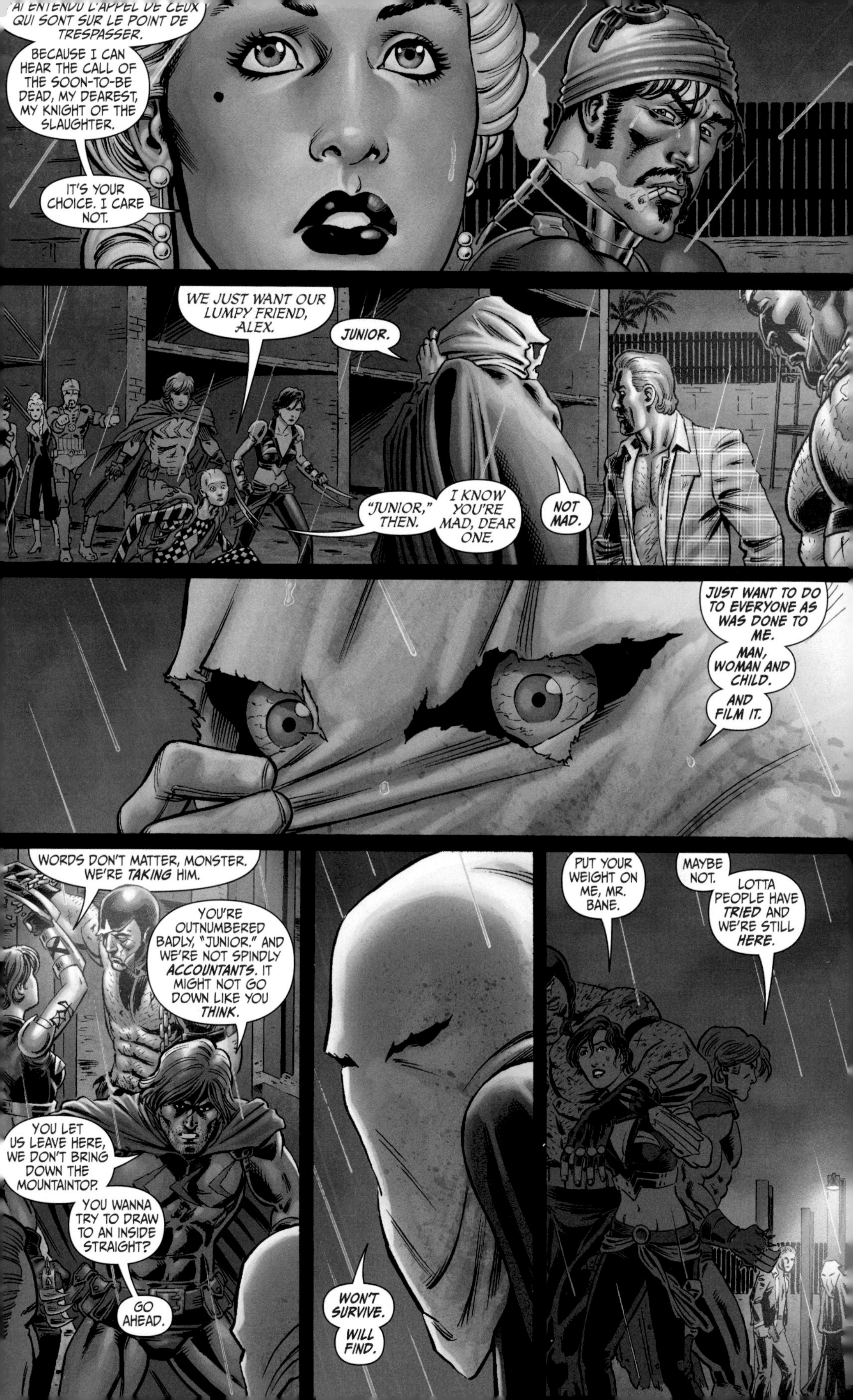
J'AI ENTENDU L'APPEL DE CEUX QUI SONT SUR LE POINT DE TRESPASSER.
BECAUSE I CAN HEAR THE CALL OF THE SOON-TO-BE DEAD, MY DEAREST, MY KNIGHT OF THE SLAUGHTER.
IT'S YOUR CHOICE. I CARE NOT.
WE JUST WANT OUR LUMPY FRIEND, ALEX.
JUNIOR.
"JUNIOR," THEN.
I KNOW YOU'RE MAD, DEAR ONE.
NOT MAD.
JUST WANT TO DO TO EVERYONE AS WAS DONE TO ME.
MAN, WOMAN AND CHILD.
AND FILM IT.
WORDS DON'T MATTER, MONSTER. WE'RE TAKING HIM.
YOU'RE OUTNUMBERED BADLY, "JUNIOR." AND WE'RE NOT SPINDLY ACCOUNTANTS. IT MIGHT NOT GO DOWN LIKE YOU THINK.
YOU LET US LEAVE HERE, WE DON'T BRING DOWN THE MOUNTAINTOP.
YOU WANNA TRY TO DRAW TO AN INSIDE STRAIGHT?
GO AHEAD.
WON'T SURVIVE.
WILL FIND.
PUT YOUR WEIGHT ON ME, MR. BANE.
MAYBE NOT.
LOTTA PEOPLE HAVE TRIED AND WE'RE STILL HERE.

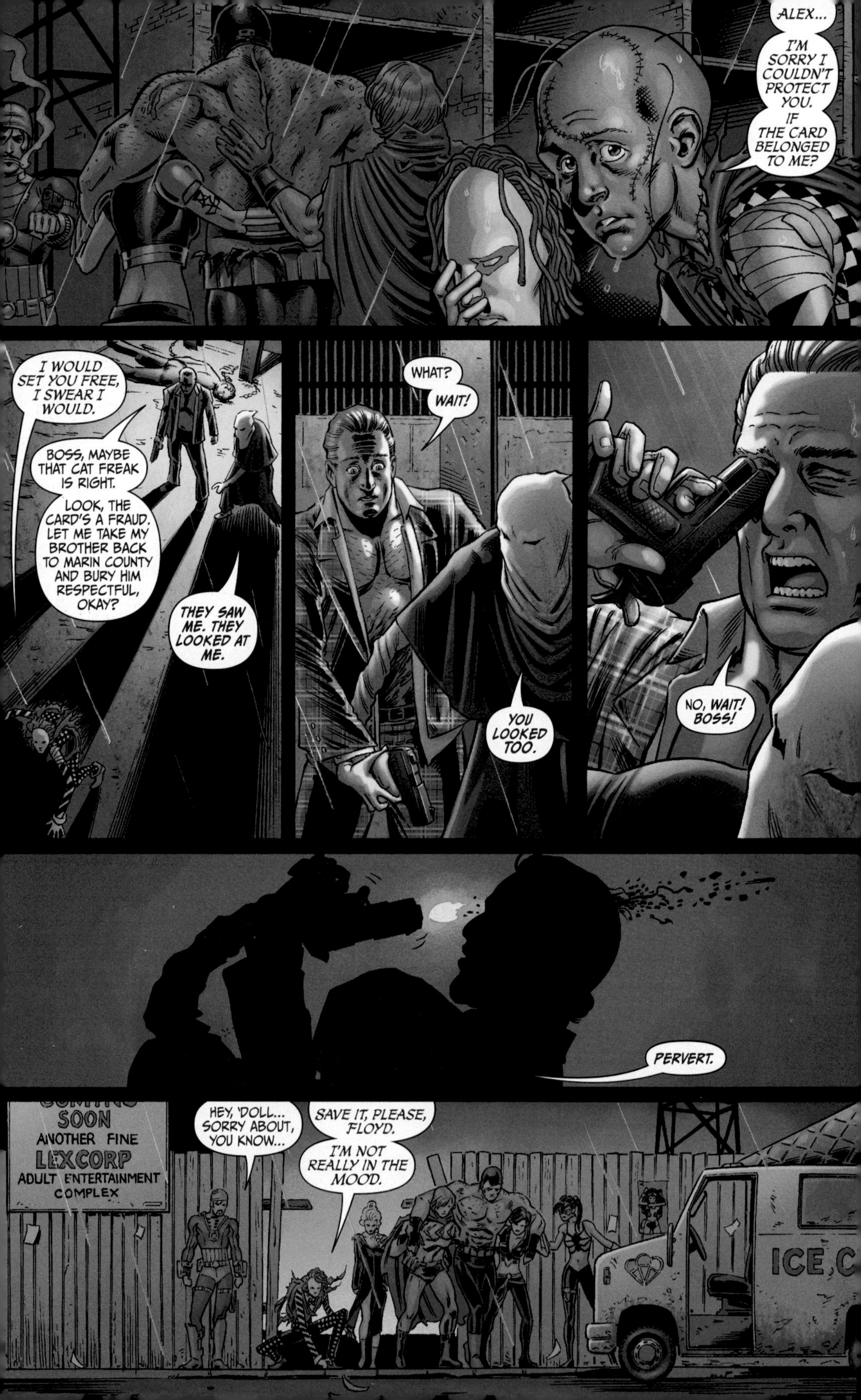
ALEX...
I'M SORRY I COULDN'T PROTECT YOU. IF THE CARD BELONGED TO ME?
I WOULD SET YOU FREE, I SWEAR I WOULD.
BOSS, MAYBE THAT CAT FREAK IS RIGHT.
LOOK, THE CARD'S A FRAUD. LET ME TAKE MY BROTHER BACK TO MARIN COUNTY AND BURY HIM RESPECTFUL, OKAY?
THEY SAW ME. THEY LOOKED AT ME.
WHAT?
WAIT!
YOU LOOKED TOO.
NO, WAIT! BOSS!
PERVERT.
SOON
ANOTHER FINE
LEXCORP
ADULT ENTERTAINMENT
COMPLEX
HEY, 'DOLL... SORRY ABOUT, YOU KNOW...
SAVE IT, PLEASE, FLOYD.
I'M NOT REALLY IN THE MOOD.

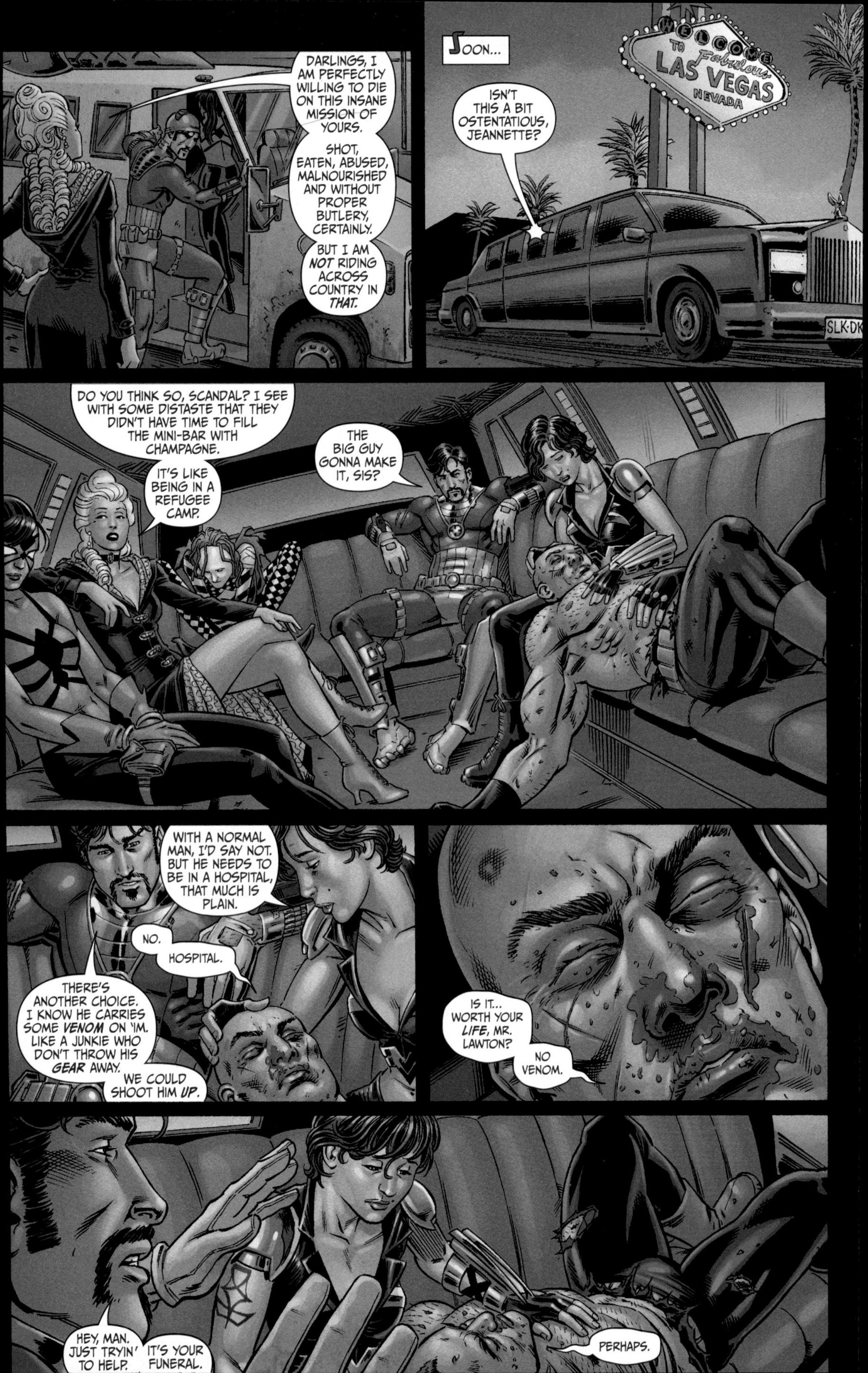
DARLINGS, I AM PERFECTLY WILLING TO DIE ON THIS INSANE MISSION OF YOURS.
SHOT, EATEN, ABUSED, MALNOURISHED AND WITHOUT PROPER BUTLERY, CERTAINLY.
BUT I AM *NOT* RIDING ACROSS COUNTRY IN *THAT.*
SOON...
WELCOME TO Fabulous LAS VEGAS NEVADA
ISN'T THIS A BIT OSTENTATIOUS, JEANNETTE?
SLK·DK
DO YOU THINK SO, SCANDAL? I SEE WITH SOME DISTASTE THAT THEY DIDN'T HAVE TIME TO FILL THE MINI-BAR WITH CHAMPAGNE.
IT'S LIKE BEING IN A REFUGEE CAMP.
THE BIG GUY GONNA MAKE IT, SIS?
WITH A NORMAL MAN, I'D SAY NOT. BUT HE NEEDS TO BE IN A HOSPITAL, THAT MUCH IS PLAIN.
NO.
HOSPITAL.
THERE'S ANOTHER CHOICE. I KNOW HE CARRIES SOME *VENOM* ON 'IM. LIKE A JUNKIE WHO DON'T THROW HIS *GEAR* AWAY.
WE COULD SHOOT HIM *UP*.
IS IT... WORTH YOUR *LIFE*, MR. LAWTON?
NO VENOM.
HEY, MAN. JUST TRYIN' TO HELP.
IT'S YOUR FUNERAL.
PERHAPS.

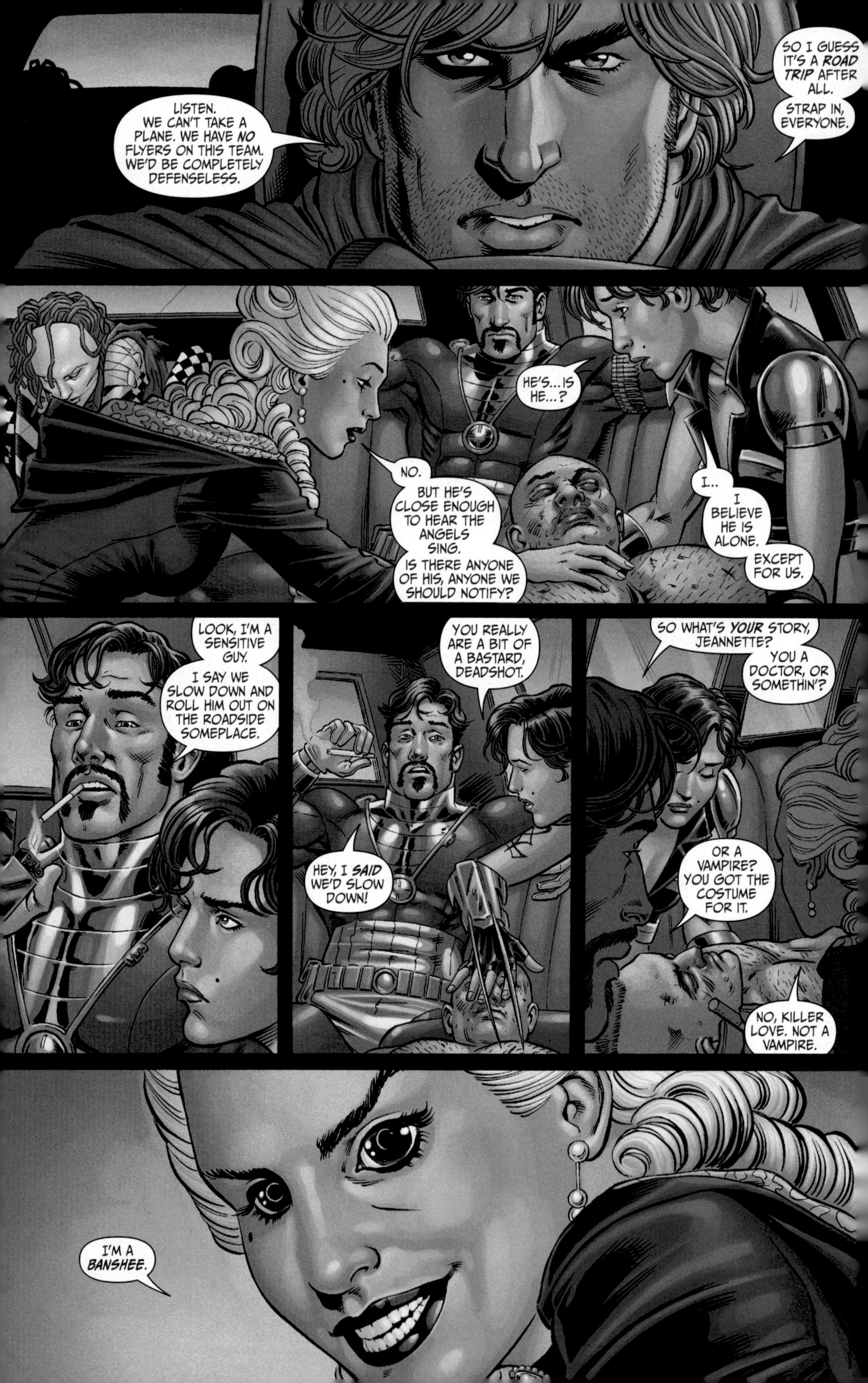
LISTEN. WE CAN'T TAKE A PLANE. WE HAVE NO FLYERS ON THIS TEAM. WE'D BE COMPLETELY DEFENSELESS.
SO I GUESS IT'S A ROAD TRIP AFTER ALL.
STRAP IN, EVERYONE.
HE'S...IS HE...?
NO.
BUT HE'S CLOSE ENOUGH TO HEAR THE ANGELS SING.
IS THERE ANYONE OF HIS, ANYONE WE SHOULD NOTIFY?
I...
I BELIEVE HE IS ALONE.
EXCEPT FOR US.
LOOK, I'M A SENSITIVE GUY.
I SAY WE SLOW DOWN AND ROLL HIM OUT ON THE ROADSIDE SOMEPLACE.
YOU REALLY ARE A BIT OF A BASTARD, DEADSHOT.
HEY, I SAID WE'D SLOW DOWN!
SO WHAT'S YOUR STORY, JEANNETTE?
YOU A DOCTOR, OR SOMETHIN'?
OR A VAMPIRE? YOU GOT THE COSTUME FOR IT.
NO, KILLER LOVE. NOT A VAMPIRE.
I'M A BANSHEE.

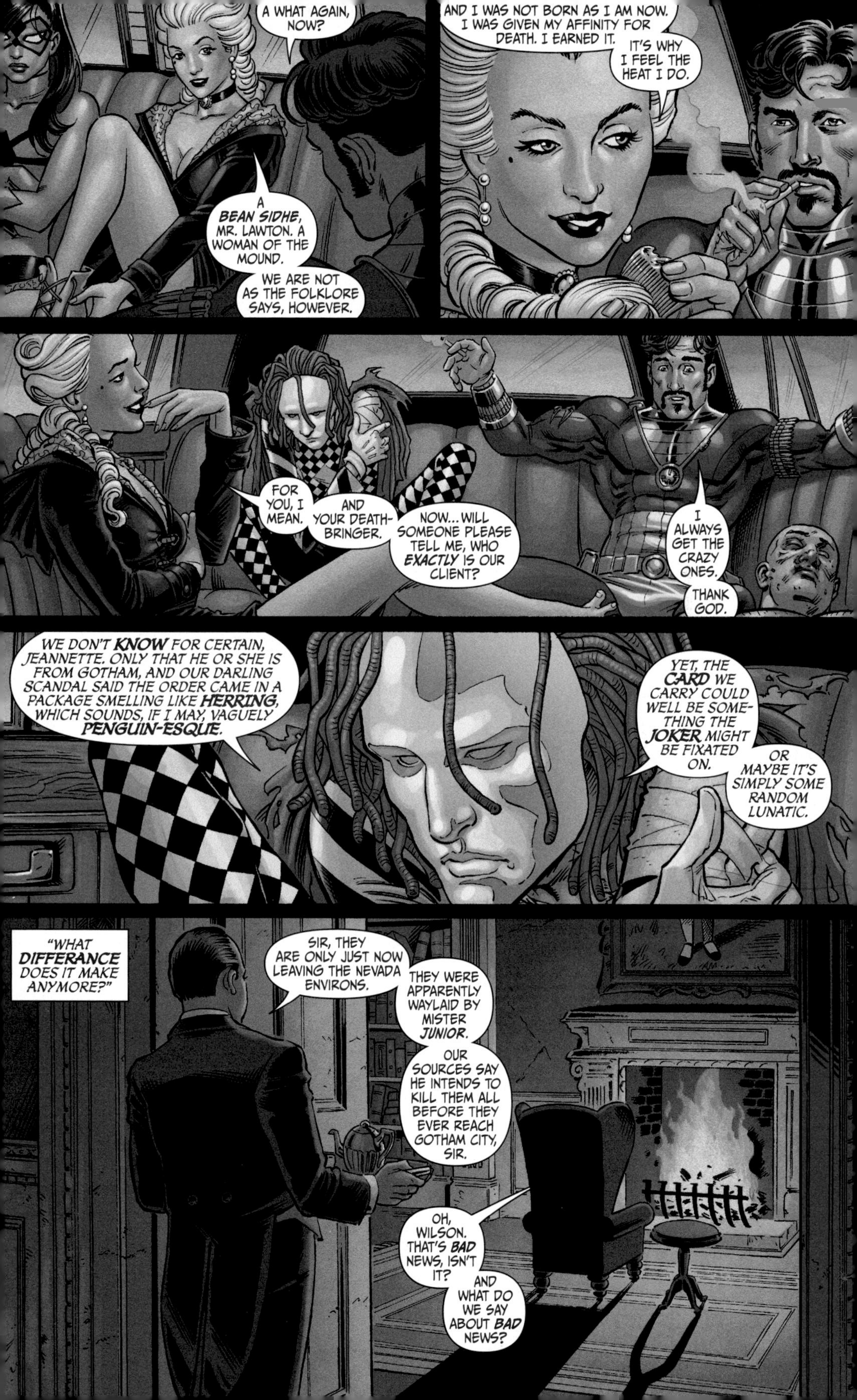
A WHAT AGAIN, NOW?
A BEAN SIDHE, MR. LAWTON. A WOMAN OF THE MOUND.
WE ARE NOT AS THE FOLKLORE SAYS, HOWEVER.
AND I WAS NOT BORN AS I AM NOW. I WAS GIVEN MY AFFINITY FOR DEATH. I EARNED IT.
IT'S WHY I FEEL THE HEAT I DO.
FOR YOU, I MEAN.
AND YOUR DEATH-BRINGER.
NOW... WILL SOMEONE PLEASE TELL ME, WHO EXACTLY IS OUR CLIENT?
I ALWAYS GET THE CRAZY ONES.
THANK GOD.
WE DON'T KNOW FOR CERTAIN, JEANNETTE. ONLY THAT HE OR SHE IS FROM GOTHAM, AND OUR DARLING SCANDAL SAID THE ORDER CAME IN A PACKAGE SMELLING LIKE HERRING, WHICH SOUNDS, IF I MAY, VAGUELY PENGUIN-ESQUE.
YET, THE CARD WE CARRY COULD WELL BE SOMETHING THE JOKER MIGHT BE FIXATED ON.
OR MAYBE IT'S SIMPLY SOME RANDOM LUNATIC.
"WHAT DIFFERANCE DOES IT MAKE ANYMORE?"
SIR, THEY ARE ONLY JUST NOW LEAVING THE NEVADA ENVIRONS.
THEY WERE APPARENTLY WAYLAID BY MISTER JUNIOR.
OUR SOURCES SAY HE INTENDS TO KILL THEM ALL BEFORE THEY EVER REACH GOTHAM CITY, SIR.
OH, WILSON. THAT'S BAD NEWS, ISN'T IT?
AND WHAT DO WE SAY ABOUT BAD NEWS?

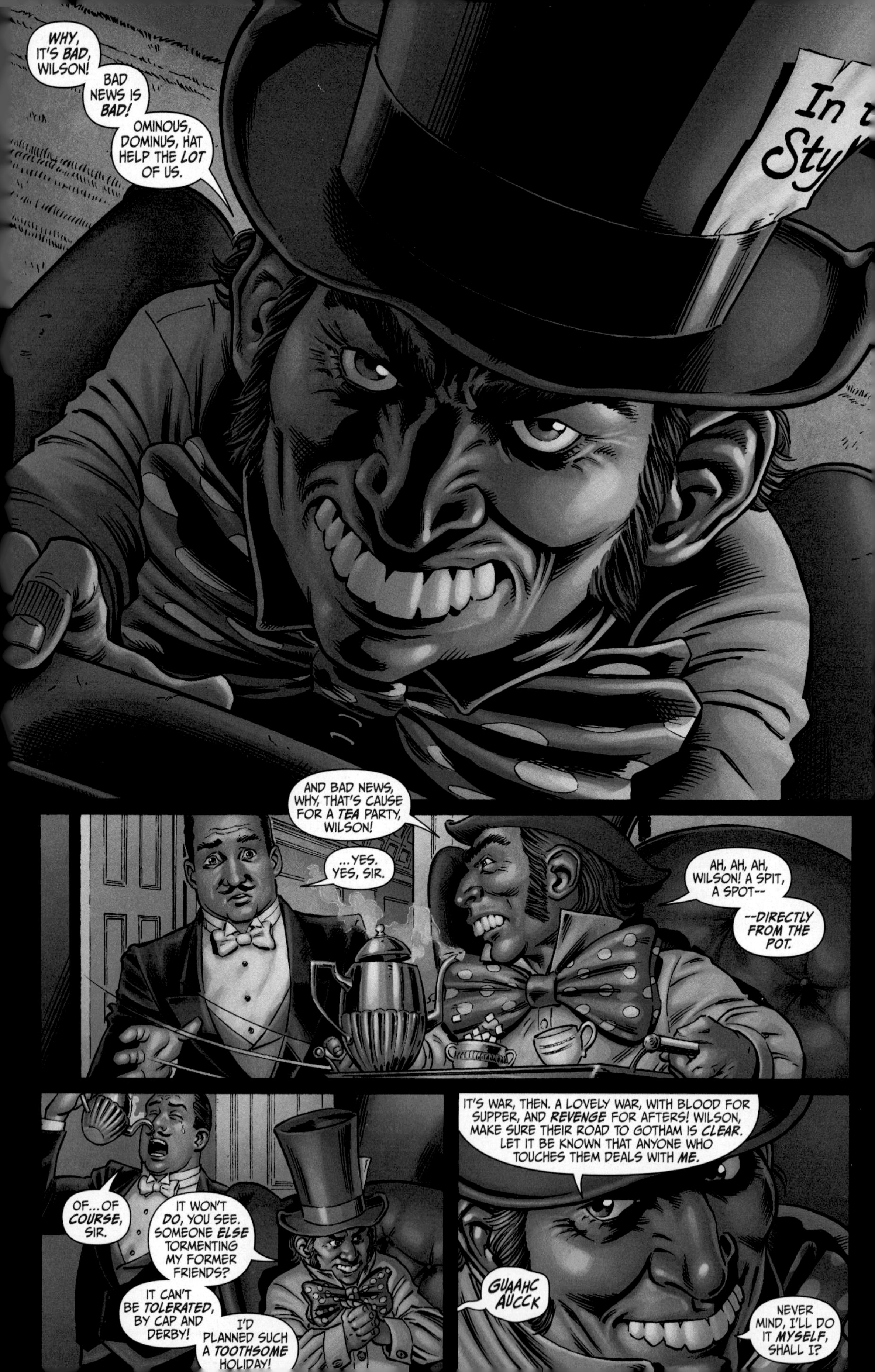

WHY, IT'S BAD, WILSON!
BAD NEWS IS BAD!
OMINOUS, DOMINUS, HAT HELP THE LOT OF US.
In t
Sty
AND BAD NEWS, WHY, THAT'S CAUSE FOR A TEA PARTY, WILSON!
...YES. YES, SIR.
AH, AH, AH, WILSON! A SPIT, A SPOT--
--DIRECTLY FROM THE POT.
OF...OF COURSE, SIR.
IT WON'T DO, YOU SEE. SOMEONE ELSE TORMENTING MY FORMER FRIENDS?
IT CAN'T BE TOLERATED, BY CAP AND DERBY!
I'D PLANNED SUCH A TOOTHSOME HOLIDAY!
IT'S WAR, THEN. A LOVELY WAR, WITH BLOOD FOR SUPPER, AND REVENGE FOR AFTERS! WILSON, MAKE SURE THEIR ROAD TO GOTHAM IS CLEAR. LET IT BE KNOWN THAT ANYONE WHO TOUCHES THEM DEALS WITH ME.
GUAAHC AUCCK
NEVER MIND, I'LL DO IT MYSELF, SHALL I?

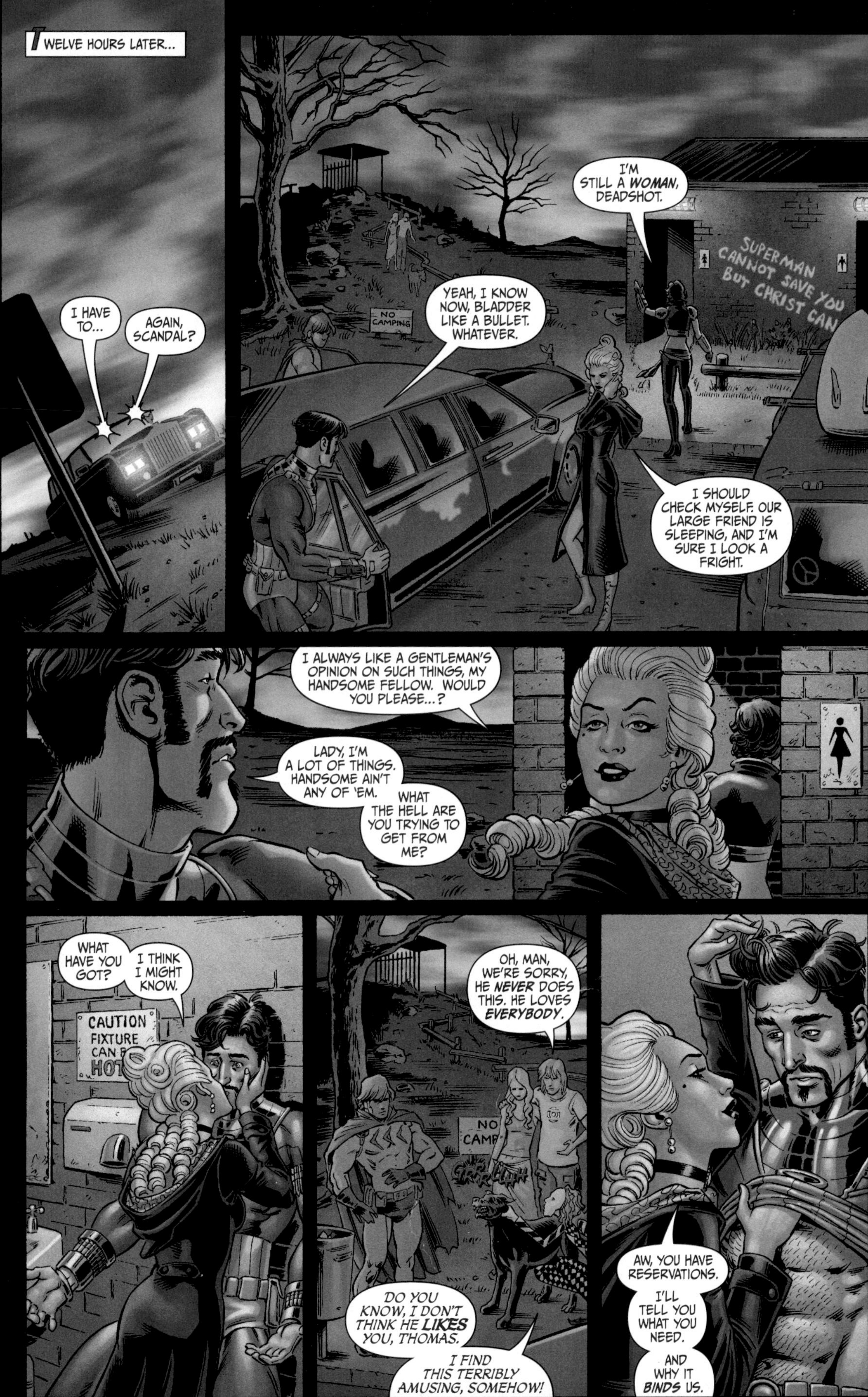

TWELVE HOURS LATER...
I HAVE TO...
AGAIN, SCANDAL?
I'M STILL A WOMAN, DEADSHOT.
SUPERMAN CANNOT SAVE YOU BUT CHRIST CAN
NO CAMPING
YEAH, I KNOW NOW, BLADDER LIKE A BULLET. WHATEVER.
I SHOULD CHECK MYSELF. OUR LARGE FRIEND IS SLEEPING, AND I'M SURE I LOOK A FRIGHT.
I ALWAYS LIKE A GENTLEMAN'S OPINION ON SUCH THINGS, MY HANDSOME FELLOW. WOULD YOU PLEASE...?
LADY, I'M A LOT OF THINGS. HANDSOME AIN'T ANY OF 'EM.
WHAT THE HELL ARE YOU TRYING TO GET FROM ME?
WHAT HAVE YOU GOT?
I THINK I MIGHT KNOW.
CAUTION FIXTURE CAN B HOT
OH, MAN, WE'RE SORRY, HE NEVER DOES THIS. HE LOVES EVERYBODY.
NO CAMP
DO YOU KNOW, I DON'T THINK HE LIKES YOU, THOMAS.
I FIND THIS TERRIBLY AMUSING, SOMEHOW!
AW, YOU HAVE RESERVATIONS.
I'LL TELL YOU WHAT YOU NEED.
AND WHY IT BINDS US.

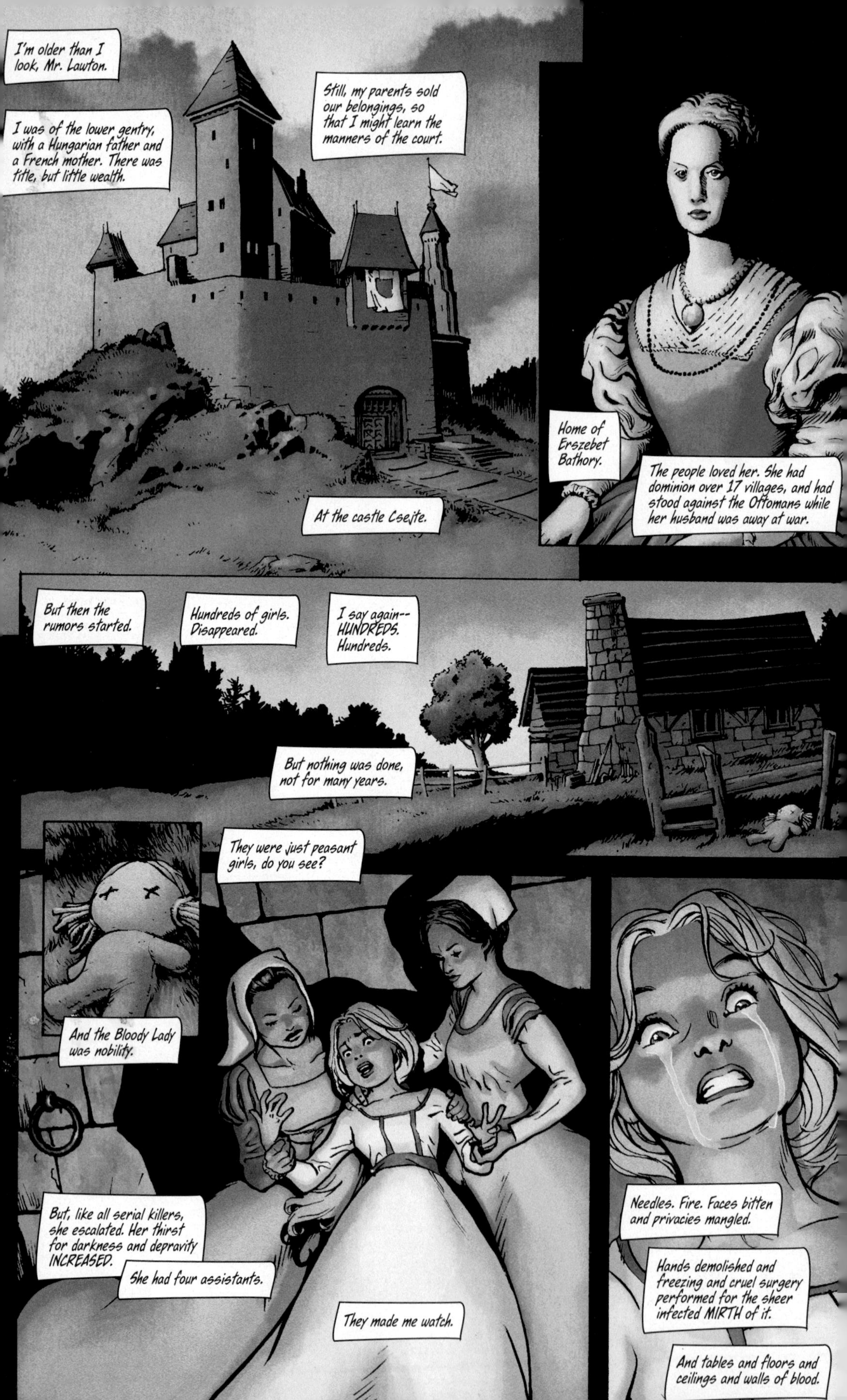
I'm older than I look, Mr. Lawton.
I was of the lower gentry, with a Hungarian father and a French mother. There was title, but little wealth.
Still, my parents sold our belongings, so that I might learn the manners of the court.
At the castle Csejte.
Home of Erszebet Bathory.
The people loved her. She had dominion over 17 villages, and had stood against the Ottomans while her husband was away at war.
But then the rumors started.
Hundreds of girls. Disappeared.
I say again--HUNDREDS. Hundreds.
But nothing was done, not for many years.
They were just peasant girls, do you see?
And the Bloody Lady was nobility.
But, like all serial killers, she escalated. Her thirst for darkness and depravity INCREASED.
She had four assistants.
They made me watch.
Needles. Fire. Faces bitten and privacies mangled.
Hands demolished and freezing and cruel surgery performed for the sheer infected MIRTH of it.
And tables and floors and ceilings and walls of blood.

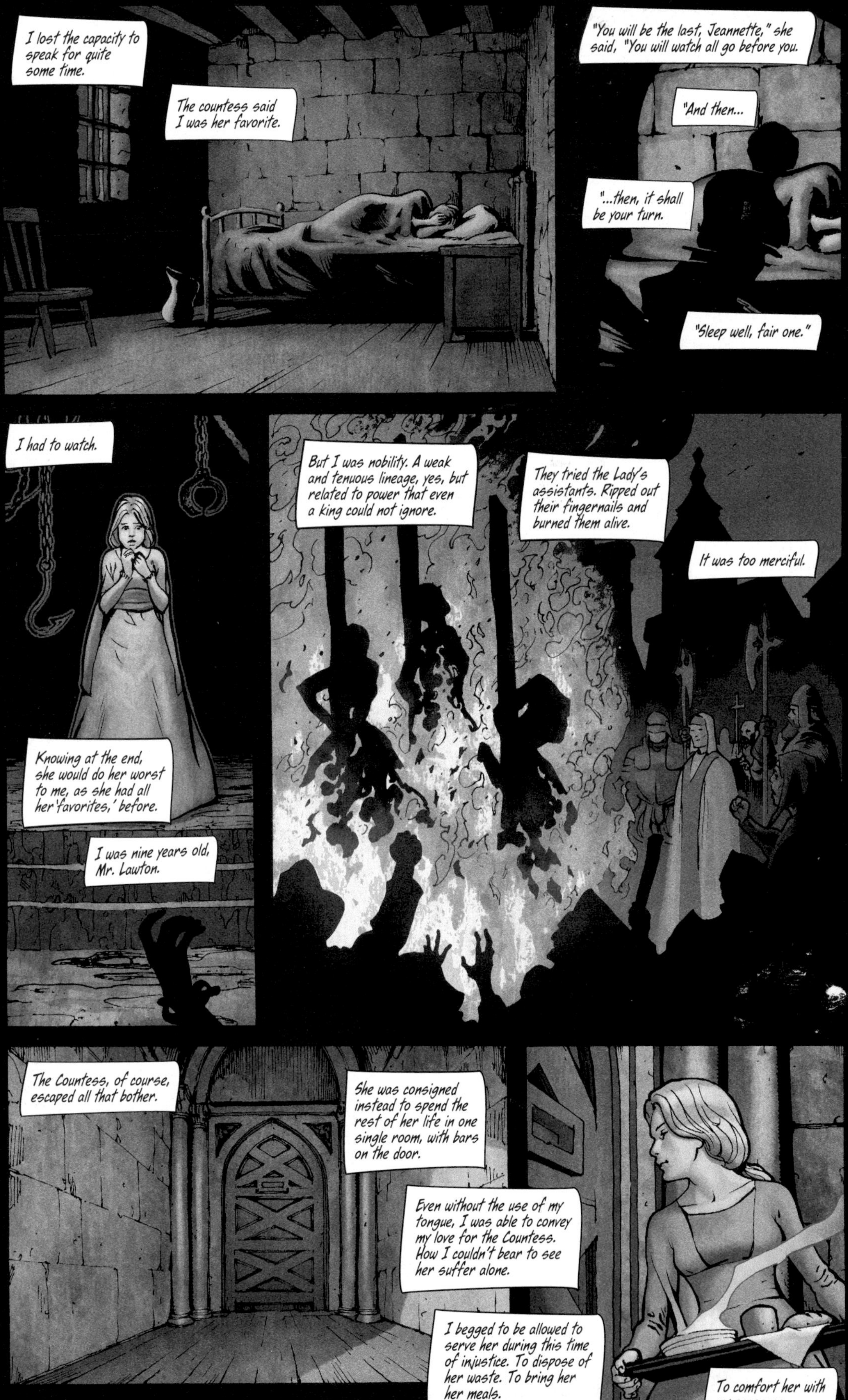
I lost the capacity to speak for quite some time.
The countess said I was her favorite.
"You will be the last, Jeannette," she said, "You will watch all go before you.
"And then...
"...then, it shall be your turn.
"Sleep well, fair one."
I had to watch.
Knowing at the end, she would do her worst to me, as she had all her 'favorites,' before.
I was nine years old, Mr. Lawton.
But I was nobility. A weak and tenuous lineage, yes, but related to power that even a king could not ignore.
They tried the Lady's assistants. Ripped out their fingernails and burned them alive.
It was too merciful.
The Countess, of course, escaped all that bother.
She was consigned instead to spend the rest of her life in one single room, with bars on the door.
Even without the use of my tongue, I was able to convey my love for the Countess. How I couldn't bear to see her suffer alone.
I begged to be allowed to serve her during this time of injustice. To dispose of her waste. To bring her her meals.
To comfort her with my presence.

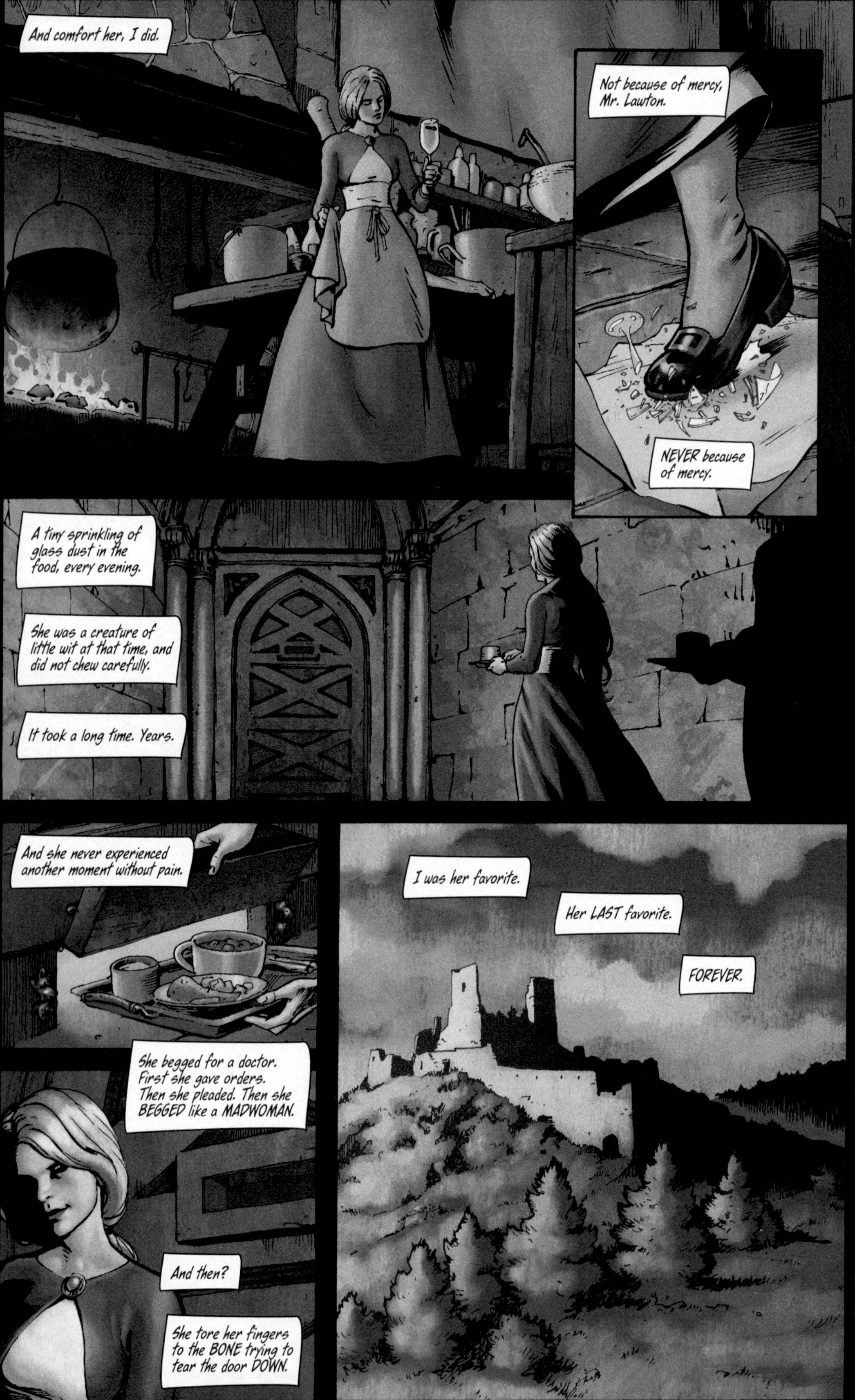
And comfort her, I did.
Not because of mercy, Mr. Lawton.
NEVER because of mercy.
A tiny sprinkling of glass dust in the food, every evening.
She was a creature of little wit at that time, and did not chew carefully.
It took a long time. Years.
And she never experienced another moment without pain.
She begged for a doctor. First she gave orders. Then she pleaded. Then she BEGGED like a MADWOMAN.
And then?
She tore her fingers to the BONE trying to tear the door DOWN.
I was her favorite.
Her LAST favorite.
FOREVER.

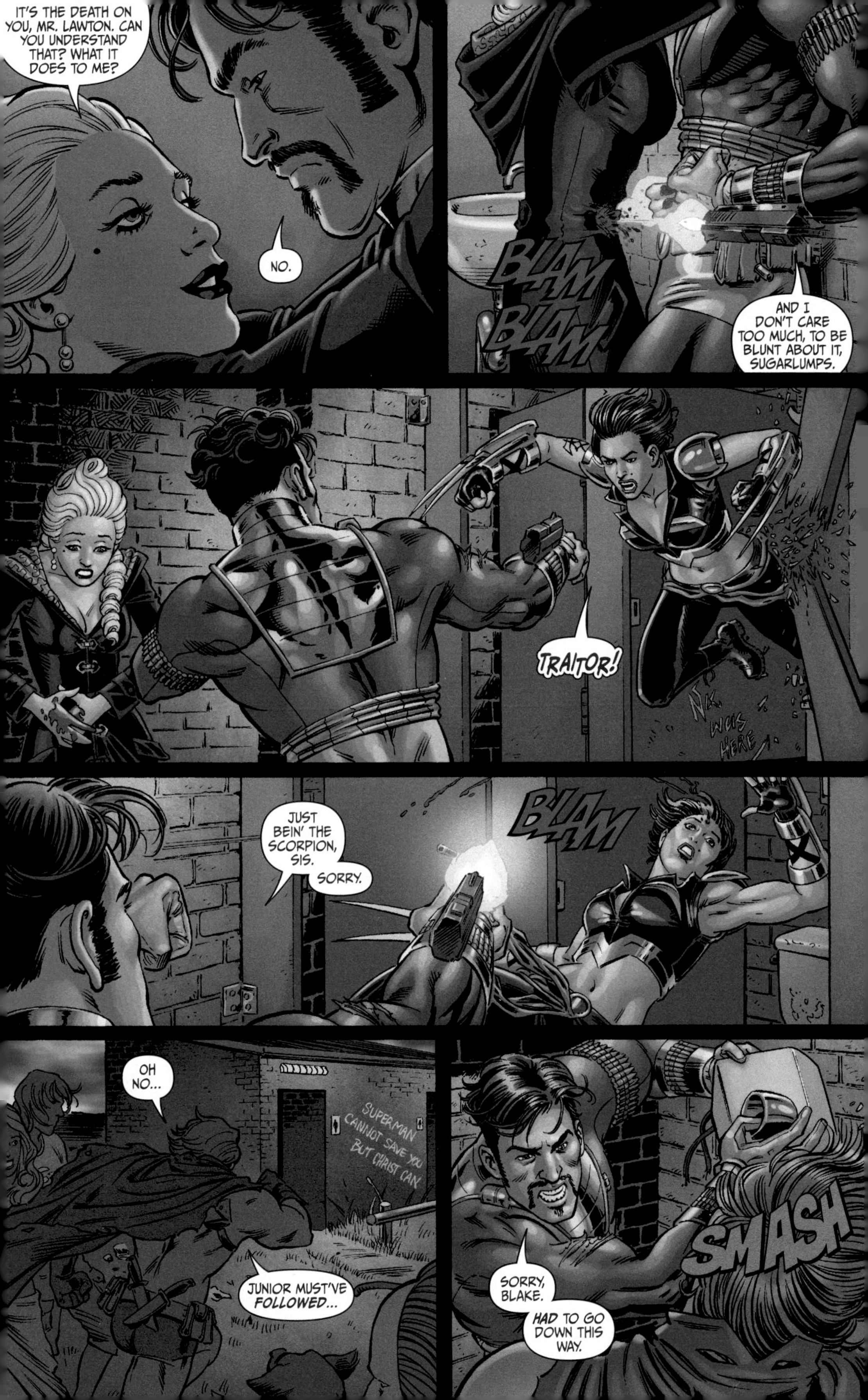
IT'S THE DEATH ON YOU, MR. LAWTON. CAN YOU UNDERSTAND THAT? WHAT IT DOES TO ME?
NO.
BLAM BLAM
AND I DON'T CARE TOO MUCH, TO BE BLUNT ABOUT IT, SUGARLUMPS.
TRAITOR!
NIK WUZ HERE
JUST BEIN' THE SCORPION, SIS.
SORRY.
BLAM
OH NO...
SUPERMAN CANNOT SAVE YOU BUT CHRIST CAN
JUNIOR MUST'VE FOLLOWED...
SORRY, BLAKE.
HAD TO GO DOWN THIS WAY.
SMASH

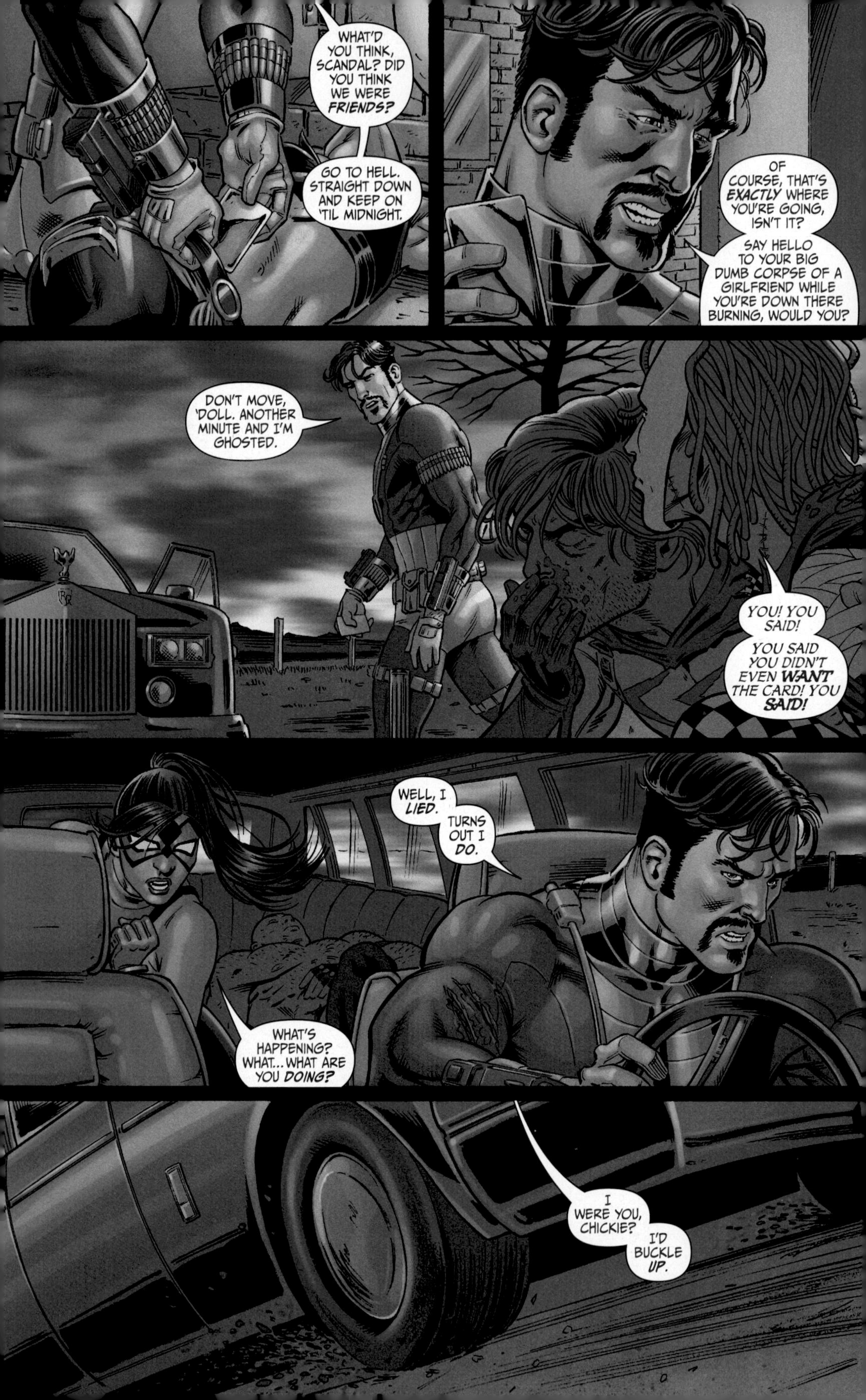
WHAT'D YOU THINK, SCANDAL? DID YOU THINK WE WERE FRIENDS?
GO TO HELL. STRAIGHT DOWN AND KEEP ON 'TIL MIDNIGHT.
OF COURSE, THAT'S EXACTLY WHERE YOU'RE GOING, ISN'T IT?
SAY HELLO TO YOUR BIG DUMB CORPSE OF A GIRLFRIEND WHILE YOU'RE DOWN THERE BURNING, WOULD YOU?
DON'T MOVE, 'DOLL. ANOTHER MINUTE AND I'M GHOSTED.
YOU! YOU SAID!
YOU SAID YOU DIDN'T EVEN WANT THE CARD! YOU SAID!
WELL, I LIED.
TURNS OUT I DO.
WHAT'S HAPPENING? WHAT... WHAT ARE YOU DOING?
I WERE YOU, CHICKIE?
I'D BUCKLE UP.

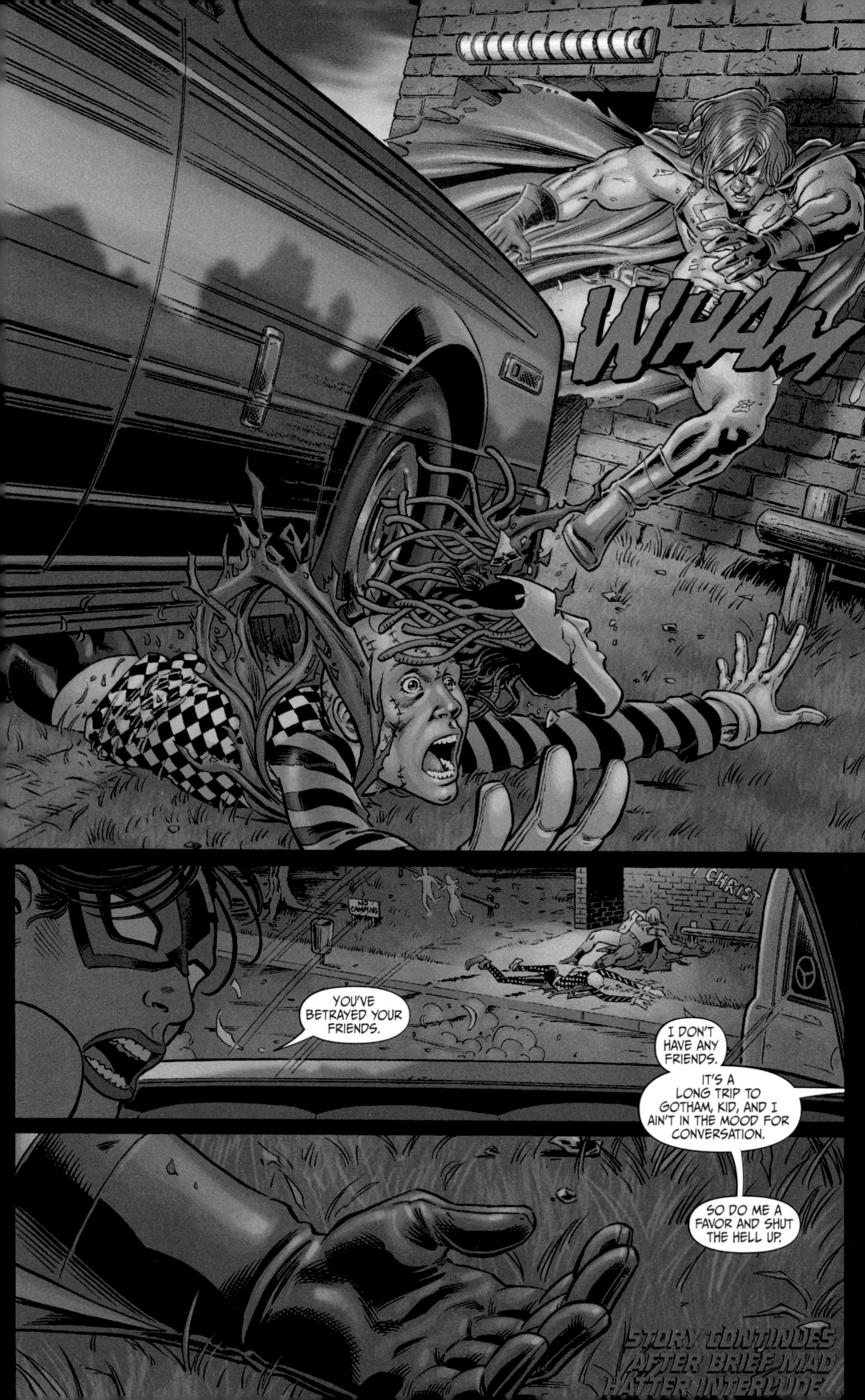
WHAM
NO CAMPING
CHRIST
YOU'VE BETRAYED YOUR FRIENDS.
I DON'T HAVE ANY FRIENDS.
IT'S A LONG TRIP TO GOTHAM, KID, AND I AIN'T IN THE MOOD FOR CONVERSATION.
SO DO ME A FAVOR AND SHUT THE HELL UP.
STORY CONTINUES AFTER BRIEF MAD HATTER INTERLUDE...

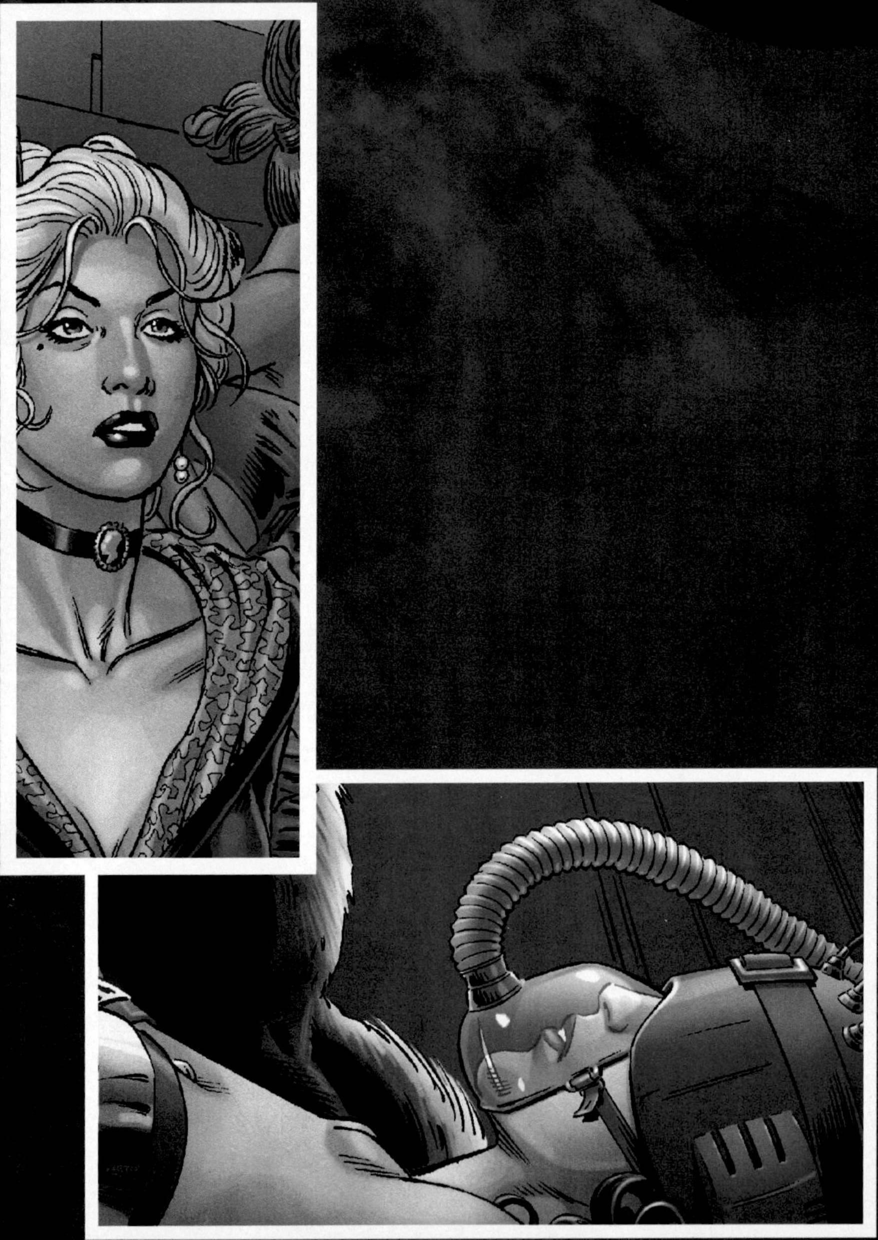

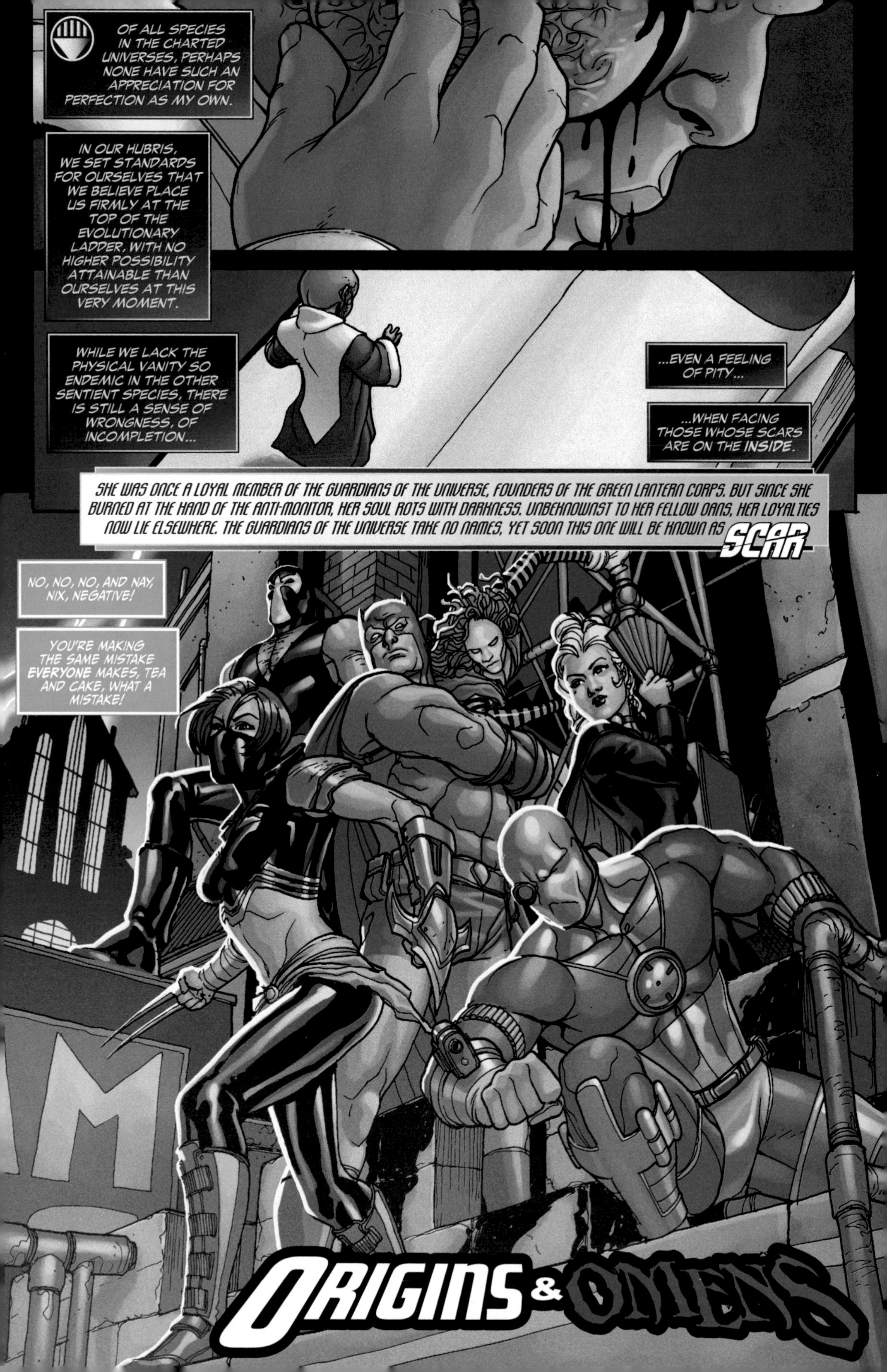
OF ALL SPECIES IN THE CHARTED UNIVERSES, PERHAPS NONE HAVE SUCH AN APPRECIATION FOR PERFECTION AS MY OWN.
IN OUR HUBRIS, WE SET STANDARDS FOR OURSELVES THAT WE BELIEVE PLACE US FIRMLY AT THE TOP OF THE EVOLUTIONARY LADDER, WITH NO HIGHER POSSIBILITY ATTAINABLE THAN OURSELVES AT THIS VERY MOMENT.
WHILE WE LACK THE PHYSICAL VANITY SO ENDEMIC IN THE OTHER SENTIENT SPECIES, THERE IS STILL A SENSE OF WRONGNESS, OF INCOMPLETION...
...EVEN A FEELING OF PITY...
...WHEN FACING THOSE WHOSE SCARS ARE ON THE INSIDE.
SHE WAS ONCE A LOYAL MEMBER OF THE GUARDIANS OF THE UNIVERSE, FOUNDERS OF THE GREEN LANTERN CORPS. BUT SINCE SHE BURNED AT THE HAND OF THE ANTI-MONITOR, HER SOUL ROTS WITH DARKNESS. UNBEKNOWNST TO HER FELLOW OANS, HER LOYALTIES NOW LIE ELSEWHERE. THE GUARDIANS OF THE UNIVERSE TAKE NO NAMES, YET SOON THIS ONE WILL BE KNOWN AS SCAR
NO, NO, NO, AND NAY, NIX, NEGATIVE!
YOU'RE MAKING THE SAME MISTAKE EVERYONE MAKES, TEA AND CAKE, WHAT A MISTAKE!
ORIGINS & OMENS

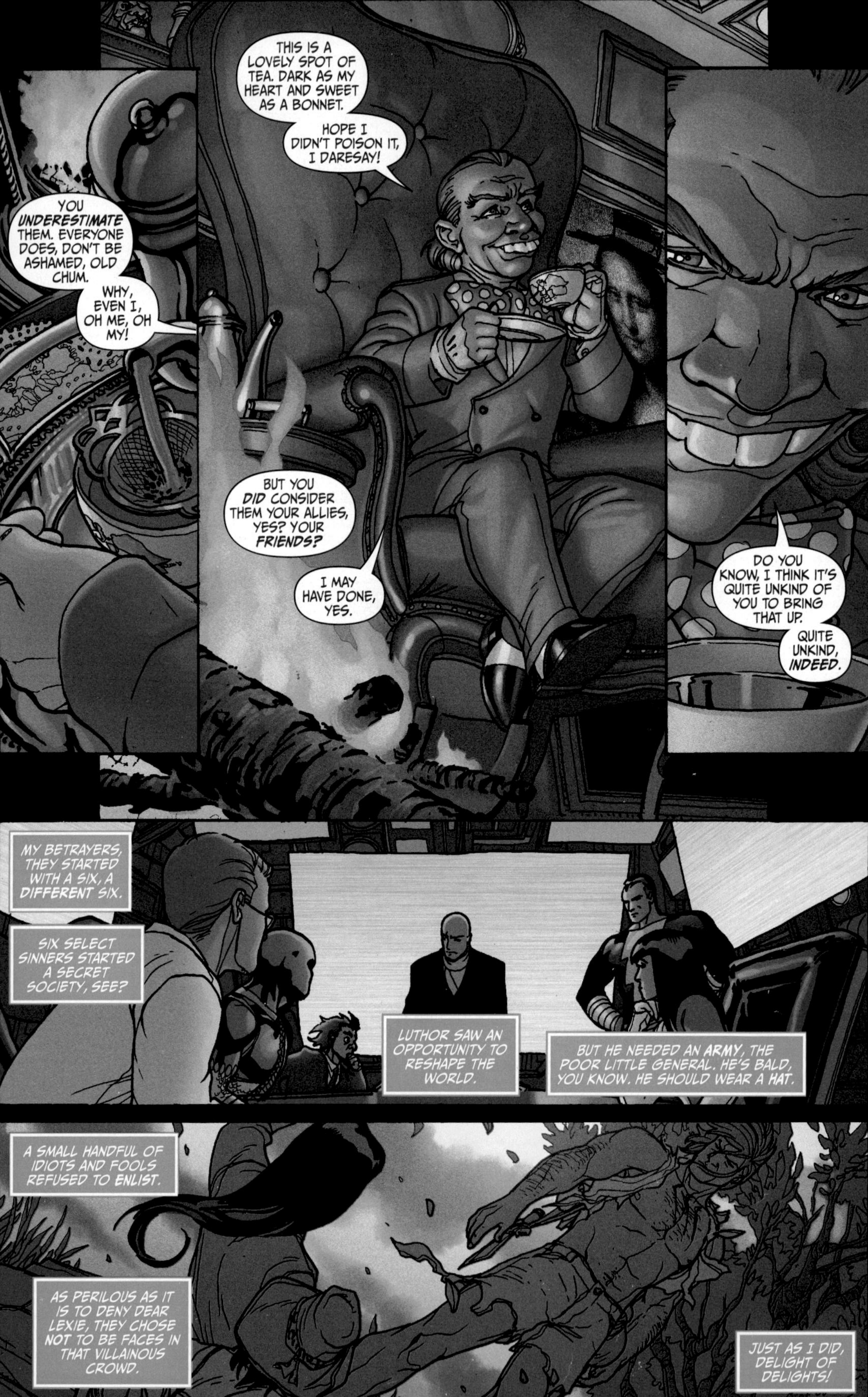
THIS IS A LOVELY SPOT OF TEA. DARK AS MY HEART AND SWEET AS A BONNET.
HOPE I DIDN'T POISON IT, I DARESAY!
YOU **UNDERESTIMATE** THEM. EVERYONE DOES, DON'T BE ASHAMED, OLD CHUM.
WHY, EVEN I, OH ME, OH MY!
BUT YOU **DID** CONSIDER THEM YOUR ALLIES, YES? YOUR **FRIENDS?**
I MAY HAVE DONE, YES.
DO YOU KNOW, I THINK IT'S QUITE UNKIND OF YOU TO BRING THAT UP.
QUITE UNKIND, **INDEED**.
MY BETRAYERS, THEY STARTED WITH A SIX, A **DIFFERENT** SIX.
SIX SELECT SINNERS STARTED A SECRET SOCIETY, SEE?
LUTHOR SAW AN OPPORTUNITY TO RESHAPE THE WORLD.
BUT HE NEEDED AN **ARMY**, THE POOR LITTLE GENERAL. HE'S BALD, YOU KNOW. HE SHOULD WEAR A **HAT**.
A SMALL HANDFUL OF IDIOTS AND FOOLS REFUSED TO **ENLIST**.
AS PERILOUS AS IT IS TO DENY DEAR LEXIE, THEY CHOSE **NOT** TO BE FACES IN THAT VILLAINOUS CROWD.
JUST AS I DID, DELIGHT OF DELIGHTS!

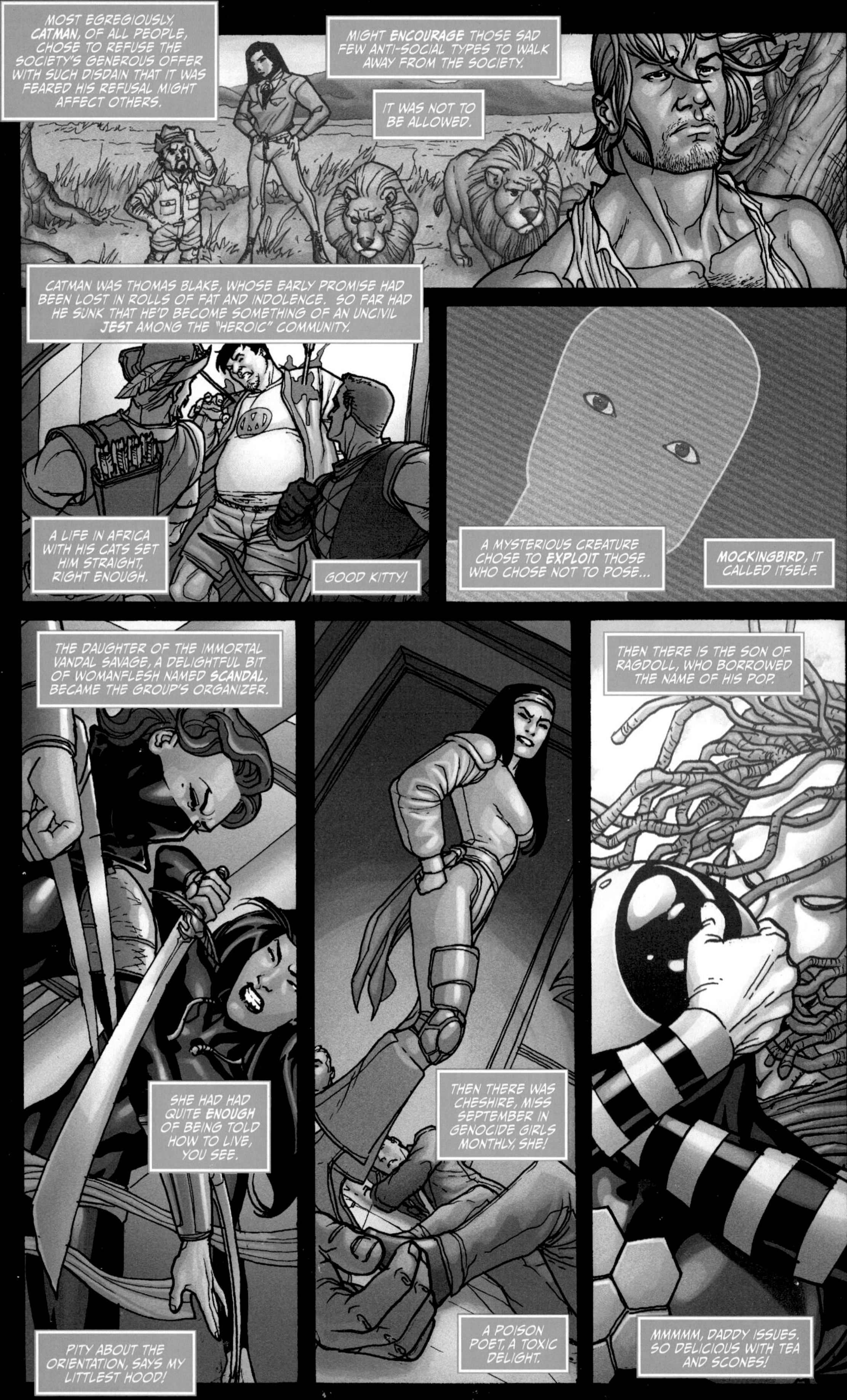
MOST EGREGIOUSLY, CATMAN, OF ALL PEOPLE, CHOSE TO REFUSE THE SOCIETY'S GENEROUS OFFER WITH SUCH DISDAIN THAT IT WAS FEARED HIS REFUSAL MIGHT AFFECT OTHERS.
MIGHT ENCOURAGE THOSE SAD FEW ANTI-SOCIAL TYPES TO WALK AWAY FROM THE SOCIETY.
IT WAS NOT TO BE ALLOWED.
CATMAN WAS THOMAS BLAKE, WHOSE EARLY PROMISE HAD BEEN LOST IN ROLLS OF FAT AND INDOLENCE. SO FAR HAD HE SUNK THAT HE'D BECOME SOMETHING OF AN UNCIVIL JEST AMONG THE "HEROIC" COMMUNITY.
A LIFE IN AFRICA WITH HIS CATS SET HIM STRAIGHT, RIGHT ENOUGH.
GOOD KITTY!
A MYSTERIOUS CREATURE CHOSE TO EXPLOIT THOSE WHO CHOSE NOT TO POSE...
MOCKINGBIRD, IT CALLED ITSELF.
THE DAUGHTER OF THE IMMORTAL VANDAL SAVAGE, A DELIGHTFUL BIT OF WOMANFLESH NAMED SCANDAL, BECAME THE GROUP'S ORGANIZER.
SHE HAD HAD QUITE ENOUGH OF BEING TOLD HOW TO LIVE, YOU SEE.
PITY ABOUT THE ORIENTATION, SAYS MY LITTLEST HOOD!
THEN THERE WAS CHESHIRE, MISS SEPTEMBER IN GENOCIDE GIRLS MONTHLY, SHE!
A POISON POET, A TOXIC DELIGHT.
THEN THERE IS THE SON OF RAGDOLL, WHO BORROWED THE NAME OF HIS POP.
MMMMM, DADDY ISSUES. SO DELICIOUS WITH TEA AND SCONES!

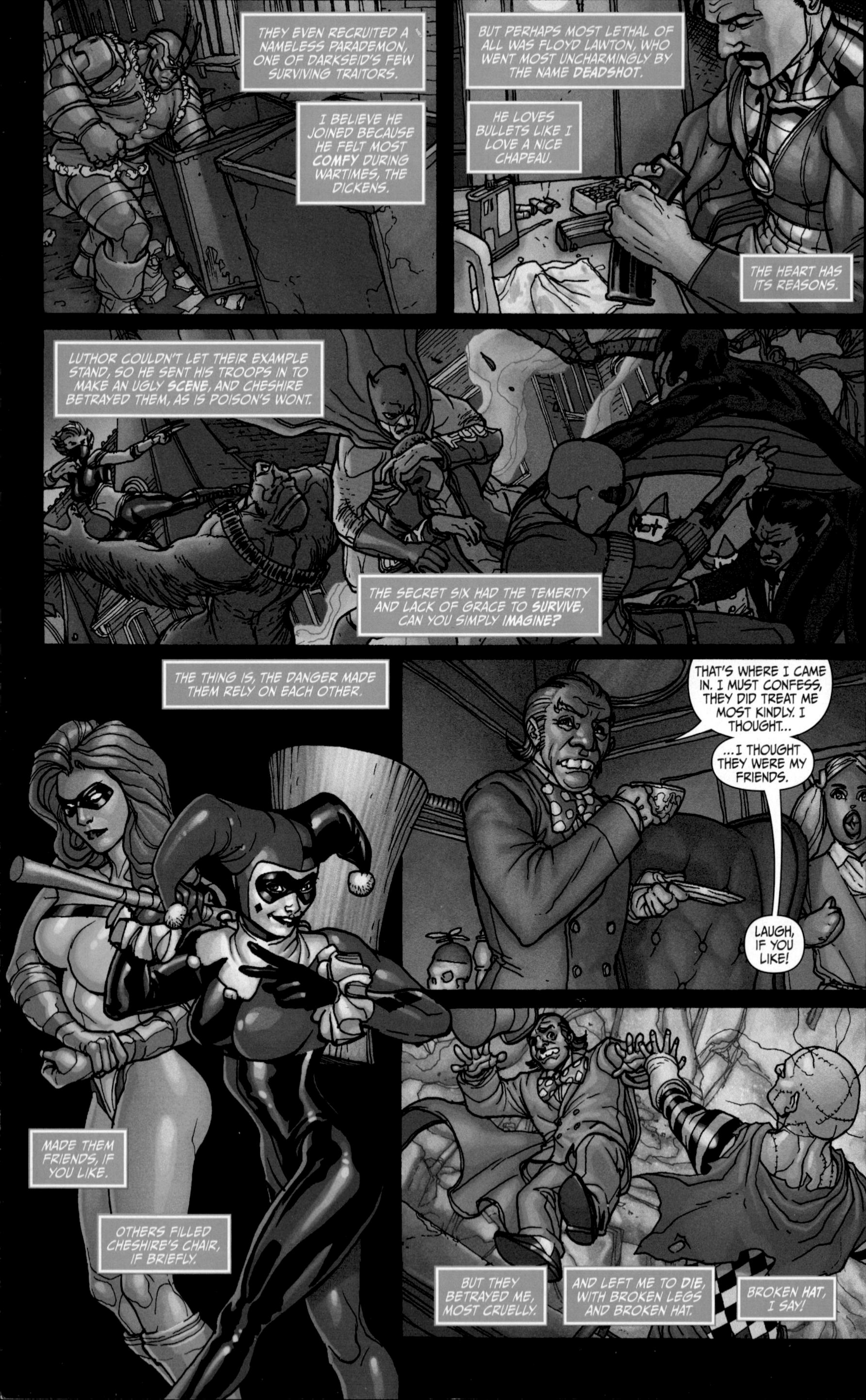
THEY EVEN RECRUITED A NAMELESS PARADEMON, ONE OF DARKSEID'S FEW SURVIVING TRAITORS.
I BELIEVE HE JOINED BECAUSE HE FELT MOST COMFY DURING WARTIMES, THE DICKENS.
BUT PERHAPS MOST LETHAL OF ALL WAS FLOYD LAWTON, WHO WENT MOST UNCHARMINGLY BY THE NAME DEADSHOT.
HE LOVES BULLETS LIKE I LOVE A NICE CHAPEAU.
THE HEART HAS ITS REASONS.
LUTHOR COULDN'T LET THEIR EXAMPLE STAND, SO HE SENT HIS TROOPS IN TO MAKE AN UGLY SCENE, AND CHESHIRE BETRAYED THEM, AS IS POISON'S WONT.
THE SECRET SIX HAD THE TEMERITY AND LACK OF GRACE TO SURVIVE, CAN YOU SIMPLY IMAGINE?
THE THING IS, THE DANGER MADE THEM RELY ON EACH OTHER.
MADE THEM FRIENDS, IF YOU LIKE.
OTHERS FILLED CHESHIRE'S CHAIR, IF BRIEFLY.
THAT'S WHERE I CAME IN. I MUST CONFESS, THEY DID TREAT ME MOST KINDLY. I THOUGHT...
...I THOUGHT THEY WERE MY FRIENDS.
LAUGH, IF YOU LIKE!
BUT THEY BETRAYED ME, MOST CRUELLY.
AND LEFT ME TO DIE, WITH BROKEN LEGS AND BROKEN HAT.
BROKEN HAT, I SAY!

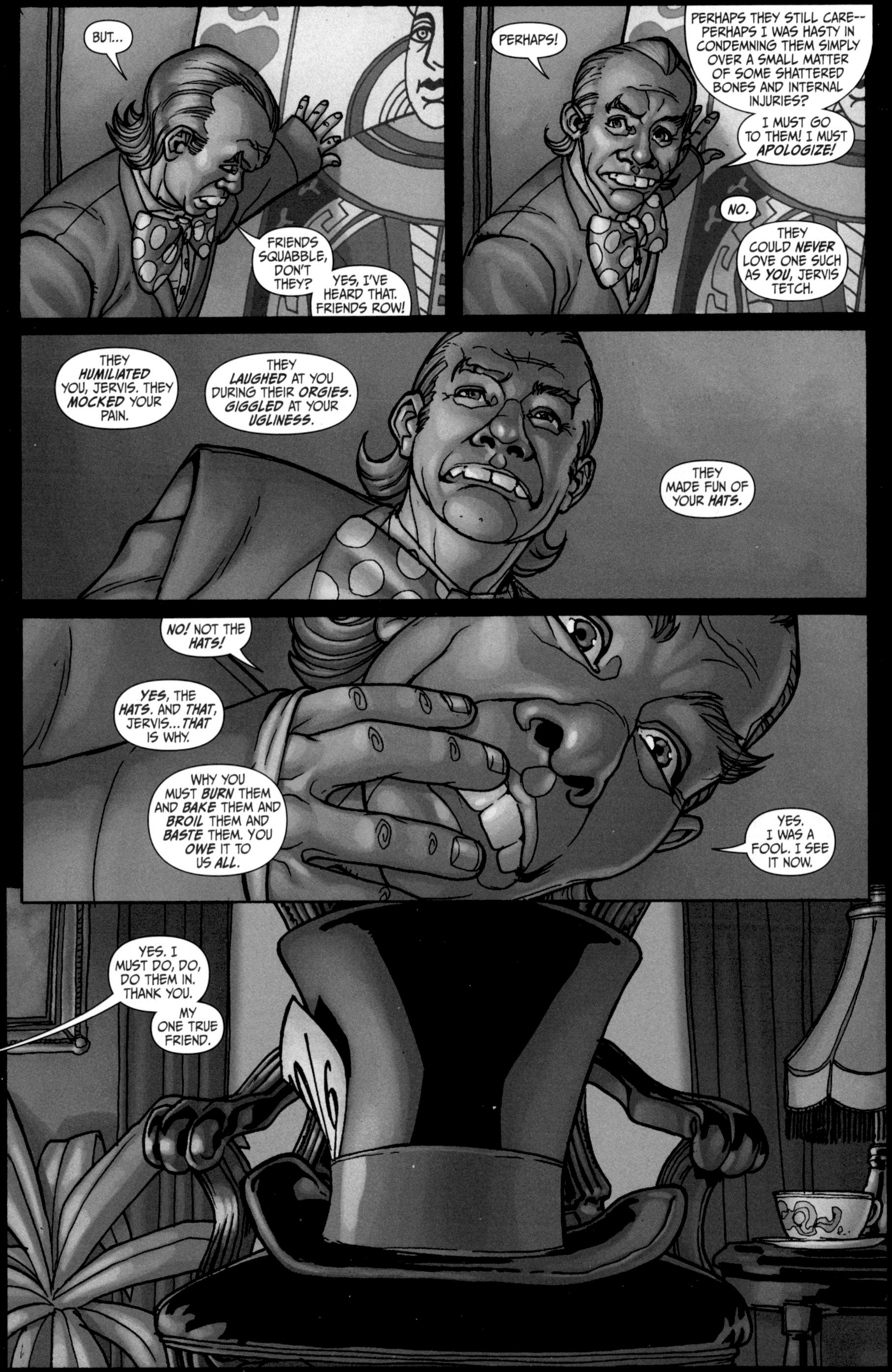
BUT...
FRIENDS SQUABBLE, DON'T THEY?
YES, I'VE HEARD THAT. FRIENDS ROW!
PERHAPS!
PERHAPS THEY STILL CARE-- PERHAPS I WAS HASTY IN CONDEMNING THEM SIMPLY OVER A SMALL MATTER OF SOME SHATTERED BONES AND INTERNAL INJURIES?
I MUST GO TO THEM! I MUST APOLOGIZE!
NO.
THEY COULD NEVER LOVE ONE SUCH AS YOU, JERVIS TETCH.
THEY HUMILIATED YOU, JERVIS. THEY MOCKED YOUR PAIN.
THEY LAUGHED AT YOU DURING THEIR ORGIES. GIGGLED AT YOUR UGLINESS.
THEY MADE FUN OF YOUR HATS.
NO! NOT THE HATS!
YES, THE HATS. AND THAT, JERVIS...THAT IS WHY.
WHY YOU MUST BURN THEM AND BAKE THEM AND BROIL THEM AND BASTE THEM. YOU OWE IT TO US ALL.
YES. I WAS A FOOL. I SEE IT NOW.
YES. I MUST DO, DO, DO THEM IN. THANK YOU.
MY ONE TRUE FRIEND.

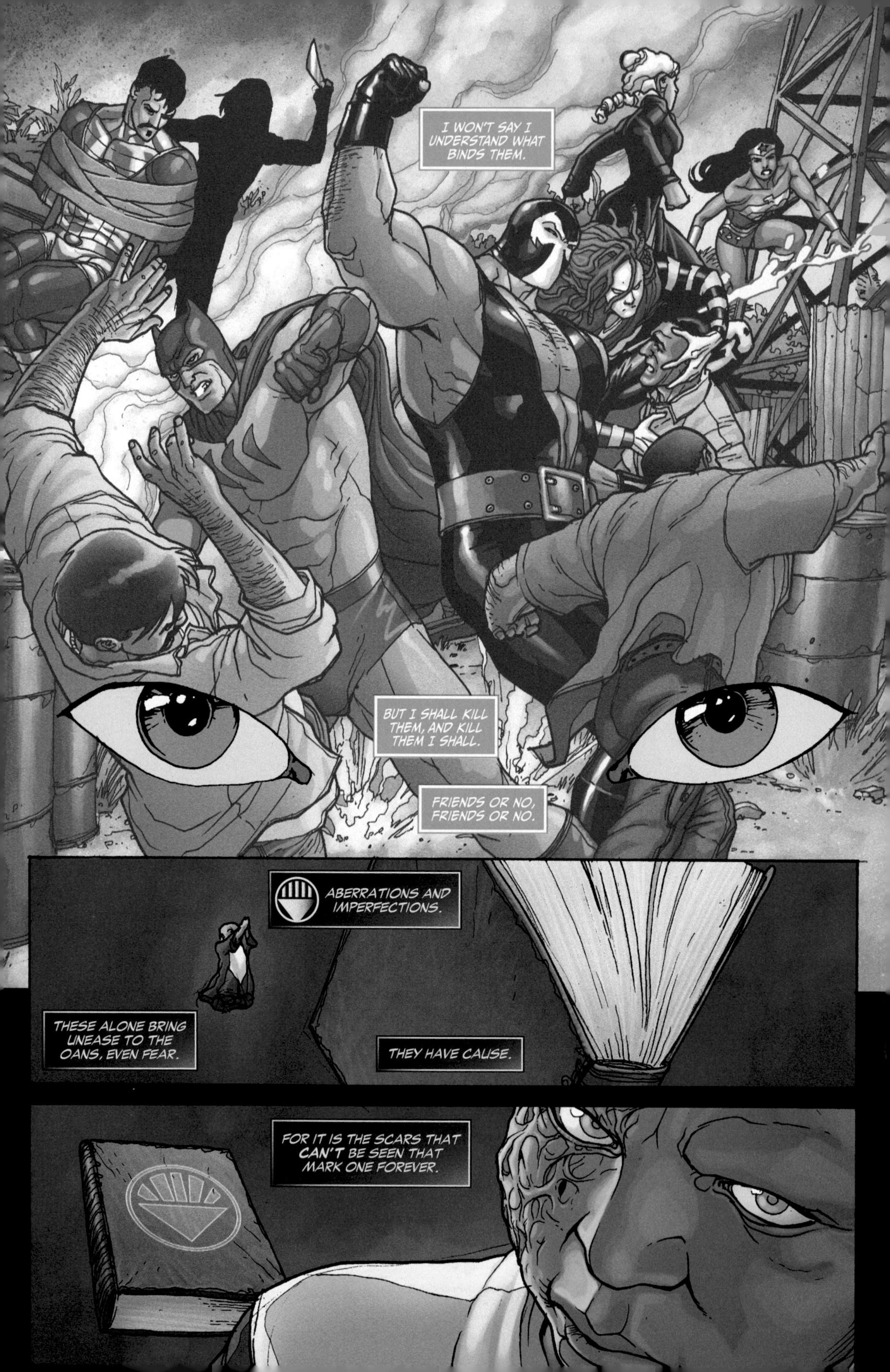
I WON'T SAY I UNDERSTAND WHAT BINDS THEM.
BUT I SHALL KILL THEM, AND KILL THEM I SHALL.
FRIENDS OR NO, FRIENDS OR NO.
ABERRATIONS AND IMPERFECTIONS.
THESE ALONE BRING UNEASE TO THE OANS, EVEN FEAR.
THEY HAVE CAUSE.
FOR IT IS THE SCARS THAT CAN'T BE SEEN THAT MARK ONE FOREVER.

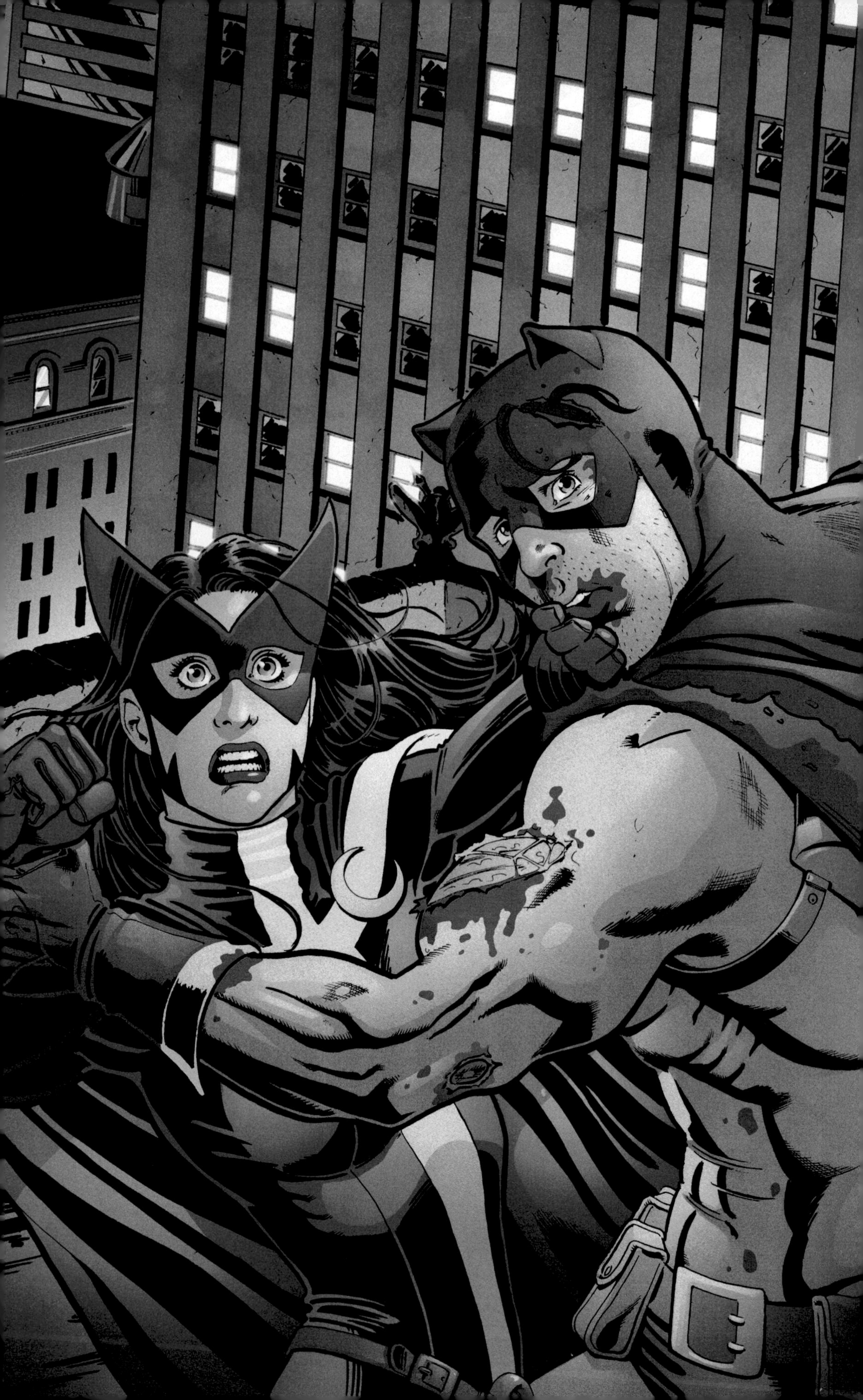

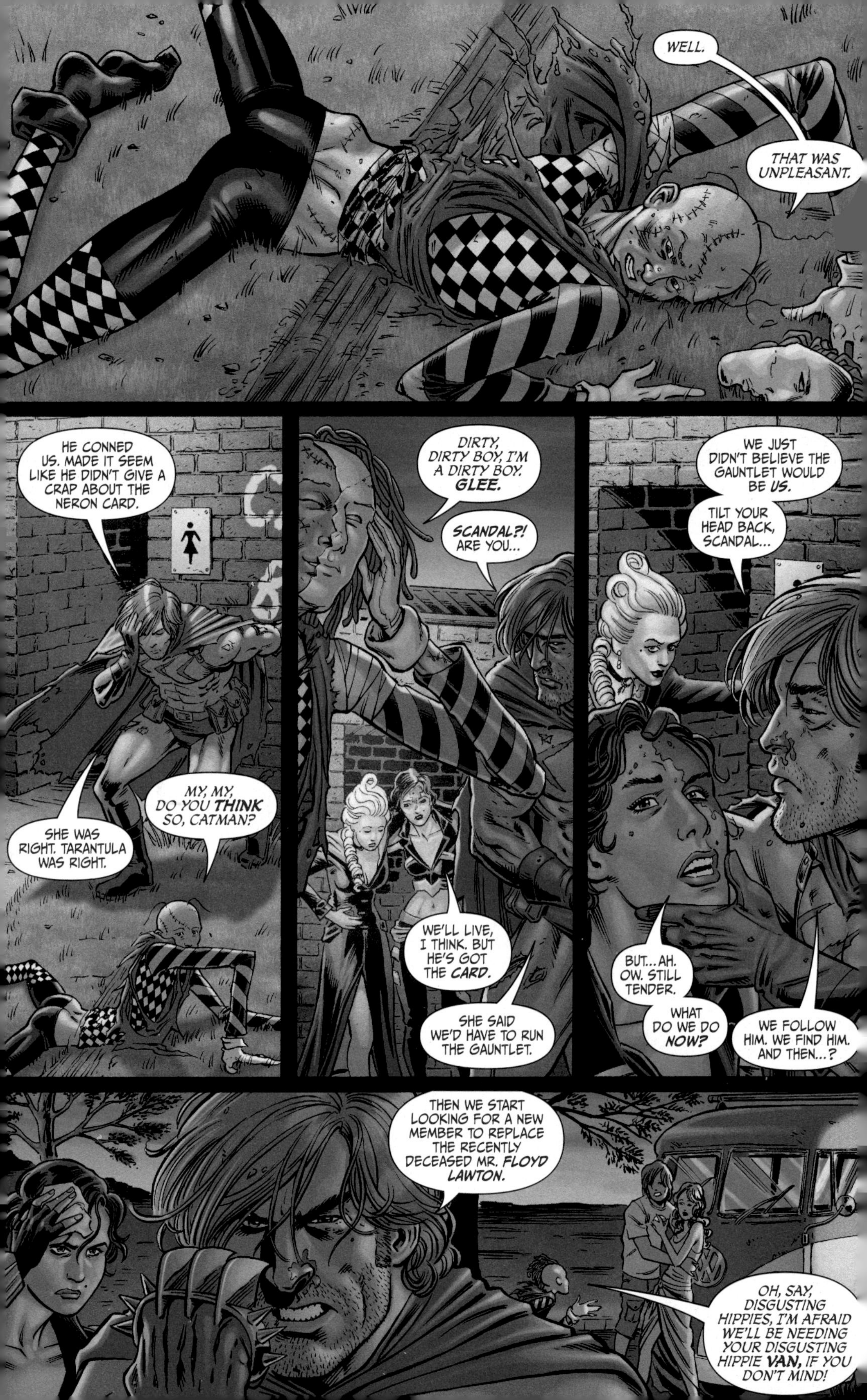
WELL.
THAT WAS UNPLEASANT.
HE CONNED US. MADE IT SEEM LIKE HE DIDN'T GIVE A CRAP ABOUT THE NERON CARD.
SHE WAS RIGHT. TARANTULA WAS RIGHT.
MY, MY, DO YOU THINK SO, CATMAN?
DIRTY, DIRTY BOY, I'M A DIRTY BOY. GLEE.
SCANDAL?! ARE YOU...
WE'LL LIVE, I THINK. BUT HE'S GOT THE CARD.
SHE SAID WE'D HAVE TO RUN THE GAUNTLET.
WE JUST DIDN'T BELIEVE THE GAUNTLET WOULD BE US.
TILT YOUR HEAD BACK, SCANDAL...
BUT...AH. OW. STILL TENDER.
WHAT DO WE DO NOW?
WE FOLLOW HIM. WE FIND HIM. AND THEN...?
THEN WE START LOOKING FOR A NEW MEMBER TO REPLACE THE RECENTLY DECEASED MR. FLOYD LAWTON.
OH, SAY, DISGUSTING HIPPIES, I'M AFRAID WE'LL BE NEEDING YOUR DISGUSTING HIPPIE VAN, IF YOU DON'T MIND!

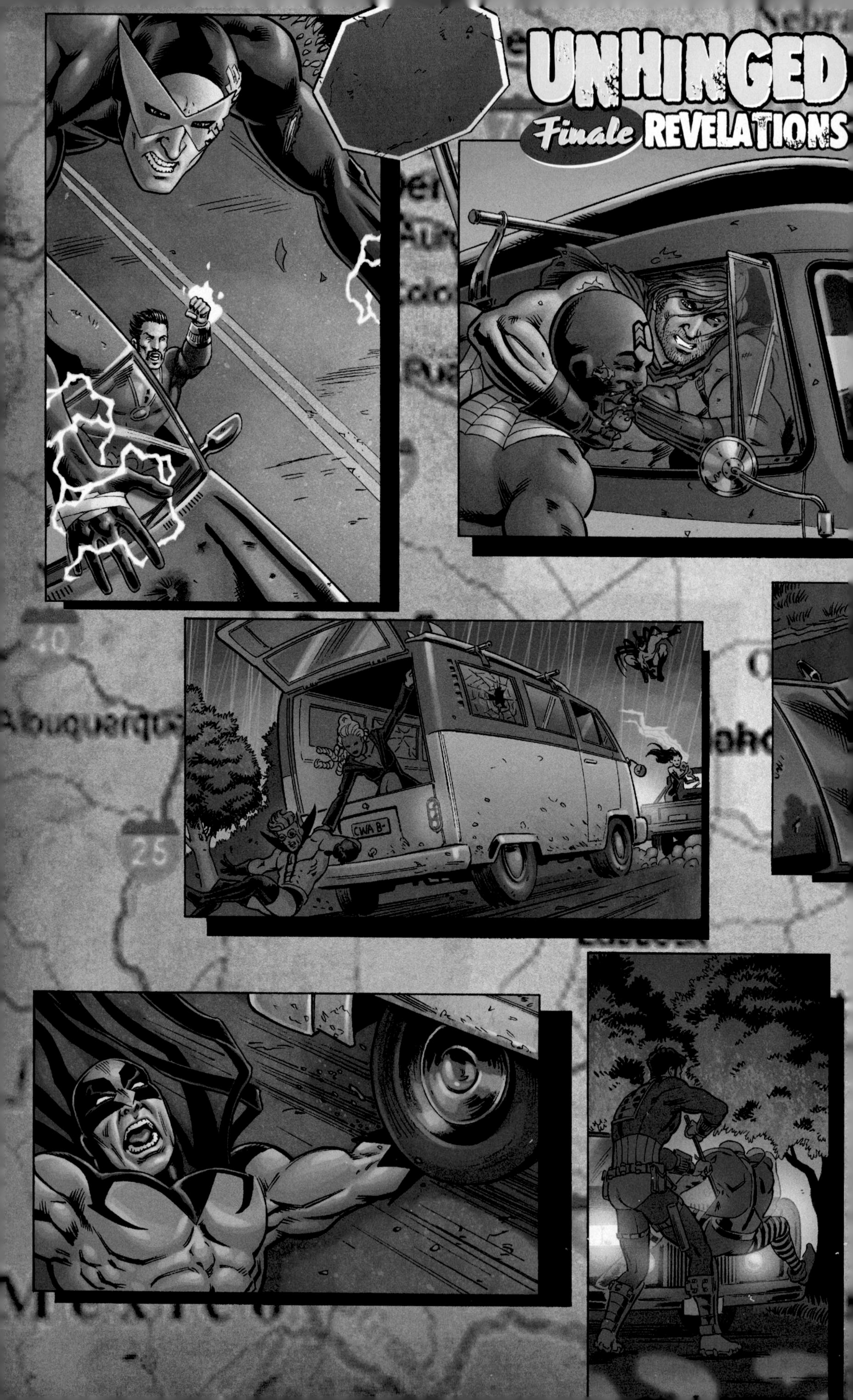
UNHINGED
Finale REVELATIONS

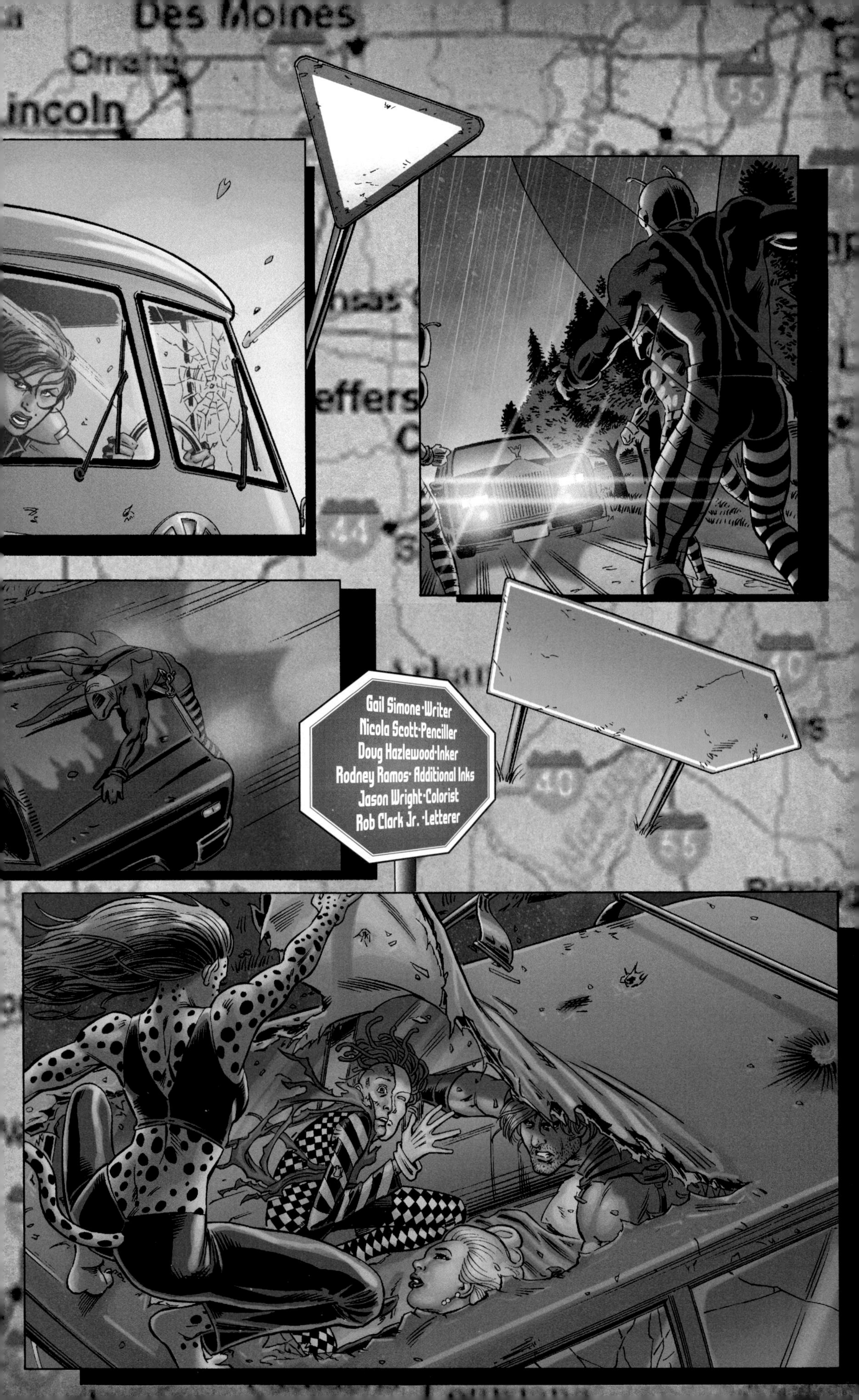
Des Moines
Gail Simone·Writer
Nicola Scott·Penciller
Doug Hazlewood·Inker
Rodney Ramos· Additional Inks
Jason Wright·Colorist
Rob Clark Jr. ·Letterer

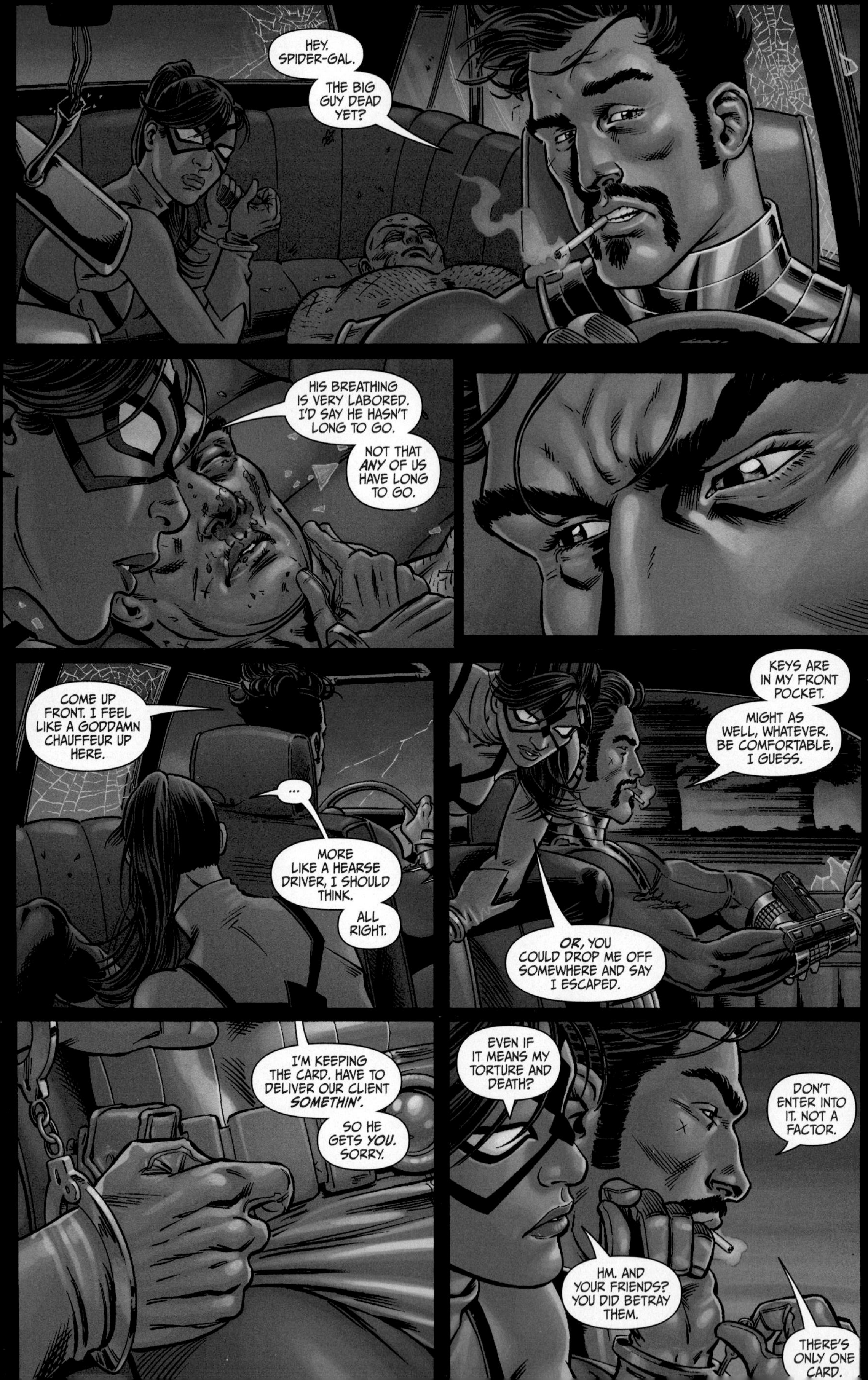
HEY. SPIDER-GAL.
THE BIG GUY DEAD YET?
HIS BREATHING IS VERY LABORED. I'D SAY HE HASN'T LONG TO GO.
NOT THAT ANY OF US HAVE LONG TO GO.
COME UP FRONT. I FEEL LIKE A GODDAMN CHAUFFEUR UP HERE.
...
MORE LIKE A HEARSE DRIVER, I SHOULD THINK.
ALL RIGHT.
KEYS ARE IN MY FRONT POCKET.
MIGHT AS WELL, WHATEVER. BE COMFORTABLE, I GUESS.
OR, YOU COULD DROP ME OFF SOMEWHERE AND SAY I ESCAPED.
I'M KEEPING THE CARD. HAVE TO DELIVER OUR CLIENT SOMETHIN'.
SO HE GETS YOU. SORRY.
EVEN IF IT MEANS MY TORTURE AND DEATH?
DON'T ENTER INTO IT. NOT A FACTOR.
HM. AND YOUR FRIENDS? YOU DID BETRAY THEM.
THERE'S ONLY ONE CARD.

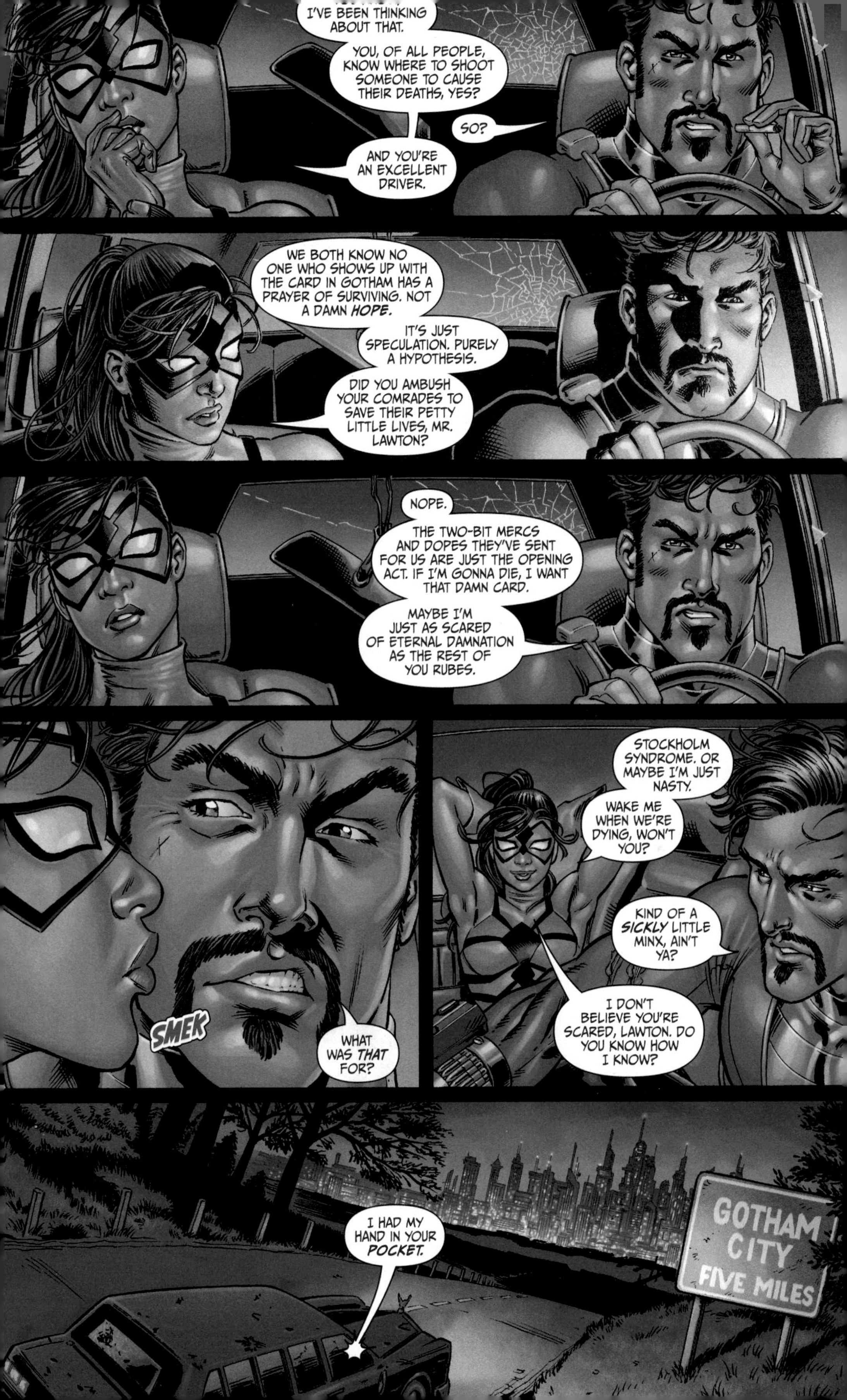
I'VE BEEN THINKING ABOUT THAT.
YOU, OF ALL PEOPLE, KNOW WHERE TO SHOOT SOMEONE TO CAUSE THEIR DEATHS, YES?
SO?
AND YOU'RE AN EXCELLENT DRIVER.
WE BOTH KNOW NO ONE WHO SHOWS UP WITH THE CARD IN GOTHAM HAS A PRAYER OF SURVIVING. NOT A DAMN HOPE.
IT'S JUST SPECULATION. PURELY A HYPOTHESIS.
DID YOU AMBUSH YOUR COMRADES TO SAVE THEIR PETTY LITTLE LIVES, MR. LAWTON?
NOPE.
THE TWO-BIT MERCS AND DOPES THEY'VE SENT FOR US ARE JUST THE OPENING ACT. IF I'M GONNA DIE, I WANT THAT DAMN CARD.
MAYBE I'M JUST AS SCARED OF ETERNAL DAMNATION AS THE REST OF YOU RUBES.
SMEK
WHAT WAS THAT FOR?
I DON'T BELIEVE YOU'RE SCARED, LAWTON. DO YOU KNOW HOW I KNOW?
STOCKHOLM SYNDROME. OR MAYBE I'M JUST NASTY.
WAKE ME WHEN WE'RE DYING, WON'T YOU?
KIND OF A SICKLY LITTLE MINX, AIN'T YA?
I HAD MY HAND IN YOUR POCKET.
GOTHAM CITY FIVE MILES

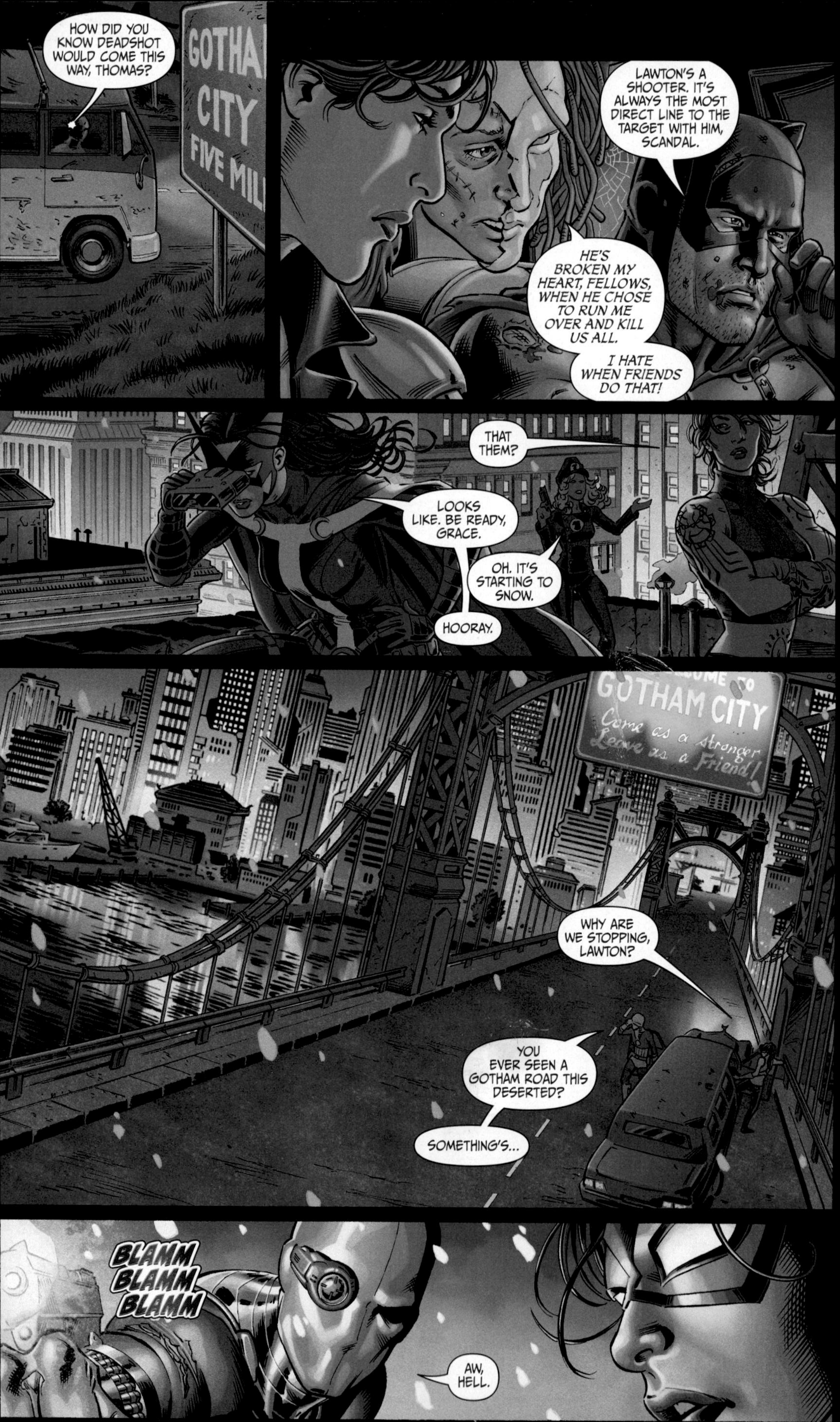
HOW DID YOU KNOW DEADSHOT WOULD COME THIS WAY, THOMAS?
GOTHAM CITY FIVE MIL
LAWTON'S A SHOOTER. IT'S ALWAYS THE MOST DIRECT LINE TO THE TARGET WITH HIM, SCANDAL.
HE'S BROKEN MY HEART, FELLOWS, WHEN HE CHOSE TO RUN ME OVER AND KILL US ALL.
I HATE WHEN FRIENDS DO THAT!
THAT THEM?
LOOKS LIKE. BE READY, GRACE.
OH. IT'S STARTING TO SNOW.
HOORAY.
GOTHAM CITY
Come as a stranger
Leave as a Friend!
WHY ARE WE STOPPING, LAWTON?
YOU EVER SEEN A GOTHAM ROAD THIS DESERTED?
SOMETHING'S...
BLAMM BLAMM BLAMM
AW, HELL.

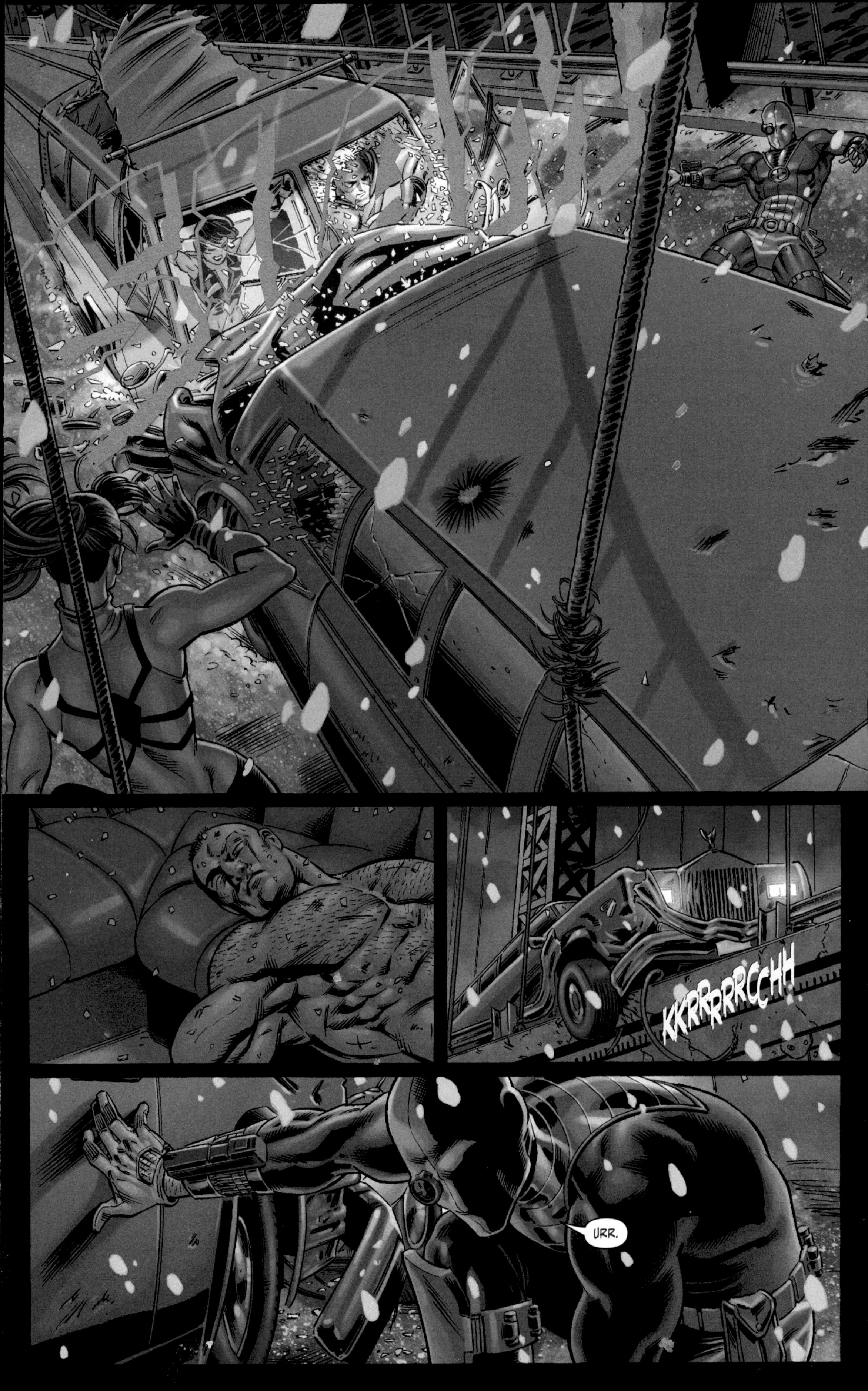
KKRRRRRCCHH
URR.

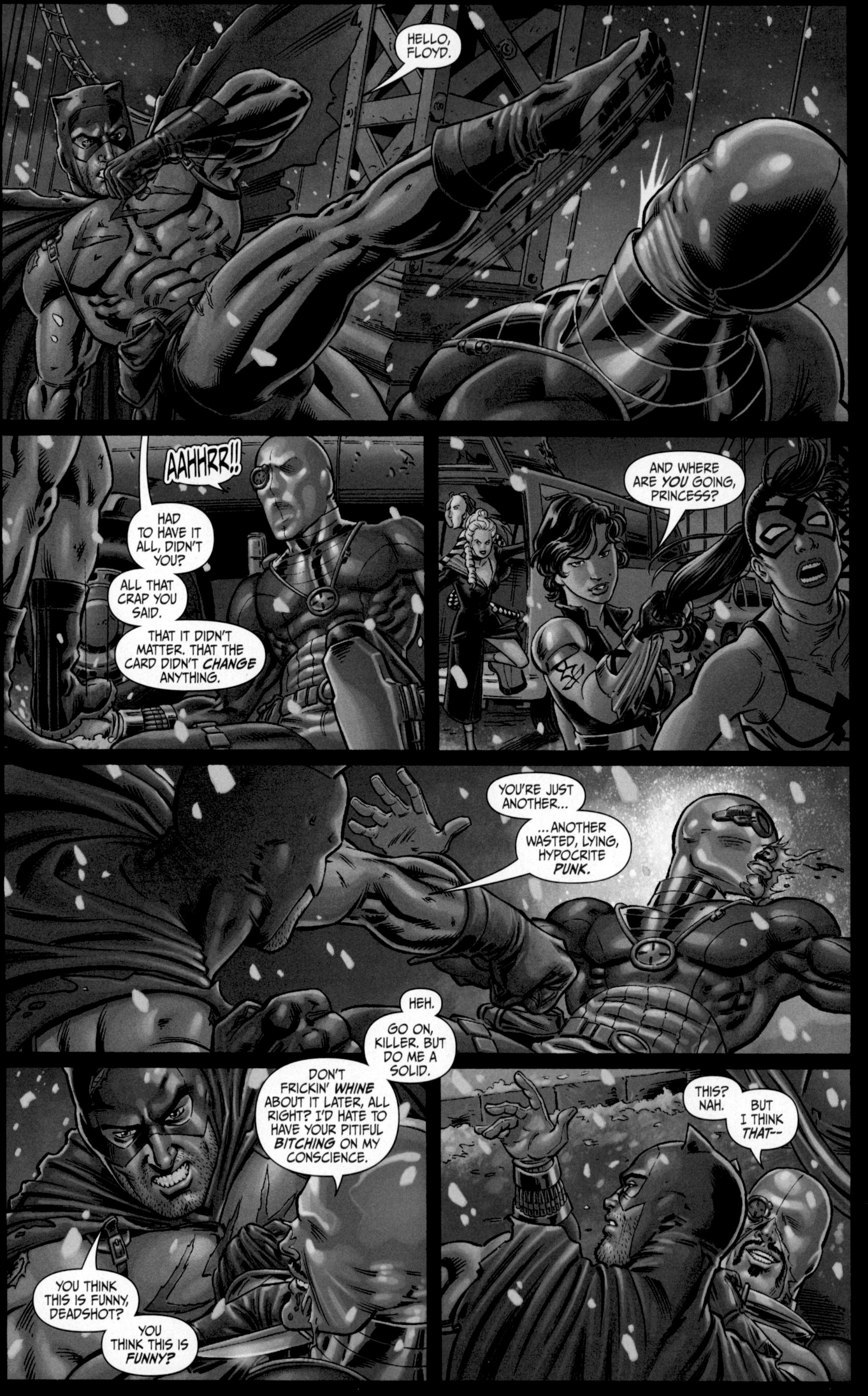
HELLO, FLOYD.
AAHHRR!!
HAD TO HAVE IT ALL, DIDN'T YOU?
ALL THAT CRAP YOU SAID.
THAT IT DIDN'T MATTER. THAT THE CARD DIDN'T CHANGE ANYTHING.
AND WHERE ARE YOU GOING, PRINCESS?
YOU'RE JUST ANOTHER...
...ANOTHER WASTED, LYING, HYPOCRITE PUNK.
HEH.
GO ON, KILLER. BUT DO ME A SOLID.
DON'T FRICKIN' WHINE ABOUT IT LATER, ALL RIGHT? I'D HATE TO HAVE YOUR PITIFUL BITCHING ON MY CONSCIENCE.
YOU THINK THIS IS FUNNY, DEADSHOT?
YOU THINK THIS IS FUNNY?
THIS? NAH.
BUT I THINK THAT--

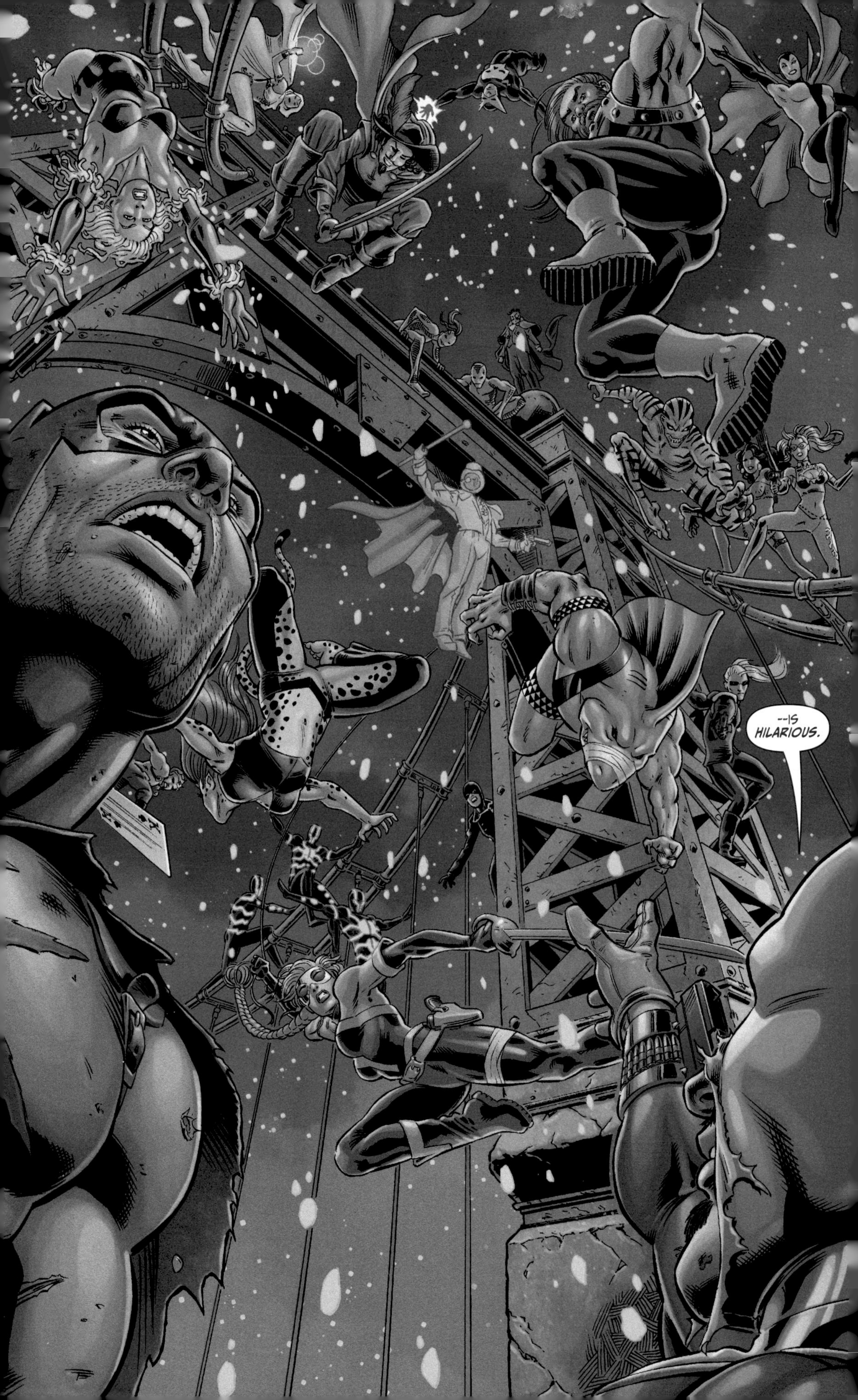
--IS HILARIOUS.

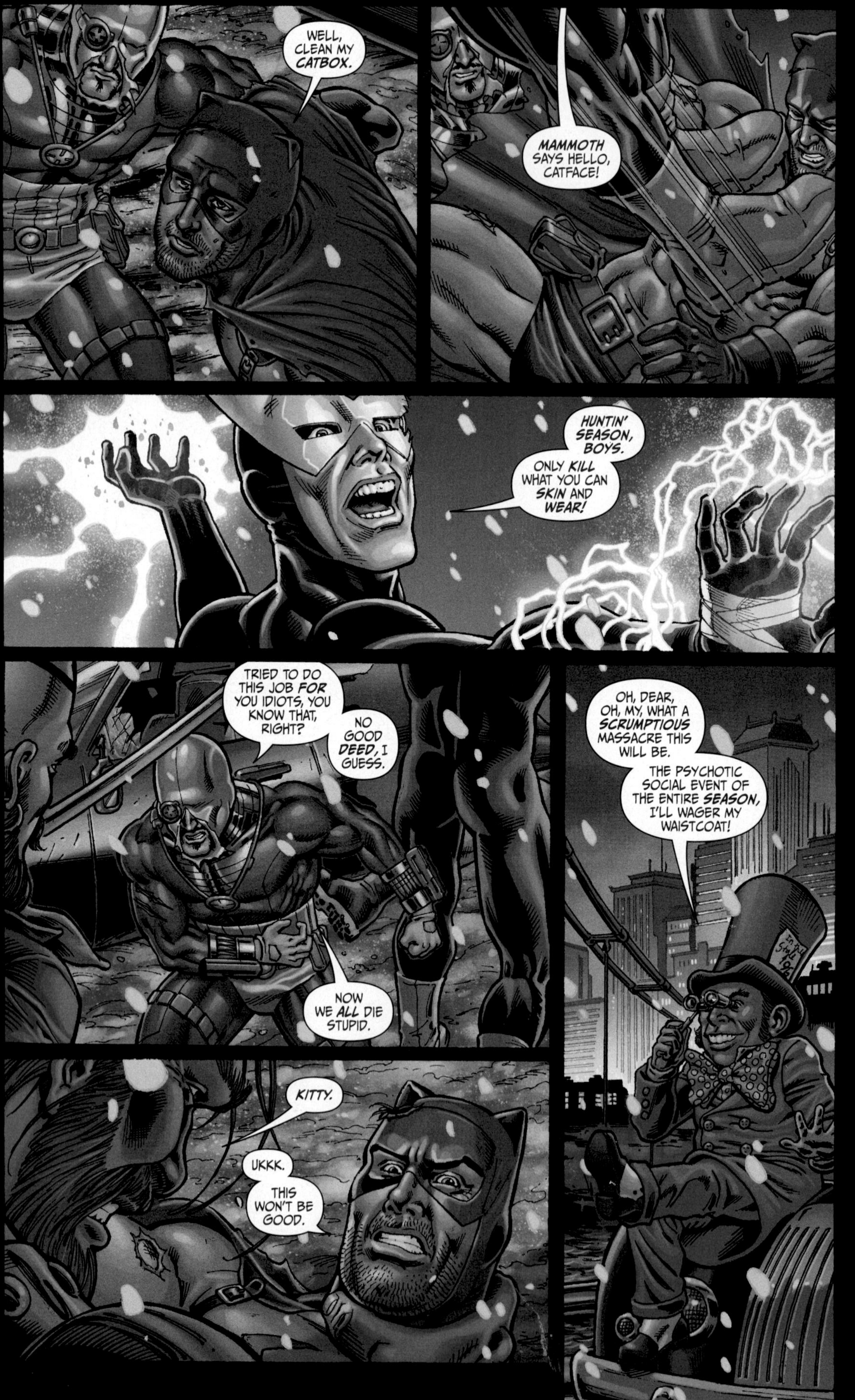
WELL, CLEAN MY *CATBOX.*
MAMMOTH SAYS HELLO, CATFACE!
HUNTIN' SEASON, BOYS.
ONLY *KILL* WHAT YOU CAN *SKIN* AND *WEAR!*
TRIED TO DO THIS JOB *FOR* YOU IDIOTS, YOU KNOW THAT, RIGHT?
NO GOOD *DEED,* I GUESS.
NOW WE *ALL* DIE STUPID.
OH, DEAR, OH, MY, WHAT A *SCRUMPTIOUS* MASSACRE THIS WILL BE.
THE PSYCHOTIC SOCIAL EVENT OF THE ENTIRE *SEASON,* I'LL WAGER MY WAISTCOAT!
KITTY.
UKKK.
THIS WON'T BE GOOD.

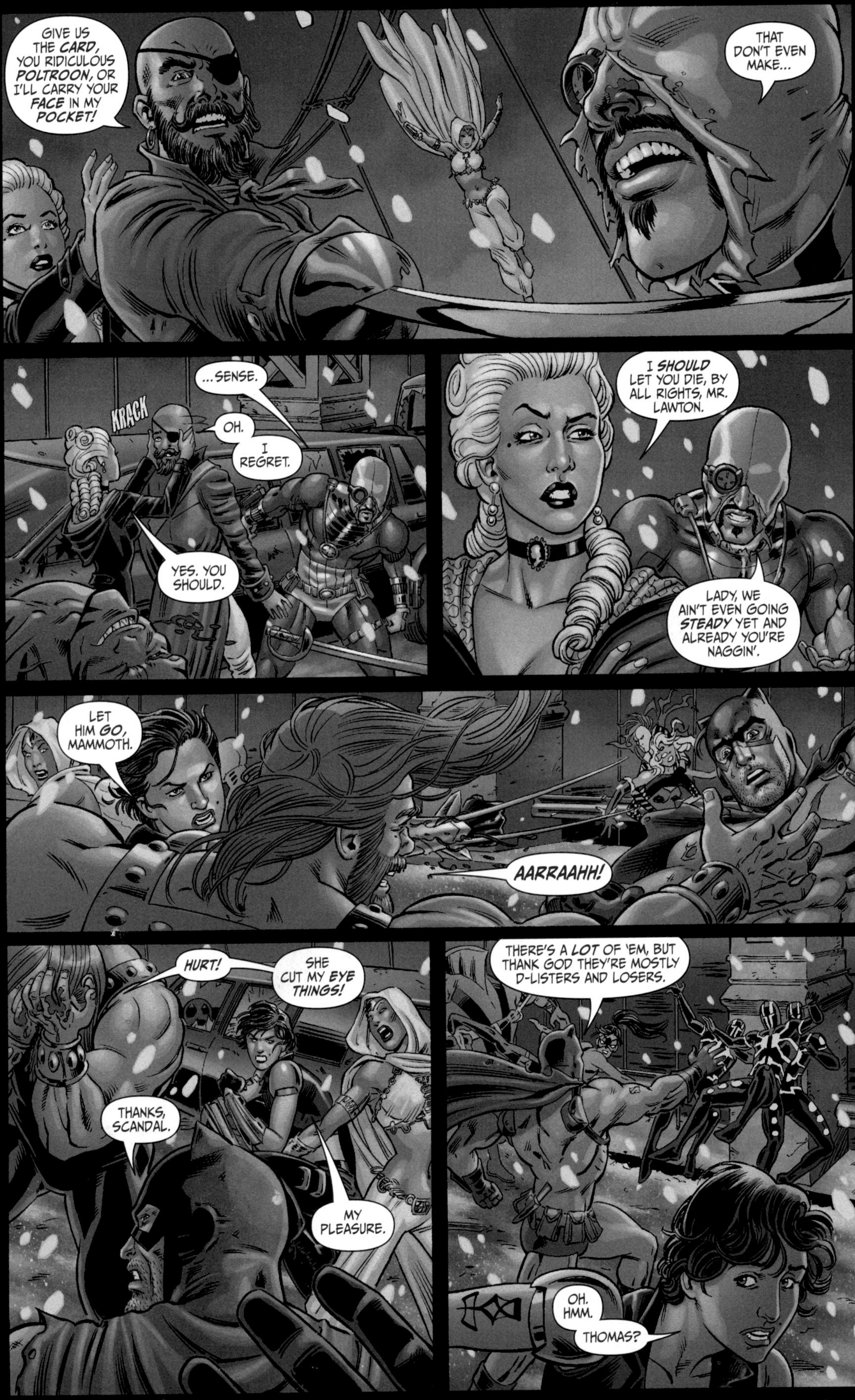
GIVE US THE CARD, YOU RIDICULOUS POLTROON, OR I'LL CARRY YOUR FACE IN MY POCKET!
THAT DON'T EVEN MAKE...
...SENSE.
KRACK
OH.
I REGRET.
YES. YOU SHOULD.
I SHOULD LET YOU DIE, BY ALL RIGHTS, MR. LAWTON.
LADY, WE AIN'T EVEN GOING STEADY YET AND ALREADY YOU'RE NAGGIN'.
LET HIM GO, MAMMOTH.
AARRAAHH!
HURT!
SHE CUT MY EYE THINGS!
THANKS, SCANDAL.
MY PLEASURE.
THERE'S A LOT OF 'EM, BUT THANK GOD THEY'RE MOSTLY D-LISTERS AND LOSERS.
OH. HMM.
THOMAS?

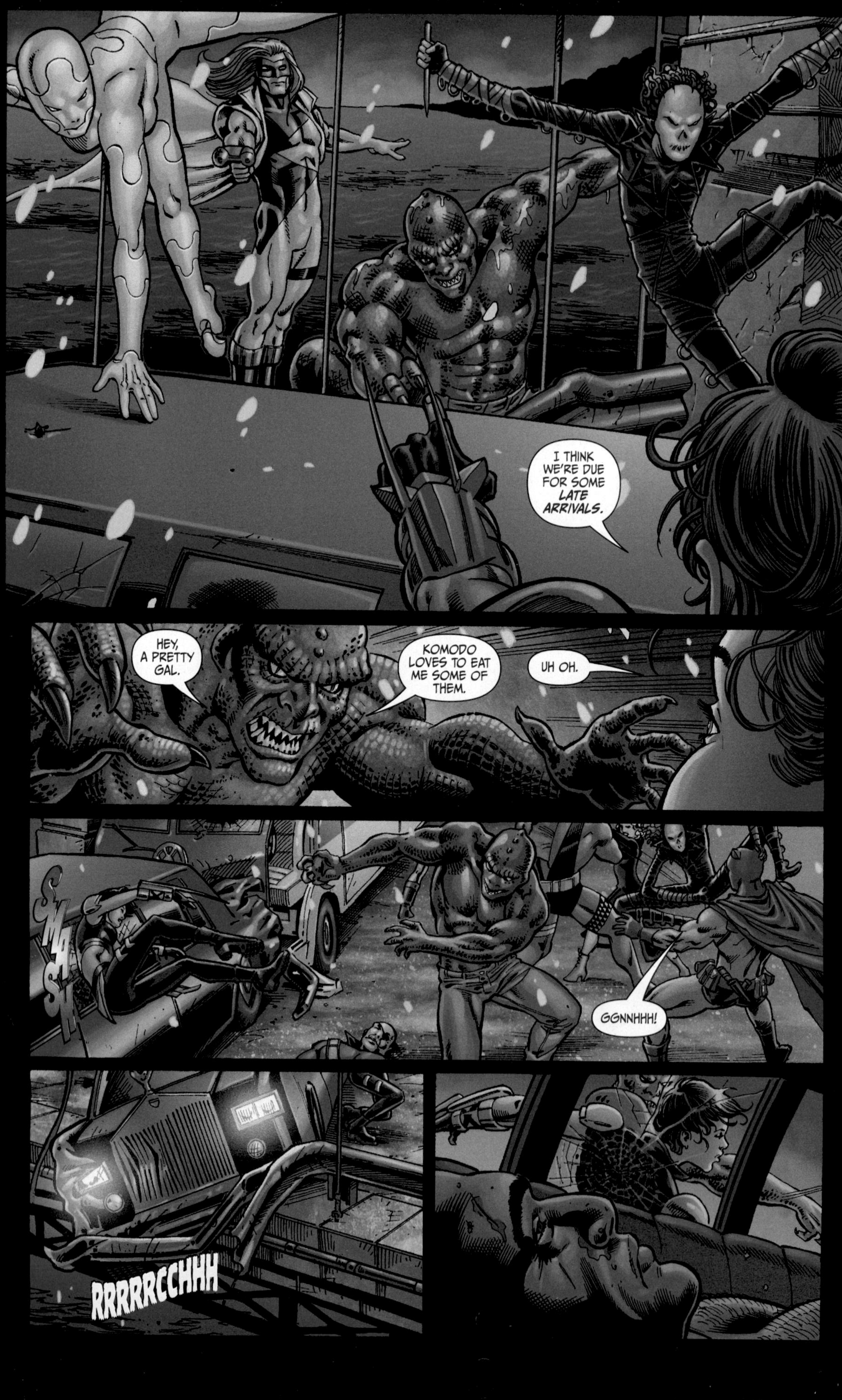
I THINK WE'RE DUE FOR SOME *LATE ARRIVALS.*
HEY, A PRETTY GAL.
KOMODO LOVES TO EAT ME SOME OF THEM.
UH OH.
SMASH
GGNNHHH!
RRRRRCCHHH

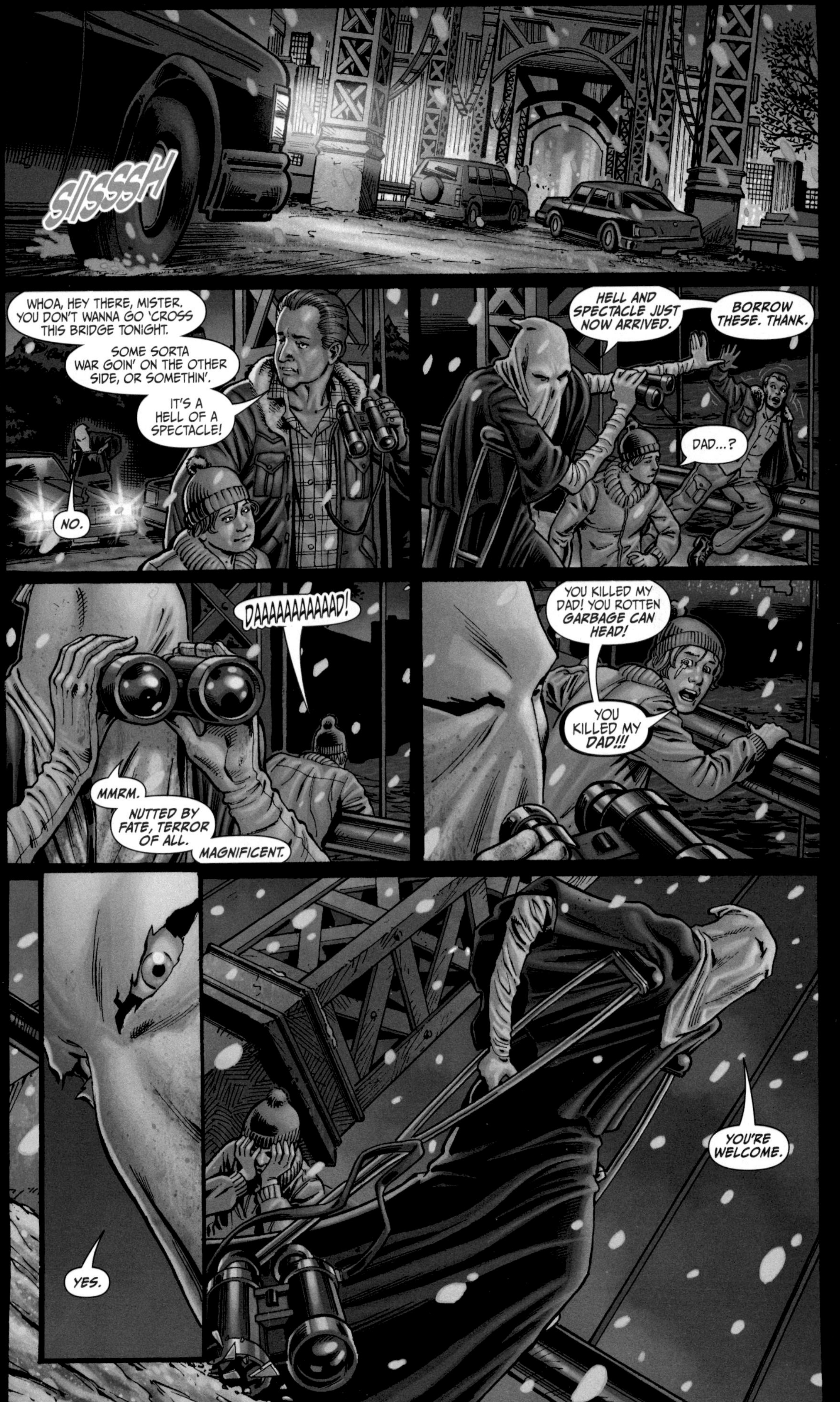
SIIISSSH
WHOA, HEY THERE, MISTER. YOU DON'T WANNA GO 'CROSS THIS BRIDGE TONIGHT.
SOME SORTA WAR GOIN' ON THE OTHER SIDE, OR SOMETHIN'.
IT'S A HELL OF A SPECTACLE!
NO.
HELL AND SPECTACLE JUST NOW ARRIVED.
BORROW THESE. THANK.
DAD...?
DAAAAAAAAAAAD!
MMRM.
NUTTED BY FATE, TERROR OF ALL.
MAGNIFICENT.
YOU KILLED MY DAD! YOU ROTTEN GARBAGE CAN HEAD!
YOU KILLED MY DAD!!!
YOU'RE WELCOME.
YES.

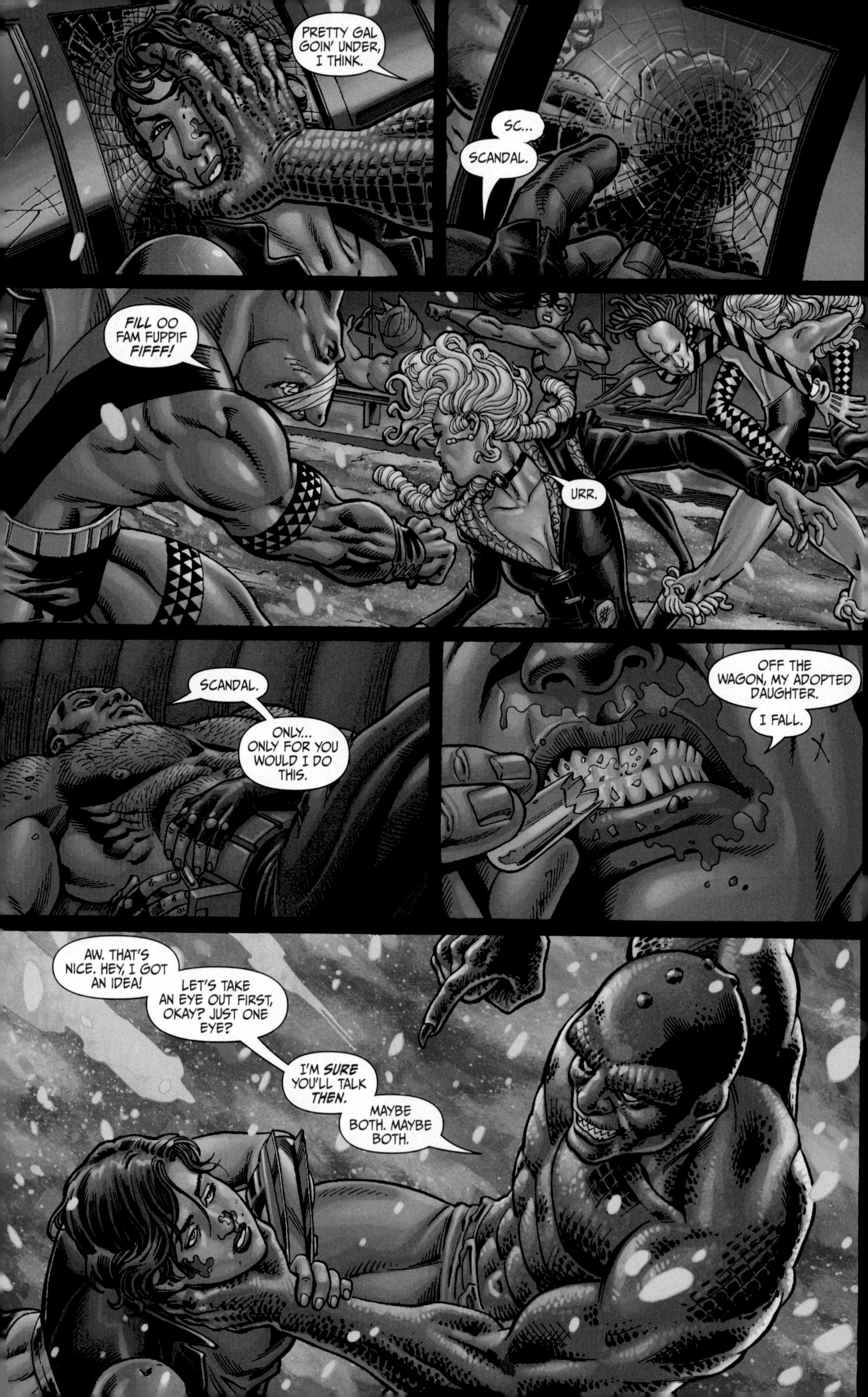
PRETTY GAL GOIN' UNDER, I THINK.
SC...
SCANDAL.
FILL OO FAM FUPPIF FIFFF!
URR.
SCANDAL.
ONLY... ONLY FOR YOU WOULD I DO THIS.
OFF THE WAGON, MY ADOPTED DAUGHTER.
I FALL.
AW. THAT'S NICE. HEY, I GOT AN IDEA!
LET'S TAKE AN EYE OUT FIRST, OKAY? JUST ONE EYE?
I'M SURE YOU'LL TALK THEN.
MAYBE BOTH. MAYBE BOTH.

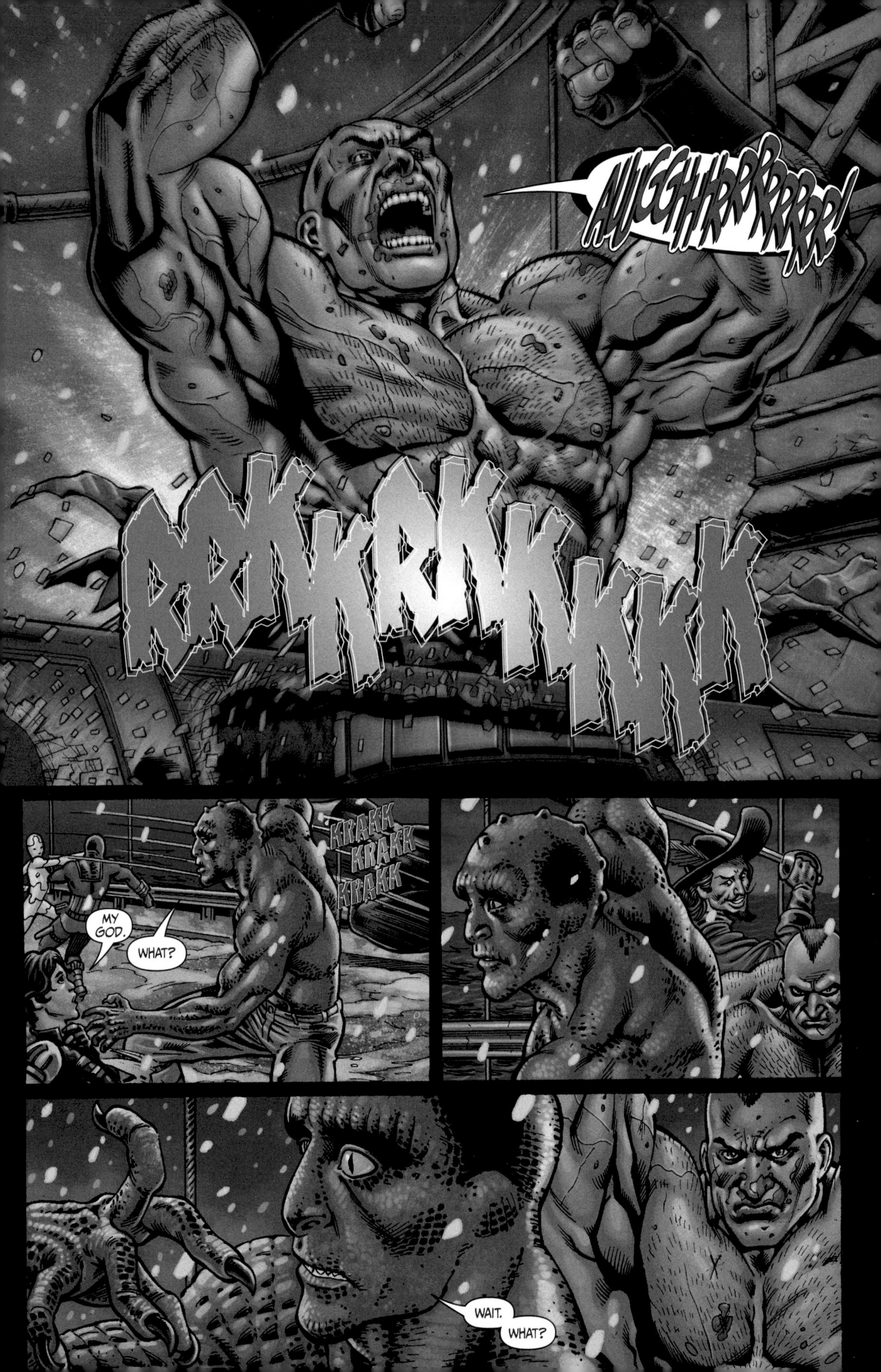
AUUGGHRRRRRRRRR!
RRAKRAKKKK
KRAKK
KRAKK
KRAKK
MY GOD.
WHAT?
WAIT.
WHAT?

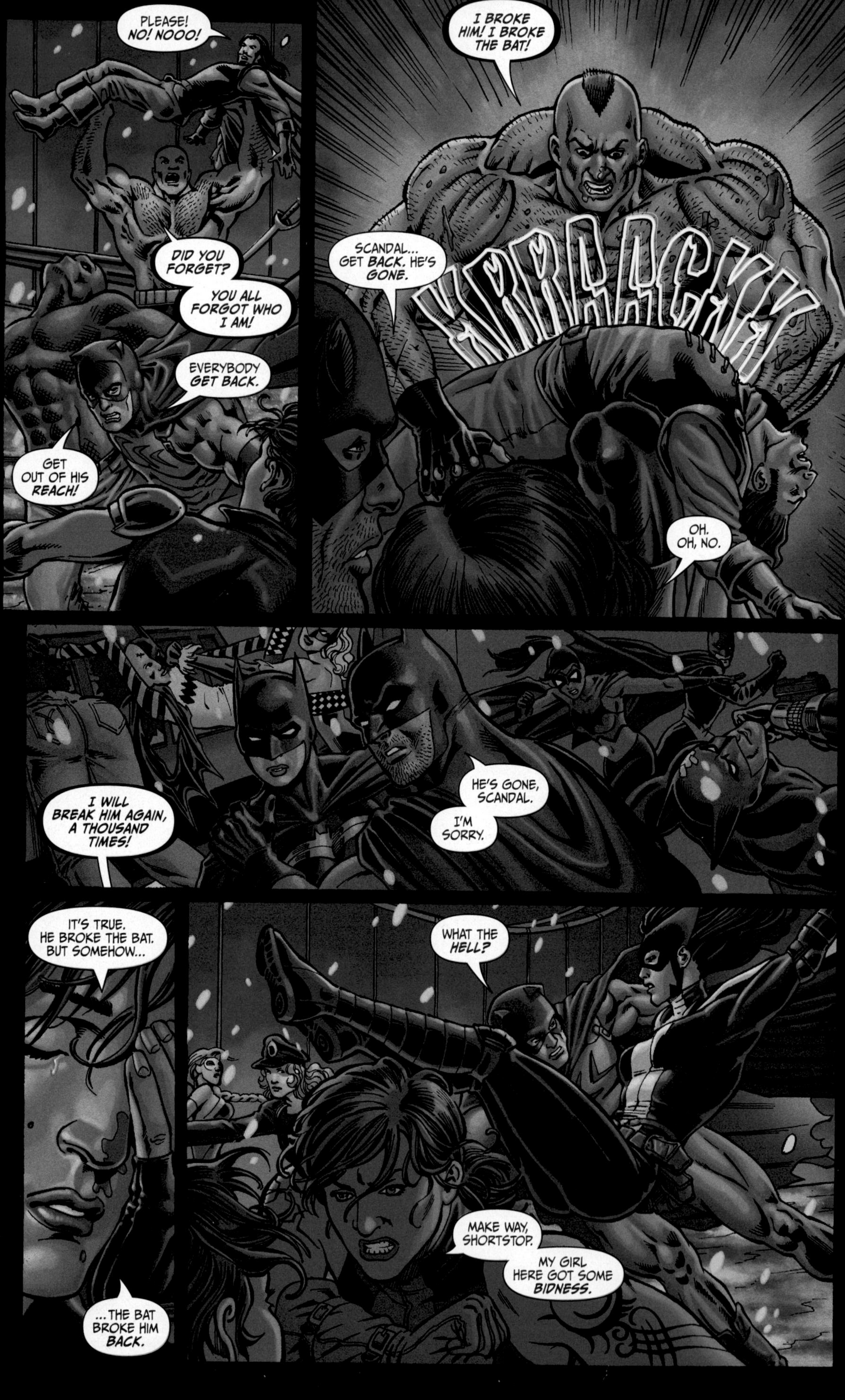
PLEASE! NO! NOOO!
DID YOU FORGET?
YOU ALL FORGOT WHO I AM!
EVERYBODY GET BACK.
GET OUT OF HIS REACH!
I BROKE HIM! I BROKE THE BAT!
KRRAACKK
SCANDAL... GET BACK. HE'S GONE.
OH. OH, NO.
I WILL BREAK HIM AGAIN, A THOUSAND TIMES!
HE'S GONE, SCANDAL.
I'M SORRY.
IT'S TRUE. HE BROKE THE BAT. BUT SOMEHOW...
...THE BAT BROKE HIM BACK.
WHAT THE HELL?
MAKE WAY, SHORTSTOP.
MY GIRL HERE GOT SOME BIDNESS.

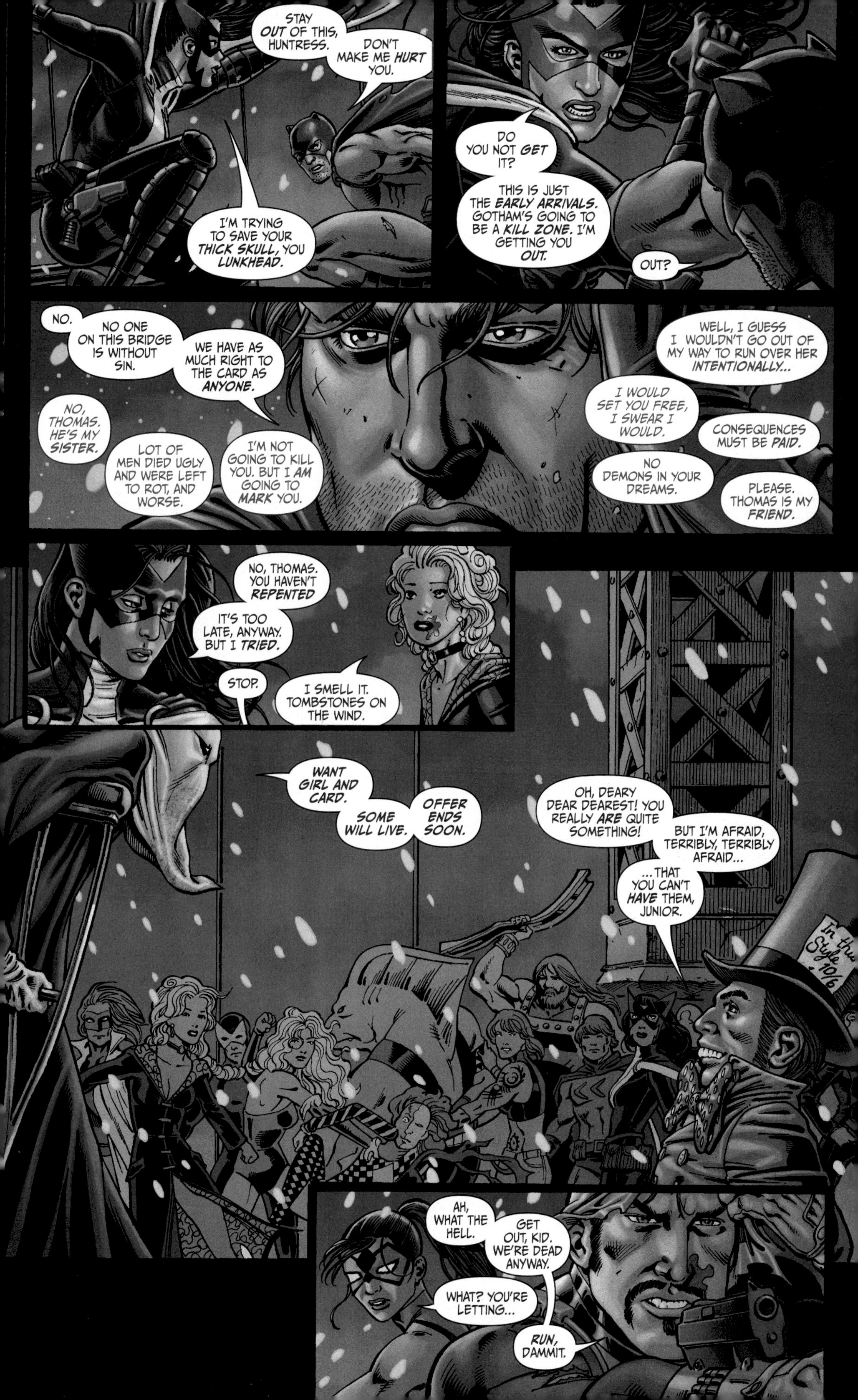
STAY OUT OF THIS, HUNTRESS.
DON'T MAKE ME HURT YOU.
I'M TRYING TO SAVE YOUR THICK SKULL, YOU LUNKHEAD.
DO YOU NOT GET IT?
THIS IS JUST THE EARLY ARRIVALS. GOTHAM'S GOING TO BE A KILL ZONE. I'M GETTING YOU OUT.
OUT?
NO.
NO ONE ON THIS BRIDGE IS WITHOUT SIN.
WE HAVE AS MUCH RIGHT TO THE CARD AS ANYONE.
NO, THOMAS. HE'S MY SISTER.
LOT OF MEN DIED UGLY AND WERE LEFT TO ROT, AND WORSE.
I'M NOT GOING TO KILL YOU. BUT I AM GOING TO MARK YOU.
WELL, I GUESS I WOULDN'T GO OUT OF MY WAY TO RUN OVER HER INTENTIONALLY...
I WOULD SET YOU FREE, I SWEAR I WOULD.
CONSEQUENCES MUST BE PAID.
NO DEMONS IN YOUR DREAMS.
PLEASE. THOMAS IS MY FRIEND.
NO, THOMAS. YOU HAVEN'T REPENTED
IT'S TOO LATE, ANYWAY. BUT I TRIED.
STOP.
I SMELL IT. TOMBSTONES ON THE WIND.
WANT GIRL AND CARD.
SOME WILL LIVE.
OFFER ENDS SOON.
OH, DEARY DEAR DEAREST! YOU REALLY ARE QUITE SOMETHING!
BUT I'M AFRAID, TERRIBLY, TERRIBLY AFRAID...
...THAT YOU CAN'T HAVE THEM, JUNIOR.
In the Style 10/6
AH, WHAT THE HELL.
GET OUT, KID. WE'RE DEAD ANYWAY.
WHAT? YOU'RE LETTING...
RUN, DAMMIT.

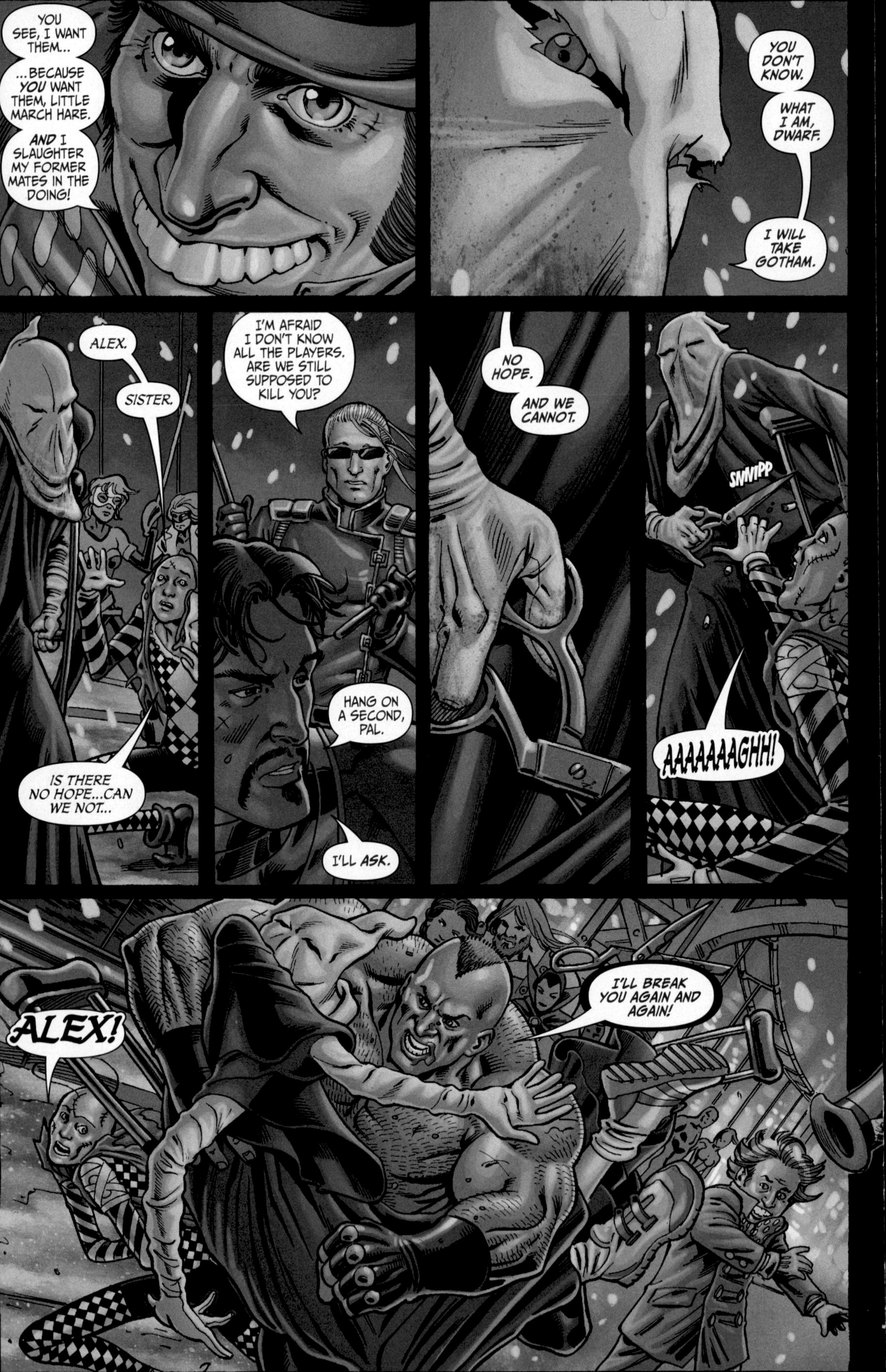
YOU SEE, I WANT THEM...
...BECAUSE YOU WANT THEM, LITTLE MARCH HARE.
AND I SLAUGHTER MY FORMER MATES IN THE DOING!
YOU DON'T KNOW.
WHAT I AM, DWARF.
I WILL TAKE GOTHAM.
ALEX.
SISTER.
IS THERE NO HOPE...CAN WE NOT...
I'M AFRAID I DON'T KNOW ALL THE PLAYERS. ARE WE STILL SUPPOSED TO KILL YOU?
HANG ON A SECOND, PAL.
I'LL ASK.
NO HOPE.
AND WE CANNOT.
SNNIPP
AAAAAAAGHH!
ALEX!
I'LL BREAK YOU AGAIN AND AGAIN!

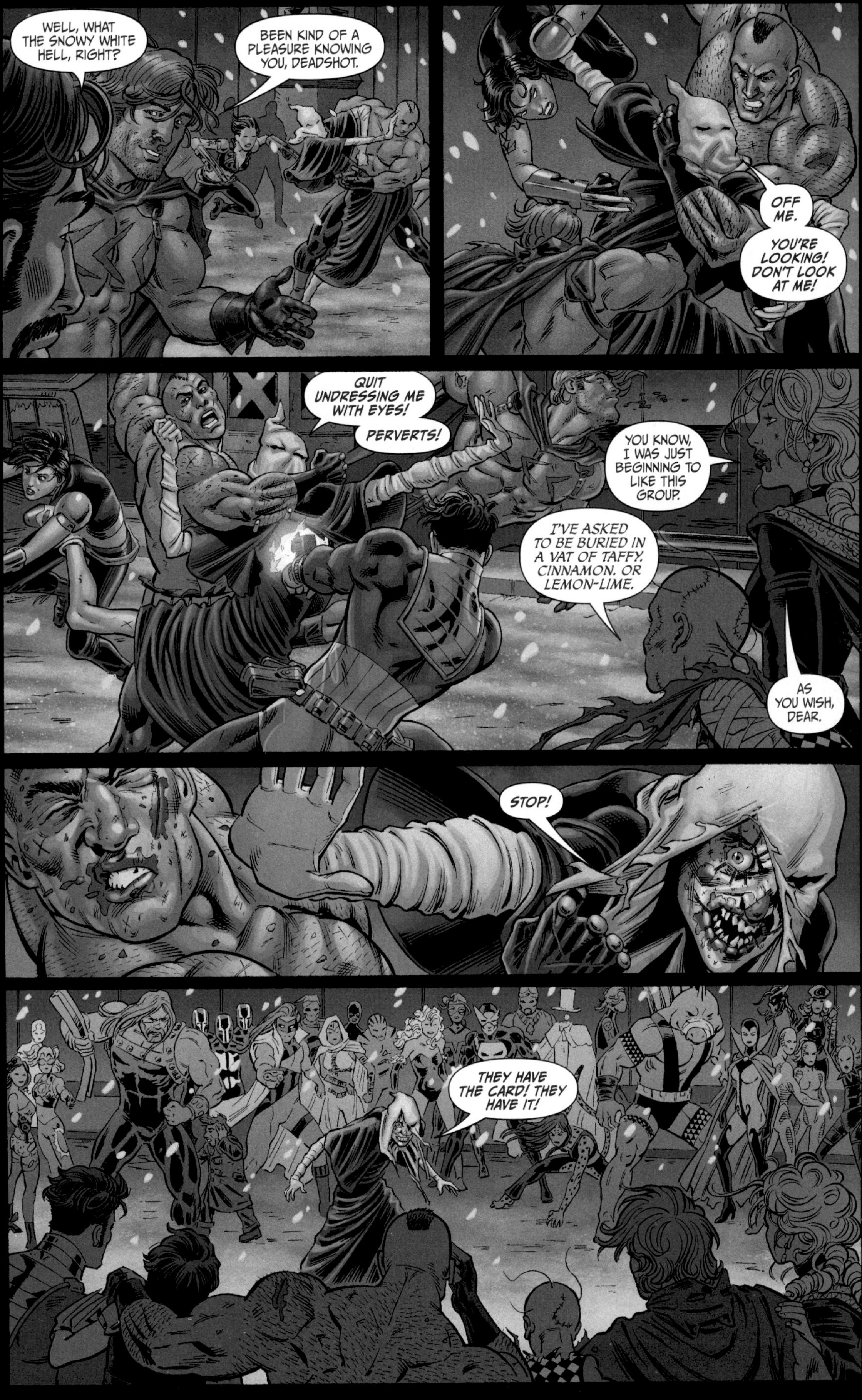
WELL, WHAT THE SNOWY WHITE HELL, RIGHT?
BEEN KIND OF A PLEASURE KNOWING YOU, DEADSHOT.
OFF ME.
YOU'RE LOOKING! DON'T LOOK AT ME!
QUIT UNDRESSING ME WITH EYES!
PERVERTS!
YOU KNOW, I WAS JUST BEGINNING TO LIKE THIS GROUP.
I'VE ASKED TO BE BURIED IN A VAT OF TAFFY. CINNAMON. OR LEMON-LIME.
AS YOU WISH, DEAR.
STOP!
THEY HAVE THE CARD! THEY HAVE IT!

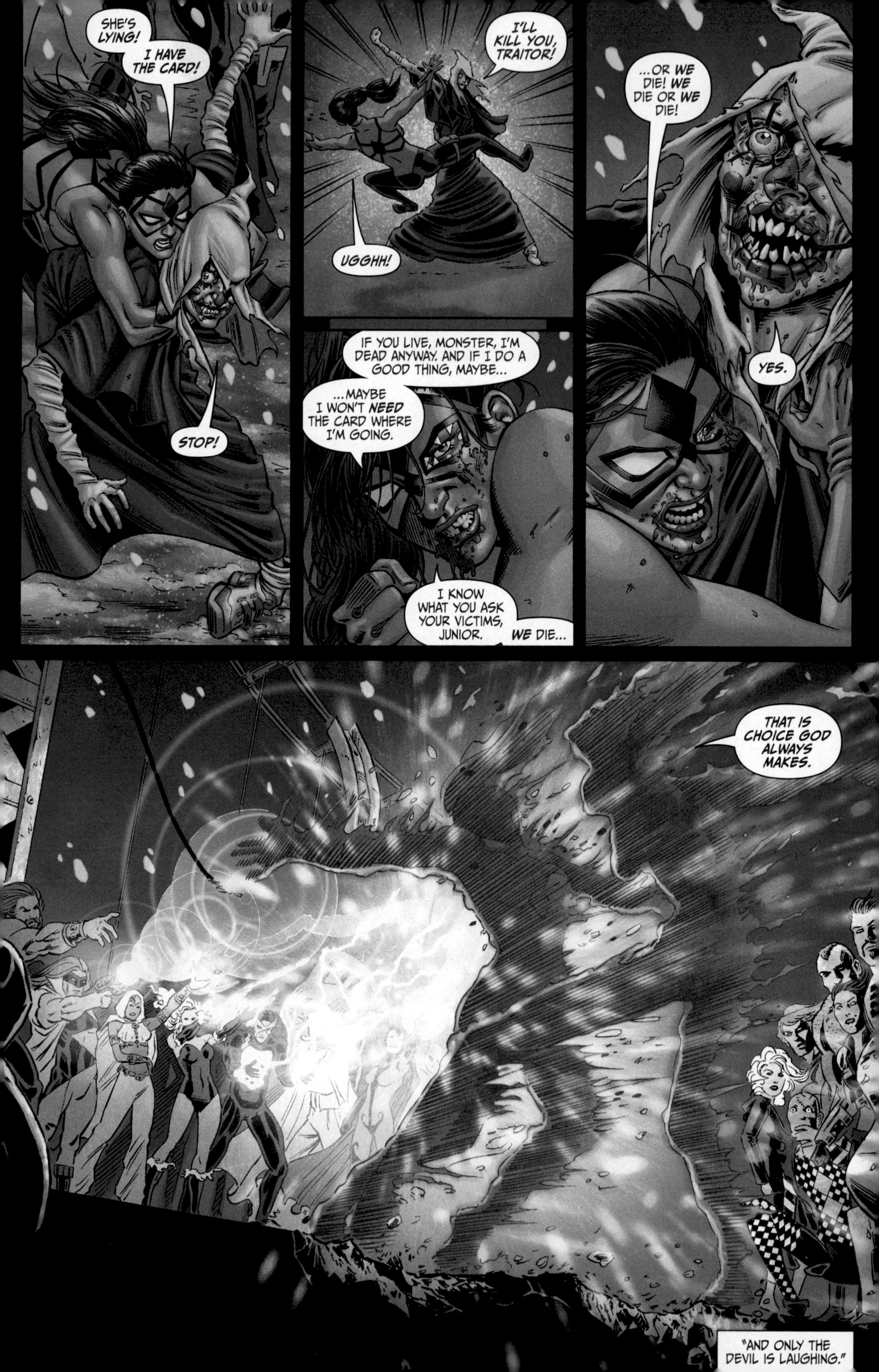
SHE'S LYING!
I HAVE THE CARD!
STOP!
I'LL KILL YOU, TRAITOR!
UGGHH!
IF YOU LIVE, MONSTER, I'M DEAD ANYWAY. AND IF I DO A GOOD THING, MAYBE...
...MAYBE I WON'T NEED THE CARD WHERE I'M GOING.
I KNOW WHAT YOU ASK YOUR VICTIMS, JUNIOR.
WE DIE...
...OR WE DIE! WE DIE OR WE DIE!
YES.
THAT IS CHOICE GOD ALWAYS MAKES.
"AND ONLY THE DEVIL IS LAUGHING."

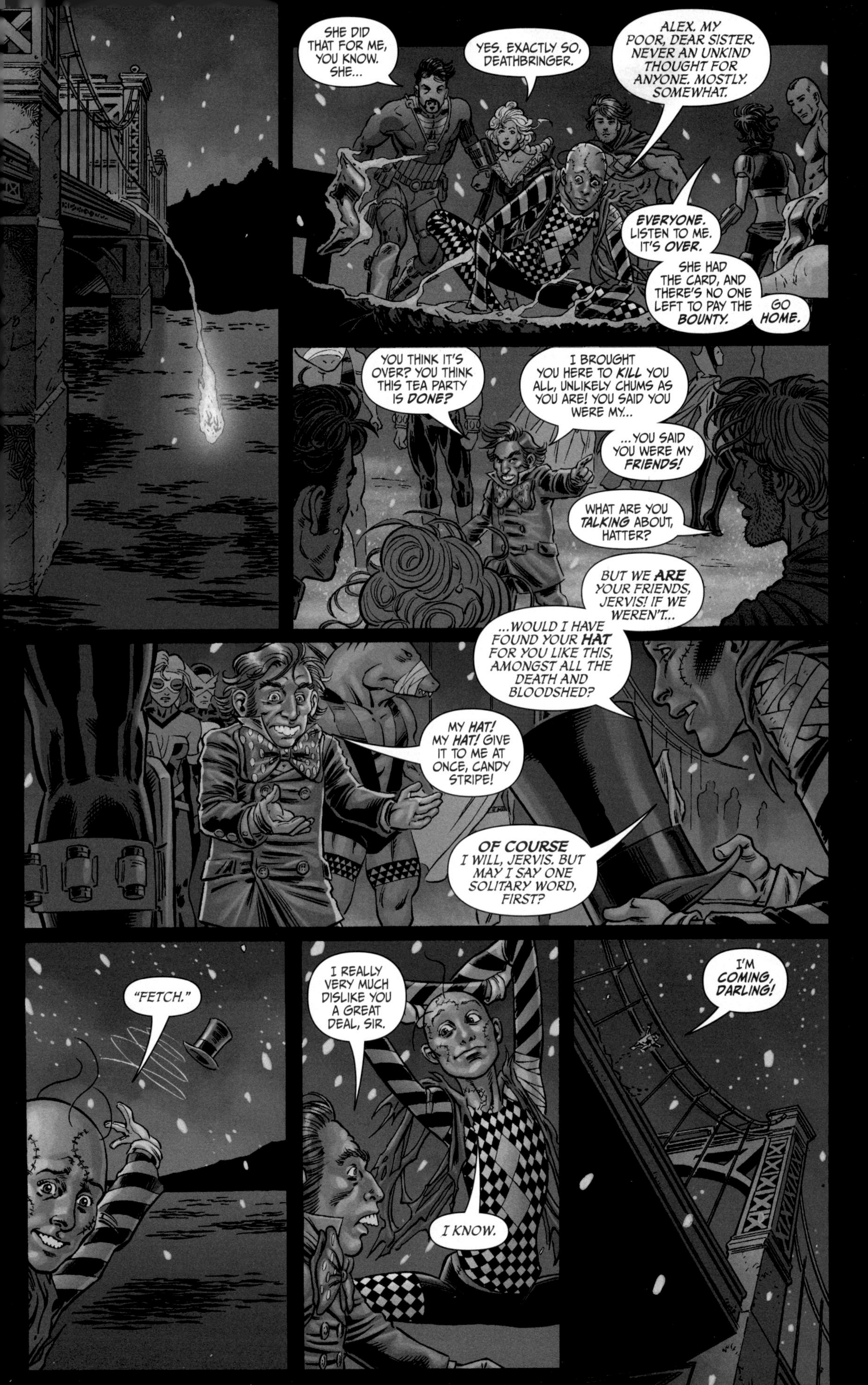

SHE DID THAT FOR ME, YOU KNOW. SHE...
YES. EXACTLY SO, DEATHBRINGER.
ALEX. MY POOR, DEAR SISTER. NEVER AN UNKIND THOUGHT FOR ANYONE. MOSTLY. SOMEWHAT.
EVERYONE. LISTEN TO ME. IT'S OVER.
SHE HAD THE CARD, AND THERE'S NO ONE LEFT TO PAY THE BOUNTY.
GO HOME.
YOU THINK IT'S OVER? YOU THINK THIS TEA PARTY IS DONE?
I BROUGHT YOU HERE TO KILL YOU ALL, UNLIKELY CHUMS AS YOU ARE! YOU SAID YOU WERE MY...
...YOU SAID YOU WERE MY FRIENDS!
WHAT ARE YOU TALKING ABOUT, HATTER?
BUT WE ARE YOUR FRIENDS, JERVIS! IF WE WEREN'T...
...WOULD I HAVE FOUND YOUR HAT FOR YOU LIKE THIS, AMONGST ALL THE DEATH AND BLOODSHED?
MY HAT! MY HAT! GIVE IT TO ME AT ONCE, CANDY STRIPE!
OF COURSE I WILL, JERVIS. BUT MAY I SAY ONE SOLITARY WORD, FIRST?
"FETCH."
I REALLY VERY MUCH DISLIKE YOU A GREAT DEAL, SIR.
I KNOW.
I'M COMING, DARLING!

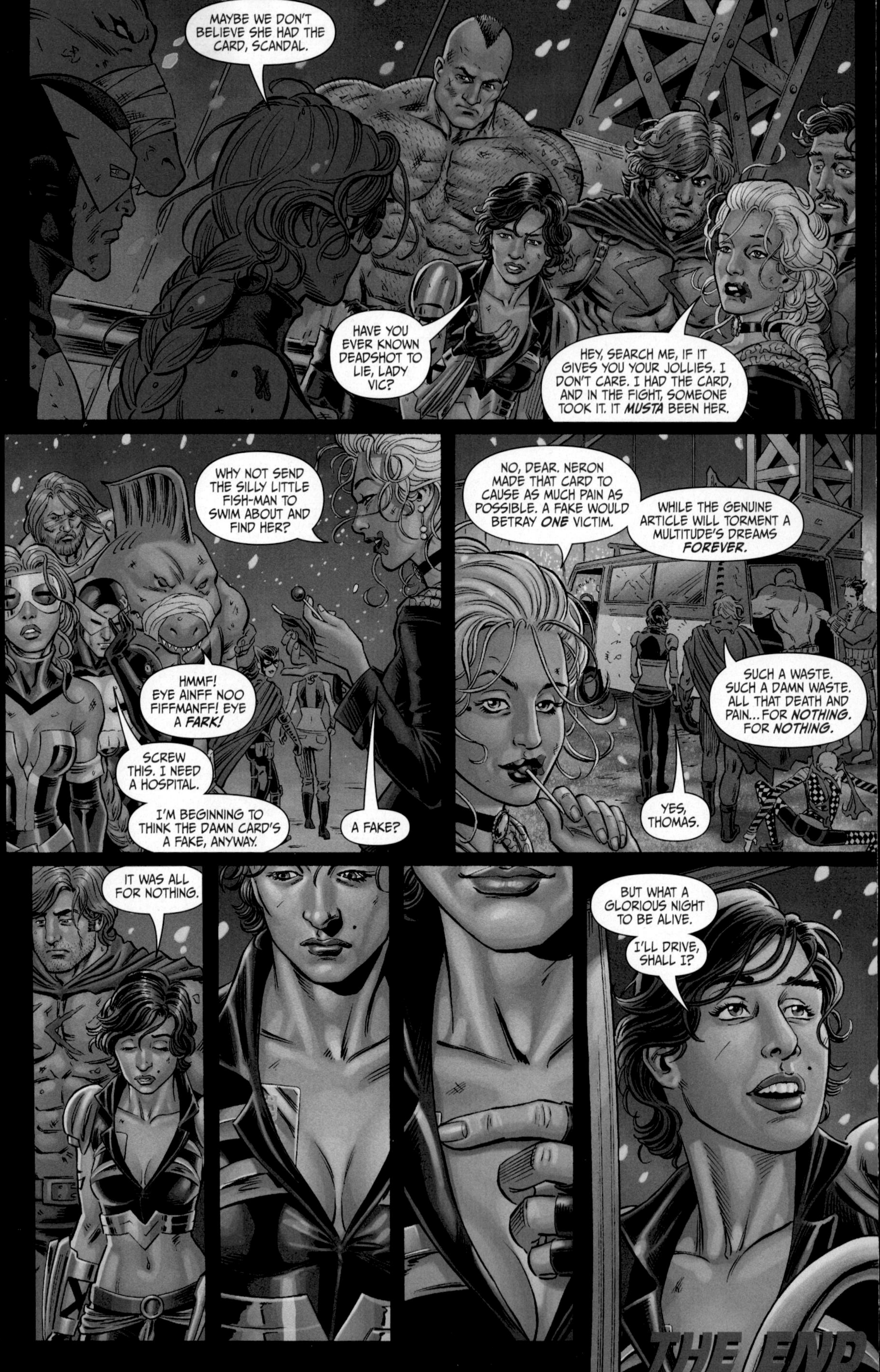
MAYBE WE DON'T BELIEVE SHE HAD THE CARD, SCANDAL.
HAVE YOU EVER KNOWN DEADSHOT TO LIE, LADY VIC?
HEY, SEARCH ME, IF IT GIVES YOU YOUR JOLLIES. I DON'T CARE. I HAD THE CARD, AND IN THE FIGHT, SOMEONE TOOK IT. IT *MUSTA* BEEN HER.
WHY NOT SEND THE SILLY LITTLE FISH-MAN TO SWIM ABOUT AND FIND HER?
HMMF! EYE AINFF NOO FIFFMANFF! EYE A *FARK!*
SCREW THIS. I NEED A HOSPITAL.
I'M BEGINNING TO THINK THE DAMN CARD'S A FAKE, ANYWAY.
A FAKE?
NO, DEAR. NERON MADE THAT CARD TO CAUSE AS MUCH PAIN AS POSSIBLE. A FAKE WOULD BETRAY *ONE* VICTIM.
WHILE THE GENUINE ARTICLE WILL TORMENT A MULTITUDE'S DREAMS *FOREVER.*
SUCH A WASTE. SUCH A DAMN WASTE. ALL THAT DEATH AND PAIN... FOR *NOTHING.* FOR *NOTHING.*
YES, THOMAS.
IT WAS ALL FOR NOTHING.
BUT WHAT A GLORIOUS NIGHT TO BE ALIVE.
I'LL DRIVE, SHALL I?
THE END

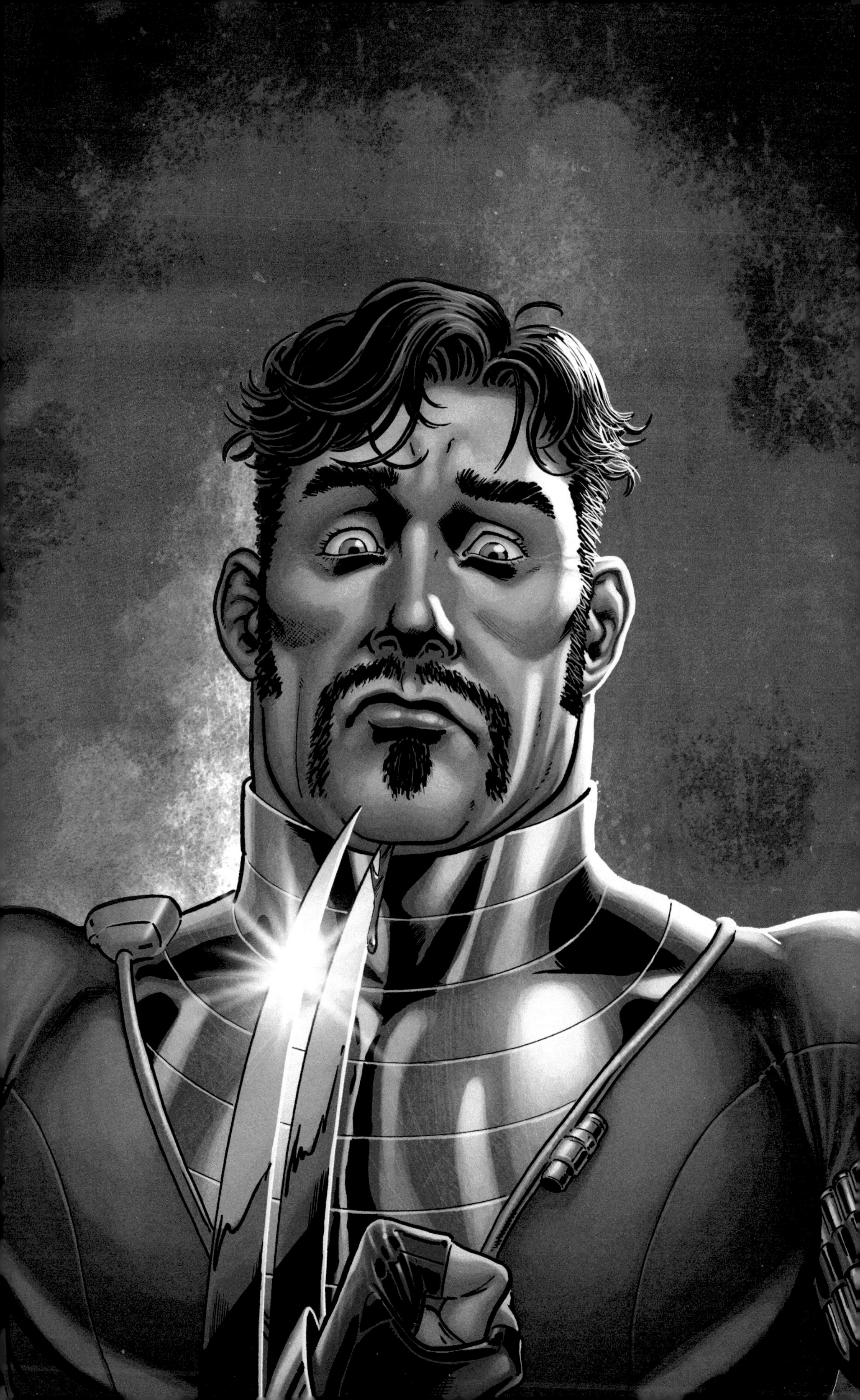

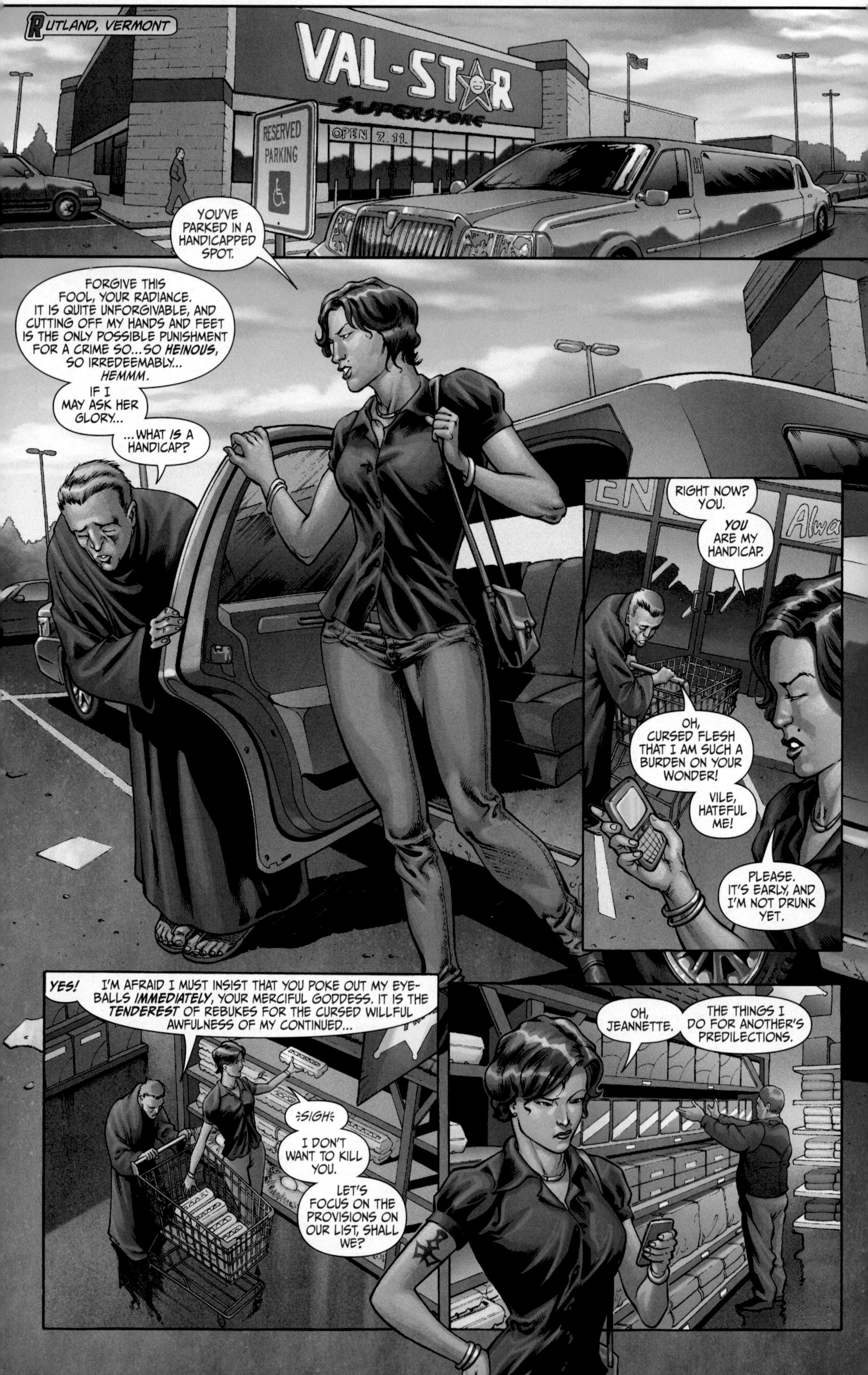
RUTLAND, VERMONT
VAL-STAR SUPERSTORE
OPEN 7-11
RESERVED PARKING
YOU'VE PARKED IN A HANDICAPPED SPOT.
FORGIVE THIS FOOL, YOUR RADIANCE. IT IS QUITE UNFORGIVABLE, AND CUTTING OFF MY HANDS AND FEET IS THE ONLY POSSIBLE PUNISHMENT FOR A CRIME SO...SO HEINOUS, SO IRREDEEMABLY... HEMMM.
IF I MAY ASK HER GLORY...
...WHAT IS A HANDICAP?
RIGHT NOW? YOU.
YOU ARE MY HANDICAP.
OH, CURSED FLESH THAT I AM SUCH A BURDEN ON YOUR WONDER!
VILE, HATEFUL ME!
PLEASE. IT'S EARLY, AND I'M NOT DRUNK YET.
YES!
I'M AFRAID I MUST INSIST THAT YOU POKE OUT MY EYEBALLS IMMEDIATELY, YOUR MERCIFUL GODDESS. IT IS THE TENDEREST OF REBUKES FOR THE CURSED WILLFUL AWFULNESS OF MY CONTINUED...
SIGH
I DON'T WANT TO KILL YOU.
LET'S FOCUS ON THE PROVISIONS ON OUR LIST, SHALL WE?
OH, JEANNETTE.
THE THINGS I DO FOR ANOTHER'S PREDILECTIONS.

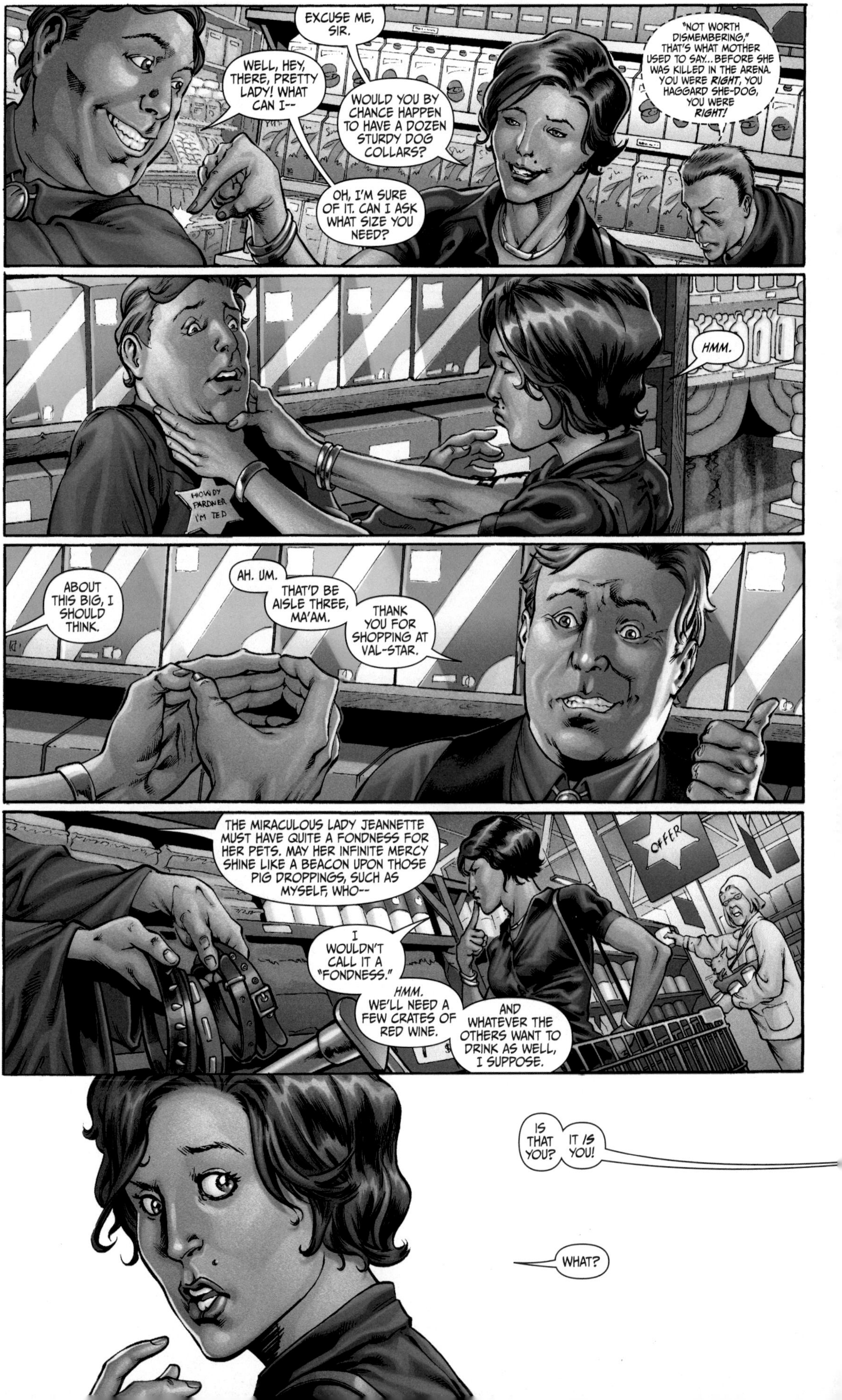
EXCUSE ME, SIR.
WELL, HEY, THERE, PRETTY LADY! WHAT CAN I--
WOULD YOU BY CHANCE HAPPEN TO HAVE A DOZEN STURDY DOG COLLARS?
OH, I'M SURE OF IT. CAN I ASK WHAT SIZE YOU NEED?
"NOT WORTH DISMEMBERING," THAT'S WHAT MOTHER USED TO SAY... BEFORE SHE WAS KILLED IN THE ARENA. YOU WERE RIGHT, YOU HAGGARD SHE-DOG, YOU WERE RIGHT!
HOWDY PARDNER I'M TED
HMM.
ABOUT THIS BIG, I SHOULD THINK.
AH. UM.
THAT'D BE AISLE THREE, MA'AM.
THANK YOU FOR SHOPPING AT VAL-STAR.
THE MIRACULOUS LADY JEANNETTE MUST HAVE QUITE A FONDNESS FOR HER PETS. MAY HER INFINITE MERCY SHINE LIKE A BEACON UPON THOSE PIG DROPPINGS, SUCH AS MYSELF, WHO--
OFFER
I WOULDN'T CALL IT A "FONDNESS."
HMM. WE'LL NEED A FEW CRATES OF RED WINE.
AND WHATEVER THE OTHERS WANT TO DRINK AS WELL, I SUPPOSE.
IS THAT YOU?
IT IS YOU!
WHAT?

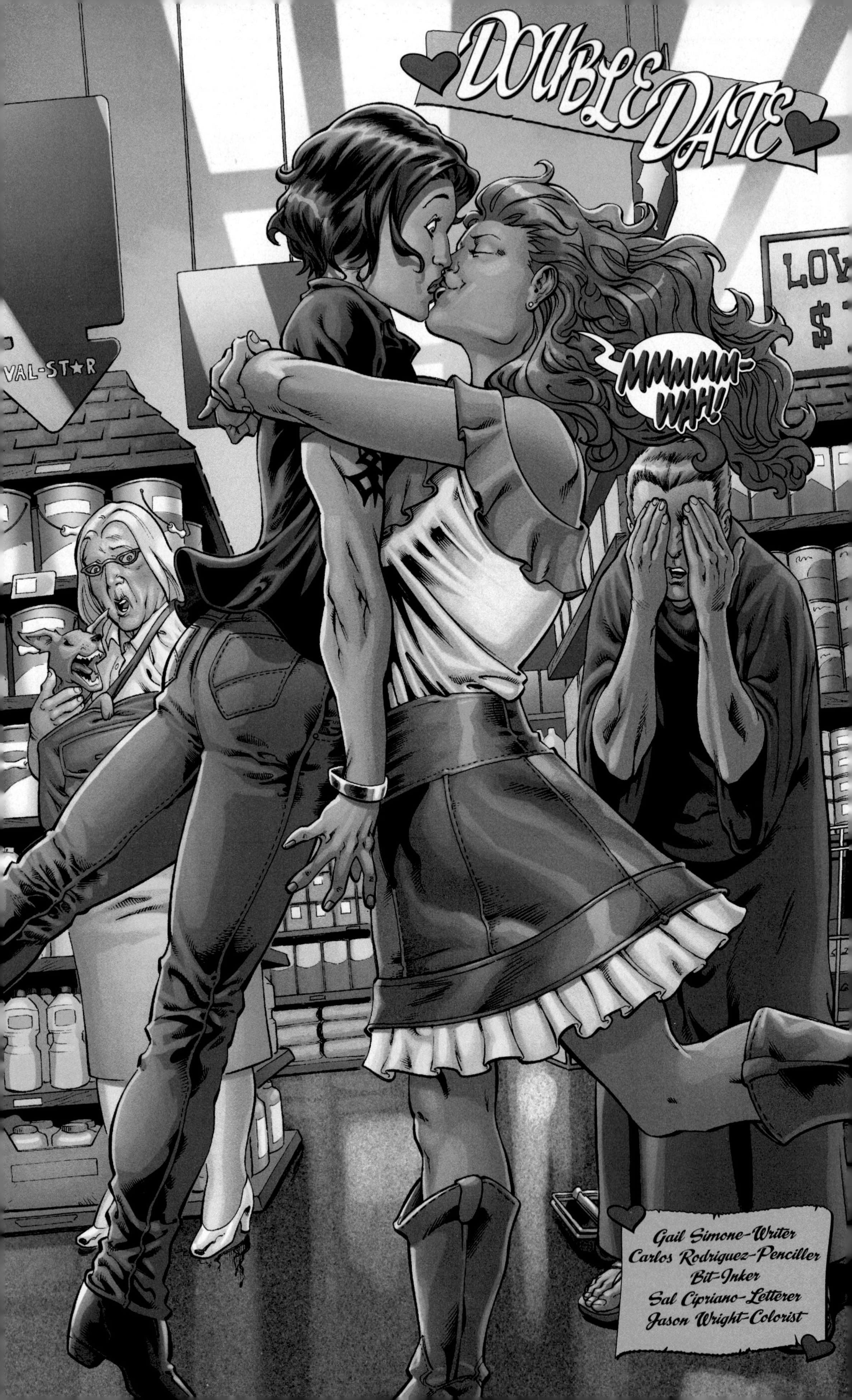
DOUBLE DATE
VAL-ST★R
MMMMM-WAH!
Gail Simone-Writer
Carlos Rodriguez-Penciller
Bit-Inker
Sal Cipriano-Letterer
Jason Wright-Colorist

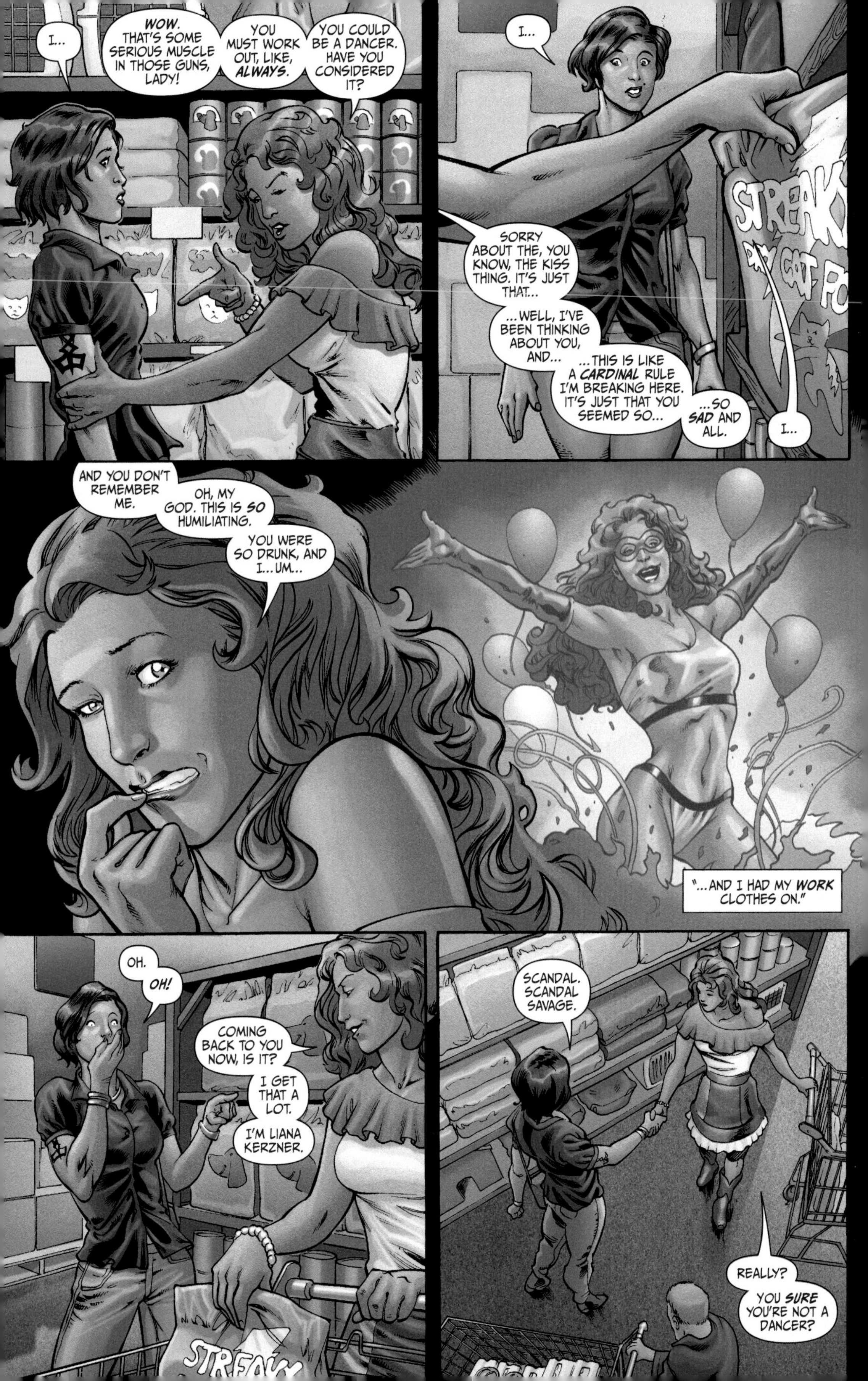
I...
WOW. THAT'S SOME SERIOUS MUSCLE IN THOSE GUNS, LADY!
YOU MUST WORK OUT, LIKE, ALWAYS.
YOU COULD BE A DANCER. HAVE YOU CONSIDERED IT?
I...
SORRY ABOUT THE, YOU KNOW, THE KISS THING. IT'S JUST THAT...
...WELL, I'VE BEEN THINKING ABOUT YOU, AND...
...THIS IS LIKE A CARDINAL RULE I'M BREAKING HERE. IT'S JUST THAT YOU SEEMED SO...
...SO SAD AND ALL.
I...
AND YOU DON'T REMEMBER ME.
OH, MY GOD. THIS IS SO HUMILIATING.
YOU WERE SO DRUNK, AND I...UM...
"...AND I HAD MY WORK CLOTHES ON."
OH.
OH!
COMING BACK TO YOU NOW, IS IT?
I GET THAT A LOT.
I'M LIANA KERZNER.
SCANDAL. SCANDAL SAVAGE.
REALLY?
YOU SURE YOU'RE NOT A DANCER?

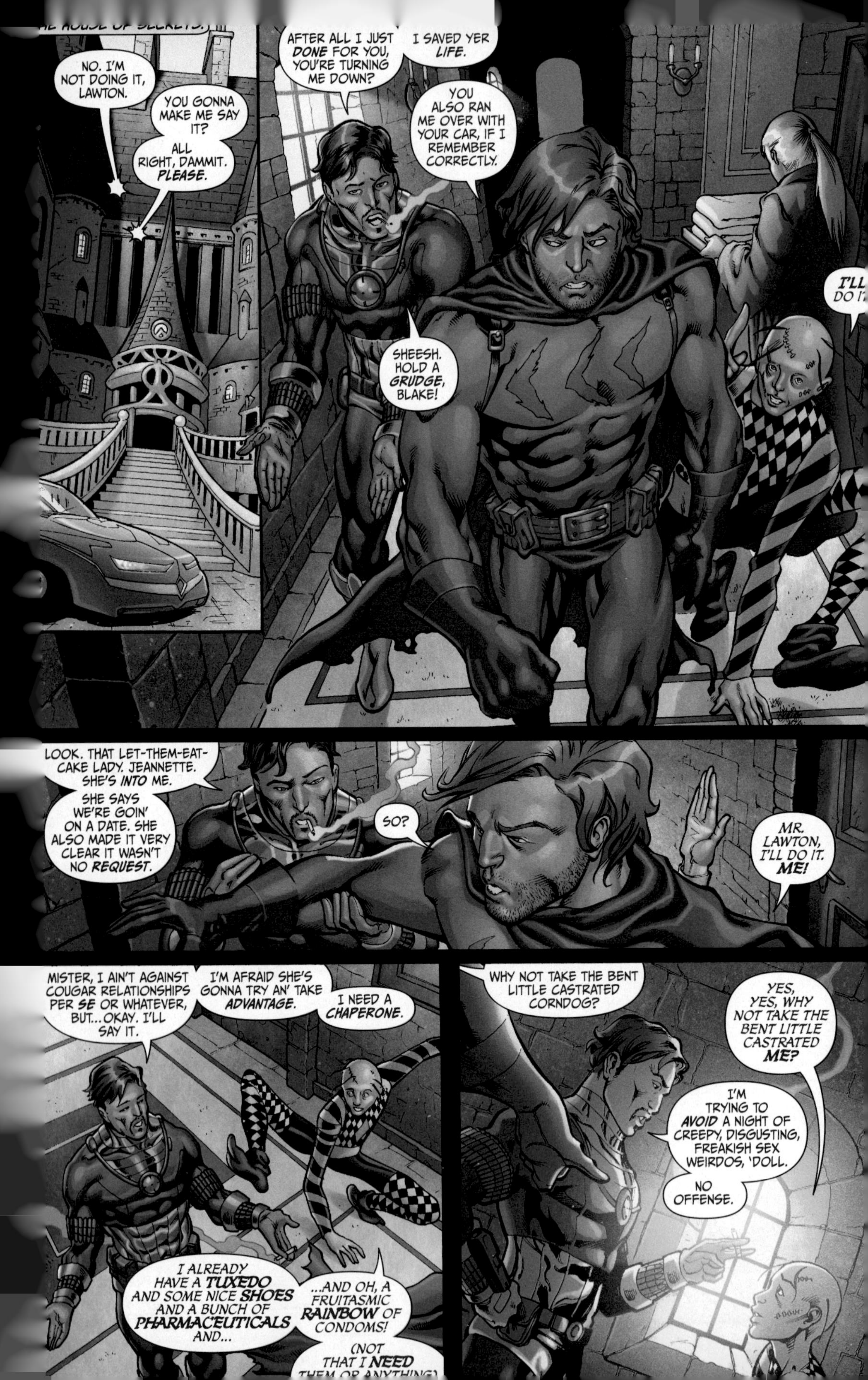

NO. I'M NOT DOING IT, LAWTON.
YOU GONNA MAKE ME SAY IT?
ALL RIGHT, DAMMIT. PLEASE.
AFTER ALL I JUST DONE FOR YOU, YOU'RE TURNING ME DOWN?
I SAVED YER LIFE.
YOU ALSO RAN ME OVER WITH YOUR CAR, IF I REMEMBER CORRECTLY.
SHEESH. HOLD A GRUDGE, BLAKE!
LOOK. THAT LET-THEM-EAT-CAKE LADY. JEANNETTE. SHE'S INTO ME.
SHE SAYS WE'RE GOIN' ON A DATE. SHE ALSO MADE IT VERY CLEAR IT WASN'T NO REQUEST.
SO?
MR. LAWTON, I'LL DO IT. ME!
MISTER, I AIN'T AGAINST COUGAR RELATIONSHIPS PER SE OR WHATEVER, BUT...OKAY. I'LL SAY IT.
I'M AFRAID SHE'S GONNA TRY AN' TAKE ADVANTAGE.
I NEED A CHAPERONE.
I ALREADY HAVE A TUXEDO AND SOME NICE SHOES AND A BUNCH OF PHARMACEUTICALS AND...
...AND OH, A FRUITASMIC RAINBOW OF CONDOMS!
(NOT THAT I NEED
WHY NOT TAKE THE BENT LITTLE CASTRATED CORNDOG?
YES, YES, WHY NOT TAKE THE BENT LITTLE CASTRATED ME?
I'M TRYING TO AVOID A NIGHT OF CREEPY, DISGUSTING, FREAKISH SEX WEIRDOS, 'DOLL.
NO OFFENSE.

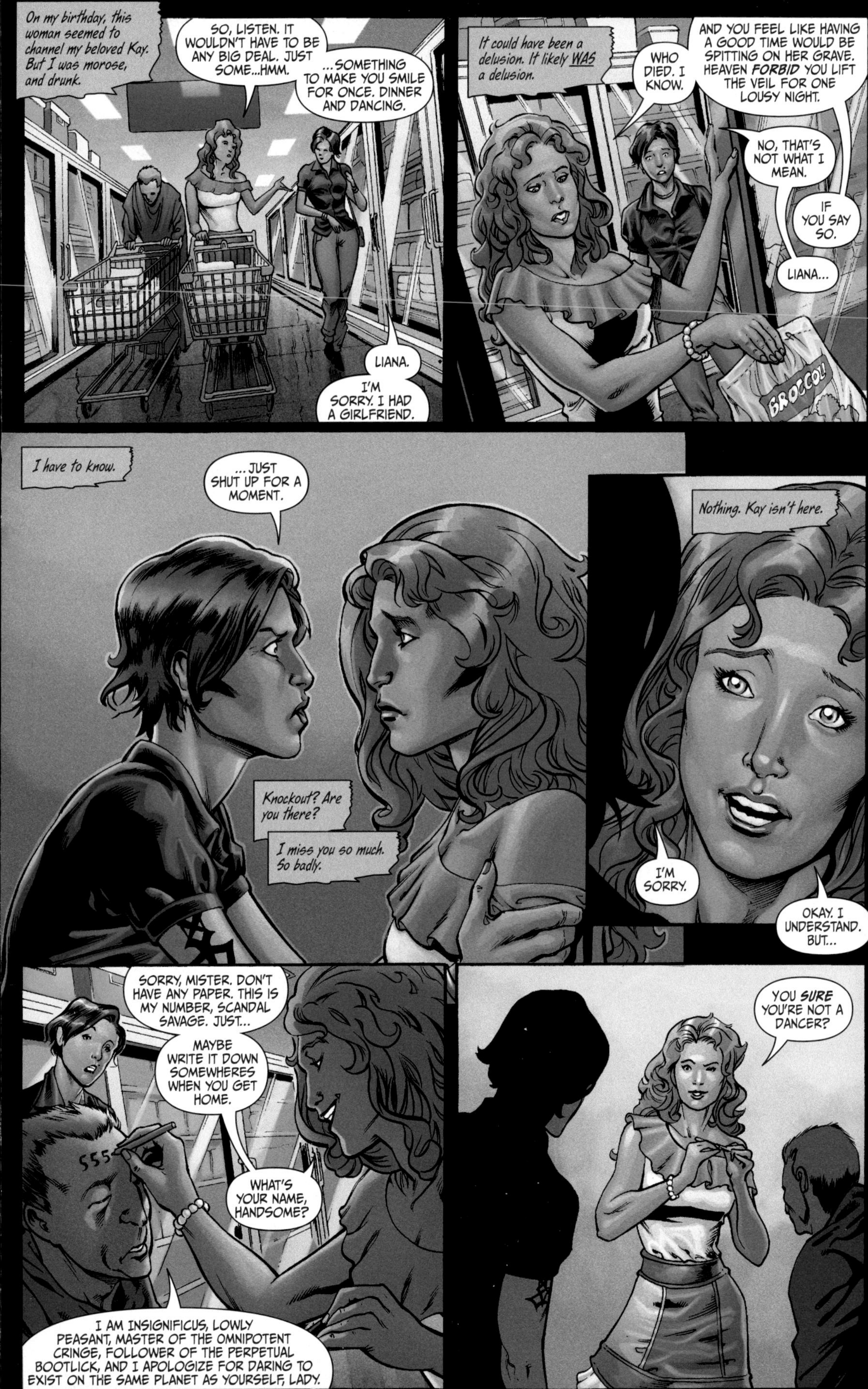
On my birthday, this woman seemed to channel my beloved Kay. But I was morose, and drunk.
SO, LISTEN. IT WOULDN'T HAVE TO BE ANY BIG DEAL. JUST SOME...HMM.
...SOMETHING TO MAKE YOU SMILE FOR ONCE. DINNER AND DANCING.
LIANA.
I'M SORRY. I HAD A GIRLFRIEND.
It could have been a delusion. It likely WAS a delusion.
WHO DIED. I KNOW.
AND YOU FEEL LIKE HAVING A GOOD TIME WOULD BE SPITTING ON HER GRAVE. HEAVEN FORBID YOU LIFT THE VEIL FOR ONE LOUSY NIGHT.
NO, THAT'S NOT WHAT I MEAN.
IF YOU SAY SO.
LIANA...
BROCCOLI
I have to know.
...JUST SHUT UP FOR A MOMENT.
Knockout? Are you there?
I miss you so much. So badly.
Nothing. Kay isn't here.
I'M SORRY.
OKAY. I UNDERSTAND. BUT...
SORRY, MISTER. DON'T HAVE ANY PAPER. THIS IS MY NUMBER, SCANDAL SAVAGE. JUST...
MAYBE WRITE IT DOWN SOMEWHERES WHEN YOU GET HOME.
555
WHAT'S YOUR NAME, HANDSOME?
I AM INSIGNIFICUS, LOWLY PEASANT, MASTER OF THE OMNIPOTENT CRINGE, FOLLOWER OF THE PERPETUAL BOOTLICK, AND I APOLOGIZE FOR DARING TO EXIST ON THE SAME PLANET AS YOURSELF, LADY.
YOU SURE YOU'RE NOT A DANCER?

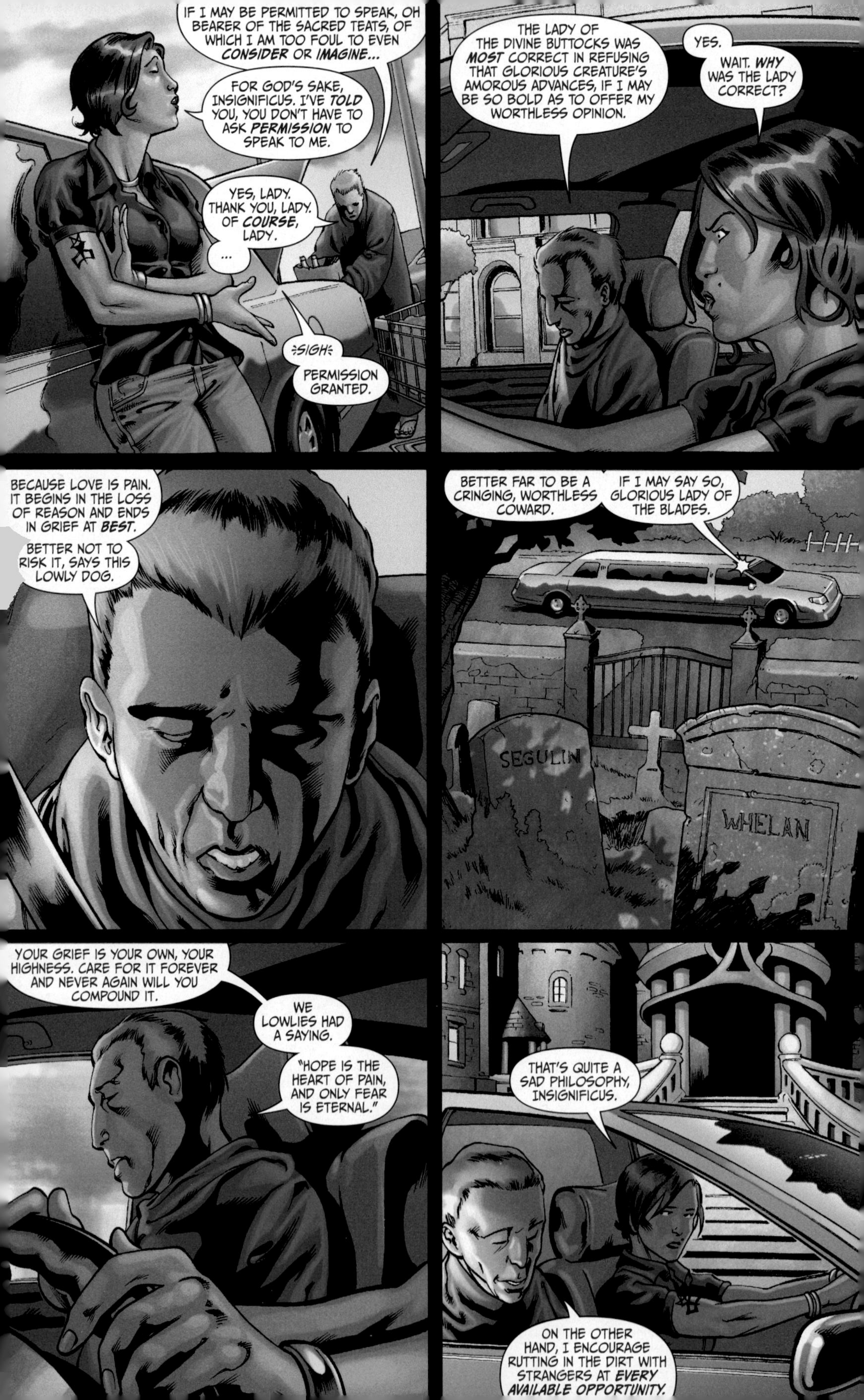
IF I MAY BE PERMITTED TO SPEAK, OH BEARER OF THE SACRED TEATS, OF WHICH I AM TOO FOUL TO EVEN *CONSIDER* OR *IMAGINE*...
FOR GOD'S SAKE, INSIGNIFICUS. I'VE *TOLD* YOU, YOU DON'T HAVE TO ASK *PERMISSION* TO SPEAK TO ME.
YES, LADY. THANK YOU, LADY. OF *COURSE*, LADY.
...
SIGH
PERMISSION GRANTED.
THE LADY OF THE DIVINE BUTTOCKS WAS *MOST* CORRECT IN REFUSING THAT GLORIOUS CREATURE'S AMOROUS ADVANCES, IF I MAY BE SO BOLD AS TO OFFER MY WORTHLESS OPINION.
YES.
WAIT. *WHY* WAS THE LADY CORRECT?
BECAUSE LOVE IS PAIN. IT BEGINS IN THE LOSS OF REASON AND ENDS IN GRIEF AT *BEST*.
BETTER NOT TO RISK IT, SAYS THIS LOWLY DOG.
BETTER FAR TO BE A CRINGING, WORTHLESS COWARD.
IF I MAY SAY SO, GLORIOUS LADY OF THE BLADES.
SEGULIN
WHELAN
YOUR GRIEF IS YOUR OWN, YOUR HIGHNESS. CARE FOR IT FOREVER AND NEVER AGAIN WILL YOU COMPOUND IT.
WE LOWLIES HAD A SAYING.
"HOPE IS THE HEART OF PAIN, AND ONLY FEAR IS ETERNAL."
THAT'S QUITE A SAD PHILOSOPHY, INSIGNIFICUS.
ON THE OTHER HAND, I ENCOURAGE RUTTING IN THE DIRT WITH STRANGERS AT *EVERY AVAILABLE OPPORTUNITY*.

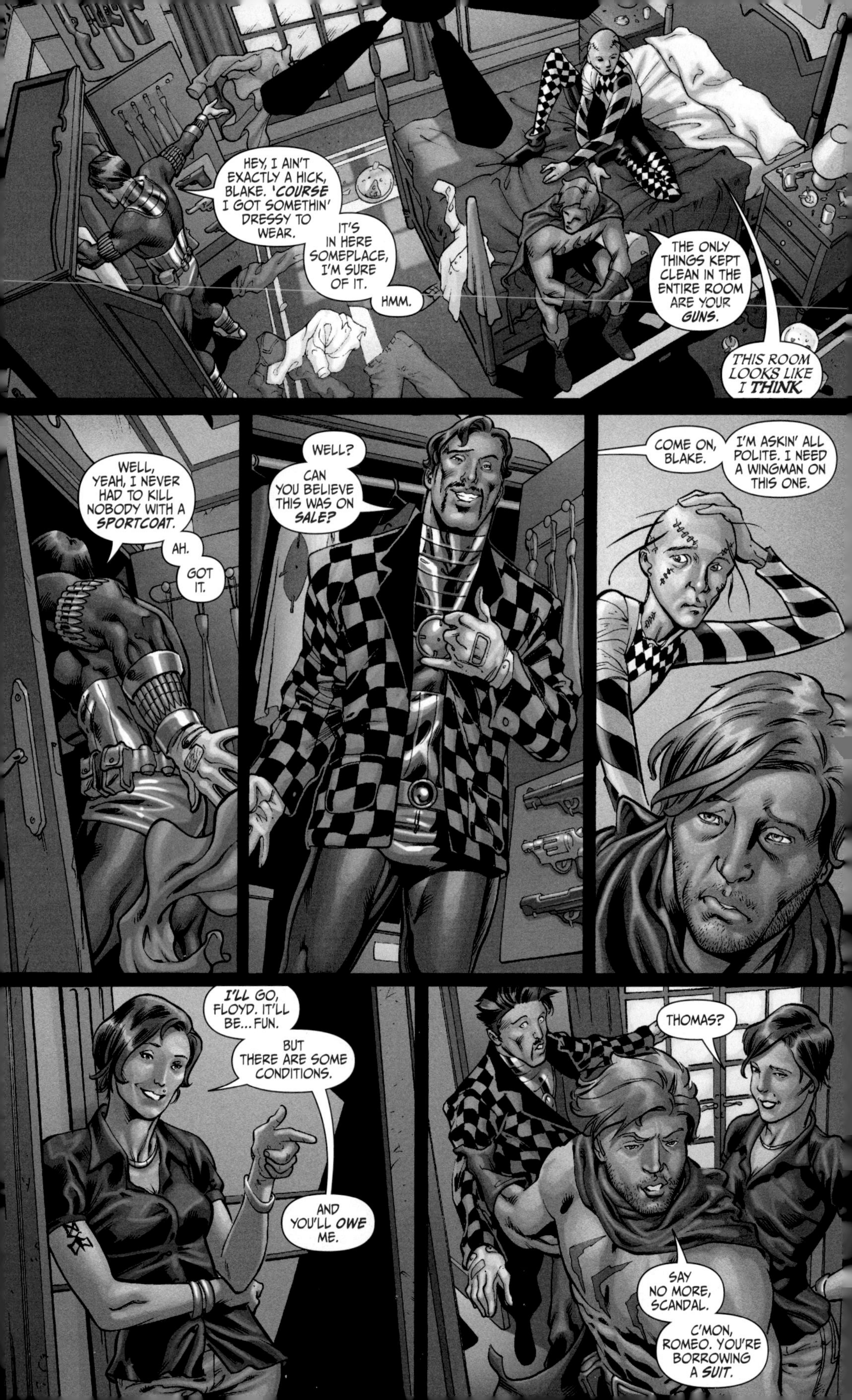
HEY, I AIN'T EXACTLY A HICK, BLAKE. 'COURSE I GOT SOMETHIN' DRESSY TO WEAR.
IT'S IN HERE SOMEPLACE, I'M SURE OF IT.
HMM.
THE ONLY THINGS KEPT CLEAN IN THE ENTIRE ROOM ARE YOUR GUNS.
THIS ROOM LOOKS LIKE I THINK.
WELL, YEAH, I NEVER HAD TO KILL NOBODY WITH A SPORTCOAT.
AH.
GOT IT.
WELL?
CAN YOU BELIEVE THIS WAS ON SALE?
COME ON, BLAKE.
I'M ASKIN' ALL POLITE. I NEED A WINGMAN ON THIS ONE.
I'LL GO, FLOYD. IT'LL BE... FUN.
BUT THERE ARE SOME CONDITIONS.
AND YOU'LL OWE ME.
THOMAS?
SAY NO MORE, SCANDAL.
C'MON, ROMEO. YOU'RE BORROWING A SUIT.

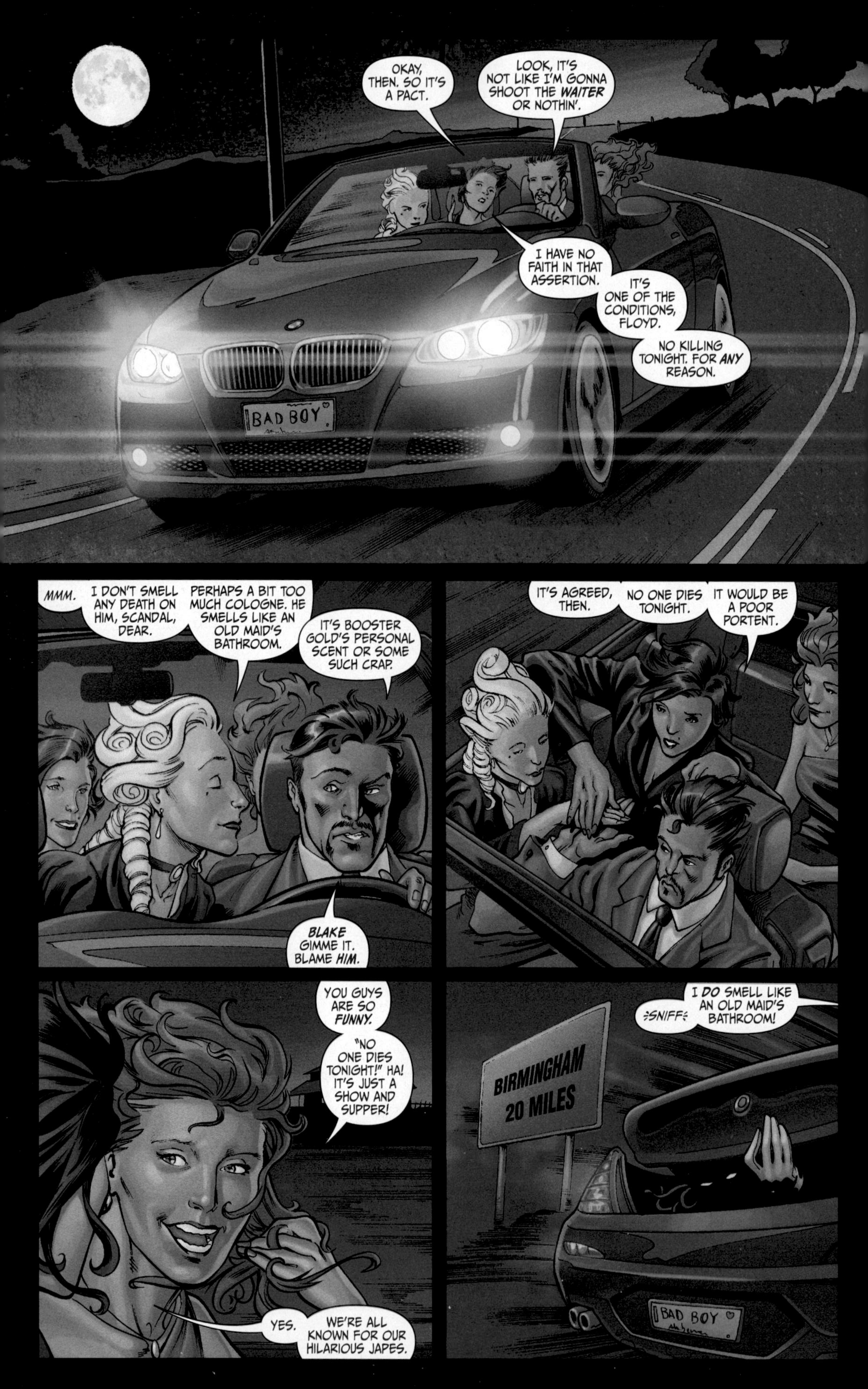
OKAY, THEN. SO IT'S A PACT.
LOOK, IT'S NOT LIKE I'M GONNA SHOOT THE WAITER OR NOTHIN'.
I HAVE NO FAITH IN THAT ASSERTION.
IT'S ONE OF THE CONDITIONS, FLOYD.
NO KILLING TONIGHT. FOR ANY REASON.
BAD BOY
MMM.
I DON'T SMELL ANY DEATH ON HIM, SCANDAL, DEAR.
PERHAPS A BIT TOO MUCH COLOGNE. HE SMELLS LIKE AN OLD MAID'S BATHROOM.
IT'S BOOSTER GOLD'S PERSONAL SCENT OR SOME SUCH CRAP.
BLAKE GIMME IT. BLAME HIM.
IT'S AGREED, THEN.
NO ONE DIES TONIGHT.
IT WOULD BE A POOR PORTENT.
YOU GUYS ARE SO FUNNY.
"NO ONE DIES TONIGHT!" HA! IT'S JUST A SHOW AND SUPPER!
YES.
WE'RE ALL KNOWN FOR OUR HILARIOUS JAPES.
SNIFF
I DO SMELL LIKE AN OLD MAID'S BATHROOM!
BIRMINGHAM 20 MILES
BAD BOY

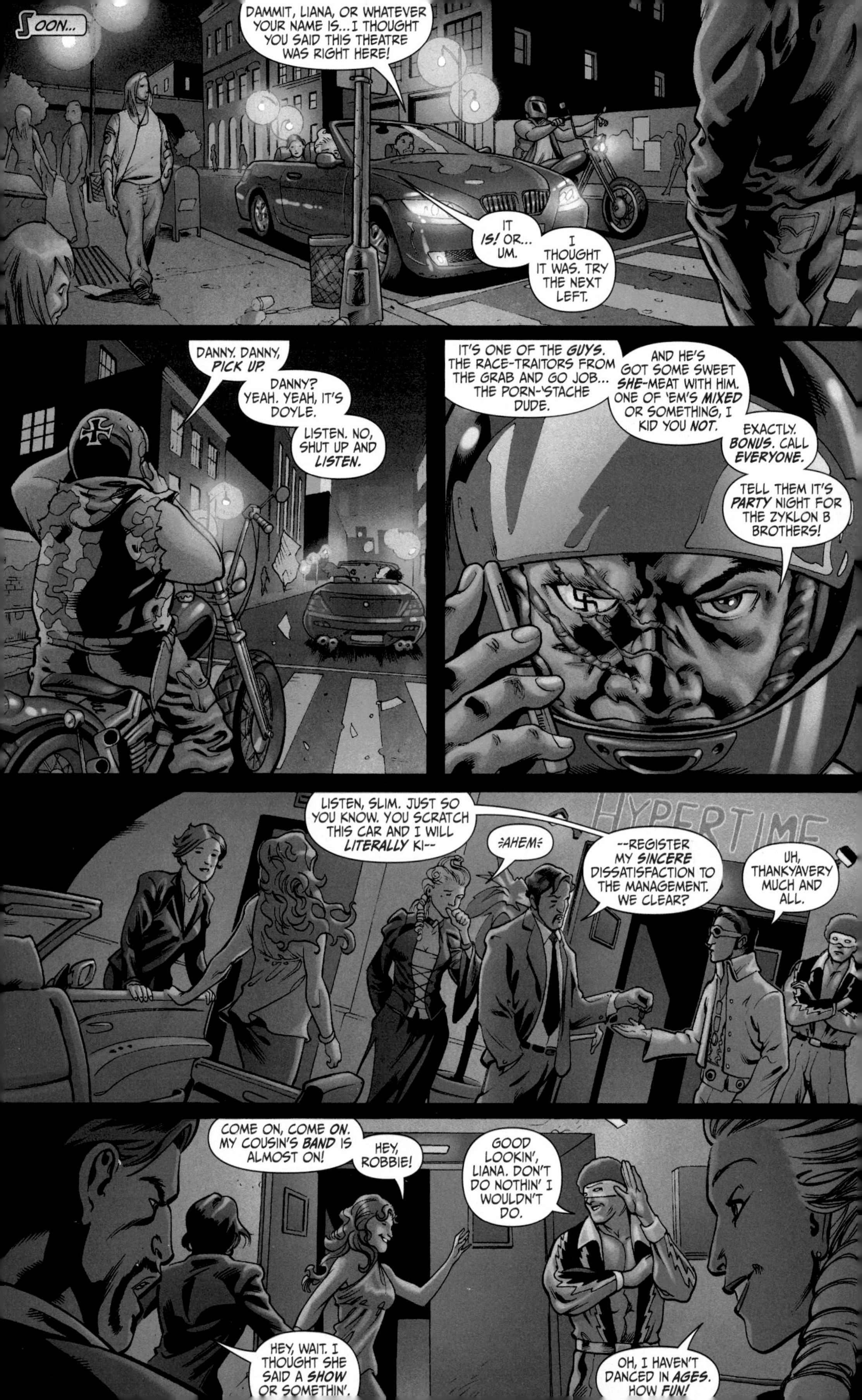
SOON...
DAMMIT, LIANA, OR WHATEVER YOUR NAME IS...I THOUGHT YOU SAID THIS THEATRE WAS RIGHT HERE!
IT IS! OR... UM.
I THOUGHT IT WAS. TRY THE NEXT LEFT.
DANNY. DANNY, PICK UP.
DANNY? YEAH. YEAH, IT'S DOYLE.
LISTEN. NO, SHUT UP AND LISTEN.
IT'S ONE OF THE GUYS. THE RACE-TRAITORS FROM THE GRAB AND GO JOB... THE PORN-'STACHE DUDE.
AND HE'S GOT SOME SWEET SHE-MEAT WITH HIM. ONE OF 'EM'S MIXED OR SOMETHING, I KID YOU NOT.
EXACTLY. BONUS. CALL EVERYONE.
TELL THEM IT'S PARTY NIGHT FOR THE ZYKLON B BROTHERS!
LISTEN, SLIM. JUST SO YOU KNOW. YOU SCRATCH THIS CAR AND I WILL LITERALLY KI--
AHEM
--REGISTER MY SINCERE DISSATISFACTION TO THE MANAGEMENT. WE CLEAR?
UH, THANKYAVERY MUCH AND ALL.
HYPERTIME
COME ON, COME ON. MY COUSIN'S BAND IS ALMOST ON!
HEY, ROBBIE!
GOOD LOOKIN', LIANA. DON'T DO NOTHIN' I WOULDN'T DO.
HEY, WAIT. I THOUGHT SHE SAID A SHOW OR SOMETHIN'.
OH, I HAVEN'T DANCED IN AGES. HOW FUN!

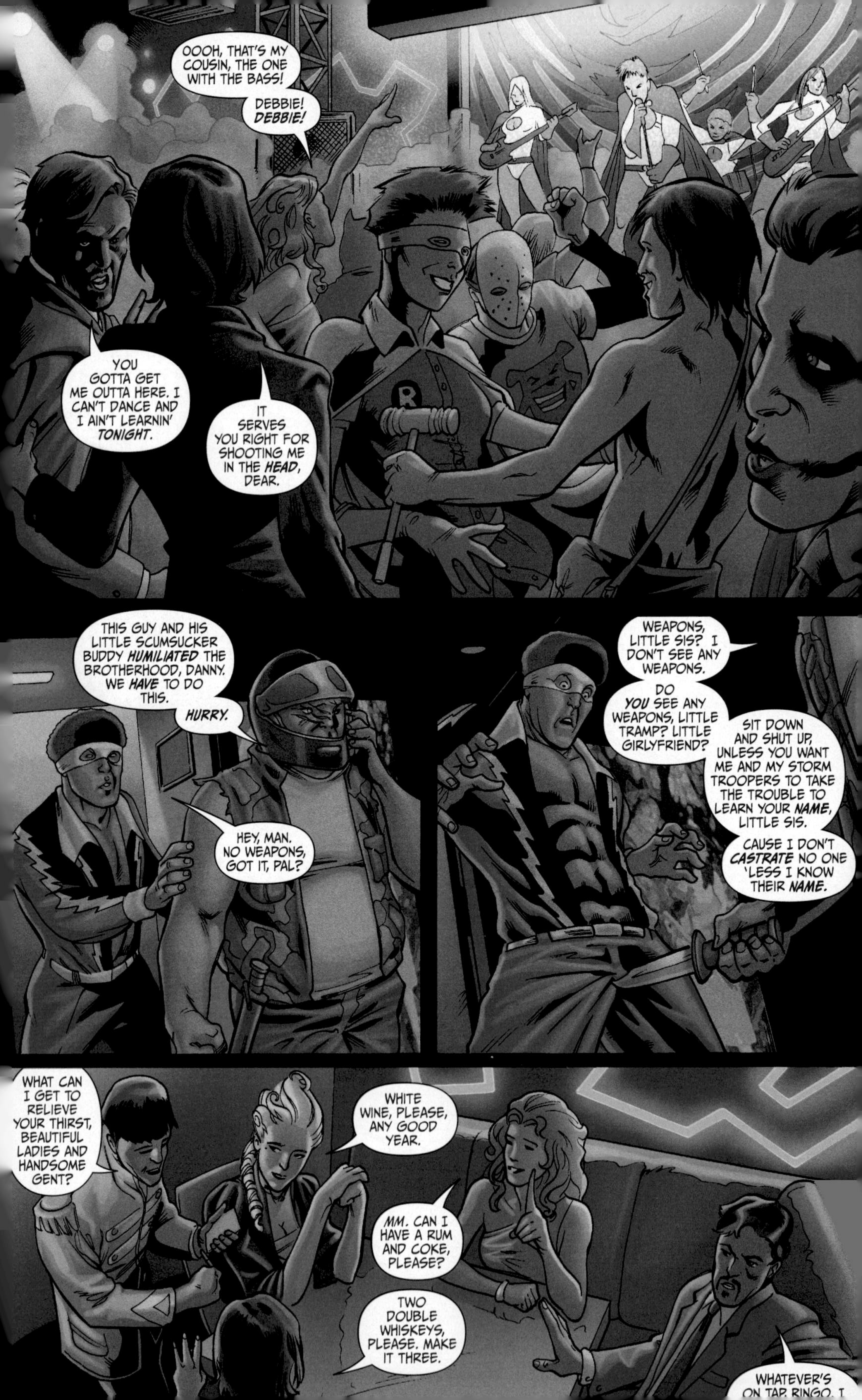
OOOH, THAT'S MY COUSIN, THE ONE WITH THE BASS!
DEBBIE! *DEBBIE!*
YOU GOTTA GET ME OUTTA HERE. I CAN'T DANCE AND I AIN'T LEARNIN' *TONIGHT*.
IT SERVES YOU RIGHT FOR SHOOTING ME IN THE *HEAD*, DEAR.
THIS GUY AND HIS LITTLE SCUMSUCKER BUDDY *HUMILIATED* THE BROTHERHOOD, DANNY. WE *HAVE* TO DO THIS.
HURRY.
HEY, MAN. NO WEAPONS, GOT IT, PAL?
WEAPONS, LITTLE SIS? I DON'T SEE ANY WEAPONS.
DO *YOU* SEE ANY WEAPONS, LITTLE TRAMP? LITTLE GIRLYFRIEND?
SIT DOWN AND SHUT UP, UNLESS YOU WANT ME AND MY STORM TROOPERS TO TAKE THE TROUBLE TO LEARN YOUR *NAME*, LITTLE SIS.
CAUSE I DON'T *CASTRATE* NO ONE 'LESS I KNOW THEIR *NAME.*
WHAT CAN I GET TO RELIEVE YOUR THIRST, BEAUTIFUL LADIES AND HANDSOME GENT?
WHITE WINE, PLEASE, ANY GOOD YEAR.
MM. CAN I HAVE A RUM AND COKE, PLEASE?
TWO DOUBLE WHISKEYS, PLEASE. MAKE IT THREE.
WHATEVER'S ON TAP, RINGO. I

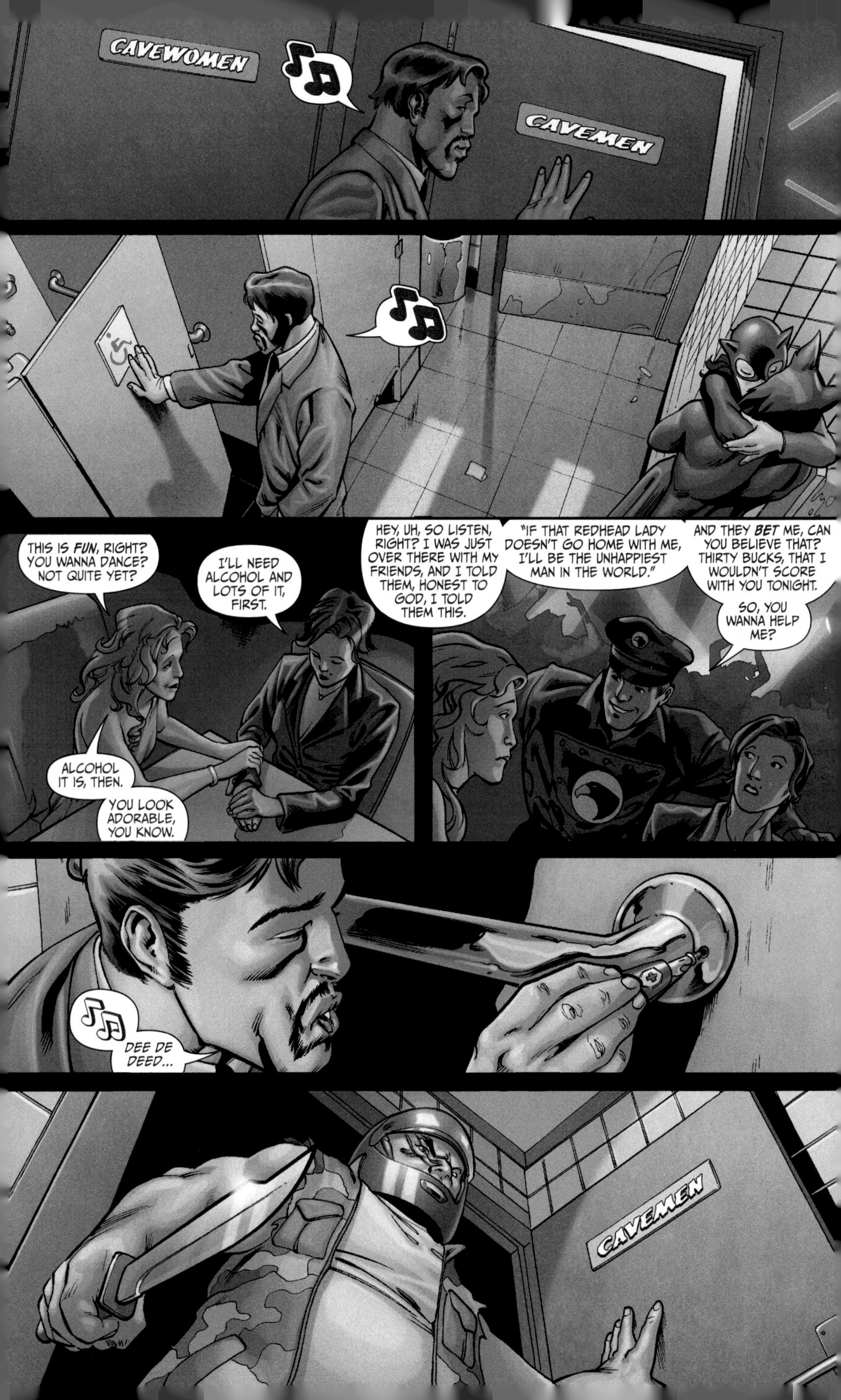
CAVEWOMEN
CAVEMEN
THIS IS FUN, RIGHT? YOU WANNA DANCE? NOT QUITE YET?
I'LL NEED ALCOHOL AND LOTS OF IT, FIRST.
ALCOHOL IT IS, THEN.
YOU LOOK ADORABLE, YOU KNOW.
HEY, UH, SO LISTEN, RIGHT? I WAS JUST OVER THERE WITH MY FRIENDS, AND I TOLD THEM, HONEST TO GOD, I TOLD THEM THIS.
"IF THAT REDHEAD LADY DOESN'T GO HOME WITH ME, I'LL BE THE UNHAPPIEST MAN IN THE WORLD."
AND THEY BET ME, CAN YOU BELIEVE THAT? THIRTY BUCKS, THAT I WOULDN'T SCORE WITH YOU TONIGHT.
SO, YOU WANNA HELP ME?
DEE DE DEED...
CAVEMEN

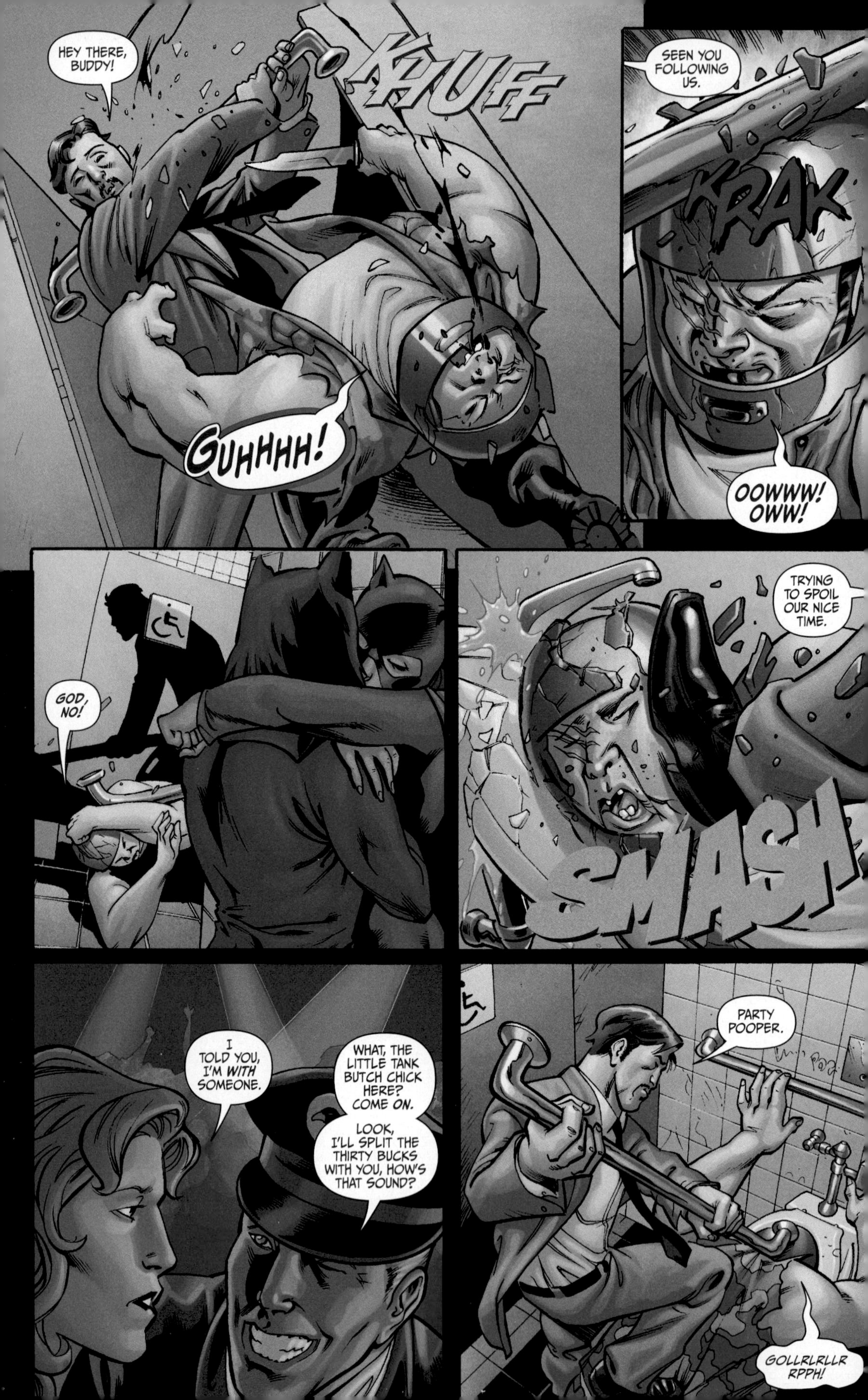
HEY THERE, BUDDY!
KTUFF
GUHHHH!
SEEN YOU FOLLOWING US.
KRAK
OOWWW! OWW!
GOD, NO!
TRYING TO SPOIL OUR NICE TIME.
SMASH
I TOLD YOU, I'M WITH SOMEONE.
WHAT, THE LITTLE TANK BUTCH CHICK HERE? COME ON.
LOOK, I'LL SPLIT THE THIRTY BUCKS WITH YOU, HOW'S THAT SOUND?
PARTY POOPER.
GOLLRLRLLR RPPH!

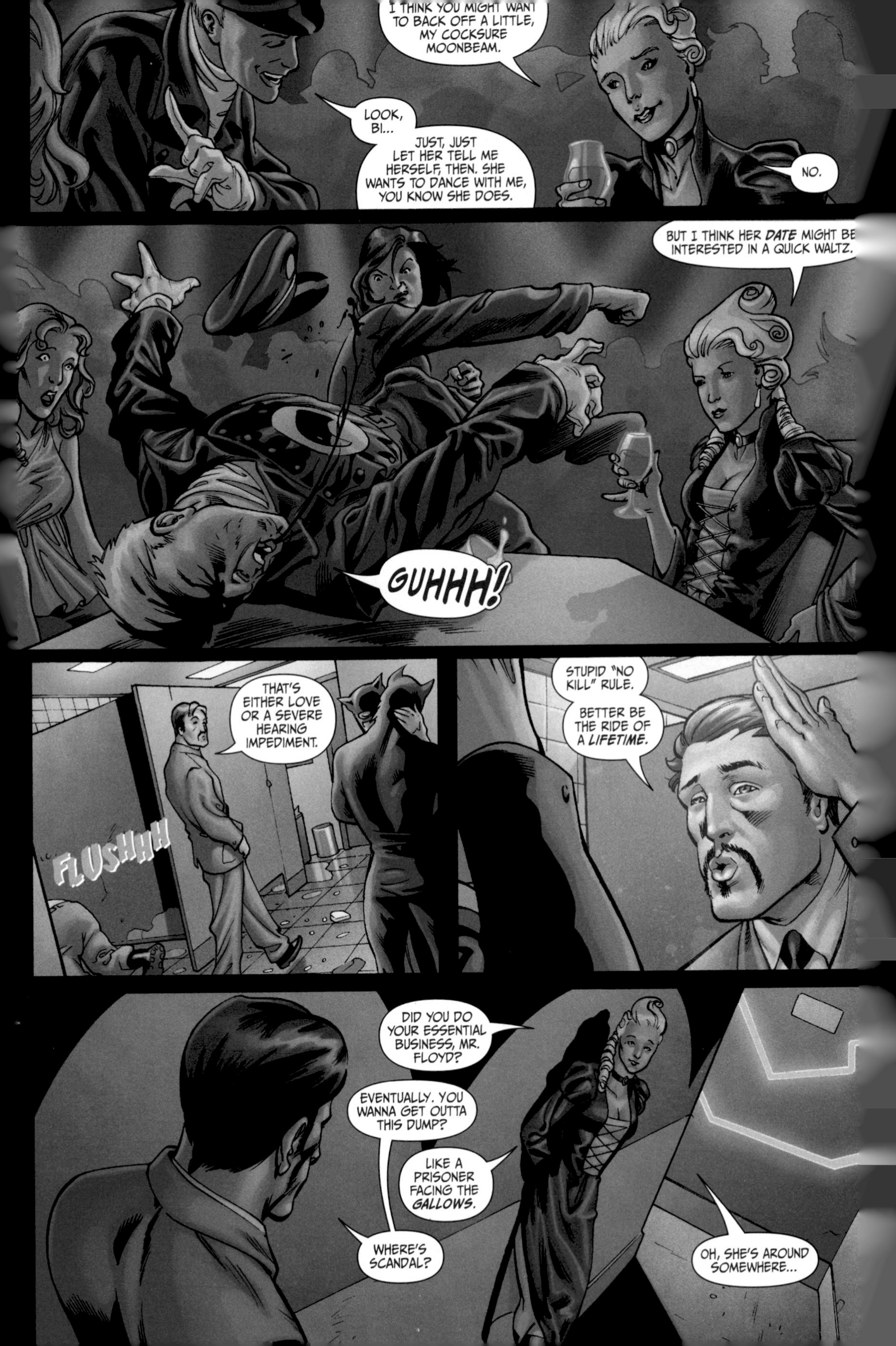
I THINK YOU MIGHT WANT TO BACK OFF A LITTLE, MY COCKSURE MOONBEAM.
LOOK, BI...
JUST, JUST LET HER TELL ME HERSELF, THEN. SHE WANTS TO DANCE WITH ME, YOU KNOW SHE DOES.
NO.
BUT I THINK HER DATE MIGHT BE INTERESTED IN A QUICK WALTZ.
GUHHH!
THAT'S EITHER LOVE OR A SEVERE HEARING IMPEDIMENT.
FLUSHHH
STUPID "NO KILL" RULE.
BETTER BE THE RIDE OF A LIFETIME.
DID YOU DO YOUR ESSENTIAL BUSINESS, MR. FLOYD?
EVENTUALLY. YOU WANNA GET OUTTA THIS DUMP?
LIKE A PRISONER FACING THE GALLOWS.
WHERE'S SCANDAL?
OH, SHE'S AROUND SOMEWHERE...

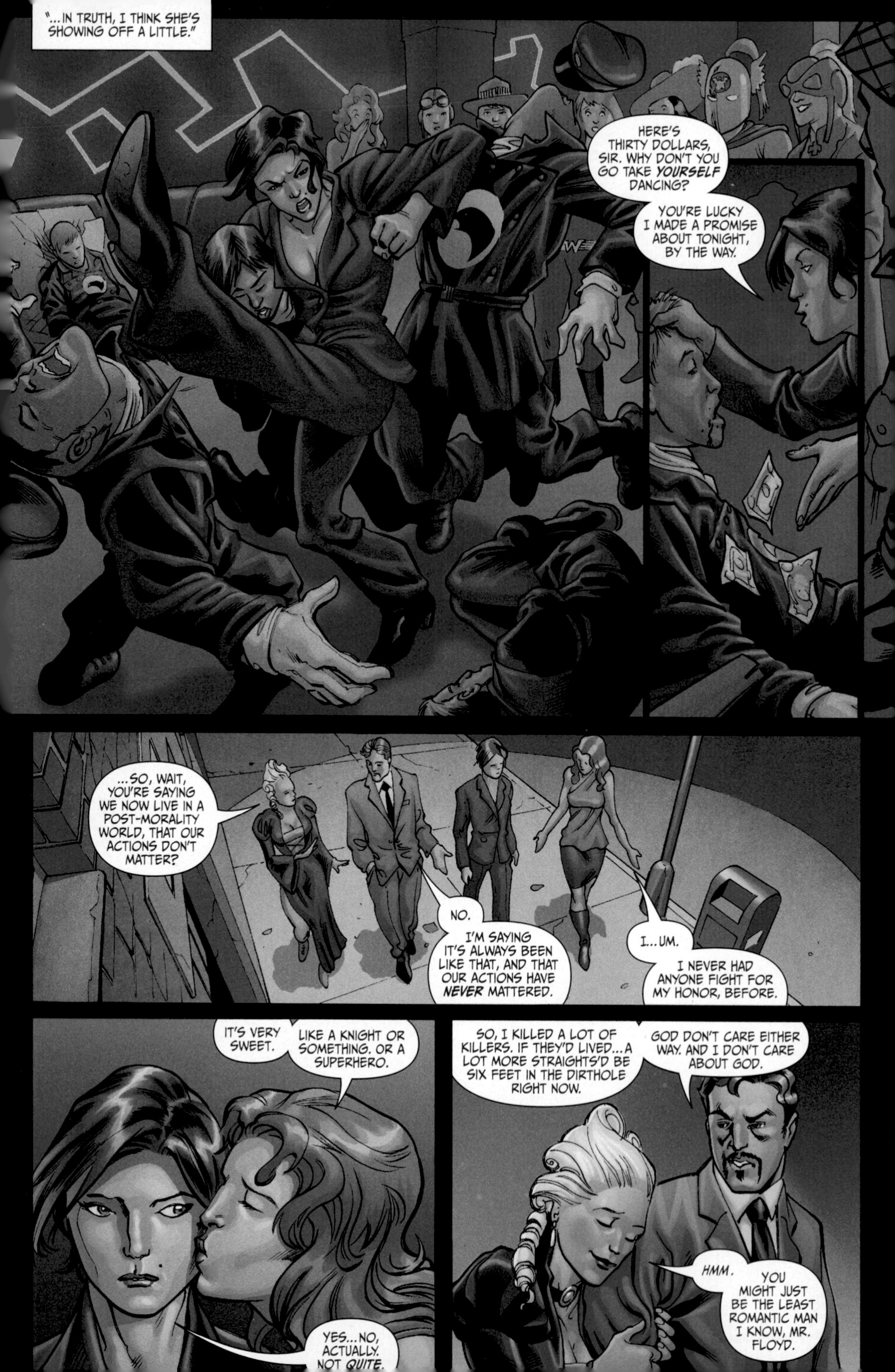

"...IN TRUTH, I THINK SHE'S SHOWING OFF A LITTLE."
HERE'S THIRTY DOLLARS, SIR. WHY DON'T YOU GO TAKE *YOURSELF* DANCING?
YOU'RE LUCKY I MADE A PROMISE ABOUT TONIGHT, BY THE WAY.
...SO, WAIT, YOU'RE SAYING WE NOW LIVE IN A POST-MORALITY WORLD, THAT OUR ACTIONS DON'T MATTER?
NO.
I'M SAYING IT'S ALWAYS BEEN LIKE THAT, AND THAT OUR ACTIONS HAVE *NEVER* MATTERED.
I...UM.
I NEVER HAD ANYONE FIGHT FOR MY HONOR, BEFORE.
IT'S VERY SWEET.
LIKE A KNIGHT OR SOMETHING. OR A SUPERHERO.
YES...NO, ACTUALLY. NOT *QUITE*.
SO, I KILLED A LOT OF KILLERS. IF THEY'D LIVED...A LOT MORE STRAIGHTS'D BE SIX FEET IN THE DIRTHOLE RIGHT NOW.
GOD DON'T CARE EITHER WAY. AND I DON'T CARE ABOUT GOD.
HMM.
YOU MIGHT JUST BE THE LEAST ROMANTIC MAN I KNOW, MR. FLOYD.

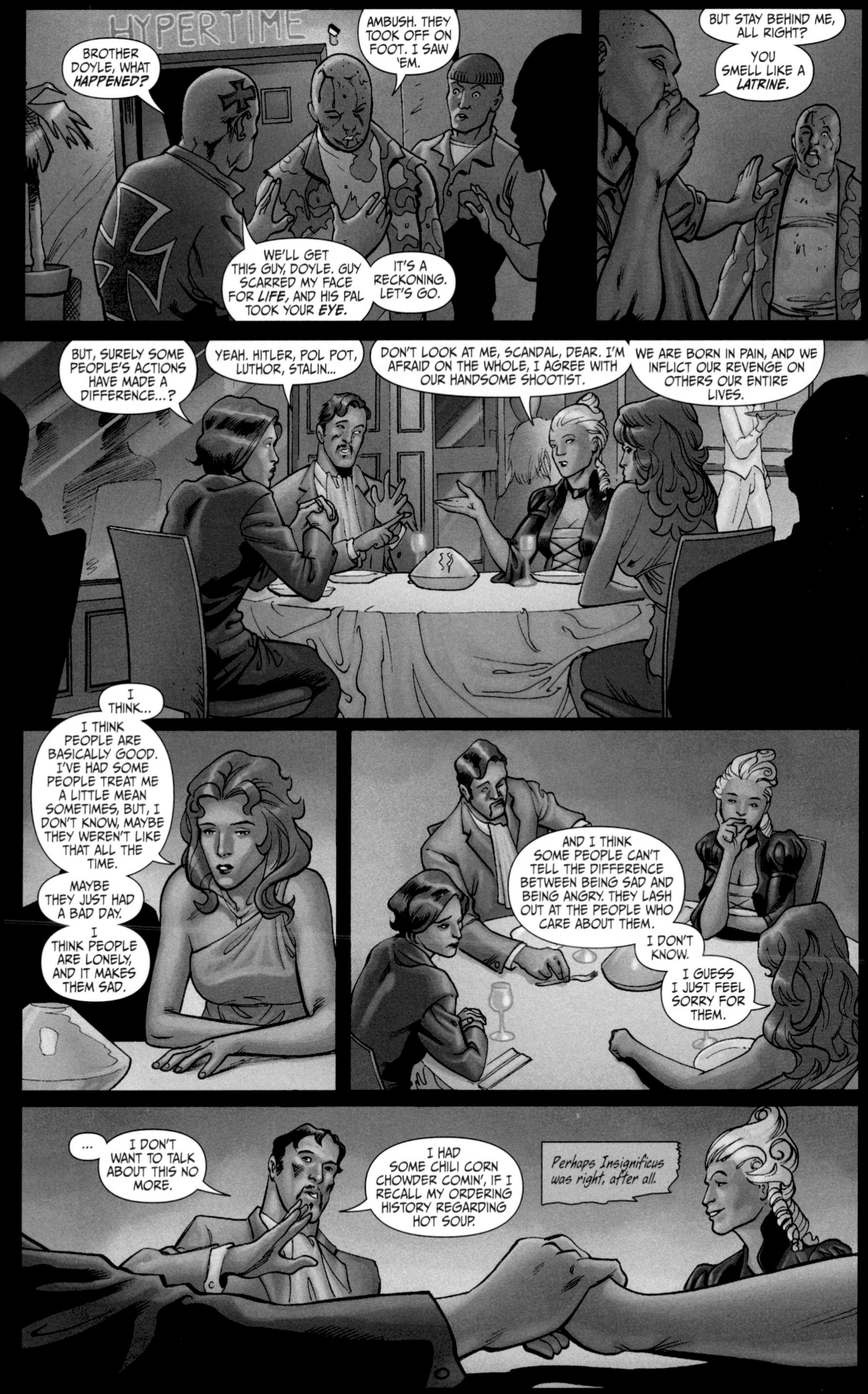
HYPERTIME
BROTHER DOYLE, WHAT HAPPENED?
AMBUSH. THEY TOOK OFF ON FOOT. I SAW 'EM.
WE'LL GET THIS GUY, DOYLE. GUY SCARRED MY FACE FOR LIFE, AND HIS PAL TOOK YOUR EYE.
IT'S A RECKONING. LET'S GO.
BUT STAY BEHIND ME, ALL RIGHT?
YOU SMELL LIKE A LATRINE.
BUT, SURELY SOME PEOPLE'S ACTIONS HAVE MADE A DIFFERENCE...?
YEAH. HITLER, POL POT, LUTHOR, STALIN...
DON'T LOOK AT ME, SCANDAL, DEAR. I'M AFRAID ON THE WHOLE, I AGREE WITH OUR HANDSOME SHOOTIST.
WE ARE BORN IN PAIN, AND WE INFLICT OUR REVENGE ON OTHERS OUR ENTIRE LIVES.
I THINK...
I THINK PEOPLE ARE BASICALLY GOOD. I'VE HAD SOME PEOPLE TREAT ME A LITTLE MEAN SOMETIMES, BUT, I DON'T KNOW, MAYBE THEY WEREN'T LIKE THAT ALL THE TIME.
MAYBE THEY JUST HAD A BAD DAY.
I THINK PEOPLE ARE LONELY, AND IT MAKES THEM SAD.
AND I THINK SOME PEOPLE CAN'T TELL THE DIFFERENCE BETWEEN BEING SAD AND BEING ANGRY. THEY LASH OUT AT THE PEOPLE WHO CARE ABOUT THEM.
I DON'T KNOW.
I GUESS I JUST FEEL SORRY FOR THEM.
...
I DON'T WANT TO TALK ABOUT THIS NO MORE.
I HAD SOME CHILI CORN CHOWDER COMIN', IF I RECALL MY ORDERING HISTORY REGARDING HOT SOUP.
Perhaps Insignificus was right, after all.

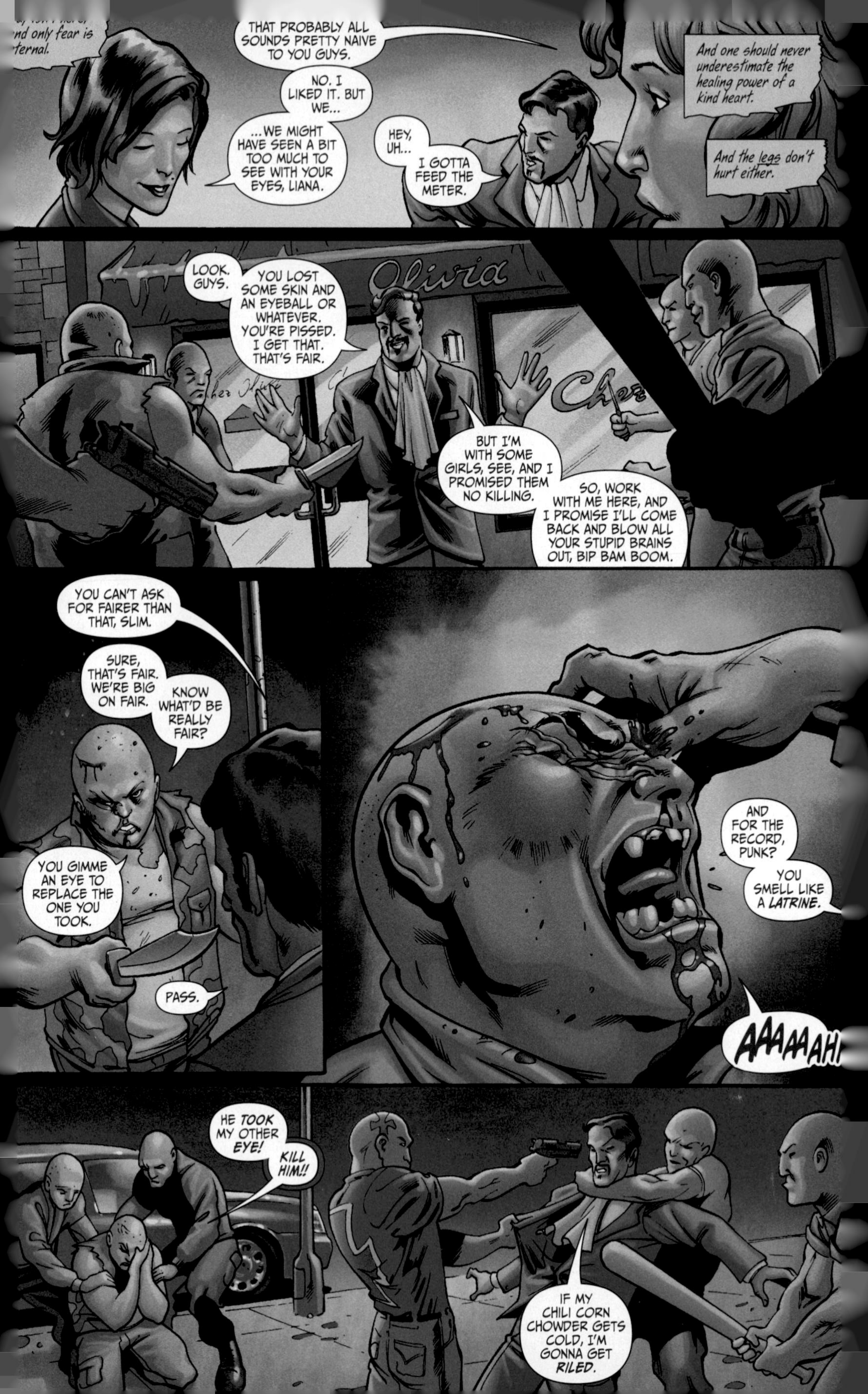
...nd only fear is ...ternal.
THAT PROBABLY ALL SOUNDS PRETTY NAIVE TO YOU GUYS.
NO. I LIKED IT. BUT WE...
...WE MIGHT HAVE SEEN A BIT TOO MUCH TO SEE WITH YOUR EYES, LIANA.
HEY, UH...
I GOTTA FEED THE METER.
And one should never underestimate the healing power of a kind heart.
And the legs don't hurt either.
LOOK. GUYS.
YOU LOST SOME SKIN AND AN EYEBALL OR WHATEVER. YOU'RE PISSED. I GET THAT. THAT'S FAIR.
BUT I'M WITH SOME GIRLS, SEE, AND I PROMISED THEM NO KILLING.
SO, WORK WITH ME HERE, AND I PROMISE I'LL COME BACK AND BLOW ALL YOUR STUPID BRAINS OUT, BIP BAM BOOM.
YOU CAN'T ASK FOR FAIRER THAN THAT, SLIM.
SURE, THAT'S FAIR. WE'RE BIG ON FAIR.
KNOW WHAT'D BE REALLY FAIR?
YOU GIMME AN EYE TO REPLACE THE ONE YOU TOOK.
PASS.
AND FOR THE RECORD, PUNK?
YOU SMELL LIKE A LATRINE.
AAAAAAH!
HE TOOK MY OTHER EYE!
KILL HIM!!
IF MY CHILI CORN CHOWDER GETS COLD, I'M GONNA GET RILED.

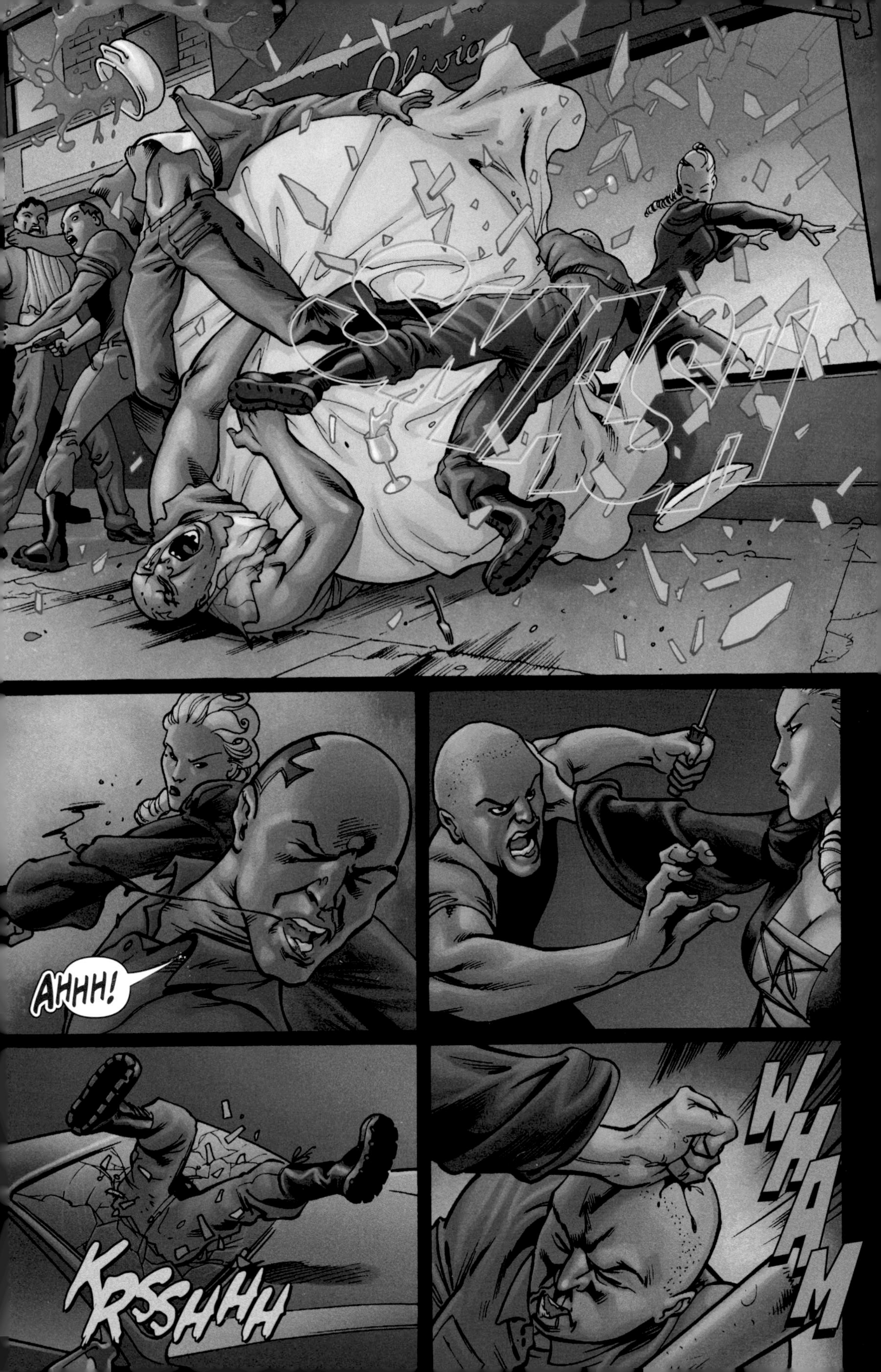
Olivia
SMASH
AHHH!
KRSSHHH
WHAAM

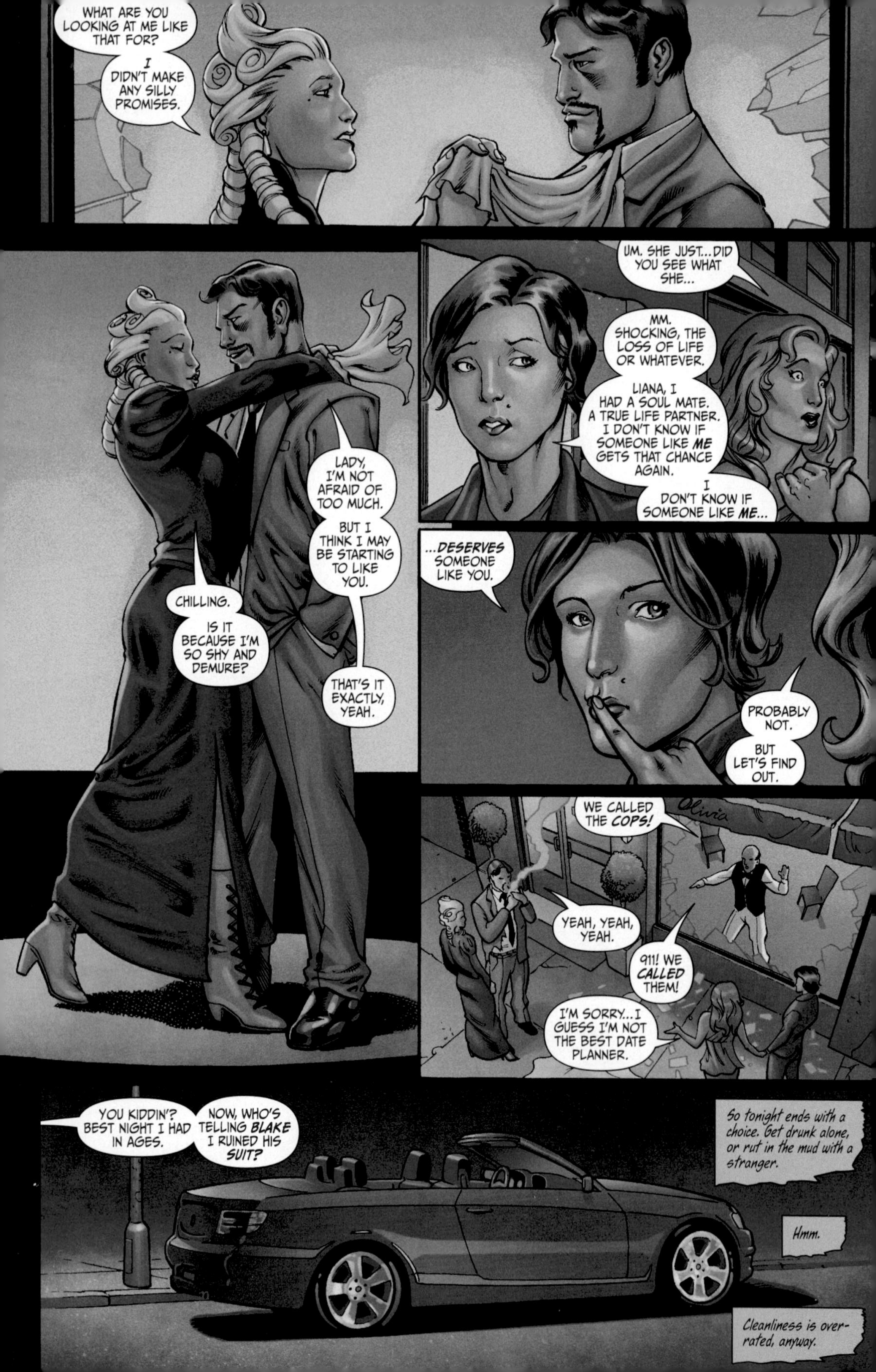
WHAT ARE YOU LOOKING AT ME LIKE THAT FOR?
I DIDN'T MAKE ANY SILLY PROMISES.
LADY, I'M NOT AFRAID OF TOO MUCH.
BUT I THINK I MAY BE STARTING TO LIKE YOU.
CHILLING.
IS IT BECAUSE I'M SO SHY AND DEMURE?
THAT'S IT EXACTLY, YEAH.
UM. SHE JUST...DID YOU SEE WHAT SHE...
MM. SHOCKING, THE LOSS OF LIFE OR WHATEVER.
LIANA, I HAD A SOUL MATE. A TRUE LIFE PARTNER. I DON'T KNOW IF SOMEONE LIKE ME GETS THAT CHANCE AGAIN.
I DON'T KNOW IF SOMEONE LIKE ME...
...DESERVES SOMEONE LIKE YOU.
PROBABLY NOT.
BUT LET'S FIND OUT.
Olivia
WE CALLED THE COPS!
YEAH, YEAH, YEAH.
911! WE CALLED THEM!
I'M SORRY...I GUESS I'M NOT THE BEST DATE PLANNER.
YOU KIDDIN'? BEST NIGHT I HAD IN AGES.
NOW, WHO'S TELLING BLAKE I RUINED HIS SUIT?
So tonight ends with a choice. Get drunk alone, or rut in the mud with a stranger.
Hmm.
Cleanliness is overrated, anyway.

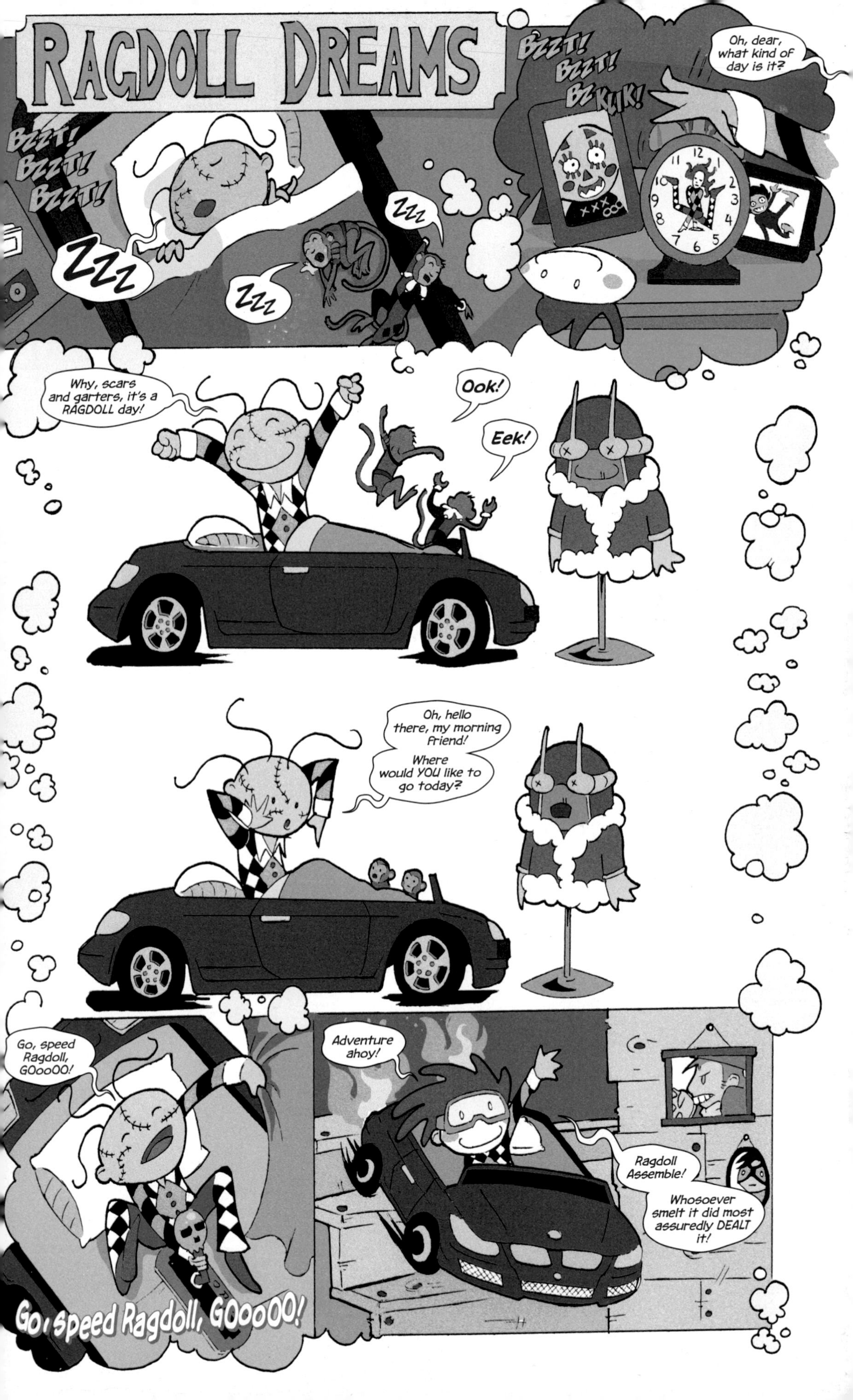

RAGDOLL DREAMS
BZZT! BZZT! BZZT!
ZZZ
ZZZ
ZZZ
BZZT! BZZT! BZ KLIK!
Oh, dear, what kind of day is it?
Why, scars and garters, it's a RAGDOLL day!
Ook!
Eek!
Oh, hello there, my morning friend!
Where would YOU like to go today?
Go, speed Ragdoll, GOooOO!
Adventure ahoy!
Ragdoll Assemble!
Whosoever smelt it did most assuredly DEALT it!
Go, speed Ragdoll, GOooOO!

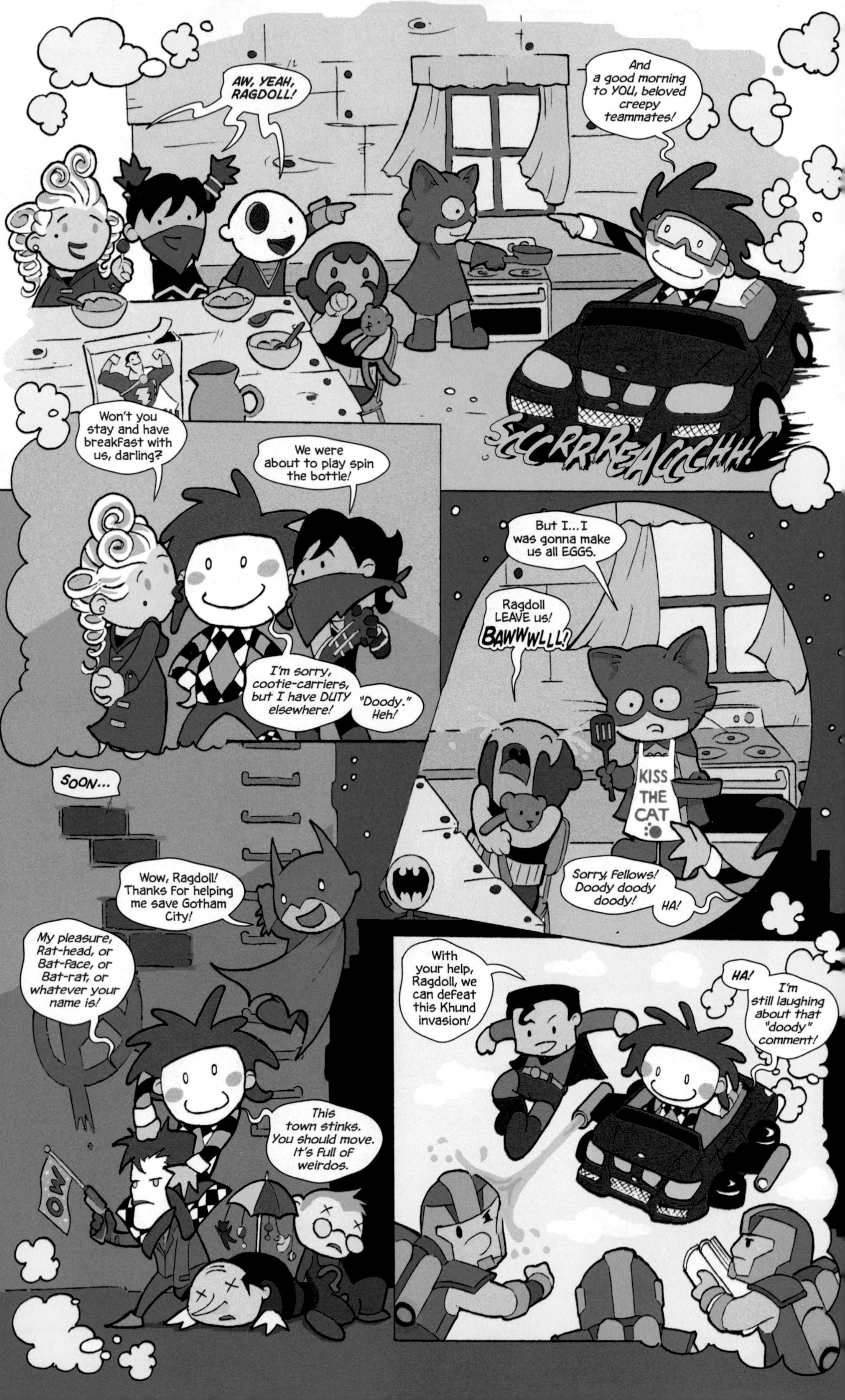
AW, YEAH, RAGDOLL!
And a good morning to YOU, beloved creepy teammates!
SCCCRRRREACCCHHH!
Won't you stay and have breakfast with us, darling?
We were about to play spin the bottle!
I'm sorry, cootie-carriers, but I have DUTY elsewhere!
"Doody." Heh!
But I...I was gonna make us all EGGS.
Ragdoll LEAVE us!
BAWWWLLL!
KISS THE CAT
Sorry, fellows! Doody doody doody!
HA!
SOON...
Wow, Ragdoll! Thanks for helping me save Gotham City!
My pleasure, Rat-head, or Bat-face, or Bat-rat, or whatever your name is!
This town stinks. You should move. It's full of weirdos.
OW
With your help, Ragdoll, we can defeat this Khund invasion!
HA!
I'm still laughing about that "doody" comment!

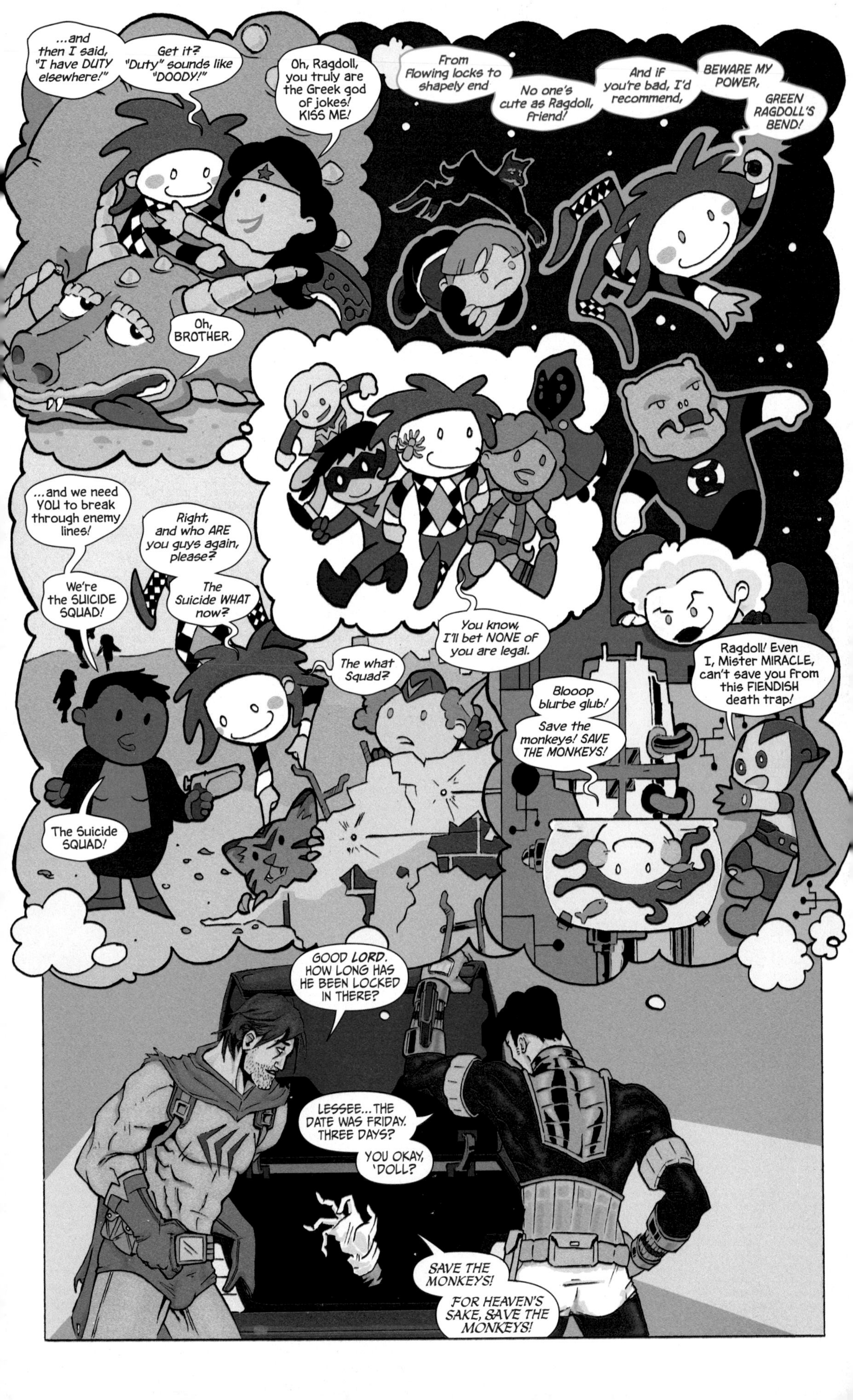

...and then I said, "I have DUTY elsewhere!"
Get it? "Duty" sounds like "DOODY!"
Oh, Ragdoll, you truly are the Greek god of jokes! KISS ME!
Oh, BROTHER.
From flowing locks to shapely end
No one's cute as Ragdoll, friend!
And if you're bad, I'd recommend,
BEWARE MY POWER,
GREEN RAGDOLL'S BEND!
...and we need YOU to break through enemy lines!
Right, and who ARE you guys again, please?
We're the SUICIDE SQUAD!
The Suicide WHAT now?
The Suicide SQUAD!
The what Squad?
You know, I'll bet NONE of you are legal.
Blooop blurbe glub!
Save the monkeys! SAVE THE MONKEYS!
Ragdoll! Even I, Mister MIRACLE, can't save you from this FIENDISH death trap!
GOOD LORD. HOW LONG HAS HE BEEN LOCKED IN THERE?
LESSEE... THE DATE WAS FRIDAY. THREE DAYS?
YOU OKAY, 'DOLL?
SAVE THE MONKEYS!
FOR HEAVEN'S SAKE, SAVE THE MONKEYS!

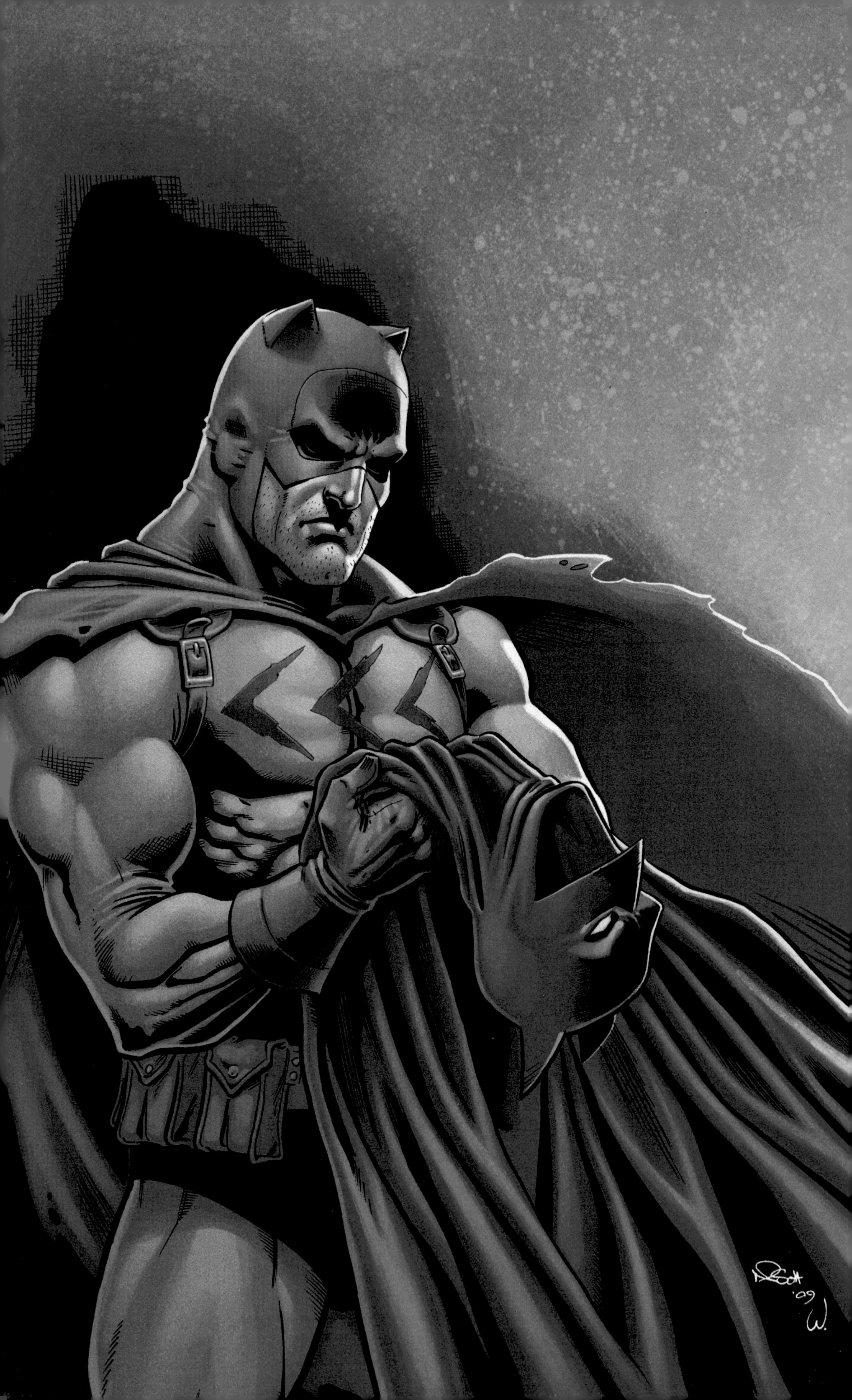

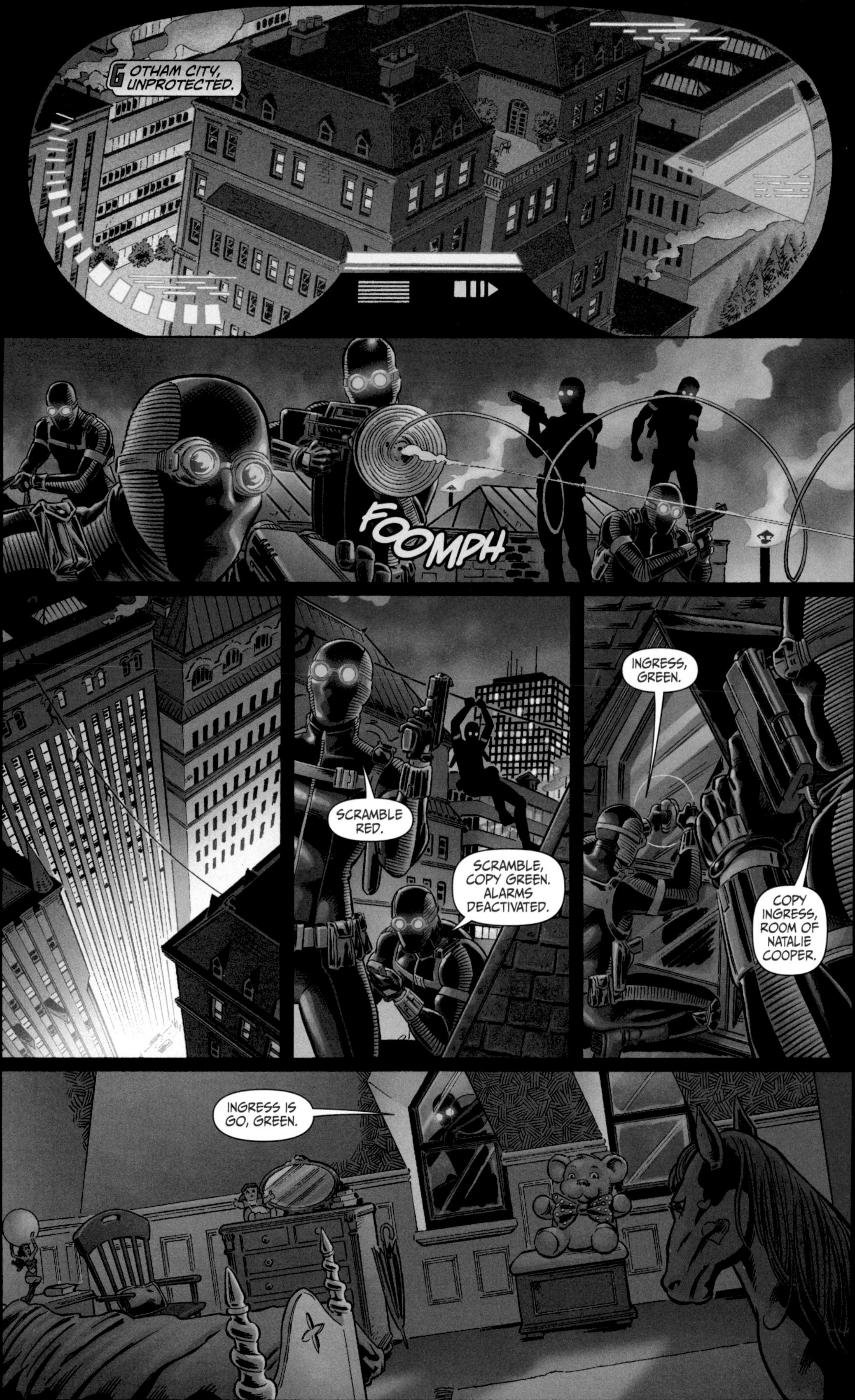
GOTHAM CITY, UNPROTECTED.
FOOMPH
SCRAMBLE RED.
SCRAMBLE, COPY GREEN. ALARMS DEACTIVATED.
INGRESS, GREEN.
COPY INGRESS, ROOM OF NATALIE COOPER.
INGRESS IS GO, GREEN.

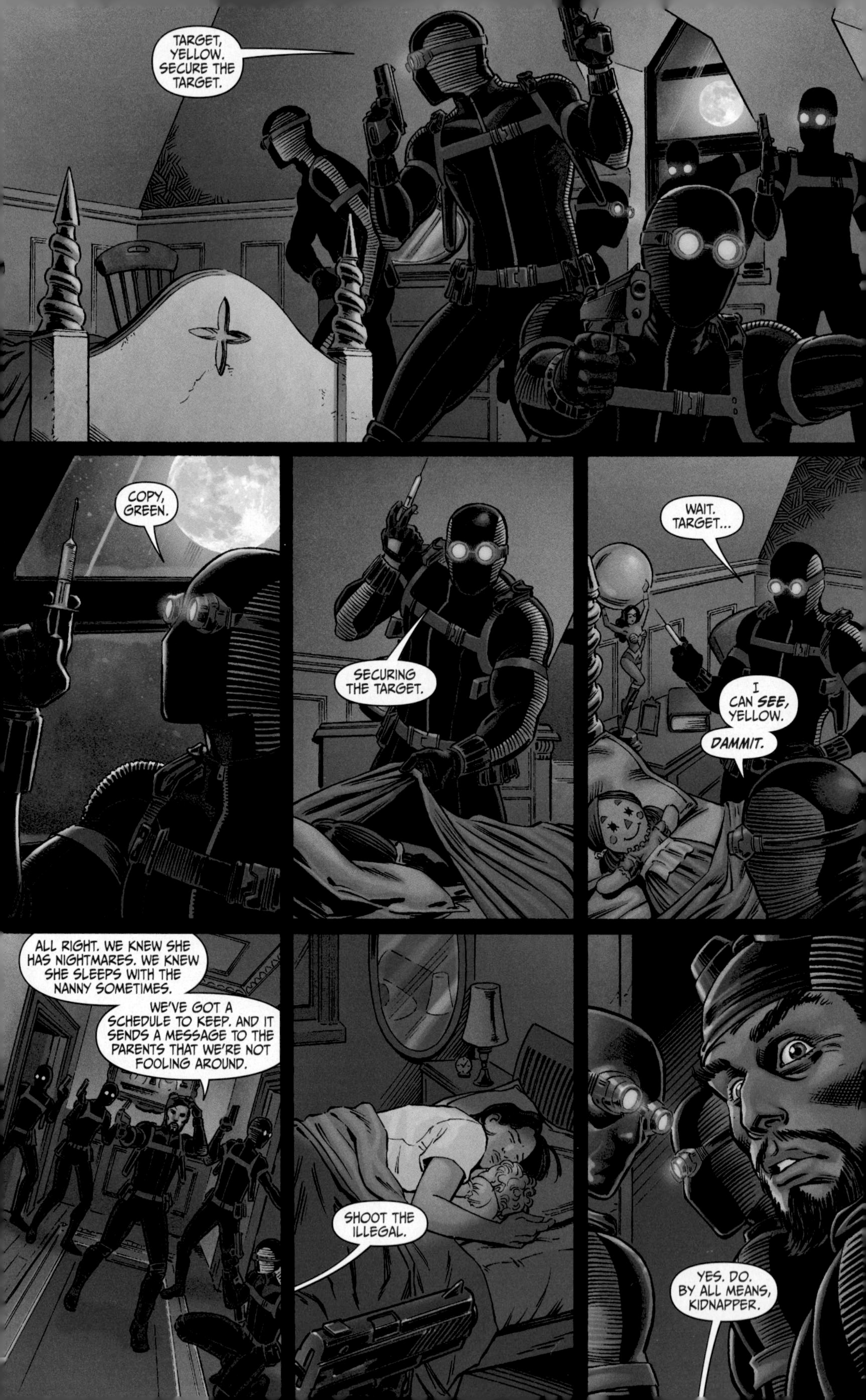
TARGET, YELLOW. SECURE THE TARGET.
COPY, GREEN.
SECURING THE TARGET.
WAIT. TARGET...
I CAN SEE, YELLOW.
DAMMIT.
ALL RIGHT. WE KNEW SHE HAS NIGHTMARES. WE KNEW SHE SLEEPS WITH THE NANNY SOMETIMES.
WE'VE GOT A SCHEDULE TO KEEP. AND IT SENDS A MESSAGE TO THE PARENTS THAT WE'RE NOT FOOLING AROUND.
SHOOT THE ILLEGAL.
YES. DO. BY ALL MEANS, KIDNAPPER.

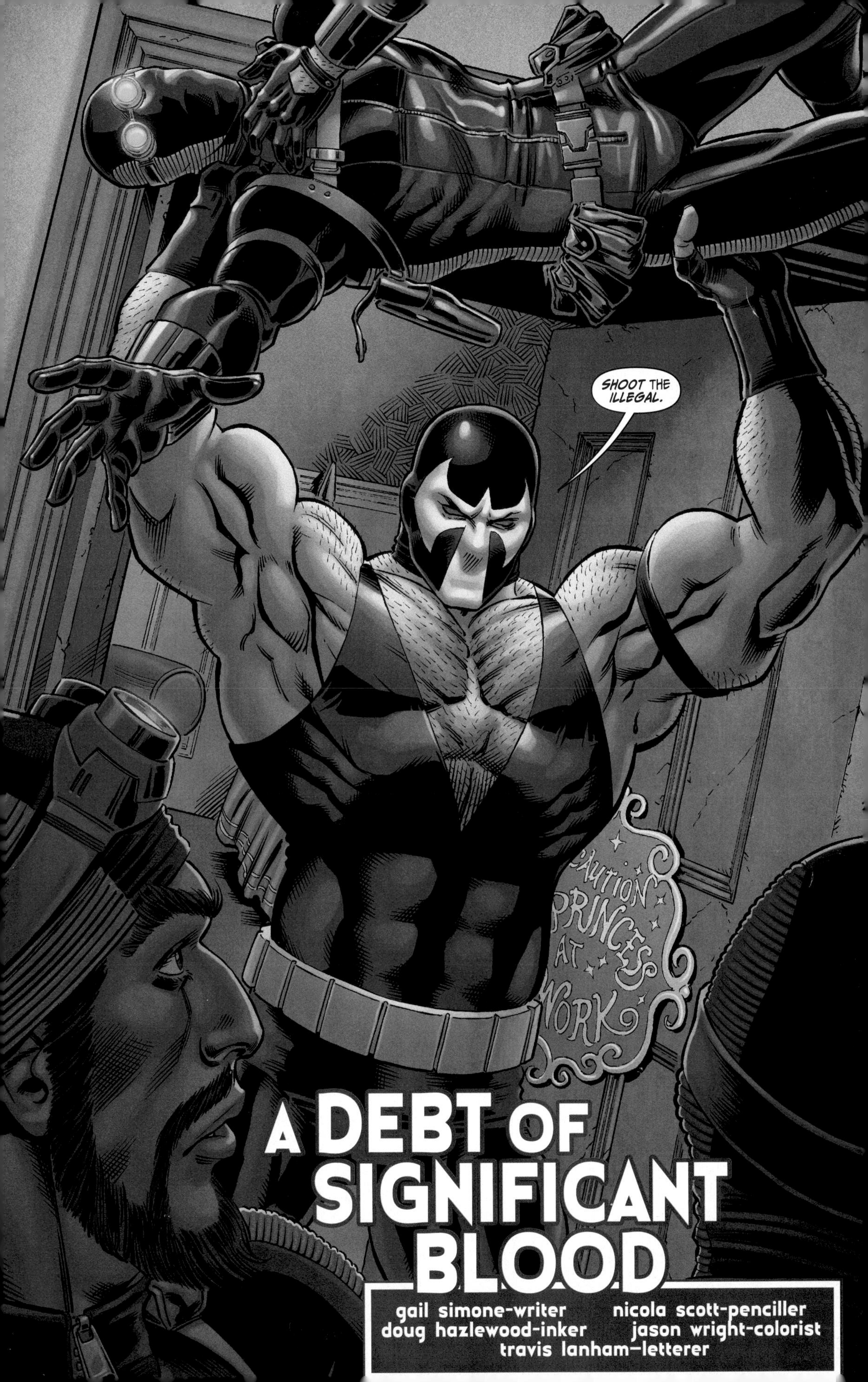
SHOOT THE ILLEGAL.
CAUTION PRINCESS AT WORK
A DEBT OF SIGNIFICANT BLOOD
gail simone-writer nicola scott-penciller
doug hazlewood-inker jason wright-colorist
travis lanham-letterer

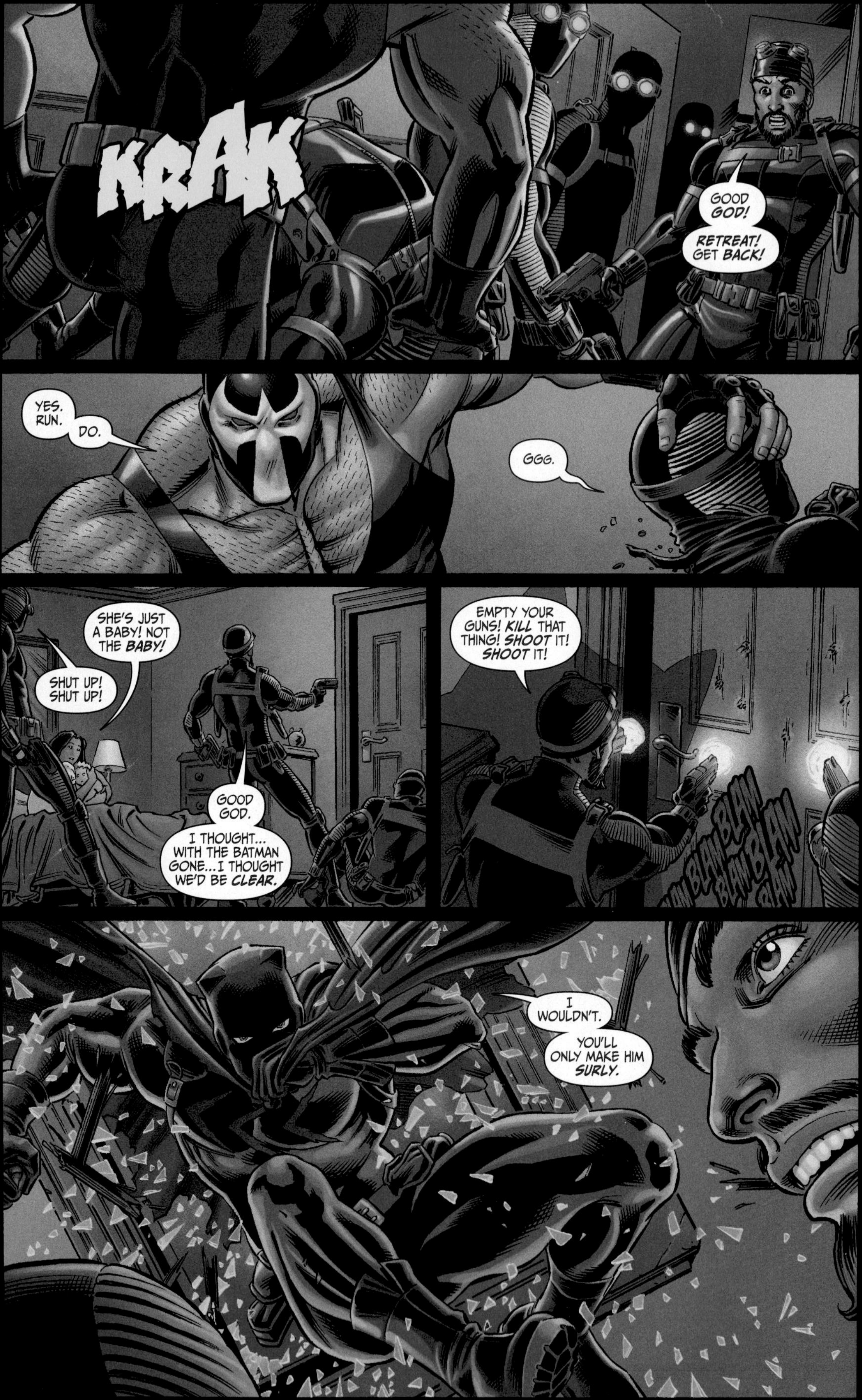
KRAK
GOOD GOD!
RETREAT! GET BACK!
YES. RUN.
DO.
GGG.
SHE'S JUST A BABY! NOT THE BABY!
SHUT UP! SHUT UP!
GOOD GOD.
I THOUGHT... WITH THE BATMAN GONE...I THOUGHT WE'D BE CLEAR.
EMPTY YOUR GUNS! KILL THAT THING! SHOOT IT! SHOOT IT!
BLAM BLAM BLAM BLAM
I WOULDN'T.
YOU'LL ONLY MAKE HIM SURLY.

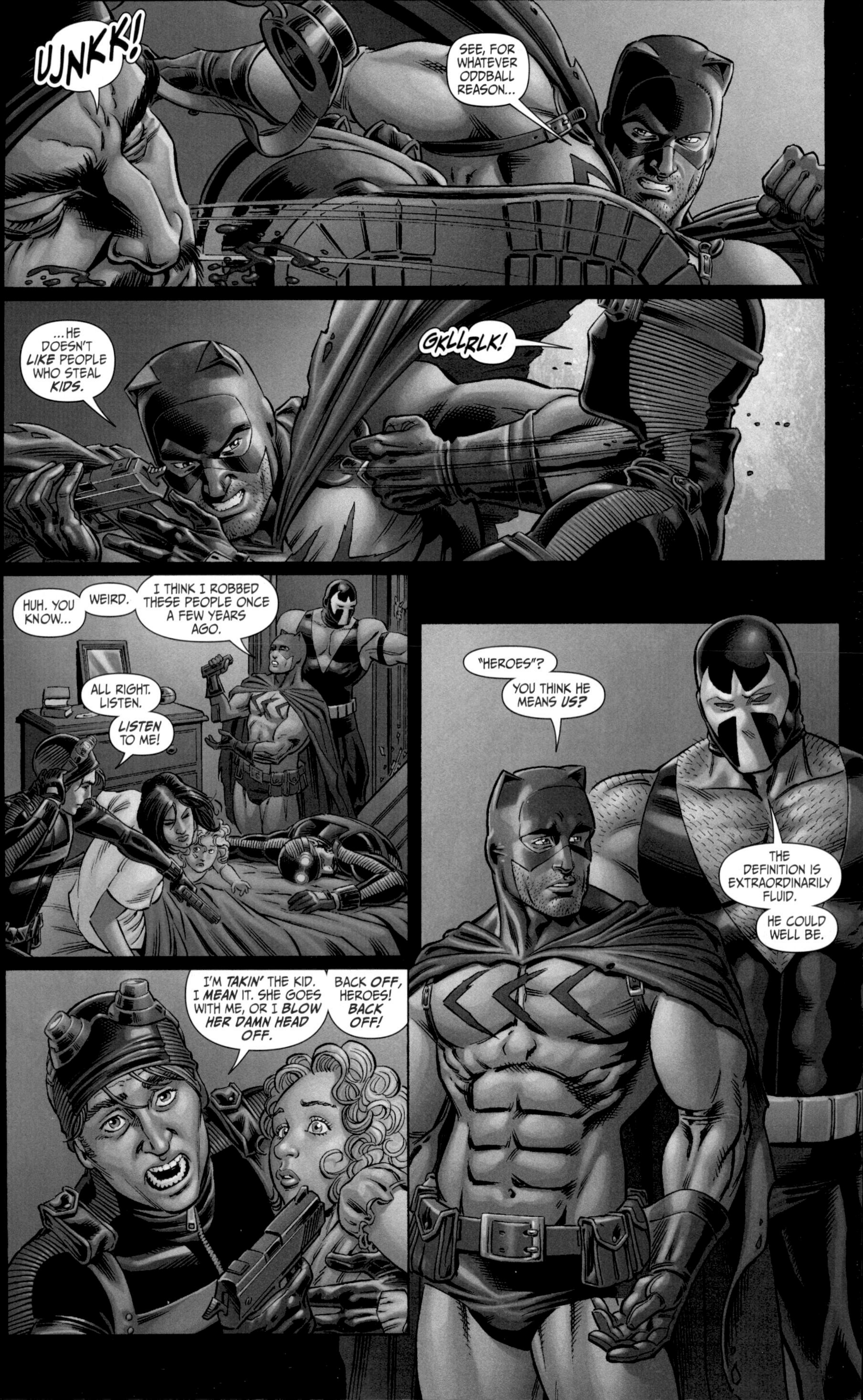
UJNKK!
SEE, FOR WHATEVER ODDBALL REASON...
...HE DOESN'T LIKE PEOPLE WHO STEAL KIDS.
GKLLRLK!
HUH. YOU KNOW...
WEIRD.
I THINK I ROBBED THESE PEOPLE ONCE A FEW YEARS AGO.
ALL RIGHT. LISTEN.
LISTEN TO ME!
I'M TAKIN' THE KID. I MEAN IT. SHE GOES WITH ME, OR I BLOW HER DAMN HEAD OFF.
BACK OFF, HEROES! BACK OFF!
"HEROES"?
YOU THINK HE MEANS US?
THE DEFINITION IS EXTRAORDINARILY FLUID.
HE COULD WELL BE.

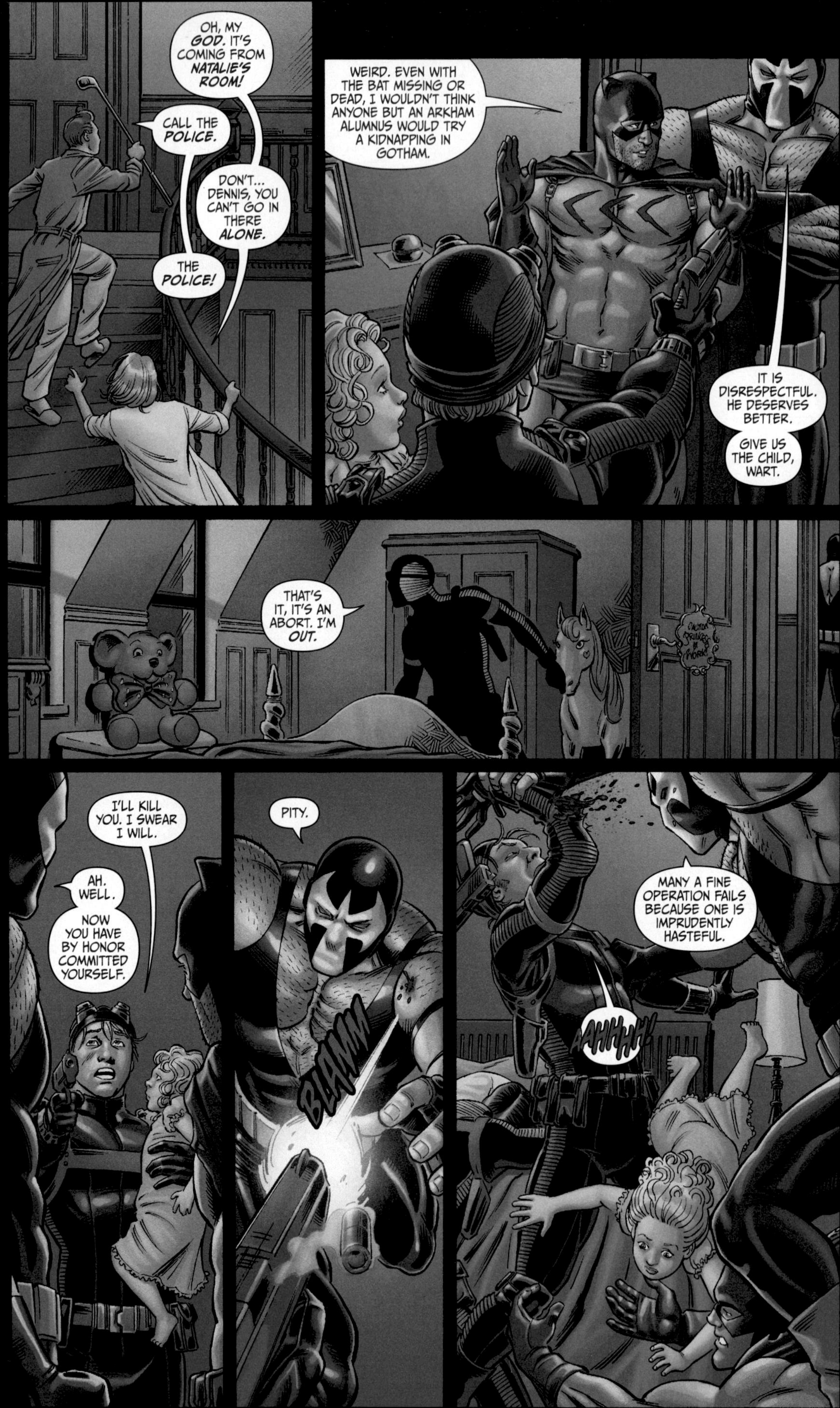
OH, MY GOD. IT'S COMING FROM NATALIE'S ROOM!
CALL THE POLICE.
DON'T... DENNIS, YOU CAN'T GO IN THERE ALONE.
THE POLICE!
WEIRD. EVEN WITH THE BAT MISSING OR DEAD, I WOULDN'T THINK ANYONE BUT AN ARKHAM ALUMNUS WOULD TRY A KIDNAPPING IN GOTHAM.
IT IS DISRESPECTFUL. HE DESERVES BETTER.
GIVE US THE CHILD, WART.
THAT'S IT, IT'S AN ABORT. I'M OUT.
I'LL KILL YOU. I SWEAR I WILL.
AH. WELL.
NOW YOU HAVE BY HONOR COMMITTED YOURSELF.
PITY.
BLAMM
MANY A FINE OPERATION FAILS BECAUSE ONE IS IMPRUDENTLY HASTEFUL.
AAHHHH!

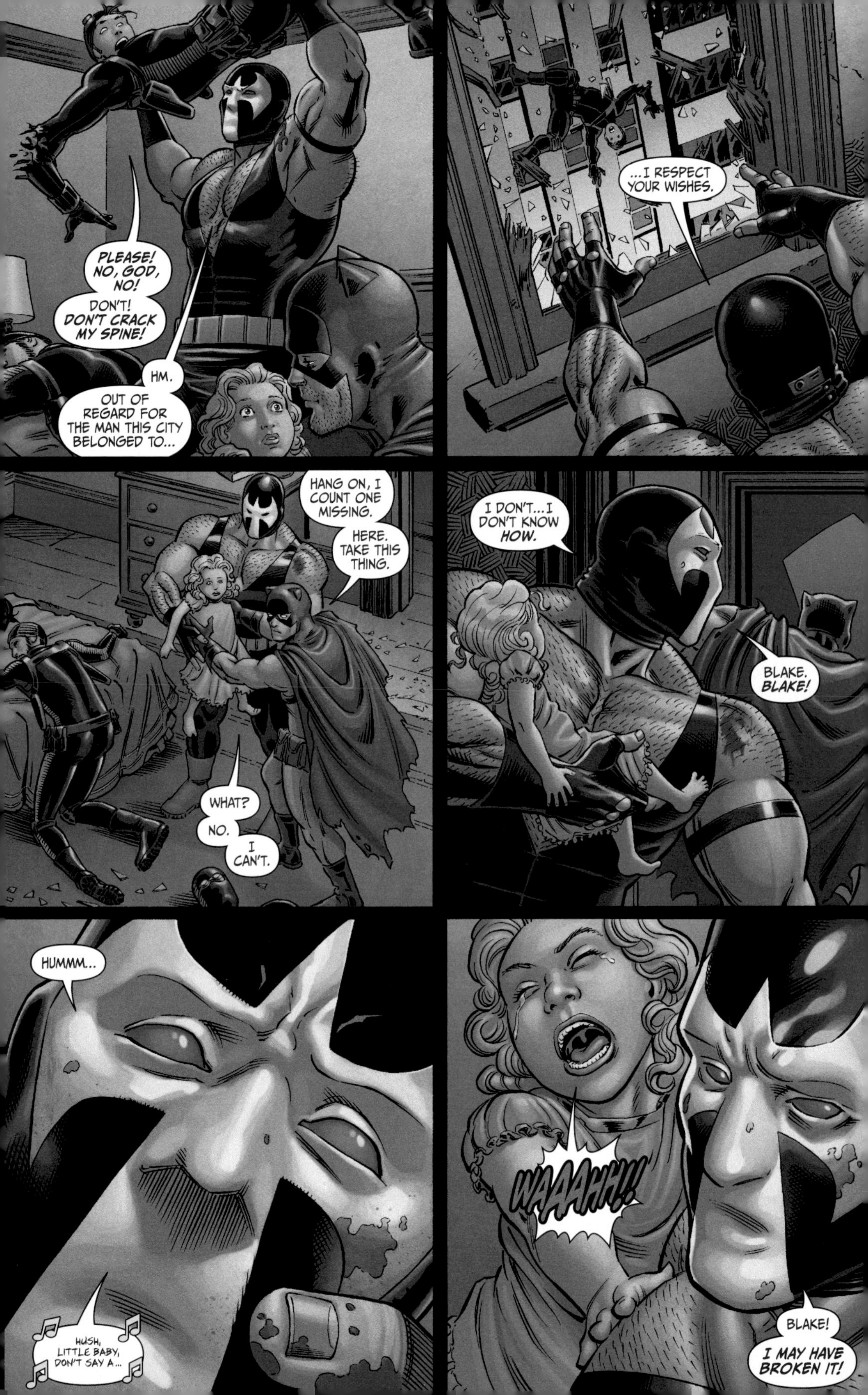
PLEASE! NO, GOD, NO!
DON'T! DON'T CRACK MY SPINE!
HM.
OUT OF REGARD FOR THE MAN THIS CITY BELONGED TO...
...I RESPECT YOUR WISHES.
HANG ON, I COUNT ONE MISSING.
HERE. TAKE THIS THING.
WHAT?
NO.
I CAN'T.
I DON'T...I DON'T KNOW HOW.
BLAKE. BLAKE!
HUMMM...
HUSH, LITTLE BABY, DON'T SAY A...
WAAAHH!!
BLAKE!
I MAY HAVE BROKEN IT!

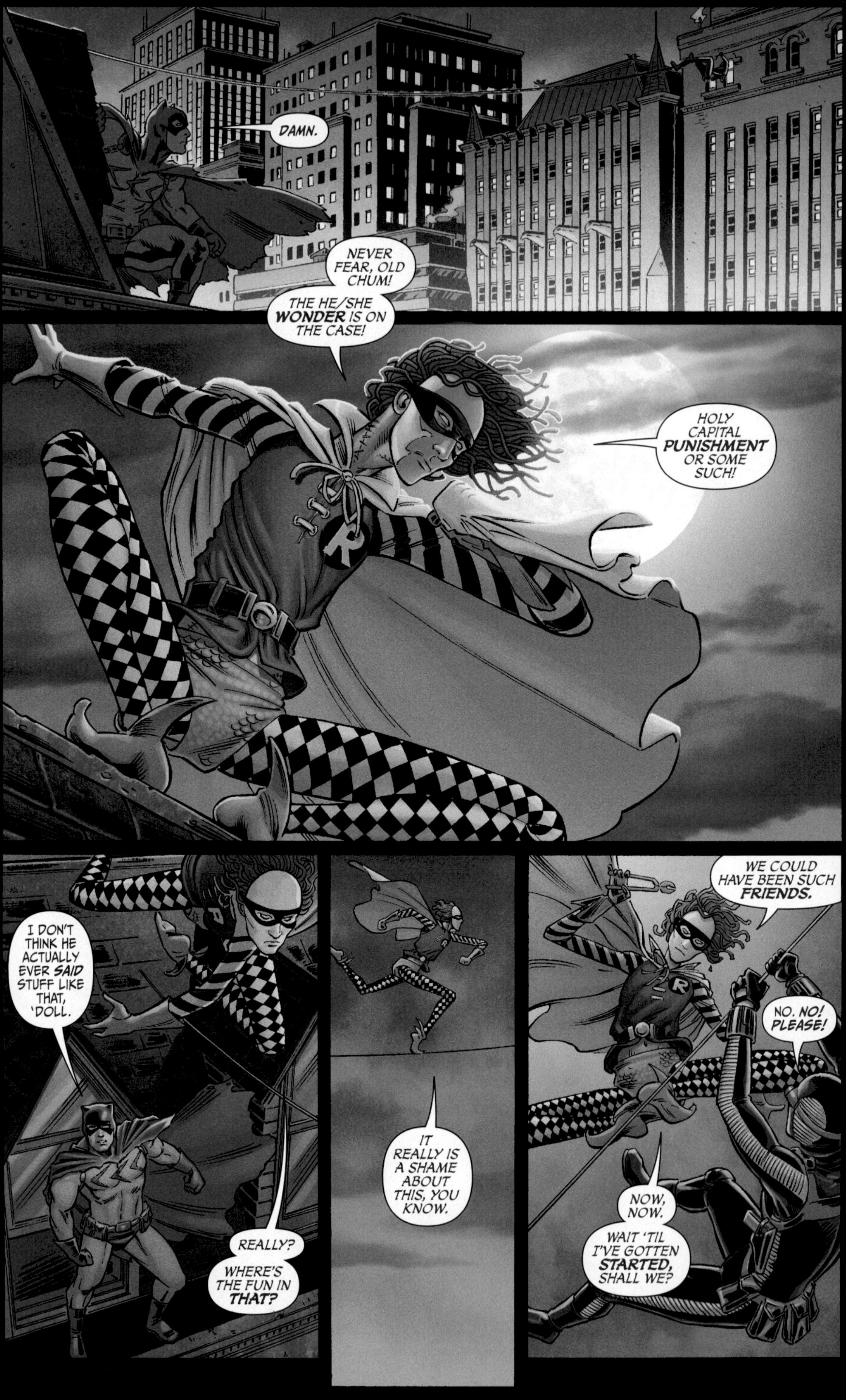
DAMN.
NEVER FEAR, OLD CHUM!
THE HE/SHE WONDER IS ON THE CASE!
HOLY CAPITAL PUNISHMENT OR SOME SUCH!
I DON'T THINK HE ACTUALLY EVER SAID STUFF LIKE THAT, 'DOLL.
REALLY?
WHERE'S THE FUN IN THAT?
IT REALLY IS A SHAME ABOUT THIS, YOU KNOW.
WE COULD HAVE BEEN SUCH FRIENDS.
NO. NO! PLEASE!
NOW, NOW.
WAIT 'TIL I'VE GOTTEN STARTED, SHALL WE?

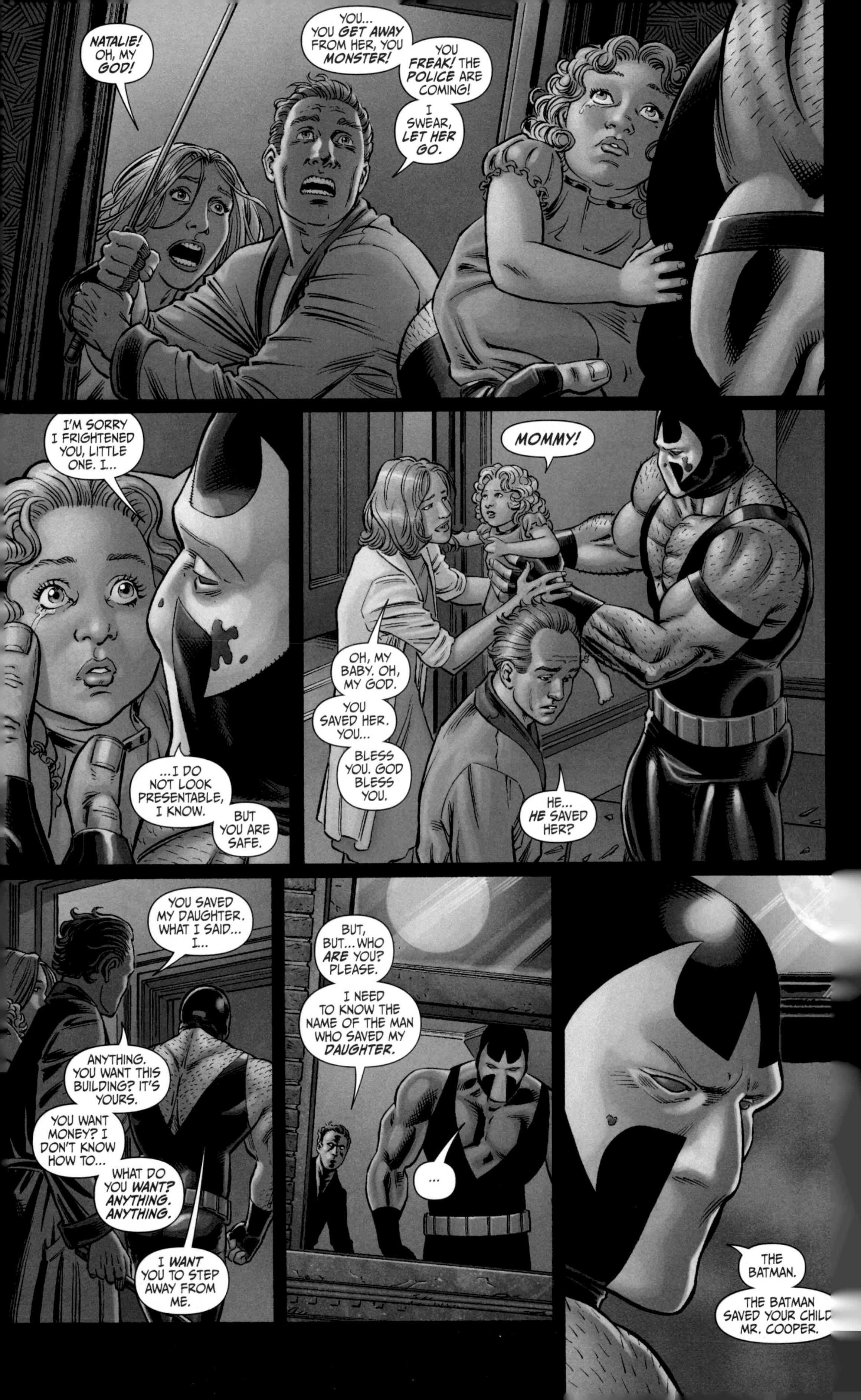
NATALIE! OH, MY GOD!
YOU... YOU GET AWAY FROM HER, YOU MONSTER!
YOU FREAK! THE POLICE ARE COMING!
I SWEAR, LET HER GO.
I'M SORRY I FRIGHTENED YOU, LITTLE ONE. I...
...I DO NOT LOOK PRESENTABLE, I KNOW.
BUT YOU ARE SAFE.
MOMMY!
OH, MY BABY. OH, MY GOD.
YOU SAVED HER. YOU...
BLESS YOU. GOD BLESS YOU.
HE... HE SAVED HER?
YOU SAVED MY DAUGHTER. WHAT I SAID... I...
ANYTHING. YOU WANT THIS BUILDING? IT'S YOURS.
YOU WANT MONEY? I DON'T KNOW HOW TO...
WHAT DO YOU WANT? ANYTHING. ANYTHING.
I WANT YOU TO STEP AWAY FROM ME.
BUT, BUT... WHO ARE YOU? PLEASE.
I NEED TO KNOW THE NAME OF THE MAN WHO SAVED MY DAUGHTER.
...
THE BATMAN.
THE BATMAN SAVED YOUR CHILD MR. COOPER.

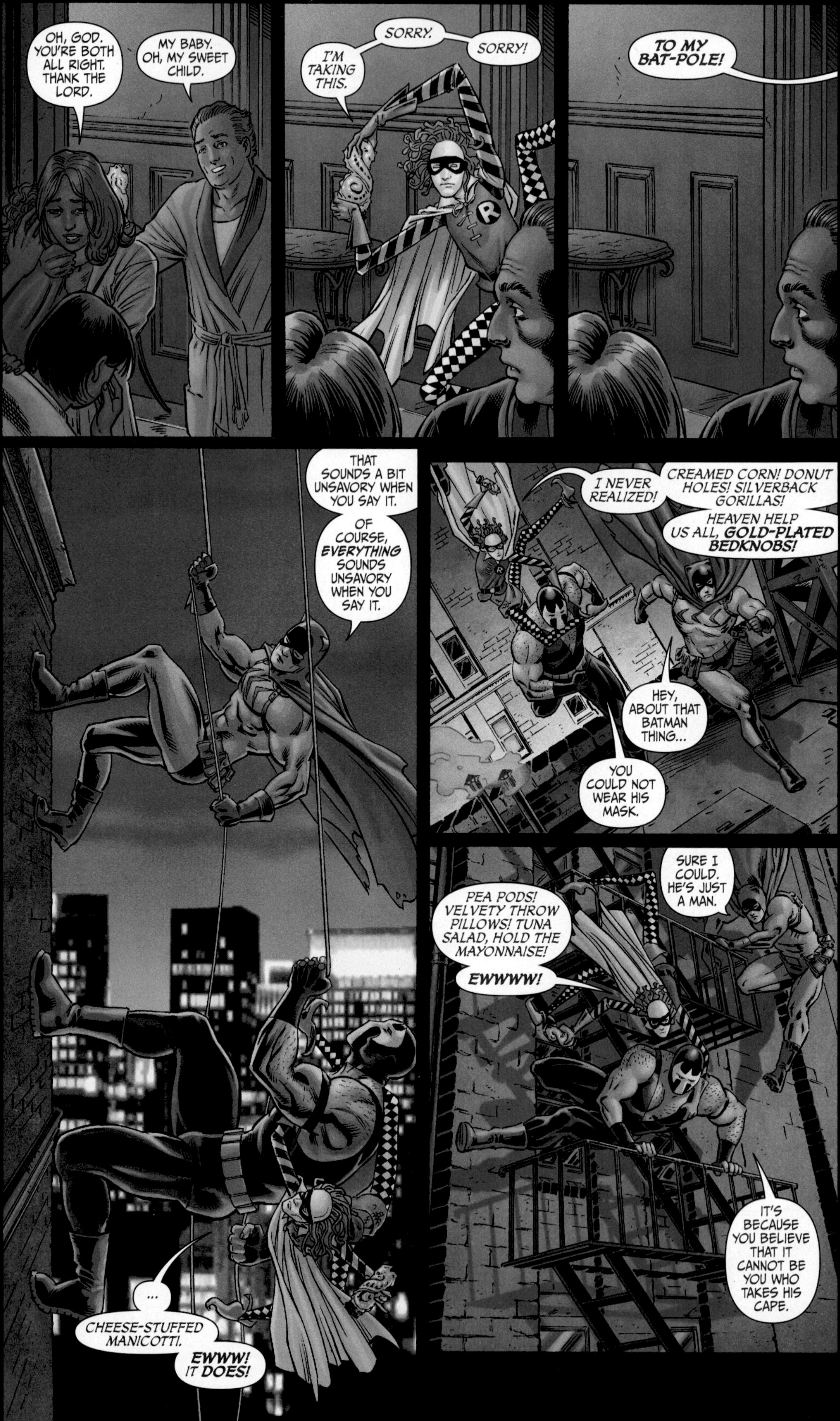

OH, GOD. YOU'RE BOTH ALL RIGHT. THANK THE LORD.
MY BABY. OH, MY SWEET CHILD.
SORRY.
SORRY!
I'M TAKING THIS.
TO MY BAT-POLE!
THAT SOUNDS A BIT UNSAVORY WHEN YOU SAY IT.
OF COURSE, EVERYTHING SOUNDS UNSAVORY WHEN YOU SAY IT.
...
CHEESE-STUFFED MANICOTTI.
EWWW! IT DOES!
I NEVER REALIZED!
CREAMED CORN! DONUT HOLES! SILVERBACK GORILLAS!
HEAVEN HELP US ALL, GOLD-PLATED BEDKNOBS!
HEY, ABOUT THAT BATMAN THING...
YOU COULD NOT WEAR HIS MASK.
SURE I COULD. HE'S JUST A MAN.
PEA PODS! VELVETY THROW PILLOWS! TUNA SALAD, HOLD THE MAYONNAISE!
EWWWW!
IT'S BECAUSE YOU BELIEVE THAT IT CANNOT BE YOU WHO TAKES HIS CAPE.

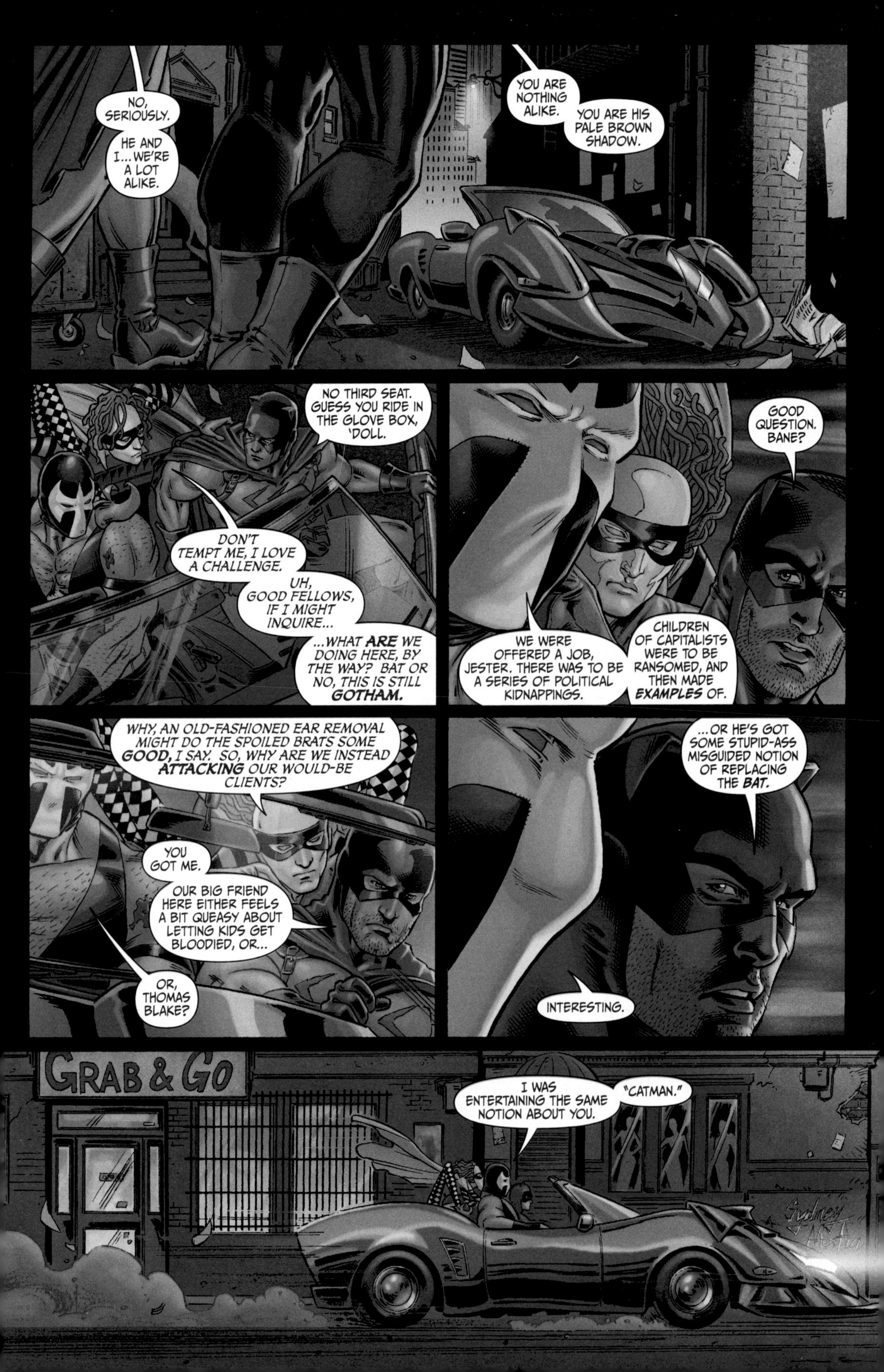
NO, SERIOUSLY.
HE AND I...WE'RE A LOT ALIKE.
YOU ARE NOTHING ALIKE.
YOU ARE HIS PALE BROWN SHADOW.
NO THIRD SEAT. GUESS YOU RIDE IN THE GLOVE BOX, 'DOLL.
DON'T TEMPT ME, I LOVE A CHALLENGE.
UH, GOOD FELLOWS, IF I MIGHT INQUIRE...
...WHAT ARE WE DOING HERE, BY THE WAY? BAT OR NO, THIS IS STILL GOTHAM.
GOOD QUESTION. BANE?
WE WERE OFFERED A JOB, JESTER. THERE WAS TO BE A SERIES OF POLITICAL KIDNAPPINGS.
CHILDREN OF CAPITALISTS WERE TO BE RANSOMED, AND THEN MADE EXAMPLES OF.
WHY, AN OLD-FASHIONED EAR REMOVAL MIGHT DO THE SPOILED BRATS SOME GOOD, I SAY. SO, WHY ARE WE INSTEAD ATTACKING OUR WOULD-BE CLIENTS?
YOU GOT ME.
OUR BIG FRIEND HERE EITHER FEELS A BIT QUEASY ABOUT LETTING KIDS GET BLOODIED, OR...
OR, THOMAS BLAKE?
...OR HE'S GOT SOME STUPID-ASS MISGUIDED NOTION OF REPLACING THE BAT.
INTERESTING.
GRAB & GO
I WAS ENTERTAINING THE SAME NOTION ABOUT YOU.
"CATMAN."

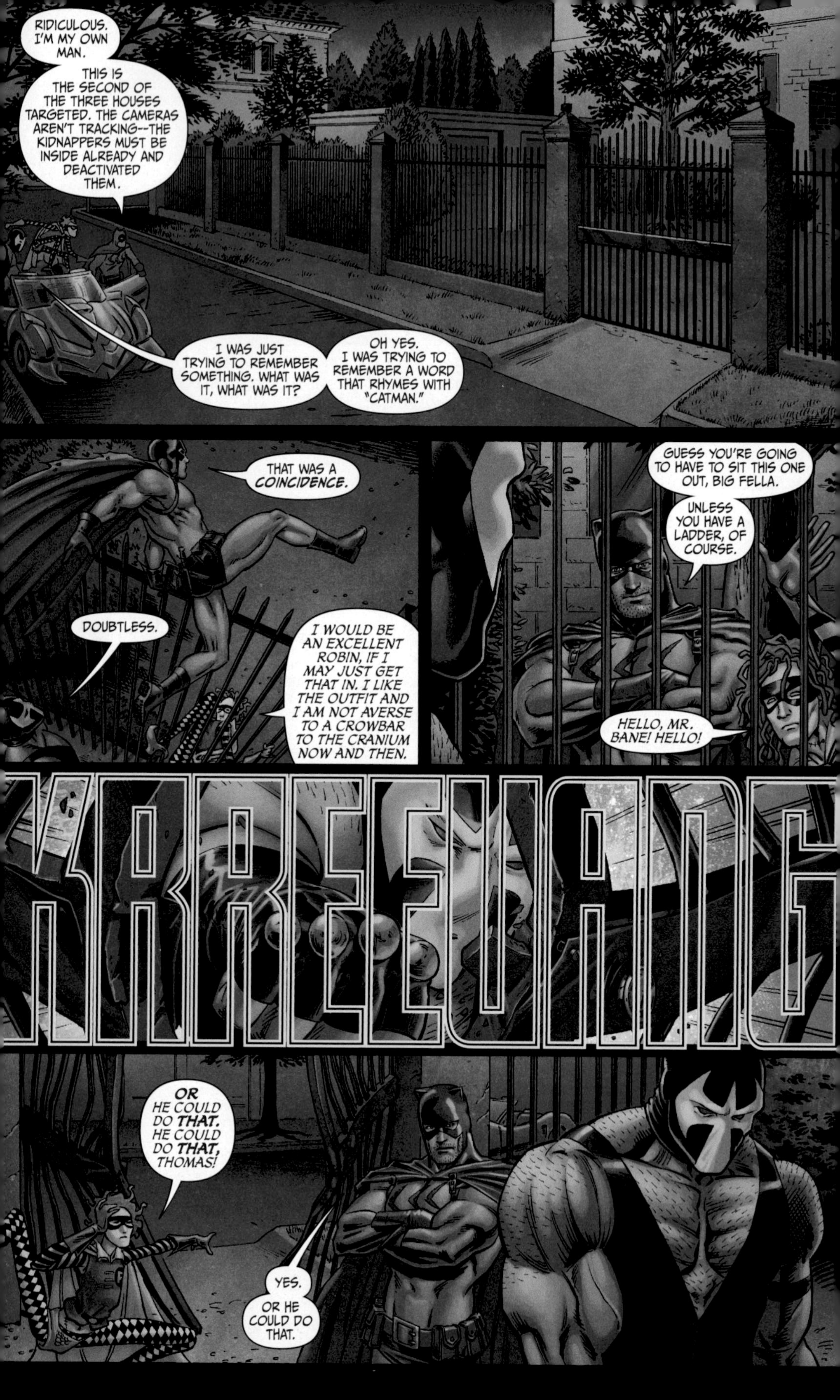
RIDICULOUS. I'M MY OWN MAN.
THIS IS THE SECOND OF THE THREE HOUSES TARGETED. THE CAMERAS AREN'T TRACKING--THE KIDNAPPERS MUST BE INSIDE ALREADY AND DEACTIVATED THEM.
I WAS JUST TRYING TO REMEMBER SOMETHING. WHAT WAS IT, WHAT WAS IT?
OH YES. I WAS TRYING TO REMEMBER A WORD THAT RHYMES WITH "CATMAN."
THAT WAS A *COINCIDENCE.*
DOUBTLESS.
I WOULD BE AN EXCELLENT ROBIN, IF I MAY JUST GET THAT IN. I LIKE THE OUTFIT AND I AM NOT AVERSE TO A CROWBAR TO THE CRANIUM NOW AND THEN.
GUESS YOU'RE GOING TO HAVE TO SIT THIS ONE OUT, BIG FELLA.
UNLESS YOU HAVE A LADDER, OF COURSE.
HELLO, MR. BANE! HELLO!
KRREEUANG
OR HE COULD DO THAT. HE COULD DO THAT, THOMAS!
YES.
OR HE COULD DO THAT.

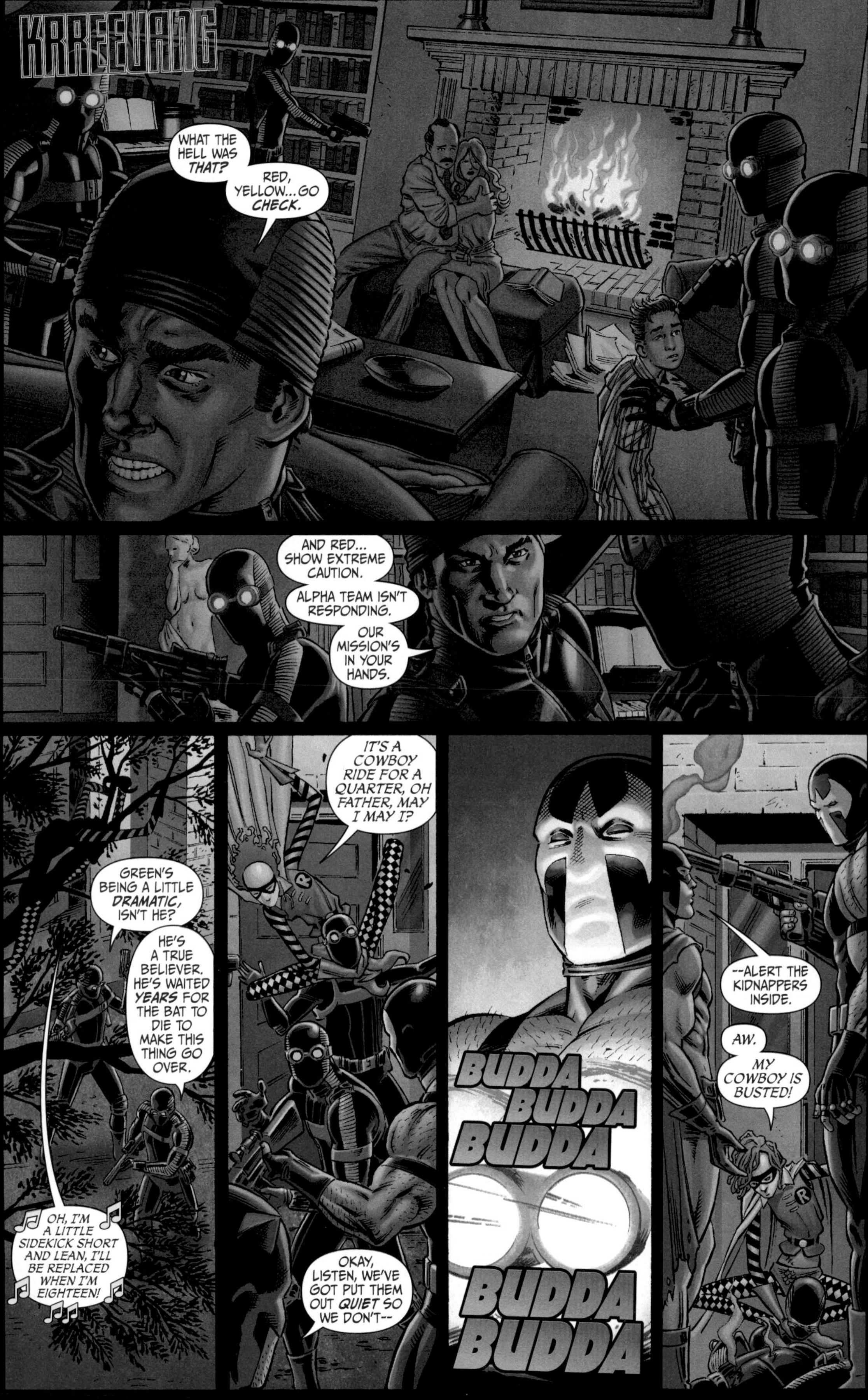
KRREEUANG
WHAT THE HELL WAS THAT?
RED, YELLOW...GO CHECK.
AND RED... SHOW EXTREME CAUTION.
ALPHA TEAM ISN'T RESPONDING.
OUR MISSION'S IN YOUR HANDS.
GREEN'S BEING A LITTLE DRAMATIC, ISN'T HE?
HE'S A TRUE BELIEVER. HE'S WAITED YEARS FOR THE BAT TO DIE TO MAKE THIS THING GO OVER.
OH, I'M A LITTLE SIDEKICK SHORT AND LEAN, I'LL BE REPLACED WHEN I'M EIGHTEEN!
IT'S A COWBOY RIDE FOR A QUARTER, OH FATHER, MAY I MAY I?
OKAY, LISTEN, WE'VE GOT PUT THEM OUT QUIET SO WE DON'T--
BUDDA BUDDA BUDDA
BUDDA BUDDA
--ALERT THE KIDNAPPERS INSIDE.
AW.
MY COWBOY IS BUSTED!

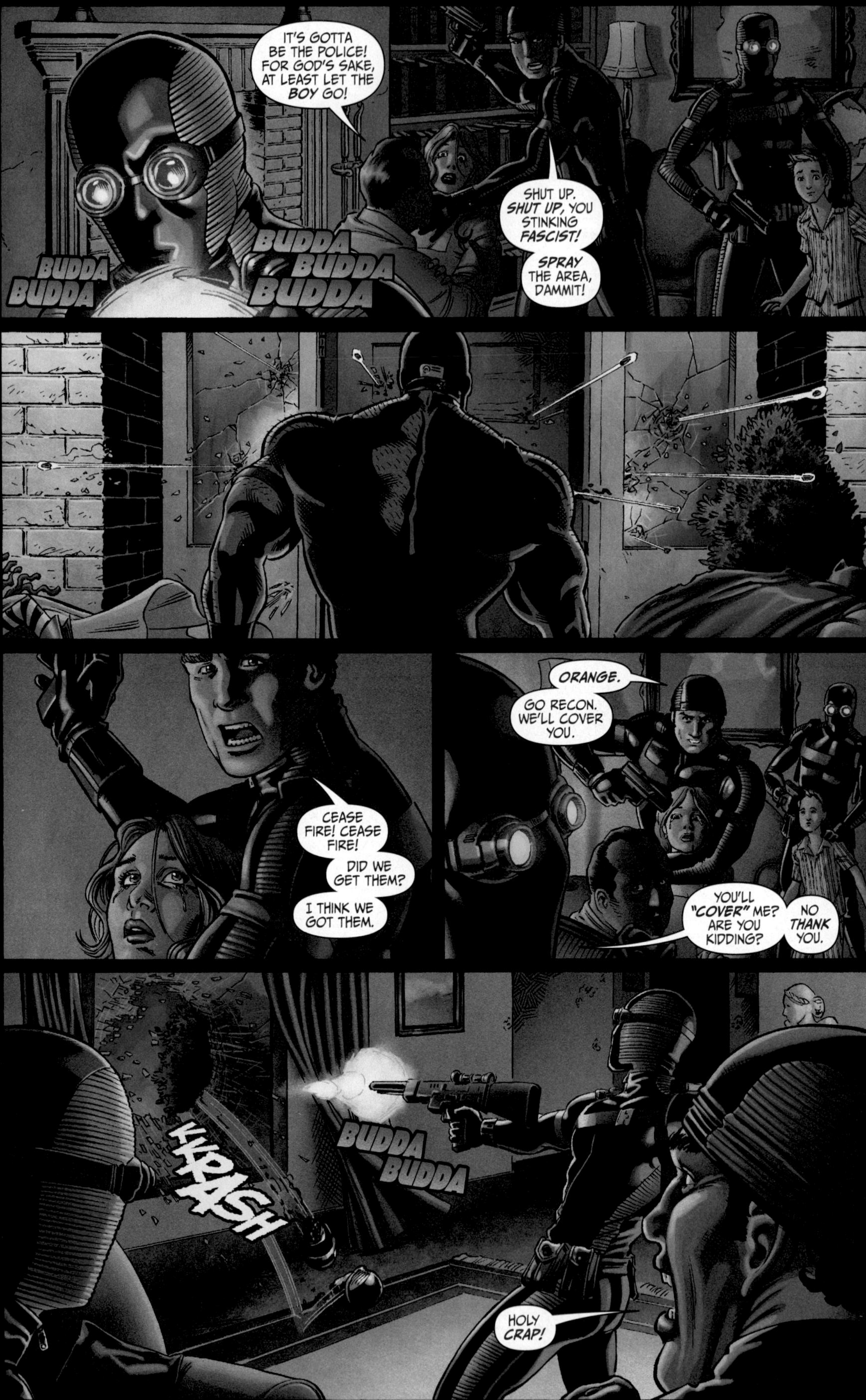
IT'S GOTTA BE THE POLICE! FOR GOD'S SAKE, AT LEAST LET THE BOY GO!
SHUT UP. SHUT UP, YOU STINKING FASCIST!
SPRAY THE AREA, DAMMIT!
BUDDA BUDDA
BUDDA BUDDA BUDDA
CEASE FIRE! CEASE FIRE!
DID WE GET THEM?
I THINK WE GOT THEM.
ORANGE.
GO RECON. WE'LL COVER YOU.
YOU'LL "COVER" ME? ARE YOU KIDDING?
NO THANK YOU.
KRASH
BUDDA BUDDA
HOLY CRAP!

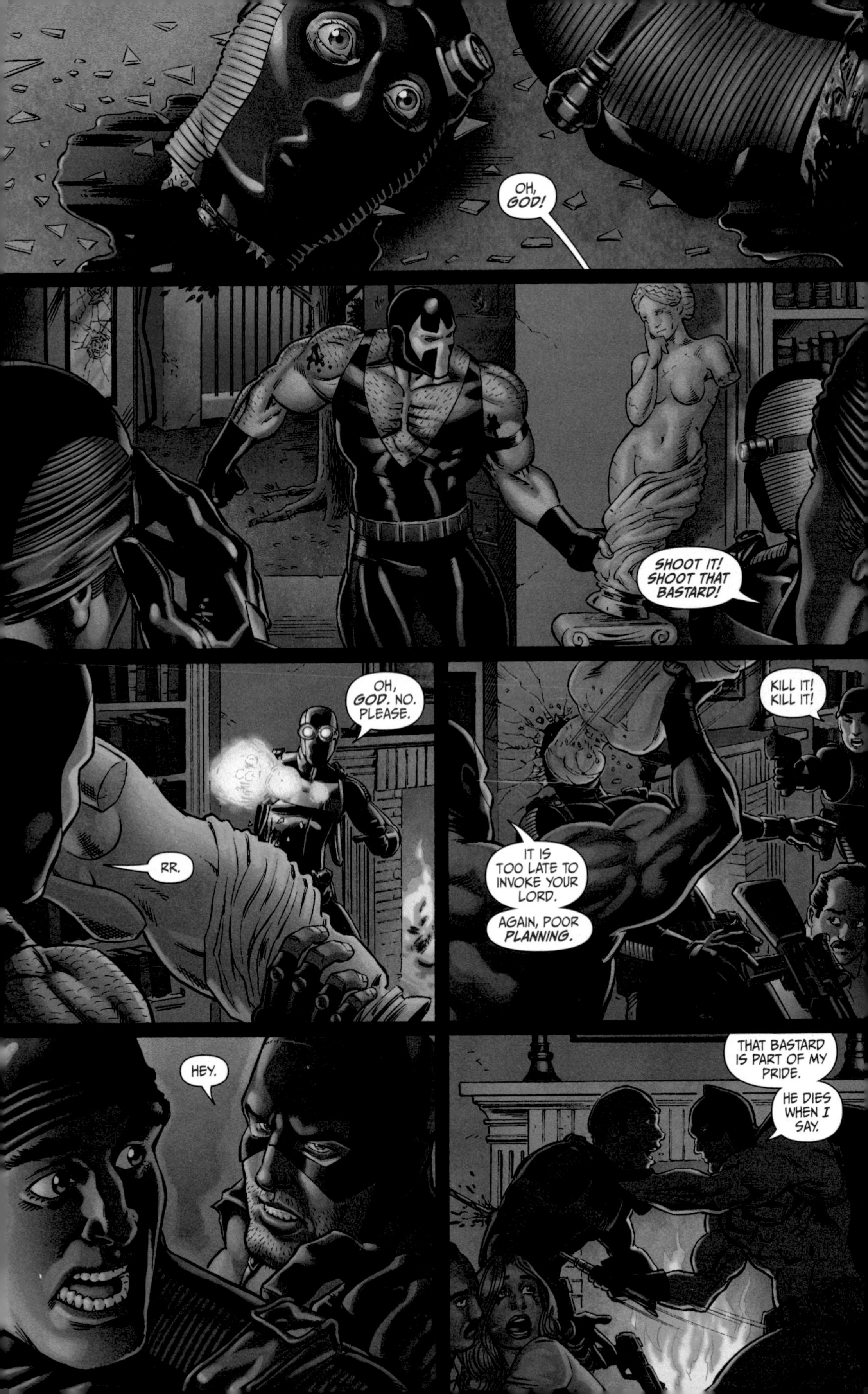
OH, GOD!
SHOOT IT! SHOOT THAT BASTARD!
OH, GOD. NO. PLEASE.
RR.
KILL IT! KILL IT!
IT IS TOO LATE TO INVOKE YOUR LORD.
AGAIN, POOR PLANNING.
HEY.
THAT BASTARD IS PART OF MY PRIDE.
HE DIES WHEN I SAY.

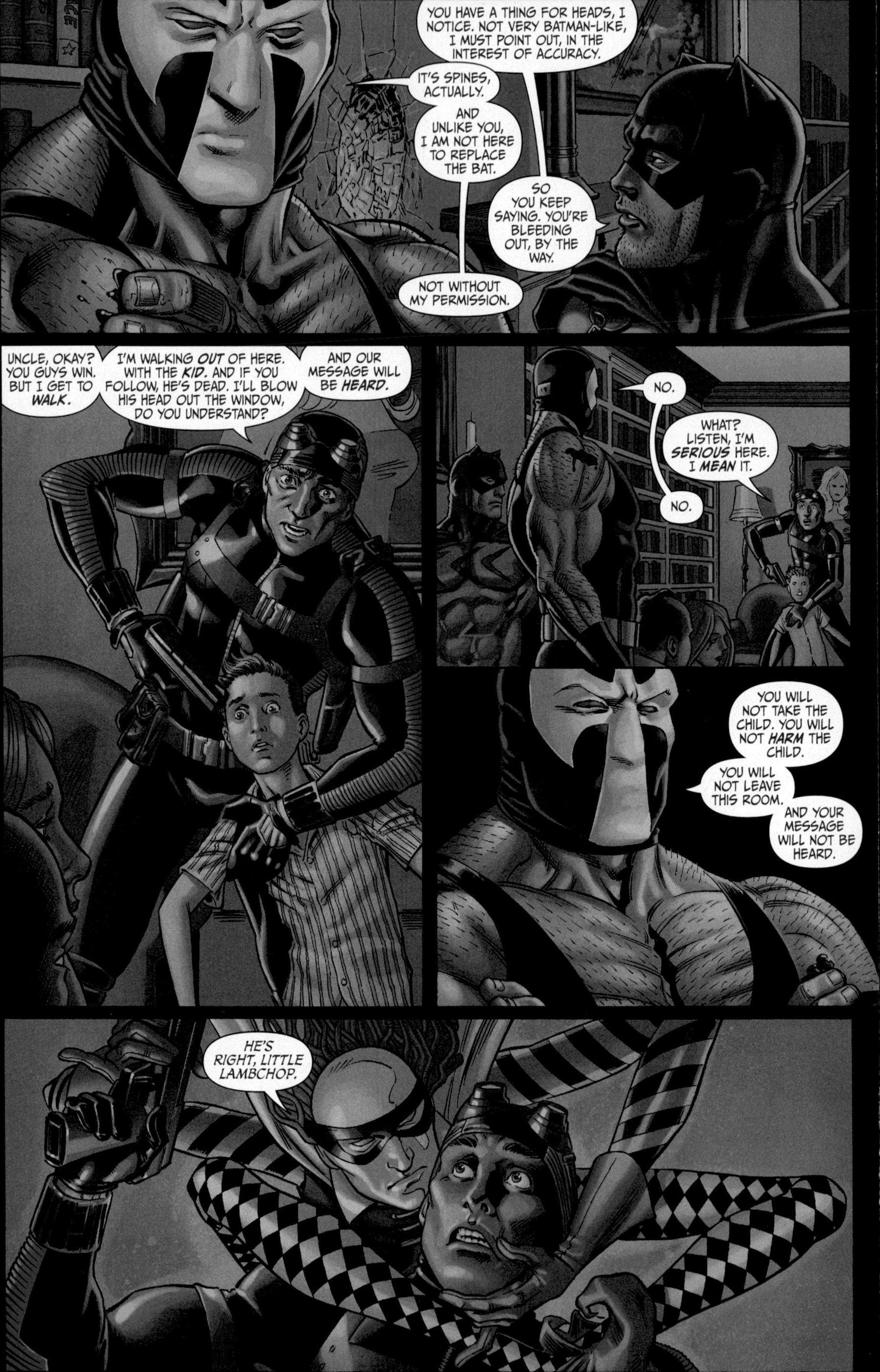
YOU HAVE A THING FOR HEADS, I NOTICE. NOT VERY BATMAN-LIKE, I MUST POINT OUT, IN THE INTEREST OF ACCURACY.
IT'S SPINES, ACTUALLY.
AND UNLIKE YOU, I AM NOT HERE TO REPLACE THE BAT.
SO YOU KEEP SAYING. YOU'RE BLEEDING OUT, BY THE WAY.
NOT WITHOUT MY PERMISSION.
UNCLE, OKAY? YOU GUYS WIN. BUT I GET TO WALK.
I'M WALKING OUT OF HERE. WITH THE KID. AND IF YOU FOLLOW, HE'S DEAD. I'LL BLOW HIS HEAD OUT THE WINDOW, DO YOU UNDERSTAND?
AND OUR MESSAGE WILL BE HEARD.
NO.
WHAT? LISTEN, I'M SERIOUS HERE. I MEAN IT.
NO.
YOU WILL NOT TAKE THE CHILD. YOU WILL NOT HARM THE CHILD.
YOU WILL NOT LEAVE THIS ROOM.
AND YOUR MESSAGE WILL NOT BE HEARD.
HE'S RIGHT, LITTLE LAMBCHOP.

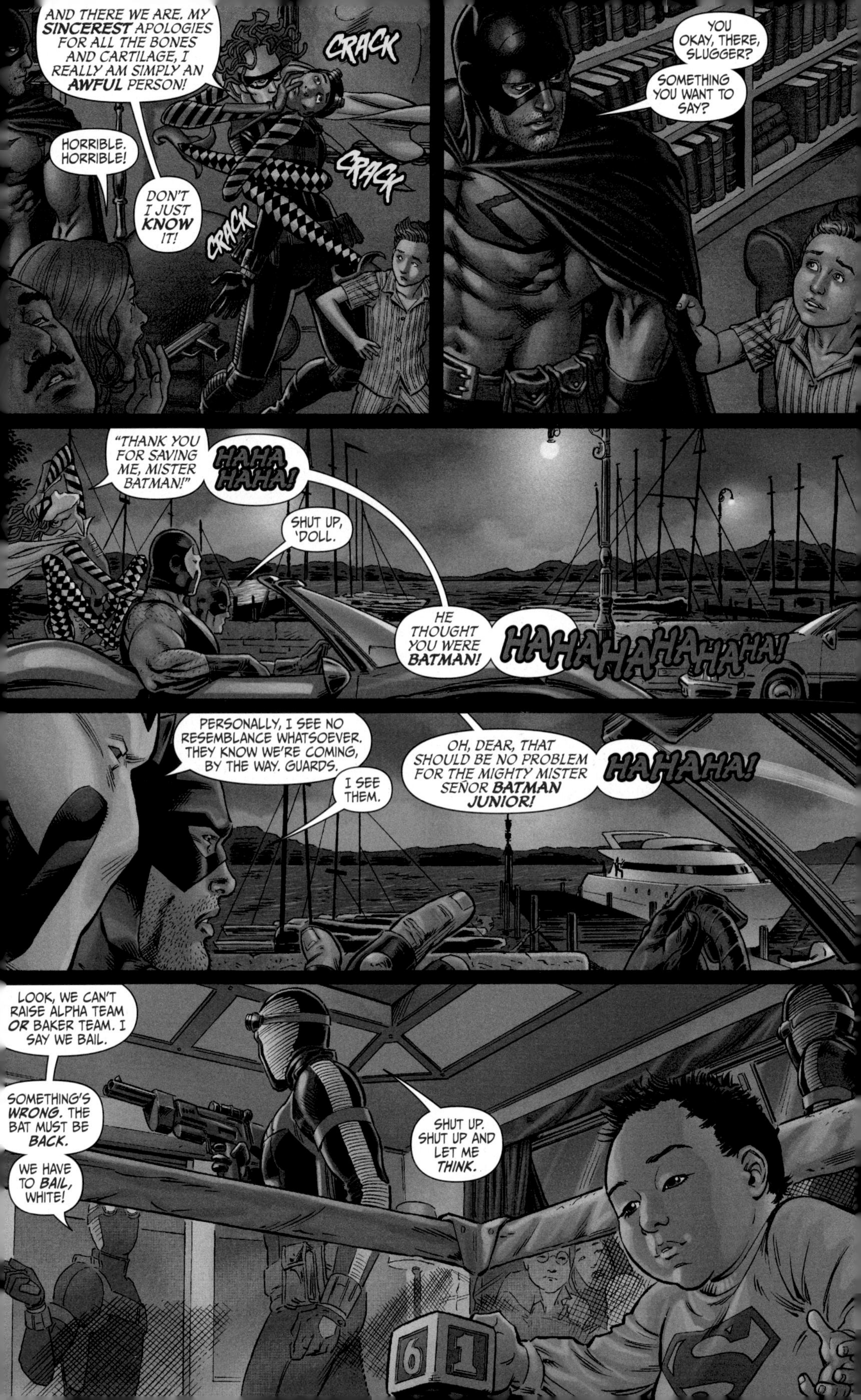
AND THERE WE ARE. MY SINCEREST APOLOGIES FOR ALL THE BONES AND CARTILAGE, I REALLY AM SIMPLY AN AWFUL PERSON!
CRACK
HORRIBLE. HORRIBLE!
CRACK
DON'T I JUST KNOW IT!
CRACK
YOU OKAY, THERE, SLUGGER?
SOMETHING YOU WANT TO SAY?
"THANK YOU FOR SAVING ME, MISTER BATMAN!"
HAHA HAHA!
SHUT UP, 'DOLL.
HE THOUGHT YOU WERE BATMAN!
HAHAHAHAHAHAHA!
PERSONALLY, I SEE NO RESEMBLANCE WHATSOEVER. THEY KNOW WE'RE COMING, BY THE WAY. GUARDS.
I SEE THEM.
OH, DEAR, THAT SHOULD BE NO PROBLEM FOR THE MIGHTY MISTER SEÑOR BATMAN JUNIOR!
HAHAHA!
LOOK, WE CAN'T RAISE ALPHA TEAM OR BAKER TEAM. I SAY WE BAIL.
SOMETHING'S WRONG. THE BAT MUST BE BACK.
WE HAVE TO BAIL, WHITE!
SHUT UP. SHUT UP AND LET ME THINK.

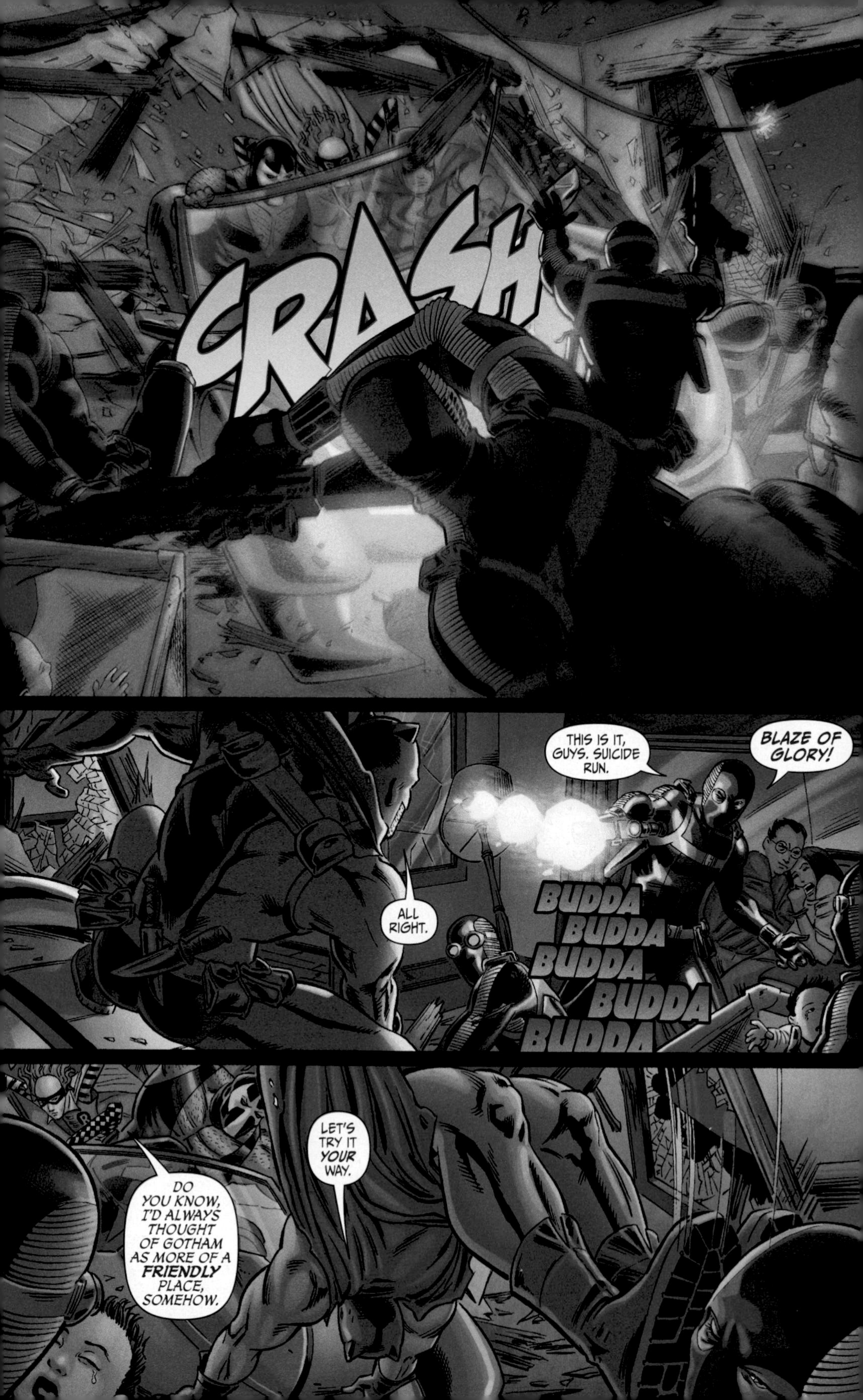
CRASH
THIS IS IT, GUYS. SUICIDE RUN.
BLAZE OF GLORY!
ALL RIGHT.
BUDDA BUDDA BUDDA BUDDA BUDDA
DO YOU KNOW, I'D ALWAYS THOUGHT OF GOTHAM AS MORE OF A FRIENDLY PLACE, SOMEHOW.
LET'S TRY IT YOUR WAY.

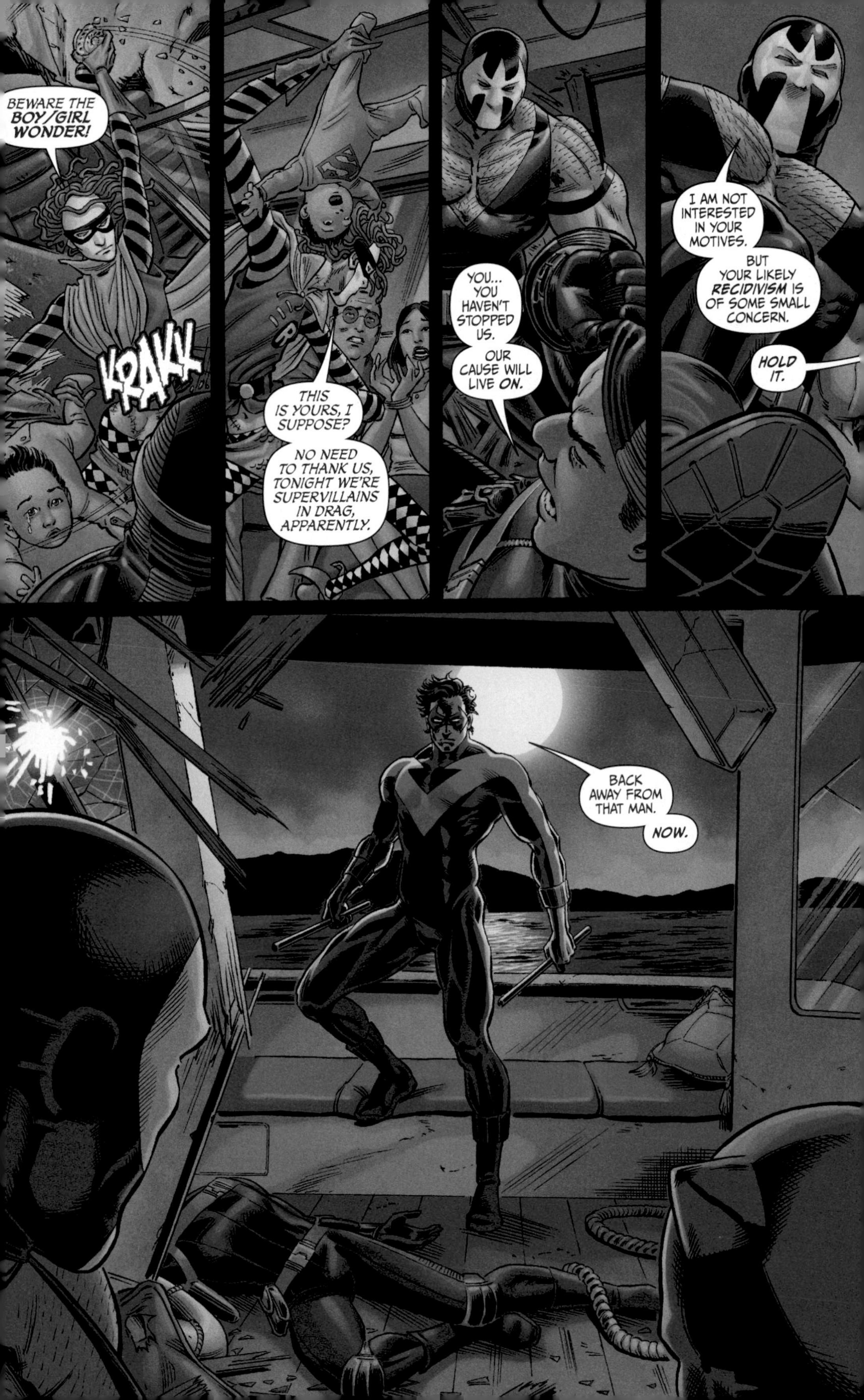

BEWARE THE BOY/GIRL WONDER!
KRAKK
THIS IS YOURS, I SUPPOSE?
NO NEED TO THANK US, TONIGHT WE'RE SUPERVILLAINS IN DRAG, APPARENTLY.
YOU... YOU HAVEN'T STOPPED US.
OUR CAUSE WILL LIVE ON.
I AM NOT INTERESTED IN YOUR MOTIVES.
BUT YOUR LIKELY RECIDIVISM IS OF SOME SMALL CONCERN.
HOLD IT.
BACK AWAY FROM THAT MAN.
NOW.

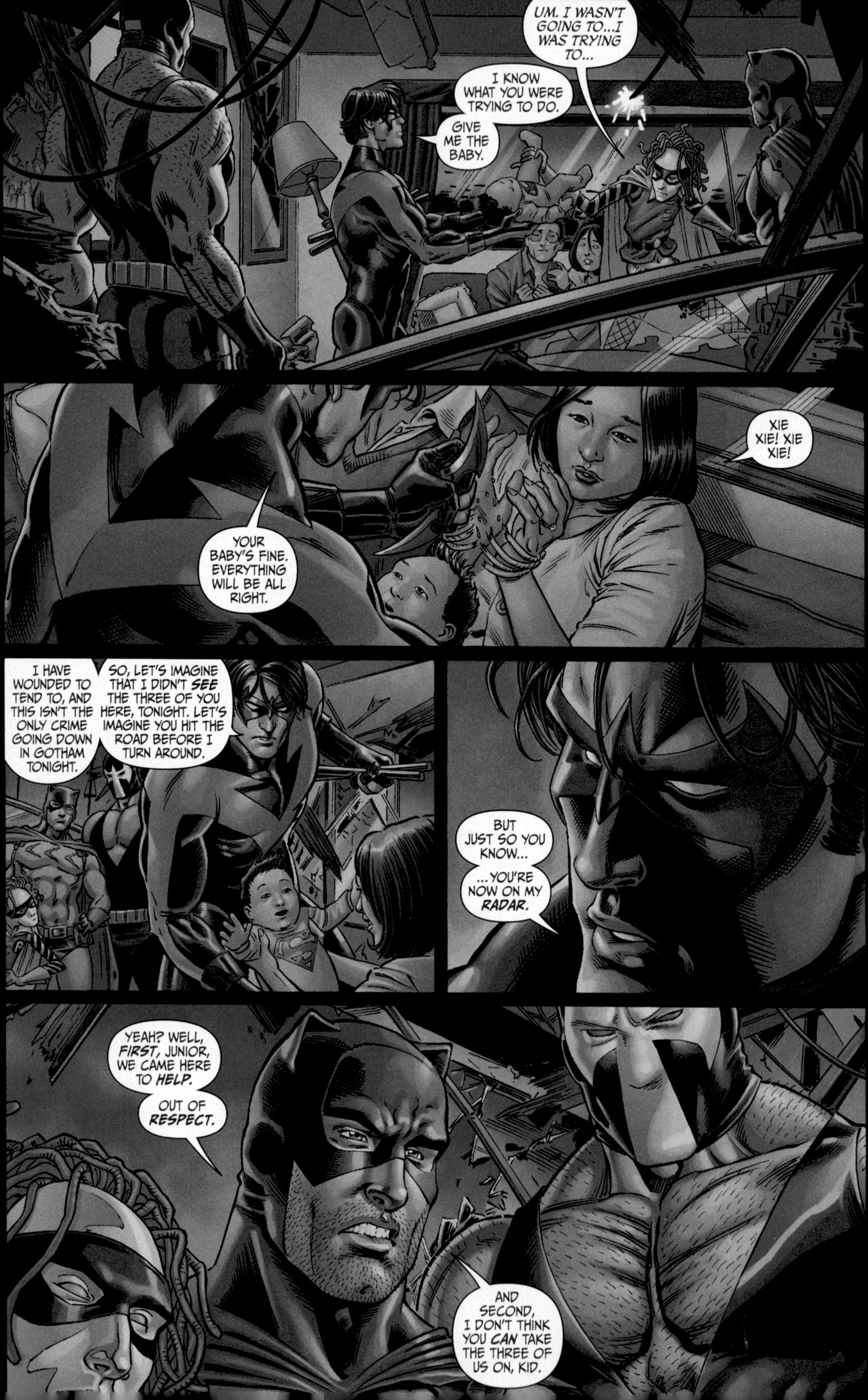
UM. I WASN'T GOING TO...I WAS TRYING TO...
I KNOW WHAT YOU WERE TRYING TO DO.
GIVE ME THE BABY.
XIE XIE! XIE XIE!
YOUR BABY'S FINE. EVERYTHING WILL BE ALL RIGHT.
I HAVE WOUNDED TO TEND TO, AND THIS ISN'T THE ONLY CRIME GOING DOWN IN GOTHAM TONIGHT.
SO, LET'S IMAGINE THAT I DIDN'T SEE THE THREE OF YOU HERE, TONIGHT. LET'S IMAGINE YOU HIT THE ROAD BEFORE I TURN AROUND.
BUT JUST SO YOU KNOW...
...YOU'RE NOW ON MY RADAR.
YEAH? WELL, FIRST, JUNIOR, WE CAME HERE TO HELP.
OUT OF RESPECT.
AND SECOND, I DON'T THINK YOU CAN TAKE THE THREE OF US ON, KID.

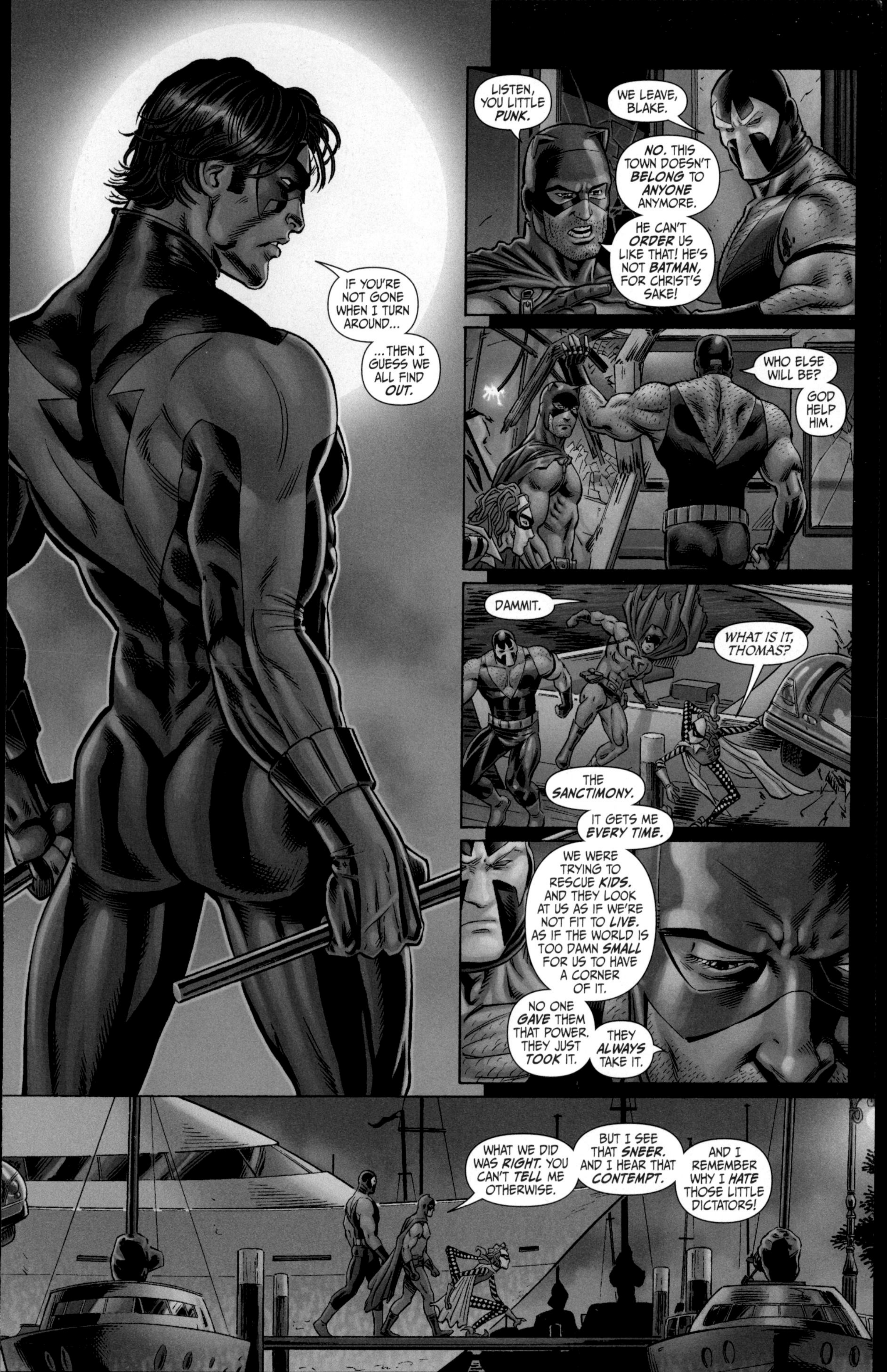
IF YOU'RE NOT GONE WHEN I TURN AROUND...
...THEN I GUESS WE ALL FIND OUT.
LISTEN, YOU LITTLE PUNK.
WE LEAVE, BLAKE.
NO. THIS TOWN DOESN'T BELONG TO ANYONE ANYMORE.
HE CAN'T ORDER US LIKE THAT! HE'S NOT BATMAN, FOR CHRIST'S SAKE!
WHO ELSE WILL BE?
GOD HELP HIM.
DAMMIT.
WHAT IS IT, THOMAS?
THE SANCTIMONY.
IT GETS ME EVERY TIME.
WE WERE TRYING TO RESCUE KIDS. AND THEY LOOK AT US AS IF WE'RE NOT FIT TO LIVE. AS IF THE WORLD IS TOO DAMN SMALL FOR US TO HAVE A CORNER OF IT.
NO ONE GAVE THEM THAT POWER. THEY JUST TOOK IT.
THEY ALWAYS TAKE IT.
WHAT WE DID WAS RIGHT. YOU CAN'T TELL ME OTHERWISE.
BUT I SEE THAT SNEER. AND I HEAR THAT CONTEMPT.
AND I REMEMBER WHY I HATE THOSE LITTLE DICTATORS!

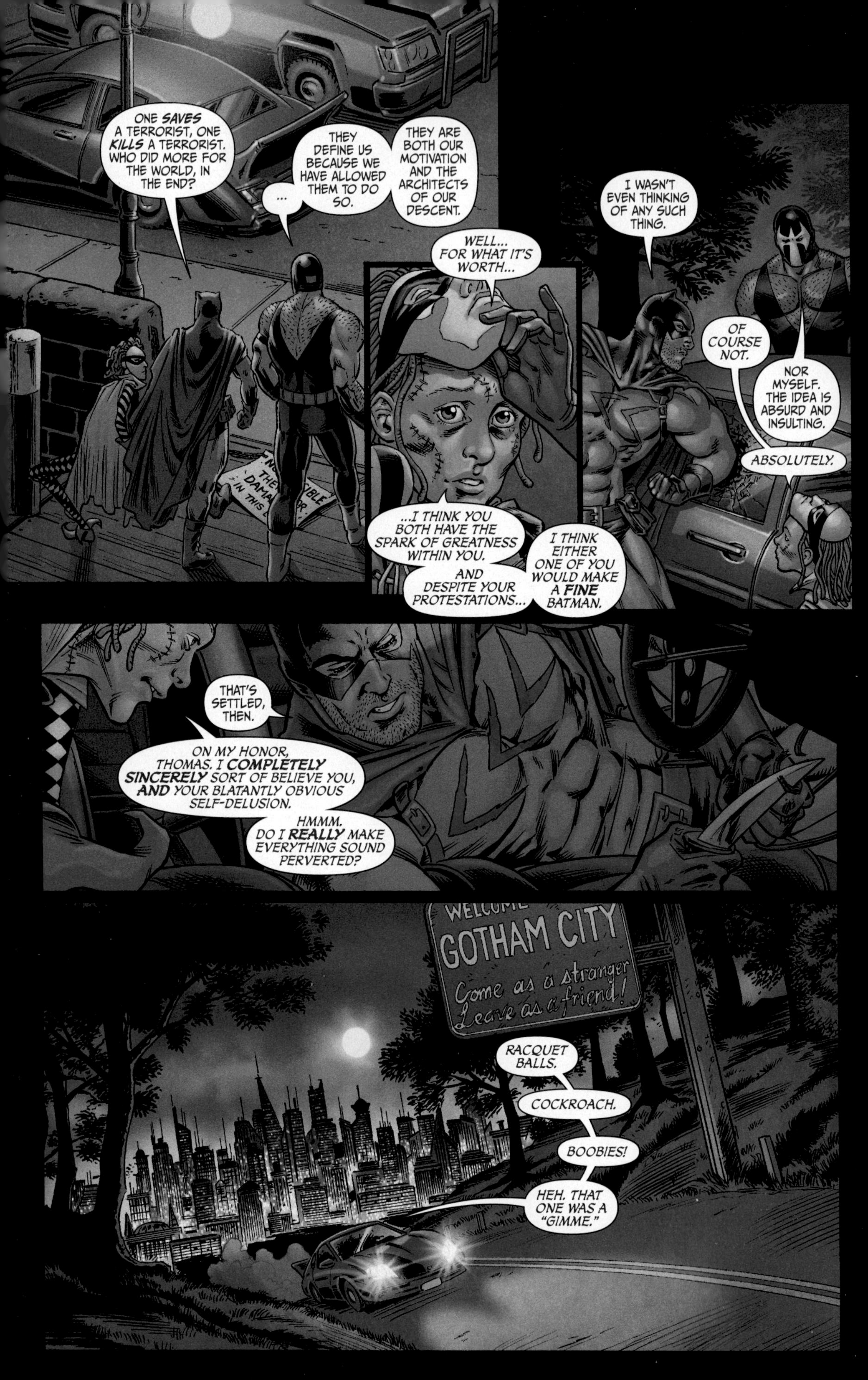
ONE SAVES A TERRORIST, ONE KILLS A TERRORIST. WHO DID MORE FOR THE WORLD, IN THE END?
...
THEY DEFINE US BECAUSE WE HAVE ALLOWED THEM TO DO SO.
THEY ARE BOTH OUR MOTIVATION AND THE ARCHITECTS OF OUR DESCENT.
I WASN'T EVEN THINKING OF ANY SUCH THING.
WELL... FOR WHAT IT'S WORTH...
...I THINK YOU BOTH HAVE THE SPARK OF GREATNESS WITHIN YOU.
AND DESPITE YOUR PROTESTATIONS...
I THINK EITHER ONE OF YOU WOULD MAKE A FINE BATMAN.
OF COURSE NOT.
NOR MYSELF. THE IDEA IS ABSURD AND INSULTING.
ABSOLUTELY.
THAT'S SETTLED, THEN.
ON MY HONOR, THOMAS. I COMPLETELY SINCERELY SORT OF BELIEVE YOU, AND YOUR BLATANTLY OBVIOUS SELF-DELUSION.
HMMM. DO I REALLY MAKE EVERYTHING SOUND PERVERTED?
GOTHAM CITY
Come as a stranger
Leave as a friend!
RACQUET BALLS.
COCKROACH.
BOOBIES!
HEH. THAT ONE WAS A "GIMME."

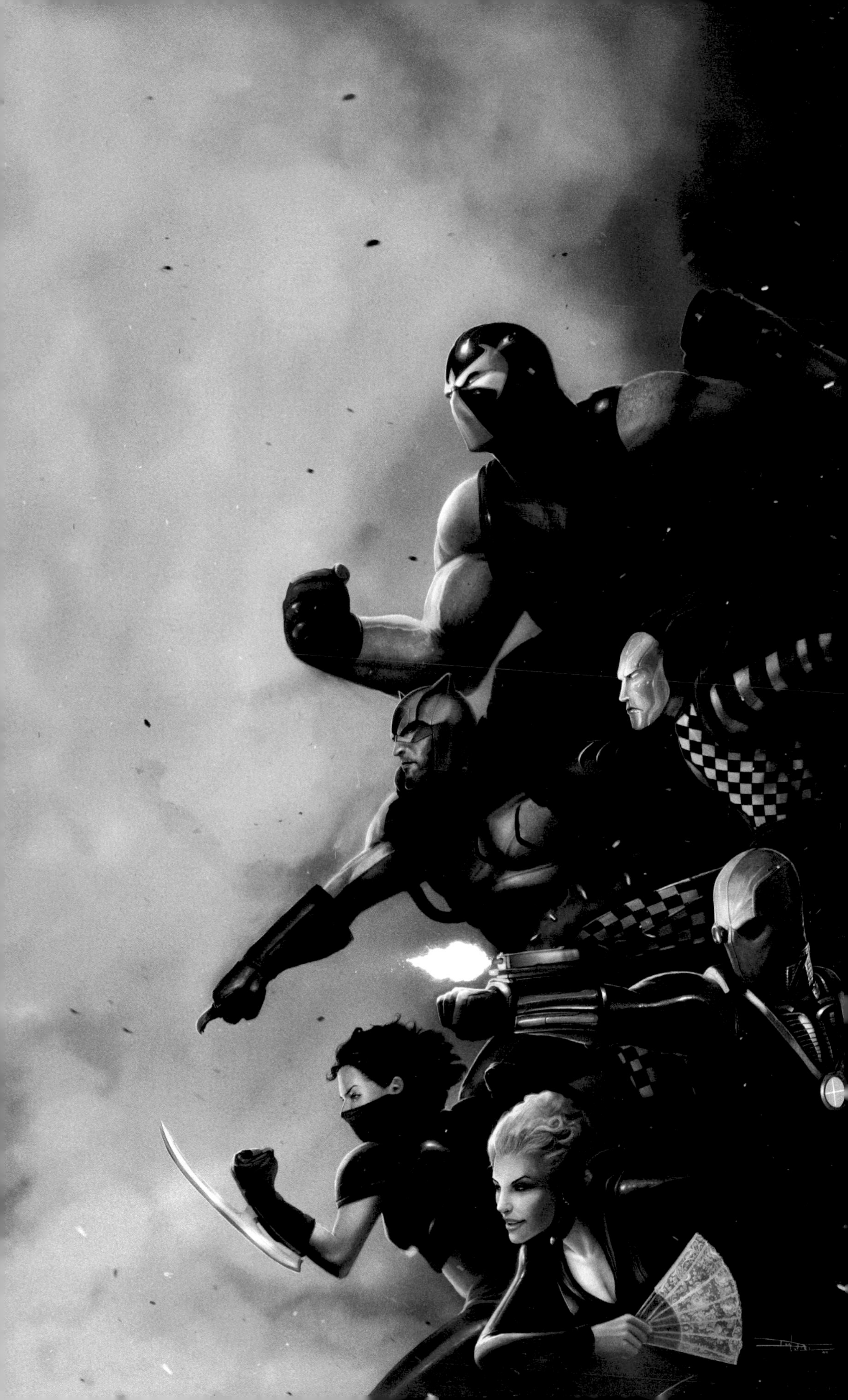

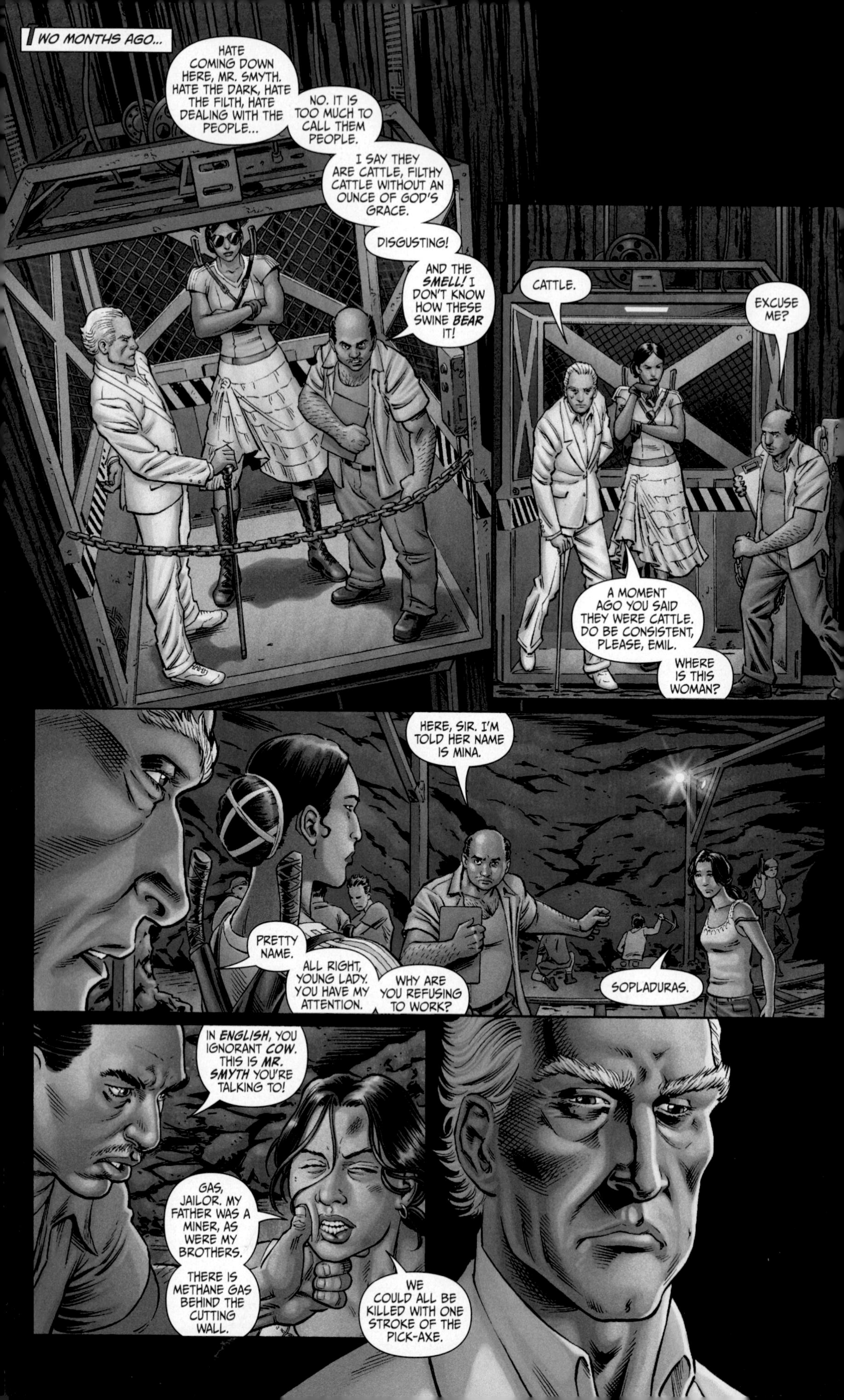
TWO MONTHS AGO...
HATE COMING DOWN HERE, MR. SMYTH. HATE THE DARK, HATE THE FILTH, HATE DEALING WITH THE PEOPLE...
NO. IT IS TOO MUCH TO CALL THEM PEOPLE.
I SAY THEY ARE CATTLE, FILTHY CATTLE WITHOUT AN OUNCE OF GOD'S GRACE.
DISGUSTING!
AND THE SMELL! I DON'T KNOW HOW THESE SWINE BEAR IT!
CATTLE.
EXCUSE ME?
A MOMENT AGO YOU SAID THEY WERE CATTLE. DO BE CONSISTENT, PLEASE, EMIL.
WHERE IS THIS WOMAN?
HERE, SIR. I'M TOLD HER NAME IS MINA.
PRETTY NAME.
ALL RIGHT, YOUNG LADY. YOU HAVE MY ATTENTION.
WHY ARE YOU REFUSING TO WORK?
SOPLADURAS.
IN ENGLISH, YOU IGNORANT COW. THIS IS MR. SMYTH YOU'RE TALKING TO!
GAS, JAILOR. MY FATHER WAS A MINER, AS WERE MY BROTHERS.
THERE IS METHANE GAS BEHIND THE CUTTING WALL.
WE COULD ALL BE KILLED WITH ONE STROKE OF THE PICK-AXE.

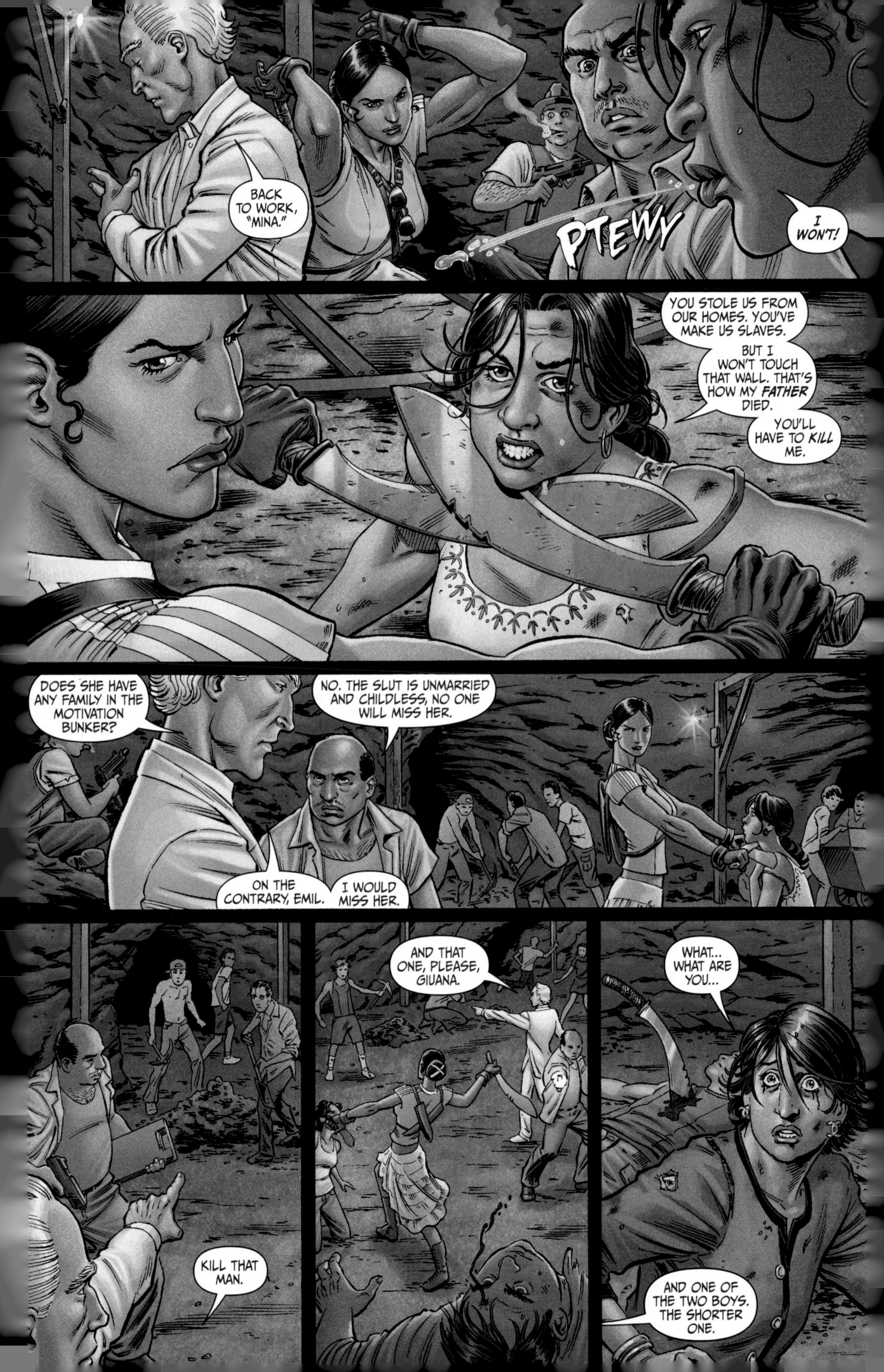
BACK TO WORK, "MINA."
PTEWY
I WON'T!
YOU STOLE US FROM OUR HOMES. YOU'VE MAKE US SLAVES.
BUT I WON'T TOUCH THAT WALL. THAT'S HOW MY FATHER DIED.
YOU'LL HAVE TO KILL ME.
DOES SHE HAVE ANY FAMILY IN THE MOTIVATION BUNKER?
NO. THE SLUT IS UNMARRIED AND CHILDLESS, NO ONE WILL MISS HER.
ON THE CONTRARY, EMIL.
I WOULD MISS HER.
KILL THAT MAN.
AND THAT ONE, PLEASE, GIUANA.
WHAT... WHAT ARE YOU...
AND ONE OF THE TWO BOYS. THE SHORTER ONE.

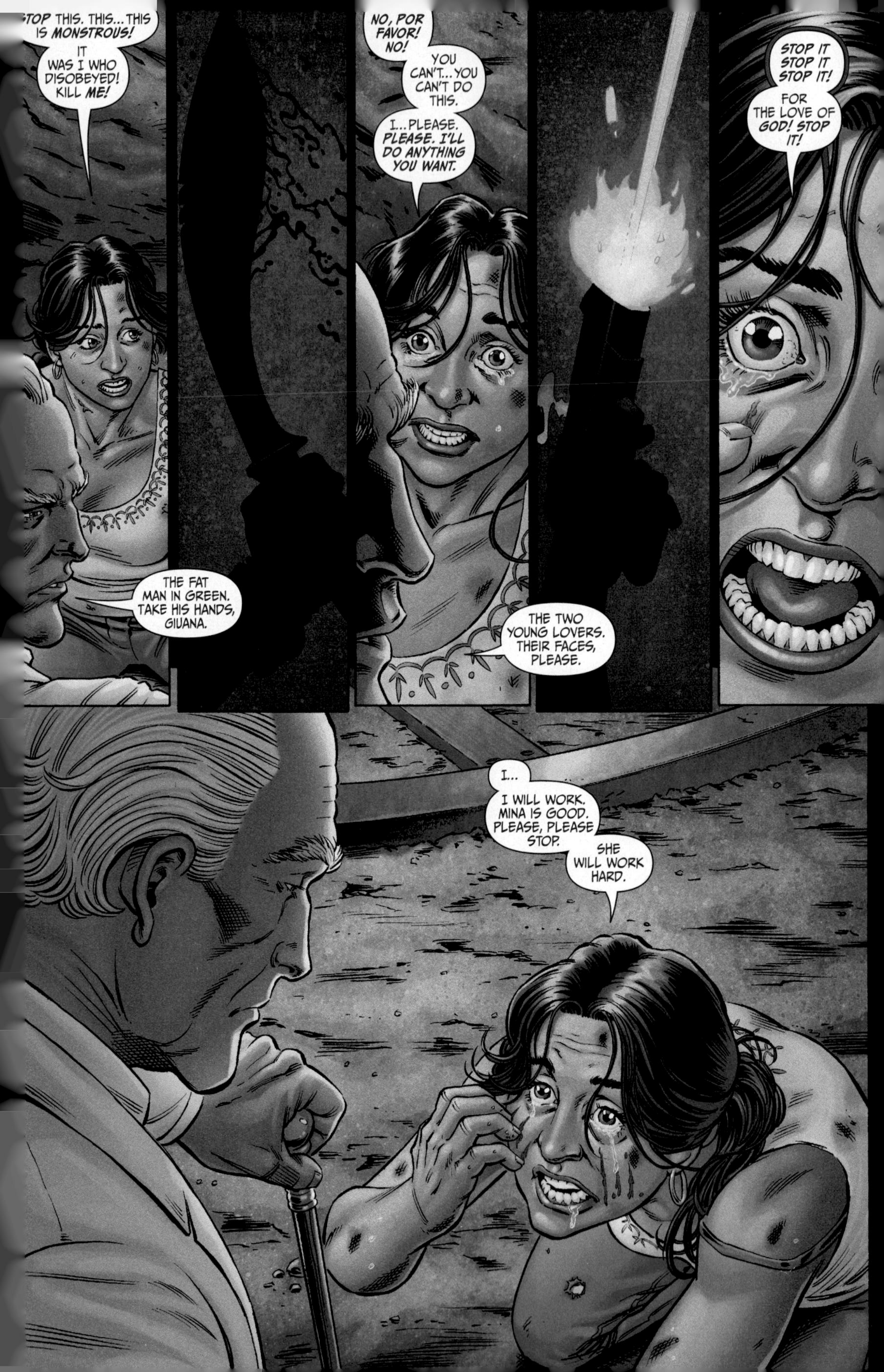
STOP THIS. THIS... THIS IS MONSTROUS!
IT WAS I WHO DISOBEYED! KILL ME!
THE FAT MAN IN GREEN. TAKE HIS HANDS, GIUANA.
NO, POR FAVOR! NO!
YOU CAN'T... YOU CAN'T DO THIS.
I... PLEASE. PLEASE. I'LL DO ANYTHING YOU WANT.
THE TWO YOUNG LOVERS. THEIR FACES, PLEASE.
STOP IT STOP IT STOP IT!
FOR THE LOVE OF GOD! STOP IT!
I...
I WILL WORK. MINA IS GOOD. PLEASE, PLEASE STOP.
SHE WILL WORK HARD.

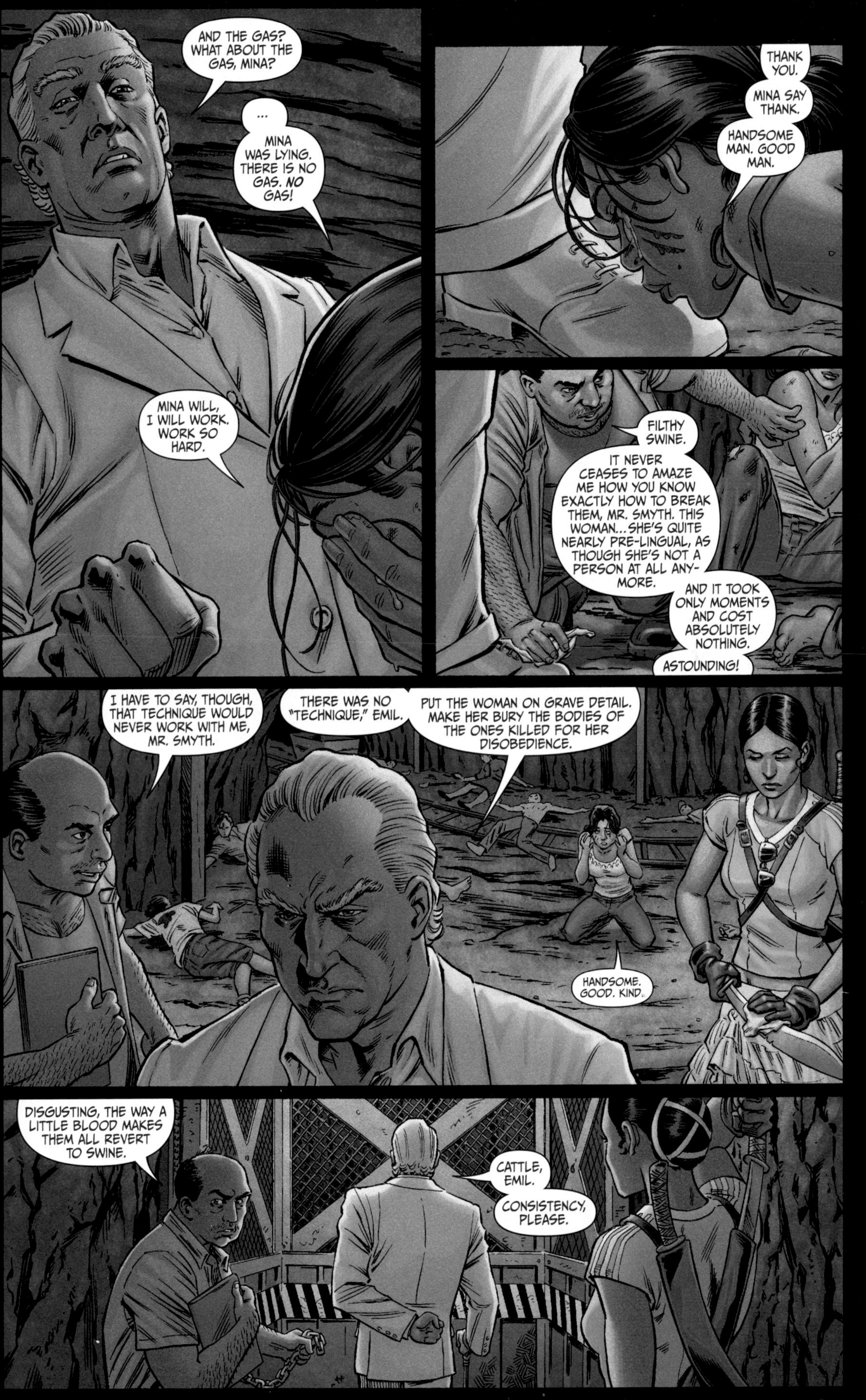
AND THE GAS? WHAT ABOUT THE GAS, MINA?
...
MINA WAS LYING. THERE IS NO GAS. NO GAS!
MINA WILL, I WILL WORK. WORK SO HARD.
THANK YOU.
MINA SAY THANK.
HANDSOME MAN. GOOD MAN.
FILTHY SWINE.
IT NEVER CEASES TO AMAZE ME HOW YOU KNOW EXACTLY HOW TO BREAK THEM, MR. SMYTH. THIS WOMAN...SHE'S QUITE NEARLY PRE-LINGUAL, AS THOUGH SHE'S NOT A PERSON AT ALL ANY-MORE.
AND IT TOOK ONLY MOMENTS AND COST ABSOLUTELY NOTHING.
ASTOUNDING!
I HAVE TO SAY, THOUGH, THAT TECHNIQUE WOULD NEVER WORK WITH ME, MR. SMYTH.
THERE WAS NO "TECHNIQUE," EMIL.
PUT THE WOMAN ON GRAVE DETAIL. MAKE HER BURY THE BODIES OF THE ONES KILLED FOR HER DISOBEDIENCE.
HANDSOME. GOOD. KIND...
DISGUSTING, THE WAY A LITTLE BLOOD MAKES THEM ALL REVERT TO SWINE.
CATTLE, EMIL.
CONSISTENCY, PLEASE.

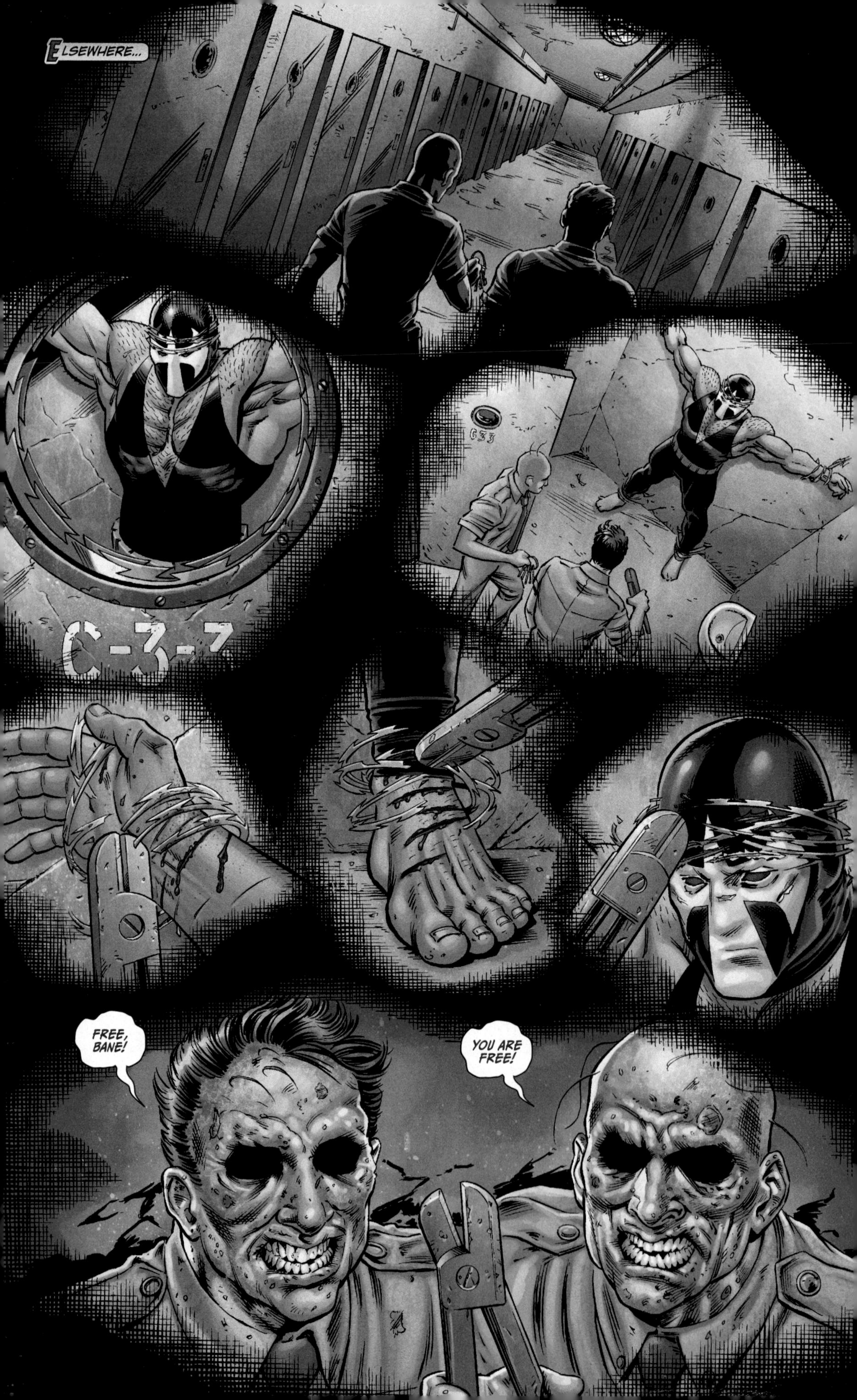
ELSEWHERE...
C33
C-3-3
FREE, BANE!
YOU ARE FREE!

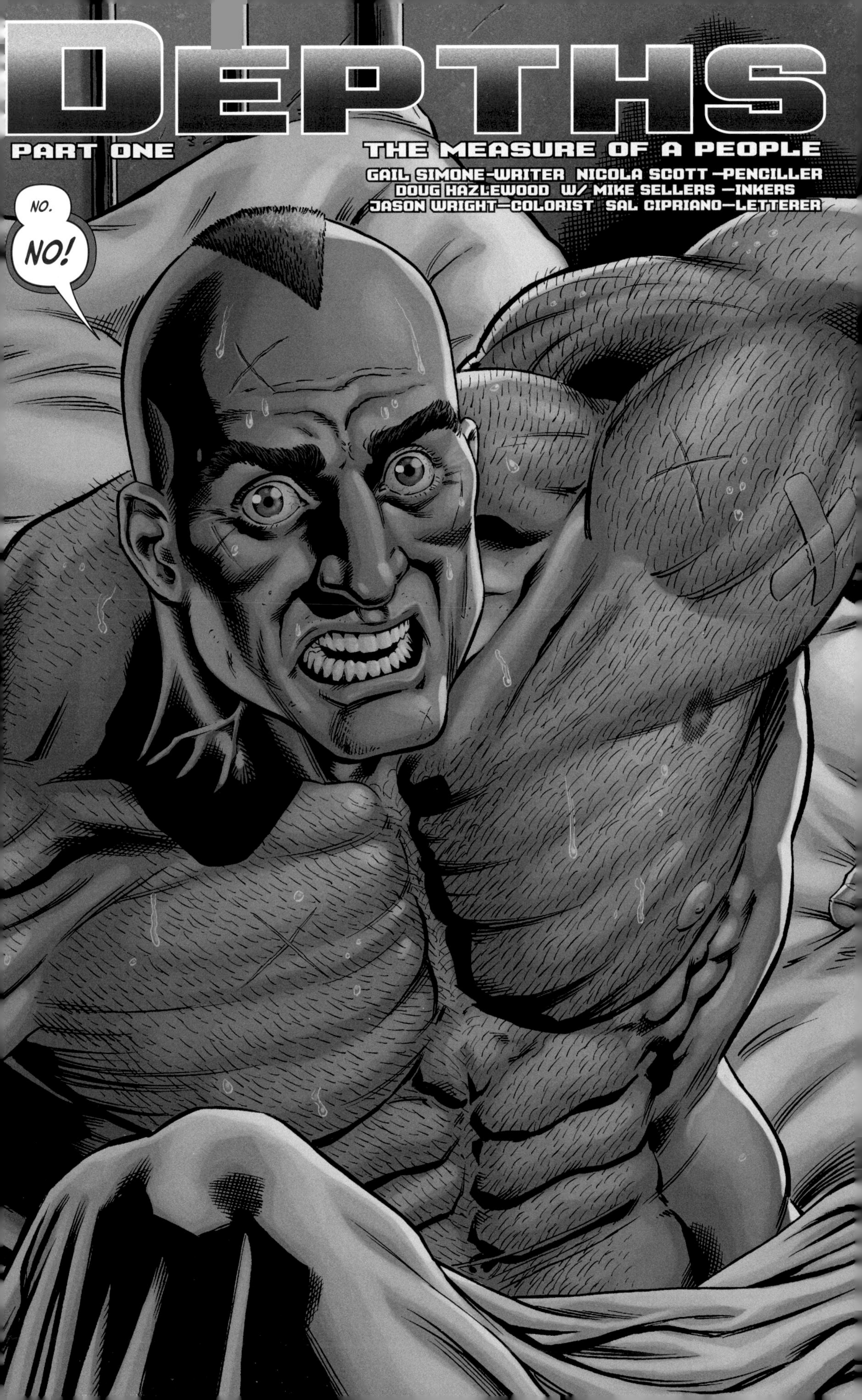
DEPTHS
PART ONE
THE MEASURE OF A PEOPLE
GAIL SIMONE-WRITER NICOLA SCOTT -PENCILLER
DOUG HAZLEWOOD W/ MIKE SELLERS -INKERS
JASON WRIGHT-COLORIST SAL CIPRIANO-LETTERER
NO.
NO!

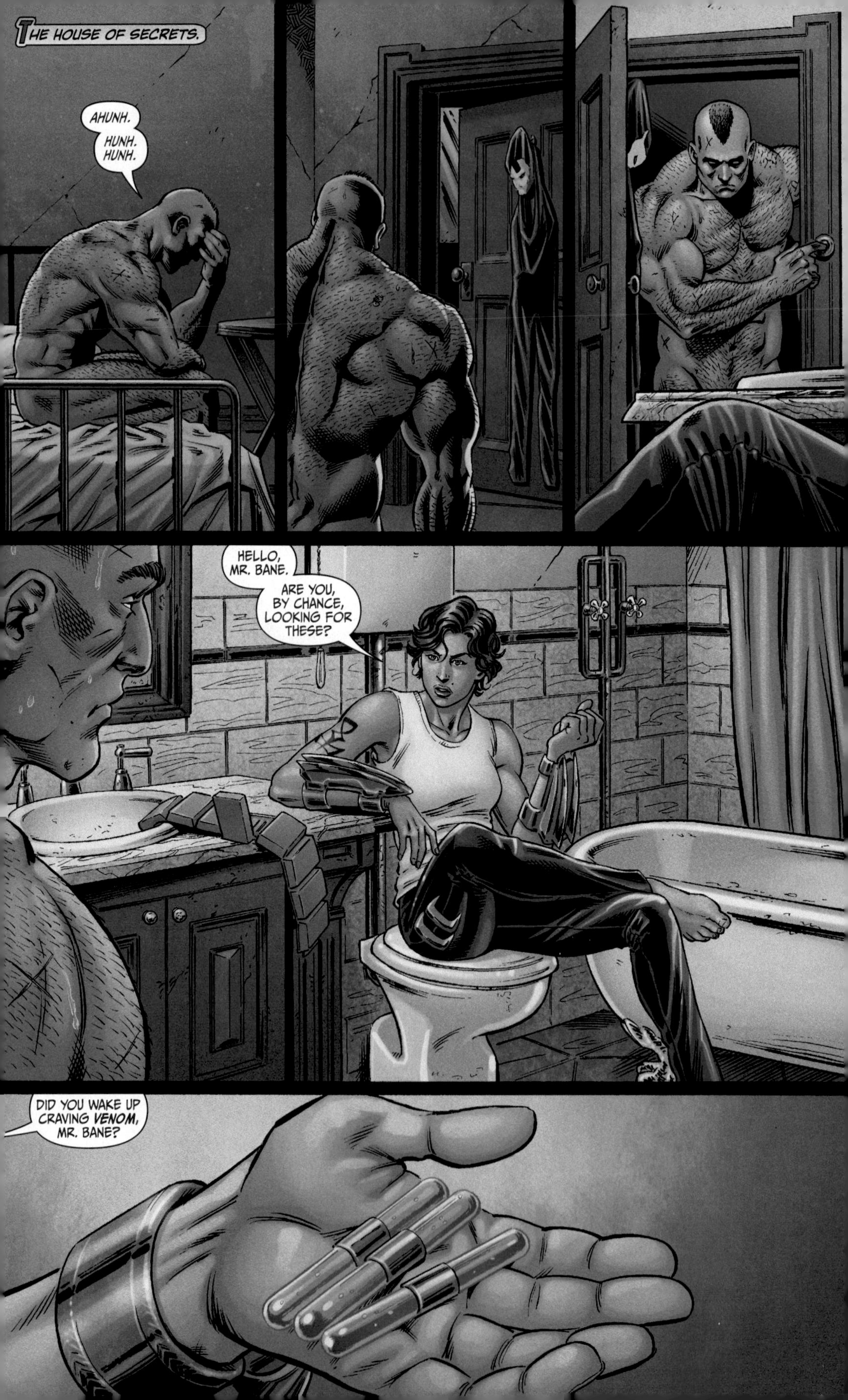
THE HOUSE OF SECRETS.
AHUNH.
HUNH. HUNH.
HELLO, MR. BANE.
ARE YOU, BY CHANCE, LOOKING FOR THESE?
DID YOU WAKE UP CRAVING VENOM, MR. BANE?

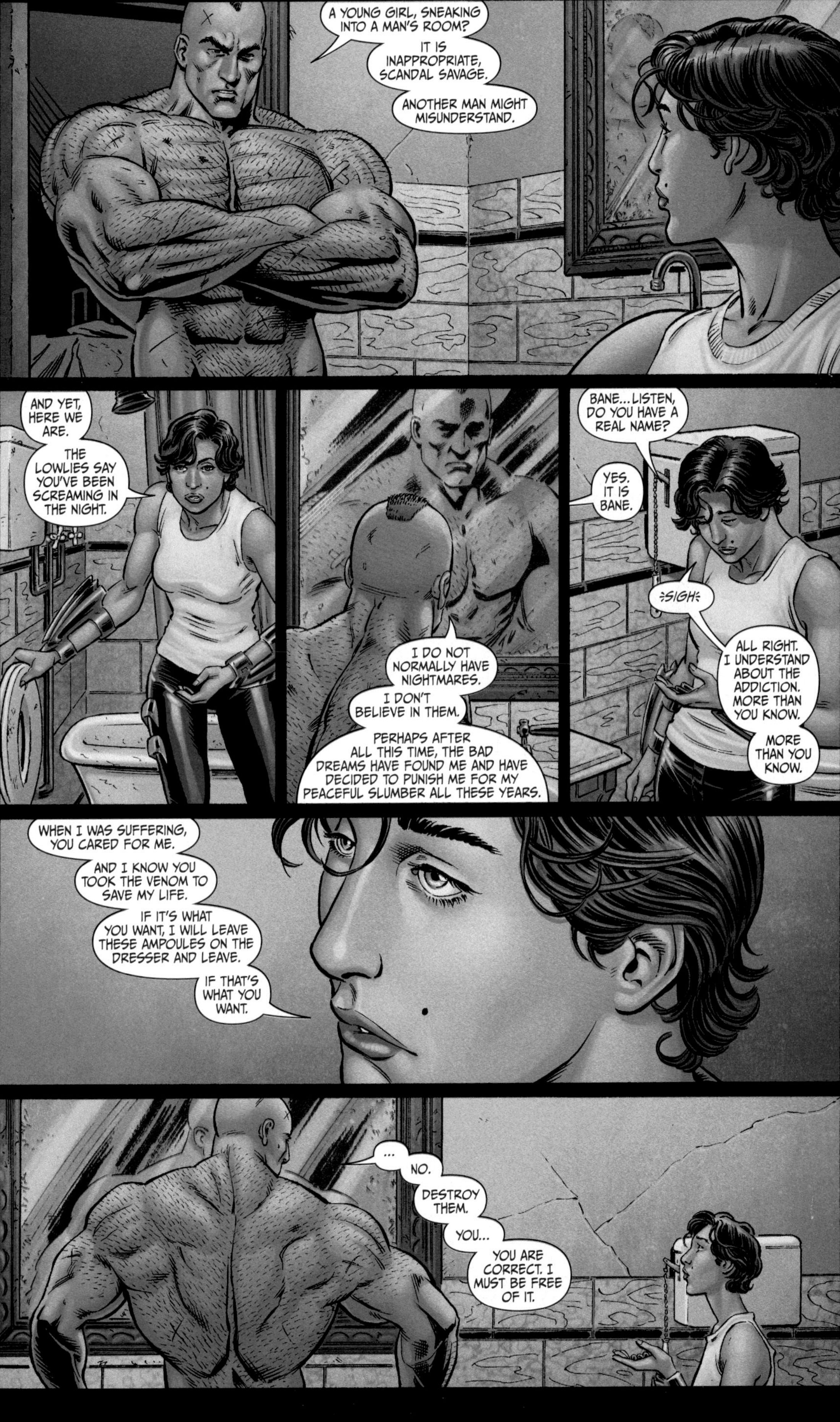

A YOUNG GIRL, SNEAKING INTO A MAN'S ROOM?
IT IS INAPPROPRIATE, SCANDAL SAVAGE.
ANOTHER MAN MIGHT MISUNDERSTAND.
AND YET, HERE WE ARE.
THE LOWLIES SAY YOU'VE BEEN SCREAMING IN THE NIGHT.
I DO NOT NORMALLY HAVE NIGHTMARES.
I DON'T BELIEVE IN THEM.
PERHAPS AFTER ALL THIS TIME, THE BAD DREAMS HAVE FOUND ME AND HAVE DECIDED TO PUNISH ME FOR MY PEACEFUL SLUMBER ALL THESE YEARS.
BANE...LISTEN, DO YOU HAVE A REAL NAME?
YES. IT IS BANE.
SIGH
ALL RIGHT. I UNDERSTAND ABOUT THE ADDICTION. MORE THAN YOU KNOW.
MORE THAN YOU KNOW.
WHEN I WAS SUFFERING, YOU CARED FOR ME.
AND I KNOW YOU TOOK THE VENOM TO SAVE MY LIFE.
IF IT'S WHAT YOU WANT, I WILL LEAVE THESE AMPOULES ON THE DRESSER AND LEAVE.
IF THAT'S WHAT YOU WANT.
...
NO.
DESTROY THEM.
YOU...
YOU ARE CORRECT. I MUST BE FREE OF IT.

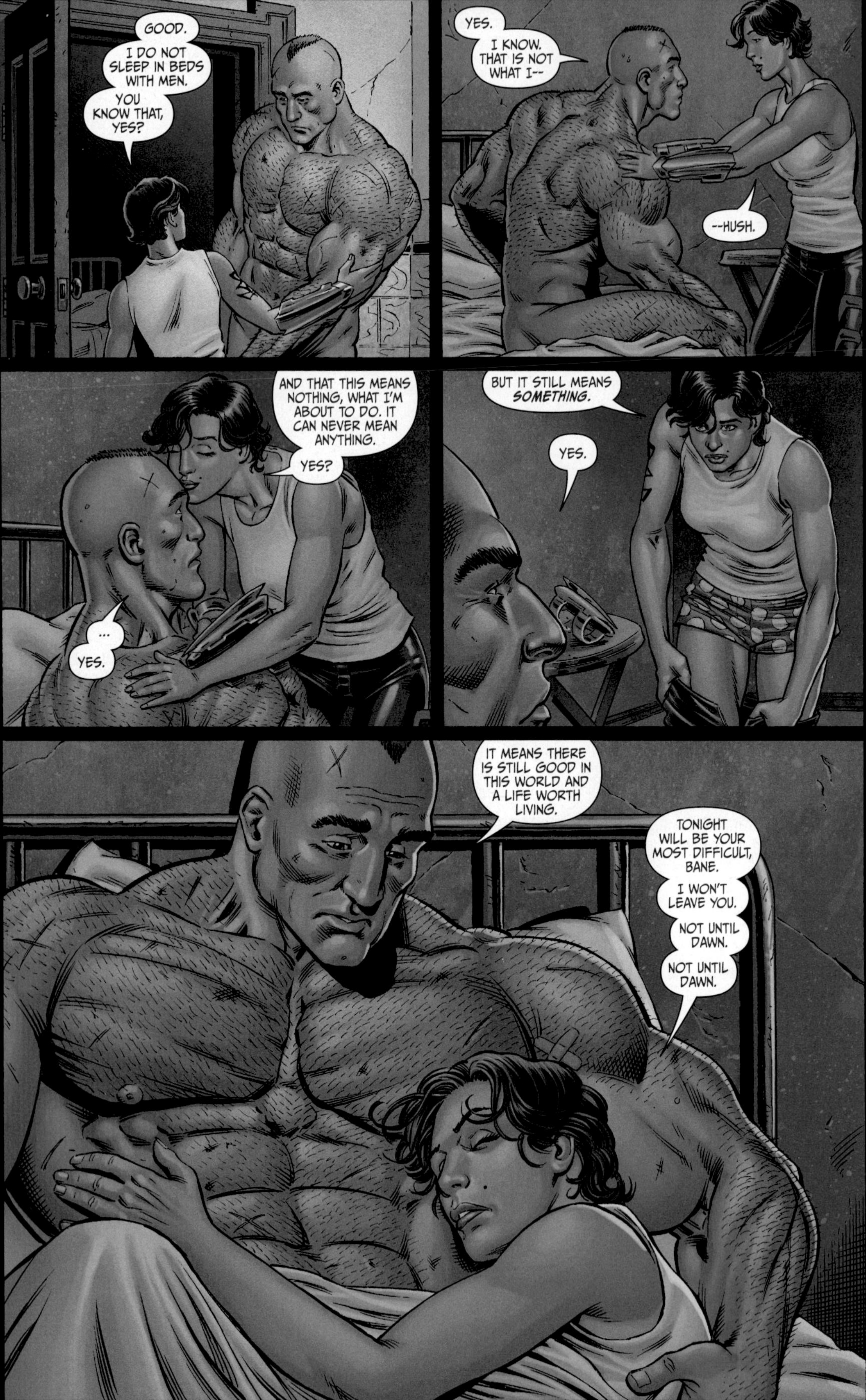
GOOD.
I DO NOT SLEEP IN BEDS WITH MEN.
YOU KNOW THAT, YES?
YES.
I KNOW. THAT IS NOT WHAT I--
--HUSH.
AND THAT THIS MEANS NOTHING, WHAT I'M ABOUT TO DO. IT CAN NEVER MEAN ANYTHING.
YES?
...
YES.
BUT IT STILL MEANS *SOMETHING.*
YES.
IT MEANS THERE IS STILL GOOD IN THIS WORLD AND A LIFE WORTH LIVING.
TONIGHT WILL BE YOUR MOST DIFFICULT, BANE.
I WON'T LEAVE YOU.
NOT UNTIL DAWN.
NOT UNTIL DAWN.

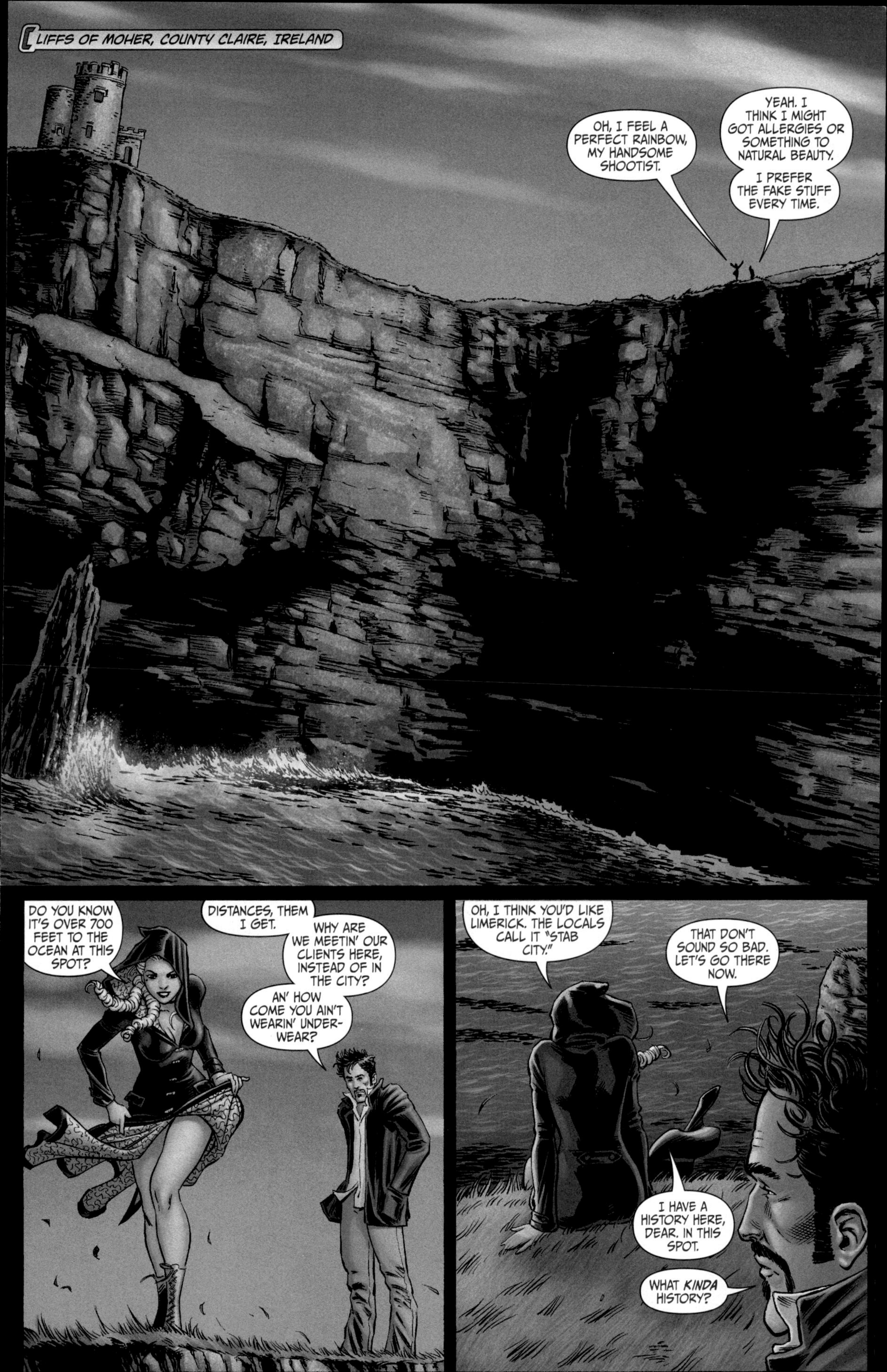
CLIFFS OF MOHER, COUNTY CLAIRE, IRELAND
OH, I FEEL A PERFECT RAINBOW, MY HANDSOME SHOOTIST.
YEAH. I THINK I MIGHT GOT ALLERGIES OR SOMETHING TO NATURAL BEAUTY.
I PREFER THE FAKE STUFF EVERY TIME.
DO YOU KNOW IT'S OVER 700 FEET TO THE OCEAN AT THIS SPOT?
DISTANCES, THEM I GET.
WHY ARE WE MEETIN' OUR CLIENTS HERE, INSTEAD OF IN THE CITY?
AN' HOW COME YOU AIN'T WEARIN' UNDER-WEAR?
OH, I THINK YOU'D LIKE LIMERICK. THE LOCALS CALL IT "STAB CITY."
THAT DON'T SOUND SO BAD. LET'S GO THERE NOW.
I HAVE A HISTORY HERE, DEAR. IN THIS SPOT.
WHAT KINDA HISTORY?

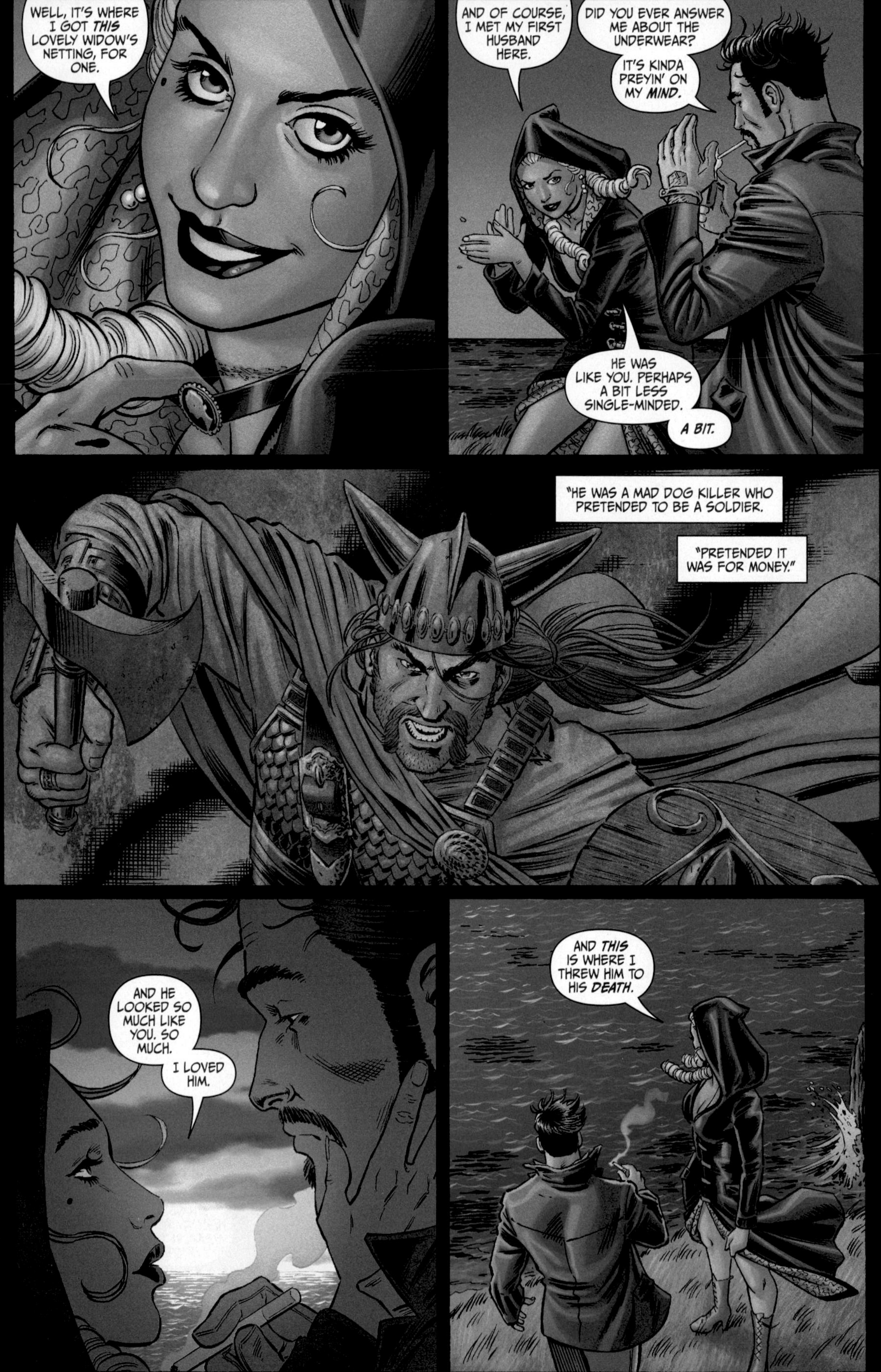
WELL, IT'S WHERE I GOT *THIS* LOVELY WIDOW'S NETTING, FOR ONE.
AND OF COURSE, I MET MY FIRST HUSBAND HERE.
DID YOU EVER ANSWER ME ABOUT THE UNDERWEAR?
IT'S KINDA PREYIN' ON MY *MIND*.
HE WAS LIKE YOU. PERHAPS A BIT LESS SINGLE-MINDED.
A BIT.
"HE WAS A MAD DOG KILLER WHO PRETENDED TO BE A SOLDIER.
"PRETENDED IT WAS FOR MONEY."
AND HE LOOKED SO MUCH LIKE YOU. SO MUCH.
I LOVED HIM.
AND *THIS* IS WHERE I THREW HIM TO HIS *DEATH*.

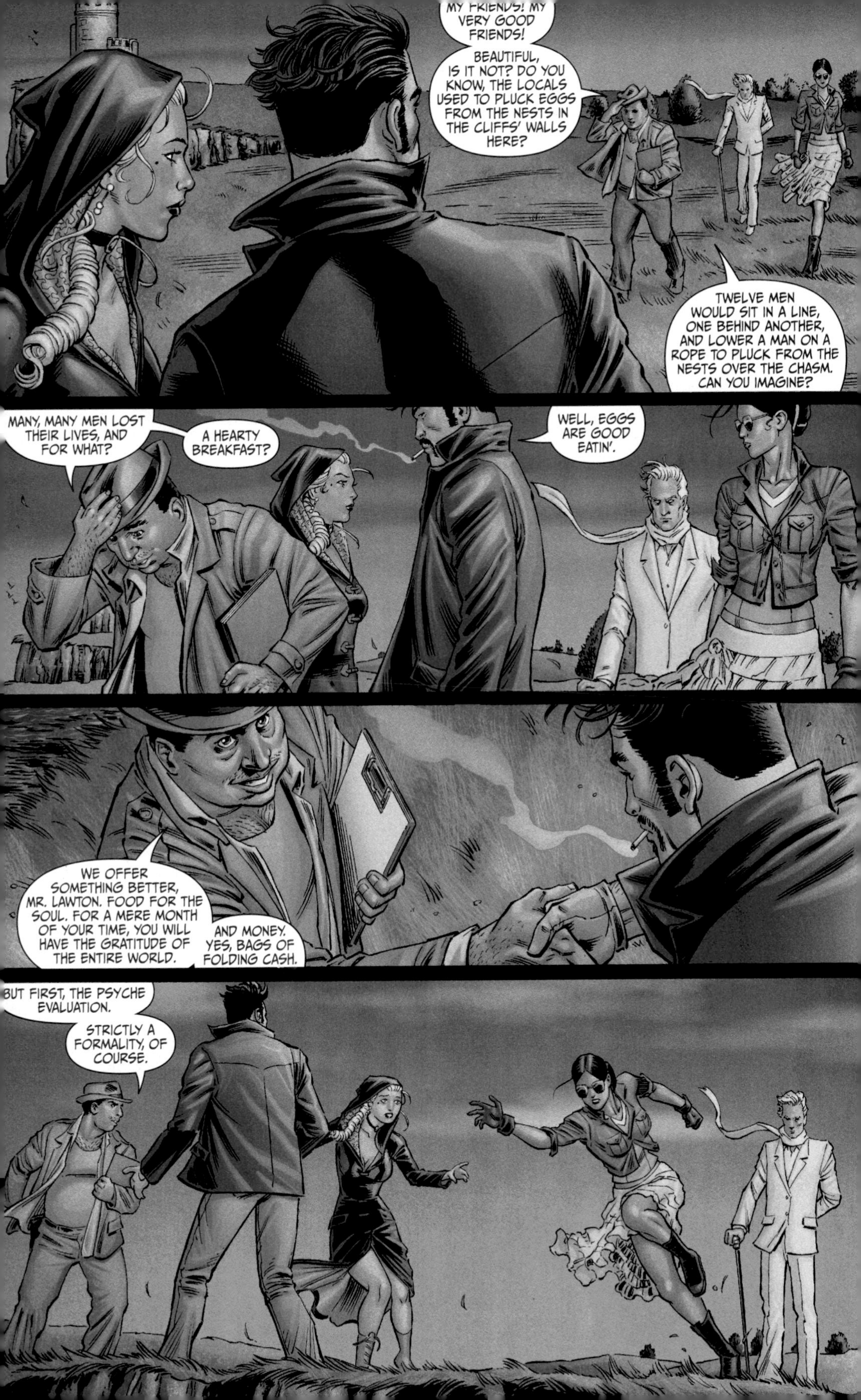
MY FRIENDS! MY VERY GOOD FRIENDS!
BEAUTIFUL, IS IT NOT? DO YOU KNOW, THE LOCALS USED TO PLUCK EGGS FROM THE NESTS IN THE CLIFFS' WALLS HERE?
TWELVE MEN WOULD SIT IN A LINE, ONE BEHIND ANOTHER, AND LOWER A MAN ON A ROPE TO PLUCK FROM THE NESTS OVER THE CHASM. CAN YOU IMAGINE?
MANY, MANY MEN LOST THEIR LIVES, AND FOR WHAT?
A HEARTY BREAKFAST?
WELL, EGGS ARE GOOD EATIN'.
WE OFFER SOMETHING BETTER, MR. LAWTON. FOOD FOR THE SOUL. FOR A MERE MONTH OF YOUR TIME, YOU WILL HAVE THE GRATITUDE OF THE ENTIRE WORLD.
AND MONEY. YES, BAGS OF FOLDING CASH.
BUT FIRST, THE PSYCHE EVALUATION.
STRICTLY A FORMALITY, OF COURSE.

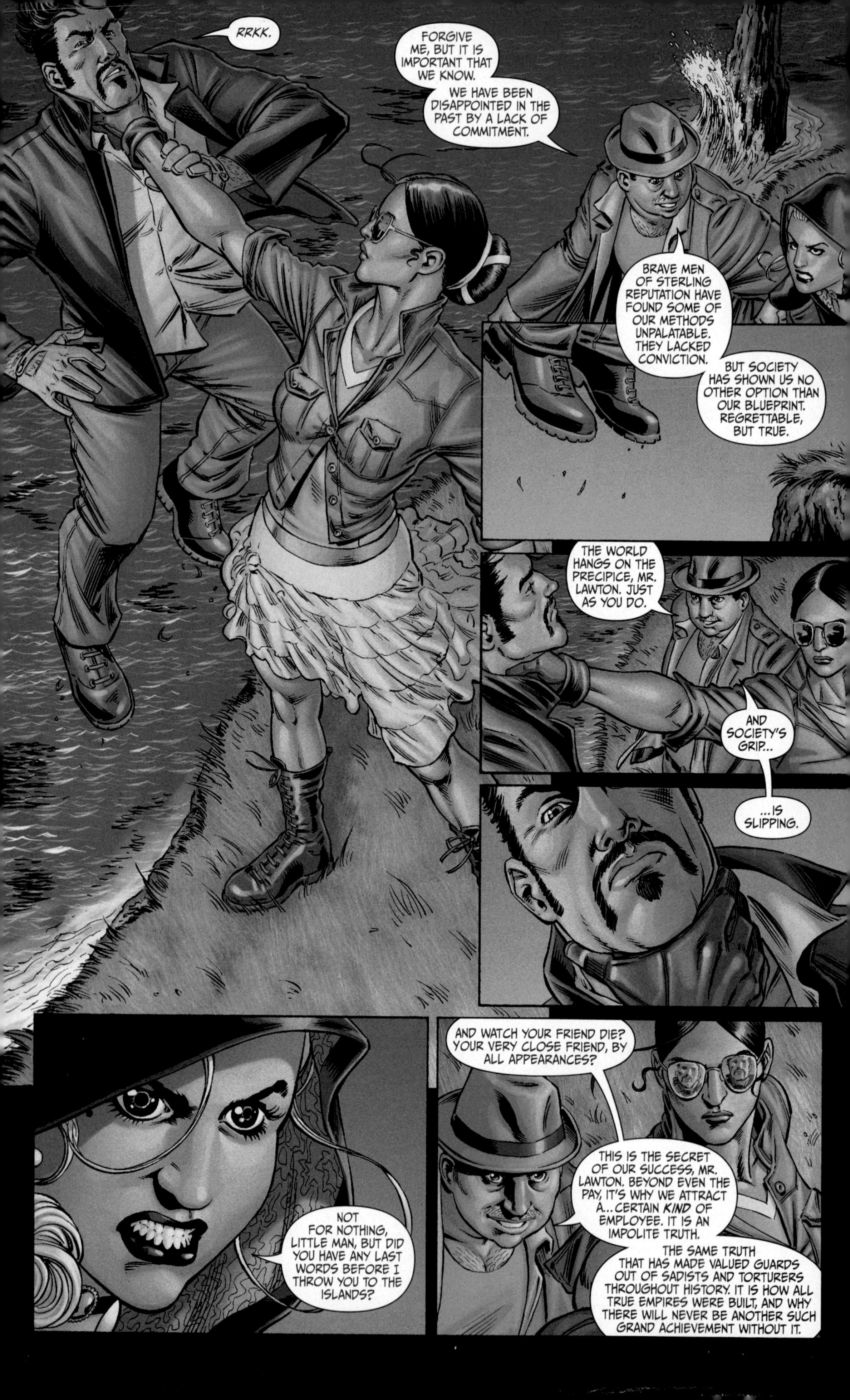
RRKK.
FORGIVE ME, BUT IT IS IMPORTANT THAT WE KNOW.
WE HAVE BEEN DISAPPOINTED IN THE PAST BY A LACK OF COMMITMENT.
BRAVE MEN OF STERLING REPUTATION HAVE FOUND SOME OF OUR METHODS UNPALATABLE. THEY LACKED CONVICTION.
BUT SOCIETY HAS SHOWN US NO OTHER OPTION THAN OUR BLUEPRINT. REGRETTABLE, BUT TRUE.
THE WORLD HANGS ON THE PRECIPICE, MR. LAWTON. JUST AS YOU DO.
AND SOCIETY'S GRIP...
...IS SLIPPING.
NOT FOR NOTHING, LITTLE MAN, BUT DID YOU HAVE ANY LAST WORDS BEFORE I THROW YOU TO THE ISLANDS?
AND WATCH YOUR FRIEND DIE? YOUR VERY CLOSE FRIEND, BY ALL APPEARANCES?
THIS IS THE SECRET OF OUR SUCCESS, MR. LAWTON. BEYOND EVEN THE PAY, IT'S WHY WE ATTRACT A...CERTAIN KIND OF EMPLOYEE. IT IS AN IMPOLITE TRUTH.
THE SAME TRUTH THAT HAS MADE VALUED GUARDS OUT OF SADISTS AND TORTURERS THROUGHOUT HISTORY. IT IS HOW ALL TRUE EMPIRES WERE BUILT, AND WHY THERE WILL NEVER BE ANOTHER SUCH GRAND ACHIEVEMENT WITHOUT IT.

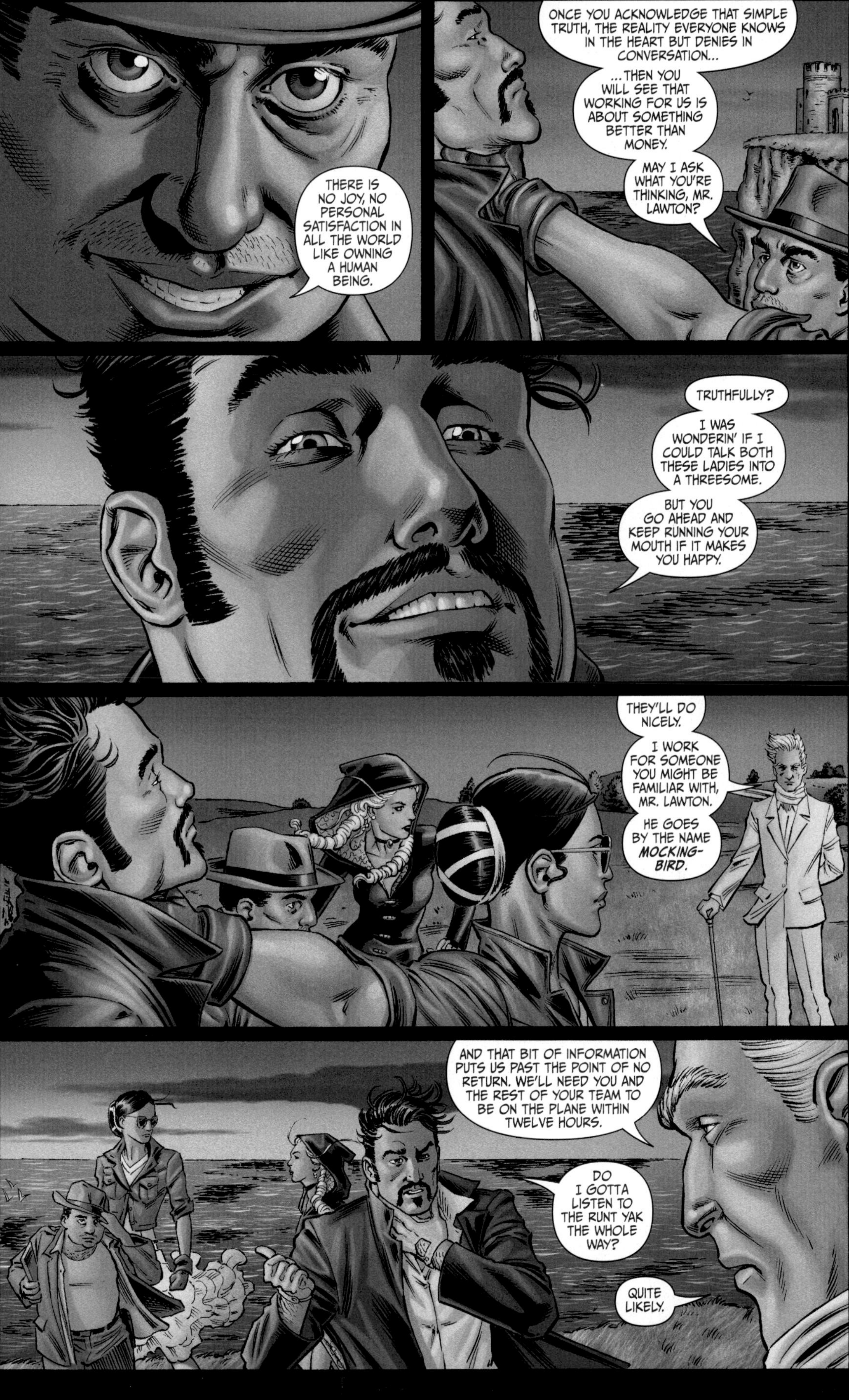
THERE IS NO JOY, NO PERSONAL SATISFACTION IN ALL THE WORLD LIKE OWNING A HUMAN BEING.
ONCE YOU ACKNOWLEDGE THAT SIMPLE TRUTH, THE REALITY EVERYONE KNOWS IN THE HEART BUT DENIES IN CONVERSATION...
...THEN YOU WILL SEE THAT WORKING FOR US IS ABOUT SOMETHING BETTER THAN MONEY.
MAY I ASK WHAT YOU'RE THINKING, MR. LAWTON?
TRUTHFULLY?
I WAS WONDERIN' IF I COULD TALK BOTH THESE LADIES INTO A THREESOME.
BUT YOU GO AHEAD AND KEEP RUNNING YOUR MOUTH IF IT MAKES YOU HAPPY.
THEY'LL DO NICELY.
I WORK FOR SOMEONE YOU MIGHT BE FAMILIAR WITH, MR. LAWTON.
HE GOES BY THE NAME ***MOCKING-BIRD***.
AND THAT BIT OF INFORMATION PUTS US PAST THE POINT OF NO RETURN. WE'LL NEED YOU AND THE REST OF YOUR TEAM TO BE ON THE PLANE WITHIN TWELVE HOURS.
DO I GOTTA LISTEN TO THE RUNT YAK THE WHOLE WAY?
QUITE LIKELY.

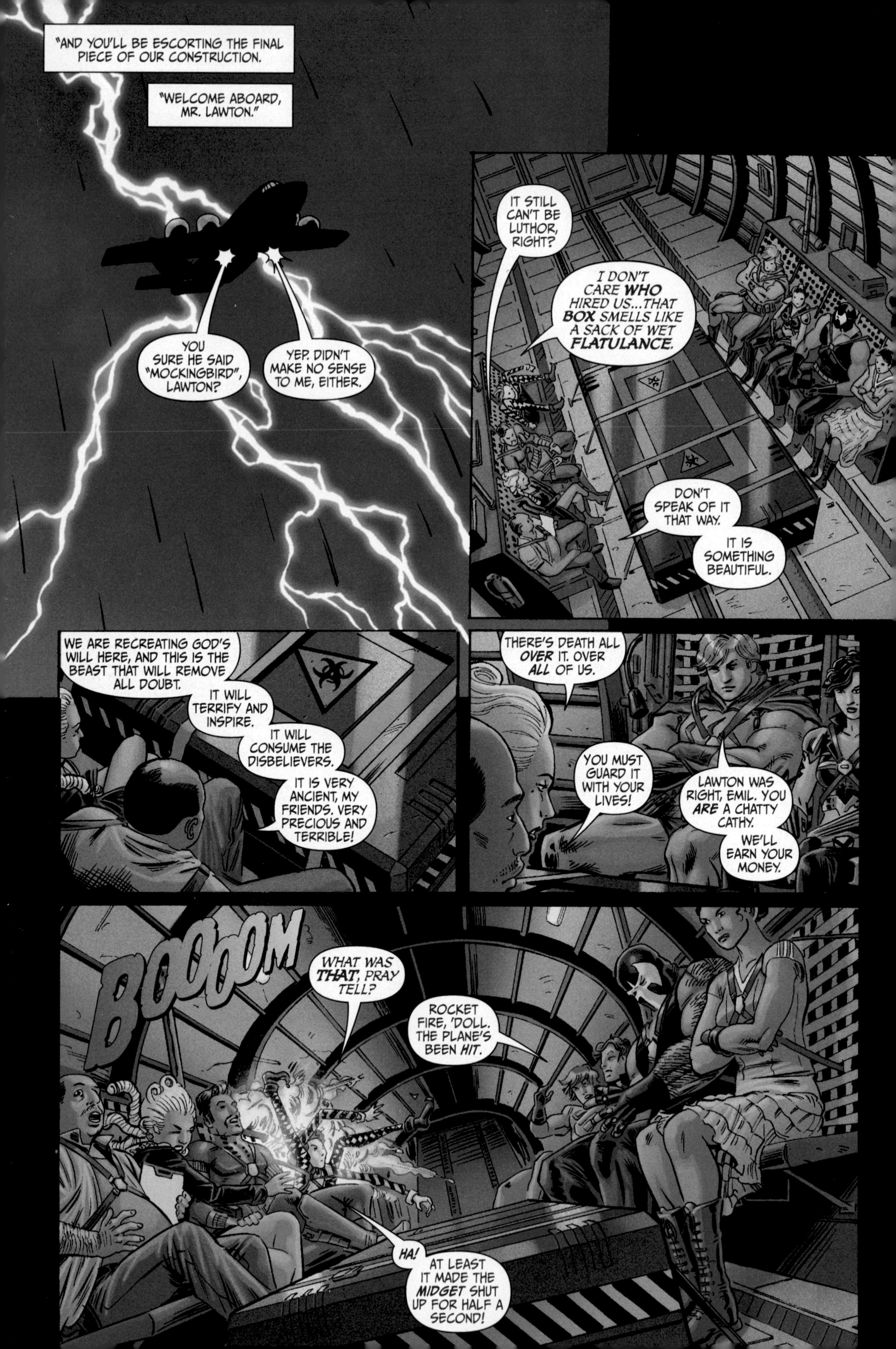
"AND YOU'LL BE ESCORTING THE FINAL PIECE OF OUR CONSTRUCTION.
"WELCOME ABOARD, MR. LAWTON."
YOU SURE HE SAID "MOCKINGBIRD", LAWTON?
YEP. DIDN'T MAKE NO SENSE TO ME, EITHER.
IT STILL CAN'T BE LUTHOR, RIGHT?
I DON'T CARE WHO HIRED US...THAT BOX SMELLS LIKE A SACK OF WET FLATULANCE.
DON'T SPEAK OF IT THAT WAY.
IT IS SOMETHING BEAUTIFUL.
WE ARE RECREATING GOD'S WILL HERE, AND THIS IS THE BEAST THAT WILL REMOVE ALL DOUBT.
IT WILL TERRIFY AND INSPIRE.
IT WILL CONSUME THE DISBELIEVERS.
IT IS VERY ANCIENT, MY FRIENDS. VERY PRECIOUS AND TERRIBLE!
THERE'S DEATH ALL OVER IT. OVER ALL OF US.
YOU MUST GUARD IT WITH YOUR LIVES!
LAWTON WAS RIGHT, EMIL. YOU ARE A CHATTY CATHY.
WE'LL EARN YOUR MONEY.
BOOOOM
WHAT WAS THAT, PRAY TELL?
ROCKET FIRE, 'DOLL. THE PLANE'S BEEN HIT.
HA!
AT LEAST IT MADE THE MIDGET SHUT UP FOR HALF A SECOND!

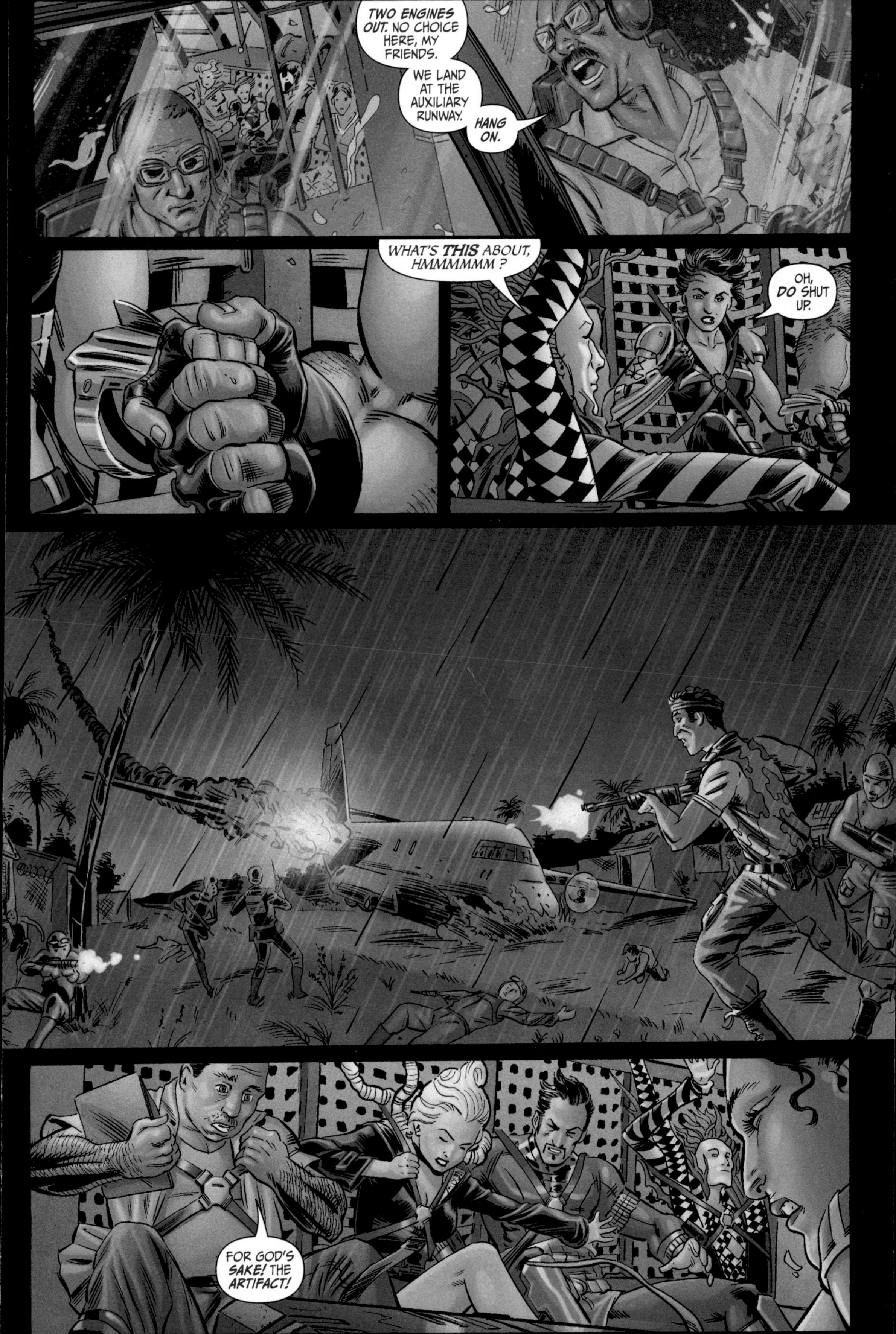
TWO ENGINES OUT. NO CHOICE HERE, MY FRIENDS.
WE LAND AT THE AUXILIARY RUNWAY.
HANG ON.
WHAT'S THIS ABOUT, HMMMMMM ?
OH, DO SHUT UP.
FOR GOD'S SAKE! THE ARTIFACT!

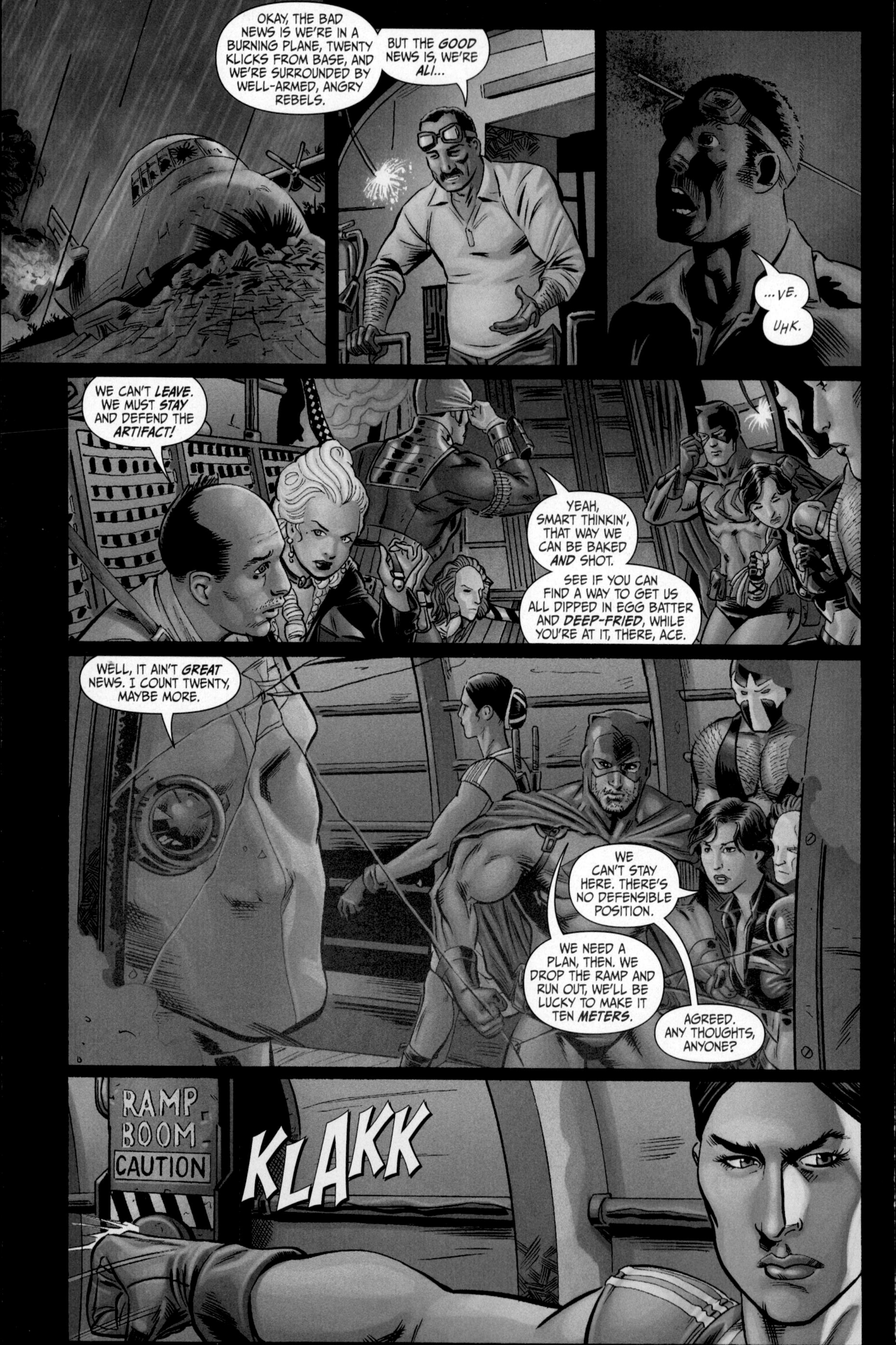
OKAY, THE BAD NEWS IS WE'RE IN A BURNING PLANE, TWENTY KLICKS FROM BASE, AND WE'RE SURROUNDED BY WELL-ARMED, ANGRY REBELS.
BUT THE GOOD NEWS IS, WE'RE ALI...
...VE.
UHK.
WE CAN'T LEAVE. WE MUST STAY AND DEFEND THE ARTIFACT!
YEAH, SMART THINKIN', THAT WAY WE CAN BE BAKED AND SHOT.
SEE IF YOU CAN FIND A WAY TO GET US ALL DIPPED IN EGG BATTER AND DEEP-FRIED, WHILE YOU'RE AT IT, THERE, ACE.
WELL, IT AIN'T GREAT NEWS. I COUNT TWENTY, MAYBE MORE.
WE CAN'T STAY HERE. THERE'S NO DEFENSIBLE POSITION.
WE NEED A PLAN, THEN. WE DROP THE RAMP AND RUN OUT, WE'LL BE LUCKY TO MAKE IT TEN METERS.
AGREED. ANY THOUGHTS, ANYONE?
RAMP BOOM
CAUTION
KLAKK

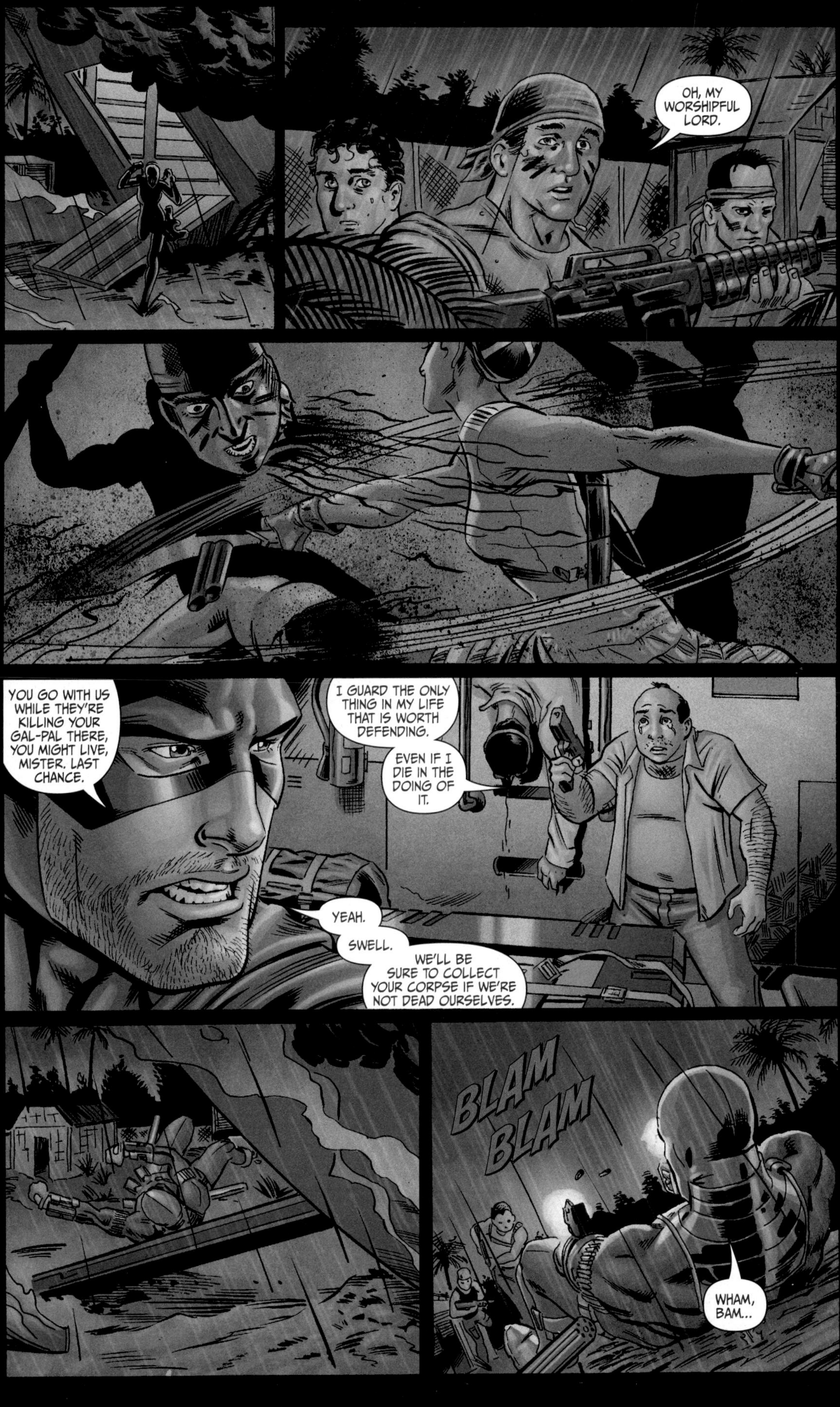
OH, MY WORSHIPFUL LORD.
YOU GO WITH US WHILE THEY'RE KILLING YOUR GAL-PAL THERE, YOU MIGHT LIVE, MISTER. LAST CHANCE.
I GUARD THE ONLY THING IN MY LIFE THAT IS WORTH DEFENDING.
EVEN IF I DIE IN THE DOING OF IT.
YEAH.
SWELL.
WE'LL BE SURE TO COLLECT YOUR CORPSE IF WE'RE NOT DEAD OURSELVES.
BLAM BLAM
WHAM, BAM...

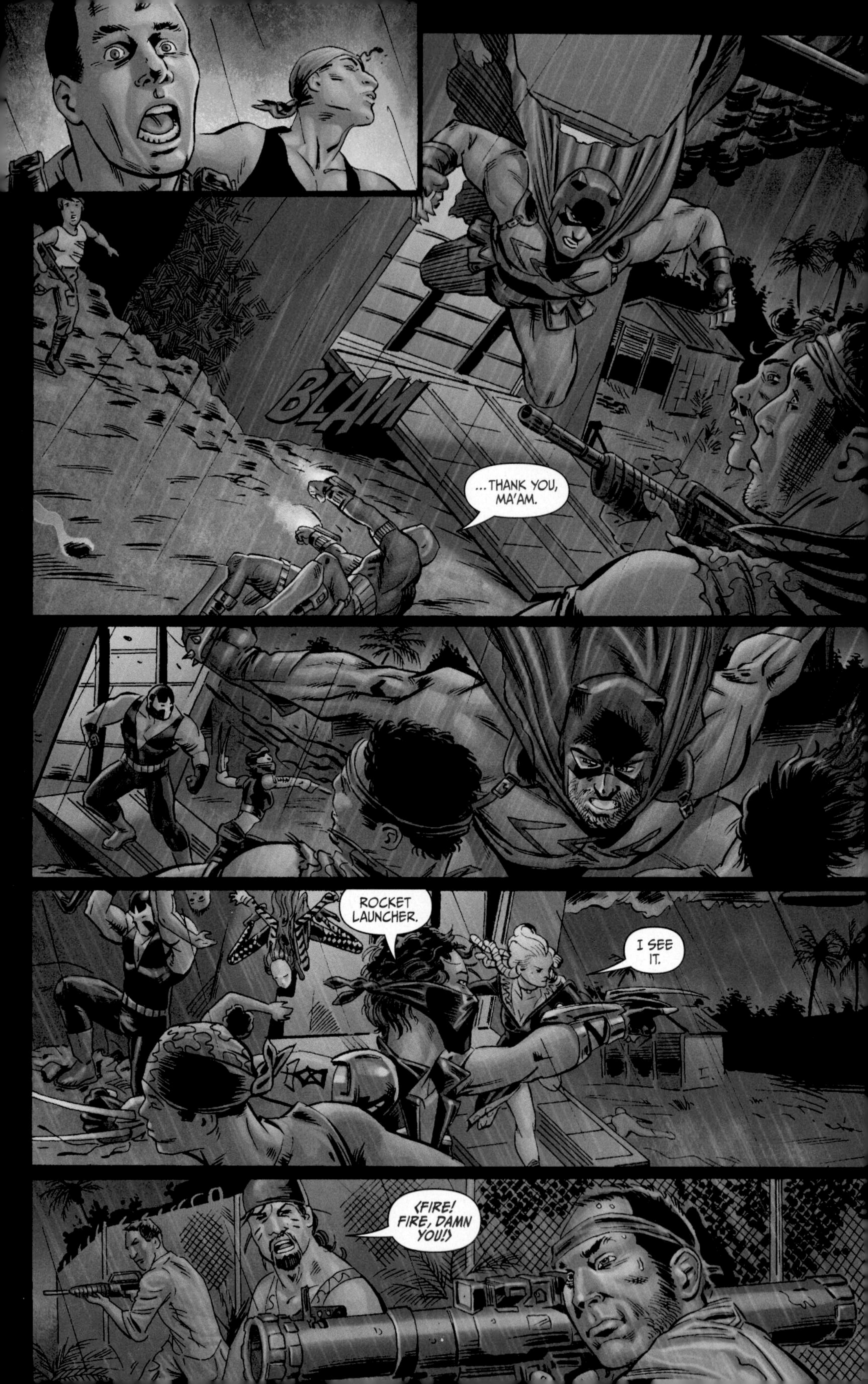
BLAM
...THANK YOU, MA'AM.
ROCKET LAUNCHER.
I SEE IT.
‹FIRE! FIRE, DAMN YOU!›

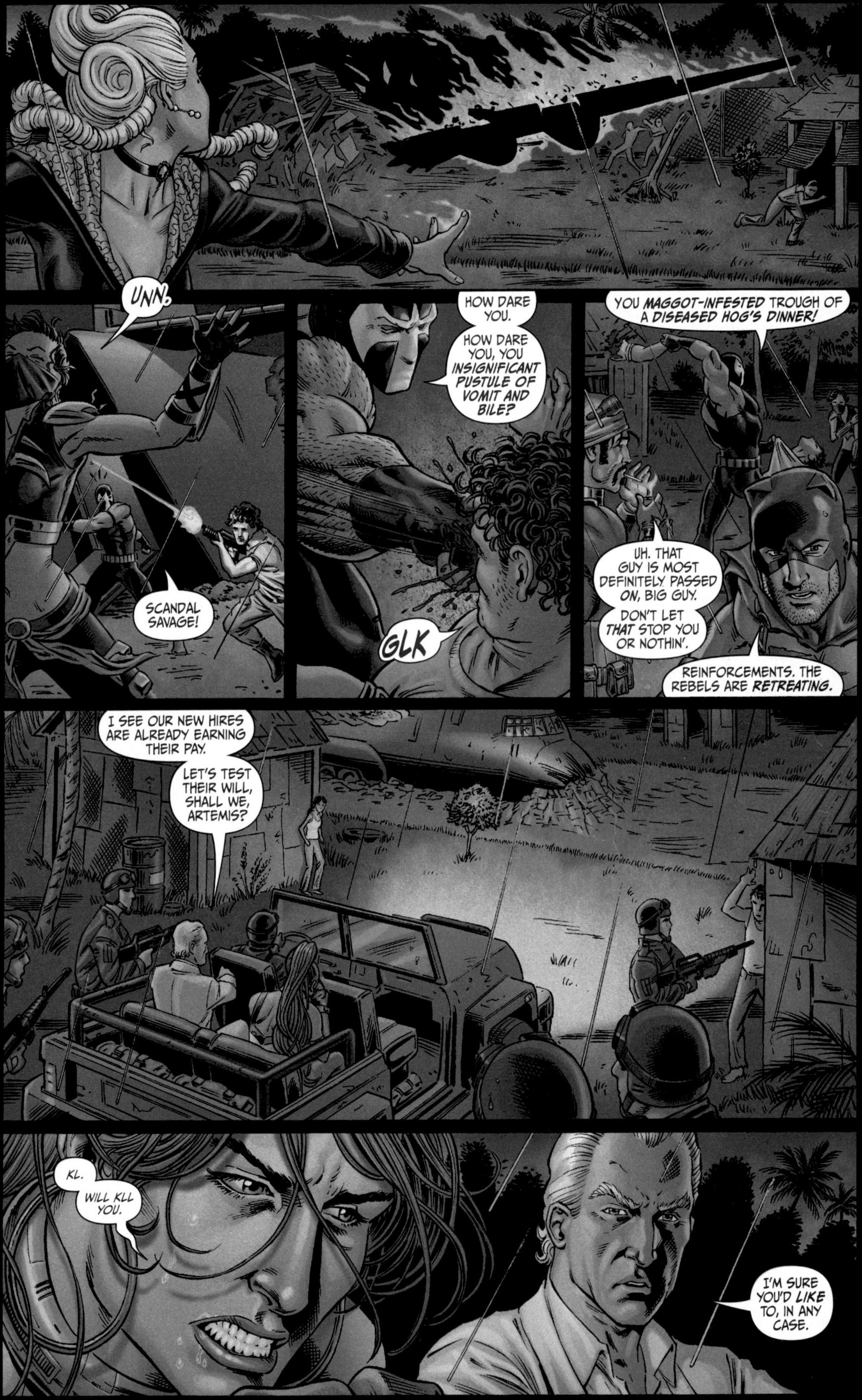
UNN.
SCANDAL SAVAGE!
HOW DARE YOU.
HOW DARE YOU, YOU INSIGNIFICANT PUSTULE OF VOMIT AND BILE?
GLK
YOU MAGGOT-INFESTED TROUGH OF A DISEASED HOG'S DINNER!
UH. THAT GUY IS MOST DEFINITELY PASSED ON, BIG GUY.
DON'T LET THAT STOP YOU OR NOTHIN'.
REINFORCEMENTS. THE REBELS ARE RETREATING.
I SEE OUR NEW HIRES ARE ALREADY EARNING THEIR PAY.
LET'S TEST THEIR WILL, SHALL WE, ARTEMIS?
KL.
WILL KLL YOU.
I'M SURE YOU'D LIKE TO, IN ANY CASE.

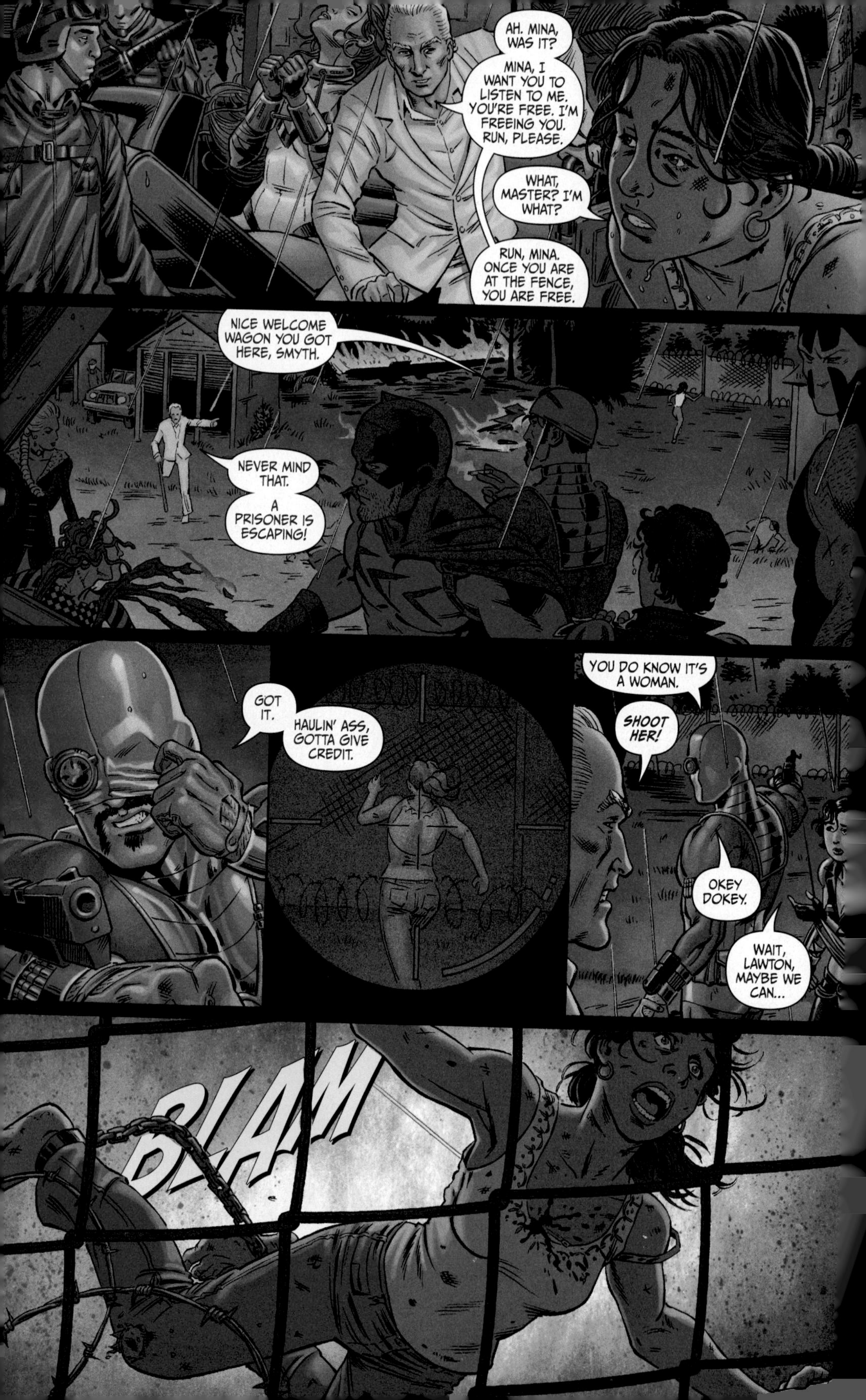
AH. MINA, WAS IT?
MINA, I WANT YOU TO LISTEN TO ME. YOU'RE FREE. I'M FREEING YOU. RUN, PLEASE.
WHAT, MASTER? I'M WHAT?
RUN, MINA. ONCE YOU ARE AT THE FENCE, YOU ARE FREE.
NICE WELCOME WAGON YOU GOT HERE, SMYTH.
NEVER MIND THAT.
A PRISONER IS ESCAPING!
GOT IT.
HAULIN' ASS, GOTTA GIVE CREDIT.
YOU DO KNOW IT'S A WOMAN.
SHOOT HER!
OKEY DOKEY.
WAIT, LAWTON, MAYBE WE CAN...
BLAM

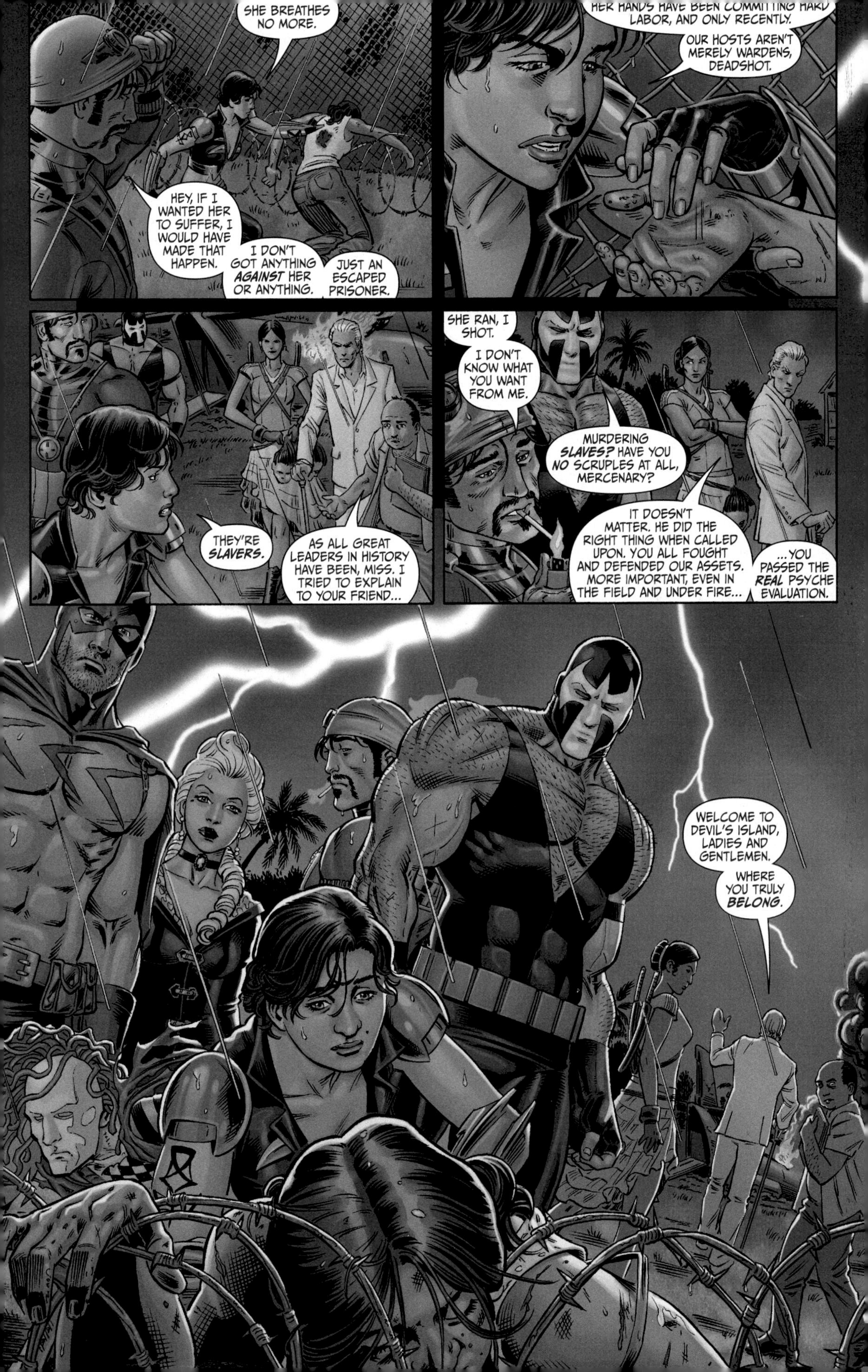
SHE BREATHES NO MORE.
HEY, IF I WANTED HER TO SUFFER, I WOULD HAVE MADE THAT HAPPEN.
I DON'T GOT ANYTHING AGAINST HER OR ANYTHING.
JUST AN ESCAPED PRISONER.
HER HANDS HAVE BEEN COMMITTING HARD LABOR, AND ONLY RECENTLY.
OUR HOSTS AREN'T MERELY WARDENS, DEADSHOT.
THEY'RE SLAVERS.
AS ALL GREAT LEADERS IN HISTORY HAVE BEEN, MISS. I TRIED TO EXPLAIN TO YOUR FRIEND...
SHE RAN, I SHOT.
I DON'T KNOW WHAT YOU WANT FROM ME.
MURDERING SLAVES? HAVE YOU NO SCRUPLES AT ALL, MERCENARY?
IT DOESN'T MATTER. HE DID THE RIGHT THING WHEN CALLED UPON. YOU ALL FOUGHT AND DEFENDED OUR ASSETS. MORE IMPORTANT, EVEN IN THE FIELD AND UNDER FIRE...
...YOU PASSED THE REAL PSYCHE EVALUATION.
WELCOME TO DEVIL'S ISLAND, LADIES AND GENTLEMEN.
WHERE YOU TRULY BELONG.

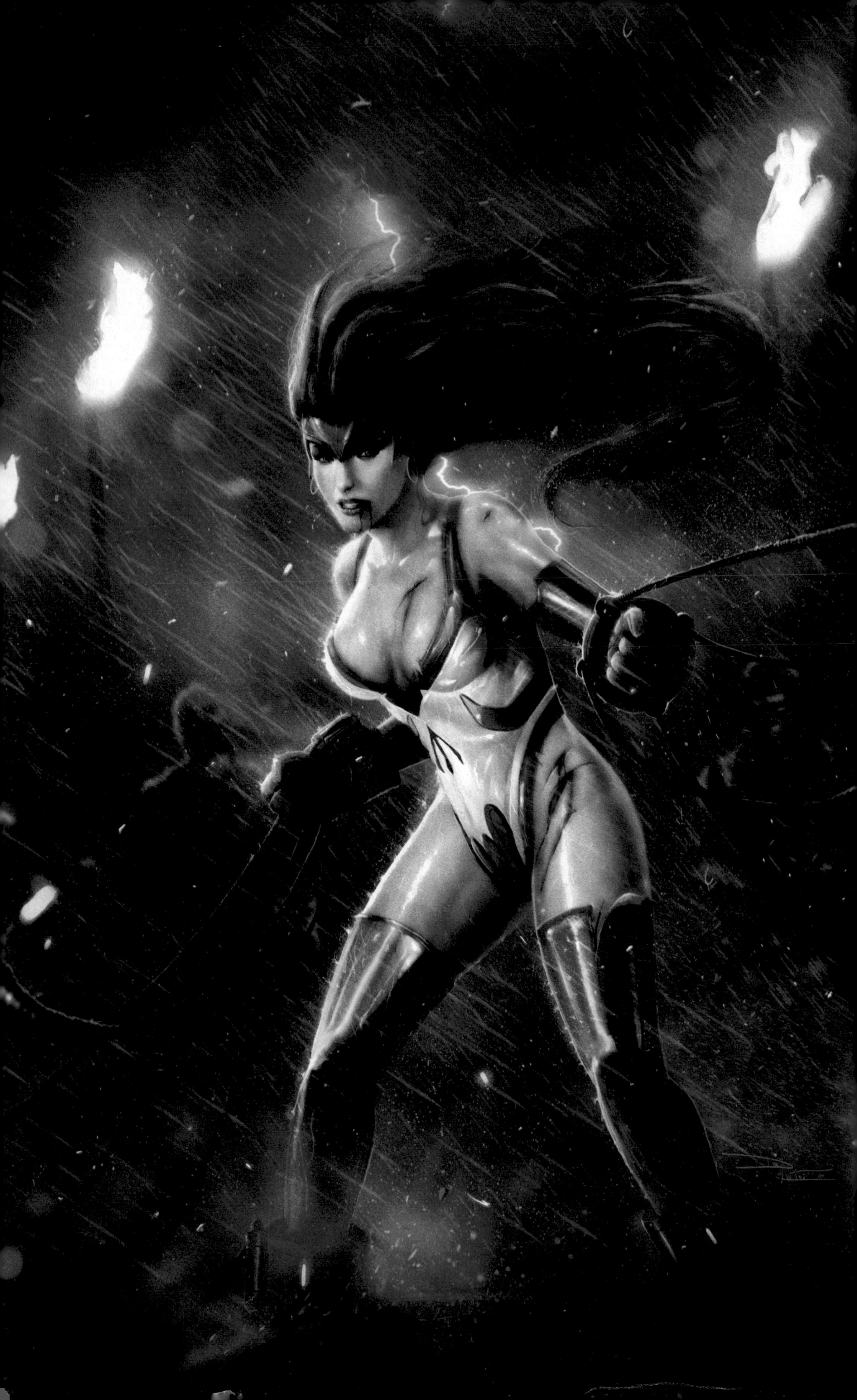

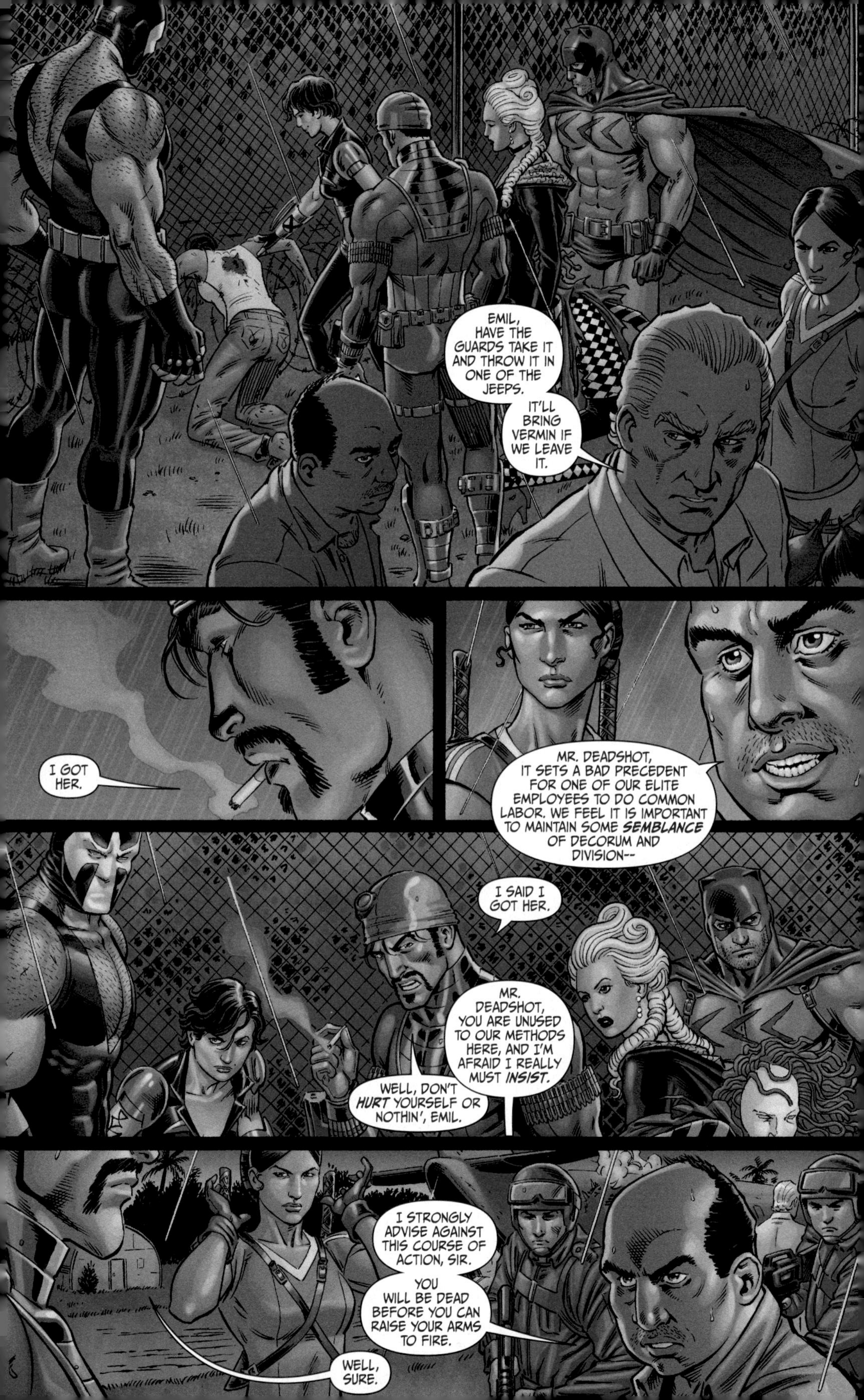
EMIL, HAVE THE GUARDS TAKE IT AND THROW IT IN ONE OF THE JEEPS.
IT'LL BRING VERMIN IF WE LEAVE IT.
I GOT HER.
MR. DEADSHOT, IT SETS A BAD PRECEDENT FOR ONE OF OUR ELITE EMPLOYEES TO DO COMMON LABOR. WE FEEL IT IS IMPORTANT TO MAINTAIN SOME *SEMBLANCE* OF DECORUM AND DIVISION--
I SAID I GOT HER.
MR. DEADSHOT, YOU ARE UNUSED TO OUR METHODS HERE, AND I'M AFRAID I REALLY MUST *INSIST.*
WELL, DON'T *HURT* YOURSELF OR NOTHIN', EMIL.
I STRONGLY ADVISE AGAINST THIS COURSE OF ACTION, SIR.
YOU WILL BE DEAD BEFORE YOU CAN RAISE YOUR ARMS TO FIRE.
WELL, SURE.

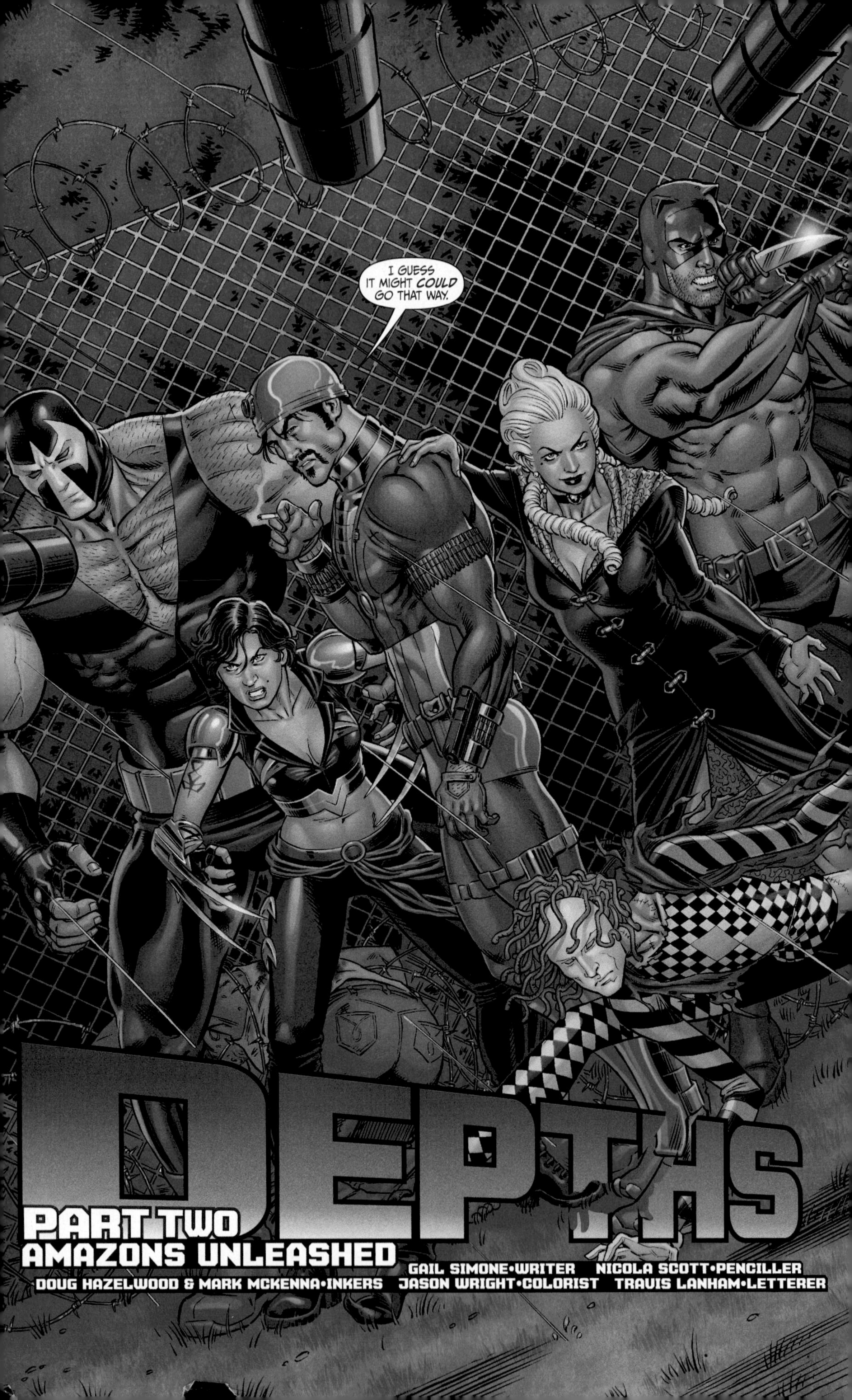
I GUESS IT MIGHT *COULD* GO THAT WAY.
DEPTHS
PART TWO
AMAZONS UNLEASHED
GAIL SIMONE•WRITER NICOLA SCOTT•PENCILLER
DOUG HAZELWOOD & MARK MCKENNA•INKERS JASON WRIGHT•COLORIST TRAVIS LANHAM•LETTERER

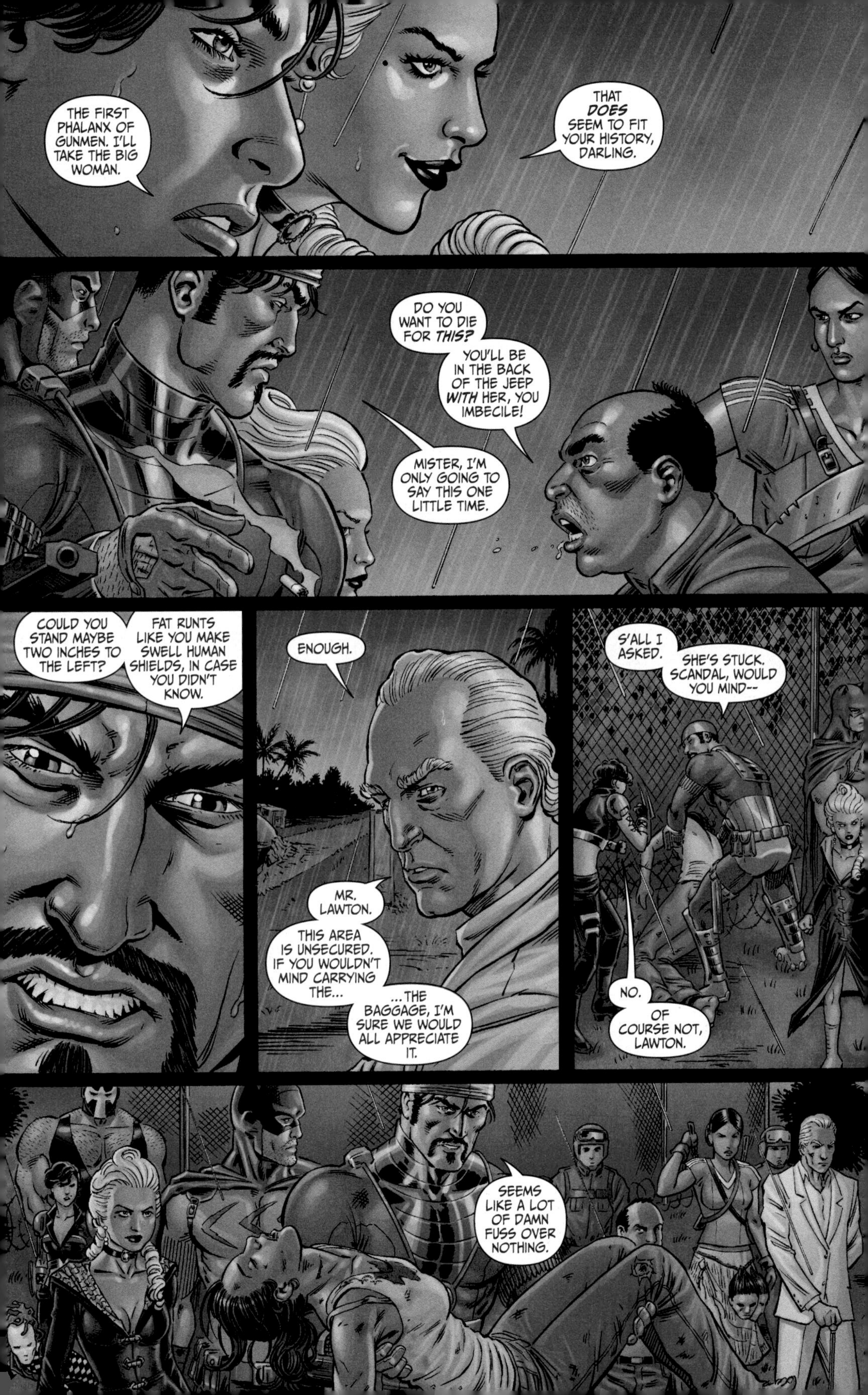
THE FIRST PHALANX OF GUNMEN. I'LL TAKE THE BIG WOMAN.
THAT DOES SEEM TO FIT YOUR HISTORY, DARLING.
DO YOU WANT TO DIE FOR THIS?
YOU'LL BE IN THE BACK OF THE JEEP WITH HER, YOU IMBECILE!
MISTER, I'M ONLY GOING TO SAY THIS ONE LITTLE TIME.
COULD YOU STAND MAYBE TWO INCHES TO THE LEFT?
FAT RUNTS LIKE YOU MAKE SWELL HUMAN SHIELDS, IN CASE YOU DIDN'T KNOW.
ENOUGH.
MR. LAWTON.
THIS AREA IS UNSECURED. IF YOU WOULDN'T MIND CARRYING THE...
...THE BAGGAGE, I'M SURE WE WOULD ALL APPRECIATE IT.
S'ALL I ASKED.
SHE'S STUCK. SCANDAL, WOULD YOU MIND--
NO.
OF COURSE NOT, LAWTON.
SEEMS LIKE A LOT OF DAMN FUSS OVER NOTHING.

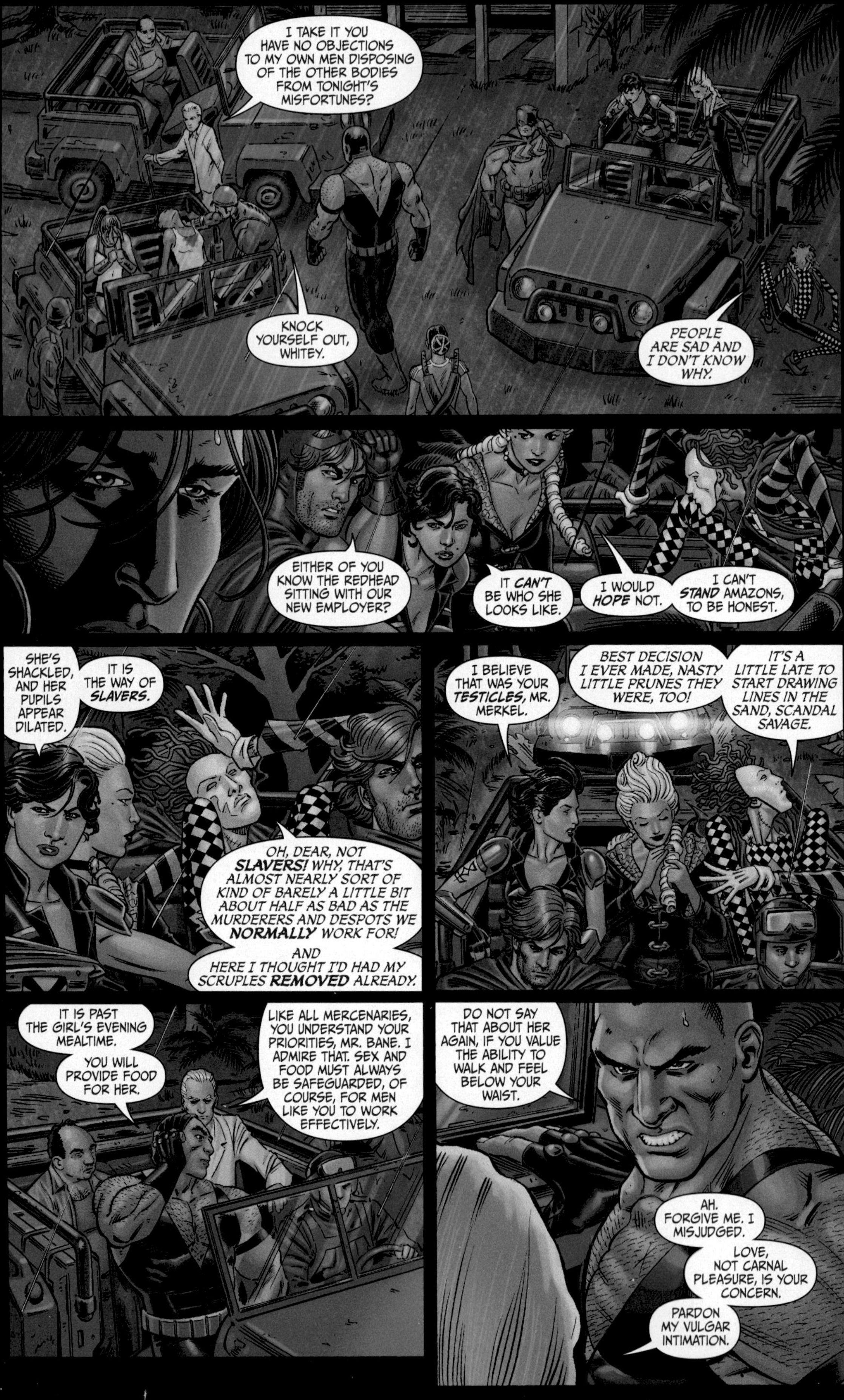
I TAKE IT YOU HAVE NO OBJECTIONS TO MY OWN MEN DISPOSING OF THE OTHER BODIES FROM TONIGHT'S MISFORTUNES?
KNOCK YOURSELF OUT, WHITEY.
PEOPLE ARE SAD AND I DON'T KNOW WHY.
EITHER OF YOU KNOW THE REDHEAD SITTING WITH OUR NEW EMPLOYER?
IT CAN'T BE WHO SHE LOOKS LIKE.
I WOULD HOPE NOT.
I CAN'T STAND AMAZONS, TO BE HONEST.
SHE'S SHACKLED, AND HER PUPILS APPEAR DILATED.
IT IS THE WAY OF SLAVERS.
OH, DEAR, NOT SLAVERS! WHY, THAT'S ALMOST NEARLY SORT OF KIND OF BARELY A LITTLE BIT ABOUT HALF AS BAD AS THE MURDERERS AND DESPOTS WE NORMALLY WORK FOR!
AND HERE I THOUGHT I'D HAD MY SCRUPLES REMOVED ALREADY.
I BELIEVE THAT WAS YOUR TESTICLES, MR. MERKEL.
BEST DECISION I EVER MADE, NASTY LITTLE PRUNES THEY WERE, TOO!
IT'S A LITTLE LATE TO START DRAWING LINES IN THE SAND, SCANDAL SAVAGE.
IT IS PAST THE GIRL'S EVENING MEALTIME.
YOU WILL PROVIDE FOOD FOR HER.
LIKE ALL MERCENARIES, YOU UNDERSTAND YOUR PRIORITIES, MR. BANE. I ADMIRE THAT. SEX AND FOOD MUST ALWAYS BE SAFEGUARDED, OF COURSE, FOR MEN LIKE YOU TO WORK EFFECTIVELY.
DO NOT SAY THAT ABOUT HER AGAIN, IF YOU VALUE THE ABILITY TO WALK AND FEEL BELOW YOUR WAIST.
AH. FORGIVE ME. I MISJUDGED.
LOVE, NOT CARNAL PLEASURE, IS YOUR CONCERN.
PARDON MY VULGAR INTIMATION.

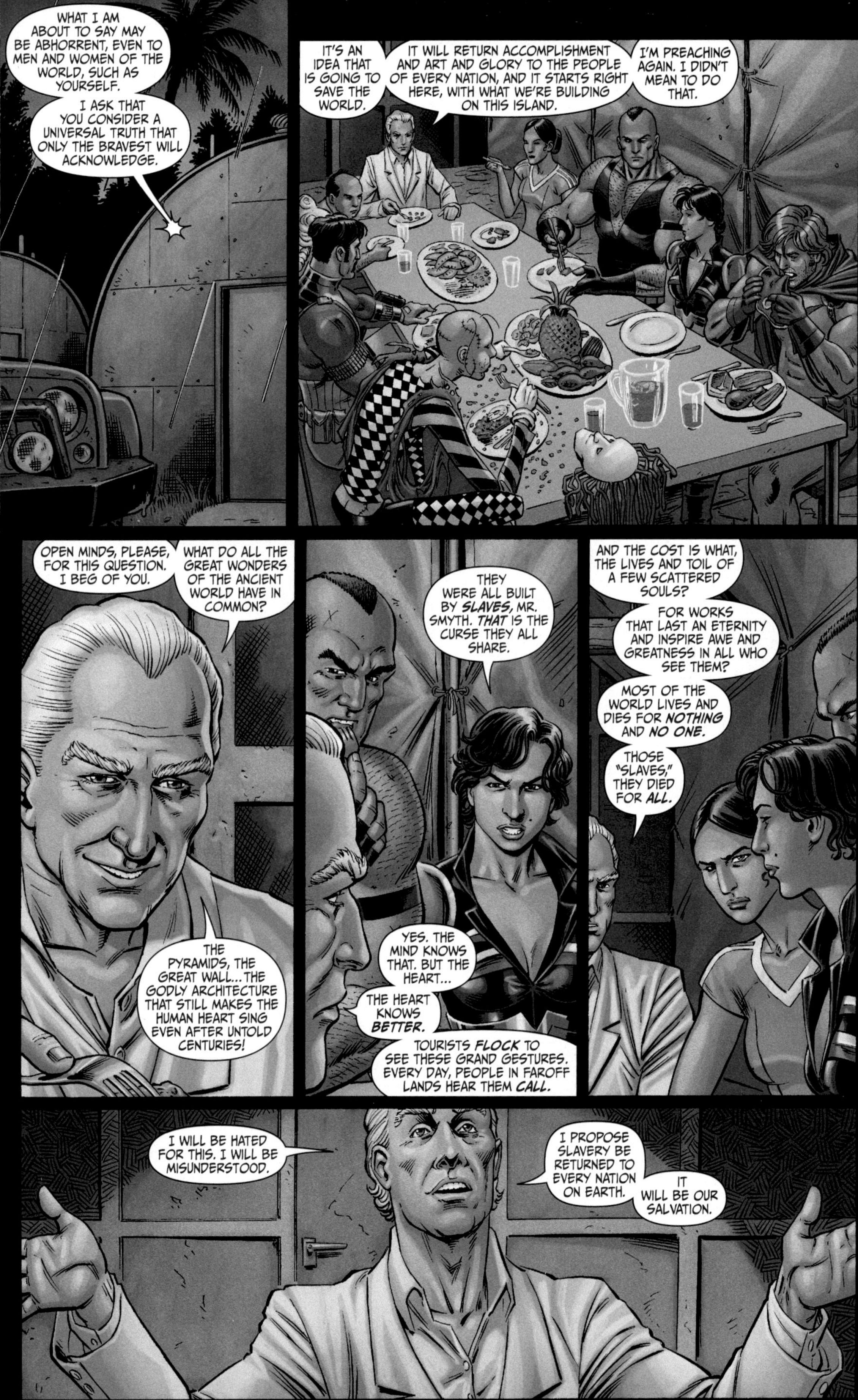
WHAT I AM ABOUT TO SAY MAY BE ABHORRENT, EVEN TO MEN AND WOMEN OF THE WORLD, SUCH AS YOURSELF.
I ASK THAT YOU CONSIDER A UNIVERSAL TRUTH THAT ONLY THE BRAVEST WILL ACKNOWLEDGE.
IT'S AN IDEA THAT IS GOING TO SAVE THE WORLD.
IT WILL RETURN ACCOMPLISHMENT AND ART AND GLORY TO THE PEOPLE OF EVERY NATION, AND IT STARTS RIGHT HERE, WITH WHAT WE'RE BUILDING ON THIS ISLAND.
I'M PREACHING AGAIN. I DIDN'T MEAN TO DO THAT.
OPEN MINDS, PLEASE, FOR THIS QUESTION. I BEG OF YOU.
WHAT DO ALL THE GREAT WONDERS OF THE ANCIENT WORLD HAVE IN COMMON?
THE PYRAMIDS, THE GREAT WALL...THE GODLY ARCHITECTURE THAT STILL MAKES THE HUMAN HEART SING EVEN AFTER UNTOLD CENTURIES!
THEY WERE ALL BUILT BY *SLAVES,* MR. SMYTH. *THAT* IS THE CURSE THEY ALL SHARE.
YES. THE MIND KNOWS THAT. BUT THE HEART...
THE HEART KNOWS *BETTER.*
TOURISTS *FLOCK* TO SEE THESE GRAND GESTURES. EVERY DAY, PEOPLE IN FAROFF LANDS HEAR THEM *CALL.*
AND THE COST IS WHAT, THE LIVES AND TOIL OF A FEW SCATTERED SOULS?
FOR WORKS THAT LAST AN ETERNITY AND INSPIRE AWE AND GREATNESS IN ALL WHO SEE THEM?
MOST OF THE WORLD LIVES AND DIES FOR *NOTHING* AND *NO ONE.*
THOSE "SLAVES," THEY DIED FOR *ALL.*
I WILL BE HATED FOR THIS. I WILL BE MISUNDERSTOOD.
I PROPOSE SLAVERY BE RETURNED TO EVERY NATION ON EARTH.
IT WILL BE OUR SALVATION.

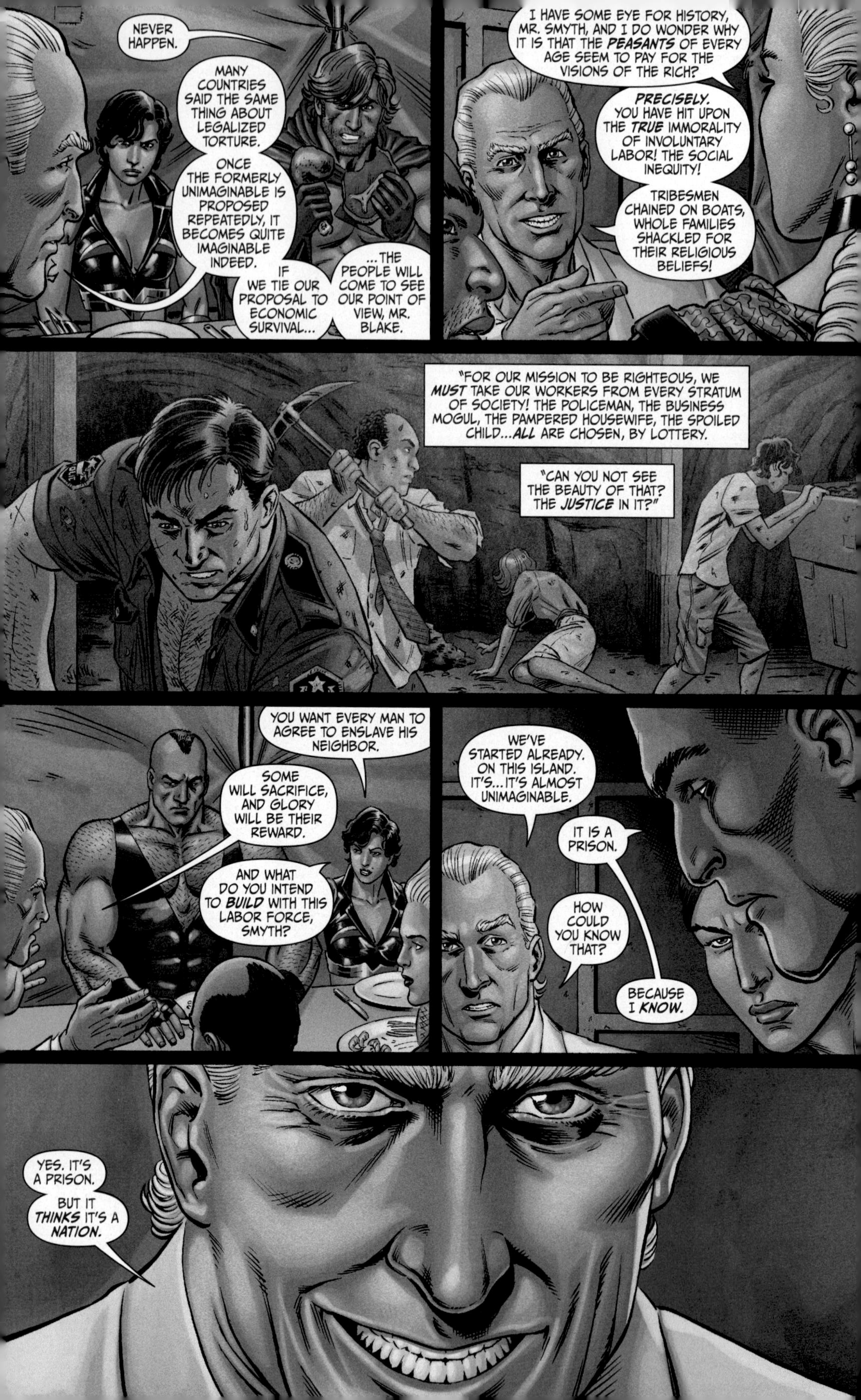
NEVER HAPPEN.
MANY COUNTRIES SAID THE SAME THING ABOUT LEGALIZED TORTURE.
ONCE THE FORMERLY UNIMAGINABLE IS PROPOSED REPEATEDLY, IT BECOMES QUITE IMAGINABLE INDEED.
IF WE TIE OUR PROPOSAL TO ECONOMIC SURVIVAL...
...THE PEOPLE WILL COME TO SEE OUR POINT OF VIEW, MR. BLAKE.
I HAVE SOME EYE FOR HISTORY, MR. SMYTH, AND I DO WONDER WHY IT IS THAT THE PEASANTS OF EVERY AGE SEEM TO PAY FOR THE VISIONS OF THE RICH?
PRECISELY. YOU HAVE HIT UPON THE TRUE IMMORALITY OF INVOLUNTARY LABOR! THE SOCIAL INEQUITY!
TRIBESMEN CHAINED ON BOATS, WHOLE FAMILIES SHACKLED FOR THEIR RELIGIOUS BELIEFS!
"FOR OUR MISSION TO BE RIGHTEOUS, WE MUST TAKE OUR WORKERS FROM EVERY STRATUM OF SOCIETY! THE POLICEMAN, THE BUSINESS MOGUL, THE PAMPERED HOUSEWIFE, THE SPOILED CHILD...ALL ARE CHOSEN, BY LOTTERY.
"CAN YOU NOT SEE THE BEAUTY OF THAT? THE JUSTICE IN IT?"
YOU WANT EVERY MAN TO AGREE TO ENSLAVE HIS NEIGHBOR.
SOME WILL SACRIFICE, AND GLORY WILL BE THEIR REWARD.
AND WHAT DO YOU INTEND TO BUILD WITH THIS LABOR FORCE, SMYTH?
WE'VE STARTED ALREADY. ON THIS ISLAND. IT'S...IT'S ALMOST UNIMAGINABLE.
IT IS A PRISON.
HOW COULD YOU KNOW THAT?
BECAUSE I KNOW.
YES. IT'S A PRISON.
BUT IT THINKS IT'S A NATION.

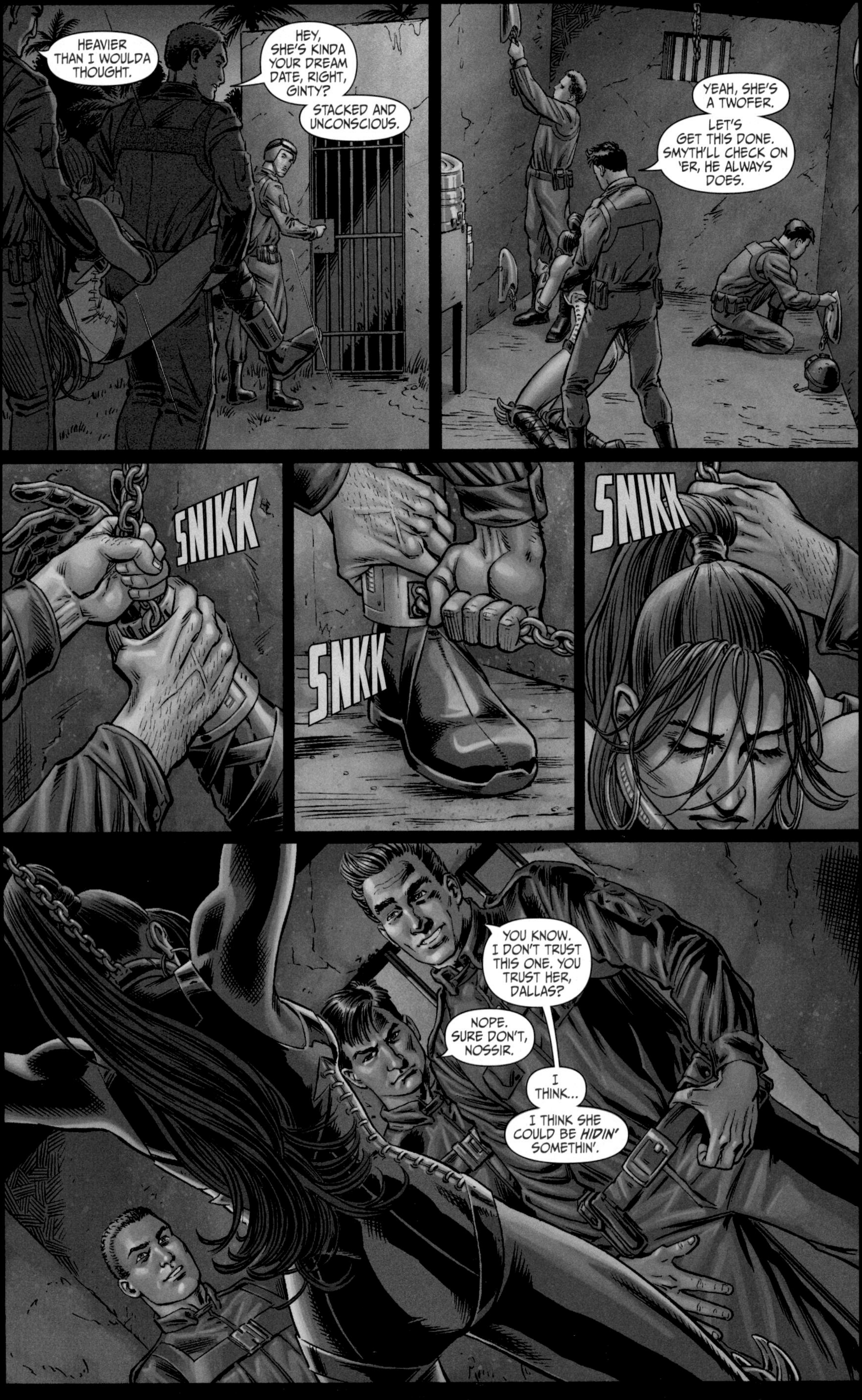
HEAVIER THAN I WOULDA THOUGHT.
HEY, SHE'S KINDA YOUR DREAM DATE, RIGHT, GINTY?
STACKED AND UNCONSCIOUS.
YEAH, SHE'S A TWOFER.
LET'S GET THIS DONE. SMYTH'LL CHECK ON 'ER, HE ALWAYS DOES.
SNIKK
SNKK
SNIKK
YOU KNOW. I DON'T TRUST THIS ONE. YOU TRUST HER, DALLAS?
NOPE. SURE DON'T, NOSSIR.
I THINK...
I THINK SHE COULD BE *HIDIN'* SOMETHIN'.

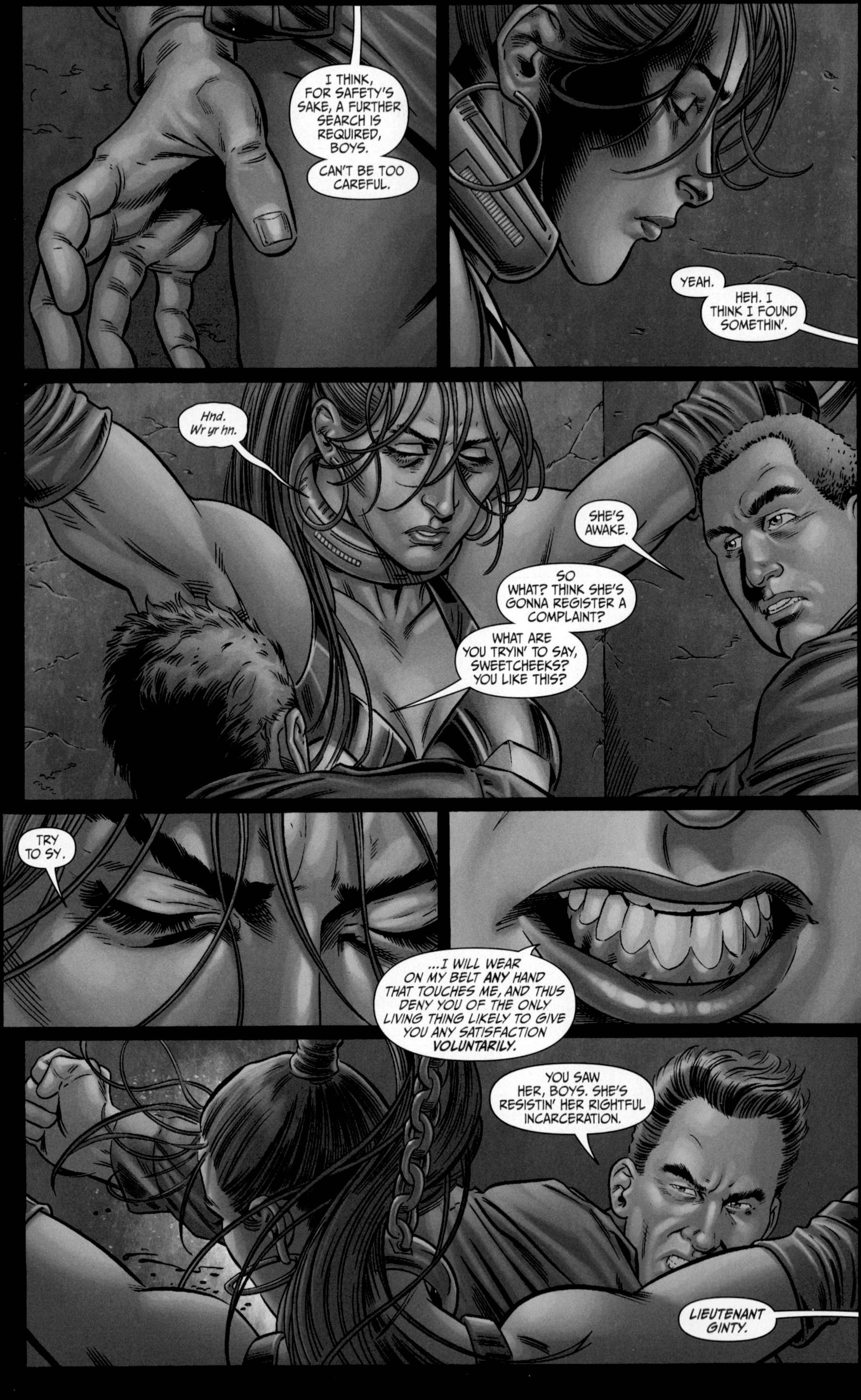
I THINK, FOR SAFETY'S SAKE, A FURTHER SEARCH IS REQUIRED, BOYS.
CAN'T BE TOO CAREFUL.
YEAH.
HEH. I THINK I FOUND SOMETHIN'.
Hnd. Wr yr hn.
SHE'S AWAKE.
SO WHAT? THINK SHE'S GONNA REGISTER A COMPLAINT?
WHAT ARE YOU TRYIN' TO SAY, SWEETCHEEKS? YOU LIKE THIS?
TRY TO SY.
...I WILL WEAR ON MY BELT ANY HAND THAT TOUCHES ME, AND THUS DENY YOU OF THE ONLY LIVING THING LIKELY TO GIVE YOU ANY SATISFACTION VOLUNTARILY.
YOU SAW HER, BOYS. SHE'S RESISTIN' HER RIGHTFUL INCARCERATION.
LIEUTENANT GINTY.

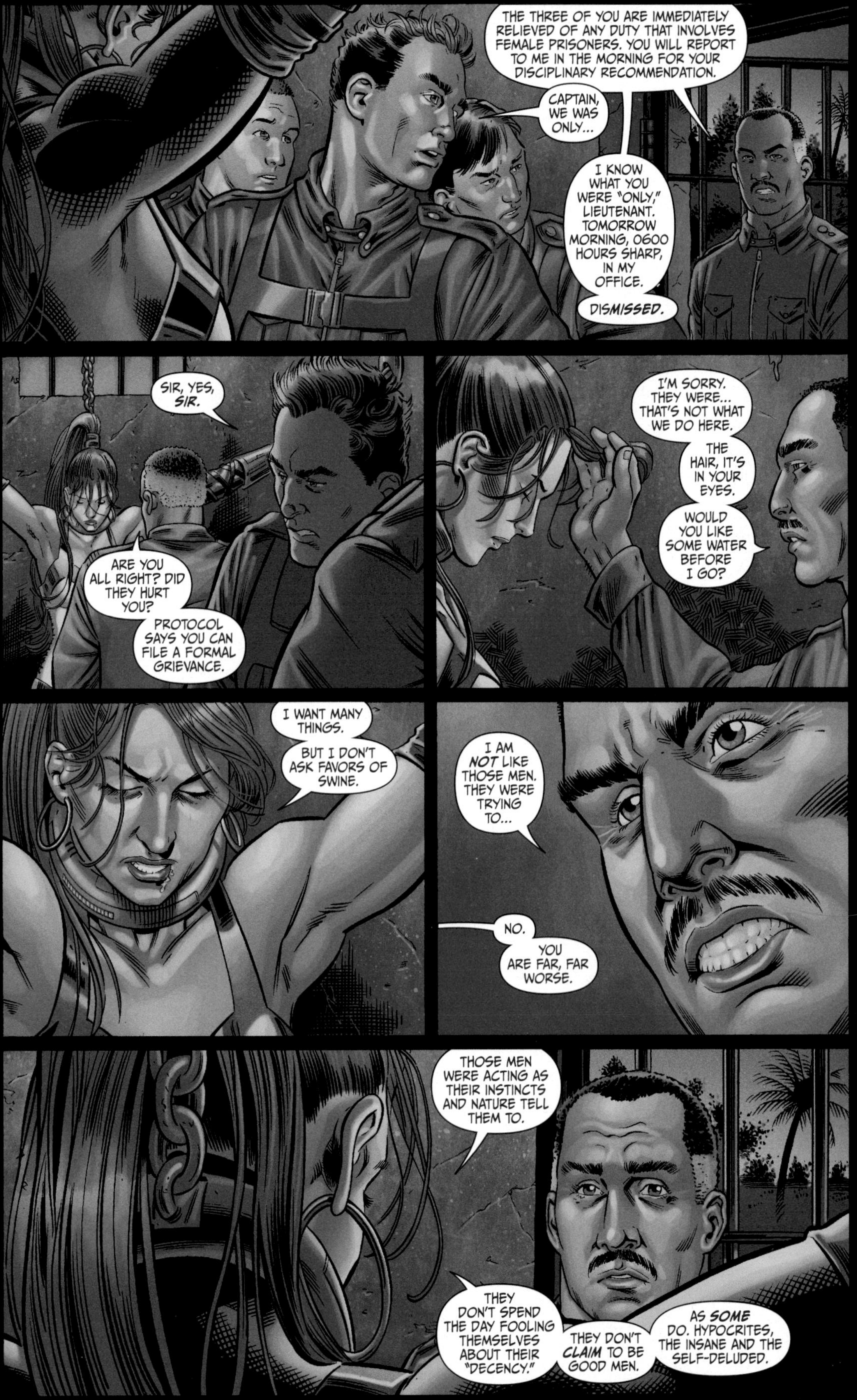
THE THREE OF YOU ARE IMMEDIATELY RELIEVED OF ANY DUTY THAT INVOLVES FEMALE PRISONERS. YOU WILL REPORT TO ME IN THE MORNING FOR YOUR DISCIPLINARY RECOMMENDATION.
CAPTAIN, WE WAS ONLY...
I KNOW WHAT YOU WERE "ONLY," LIEUTENANT. TOMORROW MORNING, 0600 HOURS SHARP, IN MY OFFICE.
DISMISSED.
SIR, YES, SIR.
ARE YOU ALL RIGHT? DID THEY HURT YOU?
PROTOCOL SAYS YOU CAN FILE A FORMAL GRIEVANCE.
I'M SORRY. THEY WERE... THAT'S NOT WHAT WE DO HERE.
THE HAIR, IT'S IN YOUR EYES.
WOULD YOU LIKE SOME WATER BEFORE I GO?
I WANT MANY THINGS.
BUT I DON'T ASK FAVORS OF SWINE.
I AM NOT LIKE THOSE MEN. THEY WERE TRYING TO...
NO.
YOU ARE FAR, FAR WORSE.
THOSE MEN WERE ACTING AS THEIR INSTINCTS AND NATURE TELL THEM TO.
THEY DON'T SPEND THE DAY FOOLING THEMSELVES ABOUT THEIR "DECENCY."
THEY DON'T CLAIM TO BE GOOD MEN.
AS SOME DO. HYPOCRITES, THE INSANE AND THE SELF-DELUDED.

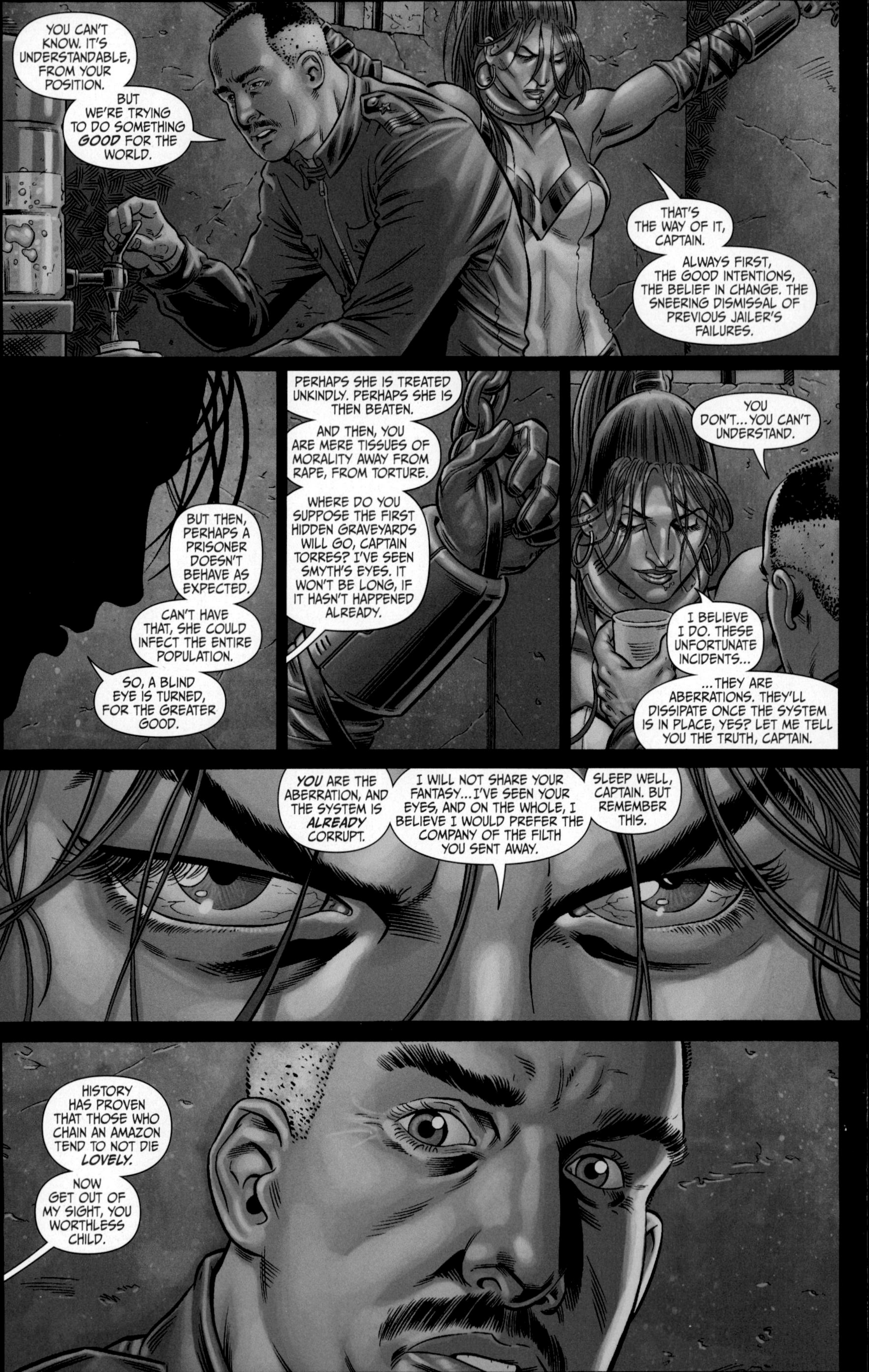
YOU CAN'T KNOW. IT'S UNDERSTANDABLE, FROM YOUR POSITION.
BUT WE'RE TRYING TO DO SOMETHING GOOD FOR THE WORLD.
THAT'S THE WAY OF IT, CAPTAIN.
ALWAYS FIRST, THE GOOD INTENTIONS, THE BELIEF IN CHANGE. THE SNEERING DISMISSAL OF PREVIOUS JAILER'S FAILURES.
BUT THEN, PERHAPS A PRISONER DOESN'T BEHAVE AS EXPECTED.
CAN'T HAVE THAT, SHE COULD INFECT THE ENTIRE POPULATION.
SO, A BLIND EYE IS TURNED, FOR THE GREATER GOOD.
PERHAPS SHE IS TREATED UNKINDLY. PERHAPS SHE IS THEN BEATEN.
AND THEN, YOU ARE MERE TISSUES OF MORALITY AWAY FROM RAPE, FROM TORTURE.
WHERE DO YOU SUPPOSE THE FIRST HIDDEN GRAVEYARDS WILL GO, CAPTAIN TORRES? I'VE SEEN SMYTH'S EYES. IT WON'T BE LONG, IF IT HASN'T HAPPENED ALREADY.
YOU DON'T...YOU CAN'T UNDERSTAND.
I BELIEVE I DO. THESE UNFORTUNATE INCIDENTS...
...THEY ARE ABERRATIONS. THEY'LL DISSIPATE ONCE THE SYSTEM IS IN PLACE, YES? LET ME TELL YOU THE TRUTH, CAPTAIN.
YOU ARE THE ABERRATION, AND THE SYSTEM IS ALREADY CORRUPT.
I WILL NOT SHARE YOUR FANTASY...I'VE SEEN YOUR EYES, AND ON THE WHOLE, I BELIEVE I WOULD PREFER THE COMPANY OF THE FILTH YOU SENT AWAY.
SLEEP WELL, CAPTAIN. BUT REMEMBER THIS.
HISTORY HAS PROVEN THAT THOSE WHO CHAIN AN AMAZON TEND TO NOT DIE LOVELY.
NOW GET OUT OF MY SIGHT, YOU WORTHLESS CHILD.

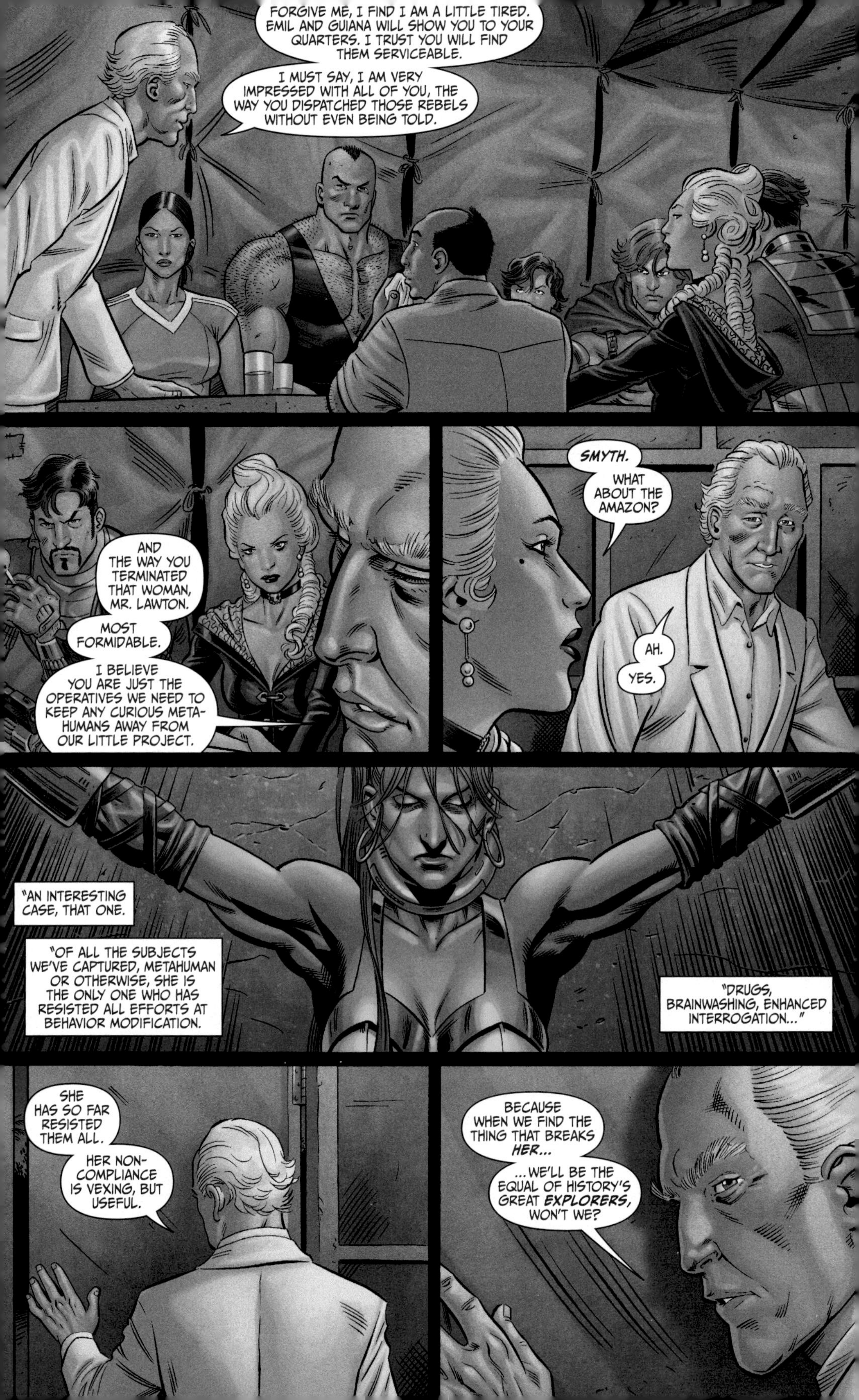
FORGIVE ME, I FIND I AM A LITTLE TIRED. EMIL AND GUIANA WILL SHOW YOU TO YOUR QUARTERS. I TRUST YOU WILL FIND THEM SERVICEABLE.
I MUST SAY, I AM VERY IMPRESSED WITH ALL OF YOU, THE WAY YOU DISPATCHED THOSE REBELS WITHOUT EVEN BEING TOLD.
AND THE WAY YOU TERMINATED THAT WOMAN, MR. LAWTON.
MOST FORMIDABLE.
I BELIEVE YOU ARE JUST THE OPERATIVES WE NEED TO KEEP ANY CURIOUS META-HUMANS AWAY FROM OUR LITTLE PROJECT.
SMYTH.
WHAT ABOUT THE AMAZON?
AH.
YES.
"AN INTERESTING CASE, THAT ONE.
"OF ALL THE SUBJECTS WE'VE CAPTURED, METAHUMAN OR OTHERWISE, SHE IS THE ONLY ONE WHO HAS RESISTED ALL EFFORTS AT BEHAVIOR MODIFICATION.
"DRUGS, BRAINWASHING, ENHANCED INTERROGATION..."
SHE HAS SO FAR RESISTED THEM ALL.
HER NON-COMPLIANCE IS VEXING, BUT USEFUL.
BECAUSE WHEN WE FIND THE THING THAT BREAKS HER...
...WE'LL BE THE EQUAL OF HISTORY'S GREAT EXPLORERS, WON'T WE?

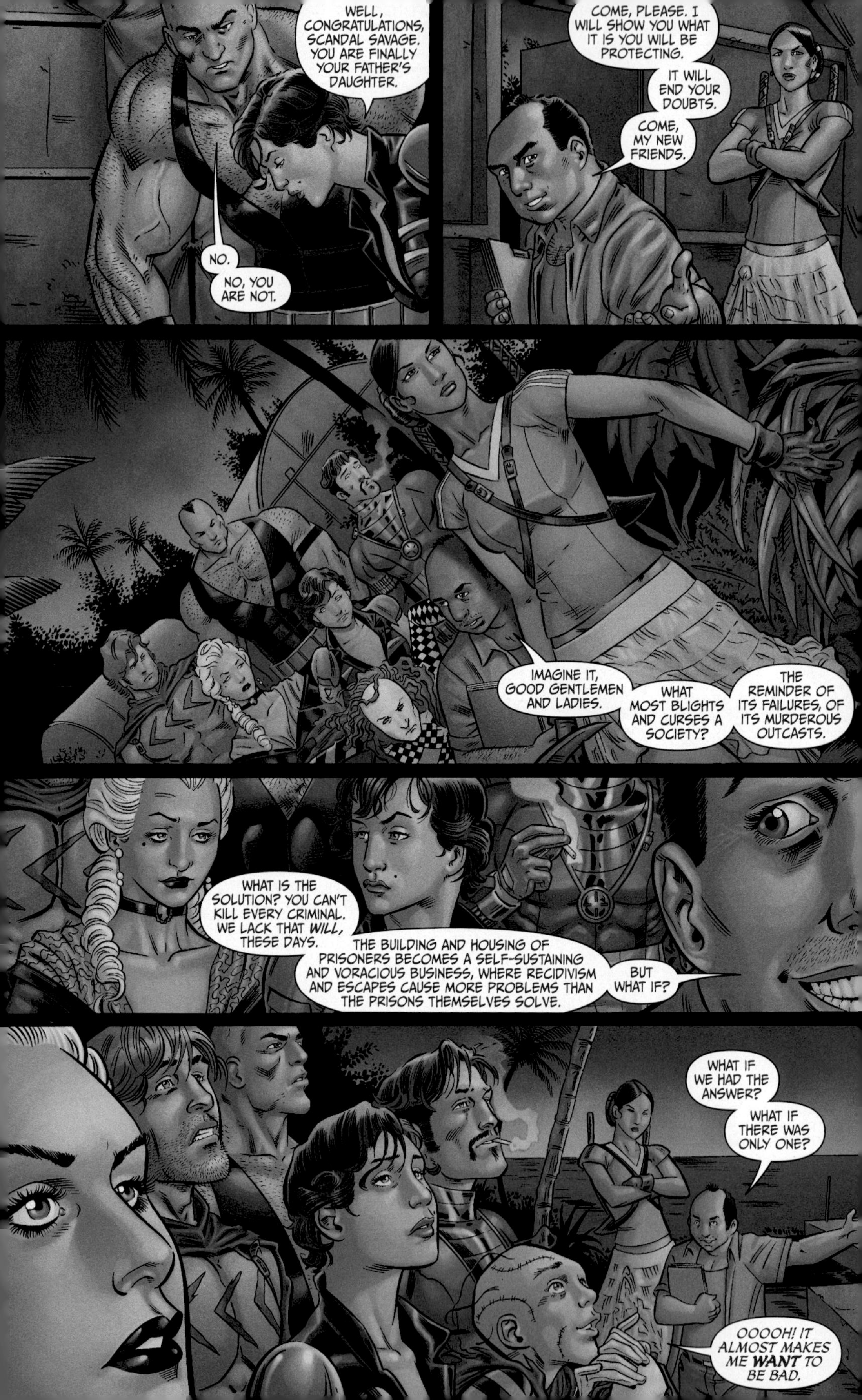
WELL, CONGRATULATIONS, SCANDAL SAVAGE. YOU ARE FINALLY YOUR FATHER'S DAUGHTER.
NO.
NO, YOU ARE NOT.
COME, PLEASE. I WILL SHOW YOU WHAT IT IS YOU WILL BE PROTECTING.
IT WILL END YOUR DOUBTS.
COME, MY NEW FRIENDS.
IMAGINE IT, GOOD GENTLEMEN AND LADIES.
WHAT MOST BLIGHTS AND CURSES A SOCIETY?
THE REMINDER OF ITS FAILURES, OF ITS MURDEROUS OUTCASTS.
WHAT IS THE SOLUTION? YOU CAN'T KILL EVERY CRIMINAL. WE LACK THAT *WILL*, THESE DAYS.
THE BUILDING AND HOUSING OF PRISONERS BECOMES A SELF-SUSTAINING AND VORACIOUS BUSINESS, WHERE RECIDIVISM AND ESCAPES CAUSE MORE PROBLEMS THAN THE PRISONS THEMSELVES SOLVE.
BUT WHAT IF?
WHAT IF WE HAD THE ANSWER?
WHAT IF THERE WAS ONLY ONE?
OOOOH! IT ALMOST MAKES ME ***WANT*** TO BE BAD.

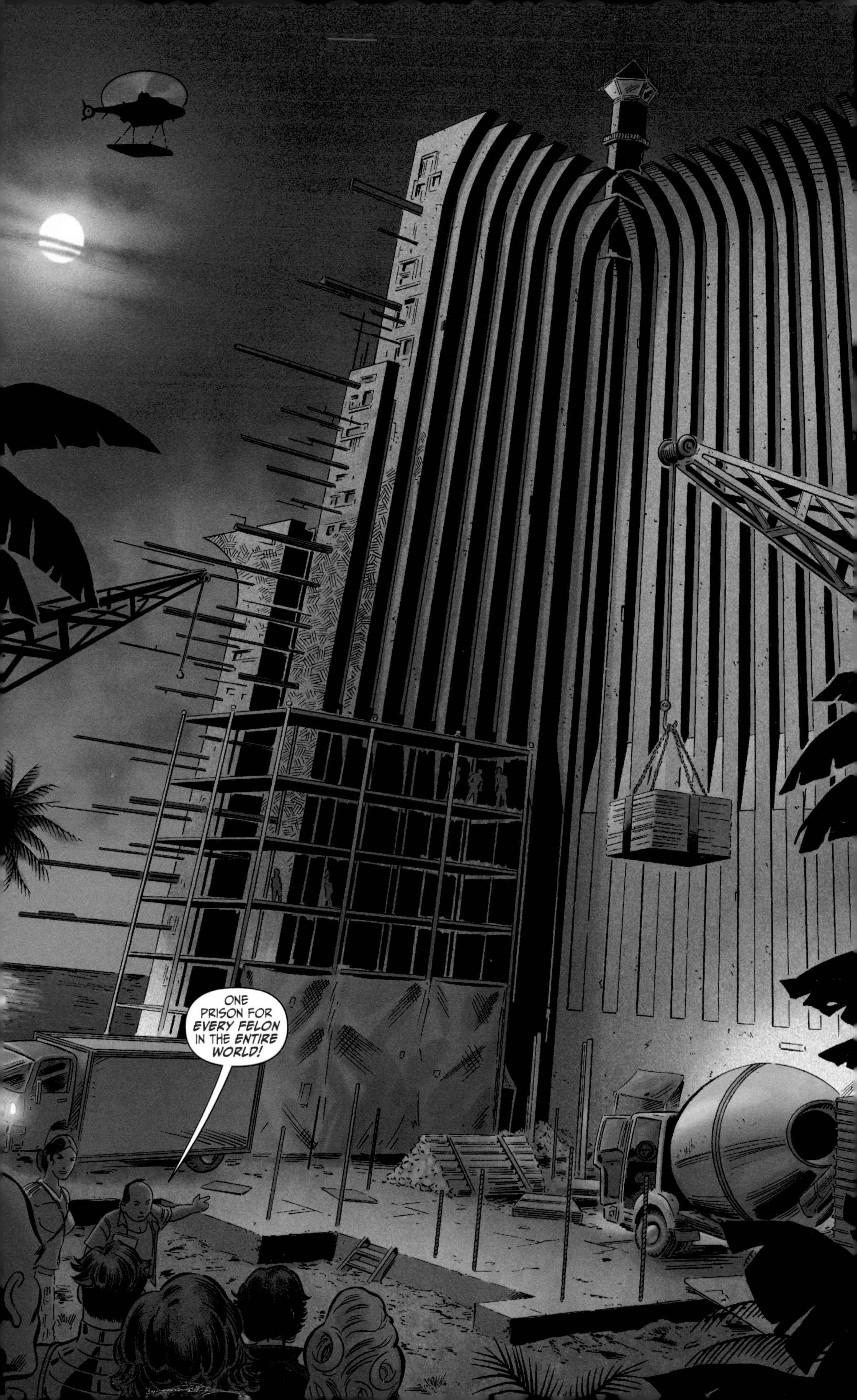
ONE PRISON FOR *EVERY FELON* IN THE *ENTIRE WORLD!*

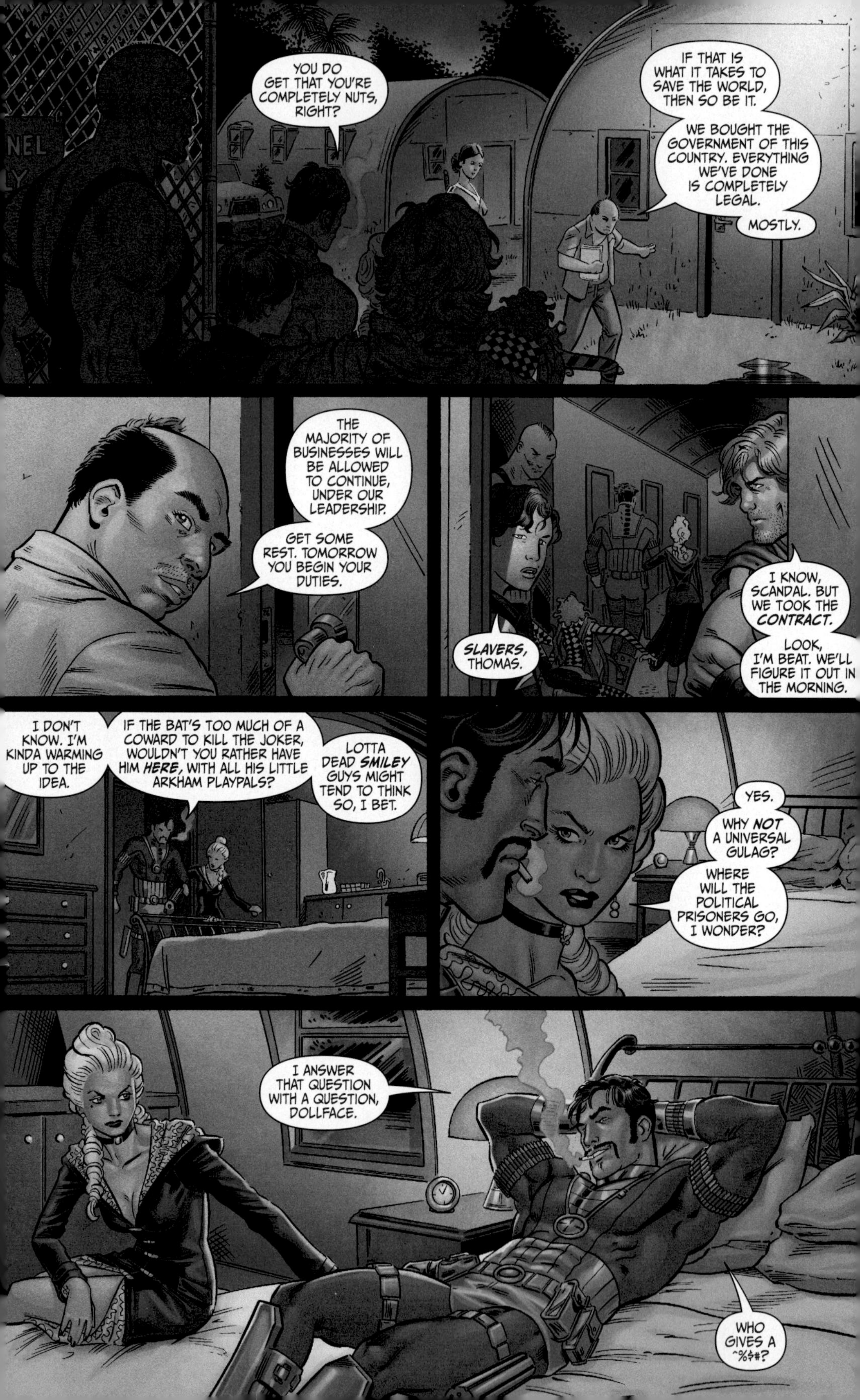
YOU DO GET THAT YOU'RE COMPLETELY NUTS, RIGHT?
IF THAT IS WHAT IT TAKES TO SAVE THE WORLD, THEN SO BE IT.
WE BOUGHT THE GOVERNMENT OF THIS COUNTRY. EVERYTHING WE'VE DONE IS COMPLETELY LEGAL.
MOSTLY.
THE MAJORITY OF BUSINESSES WILL BE ALLOWED TO CONTINUE, UNDER OUR LEADERSHIP.
GET SOME REST. TOMORROW YOU BEGIN YOUR DUTIES.
SLAVERS, THOMAS.
I KNOW, SCANDAL. BUT WE TOOK THE CONTRACT.
LOOK, I'M BEAT. WE'LL FIGURE IT OUT IN THE MORNING.
I DON'T KNOW. I'M KINDA WARMING UP TO THE IDEA.
IF THE BAT'S TOO MUCH OF A COWARD TO KILL THE JOKER, WOULDN'T YOU RATHER HAVE HIM HERE, WITH ALL HIS LITTLE ARKHAM PLAYPALS?
LOTTA DEAD SMILEY GUYS MIGHT TEND TO THINK SO, I BET.
YES.
WHY NOT A UNIVERSAL GULAG?
WHERE WILL THE POLITICAL PRISONERS GO, I WONDER?
I ANSWER THAT QUESTION WITH A QUESTION, DOLLFACE.
WHO GIVES A ^%$#?

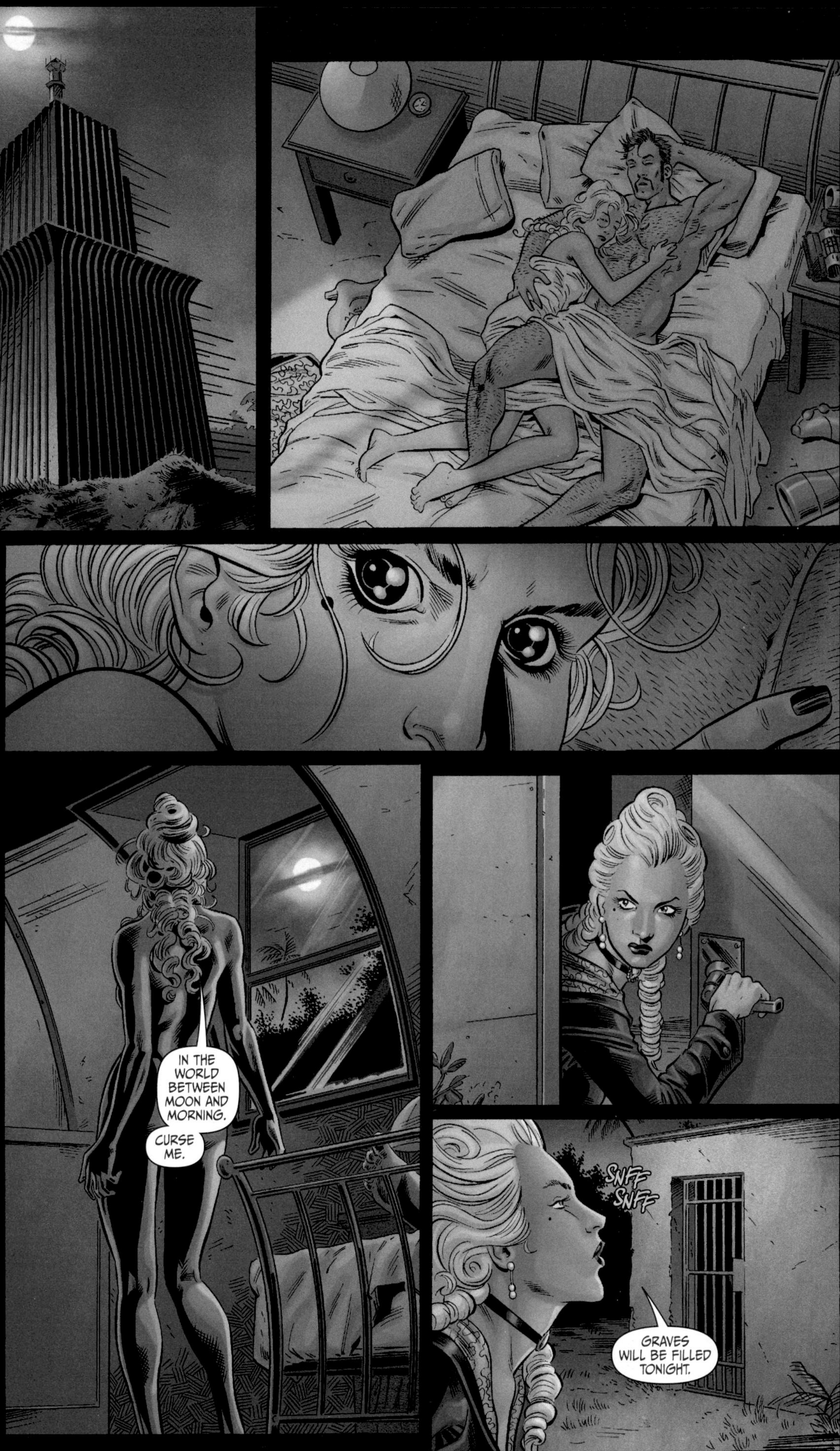
IN THE WORLD BETWEEN MOON AND MORNING.
CURSE ME.
SNFF SNFF
GRAVES WILL BE FILLED TONIGHT.

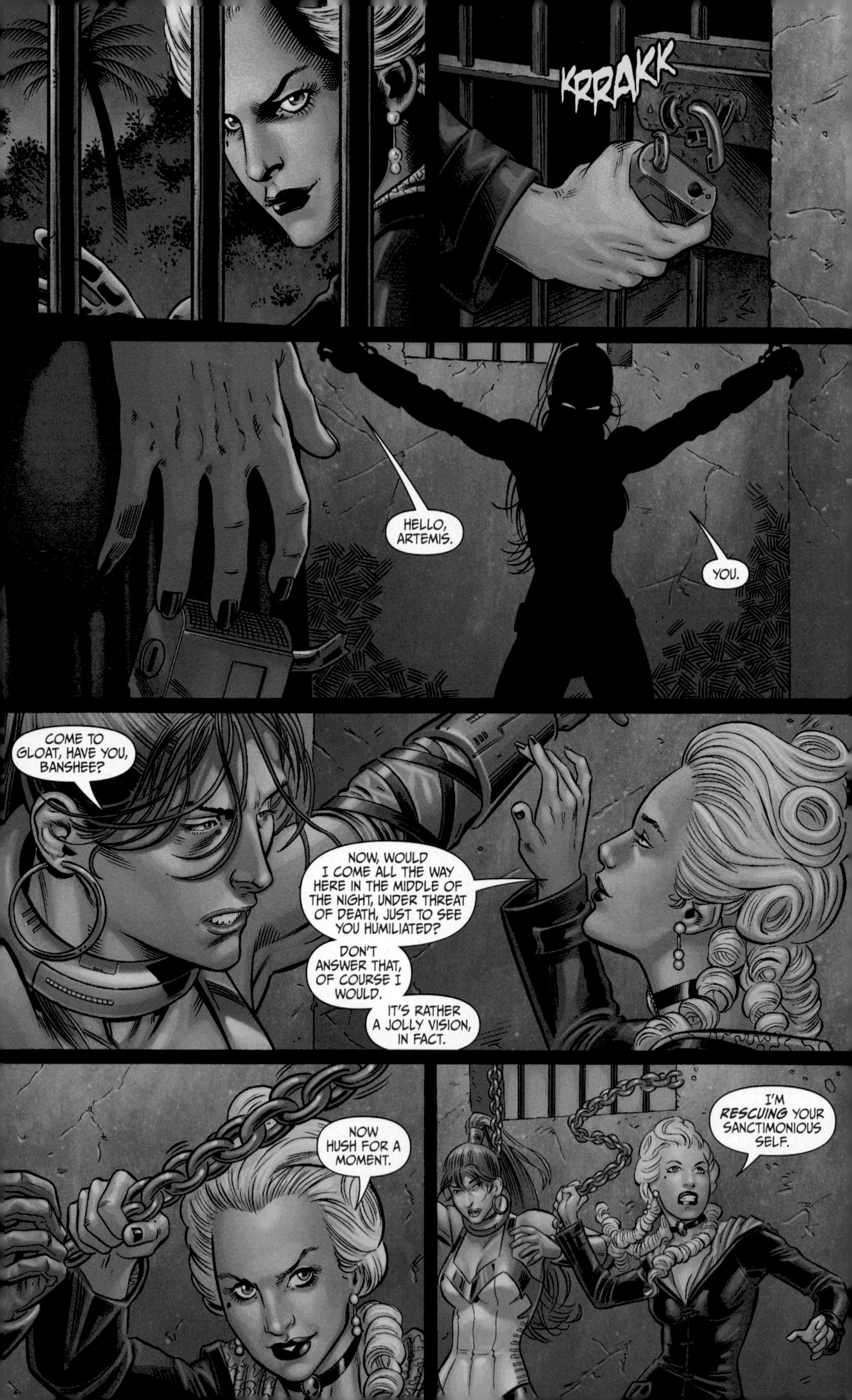
KRRAKK
HELLO, ARTEMIS.
YOU.
COME TO GLOAT, HAVE YOU, BANSHEE?
NOW, WOULD I COME ALL THE WAY HERE IN THE MIDDLE OF THE NIGHT, UNDER THREAT OF DEATH, JUST TO SEE YOU HUMILIATED?
DON'T ANSWER THAT, OF COURSE I WOULD.
IT'S RATHER A JOLLY VISION, IN FACT.
NOW HUSH FOR A MOMENT.
I'M *RESCUING* YOUR SANCTIMONIOUS SELF.

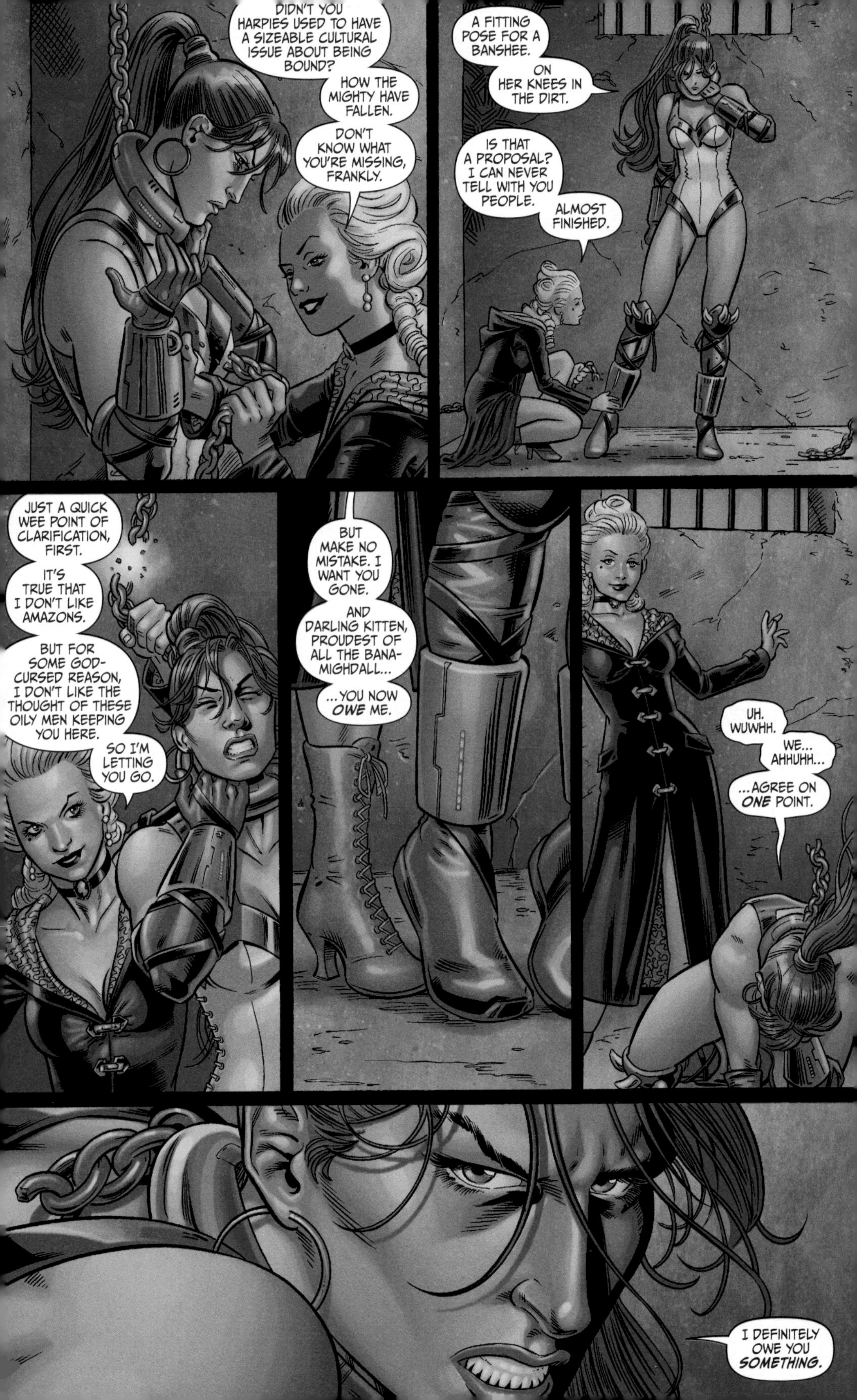
DIDN'T YOU HARPIES USED TO HAVE A SIZEABLE CULTURAL ISSUE ABOUT BEING BOUND?
HOW THE MIGHTY HAVE FALLEN.
DON'T KNOW WHAT YOU'RE MISSING, FRANKLY.
A FITTING POSE FOR A BANSHEE.
ON HER KNEES IN THE DIRT.
IS THAT A PROPOSAL? I CAN NEVER TELL WITH YOU PEOPLE.
ALMOST FINISHED.
JUST A QUICK WEE POINT OF CLARIFICATION, FIRST.
IT'S TRUE THAT I DON'T LIKE AMAZONS.
BUT FOR SOME GOD-CURSED REASON, I DON'T LIKE THE THOUGHT OF THESE OILY MEN KEEPING YOU HERE.
SO I'M LETTING YOU GO.
BUT MAKE NO MISTAKE. I WANT YOU GONE.
AND DARLING KITTEN, PROUDEST OF ALL THE BANA-MIGHDALL...
...YOU NOW *OWE* ME.
UH. WUWHH.
WE... AHHUHH...
...AGREE ON *ONE* POINT.
I DEFINITELY OWE YOU *SOMETHING.*

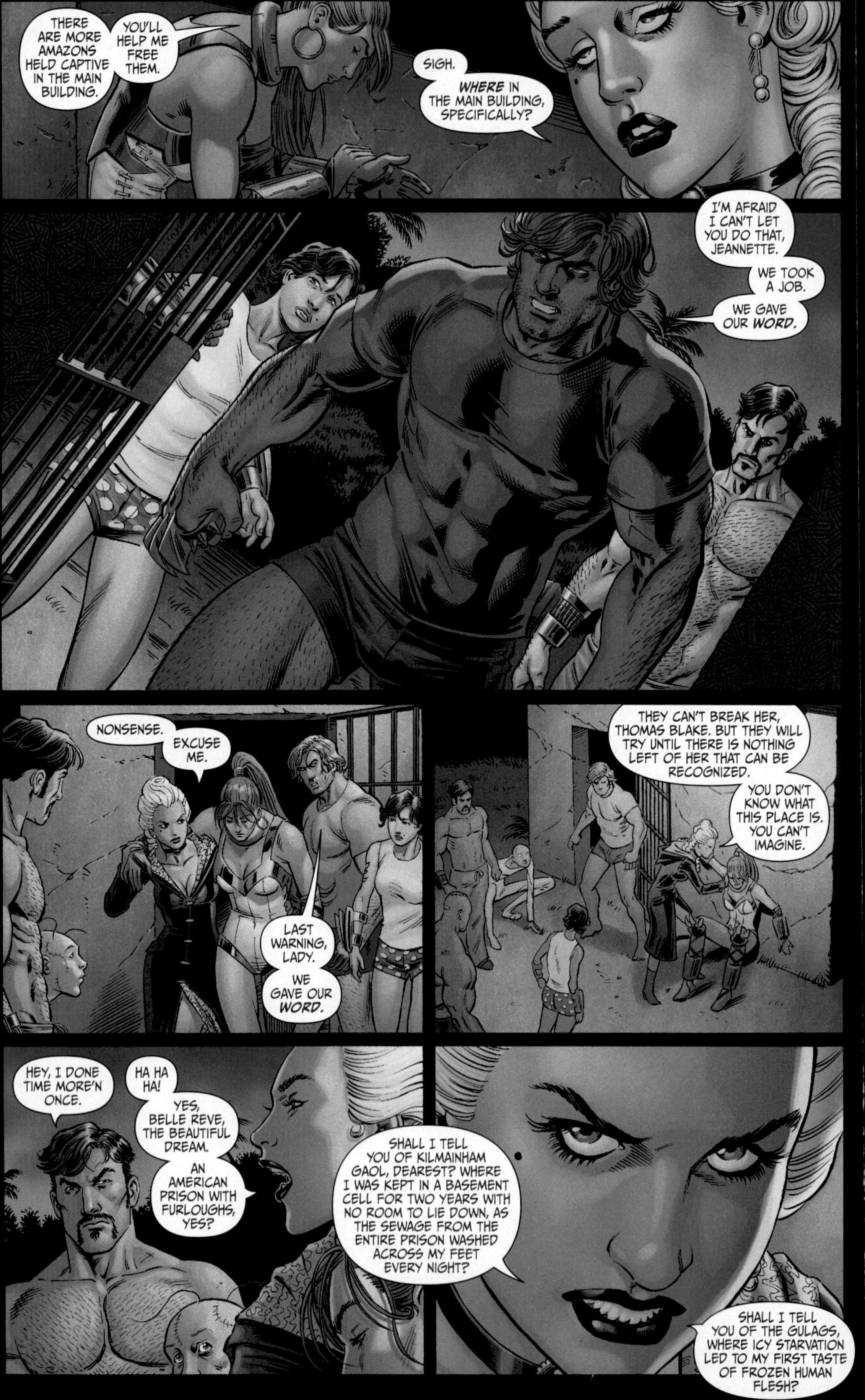
THERE ARE MORE AMAZONS HELD CAPTIVE IN THE MAIN BUILDING.
YOU'LL HELP ME FREE THEM.
SIGH.
WHERE IN THE MAIN BUILDING, SPECIFICALLY?
I'M AFRAID I CAN'T LET YOU DO THAT, JEANNETTE.
WE TOOK A JOB.
WE GAVE OUR *WORD*.
NONSENSE.
EXCUSE ME.
LAST WARNING, LADY.
WE GAVE OUR *WORD*.
THEY CAN'T BREAK HER, THOMAS BLAKE. BUT THEY WILL TRY UNTIL THERE IS NOTHING LEFT OF HER THAT CAN BE RECOGNIZED.
YOU DON'T KNOW WHAT THIS PLACE IS. YOU CAN'T IMAGINE.
HEY, I DONE TIME MORE'N ONCE.
HA HA HA!
YES, BELLE REVE, THE BEAUTIFUL DREAM.
AN AMERICAN PRISON WITH FURLOUGHS, YES?
SHALL I TELL YOU OF KILMAINHAM GAOL, DEAREST? WHERE I WAS KEPT IN A BASEMENT CELL FOR TWO YEARS WITH NO ROOM TO LIE DOWN, AS THE SEWAGE FROM THE ENTIRE PRISON WASHED ACROSS MY FEET EVERY NIGHT?
SHALL I TELL YOU OF THE GULAGS, WHERE ICY STARVATION LED TO MY FIRST TASTE OF FROZEN HUMAN FLESH?

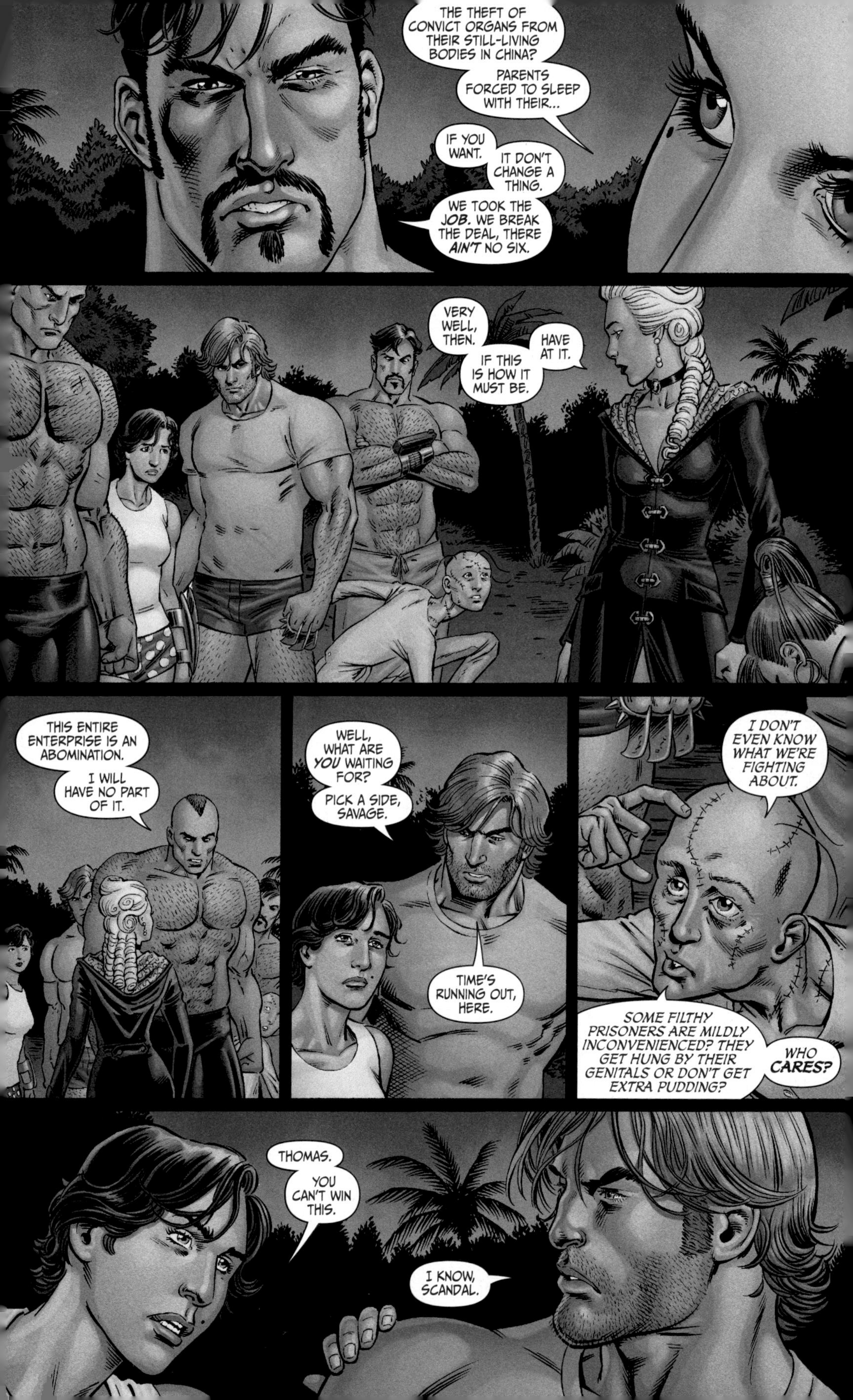
THE THEFT OF CONVICT ORGANS FROM THEIR STILL-LIVING BODIES IN CHINA?
PARENTS FORCED TO SLEEP WITH THEIR...
IF YOU WANT.
IT DON'T CHANGE A THING.
WE TOOK THE JOB. WE BREAK THE DEAL, THERE AIN'T NO SIX.
VERY WELL, THEN.
IF THIS IS HOW IT MUST BE.
HAVE AT IT.
THIS ENTIRE ENTERPRISE IS AN ABOMINATION.
I WILL HAVE NO PART OF IT.
WELL, WHAT ARE YOU WAITING FOR?
PICK A SIDE, SAVAGE.
TIME'S RUNNING OUT, HERE.
I DON'T EVEN KNOW WHAT WE'RE FIGHTING ABOUT.
SOME FILTHY PRISONERS ARE MILDLY INCONVENIENCED? THEY GET HUNG BY THEIR GENITALS OR DON'T GET EXTRA PUDDING?
WHO CARES?
THOMAS.
YOU CAN'T WIN THIS.
I KNOW, SCANDAL.

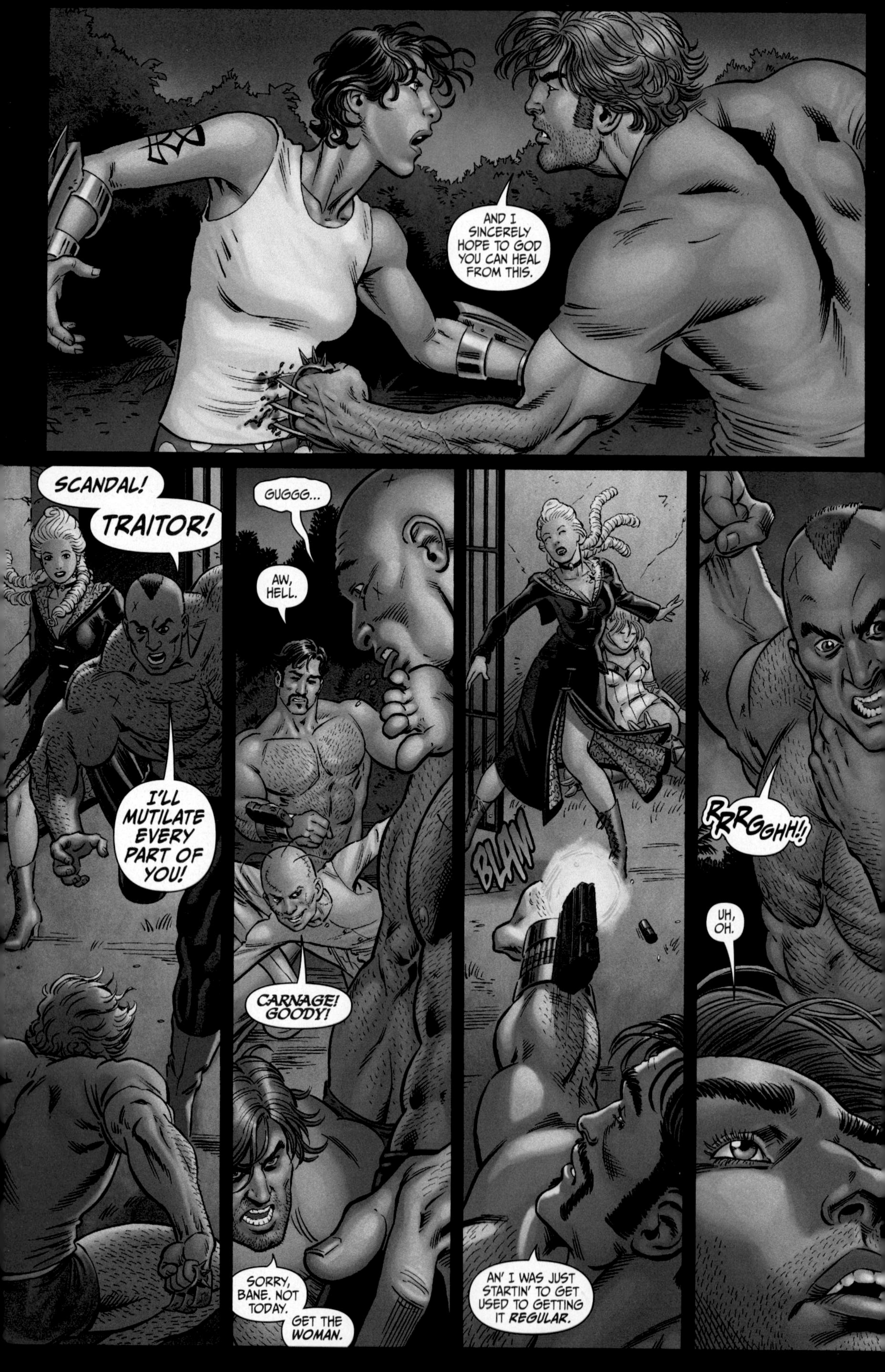
AND I SINCERELY HOPE TO GOD YOU CAN HEAL FROM THIS.
SCANDAL!
TRAITOR!
I'LL MUTILATE EVERY PART OF YOU!
GUGGG...
AW, HELL.
CARNAGE! GOODY!
SORRY, BANE. NOT TODAY.
GET THE WOMAN.
BLAM
AN' I WAS JUST STARTIN' TO GET USED TO GETTING IT REGULAR.
RRRGGHH!!
UH, OH.

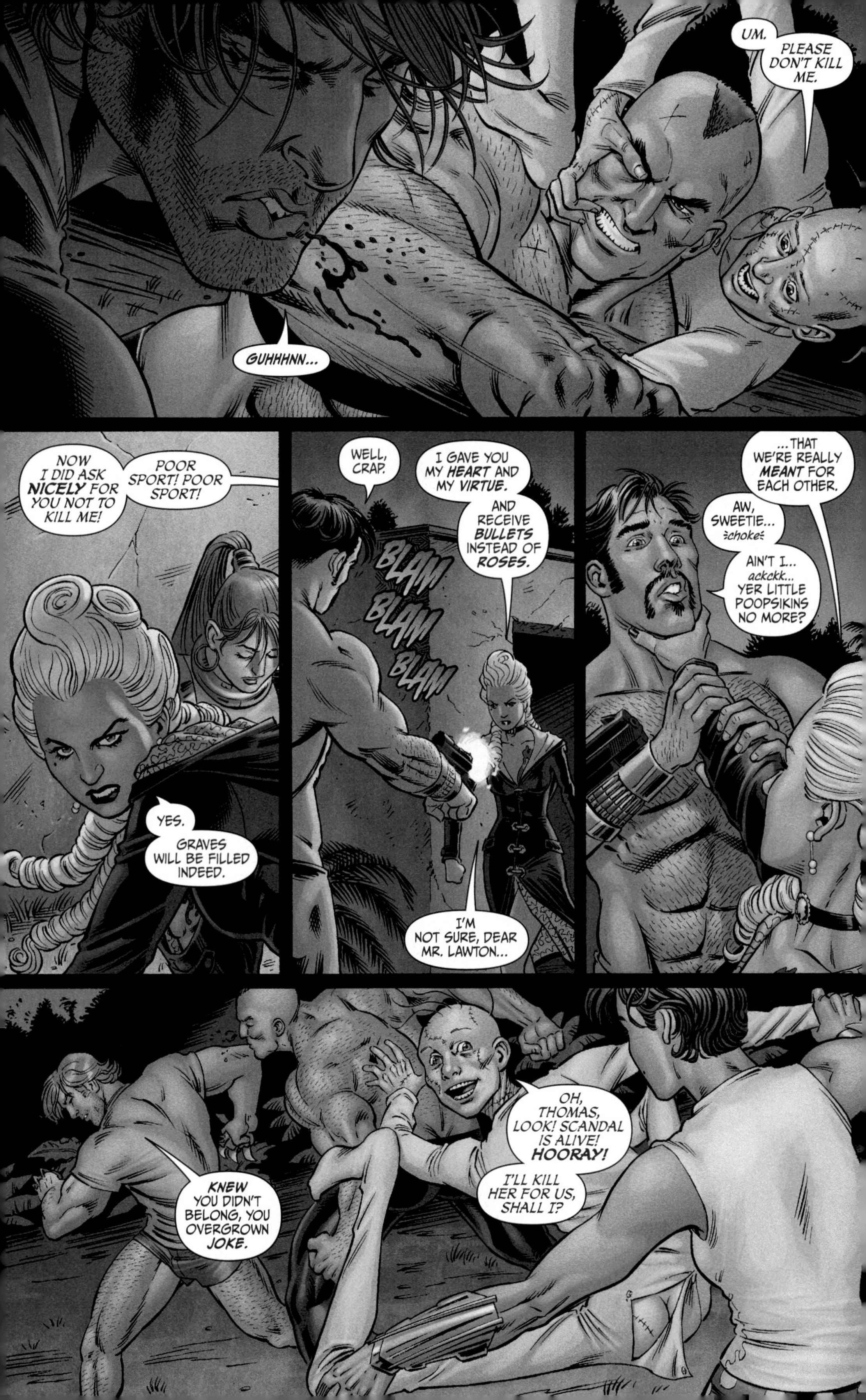
UM.
PLEASE DON'T KILL ME.
GUHHHNN...
NOW I DID ASK NICELY FOR YOU NOT TO KILL ME!
POOR SPORT! POOR SPORT!
YES.
GRAVES WILL BE FILLED INDEED.
WELL, CRAP.
I GAVE YOU MY HEART AND MY VIRTUE.
AND RECEIVE BULLETS INSTEAD OF ROSES.
BLAM
BLAM
BLAM
I'M NOT SURE, DEAR MR. LAWTON...
...THAT WE'RE REALLY MEANT FOR EACH OTHER.
AW, SWEETIE... choke
AIN'T I... ackckk... YER LITTLE POOPSIKINS NO MORE?
OH, THOMAS, LOOK! SCANDAL IS ALIVE! HOORAY!
I'LL KILL HER FOR US, SHALL I?
KNEW YOU DIDN'T BELONG, YOU OVERGROWN JOKE.

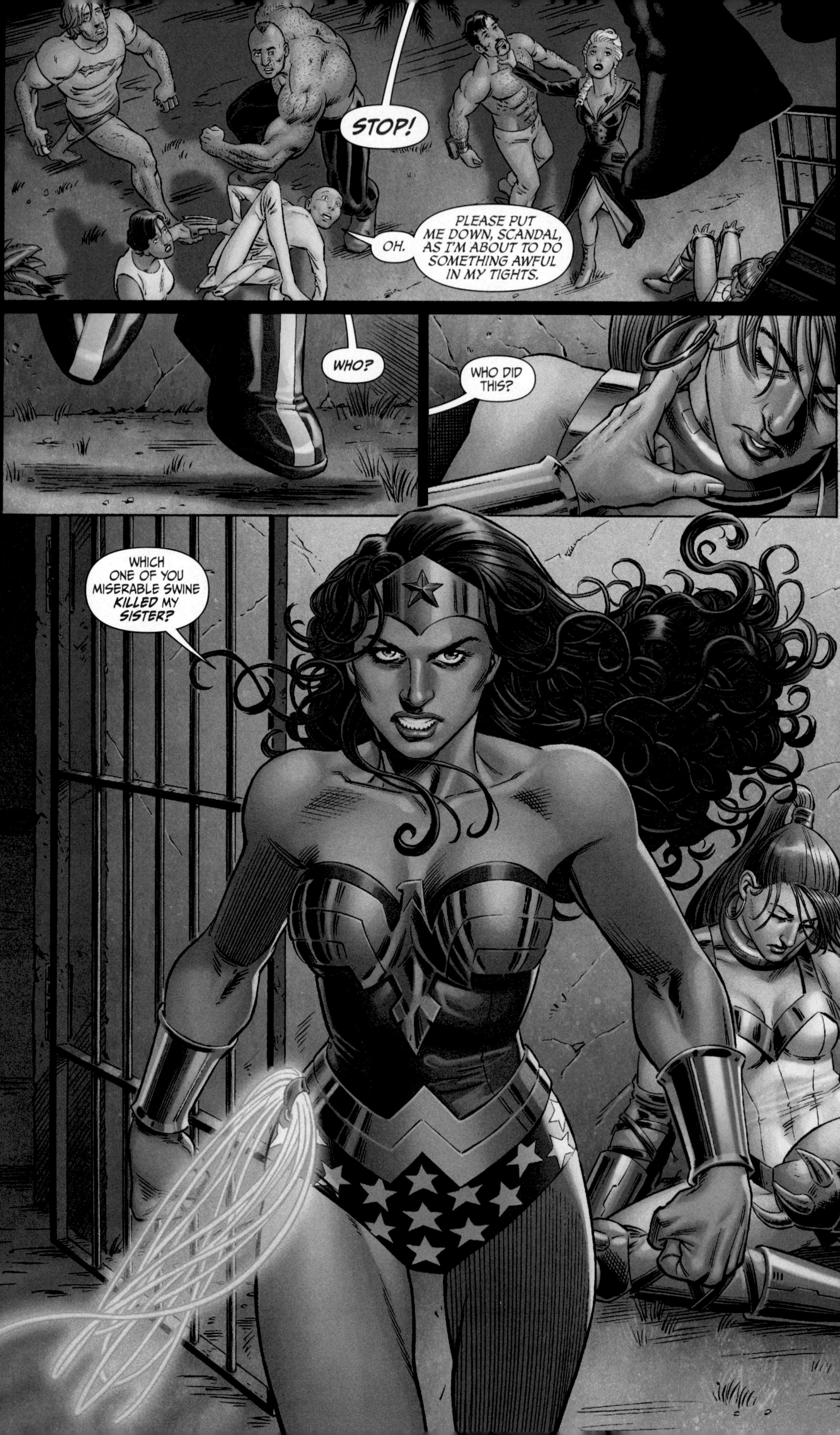
STOP!
OH.
PLEASE PUT ME DOWN, SCANDAL, AS I'M ABOUT TO DO SOMETHING AWFUL IN MY TIGHTS.
WHO?
WHO DID THIS?
WHICH ONE OF YOU MISERABLE SWINE KILLED MY SISTER?

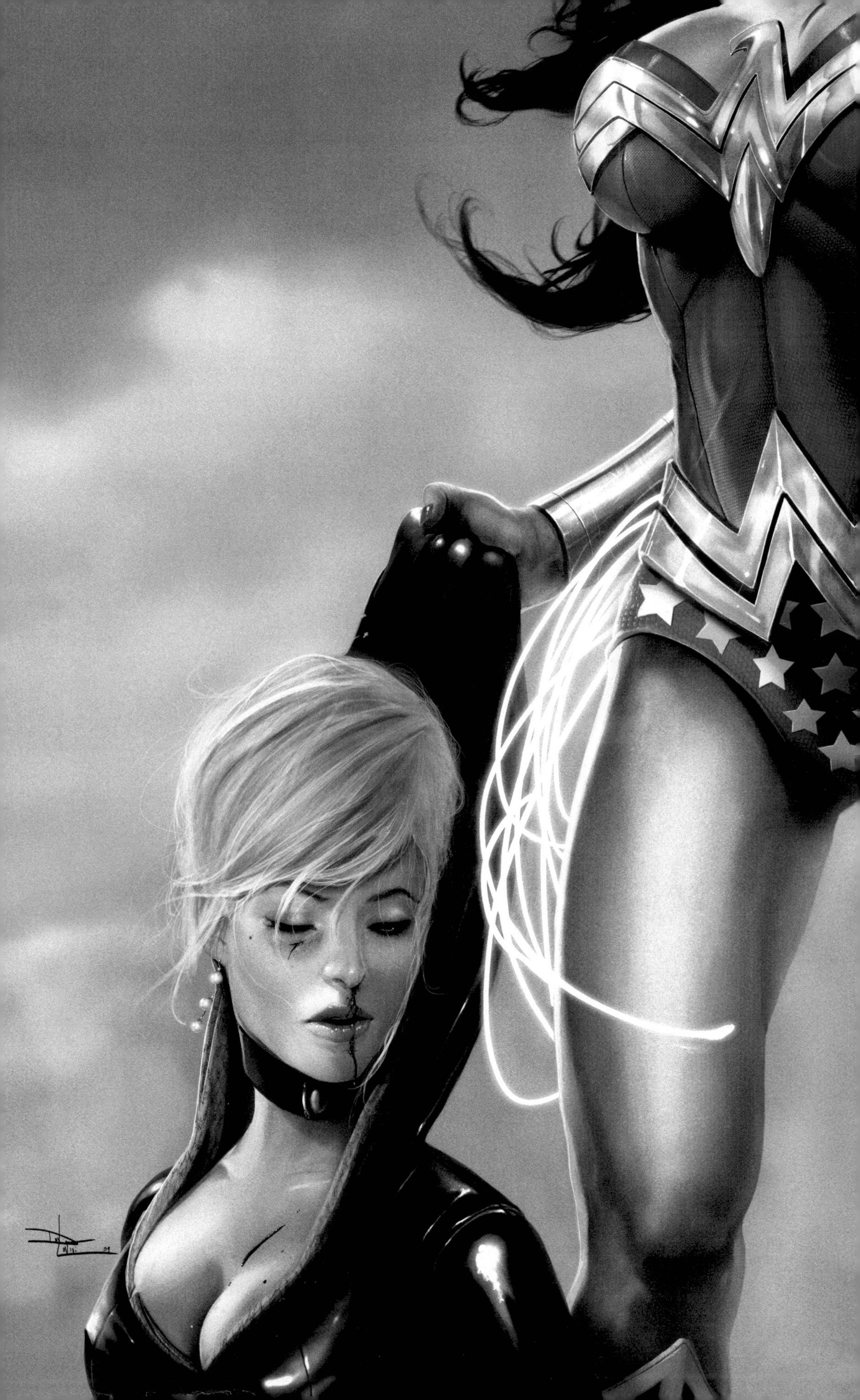

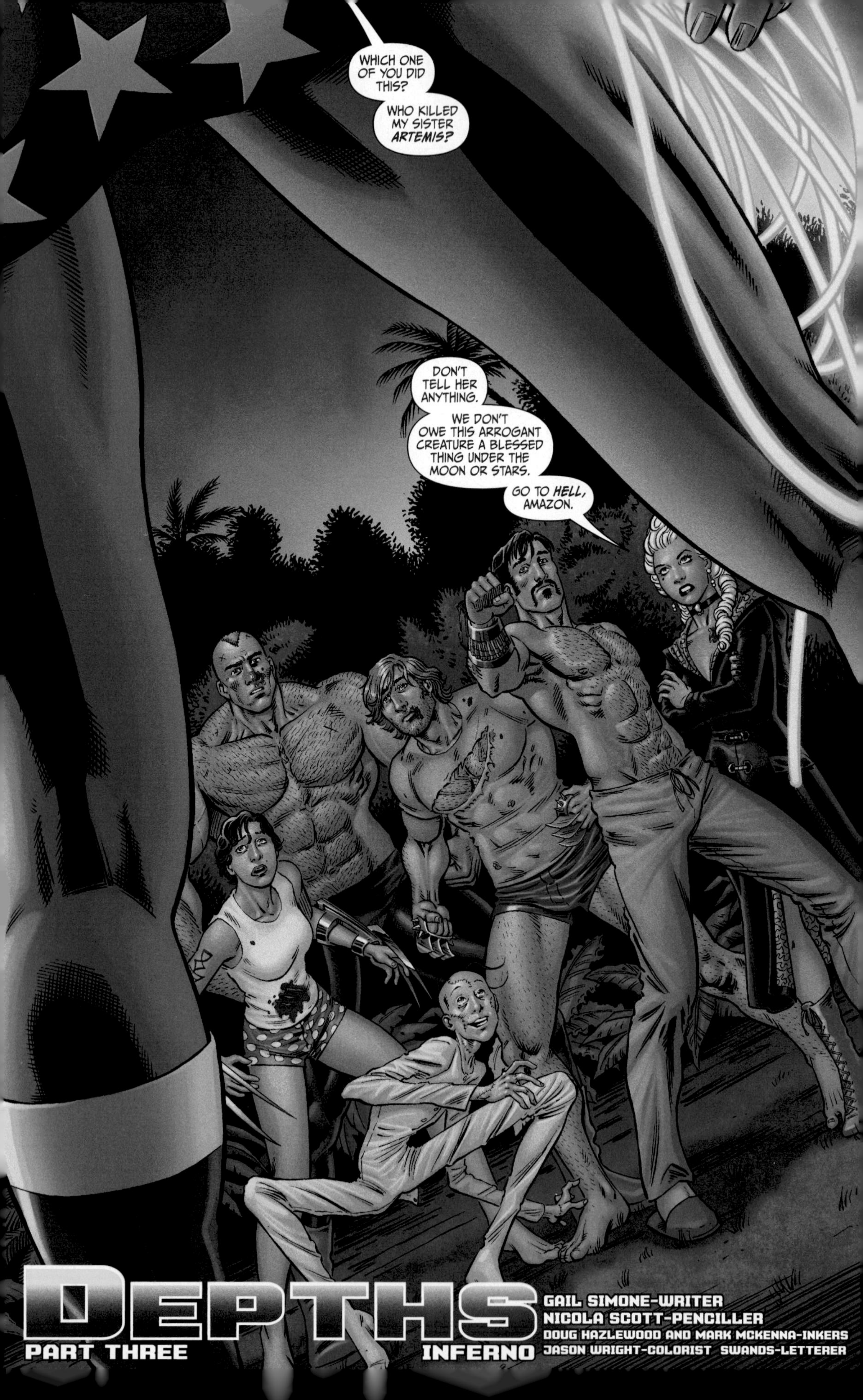
WHICH ONE OF YOU DID THIS?
WHO KILLED MY SISTER ARTEMIS?
DON'T TELL HER ANYTHING.
WE DON'T OWE THIS ARROGANT CREATURE A BLESSED THING UNDER THE MOON OR STARS.
GO TO HELL, AMAZON.
DEPTHS
PART THREE
INFERNO
GAIL SIMONE-WRITER
NICOLA SCOTT-PENCILLER
DOUG HAZLEWOOD AND MARK MCKENNA-INKERS
JASON WRIGHT-COLORIST SWANDS-LETTERER

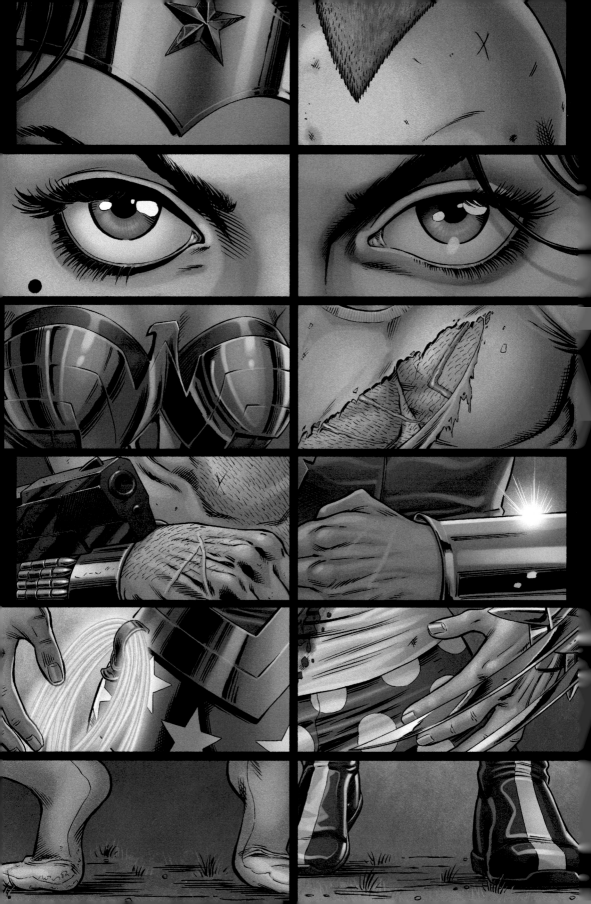

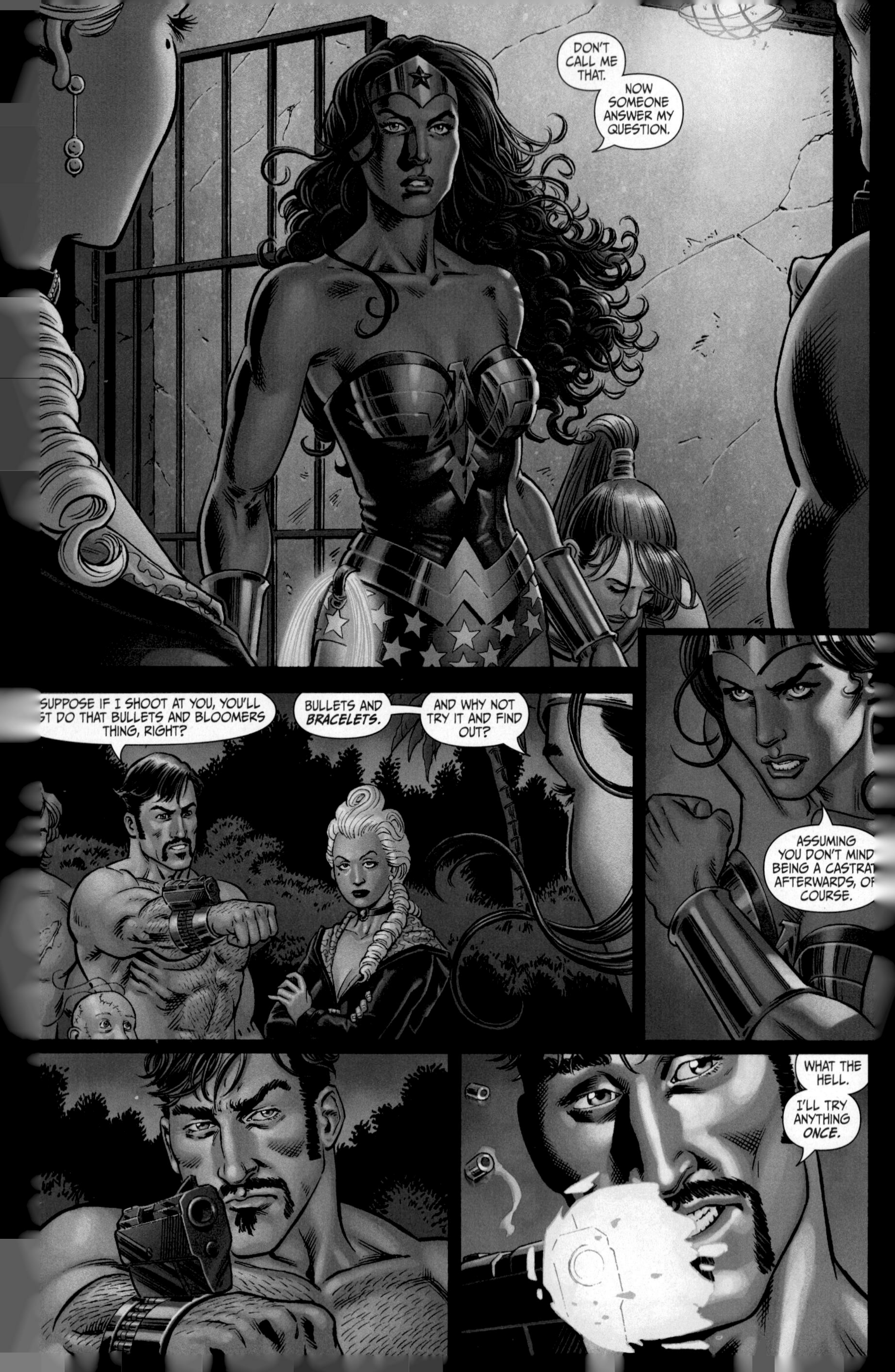
DON'T CALL ME THAT.
NOW SOMEONE ANSWER MY QUESTION.
SUPPOSE IF I SHOOT AT YOU, YOU'LL
T DO THAT BULLETS AND BLOOMERS THING, RIGHT?
BULLETS AND *BRACELETS*.
AND WHY NOT TRY IT AND FIND OUT?
ASSUMING YOU DON'T MIND BEING A CASTRAT AFTERWARDS, OF COURSE.
WHAT THE HELL.
I'LL TRY ANYTHING *ONCE*.

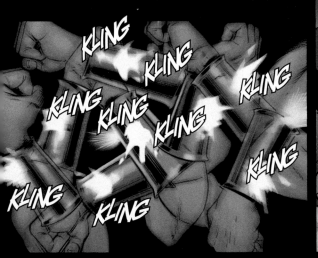

KLING **KLING** **KLING** **KLING** **KLING** **KLING** **KLING** **KLING** **KLING** **KLING** **KLING**

THAT JUST AIN'T FAIR.

LISTEN, IT'S NOT AS BAD AS IT SOUNDS.

I BARELY EVEN MISS MY LITTLE GENTLEMAN, AND MY PANTS LOOK EVER SO MUCH LESS LUMPY!

AND THEY HAVE LOOKALIKES, NOW! IN FLAVORS!

OH, DEAR.

HE'S DONE FOR, I SAY WE **RUN.**

GET AWAY FROM MY LITTLE FIRESTARTER, AMAZON.

PTT

I BELIEVE I ALREADY SAID...

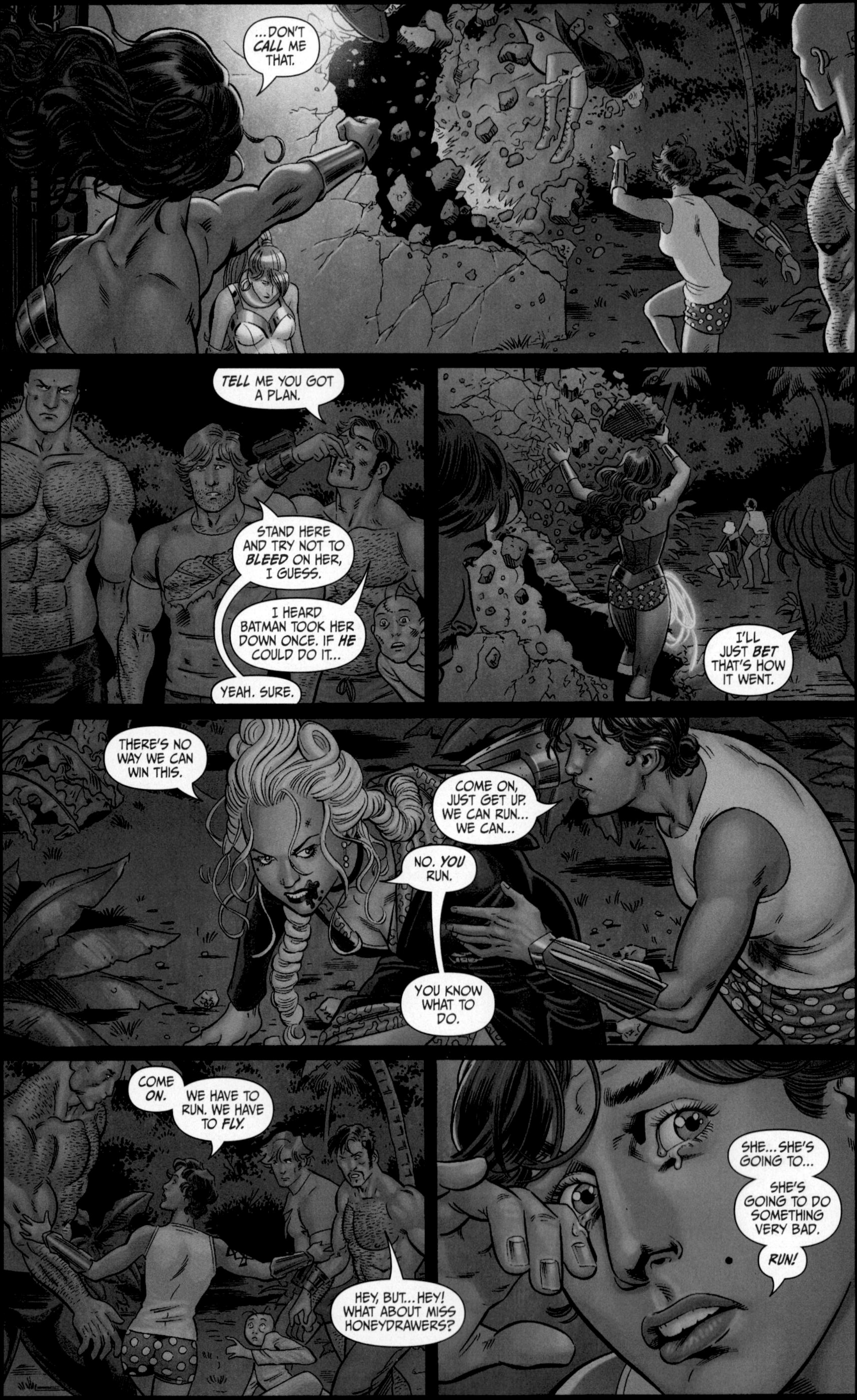
...DON'T CALL ME THAT.
TELL ME YOU GOT A PLAN.
STAND HERE AND TRY NOT TO BLEED ON HER, I GUESS.
I HEARD BATMAN TOOK HER DOWN ONCE. IF HE COULD DO IT...
YEAH. SURE.
I'LL JUST BET THAT'S HOW IT WENT.
THERE'S NO WAY WE CAN WIN THIS.
COME ON, JUST GET UP. WE CAN RUN... WE CAN...
NO. YOU RUN.
YOU KNOW WHAT TO DO.
COME ON.
WE HAVE TO RUN. WE HAVE TO FLY.
HEY, BUT... HEY! WHAT ABOUT MISS HONEYDRAWERS?
SHE... SHE'S GOING TO...
SHE'S GOING TO DO SOMETHING VERY BAD.
RUN!

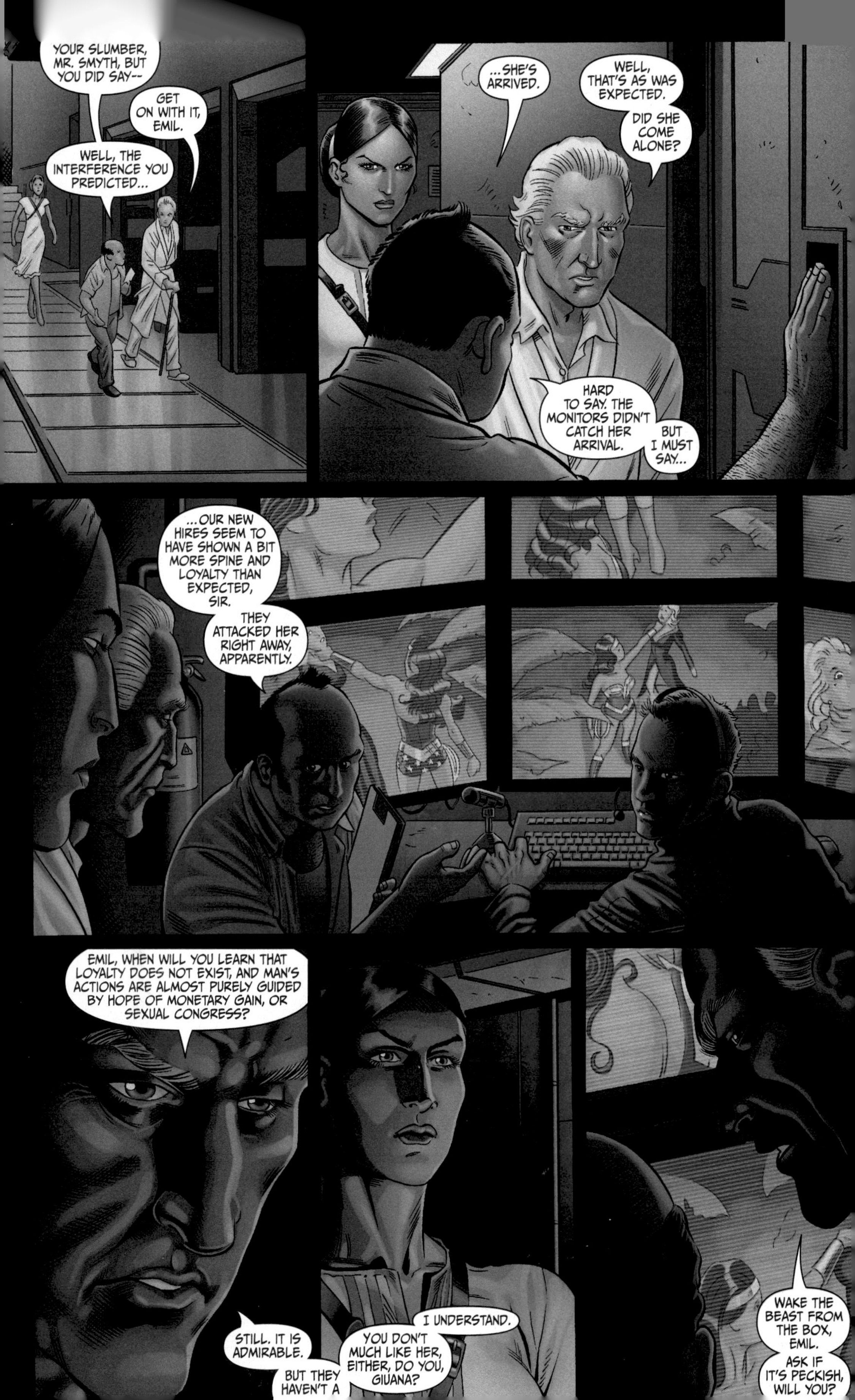
YOUR SLUMBER, MR. SMYTH, BUT YOU DID SAY--
GET ON WITH IT, EMIL.
WELL, THE INTERFERENCE YOU PREDICTED...
...SHE'S ARRIVED.
WELL, THAT'S AS WAS EXPECTED.
DID SHE COME ALONE?
HARD TO SAY. THE MONITORS DIDN'T CATCH HER ARRIVAL.
BUT I MUST SAY...
...OUR NEW HIRES SEEM TO HAVE SHOWN A BIT MORE SPINE AND LOYALTY THAN EXPECTED, SIR.
THEY ATTACKED HER RIGHT AWAY, APPARENTLY.
EMIL, WHEN WILL YOU LEARN THAT LOYALTY DOES NOT EXIST, AND MAN'S ACTIONS ARE ALMOST PURELY GUIDED BY HOPE OF MONETARY GAIN, OR SEXUAL CONGRESS?
STILL. IT IS ADMIRABLE.
BUT THEY HAVEN'T A
YOU DON'T MUCH LIKE HER, EITHER, DO YOU, GIUANA?
I UNDERSTAND.
WAKE THE BEAST FROM THE BOX, EMIL.
ASK IF IT'S PECKISH, WILL YOU?

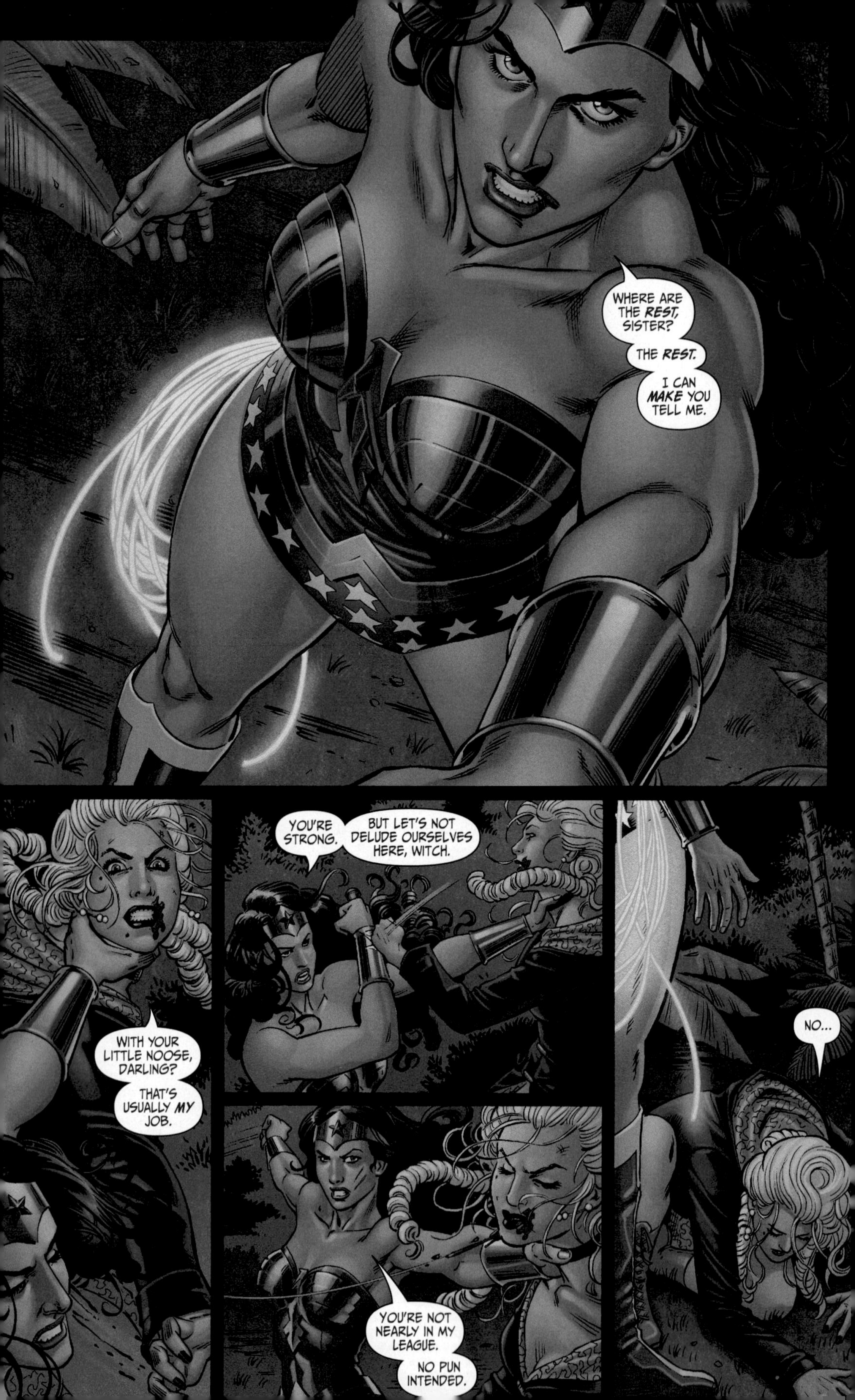
WHERE ARE THE REST, SISTER?
THE REST.
I CAN MAKE YOU TELL ME.
WITH YOUR LITTLE NOOSE, DARLING?
THAT'S USUALLY MY JOB.
YOU'RE STRONG.
BUT LET'S NOT DELUDE OURSELVES HERE, WITCH.
YOU'RE NOT NEARLY IN MY LEAGUE.
NO PUN INTENDED.
NO...

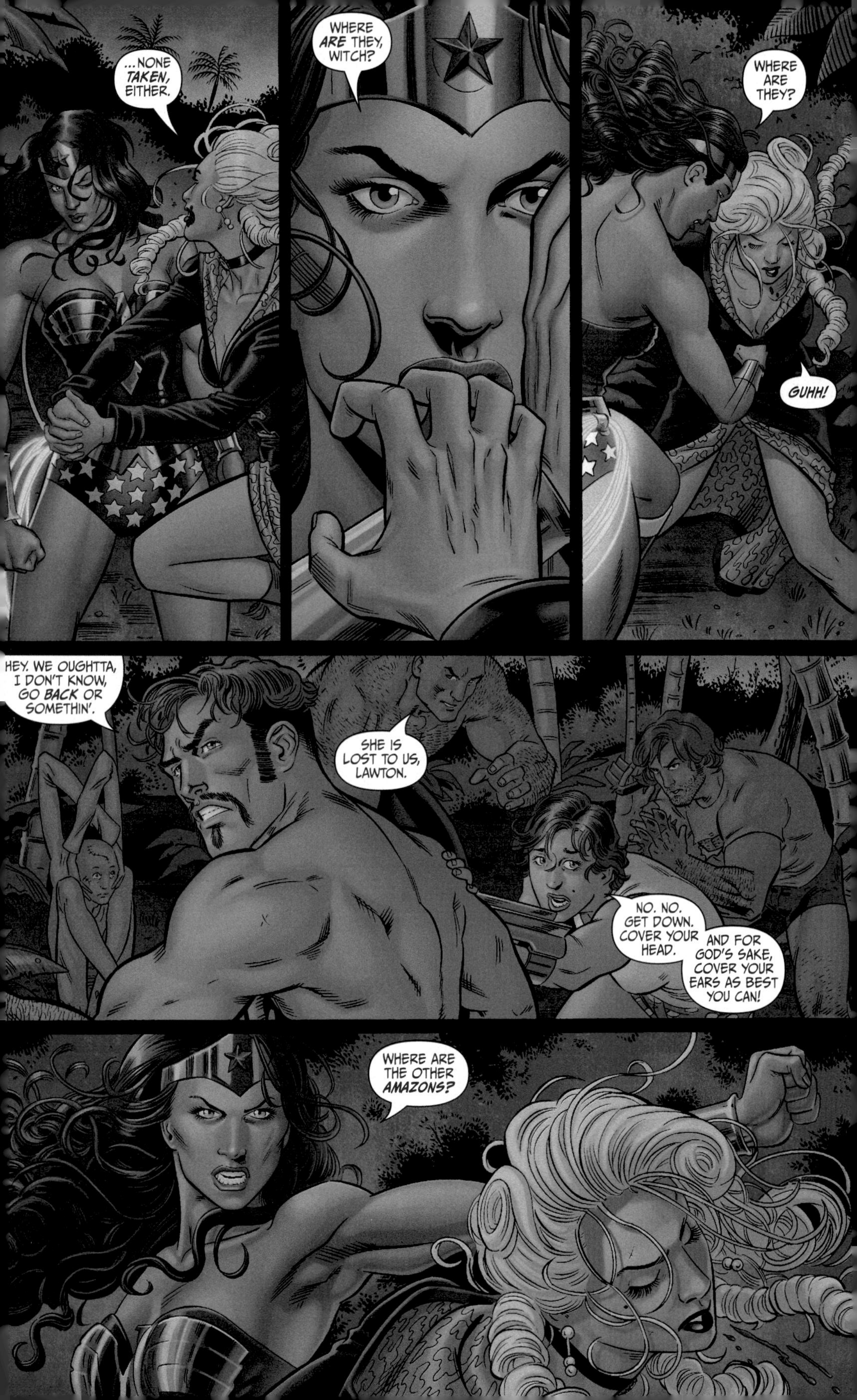

...NONE *TAKEN,* EITHER.
WHERE *ARE* THEY, WITCH?
WHERE ARE THEY?
GUHH!
HEY. WE OUGHTTA, I DON'T KNOW, GO *BACK* OR SOMETHIN'.
SHE IS LOST TO US, LAWTON.
NO. NO. GET DOWN. COVER YOUR HEAD.
AND FOR GOD'S SAKE, COVER YOUR EARS AS BEST YOU CAN!
WHERE ARE THE OTHER *AMAZONS?*

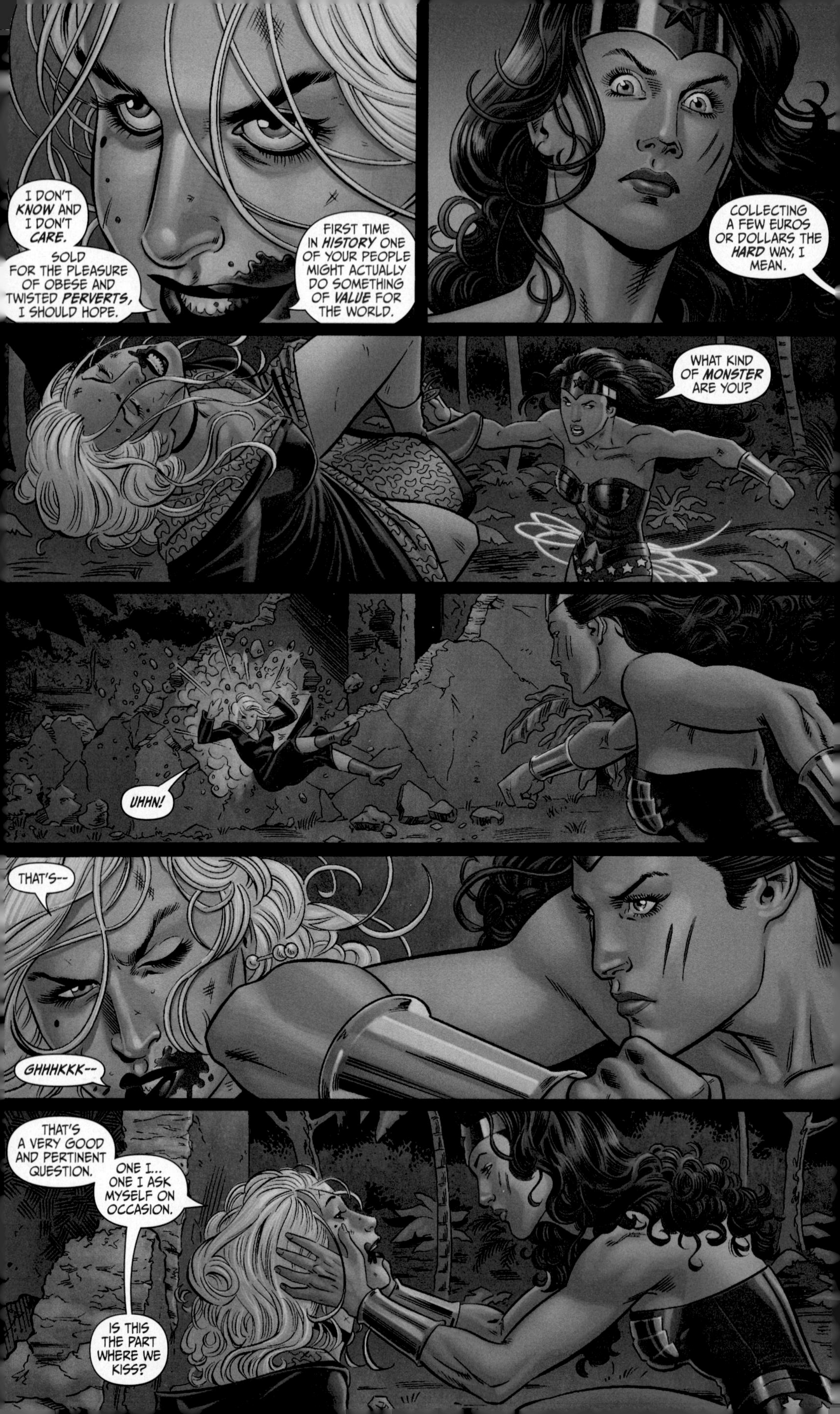
I DON'T KNOW AND I DON'T CARE.
SOLD FOR THE PLEASURE OF OBESE AND TWISTED PERVERTS, I SHOULD HOPE.
FIRST TIME IN HISTORY ONE OF YOUR PEOPLE MIGHT ACTUALLY DO SOMETHING OF VALUE FOR THE WORLD.
COLLECTING A FEW EUROS OR DOLLARS THE HARD WAY, I MEAN.
WHAT KIND OF MONSTER ARE YOU?
UHHN!
THAT'S--
GHHHKKK--
THAT'S A VERY GOOD AND PERTINENT QUESTION.
ONE I... ONE I ASK MYSELF ON OCCASION.
IS THIS THE PART WHERE WE KISS?

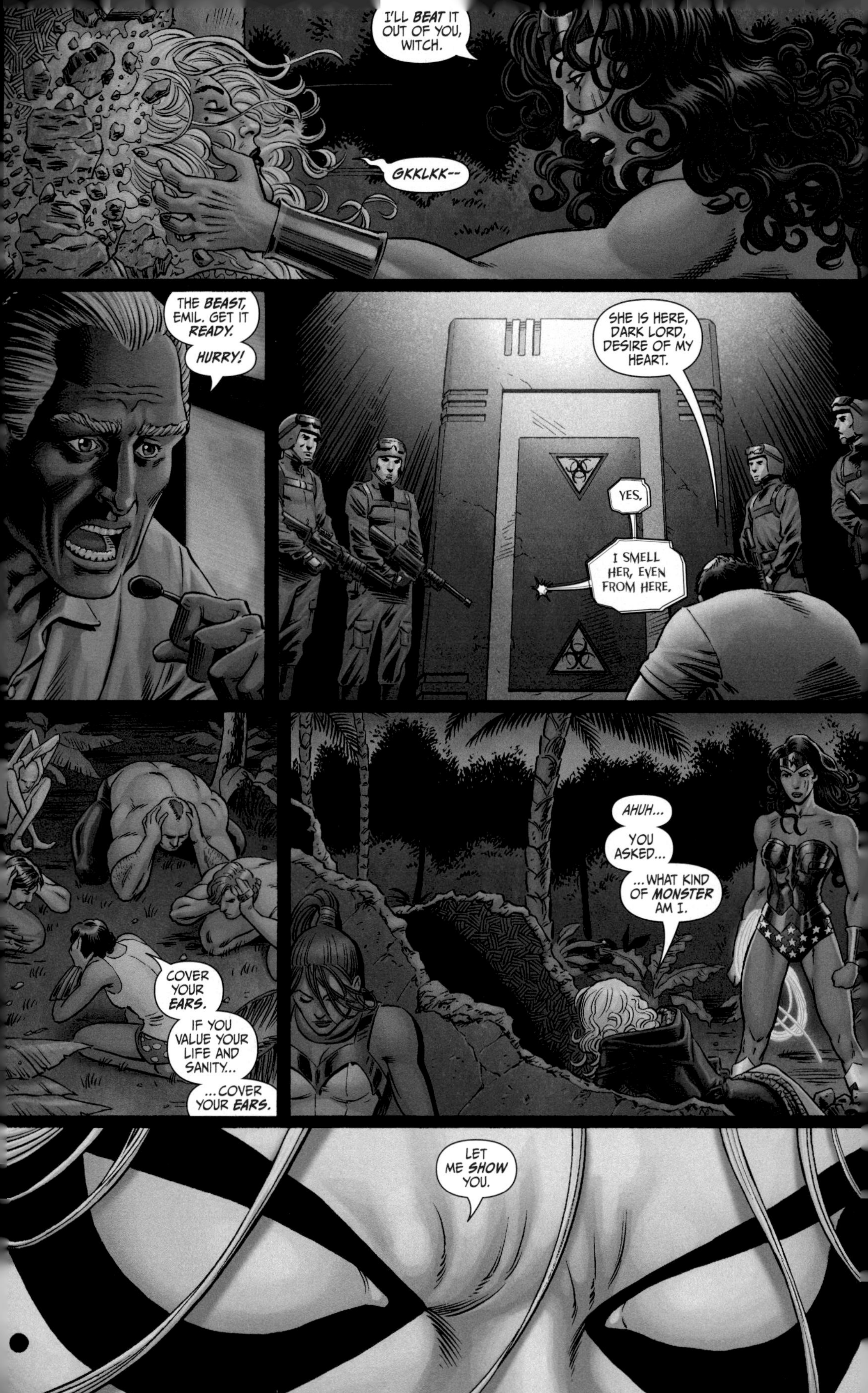

I'LL BEAT IT OUT OF YOU, WITCH.
GKKLKK--
THE BEAST, EMIL. GET IT READY.
HURRY!
SHE IS HERE, DARK LORD, DESIRE OF MY HEART.
YES.
I SMELL HER, EVEN FROM HERE.
COVER YOUR EARS.
IF YOU VALUE YOUR LIFE AND SANITY...
...COVER YOUR EARS.
AHUH...
YOU ASKED...
...WHAT KIND OF MONSTER AM I.
LET ME SHOW YOU.

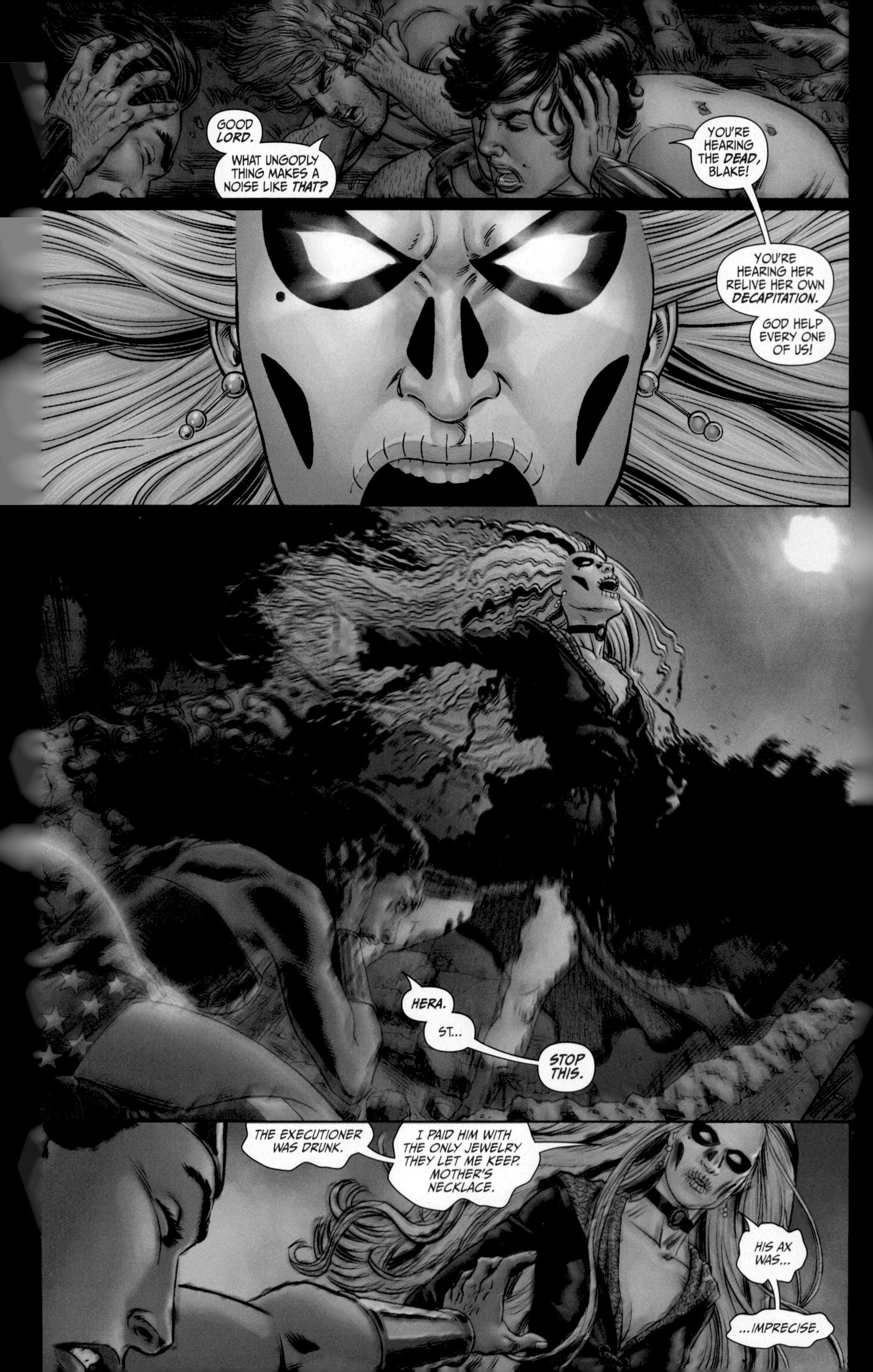
GOOD LORD.
WHAT UNGODLY THING MAKES A NOISE LIKE THAT?
YOU'RE HEARING THE DEAD, BLAKE!
YOU'RE HEARING HER RELIVE HER OWN DECAPITATION.
GOD HELP EVERY ONE OF US!
HERA.
ST...
STOP THIS.
THE EXECUTIONER WAS DRUNK.
I PAID HIM WITH THE ONLY JEWELRY THEY LET ME KEEP. MOTHER'S NECKLACE.
HIS AX WAS...
...IMPRECISE.

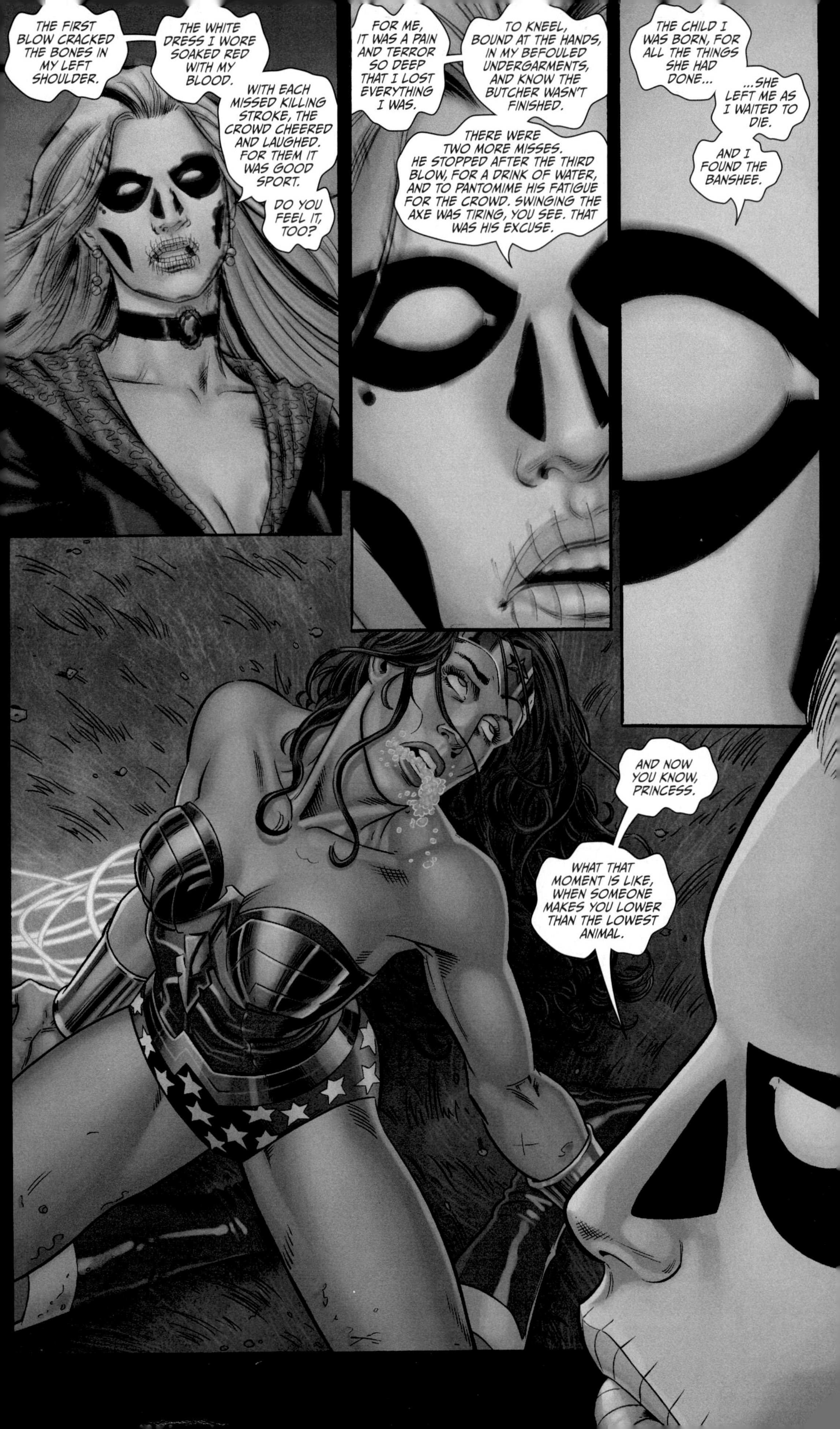
THE FIRST BLOW CRACKED THE BONES IN MY LEFT SHOULDER.
THE WHITE DRESS I WORE SOAKED RED WITH MY BLOOD.
WITH EACH MISSED KILLING STROKE, THE CROWD CHEERED AND LAUGHED. FOR THEM IT WAS GOOD SPORT.
DO YOU FEEL IT, TOO?
FOR ME, IT WAS A PAIN AND TERROR SO DEEP THAT I LOST EVERYTHING I WAS.
TO KNEEL, BOUND AT THE HANDS, IN MY BEFOULED UNDERGARMENTS, AND KNOW THE BUTCHER WASN'T FINISHED.
THERE WERE TWO MORE MISSES. HE STOPPED AFTER THE THIRD BLOW, FOR A DRINK OF WATER, AND TO PANTOMIME HIS FATIGUE FOR THE CROWD. SWINGING THE AXE WAS TIRING, YOU SEE. THAT WAS HIS EXCUSE.
THE CHILD I WAS BORN, FOR ALL THE THINGS SHE HAD DONE...
...SHE LEFT ME AS I WAITED TO DIE.
AND I FOUND THE BANSHEE.
AND NOW YOU KNOW, PRINCESS.
WHAT THAT MOMENT IS LIKE, WHEN SOMEONE MAKES YOU LOWER THAN THE LOWEST ANIMAL.

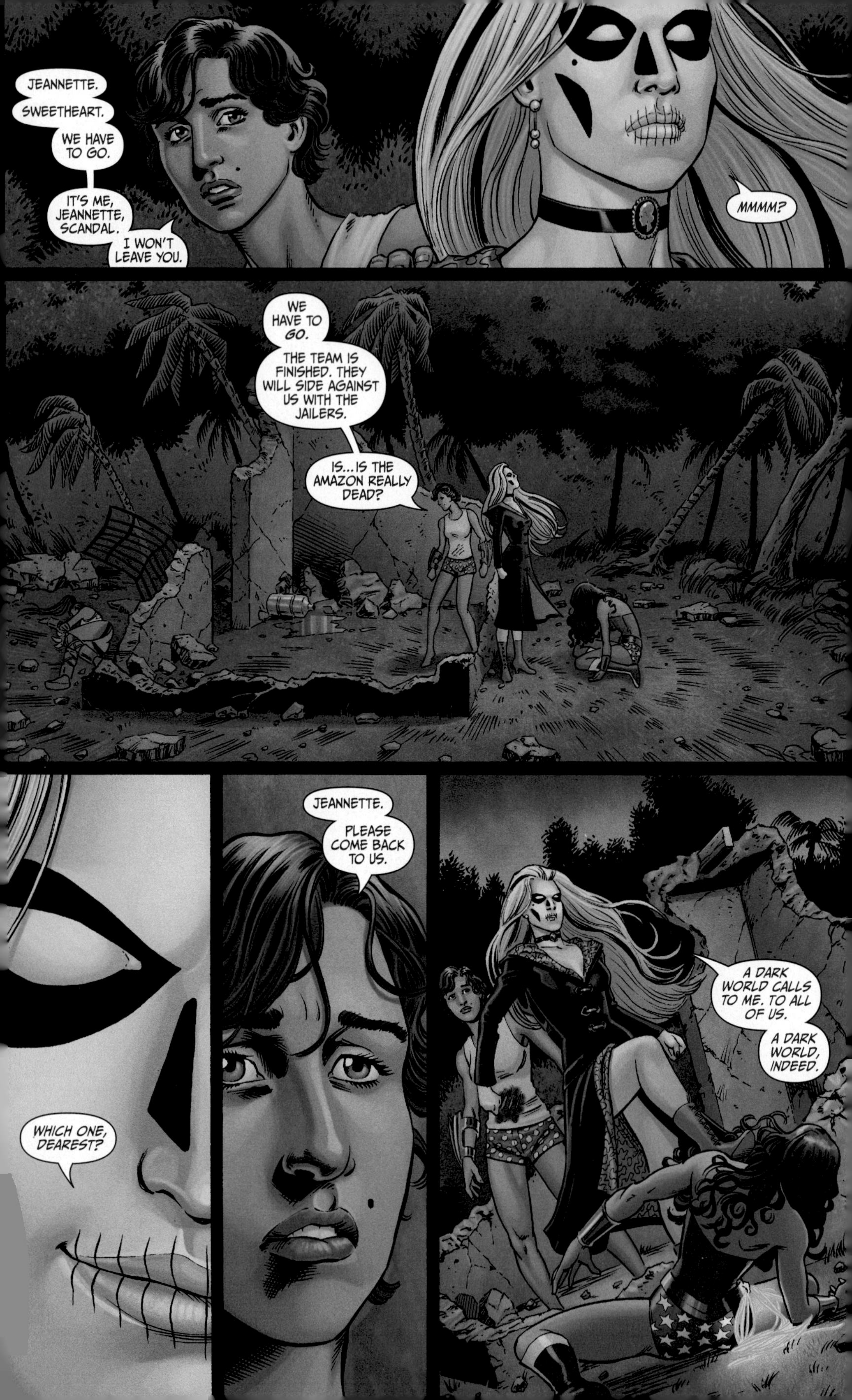
JEANNETTE.
SWEETHEART.
WE HAVE TO GO.
IT'S ME, JEANNETTE, SCANDAL.
I WON'T LEAVE YOU.
MMMM?
WE HAVE TO GO.
THE TEAM IS FINISHED. THEY WILL SIDE AGAINST US WITH THE JAILERS.
IS... IS THE AMAZON REALLY DEAD?
WHICH ONE, DEAREST?
JEANNETTE.
PLEASE COME BACK TO US.
A DARK WORLD CALLS TO ME. TO ALL OF US.
A DARK WORLD, INDEED.

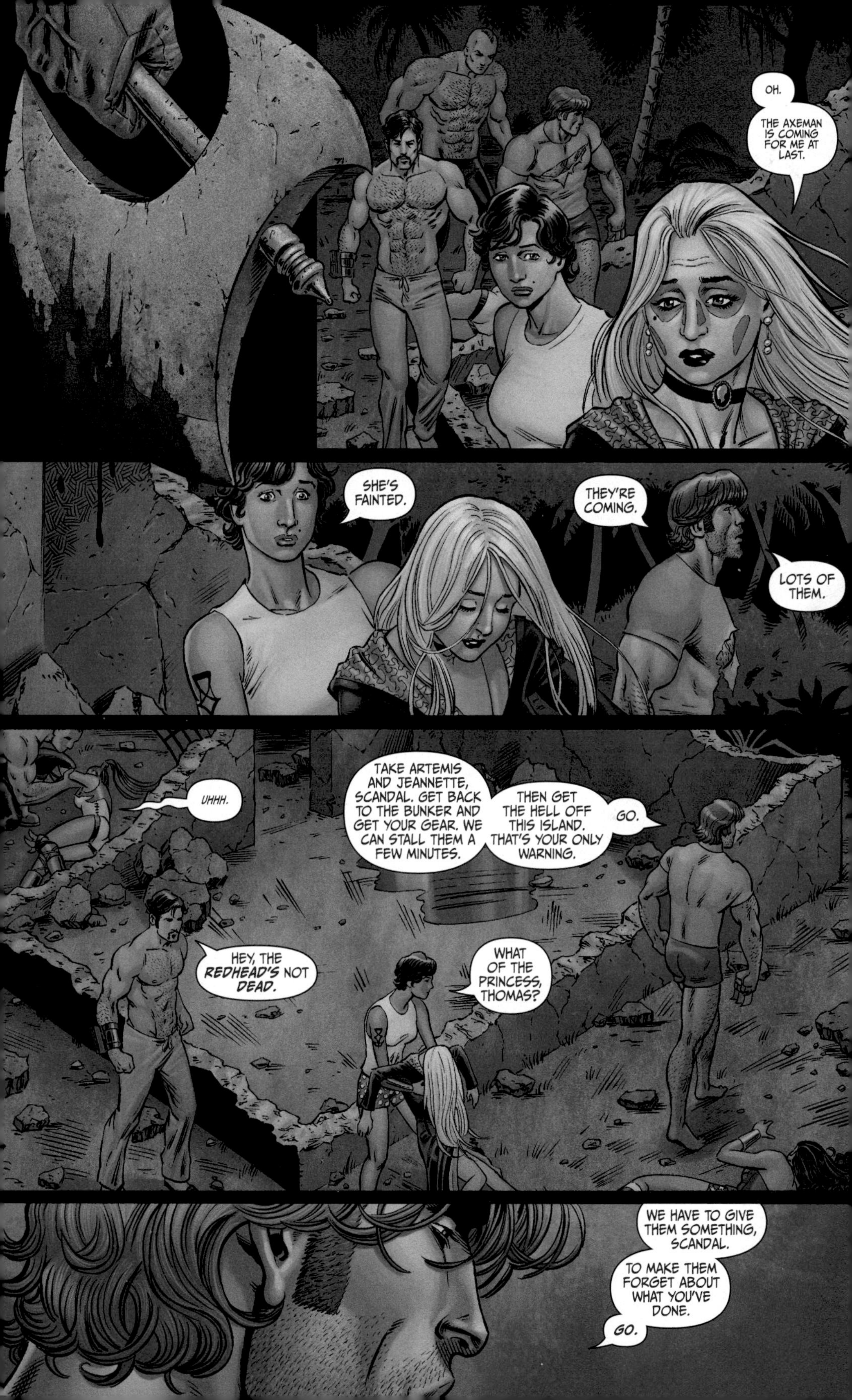
OH.
THE AXEMAN IS COMING FOR ME AT LAST.
SHE'S FAINTED.
THEY'RE COMING.
LOTS OF THEM.
UHHH.
TAKE ARTEMIS AND JEANNETTE, SCANDAL. GET BACK TO THE BUNKER AND GET YOUR GEAR. WE CAN STALL THEM A FEW MINUTES.
THEN GET THE HELL OFF THIS ISLAND. THAT'S YOUR ONLY WARNING.
GO.
HEY, THE *REDHEAD'S* NOT *DEAD.*
WHAT OF THE PRINCESS, THOMAS?
WE HAVE TO GIVE THEM SOMETHING, SCANDAL.
TO MAKE THEM FORGET ABOUT WHAT YOU'VE DONE.
GO.

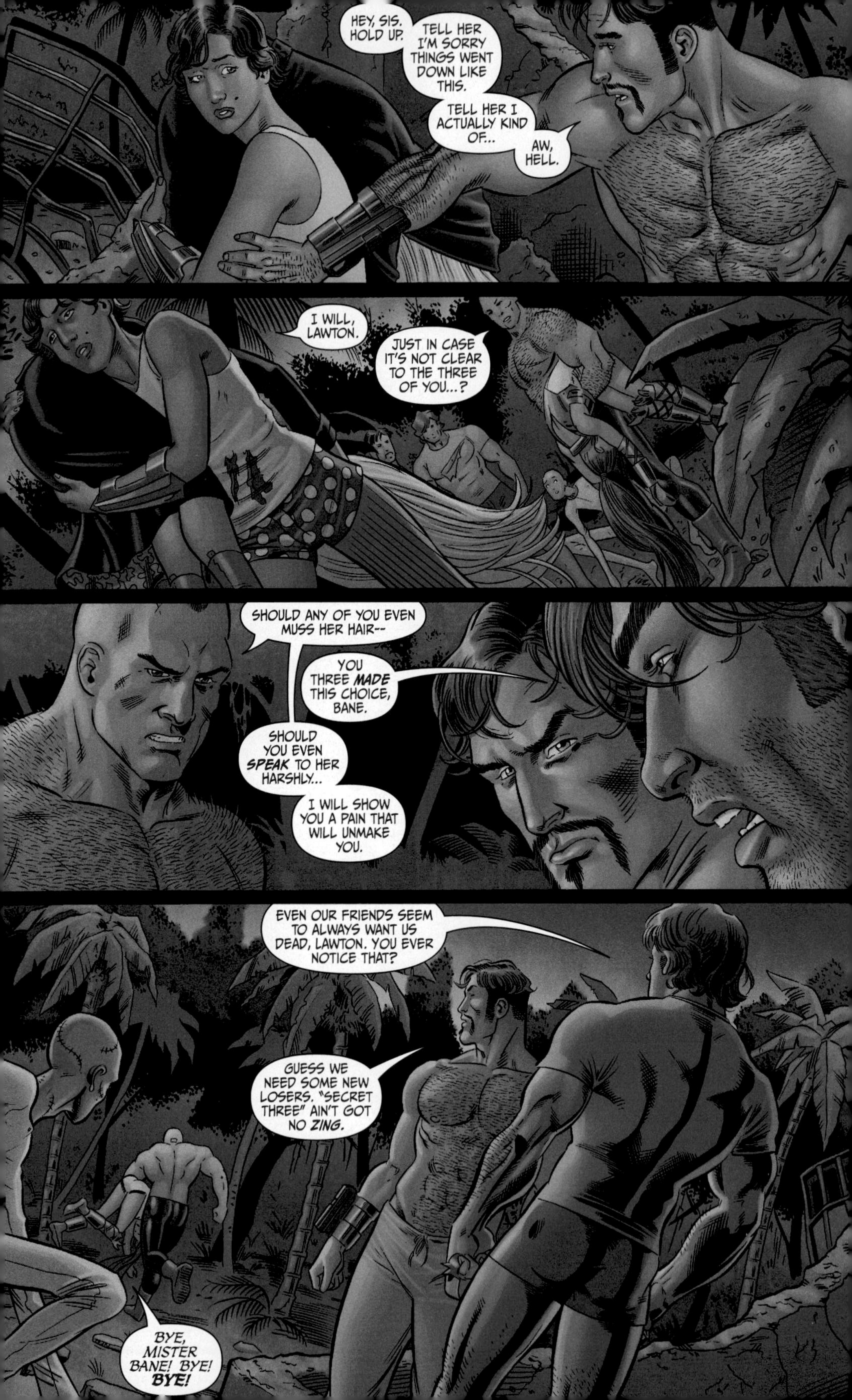
HEY, SIS. HOLD UP.
TELL HER I'M SORRY THINGS WENT DOWN LIKE THIS.
TELL HER I ACTUALLY KIND OF...
AW, HELL.
I WILL, LAWTON.
JUST IN CASE IT'S NOT CLEAR TO THE THREE OF YOU...?
SHOULD ANY OF YOU EVEN MUSS HER HAIR--
YOU THREE MADE THIS CHOICE, BANE.
SHOULD YOU EVEN SPEAK TO HER HARSHLY...
I WILL SHOW YOU A PAIN THAT WILL UNMAKE YOU.
EVEN OUR FRIENDS SEEM TO ALWAYS WANT US DEAD, LAWTON. YOU EVER NOTICE THAT?
GUESS WE NEED SOME NEW LOSERS. "SECRET THREE" AIN'T GOT NO ZING.
BYE, MISTER BANE! BYE! BYE!

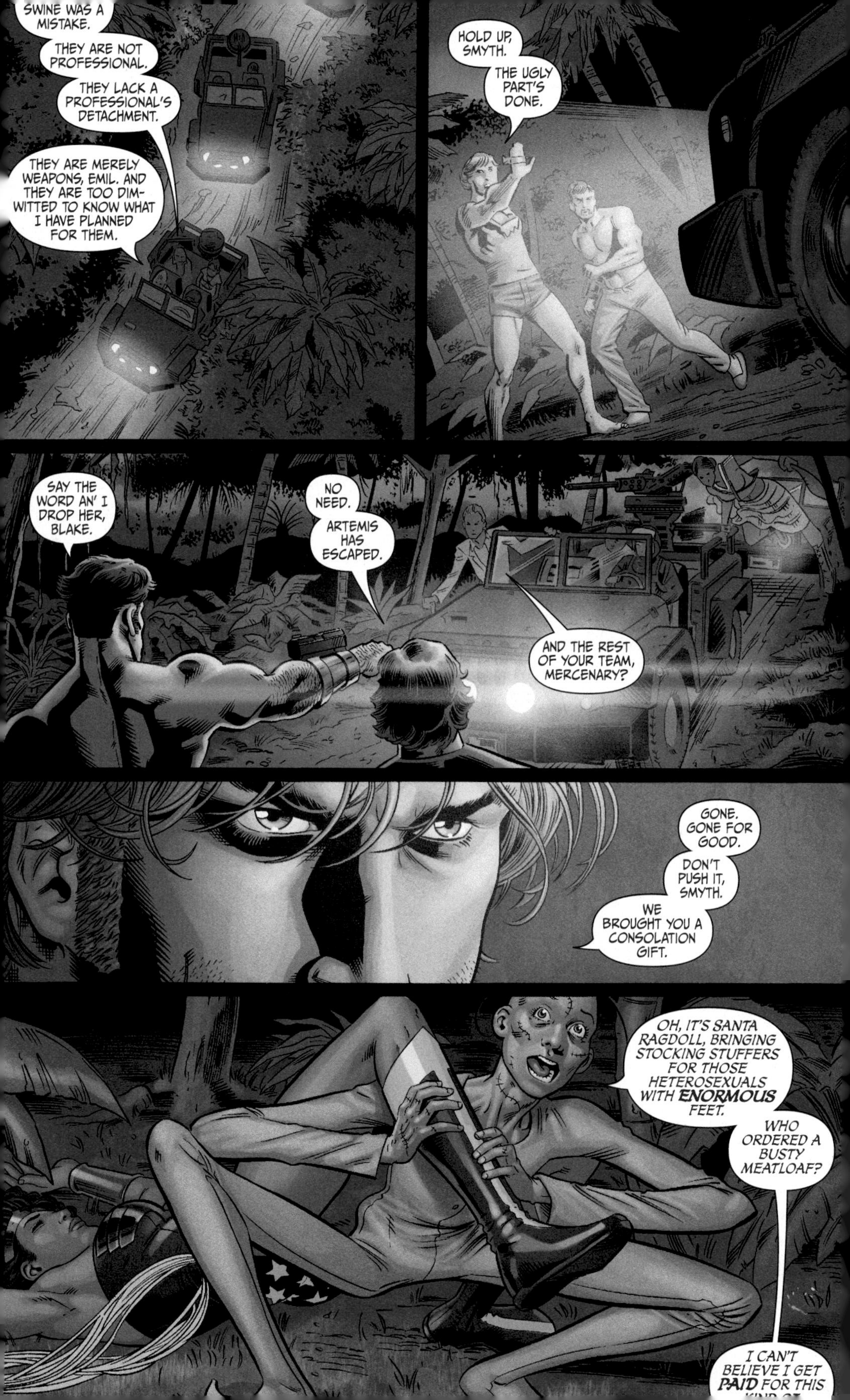
SWINE WAS A MISTAKE.
THEY ARE NOT PROFESSIONAL.
THEY LACK A PROFESSIONAL'S DETACHMENT.
THEY ARE MERELY WEAPONS, EMIL. AND THEY ARE TOO DIM-WITTED TO KNOW WHAT I HAVE PLANNED FOR THEM.
HOLD UP, SMYTH.
THE UGLY PART'S DONE.
SAY THE WORD AN' I DROP HER, BLAKE.
NO NEED.
ARTEMIS HAS ESCAPED.
AND THE REST OF YOUR TEAM, MERCENARY?
GONE. GONE FOR GOOD.
DON'T PUSH IT, SMYTH.
WE BROUGHT YOU A CONSOLATION GIFT.
OH, IT'S SANTA RAGDOLL, BRINGING STOCKING STUFFERS FOR THOSE HETEROSEXUALS WITH ENORMOUS FEET.
WHO ORDERED A BUSTY MEATLOAF?
I CAN'T BELIEVE I GET PAID FOR THIS

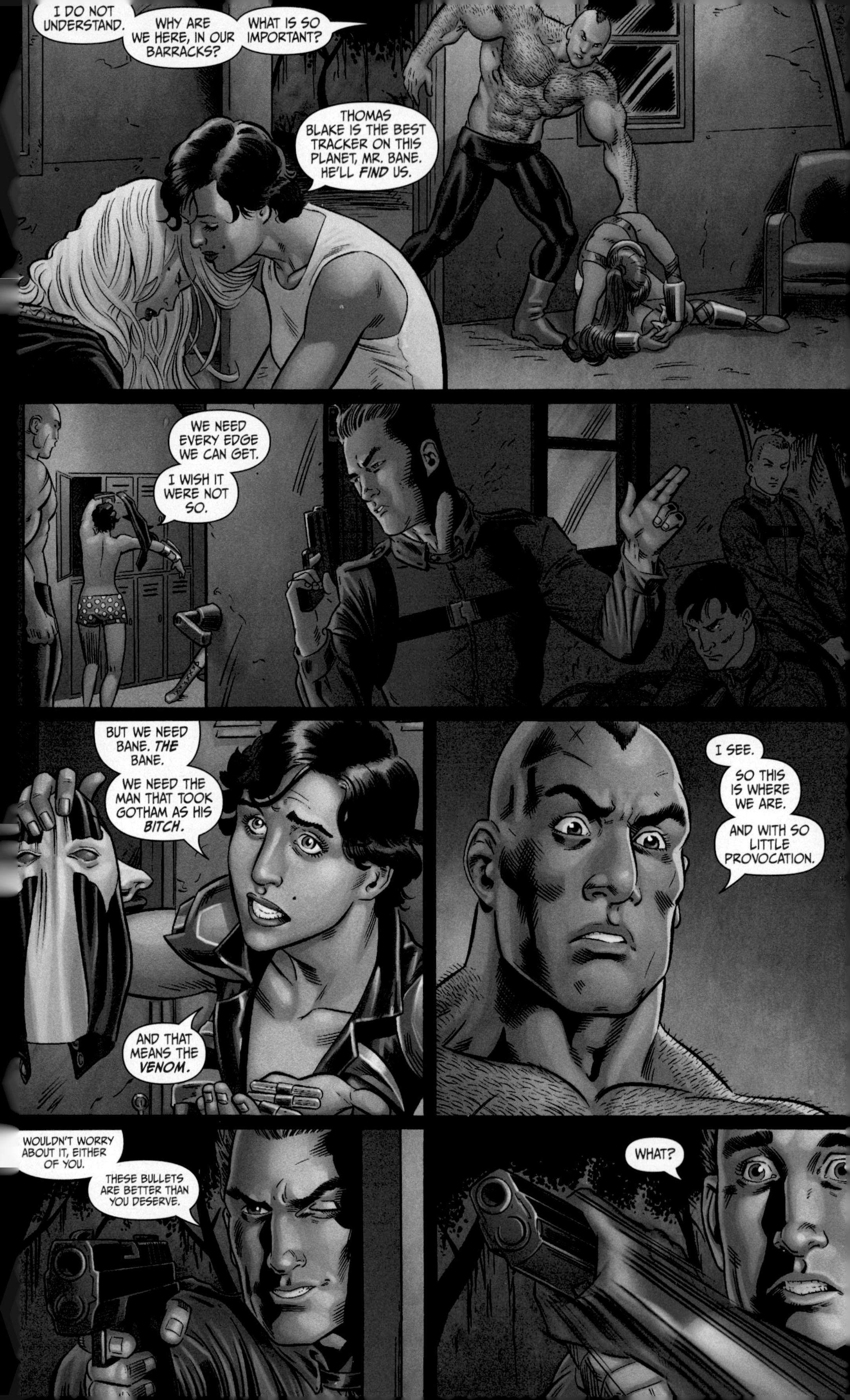
I DO NOT UNDERSTAND.
WHY ARE WE HERE, IN OUR BARRACKS?
WHAT IS SO IMPORTANT?
THOMAS BLAKE IS THE BEST TRACKER ON THIS PLANET, MR. BANE. HE'LL *FIND* US.
WE NEED EVERY EDGE WE CAN GET.
I WISH IT WERE NOT SO.
BUT WE NEED BANE. *THE* BANE.
WE NEED THE MAN THAT TOOK GOTHAM AS HIS *BITCH*.
AND THAT MEANS THE *VENOM*.
I SEE.
SO THIS IS WHERE WE ARE.
AND WITH SO LITTLE PROVOCATION.
WOULDN'T WORRY ABOUT IT, EITHER OF YOU.
THESE BULLETS ARE BETTER THAN YOU DESERVE.
WHAT?

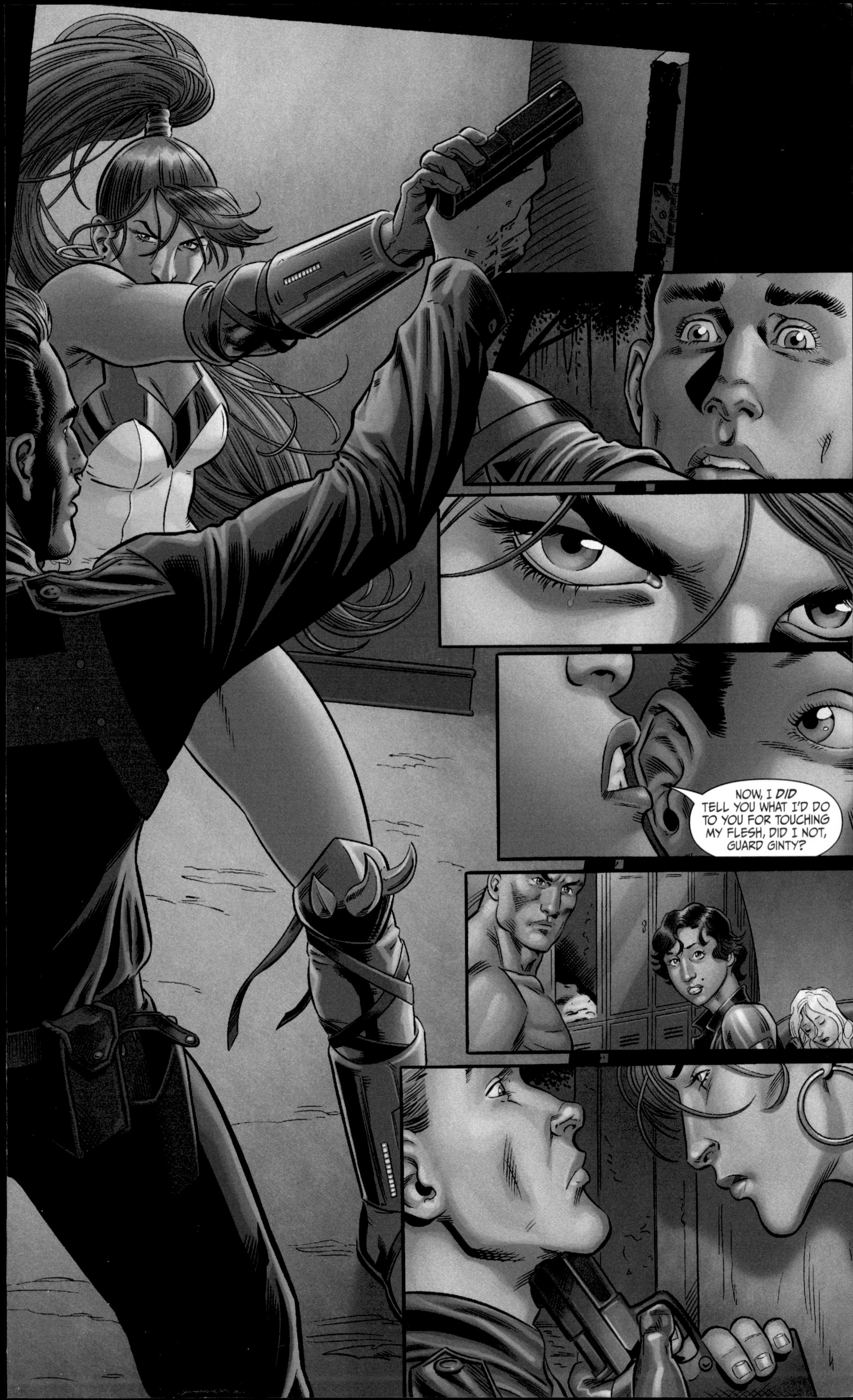
NOW, I *DID* TELL YOU WHAT I'D DO TO YOU FOR TOUCHING MY FLESH, DID I NOT, GUARD GINTY?

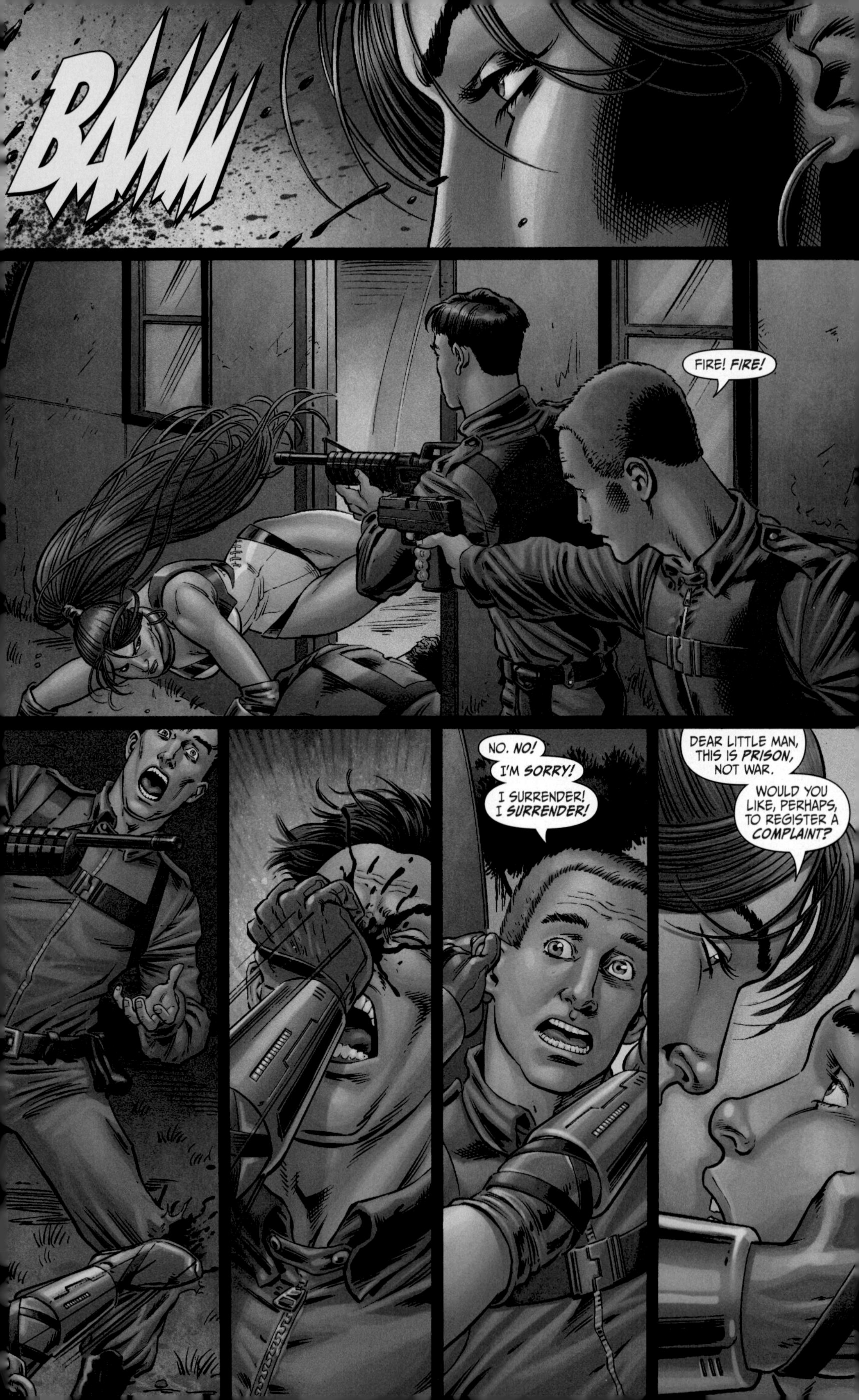
BAM
FIRE! FIRE!
NO. NO!
I'M SORRY!
I SURRENDER! I SURRENDER!
DEAR LITTLE MAN, THIS IS PRISON, NOT WAR.
WOULD YOU LIKE, PERHAPS, TO REGISTER A COMPLAINT?

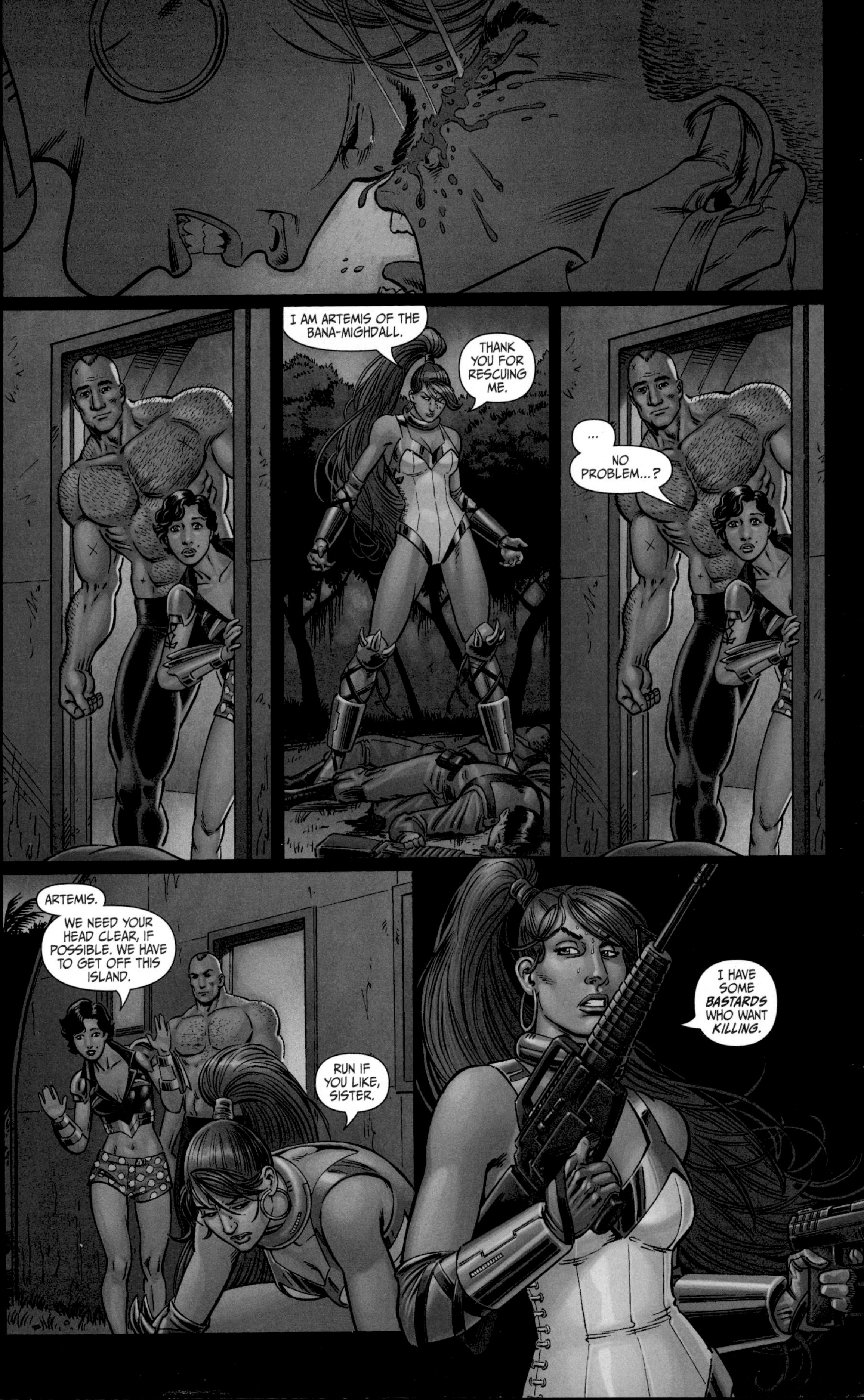

I AM ARTEMIS OF THE BANA-MIGHDALL.
THANK YOU FOR RESCUING ME.
... NO PROBLEM...?
ARTEMIS.
WE NEED YOUR HEAD CLEAR, IF POSSIBLE. WE HAVE TO GET OFF THIS ISLAND.
RUN IF YOU LIKE, SISTER.
I HAVE SOME *BASTARDS* WHO WANT *KILLING*.

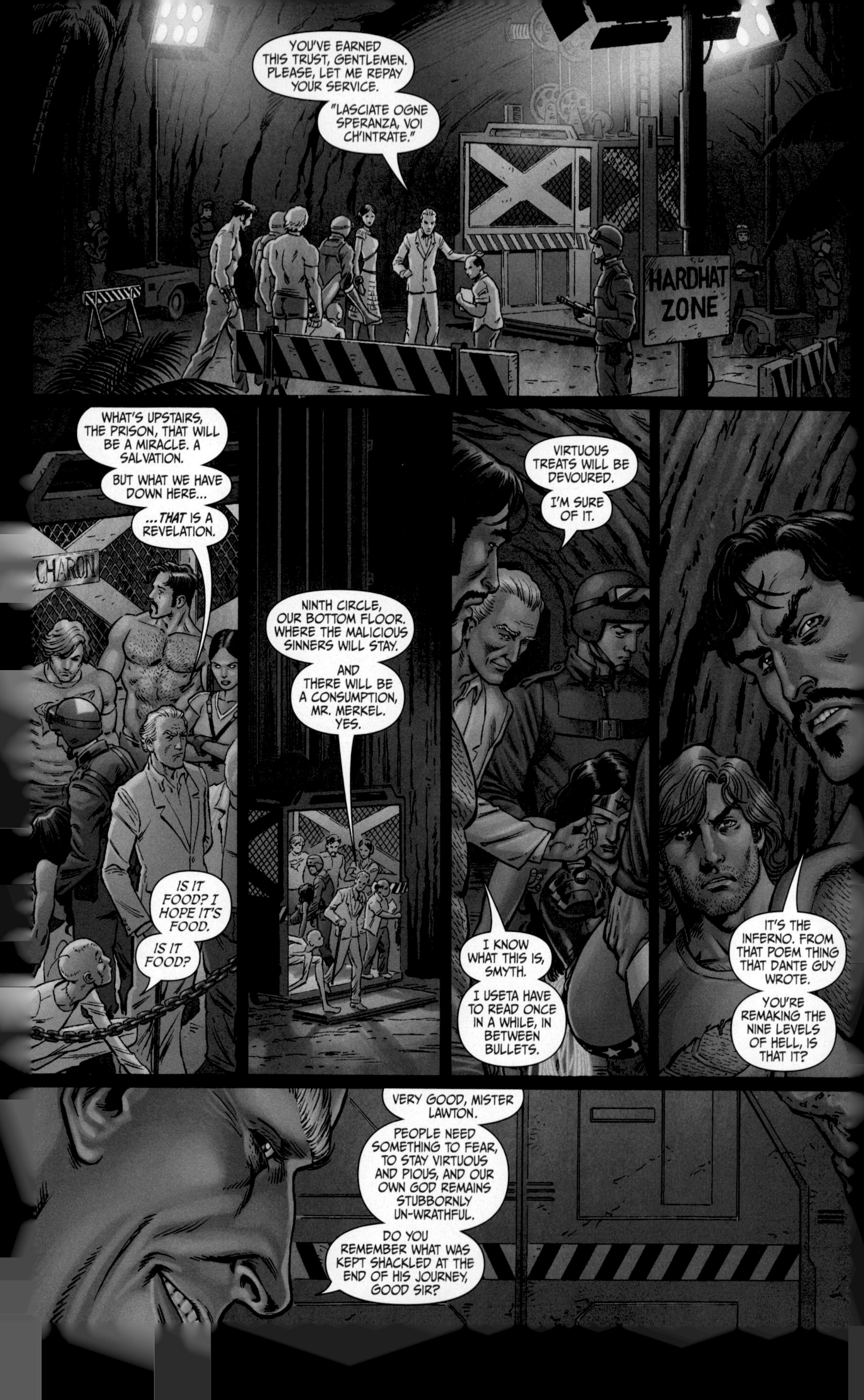
YOU'VE EARNED THIS TRUST, GENTLEMEN. PLEASE, LET ME REPAY YOUR SERVICE.
"LASCIATE OGNE SPERANZA, VOI CH'INTRATE."
HARDHAT ZONE
WHAT'S UPSTAIRS, THE PRISON, THAT WILL BE A MIRACLE. A SALVATION.
BUT WHAT WE HAVE DOWN HERE...
...*THAT* IS A REVELATION.
CHARON
IS IT FOOD? I HOPE IT'S FOOD.
IS IT FOOD?
NINTH CIRCLE, OUR BOTTOM FLOOR. WHERE THE MALICIOUS SINNERS WILL STAY.
AND THERE WILL BE A CONSUMPTION, MR. MERKEL. YES.
VIRTUOUS TREATS WILL BE DEVOURED.
I'M SURE OF IT.
I KNOW WHAT THIS IS, SMYTH.
I USETA HAVE TO READ ONCE IN A WHILE, IN BETWEEN BULLETS.
IT'S THE INFERNO. FROM THAT POEM THING THAT DANTE GUY WROTE.
YOU'RE REMAKING THE NINE LEVELS OF HELL, IS THAT IT?
VERY GOOD, MISTER LAWTON.
PEOPLE NEED SOMETHING TO FEAR, TO STAY VIRTUOUS AND PIOUS, AND OUR OWN GOD REMAINS STUBBORNLY UN-WRATHFUL.
DO YOU REMEMBER WHAT WAS KEPT SHACKLED AT THE END OF HIS JOURNEY, GOOD SIR?

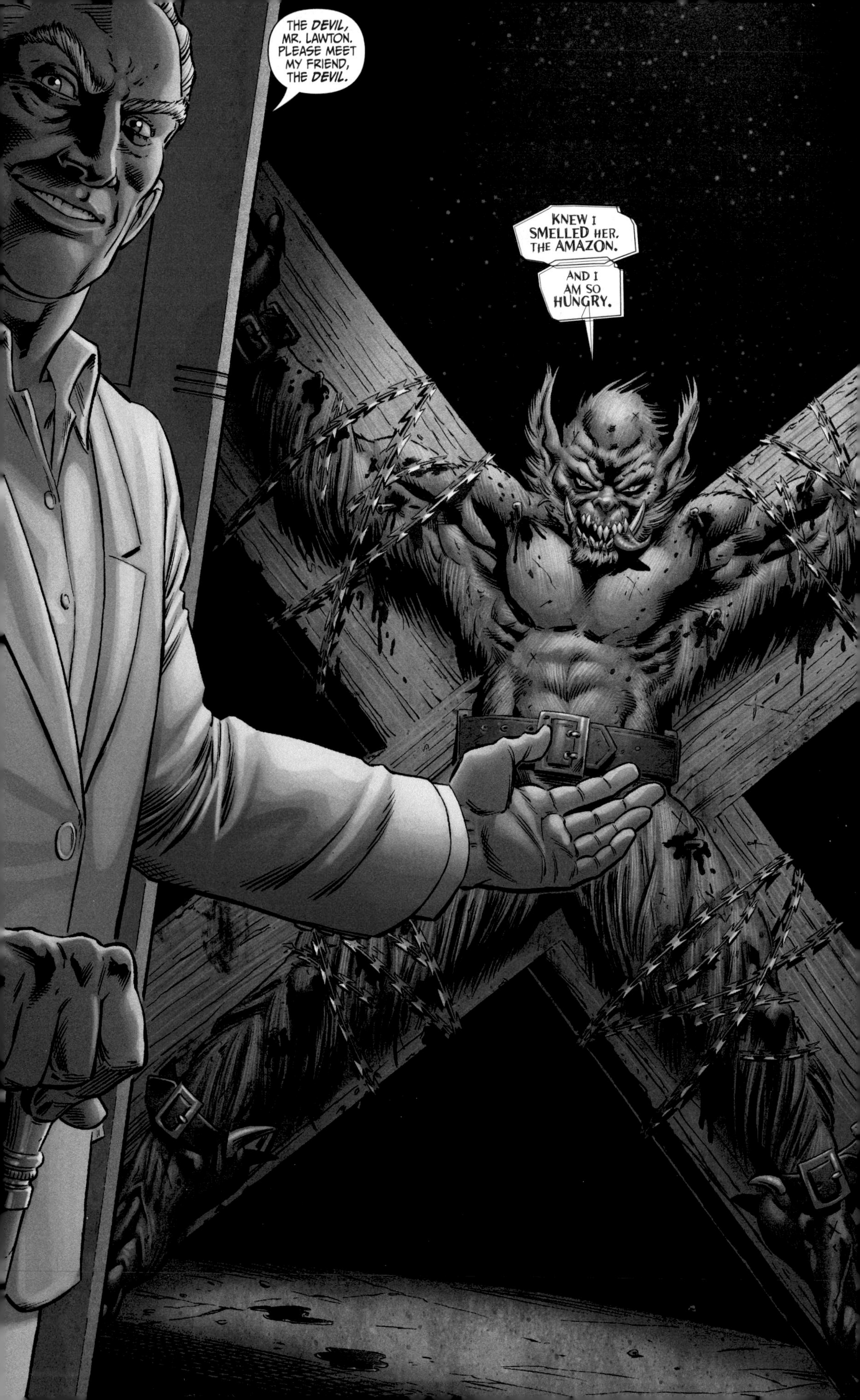
THE *DEVIL*, MR. LAWTON. PLEASE MEET MY FRIEND, THE *DEVIL*.
KNEW I SMELLED HER. THE AMAZON.
AND I AM SO HUNGRY.

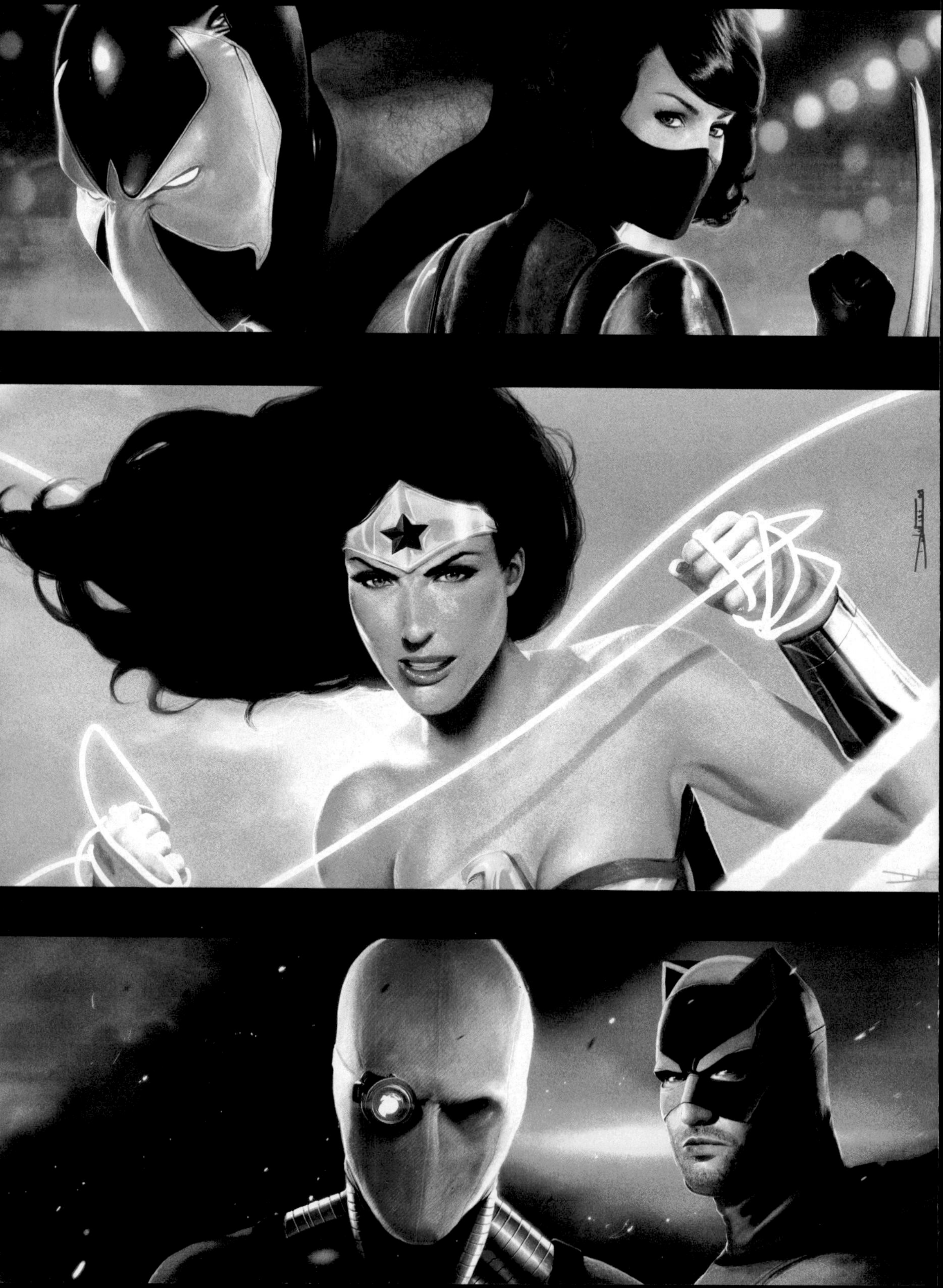

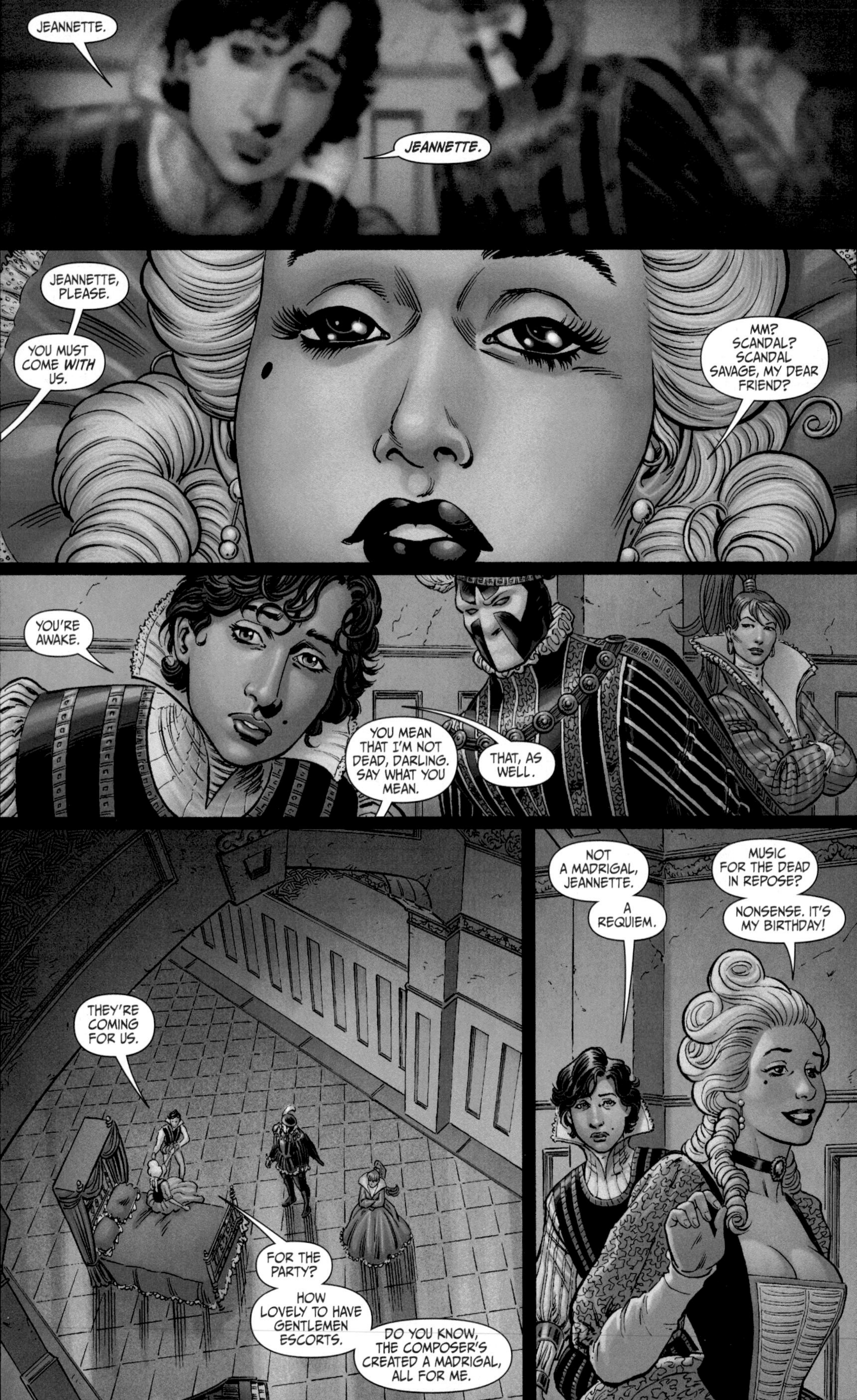
JEANNETTE.
JEANNETTE.
JEANNETTE, PLEASE.
YOU MUST COME WITH US.
MM? SCANDAL? SCANDAL SAVAGE, MY DEAR FRIEND?
YOU'RE AWAKE.
YOU MEAN THAT I'M NOT DEAD, DARLING. SAY WHAT YOU MEAN.
THAT, AS WELL.
THEY'RE COMING FOR US.
FOR THE PARTY?
HOW LOVELY TO HAVE GENTLEMEN ESCORTS.
DO YOU KNOW, THE COMPOSER'S CREATED A MADRIGAL, ALL FOR ME.
NOT A MADRIGAL, JEANNETTE.
A REQUIEM.
MUSIC FOR THE DEAD IN REPOSE?
NONSENSE. IT'S MY BIRTHDAY!

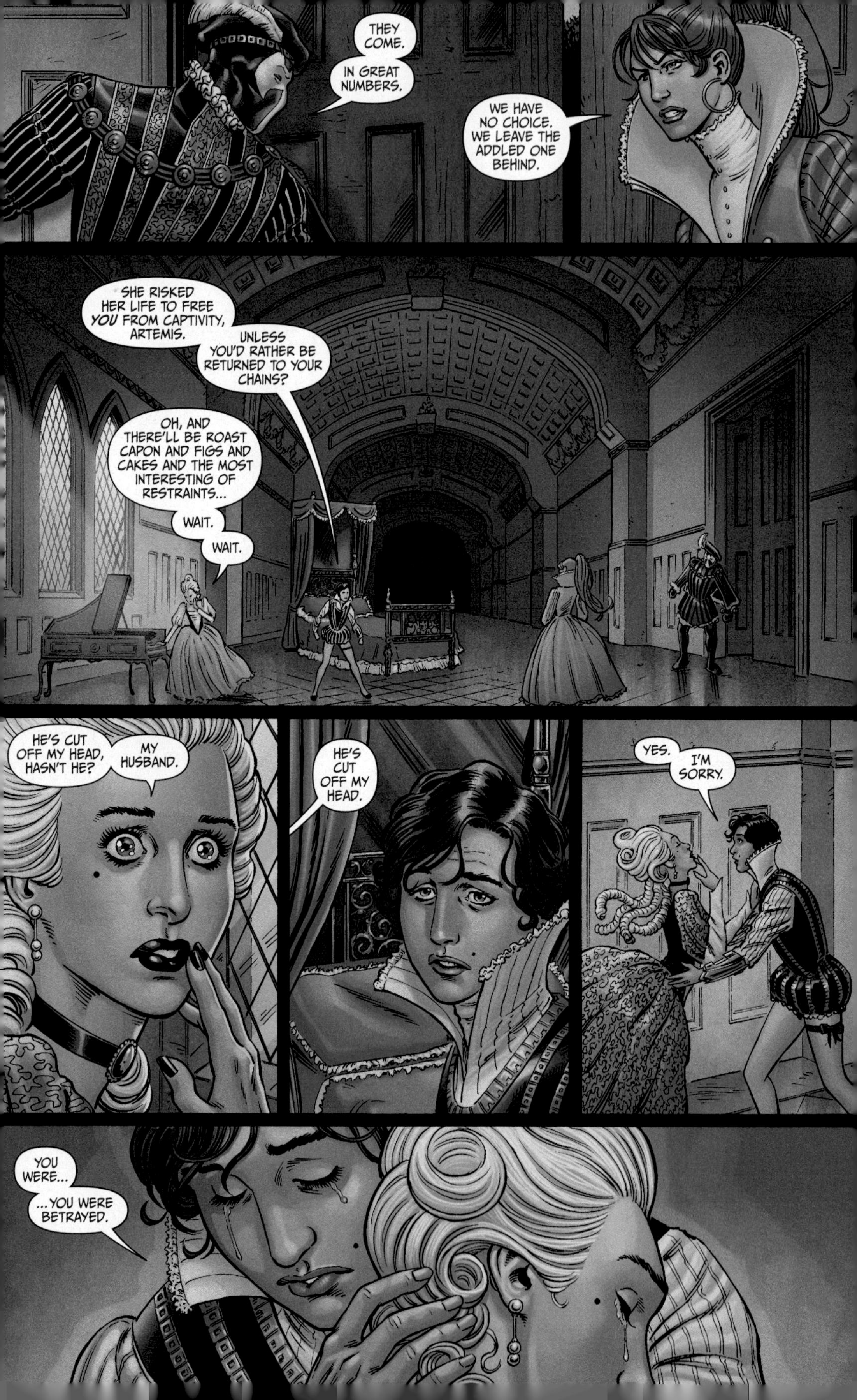
THEY COME.
IN GREAT NUMBERS.
WE HAVE NO CHOICE. WE LEAVE THE ADDLED ONE BEHIND.
SHE RISKED HER LIFE TO FREE *YOU* FROM CAPTIVITY, ARTEMIS.
UNLESS YOU'D RATHER BE RETURNED TO YOUR CHAINS?
OH, AND THERE'LL BE ROAST CAPON AND FIGS AND CAKES AND THE MOST INTERESTING OF RESTRAINTS...
WAIT.
WAIT.
HE'S CUT OFF MY HEAD, HASN'T HE?
MY HUSBAND.
HE'S CUT OFF MY HEAD.
YES.
I'M SORRY.
YOU WERE...
...YOU WERE BETRAYED.

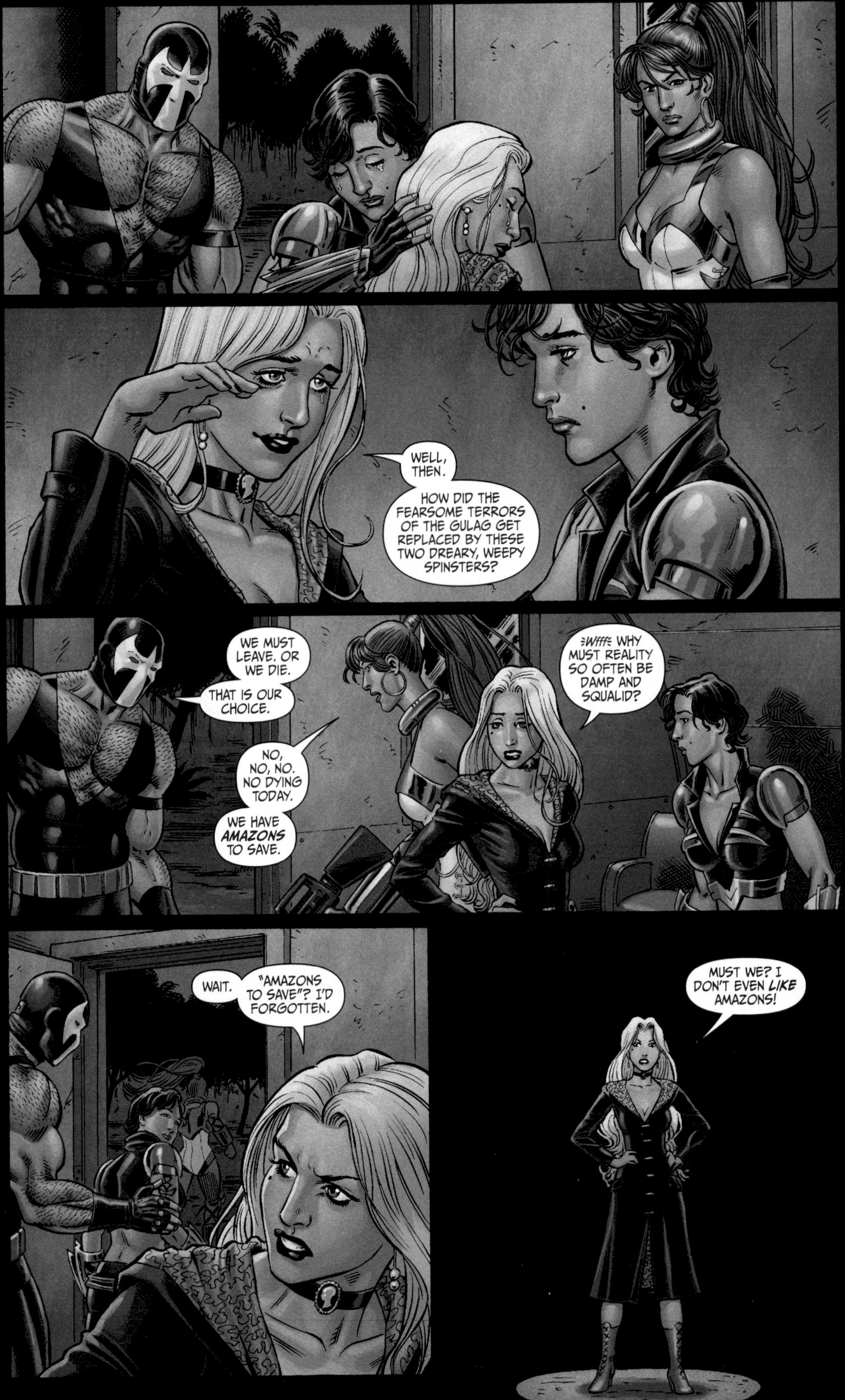
WELL, THEN.
HOW DID THE FEARSOME TERRORS OF THE GULAG GET REPLACED BY THESE TWO DREARY, WEEPY SPINSTERS?
WE MUST LEAVE. OR WE DIE.
THAT IS OUR CHOICE.
NO, NO, NO. NO DYING TODAY.
WE HAVE AMAZONS TO SAVE.
Wfff WHY MUST REALITY SO OFTEN BE DAMP AND SQUALID?
WAIT.
"AMAZONS TO SAVE"? I'D FORGOTTEN.
MUST WE? I DON'T EVEN LIKE AMAZONS!

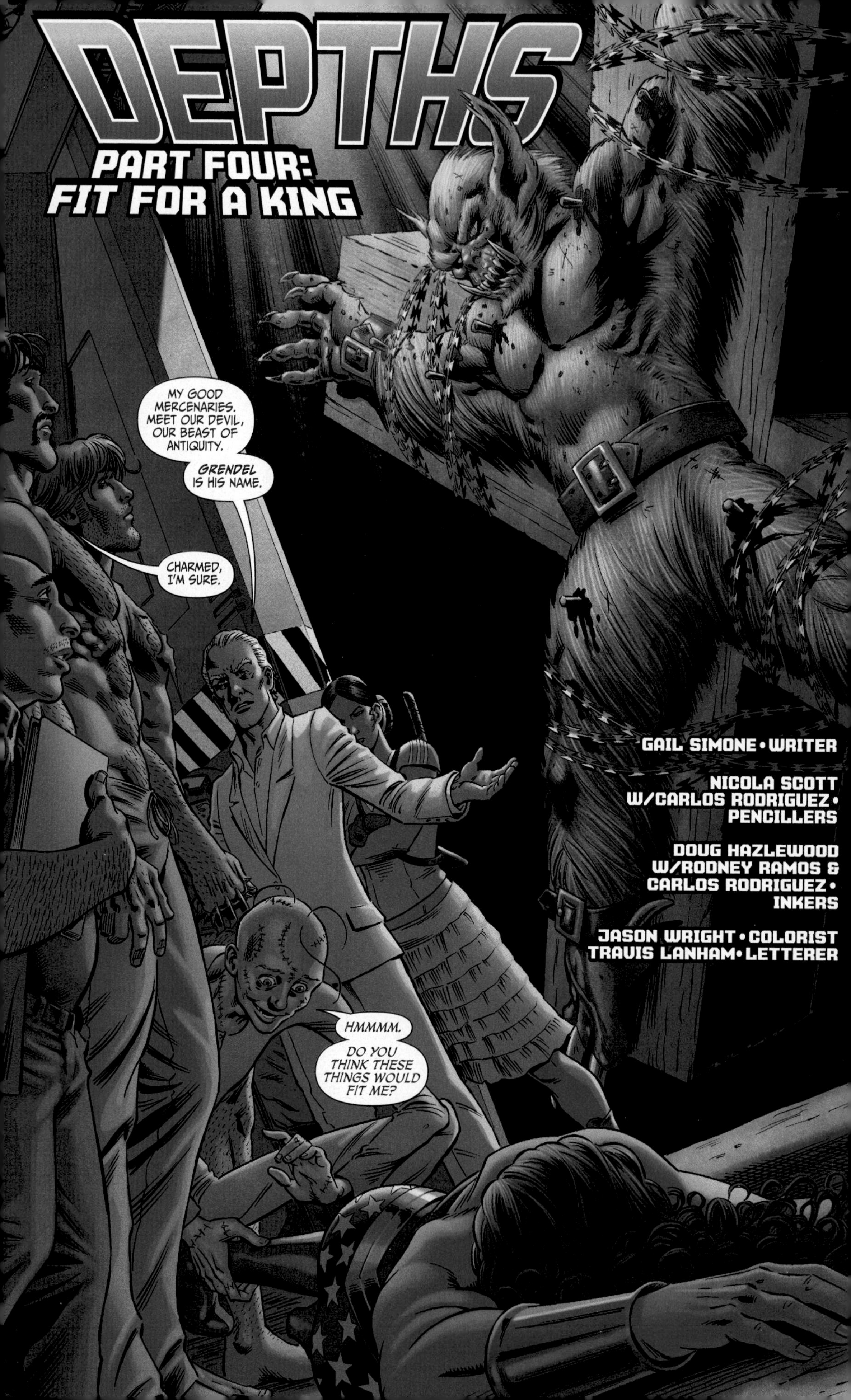
DEPTHS
PART FOUR: FIT FOR A KING
MY GOOD MERCENARIES. MEET OUR DEVIL, OUR BEAST OF ANTIQUITY.
GRENDEL IS HIS NAME.
CHARMED, I'M SURE.
GAIL SIMONE • WRITER
NICOLA SCOTT W/CARLOS RODRIGUEZ • PENCILLERS
DOUG HAZLEWOOD W/RODNEY RAMOS & CARLOS RODRIGUEZ • INKERS
JASON WRIGHT • COLORIST
TRAVIS LANHAM • LETTERER
HMMMM. DO YOU THINK THESE THINGS WOULD FIT ME?

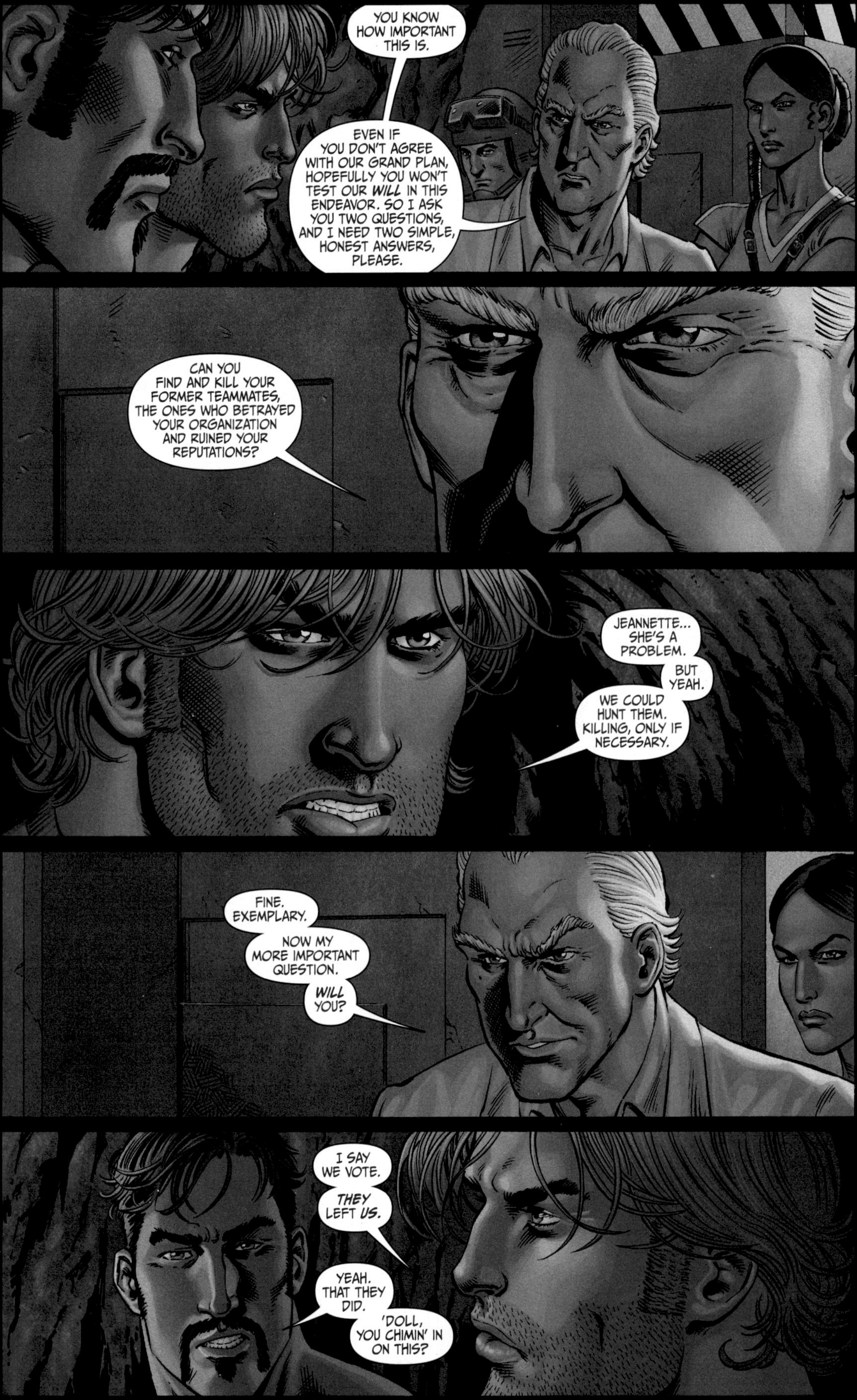
YOU KNOW HOW IMPORTANT THIS IS.
EVEN IF YOU DON'T AGREE WITH OUR GRAND PLAN, HOPEFULLY YOU WON'T TEST OUR *WILL* IN THIS ENDEAVOR. SO I ASK YOU TWO QUESTIONS, AND I NEED TWO SIMPLE, HONEST ANSWERS, PLEASE.
CAN YOU FIND AND KILL YOUR FORMER TEAMMATES, THE ONES WHO BETRAYED YOUR ORGANIZATION AND RUINED YOUR REPUTATIONS?
JEANNETTE... SHE'S A PROBLEM.
BUT YEAH.
WE COULD HUNT THEM. KILLING, ONLY IF NECESSARY.
FINE. EXEMPLARY.
NOW MY MORE IMPORTANT QUESTION.
WILL YOU?
I SAY WE VOTE.
THEY LEFT *US.*
YEAH. THAT THEY DID.
'DOLL, YOU CHIMIN' IN ON THIS?

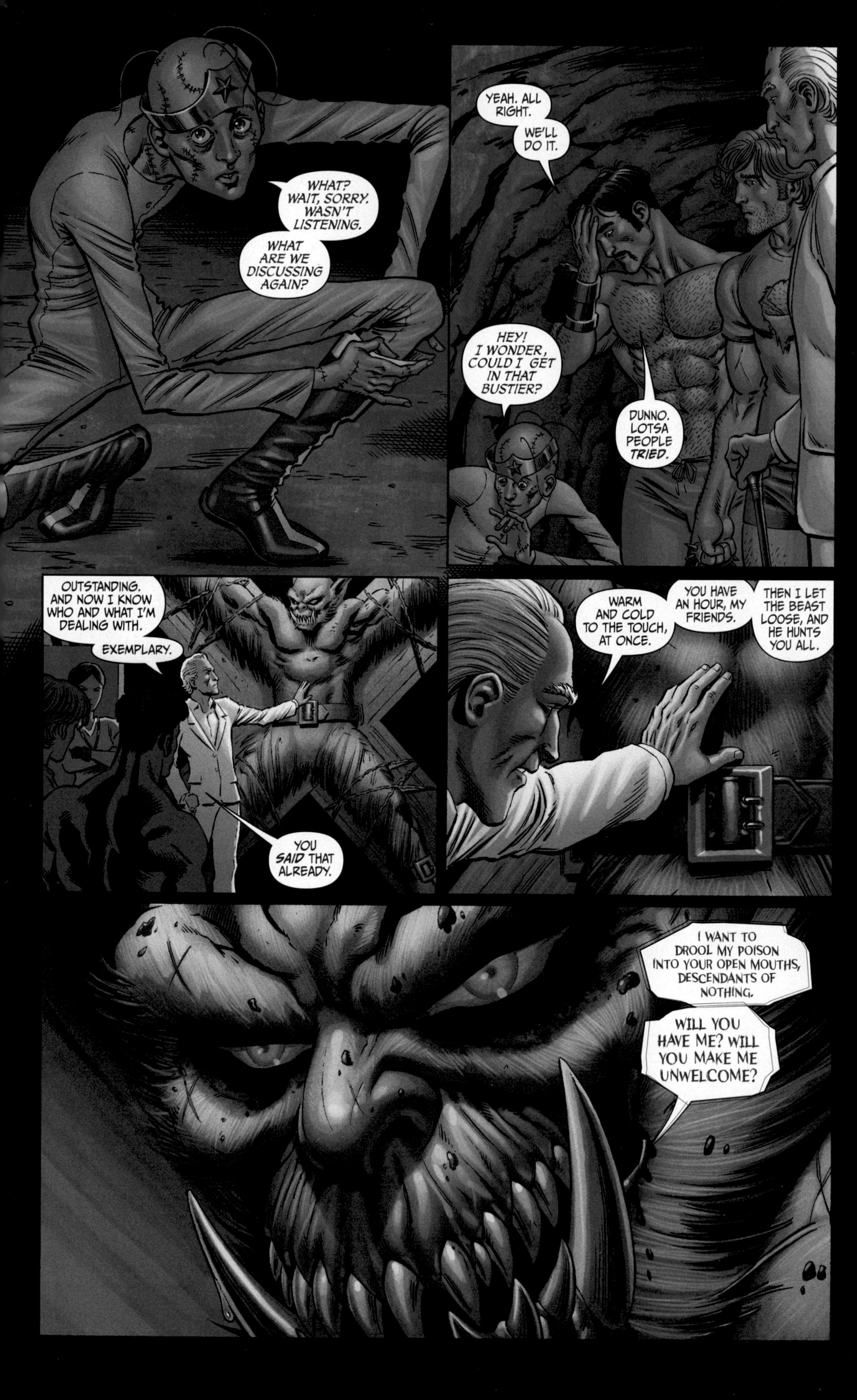
WHAT? WAIT, SORRY. WASN'T LISTENING.
WHAT ARE WE DISCUSSING AGAIN?
YEAH. ALL RIGHT.
WE'LL DO IT.
HEY! I WONDER, COULD I GET IN THAT BUSTIER?
DUNNO. LOTSA PEOPLE *TRIED*.
OUTSTANDING. AND NOW I KNOW WHO AND WHAT I'M DEALING WITH.
EXEMPLARY.
YOU *SAID* THAT ALREADY.
WARM AND COLD TO THE TOUCH, AT ONCE.
YOU HAVE AN HOUR, MY FRIENDS.
THEN I LET THE BEAST LOOSE, AND HE HUNTS YOU ALL.
I WANT TO DROOL MY POISON INTO YOUR OPEN MOUTHS, DESCENDANTS OF NOTHING.
WILL YOU HAVE ME? WILL YOU MAKE ME UNWELCOME?

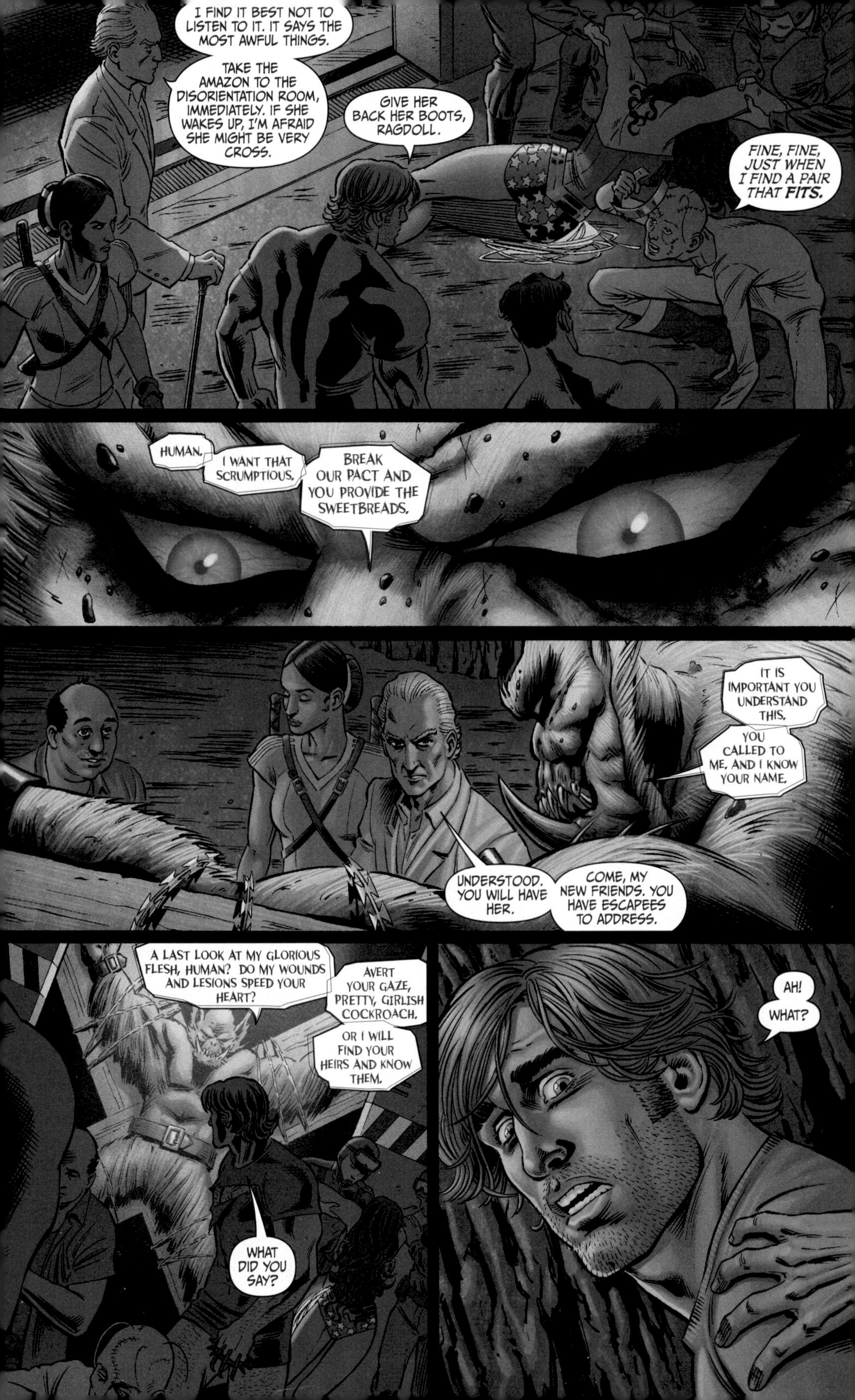
I FIND IT BEST NOT TO LISTEN TO IT. IT SAYS THE MOST AWFUL THINGS.
TAKE THE AMAZON TO THE DISORIENTATION ROOM, IMMEDIATELY. IF SHE WAKES UP, I'M AFRAID SHE MIGHT BE VERY CROSS.
GIVE HER BACK HER BOOTS, RAGDOLL.
FINE, FINE, JUST WHEN I FIND A PAIR THAT **FITS.**
HUMAN.
I WANT THAT SCRUMPTIOUS.
BREAK OUR PACT AND YOU PROVIDE THE SWEETBREADS.
IT IS IMPORTANT YOU UNDERSTAND THIS.
YOU CALLED TO ME, AND I KNOW YOUR NAME.
UNDERSTOOD. YOU WILL HAVE HER.
COME, MY NEW FRIENDS. YOU HAVE ESCAPEES TO ADDRESS.
A LAST LOOK AT MY GLORIOUS FLESH, HUMAN? DO MY WOUNDS AND LESIONS SPEED YOUR HEART?
AVERT YOUR GAZE, PRETTY, GIRLISH COCKROACH.
OR I WILL FIND YOUR HEIRS AND KNOW THEM.
WHAT DID YOU SAY?
AH!
WHAT?

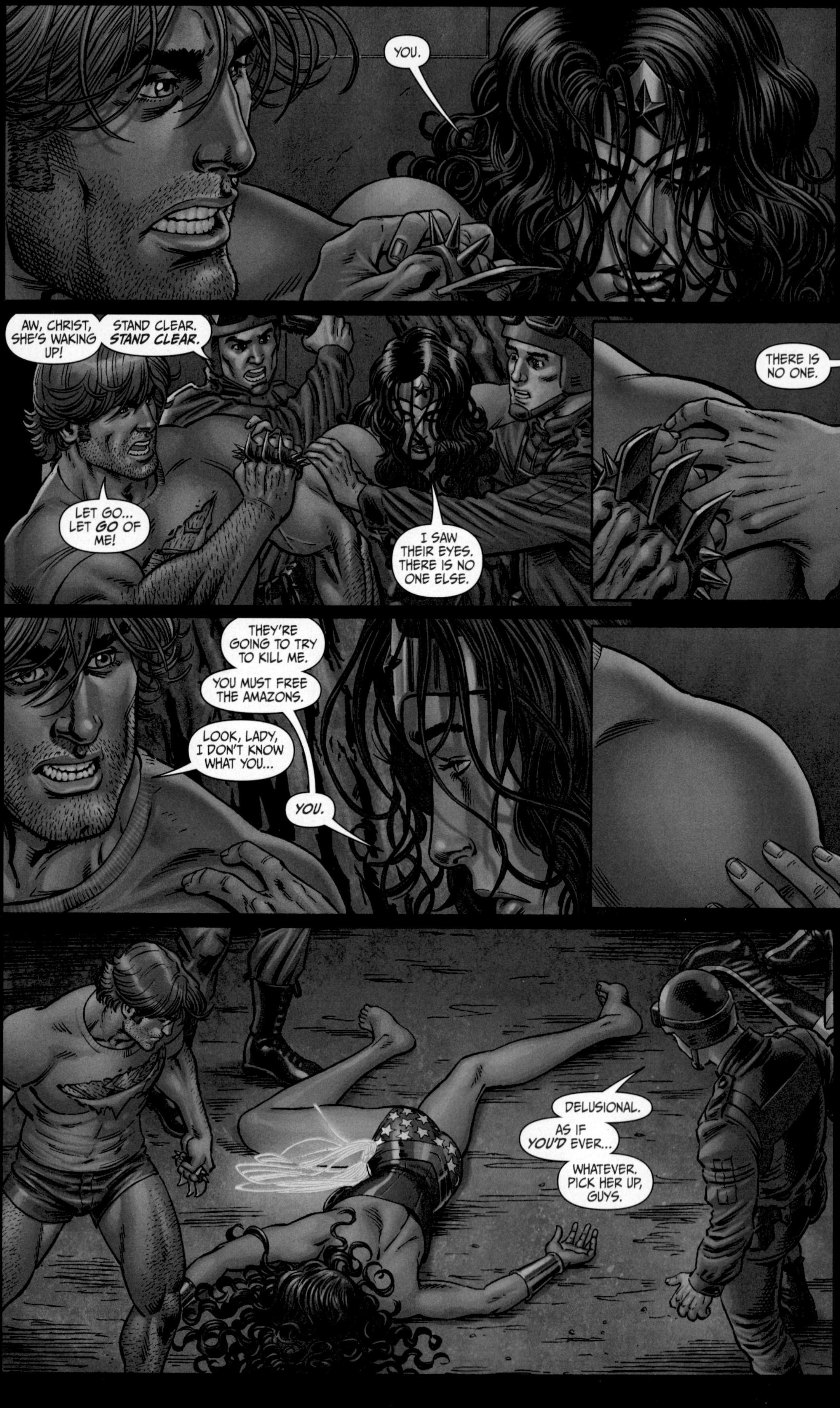
YOU.
AW, CHRIST, SHE'S WAKING UP!
STAND CLEAR. STAND CLEAR.
LET GO... LET GO OF ME!
I SAW THEIR EYES. THERE IS NO ONE ELSE.
THERE IS NO ONE.
THEY'RE GOING TO TRY TO KILL ME.
YOU MUST FREE THE AMAZONS.
LOOK, LADY, I DON'T KNOW WHAT YOU...
YOU.
DELUSIONAL.
AS IF YOU'D EVER...
WHATEVER. PICK HER UP, GUYS.

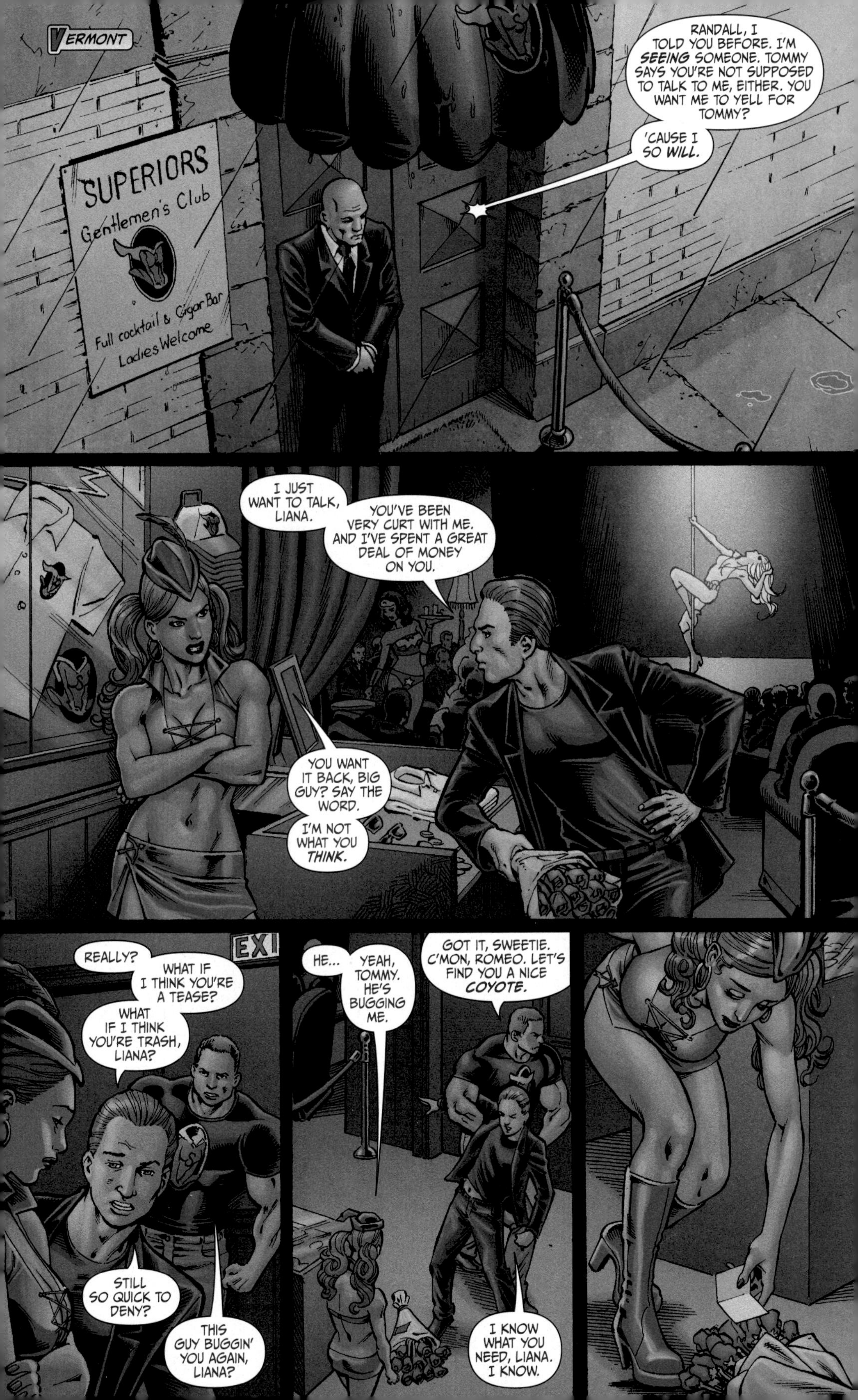
VERMONT
SUPERIORS
Gentlemen's Club
Full cocktail & Cigar Bar
Ladies Welcome
RANDALL, I TOLD YOU BEFORE. I'M SEEING SOMEONE. TOMMY SAYS YOU'RE NOT SUPPOSED TO TALK TO ME, EITHER. YOU WANT ME TO YELL FOR TOMMY?
'CAUSE I SO WILL.
I JUST WANT TO TALK, LIANA.
YOU'VE BEEN VERY CURT WITH ME. AND I'VE SPENT A GREAT DEAL OF MONEY ON YOU.
YOU WANT IT BACK, BIG GUY? SAY THE WORD.
I'M NOT WHAT YOU THINK.
EXI
REALLY?
WHAT IF I THINK YOU'RE A TEASE?
WHAT IF I THINK YOU'RE TRASH, LIANA?
STILL SO QUICK TO DENY?
THIS GUY BUGGIN' YOU AGAIN, LIANA?
HE...
YEAH, TOMMY. HE'S BUGGING ME.
GOT IT, SWEETIE. C'MON, ROMEO. LET'S FIND YOU A NICE COYOTE.
I KNOW WHAT YOU NEED, LIANA. I KNOW.

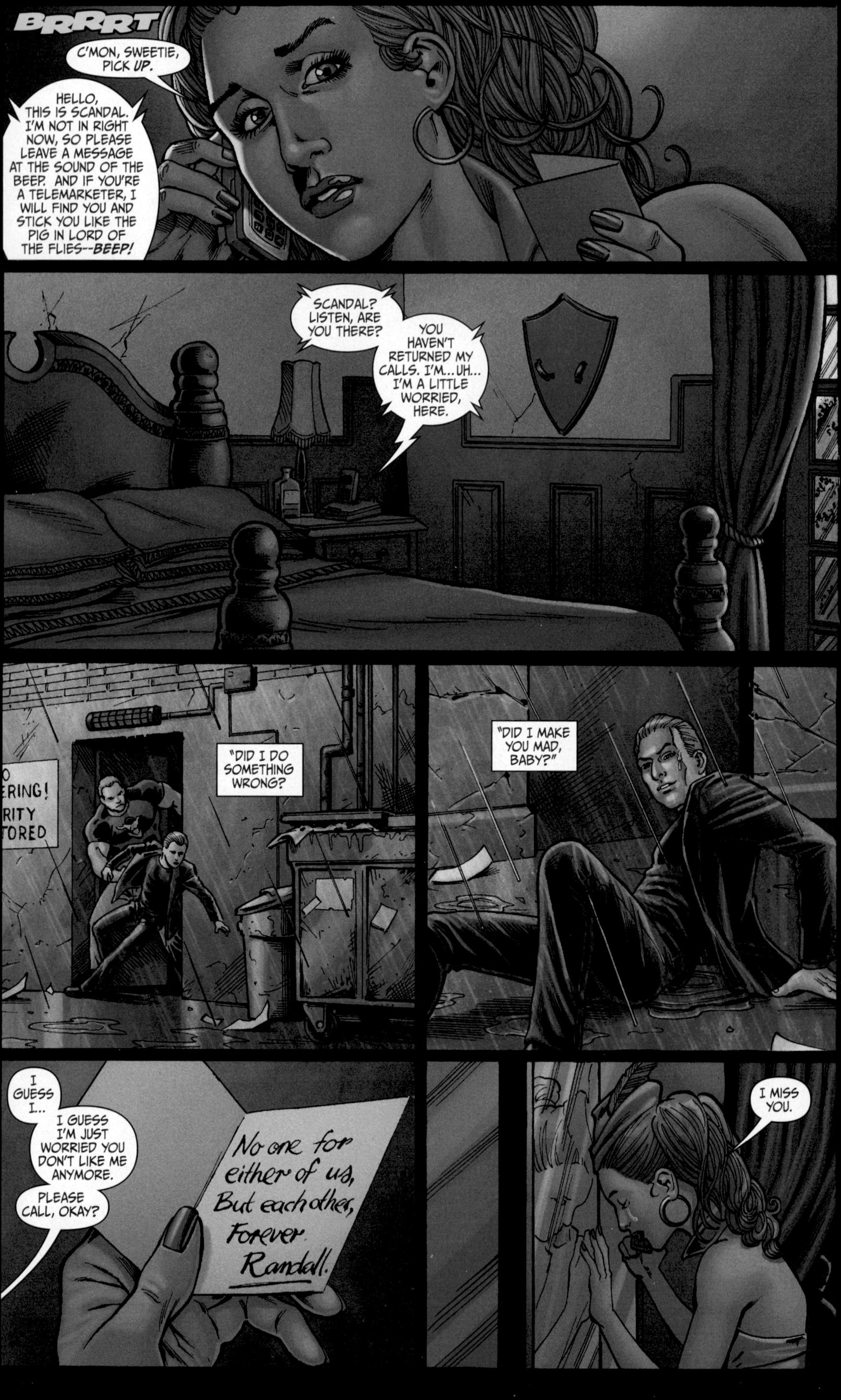
BRRRT
C'MON, SWEETIE, PICK UP.
HELLO, THIS IS SCANDAL. I'M NOT IN RIGHT NOW, SO PLEASE LEAVE A MESSAGE AT THE SOUND OF THE BEEP. AND IF YOU'RE A TELEMARKETER, I WILL FIND YOU AND STICK YOU LIKE THE PIG IN LORD OF THE FLIES--BEEP!
SCANDAL? LISTEN, ARE YOU THERE?
YOU HAVEN'T RETURNED MY CALLS. I'M...UH... I'M A LITTLE WORRIED, HERE.
"DID I DO SOMETHING WRONG?
"DID I MAKE YOU MAD, BABY?"
I GUESS I...
I GUESS I'M JUST WORRIED YOU DON'T LIKE ME ANYMORE.
PLEASE CALL, OKAY?
No one for either of us, But each other, Forever. Randall.
I MISS YOU.

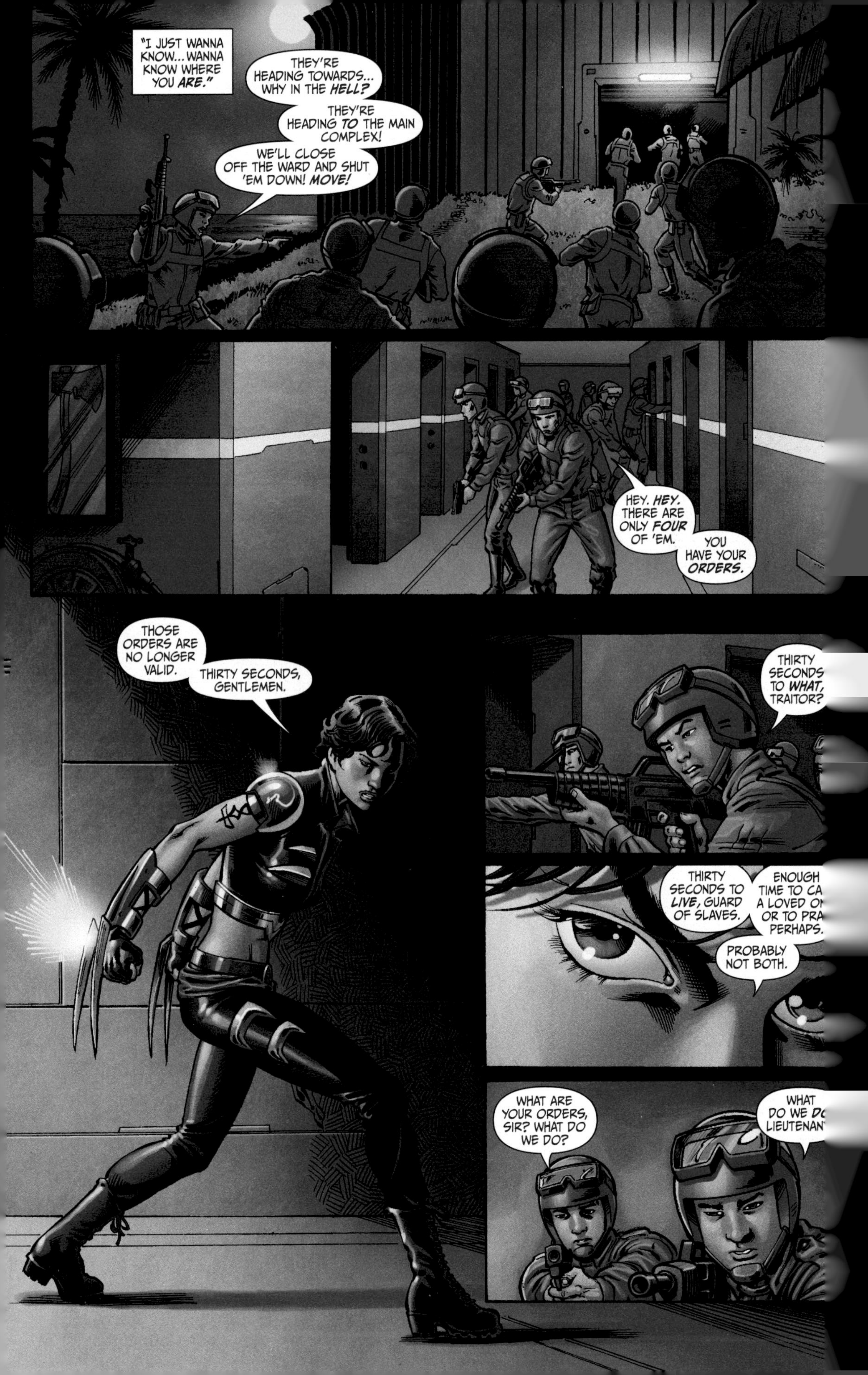

"I JUST WANNA KNOW... WANNA KNOW WHERE YOU *ARE.*"
THEY'RE HEADING TOWARDS... WHY IN THE *HELL?*
THEY'RE HEADING *TO* THE MAIN COMPLEX!
WE'LL CLOSE OFF THE WARD AND SHUT 'EM DOWN! *MOVE!*
HEY. *HEY.* THERE ARE ONLY *FOUR* OF 'EM.
YOU HAVE YOUR *ORDERS.*
THOSE ORDERS ARE NO LONGER VALID.
THIRTY SECONDS, GENTLEMEN.
THIRTY SECONDS TO *WHAT,* TRAITOR?
THIRTY SECONDS TO *LIVE,* GUARD OF SLAVES.
PROBABLY NOT BOTH.
WHAT ARE YOUR ORDERS, SIR? WHAT DO WE DO?

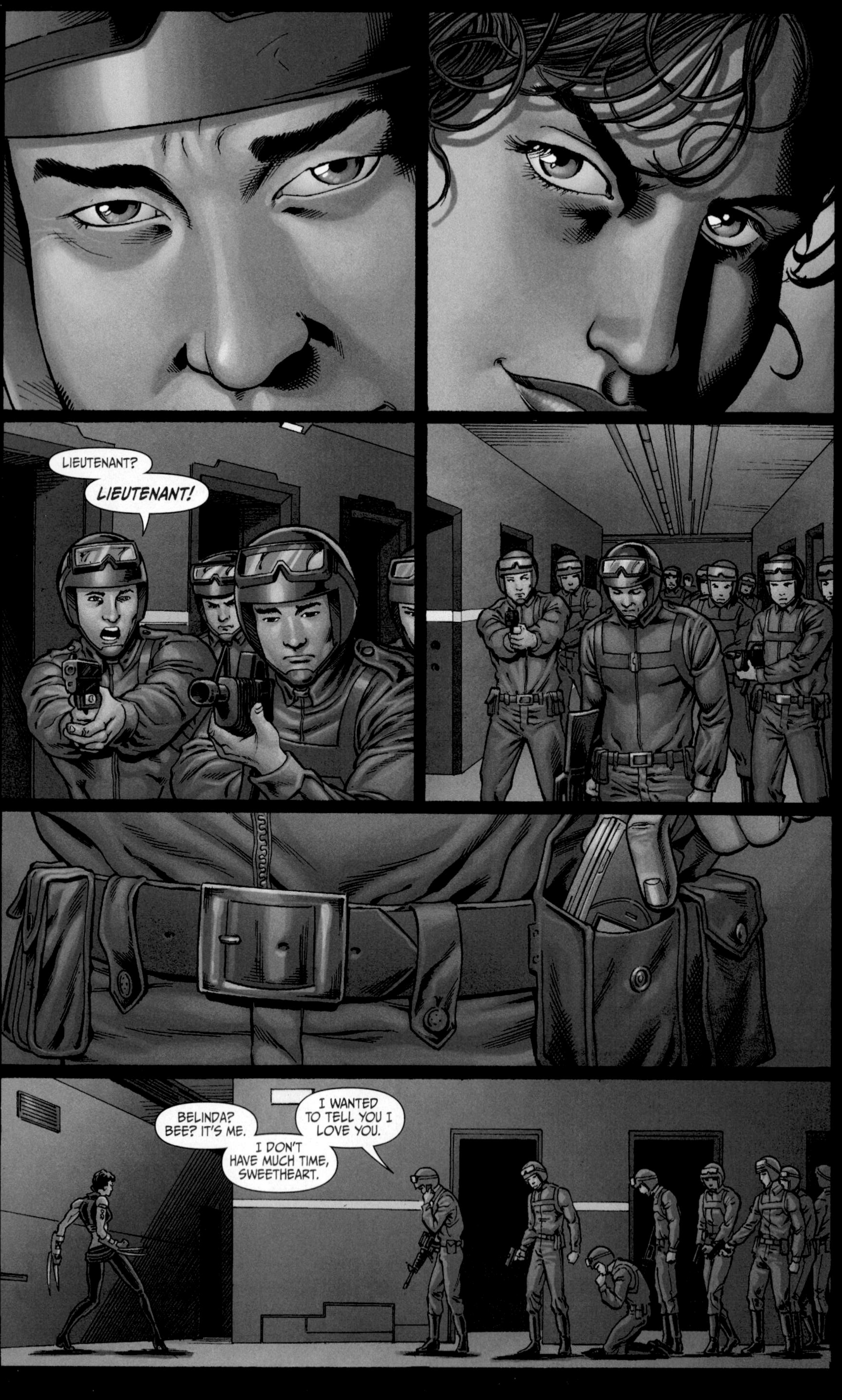

LIEUTENANT?
LIEUTENANT!
BELINDA? BEE? IT'S ME.
I DON'T HAVE MUCH TIME, SWEETHEART.
I WANTED TO TELL YOU I LOVE YOU.

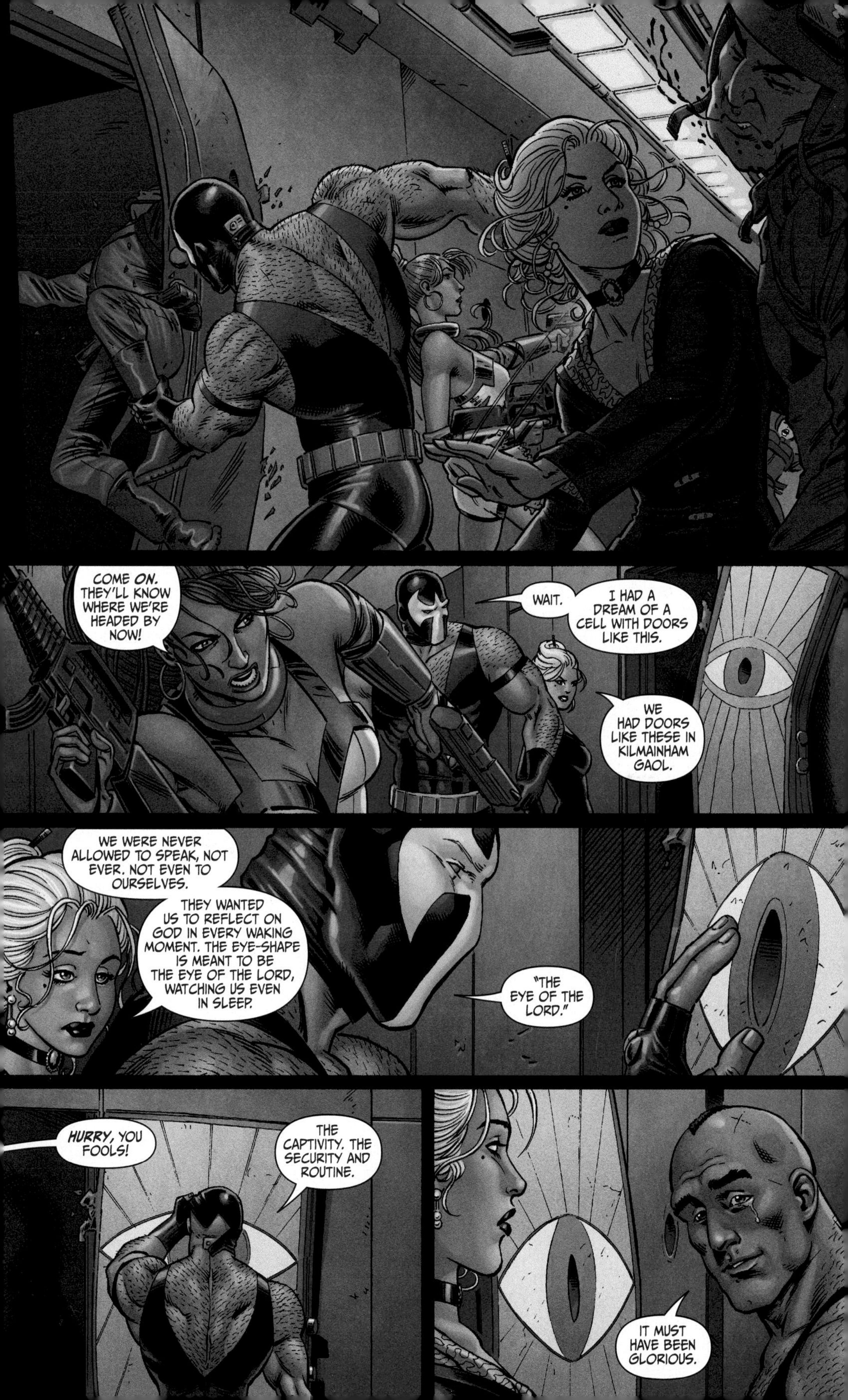
COME *ON*. THEY'LL KNOW WHERE WE'RE HEADED BY NOW!
WAIT.
I HAD A DREAM OF A CELL WITH DOORS LIKE THIS.
WE HAD DOORS LIKE THESE IN KILMAINHAM GAOL.
WE WERE NEVER ALLOWED TO SPEAK, NOT EVER. NOT EVEN TO OURSELVES.
THEY WANTED US TO REFLECT ON GOD IN EVERY WAKING MOMENT. THE EYE-SHAPE IS MEANT TO BE THE EYE OF THE LORD, WATCHING US EVEN IN SLEEP.
"THE EYE OF THE LORD."
HURRY, YOU FOOLS!
THE CAPTIVITY. THE SECURITY AND ROUTINE.
IT MUST HAVE BEEN GLORIOUS.

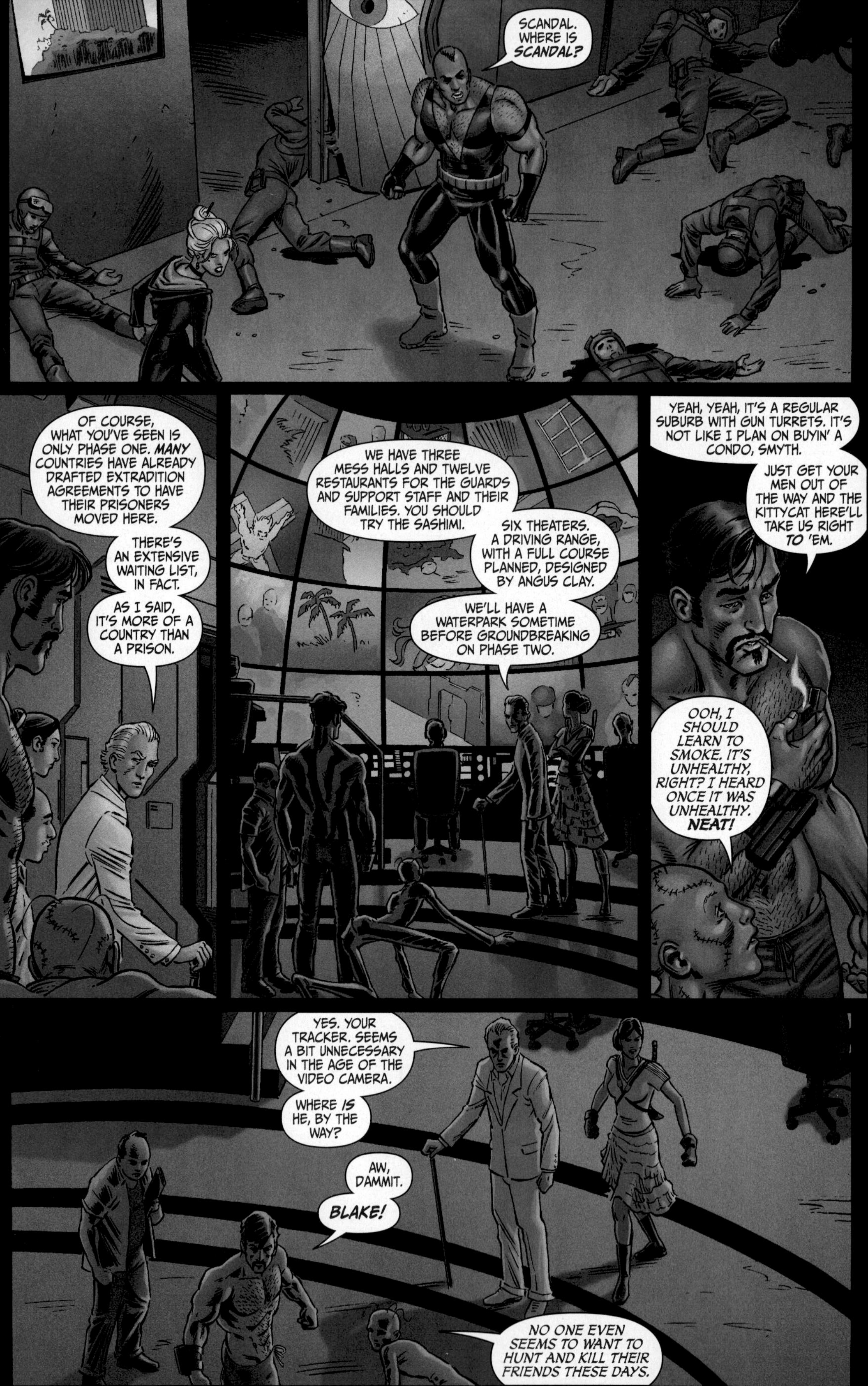
SCANDAL. WHERE IS SCANDAL?
OF COURSE, WHAT YOU'VE SEEN IS ONLY PHASE ONE. MANY COUNTRIES HAVE ALREADY DRAFTED EXTRADITION AGREEMENTS TO HAVE THEIR PRISONERS MOVED HERE.
THERE'S AN EXTENSIVE WAITING LIST, IN FACT.
AS I SAID, IT'S MORE OF A COUNTRY THAN A PRISON.
WE HAVE THREE MESS HALLS AND TWELVE RESTAURANTS FOR THE GUARDS AND SUPPORT STAFF AND THEIR FAMILIES. YOU SHOULD TRY THE SASHIMI.
SIX THEATERS. A DRIVING RANGE, WITH A FULL COURSE PLANNED, DESIGNED BY ANGUS CLAY.
WE'LL HAVE A WATERPARK SOMETIME BEFORE GROUNDBREAKING ON PHASE TWO.
YEAH, YEAH, IT'S A REGULAR SUBURB WITH GUN TURRETS. IT'S NOT LIKE I PLAN ON BUYIN' A CONDO, SMYTH.
JUST GET YOUR MEN OUT OF THE WAY AND THE KITTYCAT HERE'LL TAKE US RIGHT TO 'EM.
OOH, I SHOULD LEARN TO SMOKE. IT'S UNHEALTHY, RIGHT? I HEARD ONCE IT WAS UNHEALTHY. NEAT!
YES. YOUR TRACKER. SEEMS A BIT UNNECESSARY IN THE AGE OF THE VIDEO CAMERA.
WHERE IS HE, BY THE WAY?
AW, DAMMIT.
BLAKE!
NO ONE EVEN SEEMS TO WANT TO HUNT AND KILL THEIR FRIENDS THESE DAYS.

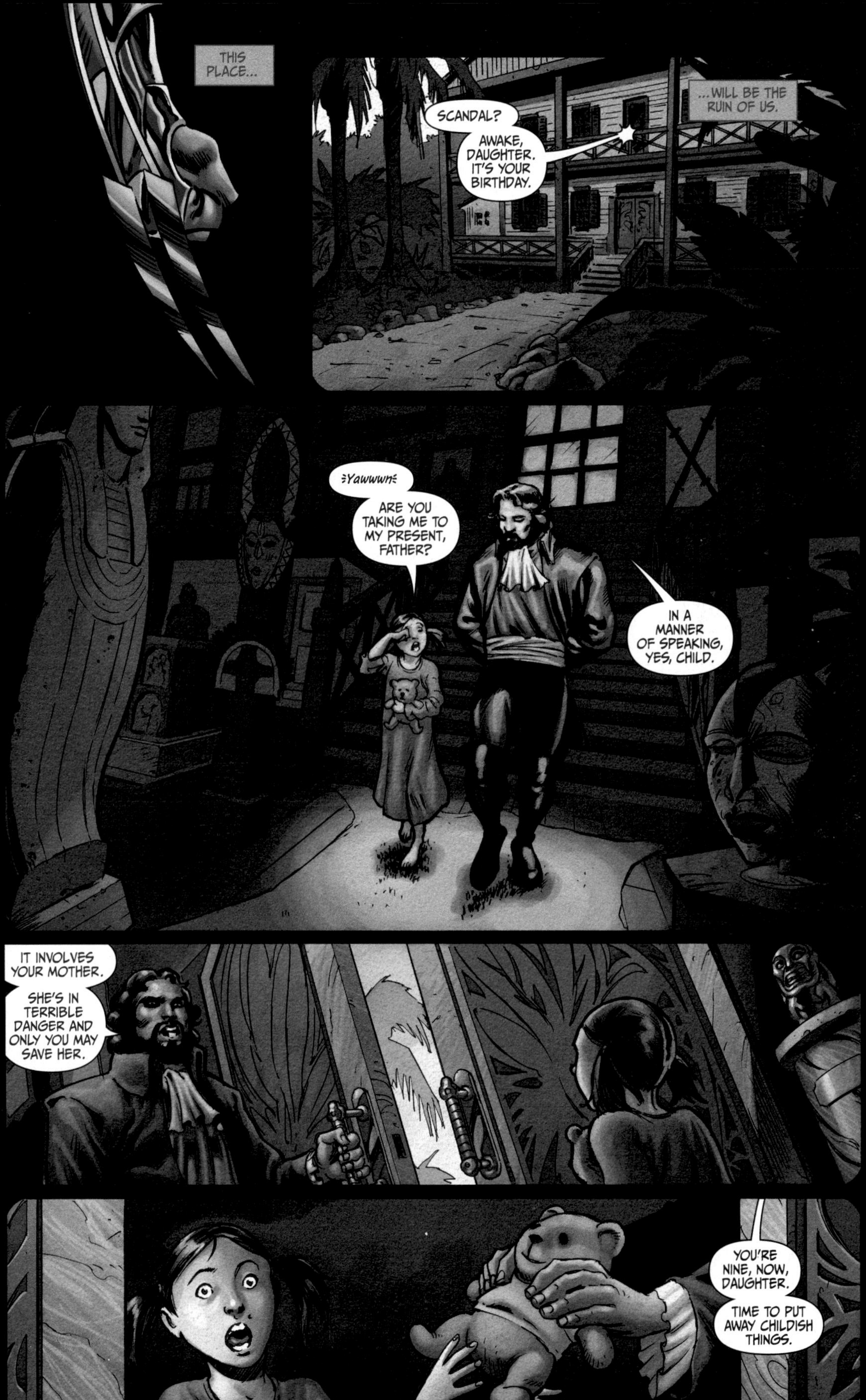
THIS PLACE...
SCANDAL?
AWAKE, DAUGHTER. IT'S YOUR BIRTHDAY.
...WILL BE THE RUIN OF US.
Yawwwn
ARE YOU TAKING ME TO MY PRESENT, FATHER?
IN A MANNER OF SPEAKING, YES, CHILD.
IT INVOLVES YOUR MOTHER.
SHE'S IN TERRIBLE DANGER AND ONLY YOU MAY SAVE HER.
YOU'RE NINE, NOW, DAUGHTER.
TIME TO PUT AWAY CHILDISH THINGS.

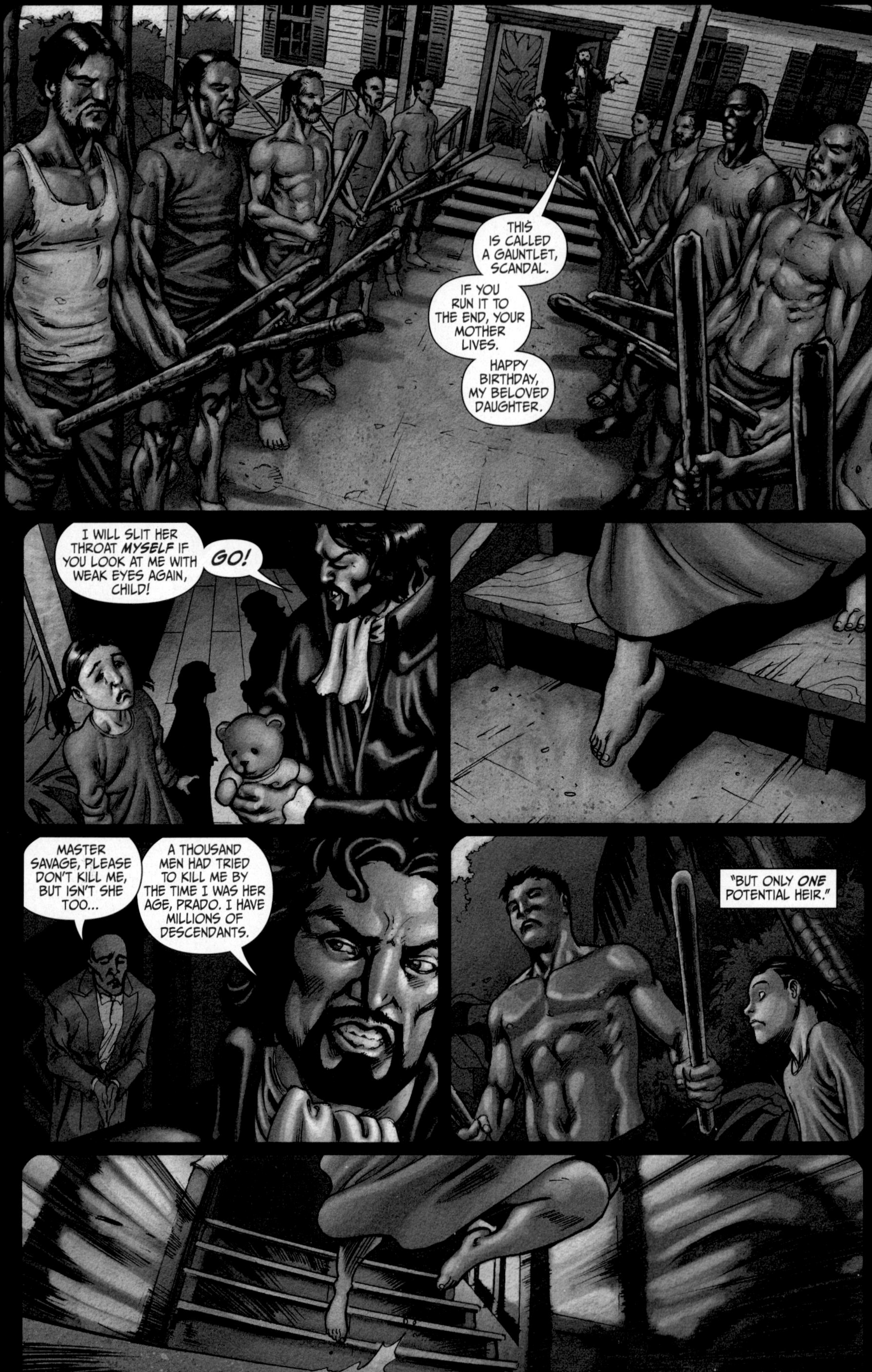
THIS IS CALLED A GAUNTLET, SCANDAL.
IF YOU RUN IT TO THE END, YOUR MOTHER LIVES.
HAPPY BIRTHDAY, MY BELOVED DAUGHTER.
I WILL SLIT HER THROAT MYSELF IF YOU LOOK AT ME WITH WEAK EYES AGAIN, CHILD!
GO!
MASTER SAVAGE, PLEASE DON'T KILL ME, BUT ISN'T SHE TOO...
A THOUSAND MEN HAD TRIED TO KILL ME BY THE TIME I WAS HER AGE, PRADO. I HAVE MILLIONS OF DESCENDANTS.
"BUT ONLY ONE POTENTIAL HEIR."

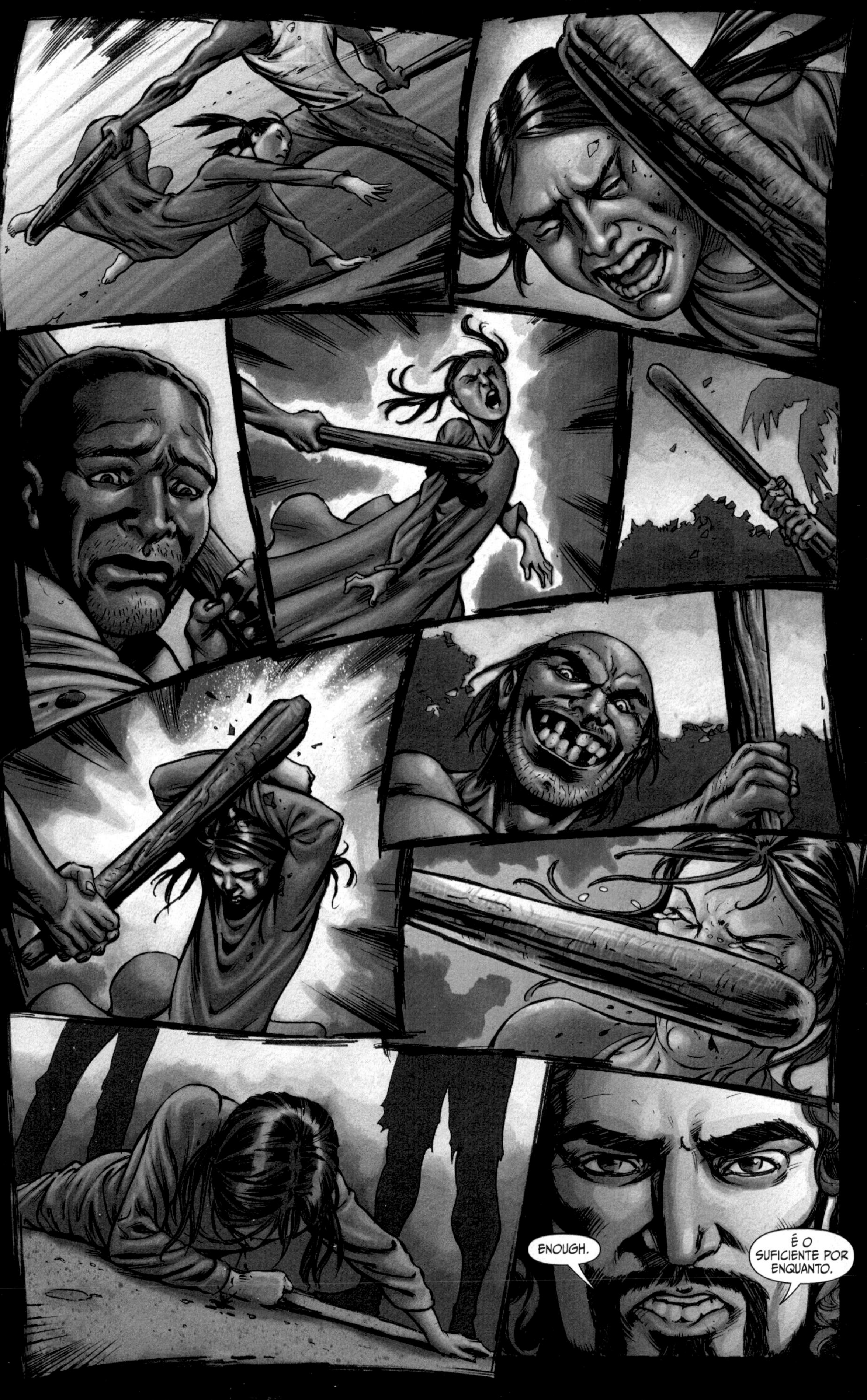
ENOUGH.
É O SUFICIENTE POR ENQUANTO.

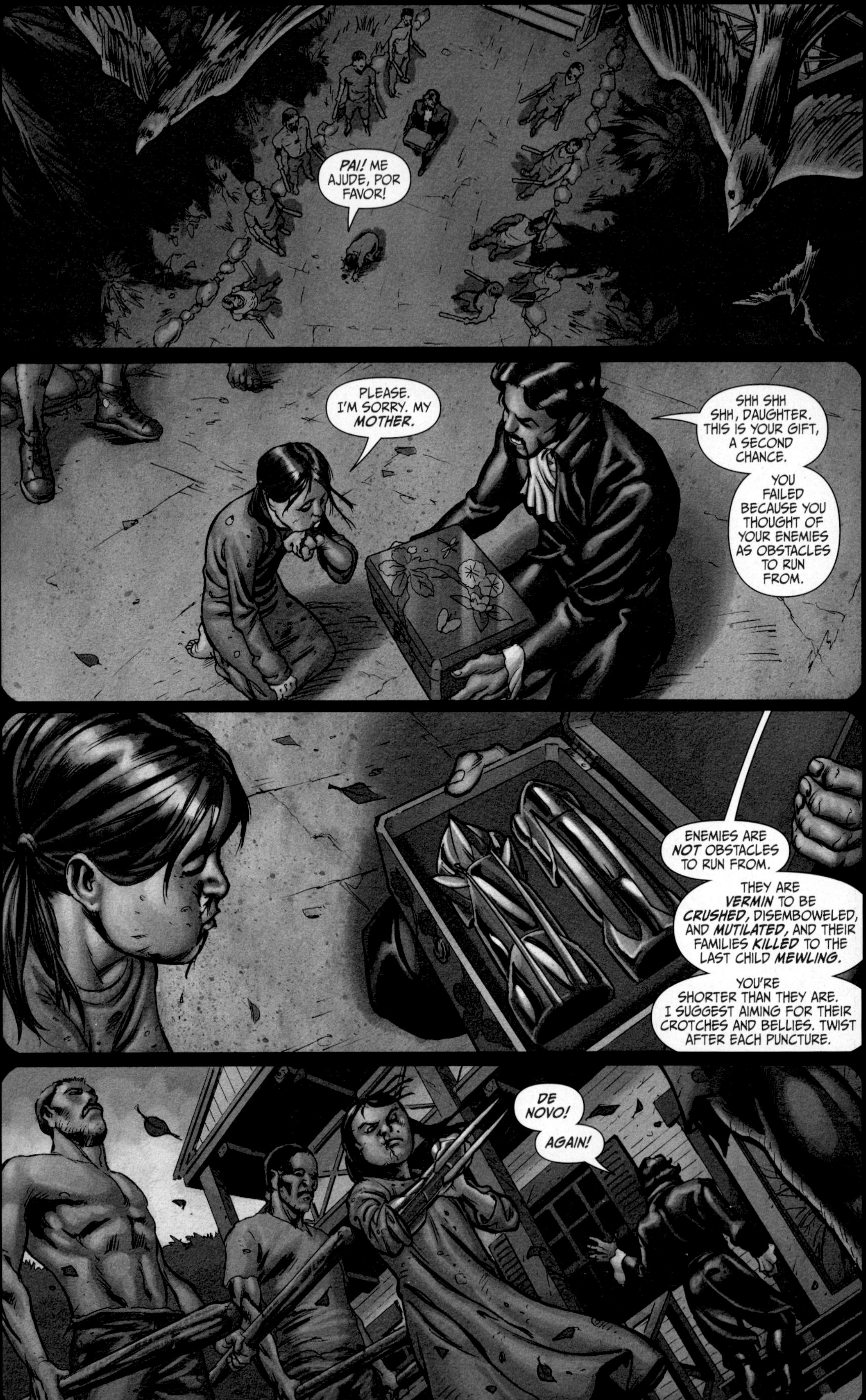
PAI! ME AJUDE, POR FAVOR!
PLEASE. I'M SORRY. MY MOTHER.
SHH SHH SHH, DAUGHTER. THIS IS YOUR GIFT, A SECOND CHANCE.
YOU FAILED BECAUSE YOU THOUGHT OF YOUR ENEMIES AS OBSTACLES TO RUN FROM.
ENEMIES ARE NOT OBSTACLES TO RUN FROM.
THEY ARE VERMIN TO BE CRUSHED, DISEMBOWELED, AND MUTILATED, AND THEIR FAMILIES KILLED TO THE LAST CHILD MEWLING.
YOU'RE SHORTER THAN THEY ARE. I SUGGEST AIMING FOR THEIR CROTCHES AND BELLIES. TWIST AFTER EACH PUNCTURE.
DE NOVO!
AGAIN!

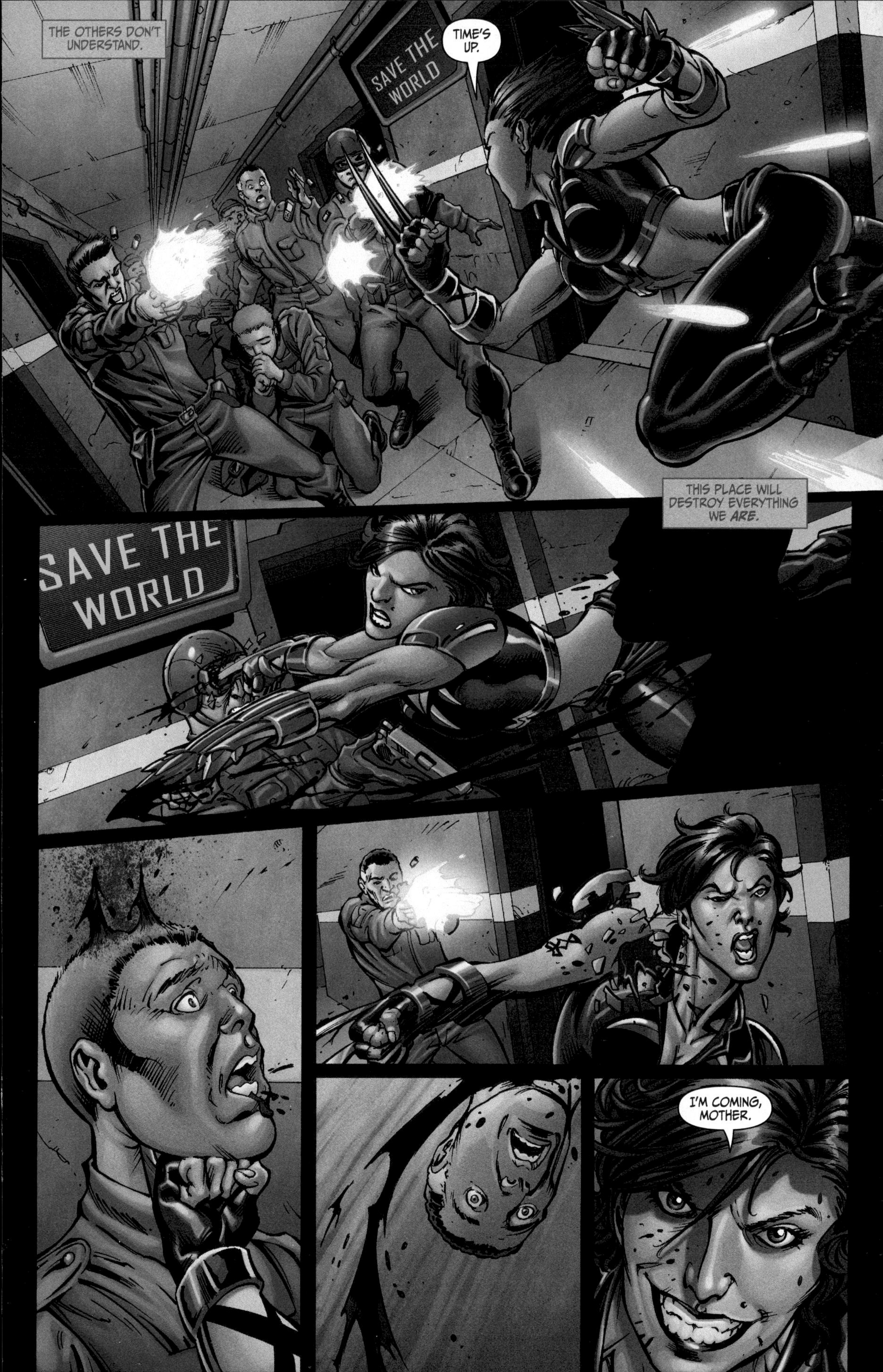
THE OTHERS DON'T UNDERSTAND.
TIME'S UP.
SAVE THE WORLD
THIS PLACE WILL DESTROY EVERYTHING WE *ARE.*
SAVE THE WORLD
I'M COMING, MOTHER.

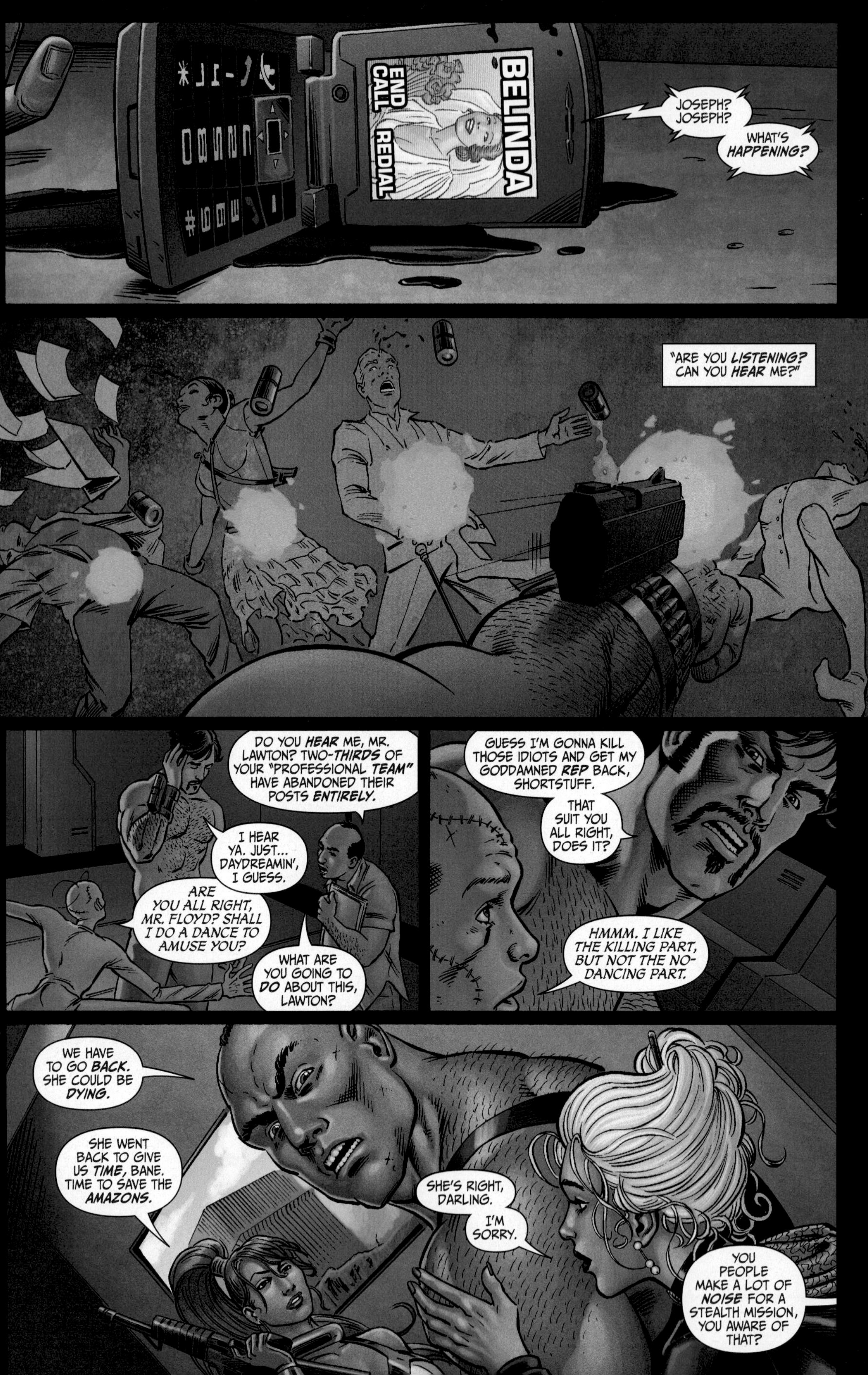
BELINDA
END CALL
REDIAL
JOSEPH? JOSEPH?
WHAT'S HAPPENING?
"ARE YOU LISTENING? CAN YOU HEAR ME?"
DO YOU HEAR ME, MR. LAWTON? TWO-THIRDS OF YOUR "PROFESSIONAL TEAM" HAVE ABANDONED THEIR POSTS ENTIRELY.
I HEAR YA. JUST... DAYDREAMIN', I GUESS.
ARE YOU ALL RIGHT, MR. FLOYD? SHALL I DO A DANCE TO AMUSE YOU?
WHAT ARE YOU GOING TO DO ABOUT THIS, LAWTON?
GUESS I'M GONNA KILL THOSE IDIOTS AND GET MY GODDAMNED REP BACK, SHORTSTUFF.
THAT SUIT YOU ALL RIGHT, DOES IT?
HMMM. I LIKE THE KILLING PART, BUT NOT THE NO-DANCING PART.
WE HAVE TO GO BACK. SHE COULD BE DYING.
SHE WENT BACK TO GIVE US TIME, BANE. TIME TO SAVE THE AMAZONS.
SHE'S RIGHT, DARLING.
I'M SORRY.
YOU PEOPLE MAKE A LOT OF NOISE FOR A STEALTH MISSION, YOU AWARE OF THAT?

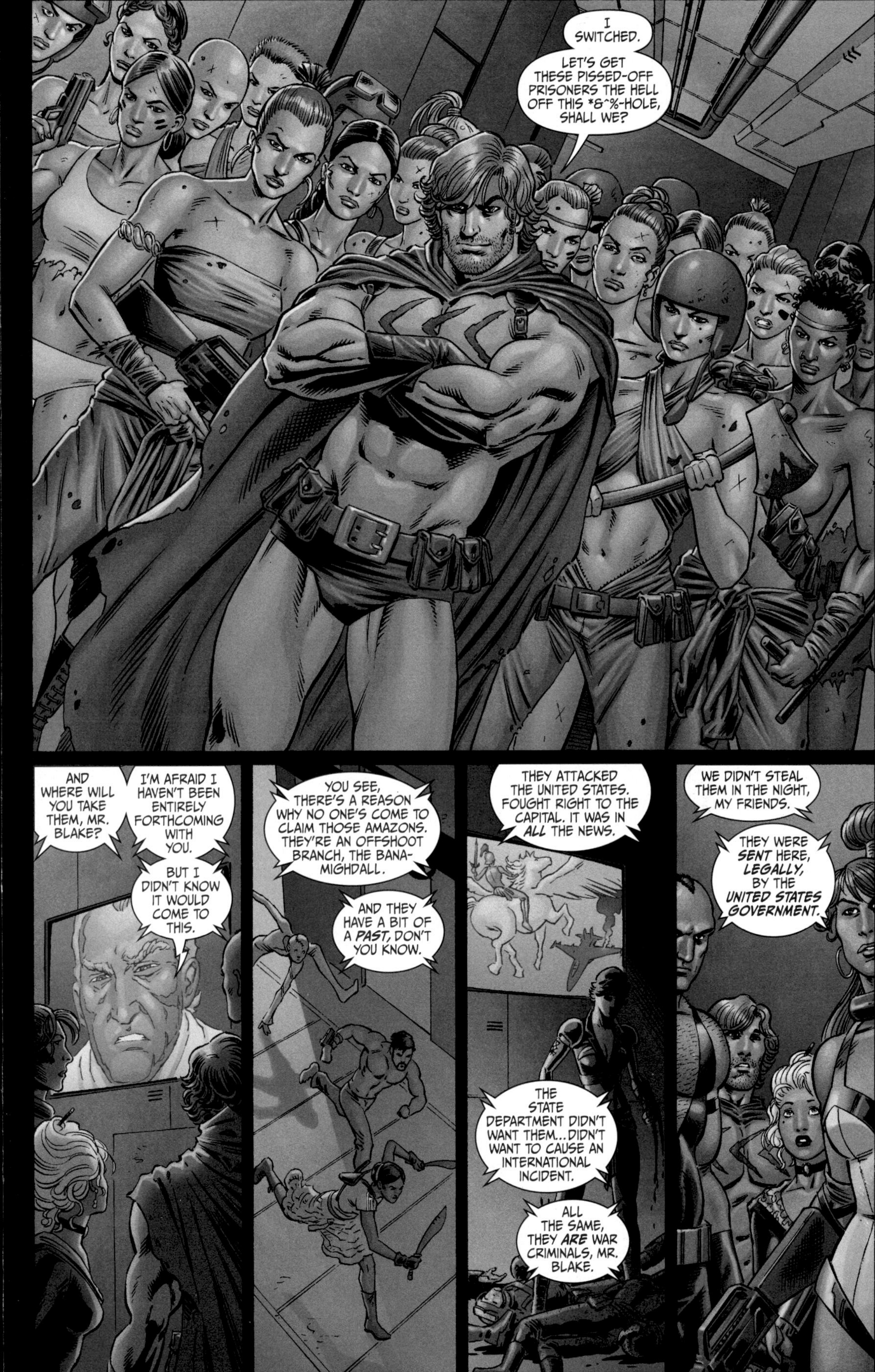
I SWITCHED.
LET'S GET THESE PISSED-OFF PRISONERS THE HELL OFF THIS *&^%-HOLE, SHALL WE?
AND WHERE WILL YOU TAKE THEM, MR. BLAKE?
I'M AFRAID I HAVEN'T BEEN ENTIRELY FORTHCOMING WITH YOU.
BUT I DIDN'T KNOW IT WOULD COME TO THIS.
YOU SEE, THERE'S A REASON WHY NO ONE'S COME TO CLAIM THOSE AMAZONS. THEY'RE AN OFFSHOOT BRANCH, THE BANA-MIGHDALL.
AND THEY HAVE A BIT OF A PAST, DON'T YOU KNOW.
THEY ATTACKED THE UNITED STATES. FOUGHT RIGHT TO THE CAPITAL. IT WAS IN ALL THE NEWS.
THE STATE DEPARTMENT DIDN'T WANT THEM...DIDN'T WANT TO CAUSE AN INTERNATIONAL INCIDENT.
ALL THE SAME, THEY ARE WAR CRIMINALS, MR. BLAKE.
WE DIDN'T STEAL THEM IN THE NIGHT, MY FRIENDS.
THEY WERE SENT HERE, LEGALLY, BY THE UNITED STATES GOVERNMENT.

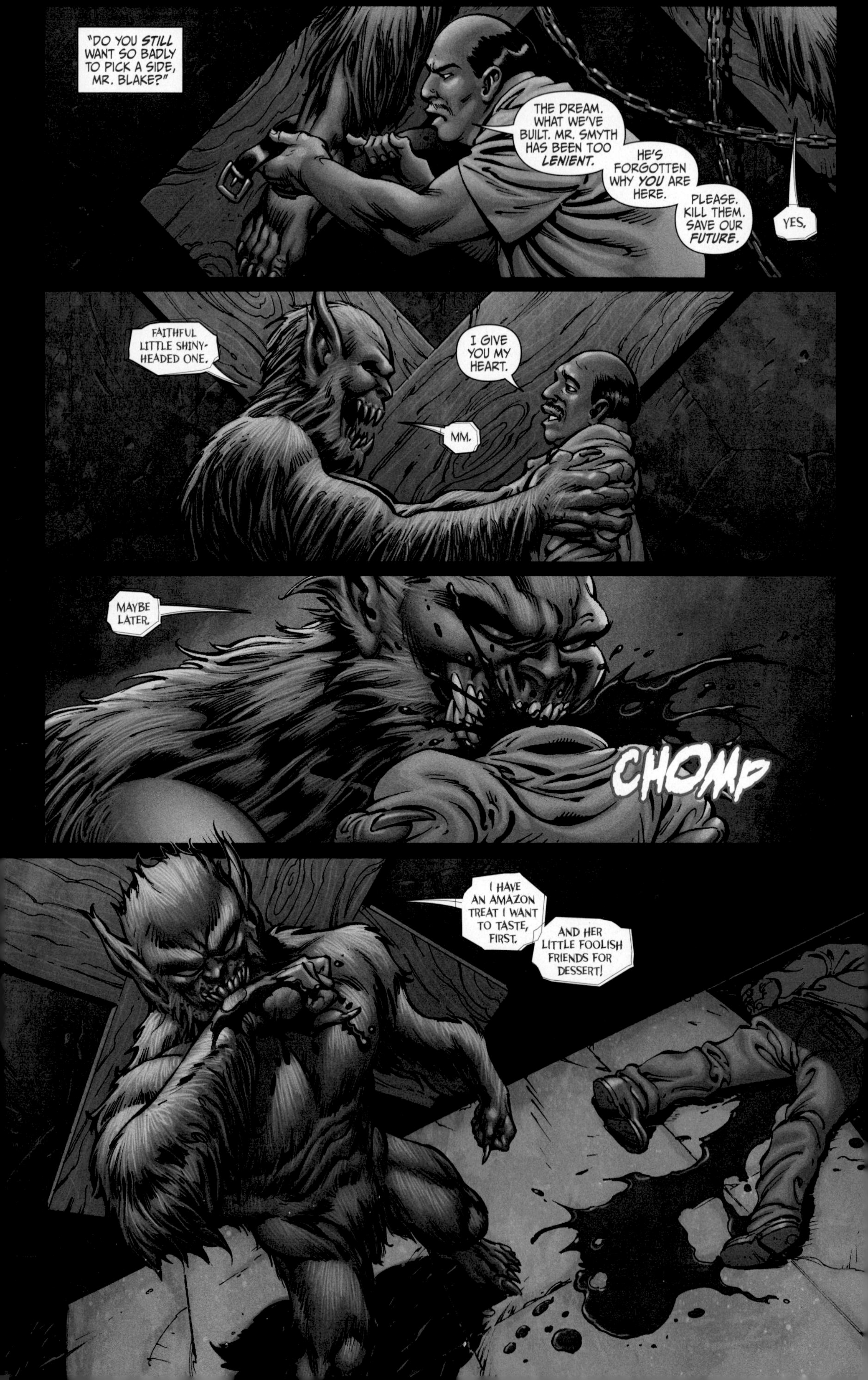
"DO YOU STILL WANT SO BADLY TO PICK A SIDE, MR. BLAKE?"
THE DREAM. WHAT WE'VE BUILT. MR. SMYTH HAS BEEN TOO LENIENT.
HE'S FORGOTTEN WHY YOU ARE HERE.
PLEASE. KILL THEM. SAVE OUR FUTURE.
YES,
FAITHFUL LITTLE SHINY-HEADED ONE.
I GIVE YOU MY HEART.
MM.
MAYBE LATER.
CHOMP
I HAVE AN AMAZON TREAT I WANT TO TASTE, FIRST.
AND HER LITTLE FOOLISH FRIENDS FOR DESSERT!

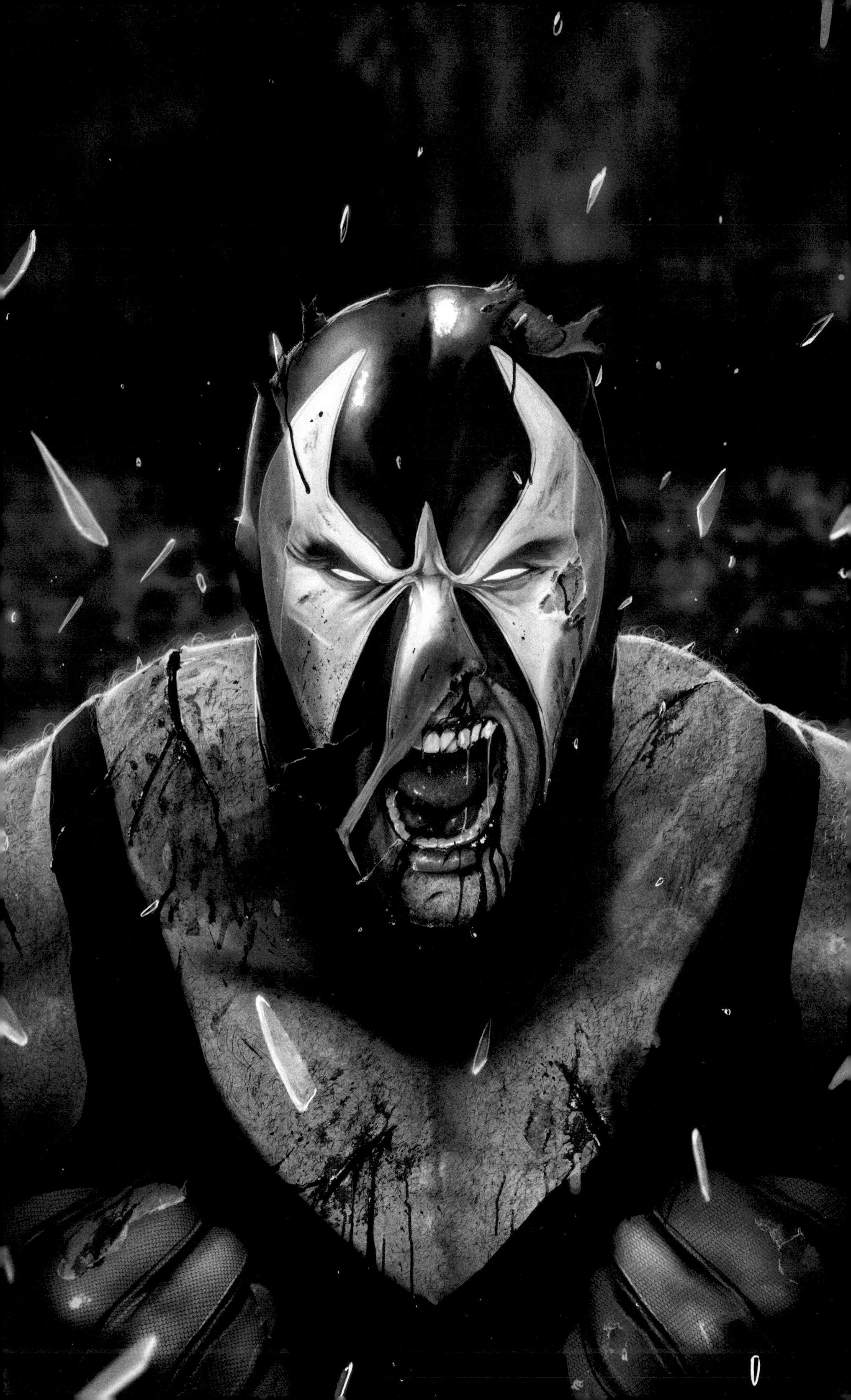

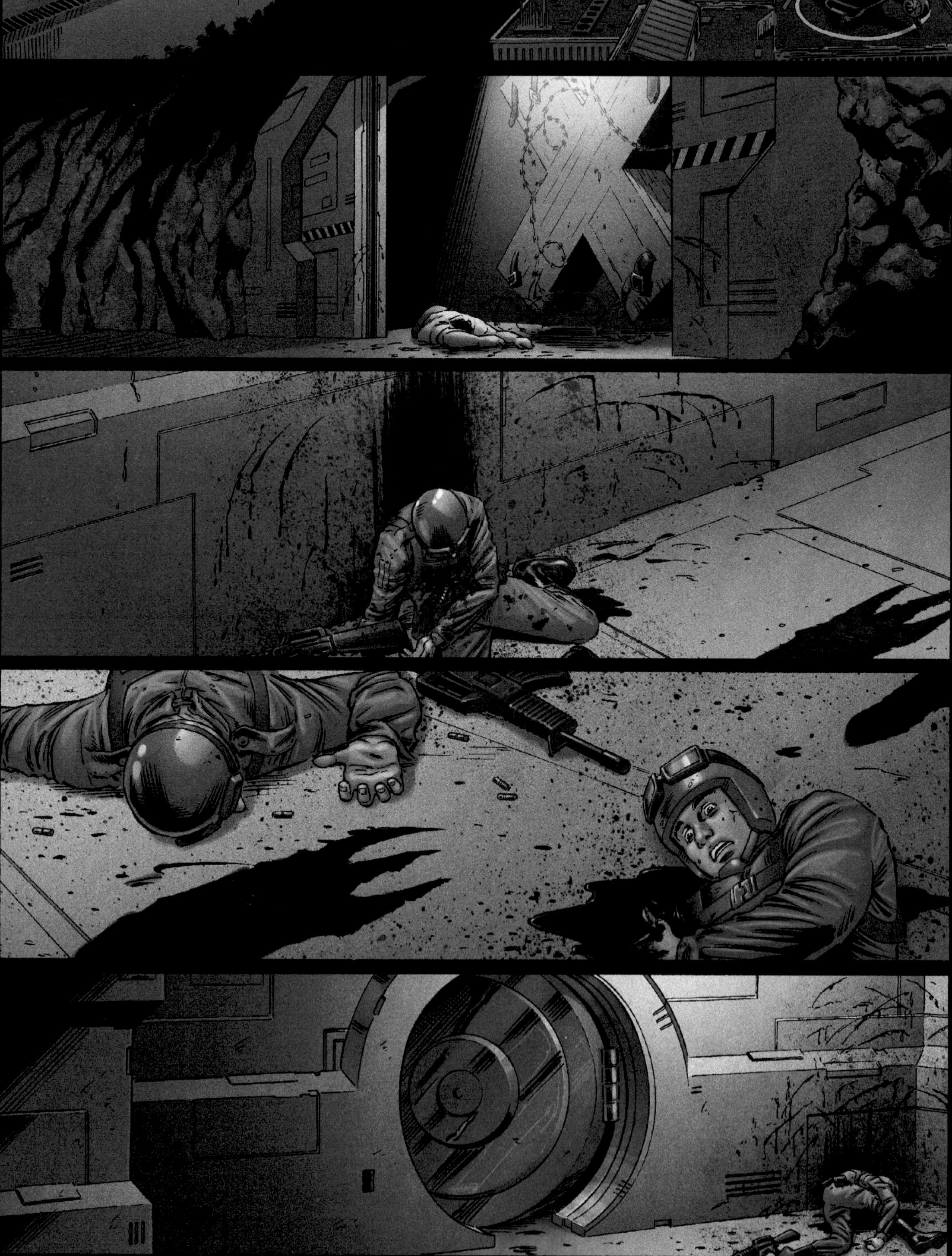

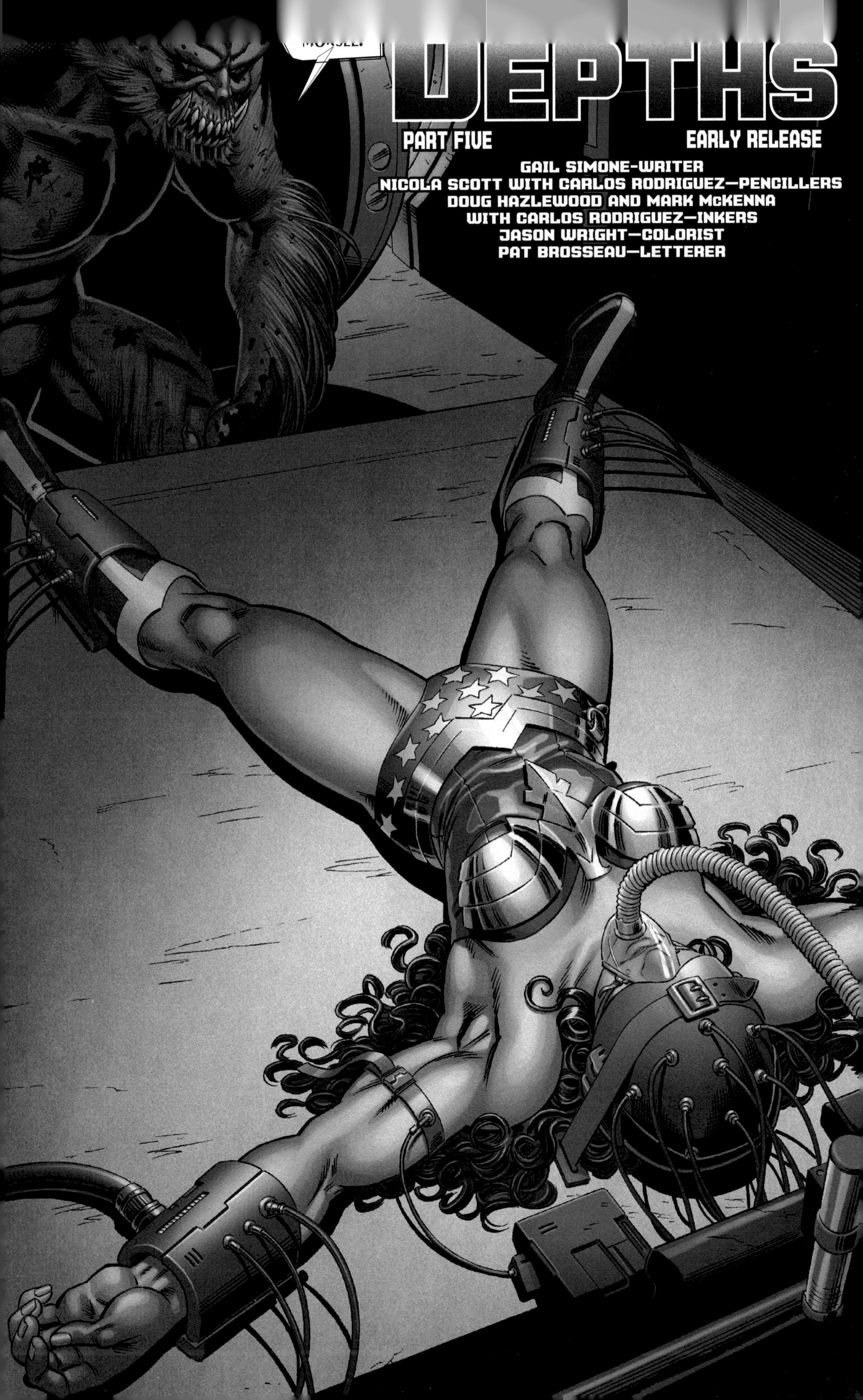
DEPTHS
PART FIVE
EARLY RELEASE
GAIL SIMONE-WRITER
NICOLA SCOTT WITH CARLOS RODRIGUEZ—PENCILLERS
DOUG HAZLEWOOD AND MARK McKENNA
WITH CARLOS RODRIGUEZ—INKERS
JASON WRIGHT—COLORIST
PAT BROSSEAU—LETTERER

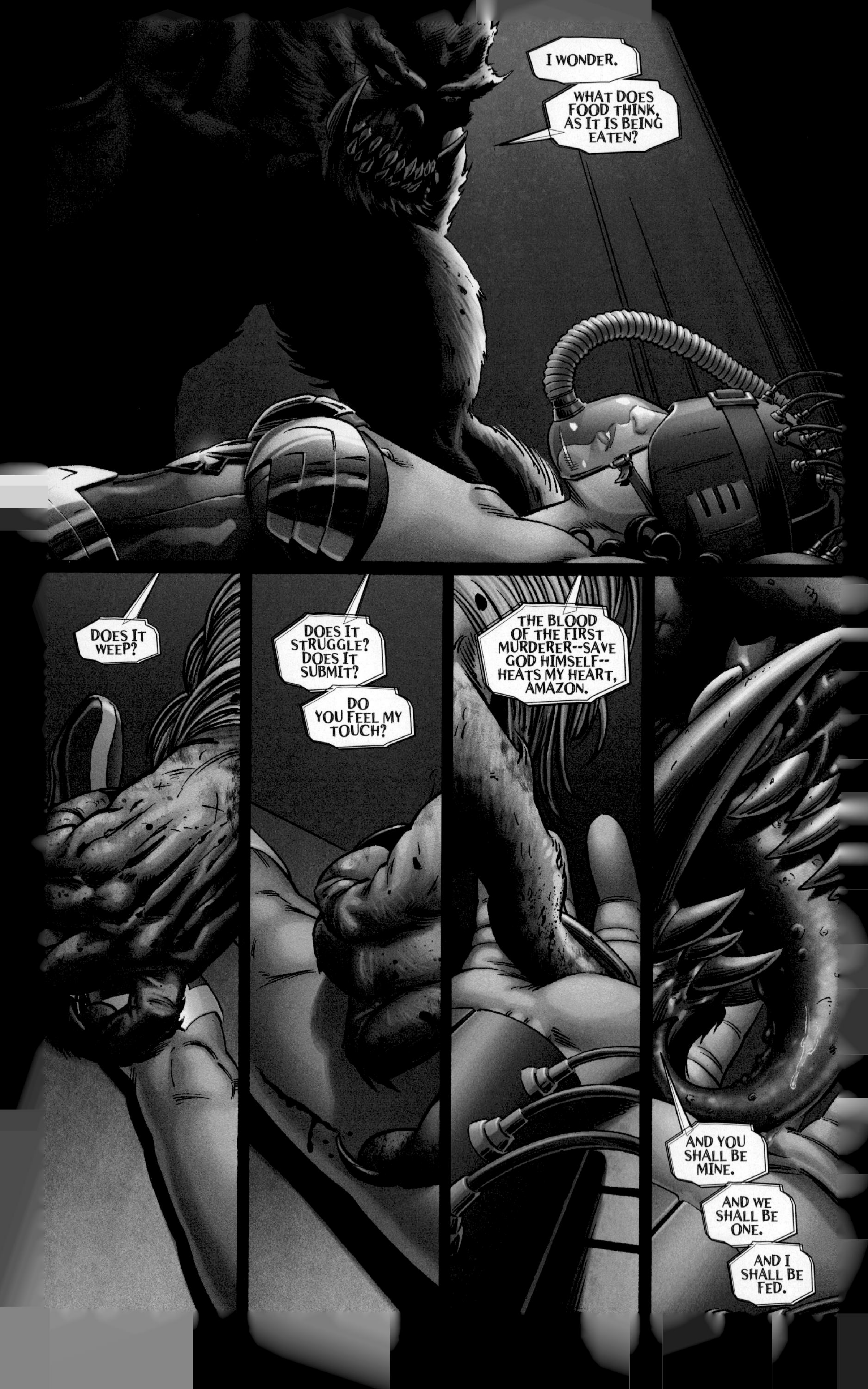
I WONDER.
WHAT DOES FOOD THINK, AS IT IS BEING EATEN?
DOES IT WEEP?
DOES IT STRUGGLE? DOES IT SUBMIT?
DO YOU FEEL MY TOUCH?
THE BLOOD OF THE FIRST MURDERER--SAVE GOD HIMSELF--HEATS MY HEART, AMAZON.
AND YOU SHALL BE MINE.
AND WE SHALL BE ONE.
AND I SHALL BE FED.

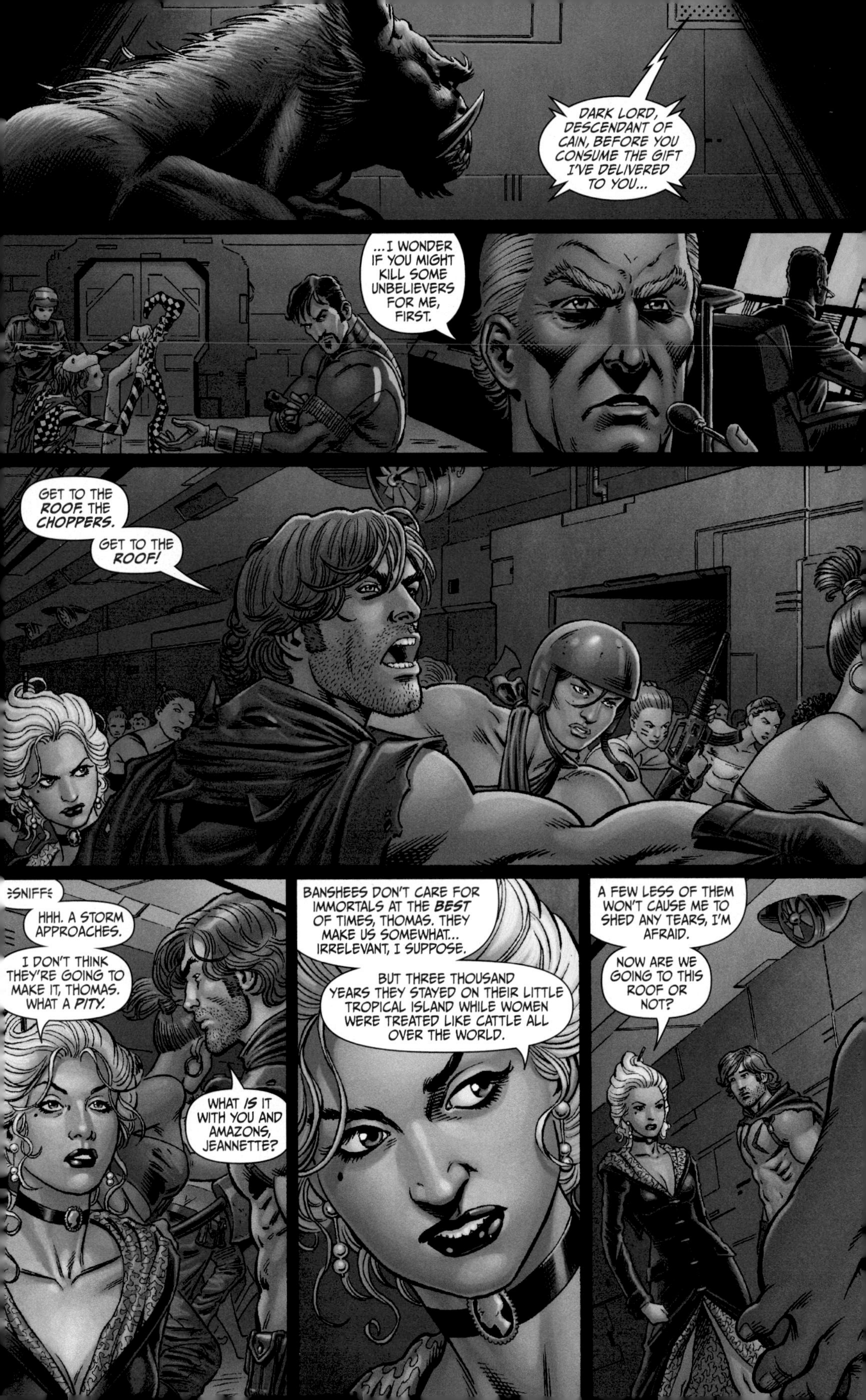
DARK LORD, DESCENDANT OF CAIN, BEFORE YOU CONSUME THE GIFT I'VE DELIVERED TO YOU...
...I WONDER IF YOU MIGHT KILL SOME UNBELIEVERS FOR ME, FIRST.
GET TO THE ROOF. THE CHOPPERS.
GET TO THE ROOF!
SNIFF
HHH. A STORM APPROACHES.
I DON'T THINK THEY'RE GOING TO MAKE IT, THOMAS. WHAT A PITY.
WHAT IS IT WITH YOU AND AMAZONS, JEANNETTE?
BANSHEES DON'T CARE FOR IMMORTALS AT THE BEST OF TIMES, THOMAS. THEY MAKE US SOMEWHAT... IRRELEVANT, I SUPPOSE.
BUT THREE THOUSAND YEARS THEY STAYED ON THEIR LITTLE TROPICAL ISLAND WHILE WOMEN WERE TREATED LIKE CATTLE ALL OVER THE WORLD.
A FEW LESS OF THEM WON'T CAUSE ME TO SHED ANY TEARS, I'M AFRAID.
NOW ARE WE GOING TO THIS ROOF OR NOT?

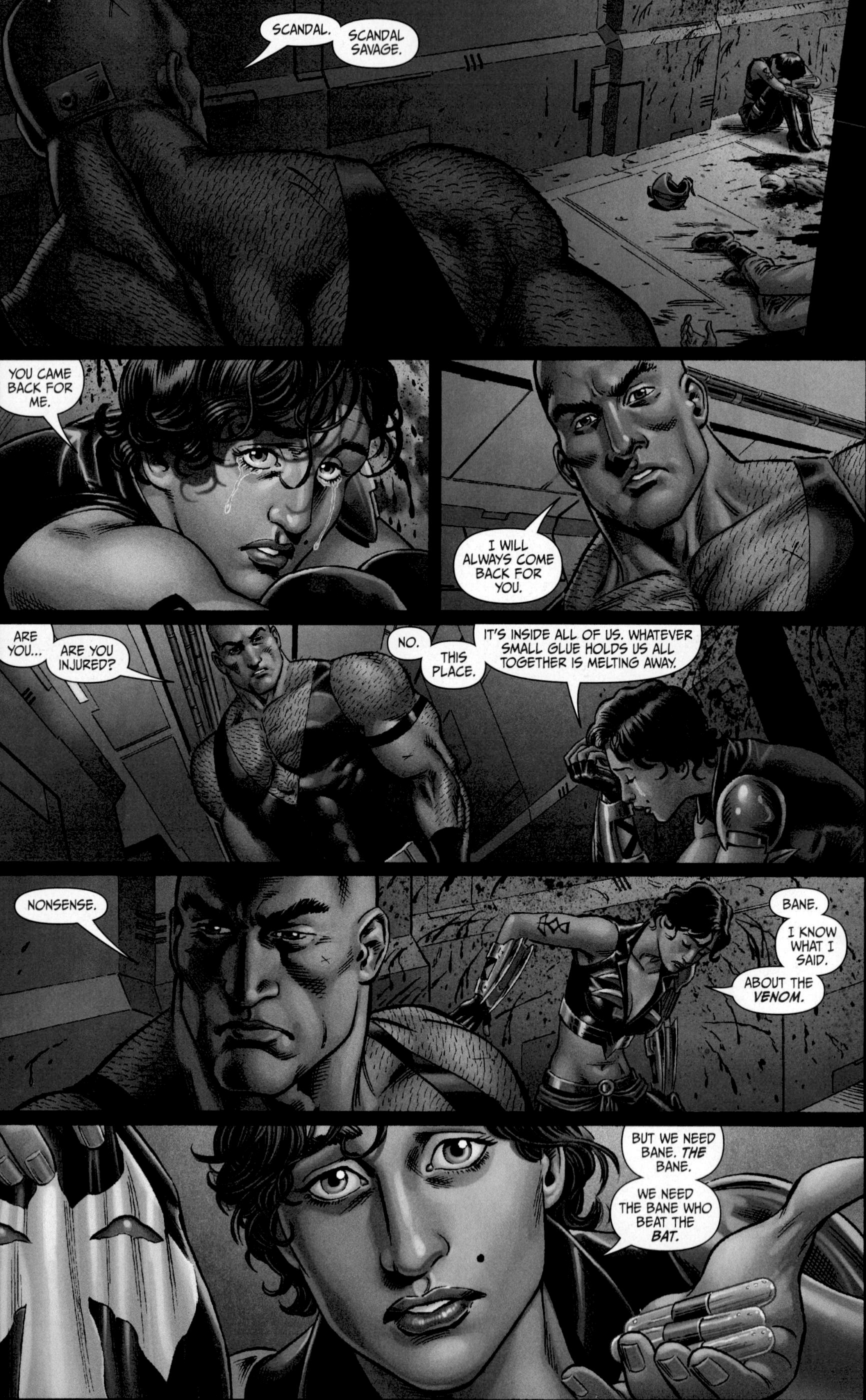
SCANDAL.
SCANDAL SAVAGE.
YOU CAME BACK FOR ME.
I WILL ALWAYS COME BACK FOR YOU.
ARE YOU...
ARE YOU INJURED?
NO.
THIS PLACE.
IT'S INSIDE ALL OF US. WHATEVER SMALL GLUE HOLDS US ALL TOGETHER IS MELTING AWAY.
NONSENSE.
BANE.
I KNOW WHAT I SAID.
ABOUT THE *VENOM.*
BUT WE NEED BANE. *THE* BANE.
WE NEED THE BANE WHO BEAT THE *BAT.*

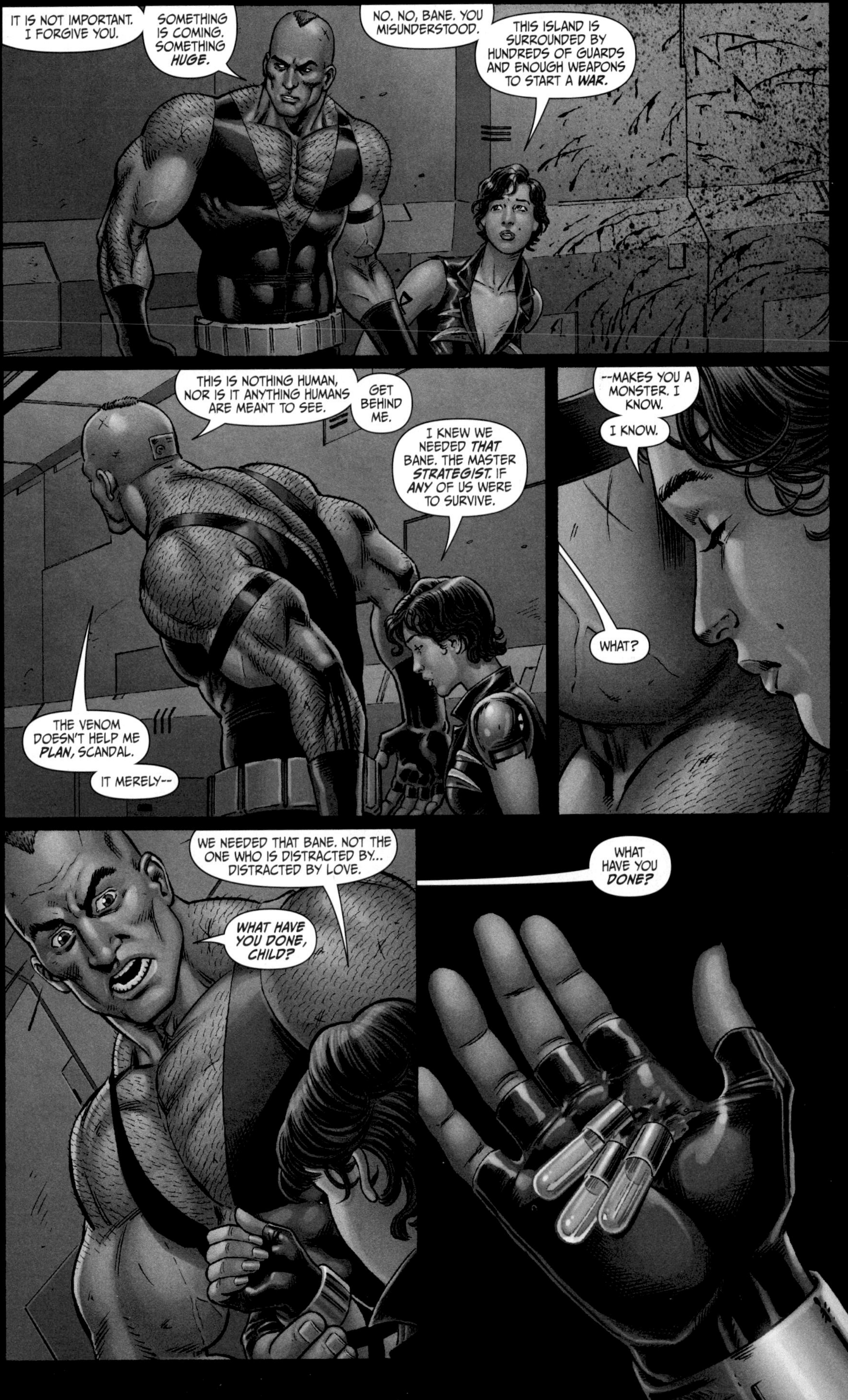
IT IS NOT IMPORTANT. I FORGIVE YOU.
SOMETHING IS COMING. SOMETHING HUGE.
NO. NO, BANE. YOU MISUNDERSTOOD.
THIS ISLAND IS SURROUNDED BY HUNDREDS OF GUARDS AND ENOUGH WEAPONS TO START A WAR.
THIS IS NOTHING HUMAN, NOR IS IT ANYTHING HUMANS ARE MEANT TO SEE.
GET BEHIND ME.
I KNEW WE NEEDED THAT BANE. THE MASTER STRATEGIST. IF ANY OF US WERE TO SURVIVE.
THE VENOM DOESN'T HELP ME PLAN, SCANDAL.
IT MERELY--
--MAKES YOU A MONSTER. I KNOW.
I KNOW.
WHAT?
WE NEEDED THAT BANE. NOT THE ONE WHO IS DISTRACTED BY... DISTRACTED BY LOVE.
WHAT HAVE YOU DONE, CHILD?
WHAT HAVE YOU DONE?

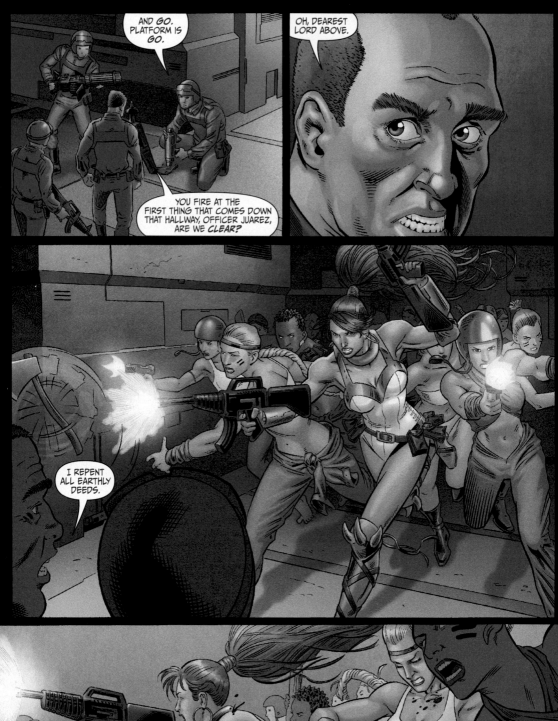

AND *GO*. PLATFORM IS *GO*.

OH, DEAREST LORD ABOVE.

YOU FIRE AT THE FIRST THING THAT COMES DOWN THAT HALLWAY, OFFICER JUAREZ, ARE WE *CLEAR*?

I REPENT ALL EARTHLY DEEDS.

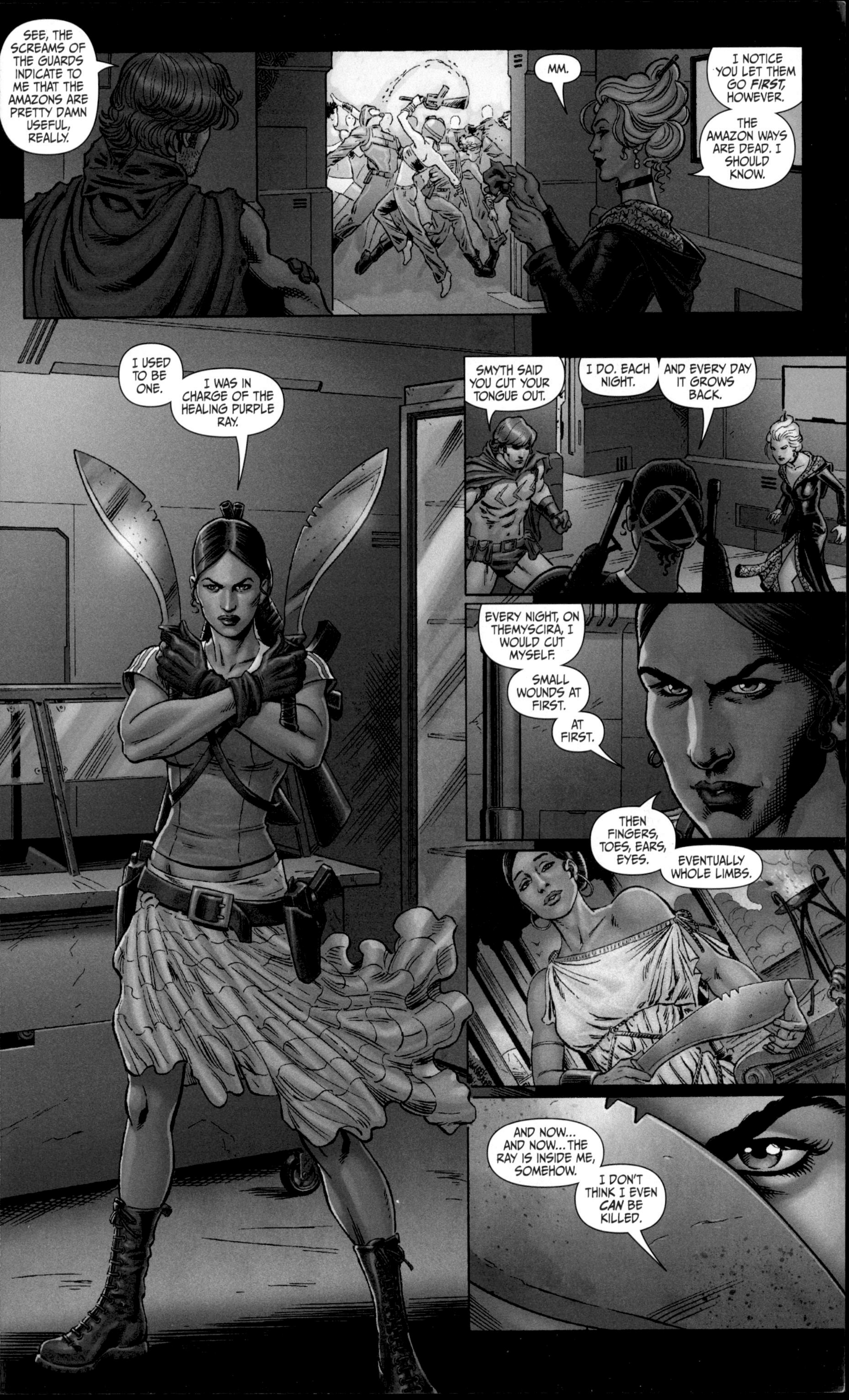
SEE, THE SCREAMS OF THE GUARDS INDICATE TO ME THAT THE AMAZONS ARE PRETTY DAMN USEFUL, REALLY.
MM.
I NOTICE YOU LET THEM GO FIRST, HOWEVER.
THE AMAZON WAYS ARE DEAD. I SHOULD KNOW.
I USED TO BE ONE.
I WAS IN CHARGE OF THE HEALING PURPLE RAY.
SMYTH SAID YOU CUT YOUR TONGUE OUT.
I DO. EACH NIGHT.
AND EVERY DAY IT GROWS BACK.
EVERY NIGHT, ON THEMYSCIRA, I WOULD CUT MYSELF.
SMALL WOUNDS AT FIRST.
AT FIRST.
THEN FINGERS, TOES, EARS, EYES.
EVENTUALLY WHOLE LIMBS.
AND NOW... AND NOW... THE RAY IS INSIDE ME, SOMEHOW.
I DON'T THINK I EVEN CAN BE KILLED.

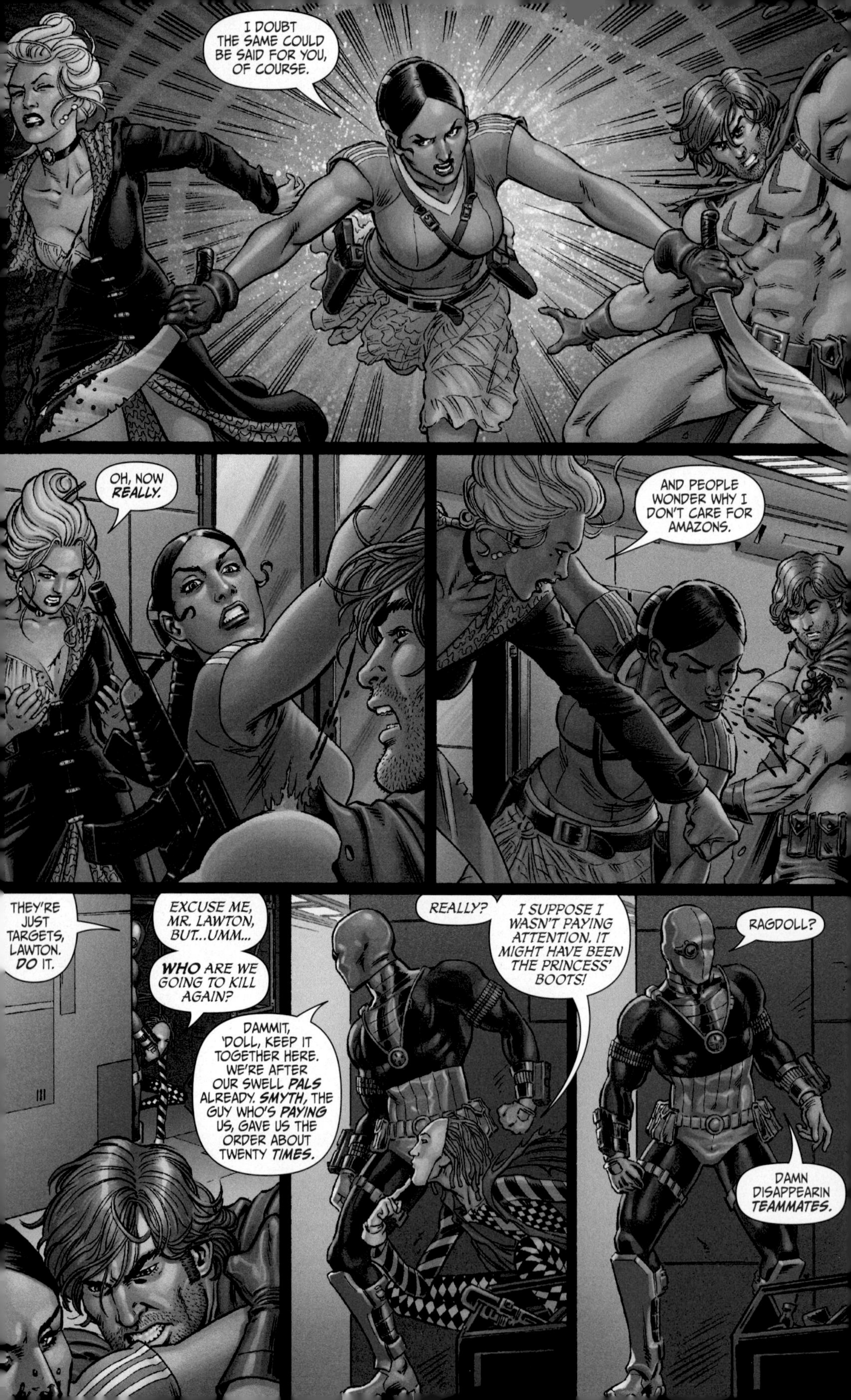
I DOUBT THE SAME COULD BE SAID FOR YOU, OF COURSE.
OH, NOW *REALLY.*
AND PEOPLE WONDER WHY I DON'T CARE FOR AMAZONS.
THEY'RE JUST TARGETS, LAWTON. *DO* IT.
EXCUSE ME, MR. LAWTON, BUT...UMM...
***WHO** ARE WE GOING TO KILL AGAIN?*
DAMMIT, 'DOLL, KEEP IT TOGETHER HERE. WE'RE AFTER OUR SWELL *PALS* ALREADY. *SMYTH,* THE GUY WHO'S *PAYING* US, GAVE US THE ORDER ABOUT TWENTY *TIMES.*
REALLY?
I SUPPOSE I WASN'T PAYING ATTENTION. IT MIGHT HAVE BEEN THE PRINCESS' BOOTS!
RAGDOLL?
DAMN DISAPPEARIN *TEAMMATES.*

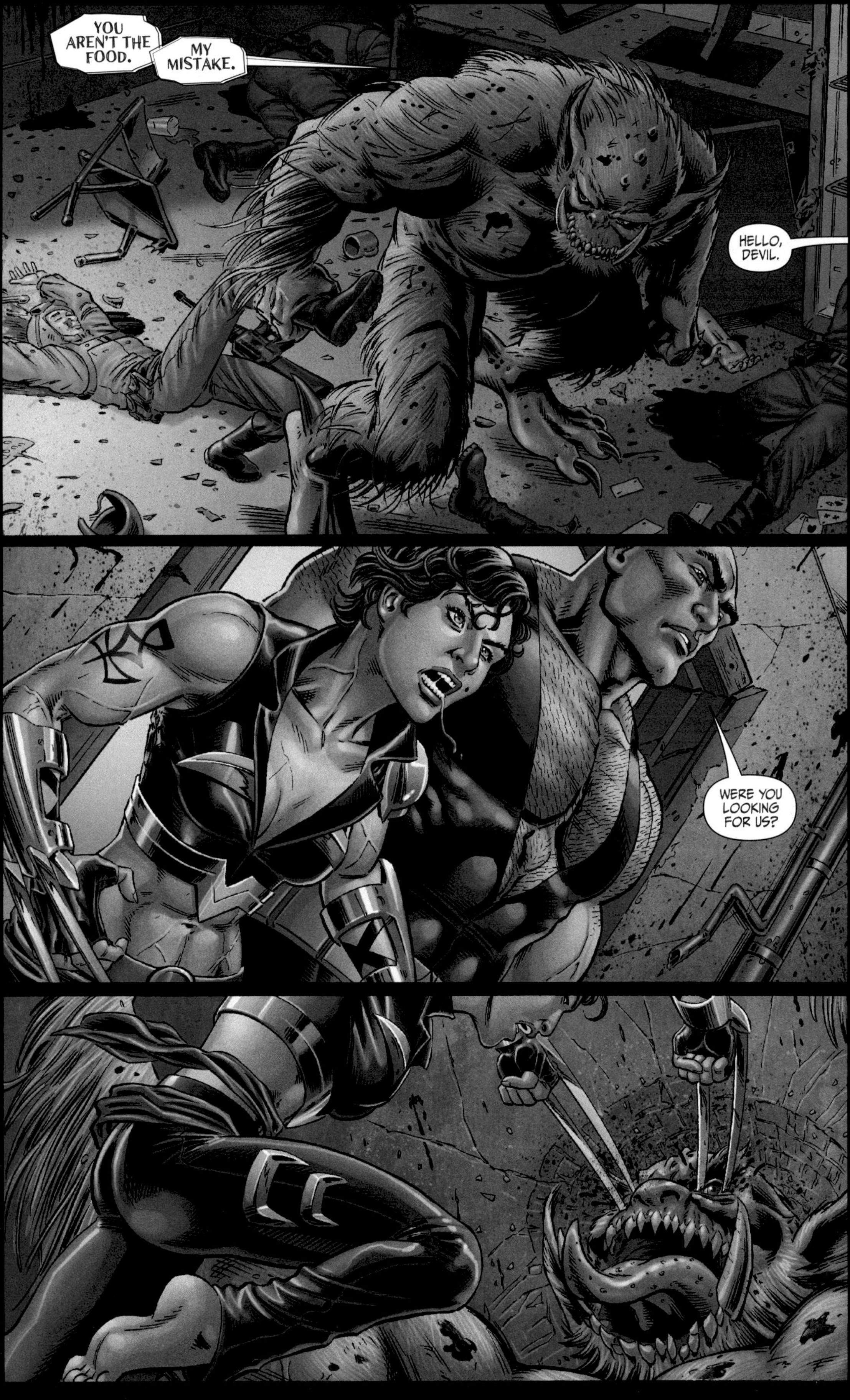

YOU AREN'T THE FOOD.
MY MISTAKE.
HELLO, DEVIL.
WERE YOU LOOKING FOR US?

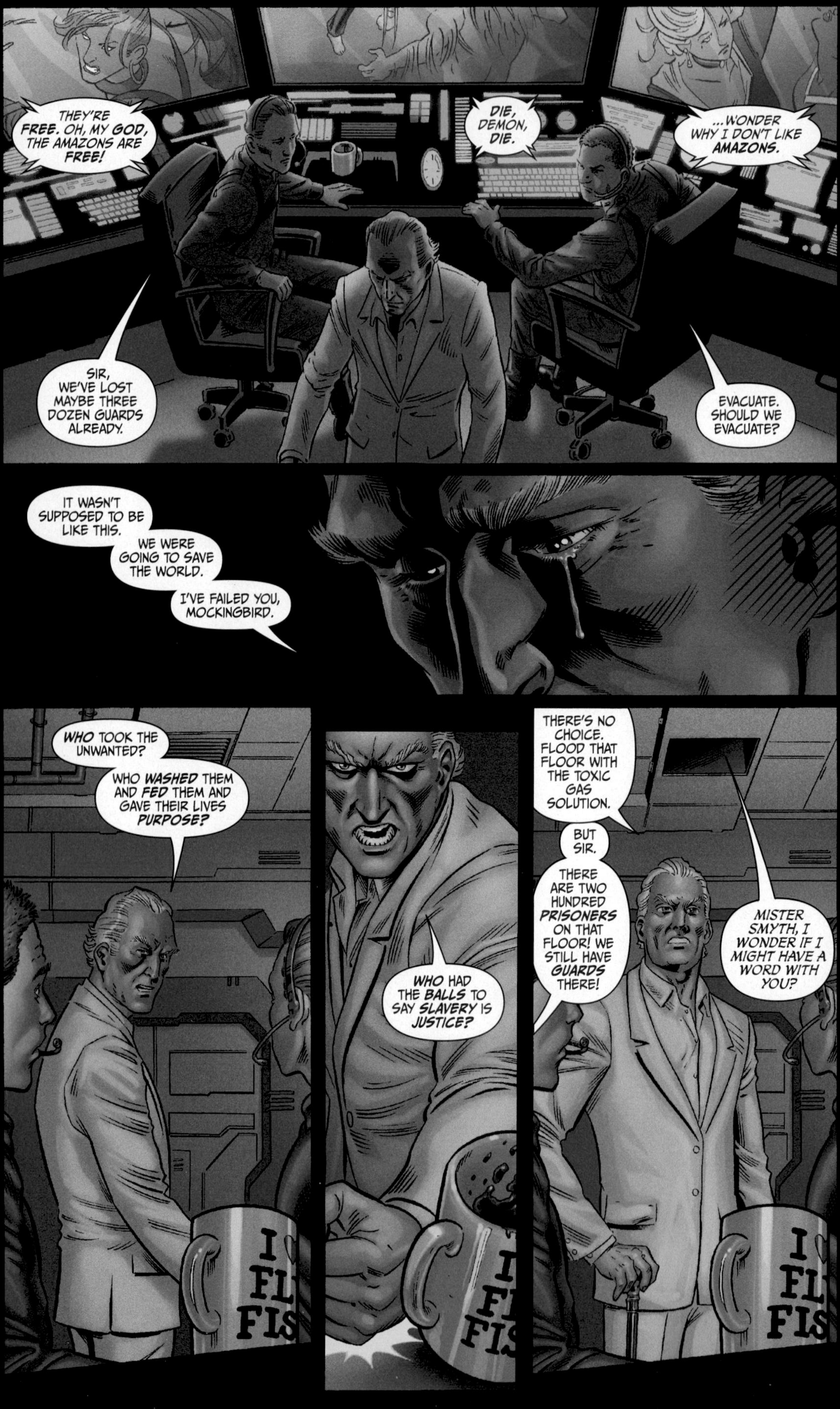
THEY'RE FREE. OH, MY GOD, THE AMAZONS ARE FREE!
DIE, DEMON, DIE.
...WONDER WHY I DON'T LIKE AMAZONS.
SIR, WE'VE LOST MAYBE THREE DOZEN GUARDS ALREADY.
EVACUATE. SHOULD WE EVACUATE?
IT WASN'T SUPPOSED TO BE LIKE THIS.
WE WERE GOING TO SAVE THE WORLD.
I'VE FAILED YOU, MOCKINGBIRD.
WHO TOOK THE UNWANTED?
WHO WASHED THEM AND FED THEM AND GAVE THEIR LIVES PURPOSE?
WHO HAD THE BALLS TO SAY SLAVERY IS JUSTICE?
THERE'S NO CHOICE. FLOOD THAT FLOOR WITH THE TOXIC GAS SOLUTION.
BUT SIR.
THERE ARE TWO HUNDRED PRISONERS ON THAT FLOOR! WE STILL HAVE GUARDS THERE!
MISTER SMYTH, I WONDER IF I MIGHT HAVE A WORD WITH YOU?

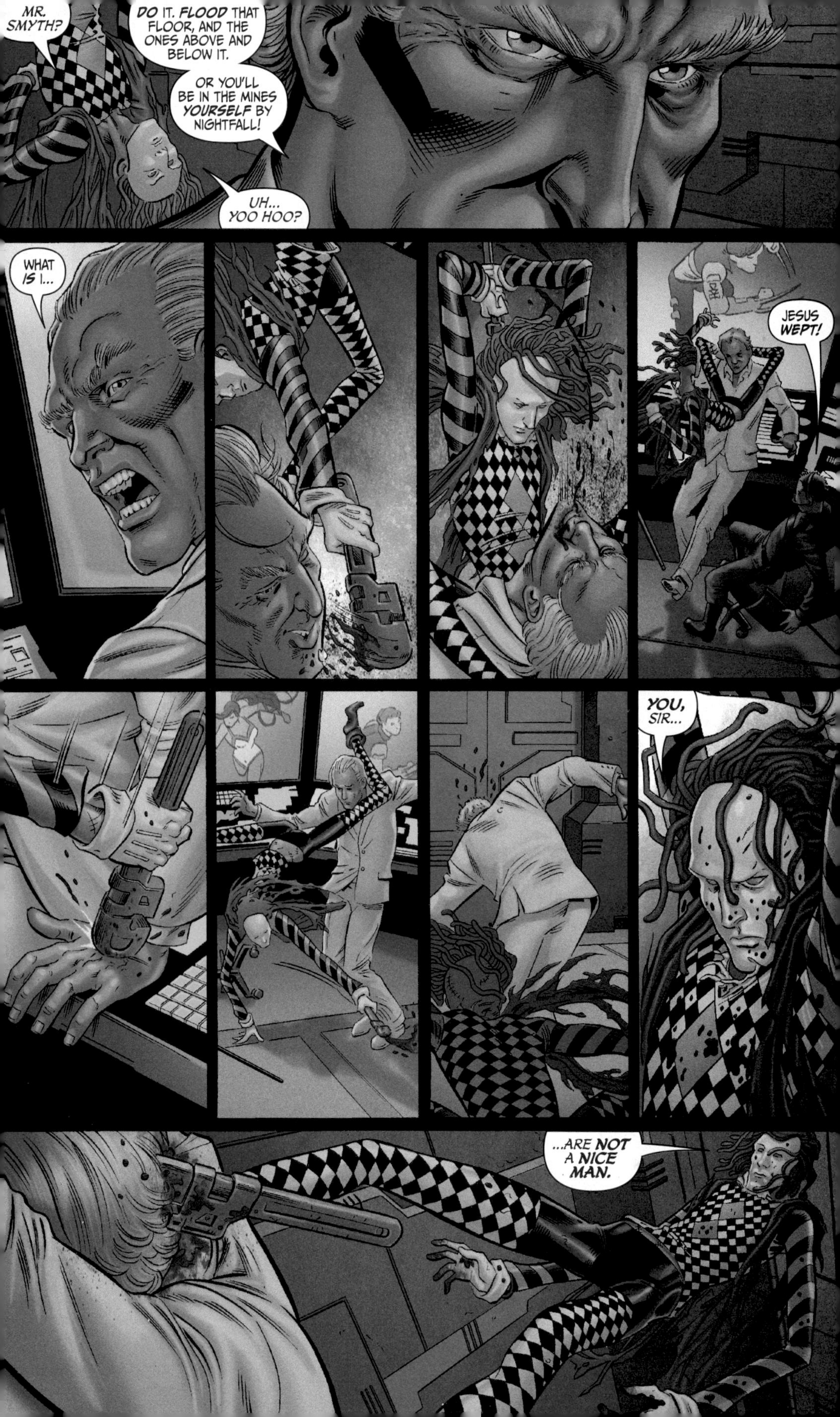
MR. SMYTH?
DO IT. FLOOD THAT FLOOR, AND THE ONES ABOVE AND BELOW IT.
OR YOU'LL BE IN THE MINES YOURSELF BY NIGHTFALL!
UH... YOO HOO?
WHAT IS I...
JESUS WEPT!
YOU, SIR...
...ARE NOT A NICE MAN.

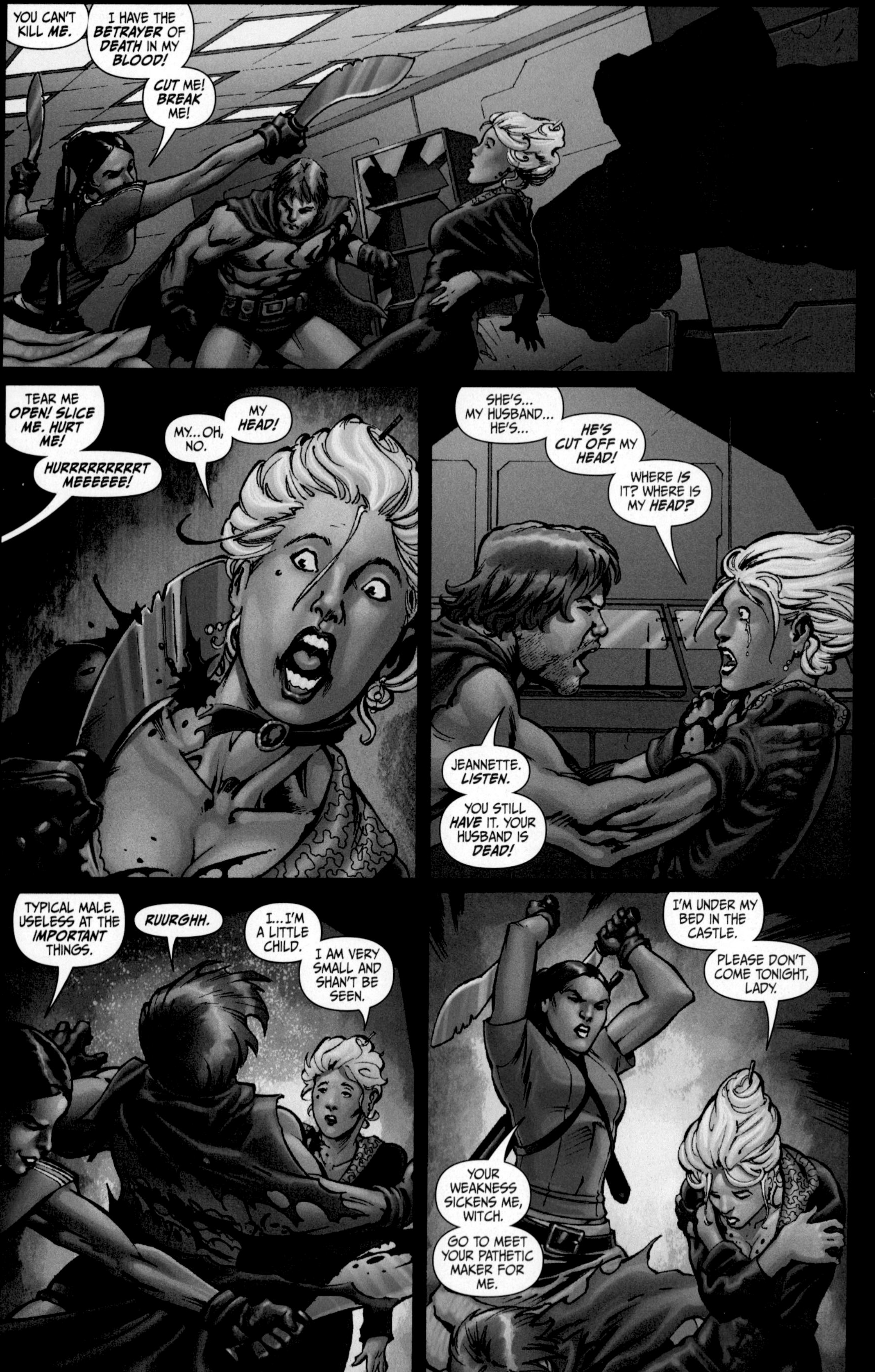
YOU CAN'T KILL ME.
I HAVE THE BETRAYER OF DEATH IN MY BLOOD!
CUT ME! BREAK ME!
TEAR ME OPEN! SLICE ME. HURT ME!
HURRRRRRRRRT MEEEEEE!
MY...OH, NO.
MY HEAD!
SHE'S... MY HUSBAND... HE'S...
HE'S CUT OFF MY HEAD!
WHERE IS IT? WHERE IS MY HEAD?
JEANNETTE. LISTEN.
YOU STILL HAVE IT. YOUR HUSBAND IS DEAD!
TYPICAL MALE. USELESS AT THE IMPORTANT THINGS.
RUURGHH.
I...I'M A LITTLE CHILD.
I AM VERY SMALL AND SHAN'T BE SEEN.
I'M UNDER MY BED IN THE CASTLE.
PLEASE DON'T COME TONIGHT, LADY.
YOUR WEAKNESS SICKENS ME, WITCH.
GO TO MEET YOUR PATHETIC MAKER FOR ME.

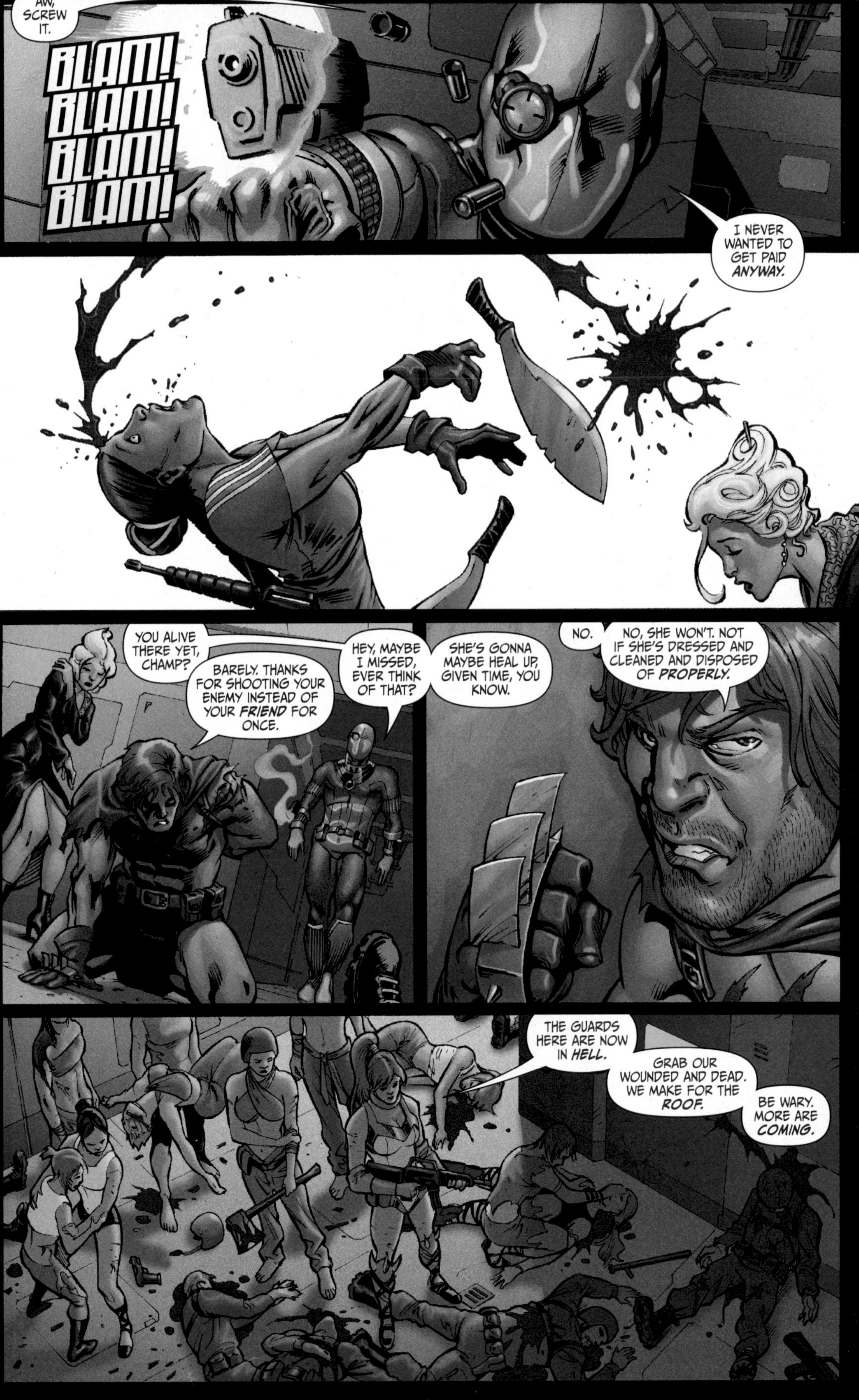
AW, SCREW IT.
BLAM! BLAM! BLAM! BLAM!
I NEVER WANTED TO GET PAID ANYWAY.
YOU ALIVE THERE YET, CHAMP?
BARELY. THANKS FOR SHOOTING YOUR ENEMY INSTEAD OF YOUR FRIEND FOR ONCE.
HEY, MAYBE I MISSED, EVER THINK OF THAT?
SHE'S GONNA MAYBE HEAL UP, GIVEN TIME, YOU KNOW.
NO.
NO, SHE WON'T. NOT IF SHE'S DRESSED AND CLEANED AND DISPOSED OF PROPERLY.
THE GUARDS HERE ARE NOW IN HELL.
GRAB OUR WOUNDED AND DEAD. WE MAKE FOR THE ROOF.
BE WARY. MORE ARE COMING.

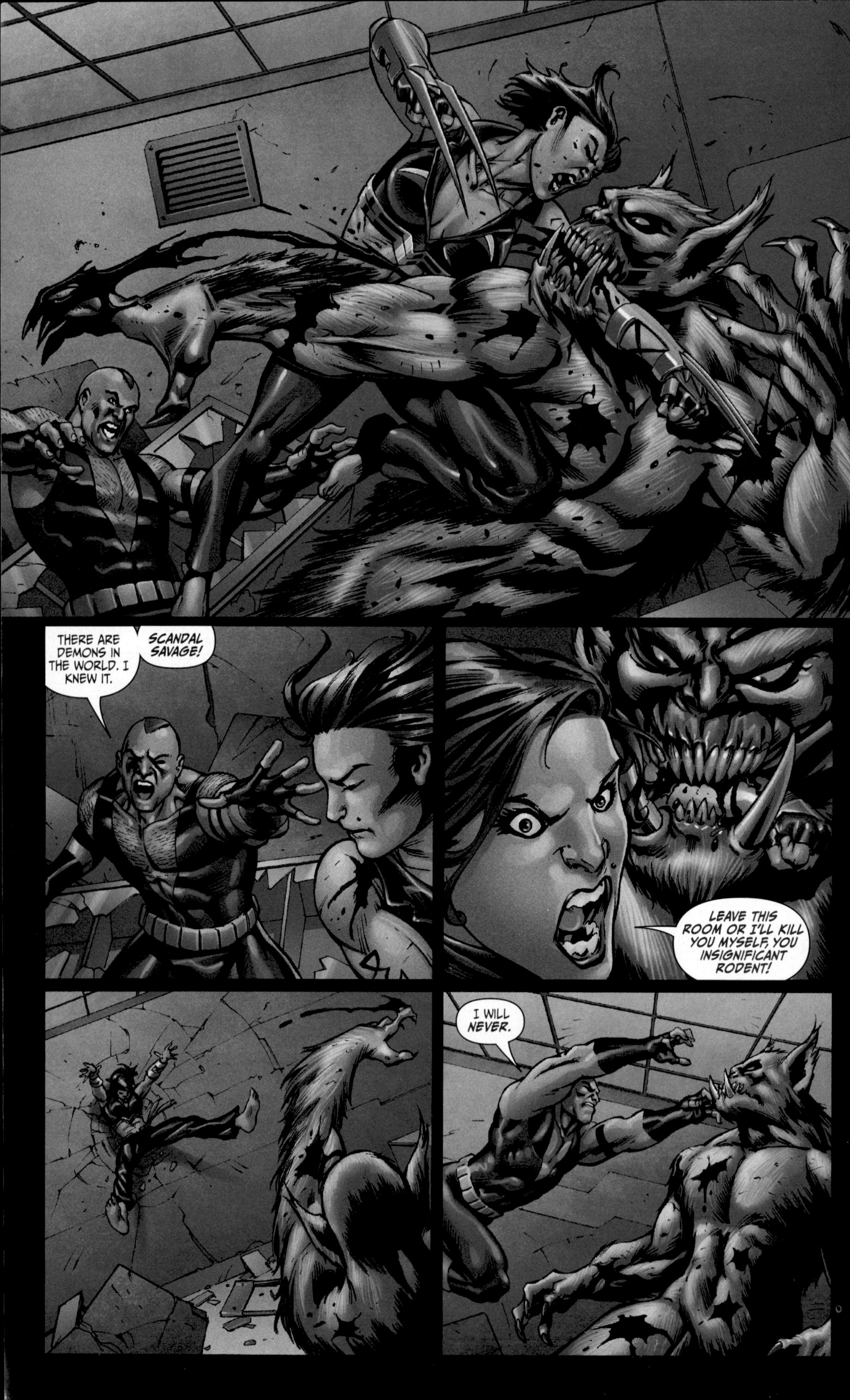
SCANDAL SAVAGE!
THERE ARE DEMONS IN THE WORLD. I KNEW IT.
LEAVE THIS ROOM OR I'LL KILL YOU MYSELF, YOU INSIGNIFICANT RODENT!
I WILL NEVER.

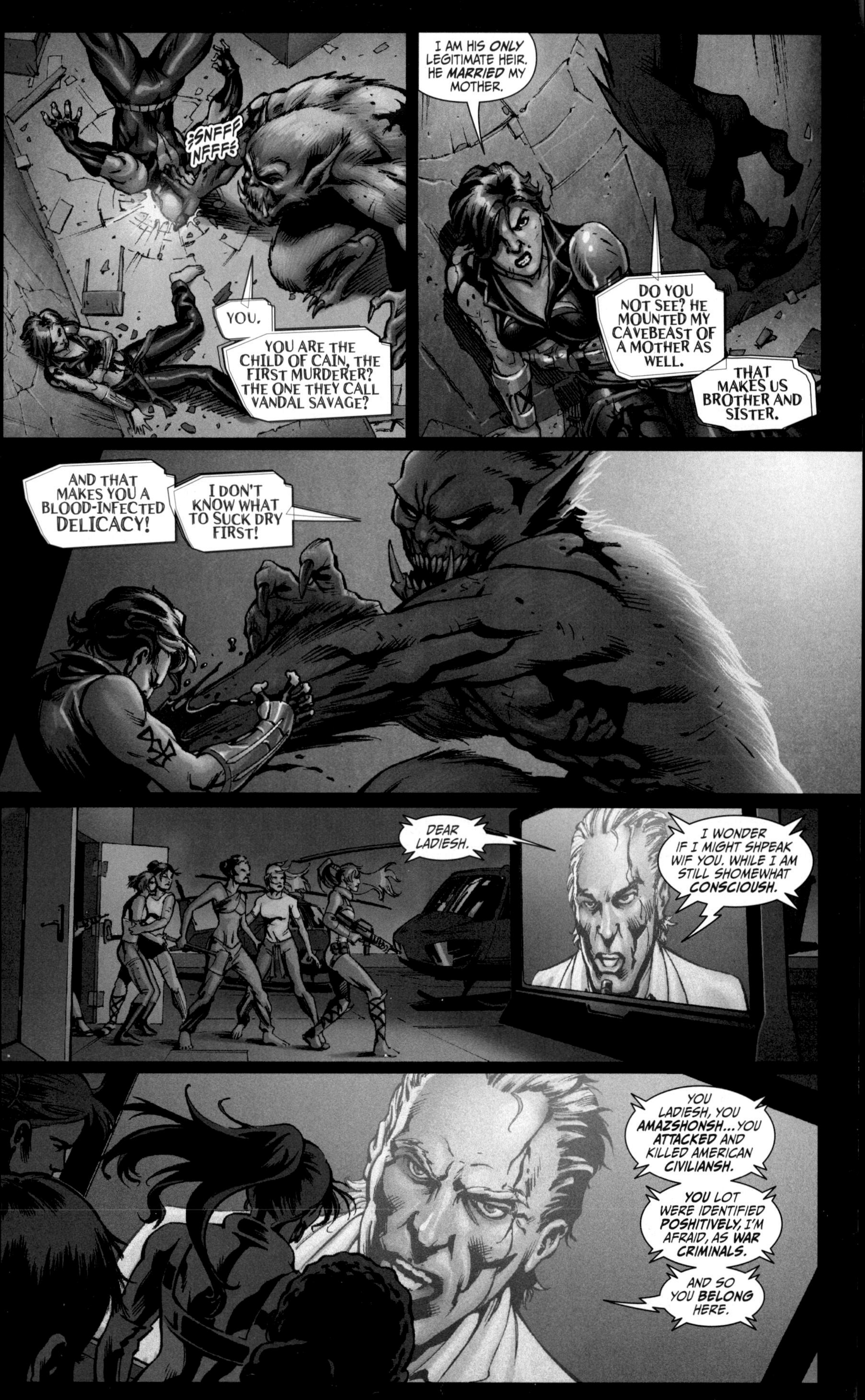

:SNFFF NFFF:
YOU.
YOU ARE THE CHILD OF CAIN, THE FIRST MURDERER? THE ONE THEY CALL VANDAL SAVAGE?
I AM HIS ONLY LEGITIMATE HEIR. HE MARRIED MY MOTHER.
DO YOU NOT SEE? HE MOUNTED MY CAVEBEAST OF A MOTHER AS WELL.
THAT MAKES US BROTHER AND SISTER.
AND THAT MAKES YOU A BLOOD-INFECTED DELICACY!
I DON'T KNOW WHAT TO SUCK DRY FIRST!
DEAR LADIESH.
I WONDER IF I MIGHT SHPEAK WIF YOU. WHILE I AM STILL SHOMEWHAT CONSCIOUSH.
YOU LADIESH, YOU AMAZSHONSH... YOU ATTACKED AND KILLED AMERICAN CIVILIANSH.
YOU LOT WERE IDENTIFIED POSHITIVELY, I'M AFRAID, AS WAR CRIMINALS.
AND SO YOU BELONG HERE.

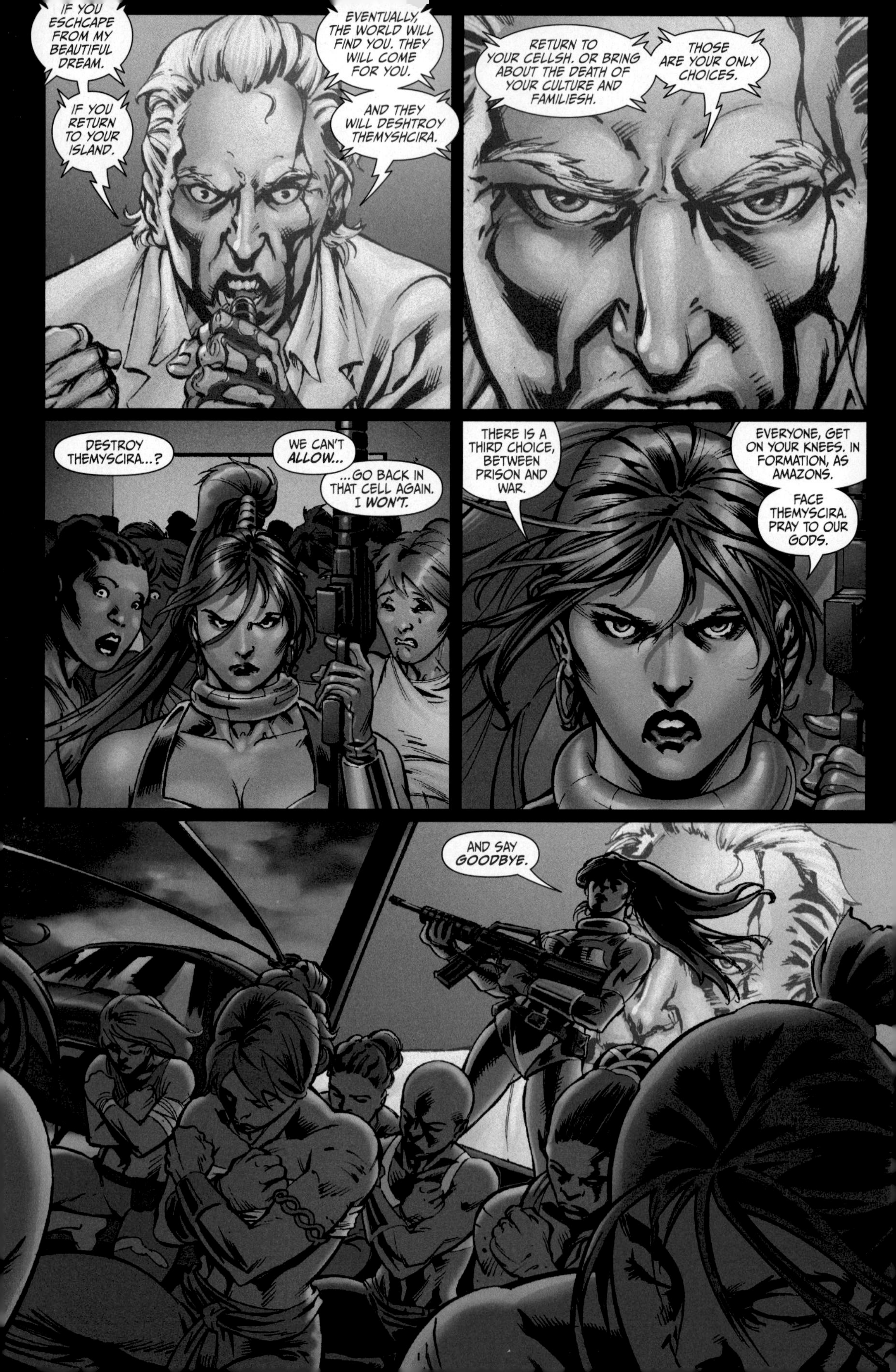
IF YOU ESCHCAPE FROM MY BEAUTIFUL DREAM.
IF YOU RETURN TO YOUR ISLAND.
EVENTUALLY, THE WORLD WILL FIND YOU. THEY WILL COME FOR YOU.
AND THEY WILL DESHTROY THEMYSHCIRA.
RETURN TO YOUR CELLSH. OR BRING ABOUT THE DEATH OF YOUR CULTURE AND FAMILIESH.
THOSE ARE YOUR ONLY CHOICES.
DESTROY THEMYSCIRA...?
WE CAN'T ALLOW...
...GO BACK IN THAT CELL AGAIN. I WON'T.
THERE IS A THIRD CHOICE, BETWEEN PRISON AND WAR.
EVERYONE, GET ON YOUR KNEES. IN FORMATION, AS AMAZONS.
FACE THEMYSCIRA. PRAY TO OUR GODS.
AND SAY GOODBYE.

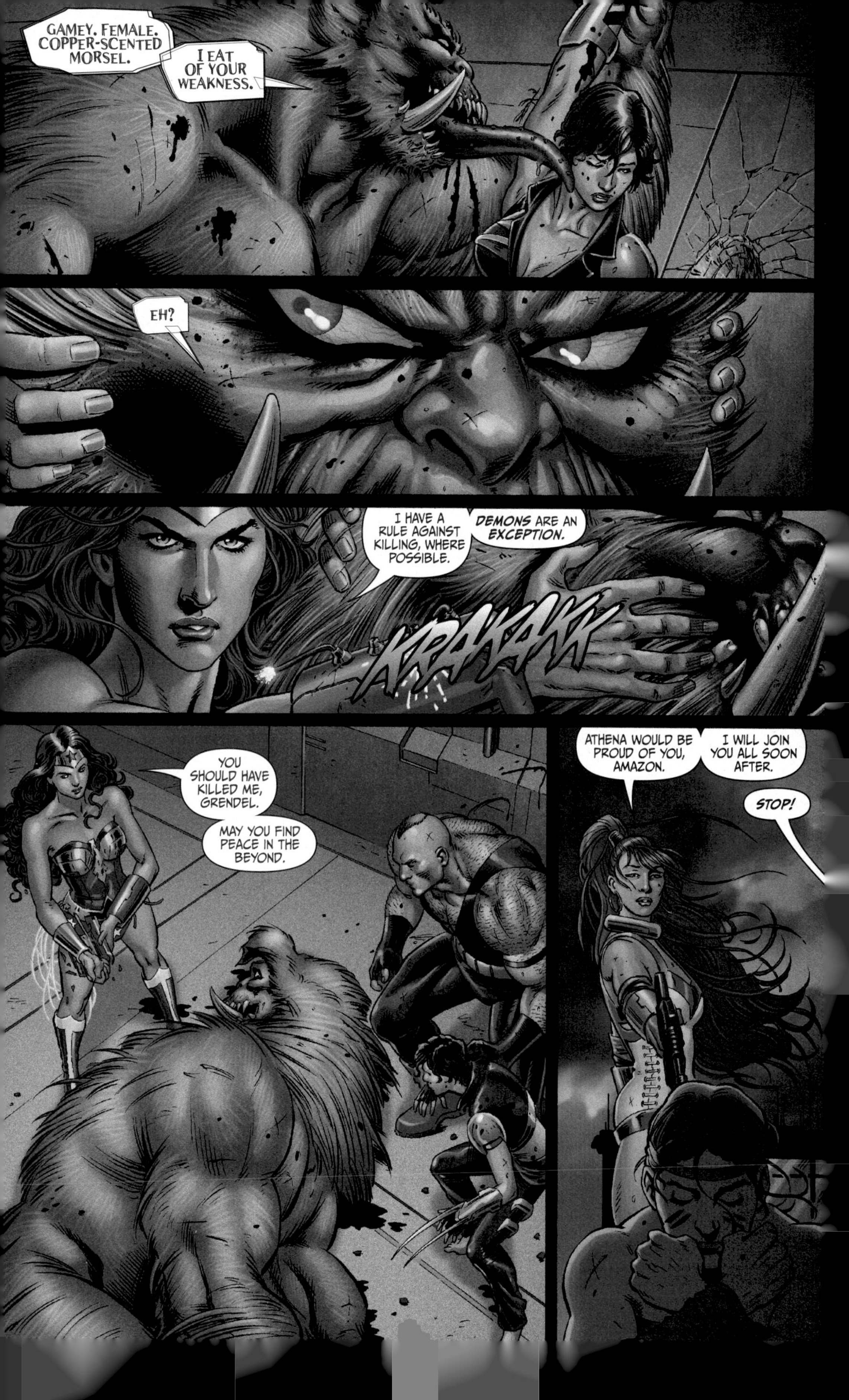
GAMEY. FEMALE. COPPER-SCENTED MORSEL.
I EAT OF YOUR WEAKNESS.
EH?
I HAVE A RULE AGAINST KILLING, WHERE POSSIBLE.
DEMONS ARE AN EXCEPTION.
KRAKAKK
YOU SHOULD HAVE KILLED ME, GRENDEL.
MAY YOU FIND PEACE IN THE BEYOND.
ATHENA WOULD BE PROUD OF YOU, AMAZON.
I WILL JOIN YOU ALL SOON AFTER.
STOP!

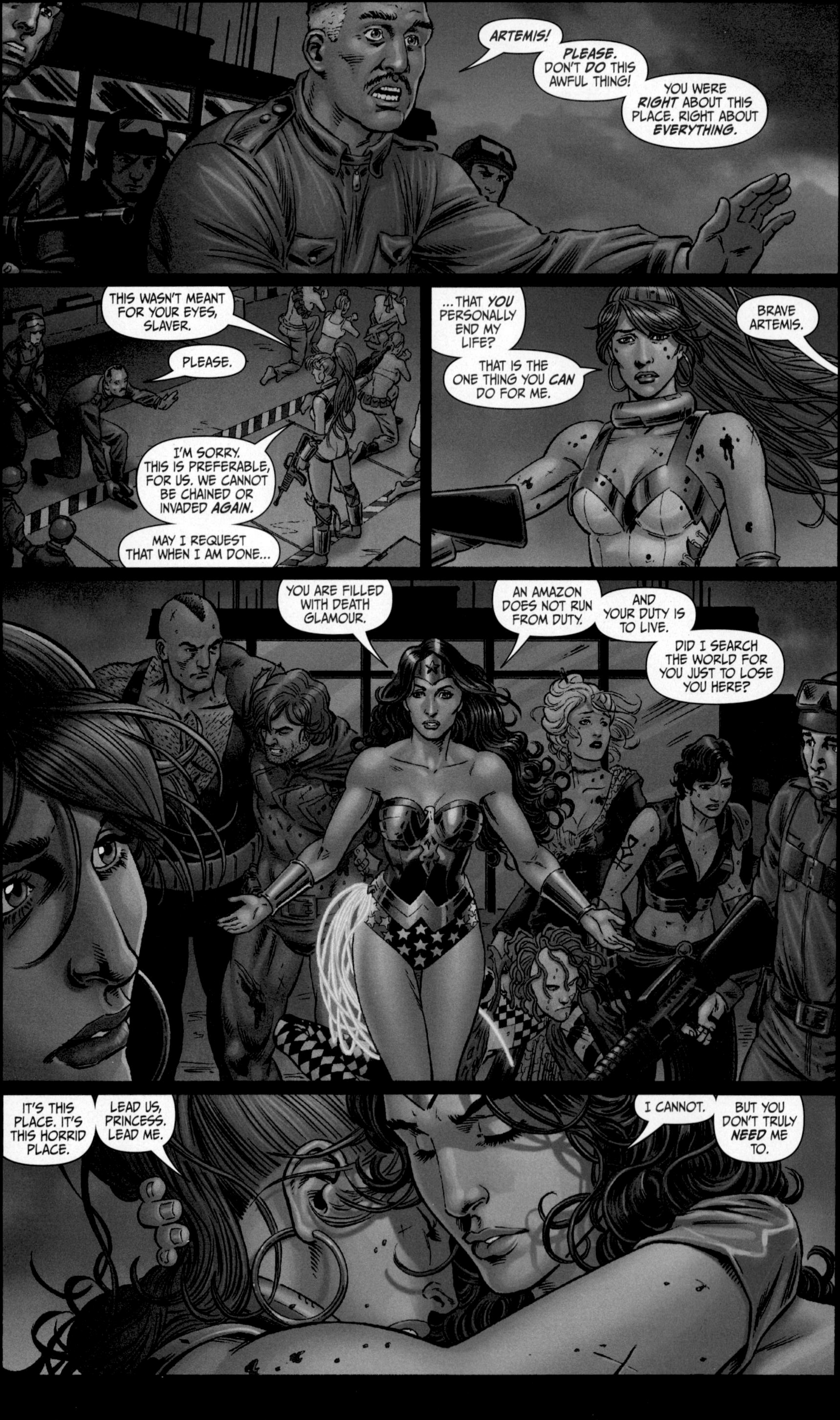
ARTEMIS!
PLEASE. DON'T DO THIS AWFUL THING!
YOU WERE RIGHT ABOUT THIS PLACE. RIGHT ABOUT EVERYTHING.
THIS WASN'T MEANT FOR YOUR EYES, SLAVER.
PLEASE.
I'M SORRY. THIS IS PREFERABLE, FOR US. WE CANNOT BE CHAINED OR INVADED AGAIN.
MAY I REQUEST THAT WHEN I AM DONE...
...THAT YOU PERSONALLY END MY LIFE?
THAT IS THE ONE THING YOU CAN DO FOR ME.
BRAVE ARTEMIS.
YOU ARE FILLED WITH DEATH GLAMOUR.
AN AMAZON DOES NOT RUN FROM DUTY.
AND YOUR DUTY IS TO LIVE.
DID I SEARCH THE WORLD FOR YOU JUST TO LOSE YOU HERE?
IT'S THIS PLACE. IT'S THIS HORRID PLACE.
LEAD US, PRINCESS. LEAD ME.
I CANNOT.
BUT YOU DON'T TRULY NEED ME TO.

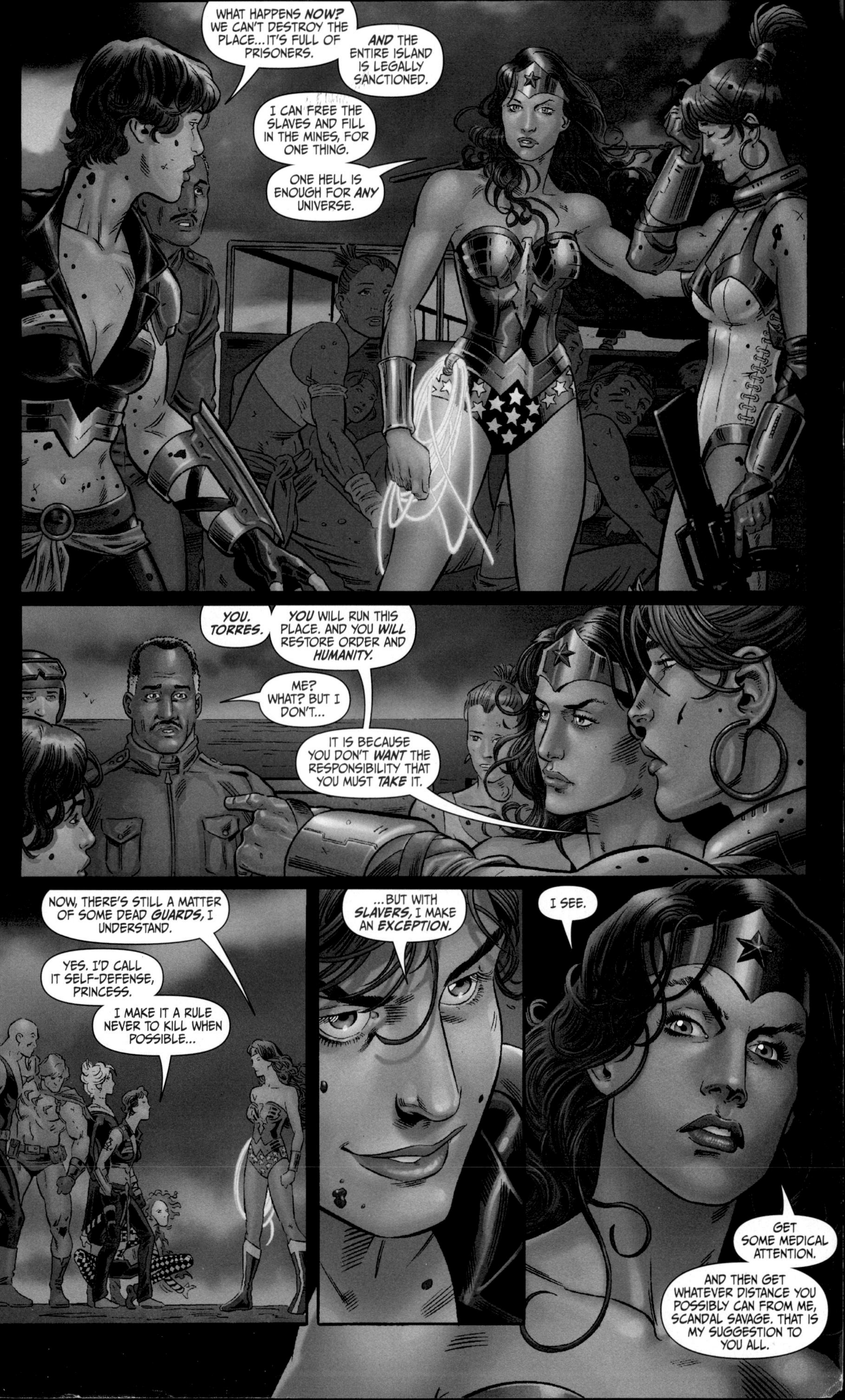
WHAT HAPPENS NOW? WE CAN'T DESTROY THE PLACE... IT'S FULL OF PRISONERS.
AND THE ENTIRE ISLAND IS LEGALLY SANCTIONED.
I CAN FREE THE SLAVES AND FILL IN THE MINES, FOR ONE THING.
ONE HELL IS ENOUGH FOR ANY UNIVERSE.
YOU. TORRES.
YOU WILL RUN THIS PLACE. AND YOU WILL RESTORE ORDER AND HUMANITY.
ME? WHAT? BUT I DON'T...
IT IS BECAUSE YOU DON'T WANT THE RESPONSIBILITY THAT YOU MUST TAKE IT.
NOW, THERE'S STILL A MATTER OF SOME DEAD GUARDS, I UNDERSTAND.
YES. I'D CALL IT SELF-DEFENSE, PRINCESS.
I MAKE IT A RULE NEVER TO KILL WHEN POSSIBLE...
...BUT WITH SLAVERS, I MAKE AN EXCEPTION.
I SEE.
GET SOME MEDICAL ATTENTION.
AND THEN GET WHATEVER DISTANCE YOU POSSIBLY CAN FROM ME, SCANDAL SAVAGE. THAT IS MY SUGGESTION TO YOU ALL.

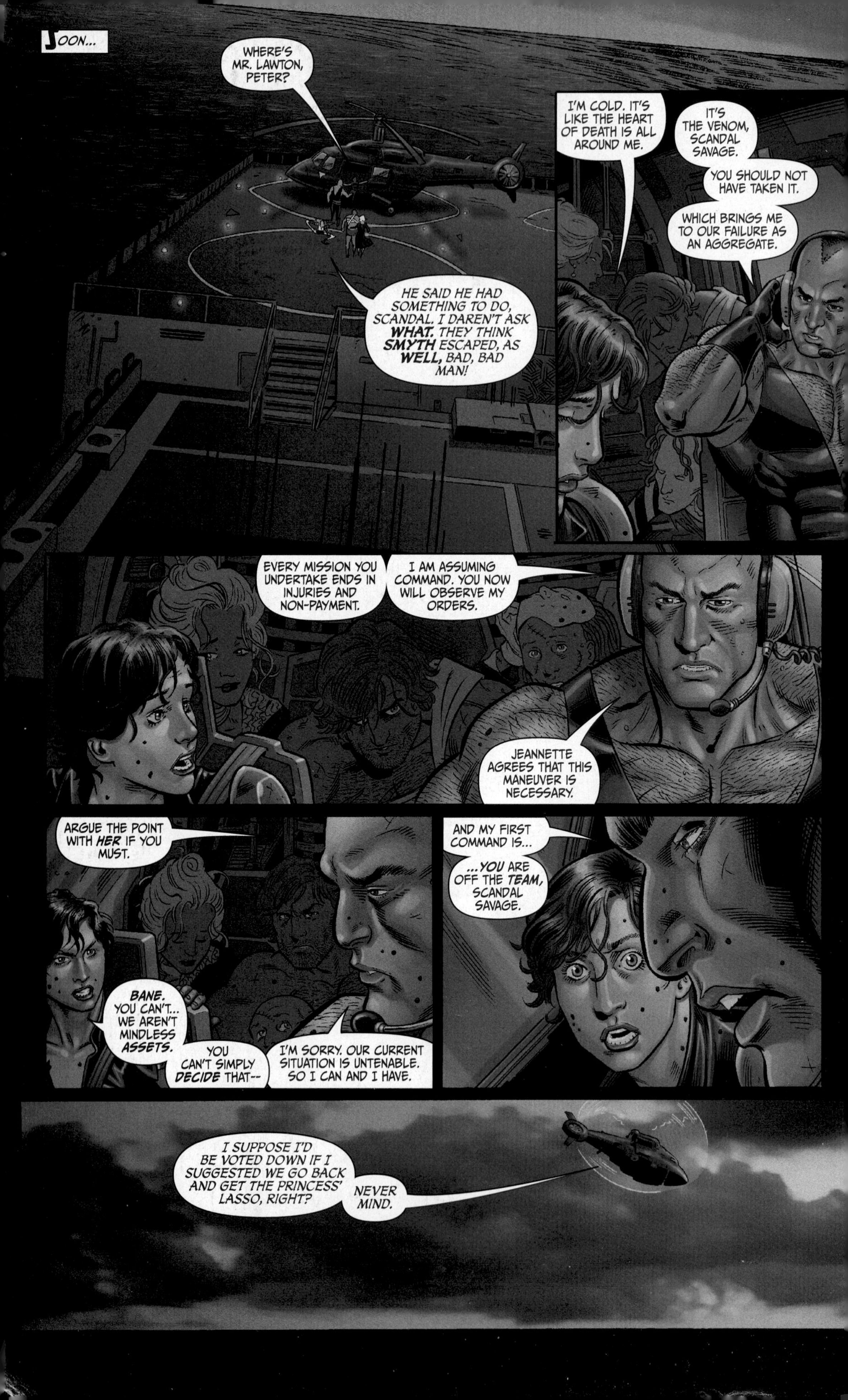
SOON...
WHERE'S MR. LAWTON, PETER?
HE SAID HE HAD SOMETHING TO DO, SCANDAL. I DAREN'T ASK WHAT. THEY THINK SMYTH ESCAPED, AS WELL, BAD, BAD MAN!
I'M COLD. IT'S LIKE THE HEART OF DEATH IS ALL AROUND ME.
IT'S THE VENOM, SCANDAL SAVAGE.
YOU SHOULD NOT HAVE TAKEN IT.
WHICH BRINGS ME TO OUR FAILURE AS AN AGGREGATE.
EVERY MISSION YOU UNDERTAKE ENDS IN INJURIES AND NON-PAYMENT.
I AM ASSUMING COMMAND. YOU NOW WILL OBSERVE MY ORDERS.
JEANNETTE AGREES THAT THIS MANEUVER IS NECESSARY.
ARGUE THE POINT WITH HER IF YOU MUST.
BANE. YOU CAN'T... WE AREN'T MINDLESS ASSETS.
YOU CAN'T SIMPLY DECIDE THAT--
I'M SORRY. OUR CURRENT SITUATION IS UNTENABLE. SO I CAN AND I HAVE.
AND MY FIRST COMMAND IS...
...YOU ARE OFF THE TEAM, SCANDAL SAVAGE.
I SUPPOSE I'D BE VOTED DOWN IF I SUGGESTED WE GO BACK AND GET THE PRINCESS' LASSO, RIGHT?
NEVER MIND.

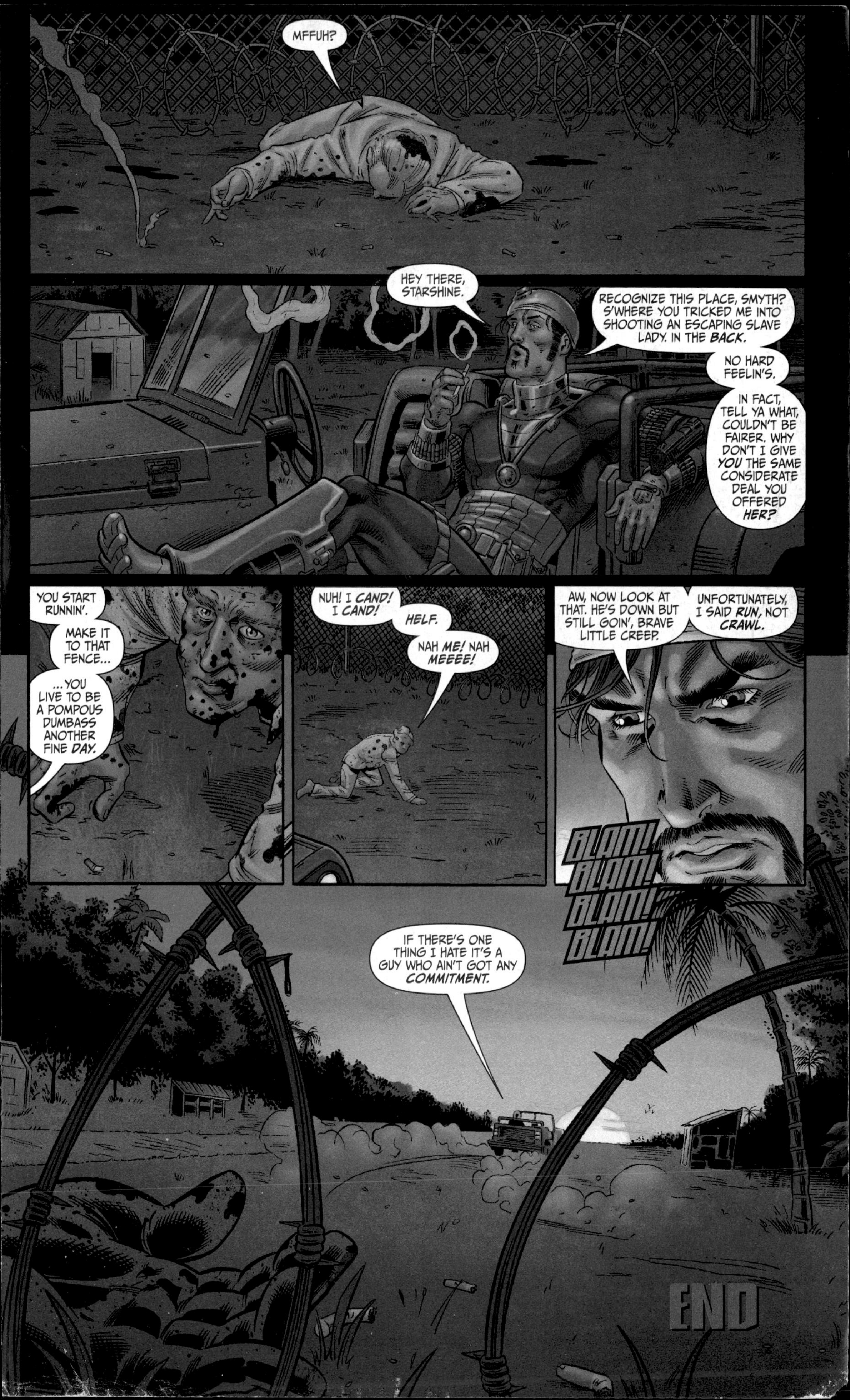

MFFUH?
HEY THERE, STARSHINE.
RECOGNIZE THIS PLACE, SMYTH? S'WHERE YOU TRICKED ME INTO SHOOTING AN ESCAPING SLAVE LADY. IN THE BACK.
NO HARD FEELIN'S.
IN FACT, TELL YA WHAT, COULDN'T BE FAIRER. WHY DON'T I GIVE YOU THE SAME CONSIDERATE DEAL YOU OFFERED HER?
YOU START RUNNIN'.
MAKE IT TO THAT FENCE...
...YOU LIVE TO BE A POMPOUS DUMBASS ANOTHER FINE DAY.
NUH! I CAND! I CAND!
HELF.
NAH ME! NAH MEEEE!
AW, NOW LOOK AT THAT. HE'S DOWN BUT STILL GOIN', BRAVE LITTLE CREEP.
UNFORTUNATELY, I SAID RUN, NOT CRAWL.
BLAM! BLAM! BLAM! BLAM!
IF THERE'S ONE THING I HATE IT'S A GUY WHO AIN'T GOT ANY COMMITMENT.
END

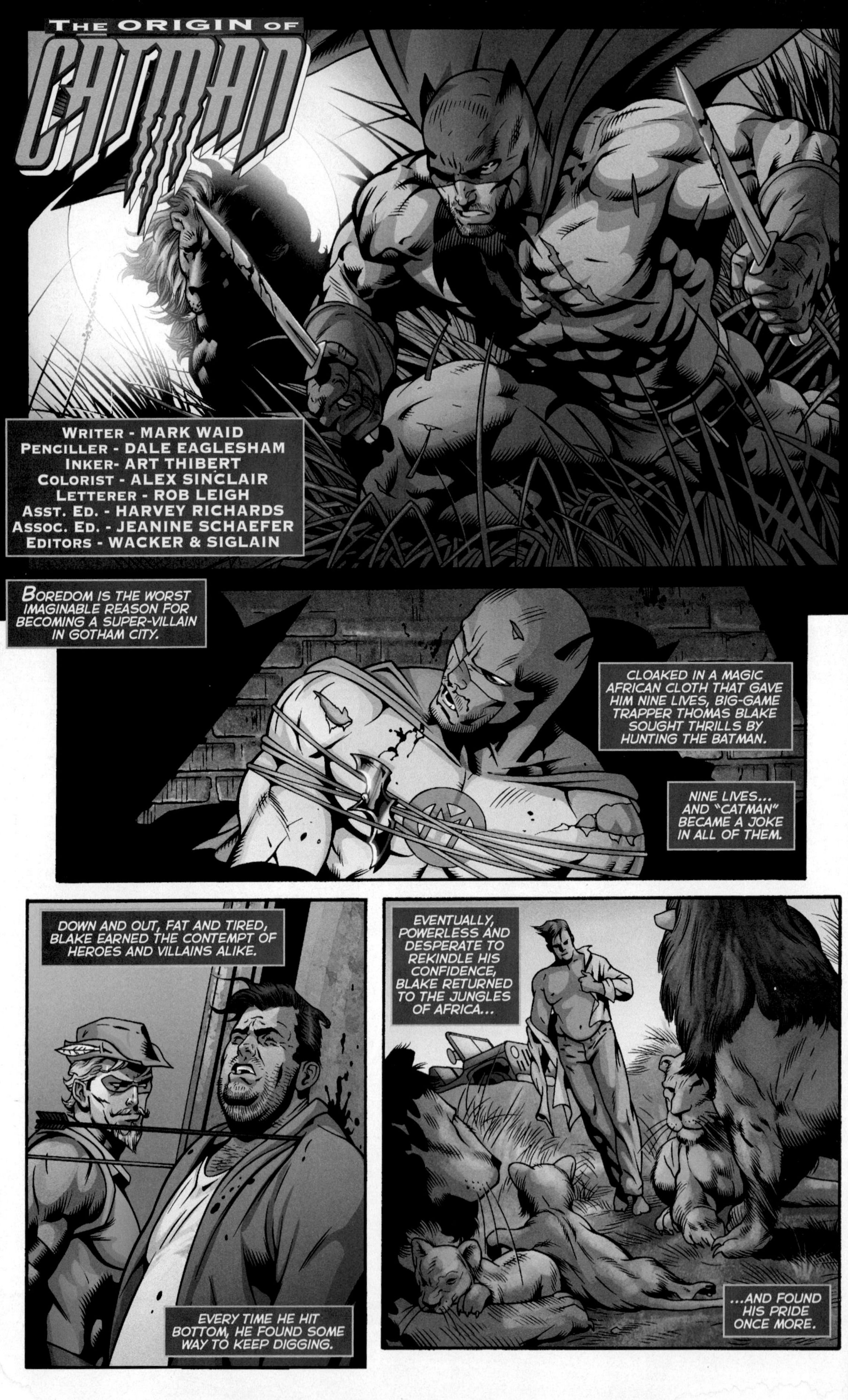
THE ORIGIN OF
CATMAN
WRITER - MARK WAID
PENCILLER - DALE EAGLESHAM
INKER- ART THIBERT
COLORIST - ALEX SINCLAIR
LETTERER - ROB LEIGH
ASST. ED. - HARVEY RICHARDS
ASSOC. ED. - JEANINE SCHAEFER
EDITORS - WACKER & SIGLAIN
BOREDOM IS THE WORST IMAGINABLE REASON FOR BECOMING A SUPER-VILLAIN IN GOTHAM CITY.
CLOAKED IN A MAGIC AFRICAN CLOTH THAT GAVE HIM NINE LIVES, BIG-GAME TRAPPER THOMAS BLAKE SOUGHT THRILLS BY HUNTING THE BATMAN.
NINE LIVES... AND "CATMAN" BECAME A JOKE IN ALL OF THEM.
DOWN AND OUT, FAT AND TIRED, BLAKE EARNED THE CONTEMPT OF HEROES AND VILLAINS ALIKE.
EVERY TIME HE HIT BOTTOM, HE FOUND SOME WAY TO KEEP DIGGING.
EVENTUALLY, POWERLESS AND DESPERATE TO REKINDLE HIS CONFIDENCE, BLAKE RETURNED TO THE JUNGLES OF AFRICA...
...AND FOUND HIS PRIDE ONCE MORE.

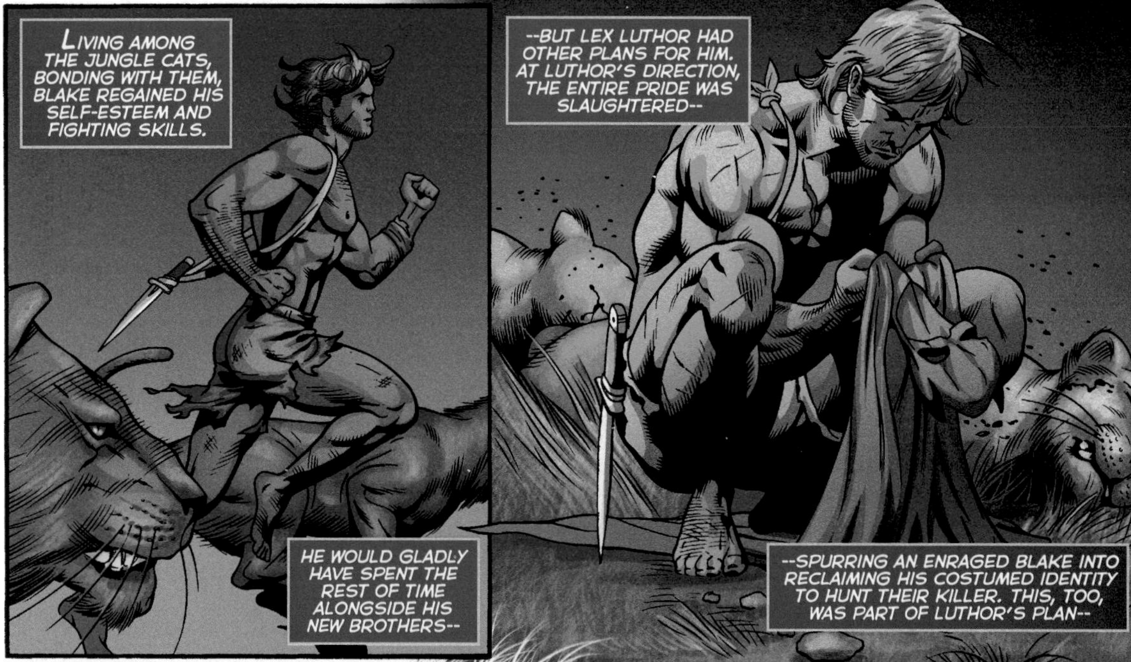
Living among the jungle cats, bonding with them, Blake regained his self-esteem and fighting skills.
He would gladly have spent the rest of time alongside his new brothers--
--But Lex Luthor had other plans for him. At Luthor's direction, the entire pride was slaughtered--
--Spurring an enraged Blake into reclaiming his costumed identity to hunt their killer. This, too, was part of Luthor's plan--

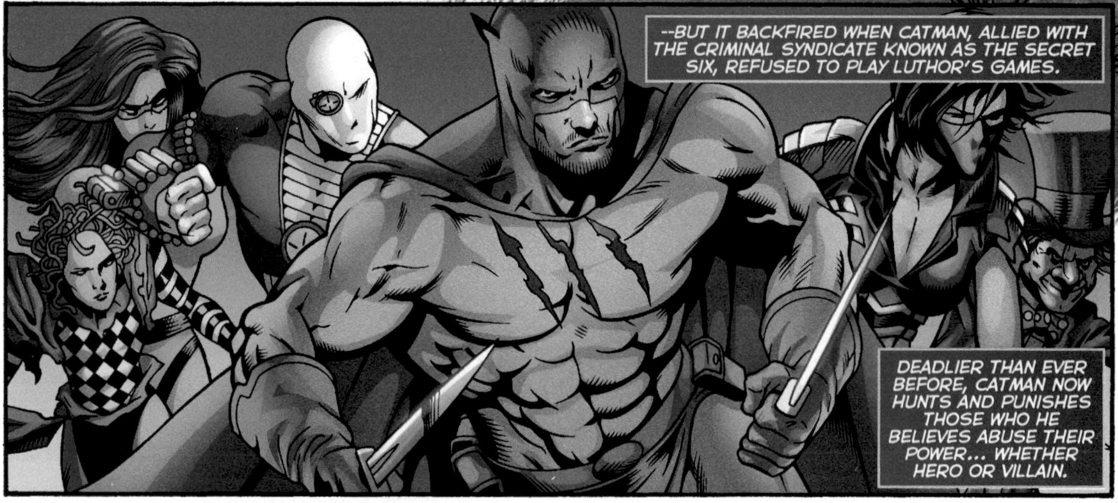
--But it backfired when Catman, allied with the criminal syndicate known as the Secret Six, refused to play Luthor's games.
Deadlier than ever before, Catman now hunts and punishes those who he believes abuse their power... whether hero or villain.

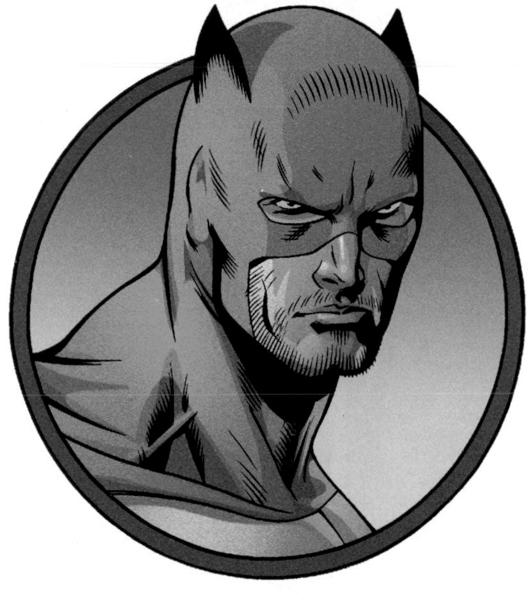

POWERS AND WEAPONS:

Catman is a fierce warrior who fights by the law of the jungle and is one of the greatest hunters and trackers alive.
He is particularly skilled in the use of bladed weapons and is uncannily stealthy and agile.

ESSENTIAL STORYLINES:

- DETECTIVE COMICS 311
- GREEN ARROW: THE ARCHER'S QUEST
- VILLAINS UNITED

ALLIANCES:

Secret Six

THE ORIGIN OF DEADSHOT

Writer
SCOTT BEATTY
Artist
FREDDIE E. WILLIAMS II
Colorist
HI-FI
Letterer
KEN LOPEZ
Editor
ELISABETH V. GEHRLEIN

IF THERE'S A BULLET WITH YOUR NAME ON IT, PRAY THAT DEADSHOT DOESN'T HAVE IT.

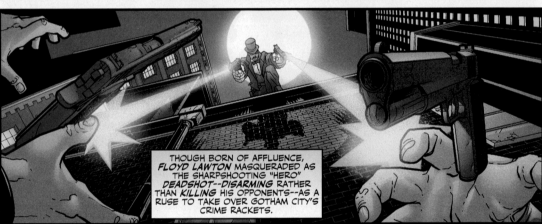

THOUGH BORN OF AFFLUENCE, *FLOYD LAWTON* MASQUERADED AS THE SHARPSHOOTING "HERO" *DEADSHOT*--*DISARMING* RATHER THAN *KILLING* HIS OPPONENTS--AS A RUSE TO TAKE OVER GOTHAM CITY'S CRIME RACKETS.

LAWTON MIGHT HAVE SUCCEEDED IF GOTHAM'S *OTHER* SELF-APPOINTED GUARDIAN HAD NOT ALTERED DEADSHOT'S GUNSIGHTS, MAKING HIS AIM--LIKE HIS INTENTIONS--*LESS* THAN TRUE.

BATTLING BATMAN ONCE IS *HUBRIS.* TARGETING HIM TWICE OR MORE IS INARGUABLY A *DEATHWISH,* WHICH EXPLAINS SO MANY OF DEADSHOT'S DECISIONS OVER THE YEARS.

WHY ELSE WOULD DEADSHOT AGREE TO COMMUTE A LENGTHY PRISON SENTENCE TO TIME-SERVED IN EXCHANGE FOR SERVICE IN THE SO-CALLED *"SUICIDE SQUAD,"* A TEAM OF *EXPENDABLE* GOVERNMENT OPERATIVES?

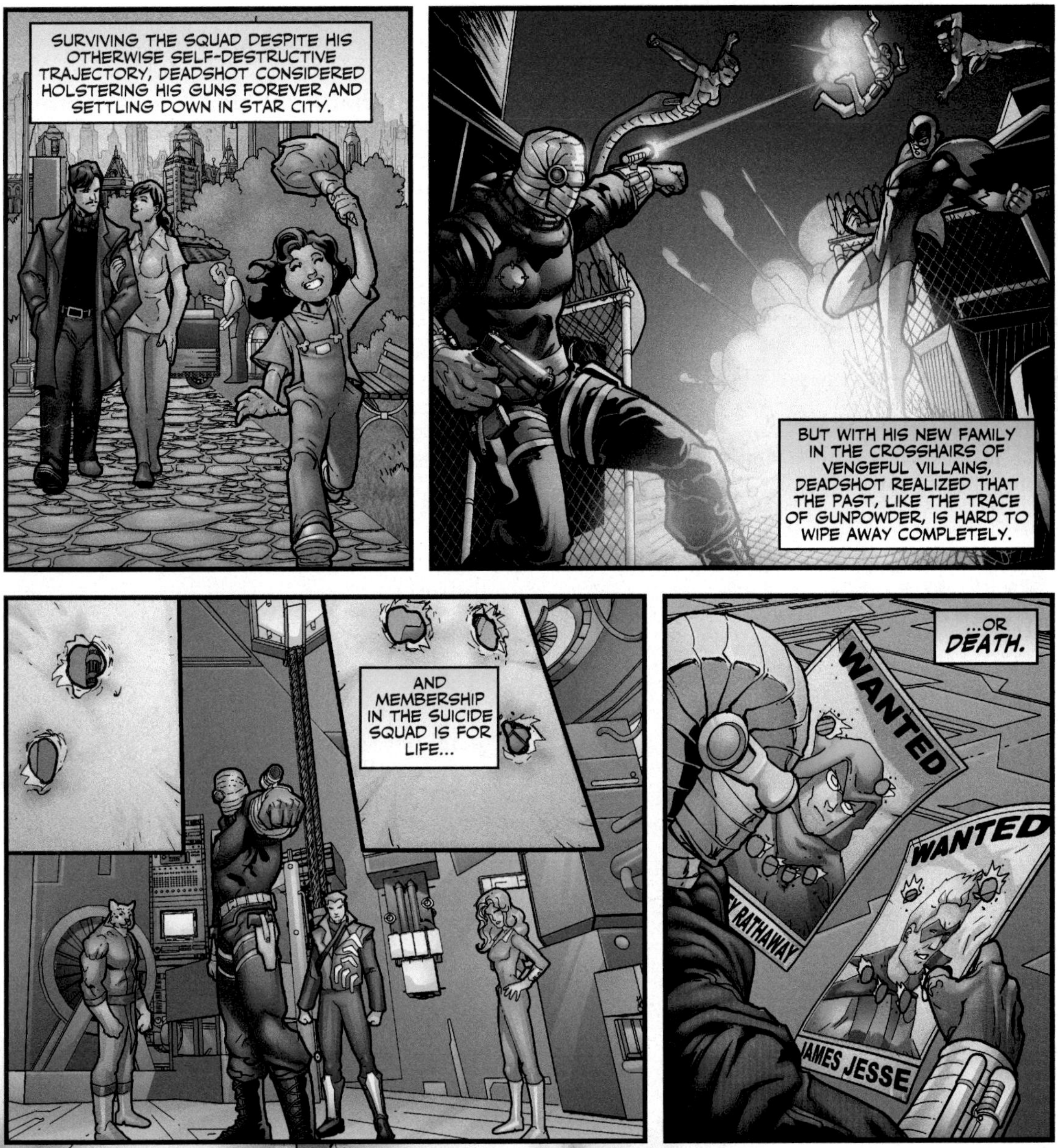
SURVIVING THE SQUAD DESPITE HIS OTHERWISE SELF-DESTRUCTIVE TRAJECTORY, DEADSHOT CONSIDERED HOLSTERING HIS GUNS FOREVER AND SETTLING DOWN IN STAR CITY.
BUT WITH HIS NEW FAMILY IN THE CROSSHAIRS OF VENGEFUL VILLAINS, DEADSHOT REALIZED THAT THE PAST, LIKE THE TRACE OF GUNPOWDER, IS HARD TO WIPE AWAY COMPLETELY.
AND MEMBERSHIP IN THE SUICIDE SQUAD IS FOR LIFE...
...OR *DEATH.*
WANTED
WANTED
JAMES JESSE

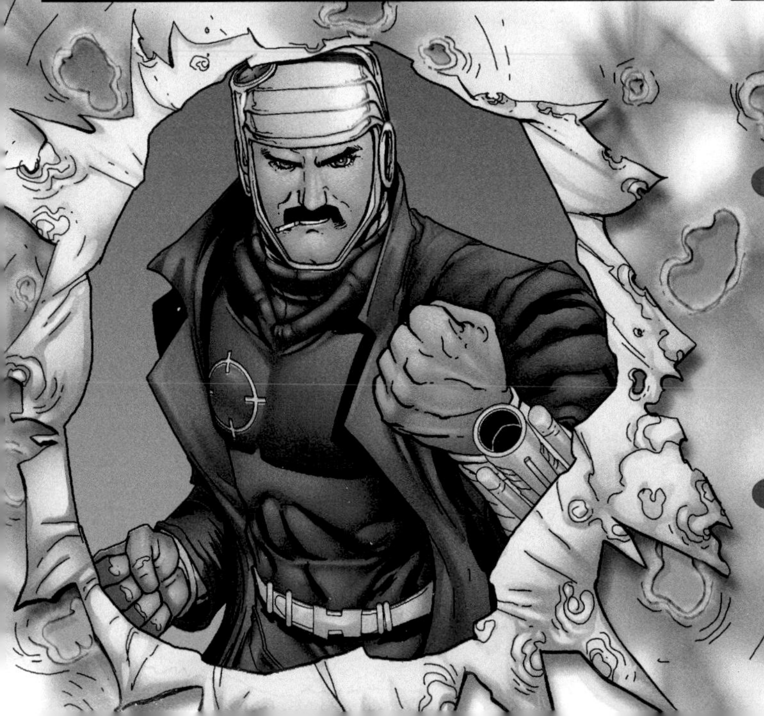

POWERS AND WEAPONS:

Gifted with unerring aim, Deadshot is likely the world's best—and deadliest—marksman, proficient with nearly every model and caliber of firearm. Deadshot prefers high-powered wrist-blaster gauntlets, as well as modified Glock 9 mm pistols able to fire grenades and other specialized projectiles.

ESSENTIAL STORYLINES:

- BATMAN: STRANGE APPARITIONS
- SHOWCASE PRESENTS: SUICIDE SQUAD 1
- DEADSHOT 1-5

"A pretty irresistible hook. What if the good guys assembled a bunch of bad guys to work as a Dirty Dozen-like superteam and do the dirty work traditional heroes would never touch (or want to know about)?"—THE ONION/AV CLUB

START AT THE BEGINNING!

SUICIDE SQUAD
VOLUME 1: KICKED IN THE TEETH

SUICIDE SQUAD VOL. 2: BASILISK RISING

SUICIDE SQUAD VOL. 3: DEATH IS FOR SUCKERS

DEATHSTROKE VOL. 1: LEGACY

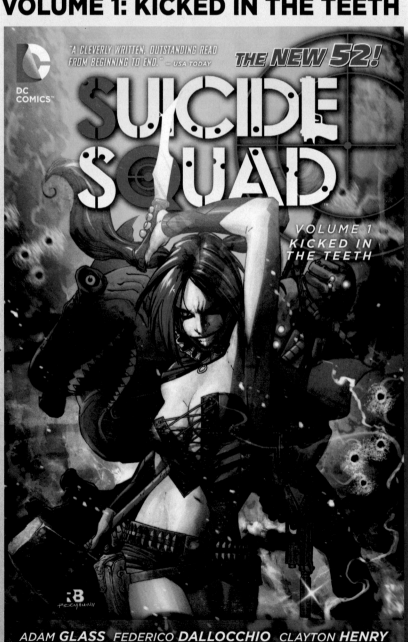

ADAM **GLASS** FEDERICO **DALLOCCHIO** CLAYTON **HENRY**